Mental Retardation in the 21st Century

Mental Retardation in the 21st Century

edited by

Michael L. Wehmeyer
James R. Patton

pro·ed
An International Publisher

8700 Shoal Creek Boulevard
Austin, Texas 78757-6897
800/897-3202   Fax 800/397-7633
Order online at http://www.proedinc.com

An International Publisher

© 2000 by PRO-ED, Inc.
8700 Shoal Creek Boulevard
Austin, Texas 78757-6897
800/897-3202   Fax 800/397-7633
Order online at http://www.proedinc.com

Publisher's Note: The Arc will receive all royalties from sales of this book.

Cover artwork reprinted with permission from *Perske: Pencil Portraits 1971–1990* by Martha Perske (Nashville, TN: Abingdon Press, 1998).

Library of Congress Cataloging-in-Publication Data
Mental retardation in the 21st century / edited by Michael L.
    Wehmeyer, James R. Patton.
            p.   cm. — (American studies series)
      ISBN 0-89079-819-2 (alk. paper).
      1. Mentally handicapped.   2. Mentally handicapped—United States.
    3. Mentally handicapped—Services for.   I. Wehmeyer, Michael L.
    II. Patton, James R.   III. Title: Mental retardation in the twenty
    first century
HV3004.M369   1999
362.3'0973—dc21   99-13073
                                                                        CIP

This book is designed in Goudy.

Production Director: Alan Grimes
Production Coordinator: Dolly Fisk Jackson
Managing Editor: Chris Olson
Art Director: Thomas Barkley
Designer: Jason Crosier
Print Buyer: Alicia Woods
Preproduction Coordinator: Chris Anne Worsham
Copy Editor: Martin Wilson
Project Editor: Debra Berman
Publishing Assistant: Jason Morris

Printed in the United States of America

1 2 3 4 5 6 7 8 9 10   03 02 01 00 99

Contents

WITHDRAWN

SECTION I
Family Issues

SECTION II
Education Issues

SECTION III
Employment and Residential Issues

SECTION IV
Issues in Psychology

SECTION V
Issues in Medicine and Health

Foreword

The beginning of the 21st century also marks the 50th anniversary of The Arc, founded in 1950 as the National Association of Parents and Friends of Mentally Retarded Children. During this 50 years, we have moved from a focus on disability to a focus on ability, from an era of institutions to an era of community supports. No one 50 years ago could have imagined the world of the end of the 20th century in which self-determination and community participation are becoming the expected norm. Even 35 years ago when my daughter was born, I could not have envisioned her living in an apartment by herself and working at a fully competitive job with a good wage and good benefits.

But The Arc has always been at its best when looking forward, not backward. As no one in 1950 could have envisaged the world for people with mental retardation as it is in 1999, no one today can truly know what it will be like throughout the 21st century. We can hardly anticipate what changes will be wrought by technology, by genetics, by behavioral research, or by government philosophy. But we can, at least, make intelligent guesses about their direction. That is why The Arc has sponsored this volume—as a challenge to us to make the 21st century a better place for children and adults with mental retardation and their families.

Quincy Abbot
President, The Arc of the United States, 1996–1998

Preface

In writing the preface for a book to be published at the end of the second millennium and focusing on the past, present, and future of mental retardation, there were several paths we, as editors, could follow. One course of action would be to provide a condensed recitation of how much has changed in the world since the turn of the present century, much as the singer Billy Joel did in his 1992 hit song "We Didn't Start the Fire." Airplanes. Automobiles. Industrial age. World Wars I and II. Korea. Vietnam. Roosevelt. Kennedy. Nixon. Spirit of St. Louis. Challenger. The Great Depression. The Great Wall of China. *The Great Gatsby*. Elvis. The Beatles. Computers. Apollo. Voyager. Malcolm X. Martin Luther King. Telephone. Hiroshima. Cold War. Berlin Wall. Polio. Salk. AIDS. Babe Ruth. Joe DiMaggio. And on and on and on. It becomes evident that such an effort would, in and of itself, become book length and likely do nothing more than illustrate the editors' lack of depth in history!

Alternatively, instead of a recitation of the events and people that mark the century, we could compare and contrast differences and similarities at the beginning and end of the century. In 1900 there were 76 million Americans; today Americans number more than 250 million. In 1900 genetic laws discovered by Mendel in 1865 become generally known for the first time because scientists rediscovered Mendel's work and made public his Mendelian laws. Today we are on the verge of mapping the entire human genome and eradicating untold diseases and conditions. In 1900 the seeds of Serbian nationalism threatened world stability, eventually resulting in World War I. Today Serbian nationalism threatens world stability in the Balkans. In 1900 the U.S. death rate from tuberculosis was 201 per 100,000 persons. During the century, tuberculosis was eliminated through vaccines but in the last few years has reemerged as a public health threat in the United States.

Alas, as with the staccato recitation of events, this comparative analysis of U.S. history in this century is too broad a task for the preface format. Instead, perhaps we could do such an analysis of the century strictly for events that impacted people with mental retardation and their families. What jumps out on the "how things are different" scale are the changes in the lives of people with mental retardation over the course of this momentous century. To catalog these changes, we could track the history of mental retardation across the century, describing the rise and fall of institutions, examining the impact of the parent movement and the passage of legislation like the Education for All Handicapped Children Act of 1975, and so forth. Such changes have been stark, as evidenced when hearing the words of Goddard who in 1912 wrote his treatise on the Kallikak family and concluded in a chapter titled "What Is To Be Done?" that

> No one interested in the progress of civilization can contemplate the facts presented in the previous chapters without having the question arise, Why isn't some-

thing done about this? What can we do? For the low-grade idiot, the loathsome unfortunate that may be sent in our institutions, some have proposed the lethal chamber. But humanity is steadily tending away from the possibility of that method, and there is no probability that it will ever be practiced. But in view of such conditions [as described about the Kallikak family in Goddard's book] we begin to realize that the idiot is not our greatest problem. He is indeed loathsome; he is somewhat difficult to take care of; nevertheless, he lives his life and is done. He does not continue the race with a line of children like himself. It is the moron type that make for us our great problem. (pp. 101–102)

These are difficult words to read at the end of the century, as venomous, insensitive, and insulting as they are. We can almost hear Goddard's regret about society's hesitancy to use the "lethal chamber" as a solution to the "problem" of idiocy and we marvel at the inhumanity of it all. Contrast this with the message of normalization, integration, inclusion, and self-determination and it is evident that this century has been one of incredible progress for people with mental retardation and their families. Then we are reminded of a recent newspaper expose of the number of people with mental retardation who have died in the 1990s as a result of the use of restraints, or we think of Blatt and Kaplan's (1966) shocking expose *Christmas in Purgatory*, published only 30 years ago, and we recognize that inhumanity is not relegated to one decade or another. It becomes increasingly evident that the task of relating even the history of mental retardation across this century looms large, and is largely unattainable within the confines of a preface.

Perhaps, instead, we could write a science-fiction type of preface, discussing the promise the future holds and identifying marvels of the coming decades. After all, futurists have prognostications by the dozens for the taking: microwave ovens that read the universal product code (the bars on every package) to obtain heating instructions, automated highways where the road and the automobile do the driving, advances in cell biology that will expand the average life span past the century mark. The possibilities seem endless, as would, probably, such a preface.

As the reader can begin to appreciate, writing a preface for a book such as this has so many possible paths that it is, frankly, overwhelming. So we will pass on the opportunity to play scribe to the events of the century or to play futurist and predict the technologies of the next century. We will leave any documentation of the history of mental retardation to the authors of the chapters in this book, and instead focus on how and why this book came to be. This book has several *raisons d'être*. First, it marks a momentous time, the turn of the century and the millennium. We'll not quibble about whether the 21st century begins on the first day of 2001 instead of 2000; we understand that explanation perfectly well and realize that it is, factually, accurate. Nonetheless, there is an allure and appeal to the three zeros in the year 2000 that is unavoidable, and so we'll join every other misinterpreter of historical timelines and unapologetically lay claim to the year 2000 as the starting point for the next millennium. Transitions from one century to another are times to reflect on the past and speculate about the future, and as we depart the 20th century and enter the 21st, it seems apropos to do so about the field of mental retardation.

A second event that precipitated the emergence of this book is the marking of a milestone for The Arc, the nation's largest voluntary association devoted exclusively to promoting the welfare of people with mental retardation and their families. At their annual convention in Nashville in October 1999, The Arc will begin the observance of its 50th anniversary. Many of the advances in service delivery and policy impacting people with mental retardation have been spearheaded by this organization and, like the turn of a century, 50th anniversary celebrations provide unique opportunities to consider where we've been, where we are now, and where we're going. The confluence of the advent of the 21st Century and The Arc's 50th Anniversary sparked this book and the latter, by and large, dictated its contents. While this book is not, per se, about The Arc, the authors were invited, and thus the topics determined, based on their relative contributions to The Arc. Some authors have received national recognition from The Arc, whereas others have been loyal volunteers and leaders in the movement.

Thus, we chose to note both the turn of the century and the 50th anniversary with a text that provided these distinguished authors the opportunity to discuss the history of mental retardation in their area or discipline, to identify the current status in that area, and, most important, to provide their vision for the future. The fact that we were starting as much from *authors* as we were from topics leads to a table of contents that has some obvious gaps in it. For example, we have no discussion of the potential life span of the term *mental retardation*. (*Editors note:* We predict a short life span. Be prepared to shift to *intellectual disability* as early as the next 5 years.) Readers should note, then, that we did not intend this book to be all encompassing and that it developed based on the contributors as much as the topics. However, we were gratified that such a wide array of distinguished contributors would dedicate their time and energy to this task. The authors and the editors have waived all compensation for their participation, and a portion of the royalties from this book will be contributed to The Arc's Research in Mental Retardation Grants Program to be used to promote research in this area. The Arc would like to acknowledge the generosity of PRO-ED Publications for this beneficial arrangement, as well as thank the authors for their generous contribution of time and effort.

The text is divided into seven sections. The first section, Family Issues, consists of two chapters. In the first, Turnbull and Turnbull discuss issues in family support. Few people are more qualified to look back on the history of family support and provide direction for the future than Rud and Ann Turnbull. They are the parents of a son, J.T., who has mental retardation; have co-directed the NIDRR-funded Rehabilitation Research and Training Center (RRTC) on families and disability (the Beach Center) for over a decade; have made substantive contributions to research, practice, and policy in education and family issues; and have contributed their time and considerable talent as volunteers for The Arc. In Chapter 2, Abeson and Davis examine the parent movement in mental retardation. Alan Abeson was, for 15 years, the executive director of The Arc and his contributions to policy and practice in the field during that tenure were considerable. He is the 1999 recipient of the American Association on Mental Retardation's Distinguished Leadership award. Prior to leading The Arc, Abeson worked at the Council for Exceptional Children, where he was one of the primary authors of federal legislation that became the Education for All Handicapped Children Act. Sharon Davis is director of The Arc's Department of Research and Program Services, where she manages the association's research and programmatic activities. In addition to her many professional contributions, Davis is also the parent of a young woman with mental retardation.

The second section explores issues in the education of students with mental retardation. Chapter 3 is authored by Michael Guralnick and discusses issues in early childhood education. Guralnick directs the Center on Human Development and Disability, a federally funded University Affiliated Program (UAP) and Mental Retardation and Developmental Disabilities Research Center (MRDDRC), and is a professor of psychology and pediatrics at the University of Washington. His research was among the first to emphasize inclusion in early childhood intervention. Among other honors, Guralnick was the recipient of The Arc's Distinguished Research Award in 1997. Chapter 4, by Cimera and Rusch, explores transition and the education of adolescents with mental retardation. Robert Cimera is an assistant professor of special education at Loyola University where he focuses his research efforts on school-to-work transition, the social relationships of supported employees, and the utilization of natural support strategies in employment. Frank Rusch was, for over a decade, director of the Transition Research Institute at the University of Illinois at Urbana–Champaign. Most recently he was principal investigator for the National Transition Alliance, a coalition of research institutes providing technical support and assistance to federally funded transition-related projects. Rusch's research over the last two decades was as influential as any such work in establishing the importance of transition services to the education of youth with disabilities.

Chapter 5, the third chapter in the education issues section, examines the education of students with mild mental retardation. Jim Patton, Ed Polloway, and Tom Smith are all former special education teachers who worked extensively with students with mild mental retardation. Currently, Jim Patton is the executive editor at PRO-ED in Austin, Texas; Ed Polloway is the vice president for institutional development at Lynchburg College in Lynchburg, Virginia; and Tom Smith is the assistant dean of the college of education at the University of Arkansas at Little Rock. Chapter 6, written by Douglas Guess, examines educational services for students with significant disabilities. Guess' involvement in the education of students with significant disabilities dates back several decades. His research on teaching communication skills to individuals with severe language delays and work on using functional approaches in the education of students with severe mental retardation was groundbreaking. He was a founding member of the Association for Persons with Severe Handicaps (now TASH) and served as editor of this organization's journal. Guess is currently a professor of special education at the University of Kansas and in 1995 was awarded The Arc's Distinguished Research Award.

Employment and residential issues form the theme for Section III. Chapter 7, authored by Wehman, Bricout, and Kregel, presents a new framework for conceptualizing supported employment focusing on workplace supports. Paul Wehman has a long and distinguished record in supported employment, originating the concept and providing research to support its utility and adoption. He directs the NIDRR Rehabilitation Research and Training Center on Supported Employment (now Workplace Supports), which, among its multiple national projects, is conducting a national examination of the implementation of supported employment with people with significant disabilities. He is the editor of the *Journal of Vocational Rehabilitation*, and received the 1990 Joseph P. Kennedy Jr. Foundation Award in Mental Retardation and the 1992 Distinguished Service Award from the President's Committee on Employment for Persons with Disabilities. In addition, Wehman has given generously of his time and expertise to volunteer for The Arc and to assist in numerous employment and transition-related activities. John Bricout is a predoctoral fellow at the RRTC on Workplace Supports and his research is in this area. John Kregel is associate director of the RRTC on Workplace Supports, and director of research. He is professor of special education at Virginia Commonwealth University and has published widely in transition and supported employment.

In Chapter 8, Kiernan examines the current and future status of employment for people with mental retardation. Bill Kiernan is a past president of the American Association on Mental Retardation and directs the Institute for Community Inclusion, a University Affiliated Program in Boston. Kiernan's research has examined the degree to which people with mental retardation or developmental disabilities have been included in employment settings in the community. In addition to volunteering his time on The Arc's national Program Services Committee, he has assisted The Arc in compiling data to inform the nation on the degree of inclusion of people with mental retardation in employment. Section III concludes with a chapter by Klein and Strully examining the movement from congregate residential settings to life in the community. Jay Klein got his feet wet in the field by joining Youth ARC, a movement in the early 1970s sponsored by the National Association for Retarded Citizens (NARC, now The Arc) to involve young people in the field. Since then he has worked on behalf of people with disabilities on issues of housing, supported employment, inclusive education policy and systems change, and coalition building. His primary focus has been in the area of supported living and he has worked at all levels to achieve community integration for people with mental retardation. Most recently he was the director of the federally funded National Home of Your Own Alliance, a technical assistance center at the University of New Hampshire's UAP, the Institute on Disability. Jeff Strully is a longtime advocate for people with developmental disabilities and the parent of a daughter with significant disabilities. He was executive director of the Association for Community Living in Colorado, the state affiliate of The Arc, and has worked in a variety of organizations to promote community inclusion. He is currently the executive director of Jay Nolan Community Services in Los Angeles, an innovative organization supporting people to live valued lives in their community. He has written and lectures extensively on topics including friendship, supported living, and organizational change.

Section IV includes chapters discussing a variety of issues in psychology as they relate to mental retardation. In Chapter 10, Robert Horner examines the past and future of positive behavior supports. Horner is professor of special education and director of the Specialized Training Program at the University of Oregon. He has contributed across a wide array of topics in special education and rehabilitation, and in 1993 received The Arc's National Distinguished Research Award for his research in the employment of people with severe disabilities, instructional design for learners with significant disabilities, and the development of the use of positive behavioral supports for people with challenging behavior. It is the latter that we have asked him to write about, and he brings to this task considerable research expertise and experience as the director of the NIDRR-funded RRTC on Positive Behavioral Support.

Reiss examines the use of psychopharmacological agents with people with mental retardation in Chapter 11. In 1995 The Arc co-sponsored a national consensus conference on the use of psychotropic medication with people with mental retardation, which resulted in the publication of the *International Consensus Handbook on Psychotropic Medication and Developmental Disabilities* (Reiss & Aman, 1998). This consensus conference was conceptualized and spearheaded by Steven Reiss, a national authority on dual diagnosis and the use of psychoactive medications with people with mental retardation. Among other national awards, Reiss was the 1991 recipient of The Arc's Distinguished Research Award for his research in these areas. He is the author of several diagnostic tools to assess emotional disorders and mental illness in people with mental retardation, and directs the Nisonger Center at Ohio State University.

Chapter 12 addresses health issues contributing to problem behavior and is co-authored by Craig Kennedy and Travis Thompson. Kennedy is associate professor of special education at Peabody College, Vanderbilt University, and Investigator at the John F. Kennedy Center. His research focuses on biobehavioral causes of antisocial behavior, the development of social relationships between adolescents with and without disabilities, and strategies for effective inclusion into general education. Thompson is professor in the departments of psychology and human development and special education at Peabody College, Vanderbilt University; professor of psychiatry, School of Medicine, Vanderbilt University; and director of the John F. Kennedy Center for Research on Human Development, a Mental Retardation/Developmental Disabilities Research Center. In 1996 he received The Arc's Distinguished Research Award for his pioneering work in the area of developmental behavioral pharmacology and his innovative work in the design and implementation of behavioral treatments for severe behavioral problems, including self-injury. Thompson's early work demonstrating behavioral change for people living in institutions was one catalyst for the eventual deinstitutionalization of people with challenging behavior who lived in Minnesota and, subsequently, across the nation.

Section V focuses on issues in medicine and health promotion. Chapter 13 examines the exploding field of genetics and gene therapy as it relates to mental retardation. The chapter is written by Hugo Moser, a noted physician and researcher who was the 1994 recipient of The Arc's Distinguished Research Award. Moser's contributions to the field of mental retardation are significant. In 1972 he was appointed professor of neurology at Harvard University. From 1963 to 1976 he served successively as director of research, assistant superintendent, and superintendent of the Walter E. Fernald State School. From 1976 to 1988 he was president of the Kennedy Institute (now the Kennedy Krieger Institute) in Baltimore and professor of neurology and pediatrics at Johns Hopkins University. Since 1988 he has been director of neurogenetics at the Kennedy Krieger Institute. He was honored by The Arc for his research on inborn errors of metabolism that cause mental retardation and he has assisted The Arc many times over the years on issues related to genetics and research.

Chapter 14 examines issues of health promotion and disability prevention. It is authored by Deborah Cohen, who has directed the New Jersey Office for Prevention of Mental Retardation and Developmental Disabilities since 1988. Cohen is a former member and chair of the American Association on Mental Retardation's (AAMR's) Health Promotion and Disability Prevention committee, and since 1988 has served on The Arc's National Prevention Committee, now the Health Promotion and Disability Prevention Committee. Cohen has chaired this committee since 1997 and has volunteered many hours to The Arc to promote prevention and health promotion issues. Issues of managed care are important in the lives of people with mental retardation, and Chapter 15 addresses these. The chapter is written by Allen Crocker, who is director of the Developmental Evaluation Center at Children's Hospital in Boston and on the faculty at Harvard Medical School. Crocker is program director for the Institute for Community Inclusion at Children's Hospital, a University Affiliated Program, and has assisted program staff at The Arc on numerous occasions.

The final chapter in this section is authored by Siegfried Pueschel and focuses on issues specific to Down syndrome. Pueschel, who is the parent of a son with Down syndrome, is among the leading authorities on this condition. He has edited and written numerous books on Down syndrome for a wide audience and in 1990 was honored for his work in this area with The Arc's Distinguished Research Award. Currently, Pueschel is director of the Child Development Center at Rhode Island Hospital and holds academic appointments at Harvard Medical School and Brown University School of Medicine.

Section VI examines life span issues pertaining to mental retardation. Chapter 17 focuses on assistive technology, particularly alternative and augmentative communication. Mary Ann Romski and Rose Sevcik have conducted extensive research in this area, are actively involved in the American Speech-Language-Hearing Association (ASHA), and hold appointments at Georgia State University. Romski is professor of communication, psychology and educational psychology at Georgia State. She is a certified speech–language pathologist, a fellow of the AAMR and ASHA, and a recent chair of ASHA's National Joint Committee on the Communication Needs of Individuals with Severe Disabilities. Among other volunteer activities, Romski has served as the chair of The Arc's National Research Committee, guiding the association's efforts to support research. Sevcik is assistant research professor in the department of psychology at Georgia State and has served as associate editor for the *Journal of Speech and Hearing Research.*

The second chapter in this section addresses issues of self-advocacy and self-determination. Michael Wehmeyer is assistant director in The Arc's Department of Research and Program Services and director of the Bill Sackter Center on Self-Determination. The Bill Sackter Center conducts research and other activities to promote the self-determination of children, youth, and adults with mental retardation. Hank Bersani is a longtime advocate for people with disabilities and past recipient of The Arc's Franklin G. Smith Award, honoring distinguished service in the field of mental retardation. Bersani has written extensively about self-advocacy and is on the faculty at Oregon Health Sciences University and affiliated with its Center on Self-Determination. Ray Gagne is a past chair of The Arc's National Self-Advocacy Committee and a past member of The Arc's Board of Directors.

The final chapter in this section focuses on issues of quality of life. The chapter's author, Robert Schalock, is a past president of AAMR and has influenced research and practice in quality of life throughout the last two decades. Schalock's work includes construct validation and theory development in quality of life, and he is the author or editor of numerous texts addressing this topic, including a recent two-volume set published by AAMR. Schalock is professor of psychology at Hastings College in Nebraska.

The final section addresses policy issues impacting people with mental retardation. Chapter 20 examines the transformation of service delivery systems in the United States. David Braddock is professor of human development, public health, and bioengineering, head of the Department of Disability and Human Development, and associate dean for research of the College of Health and Human Development Sciences at the University of Illinois at Chicago. His research has focused on the comparative study of service and resource commitments in the 50 states and by the federal government for people with developmental disabilities and their families, and his work in this area has influenced policy and practice for more than 20 years. He was the 1987 recipient of The Arc's Distinguished Research Award and is a past president of the AAMR. Richard Hemp is project director and Susan Parish is resource and policy analyst for the State of the States in Developmental Disabilities, a research project at the Department of Disability and Human Development at the University of Illinois at Chicago.

Chapter 21 examines social constructions of mental retardation. J. David Smith, professor and dean of the School of Education and Human Services at Longwood College, has written extensively about social constructions and sociopolitical aspects of mental retardation, including studies of the history of eugenics and its impact on social and educational policy. Prior to his appointment at Longwood, Smith was chair of the department of educational psychology at the University of South Carolina. Chapter 22 examines issues of criminal justice and mental retardation and is written by Robert Perske, a noted author, journalist, and advocate. Perske's work has influenced policy in and attitudes about mental retardation for several decades. His influential chapter on the dignity of risk in the 1972 book *Normalization* (Wolfensberger, 1972) was, in many ways, the precursor to current efforts to promote self-determination. His many books with illustrations by his wife Martha, including *Circles of Friends* and *Hope for the Families*, paved the way for the inclusion of people with mental retardation in their communities. In the last decade, Perske has been the national voice of consciousness for people with mental retardation ensnared in the criminal justice system, and he has written and lectured extensively about mental retardation, criminal justice, and the death penalty. He has received numerous awards, including the 1993 Humanitarian Award from the AAMR.

The book ends with not one, but two epilogues. These address the field of mental retardation as a whole instead of specific topics or disciplines within the field. The first is written by Rud and Ann Turnbull, whose credentials related to family supports were highlighted earlier. The chapter provides much food for thought, as does the final contribution by Gunnar Dybwad. Of all the voices in the field of mental retardation in this century, few are as significant as Dybwad's. He and his wife Rosemary have had as much influence on the lives of people with developmental disabilities as anyone during the century. He was born in Germany in 1909 and received the Doctor of Laws degree in 1934. He is a fellow of the AAMR, the American Sociological Association, the American Orthopsychiatric Association, and the American Public Health Association, and is an honorary fellow in the American Academy of Pediatrics. His awards are too numerous to recite, but include the AAMR's distinguished contribution award. He was executive director of the National ARC, served as a consultant to President Kennedy on mental retardation, and is considered by most to be the grandfather of the self-advocacy movement.

The American poet Ogden Nash noted cynically that each new year is the descendent of a long line of proven criminals. Yet as we move from the 20th to the 21st century, we do so not with cynicism, but with hope that the momentum will continue from the last century in acknowledging that people with intellectual disabilities are people first who deserve the same rights as other citizens to chase the American dream and to live full, rich lives in the community. So to that, we'll lift a glass and sing a song of auld lang syne.

REFERENCES

Blatt, B., & Kaplan, F. (1966). *Christmas in purgatory: A photographic essay on mental retardation.* Author.

Education for All Handicapped Children Act of 1975, 20 U.S.C. § 1400 *et seq.*

Goddard, H. H. (1912). *The Kallikak family: A study in the heredity of feeble-mindedness.* New York: Macmillan.

Perske, R. (1974). *Hope for the families: New directions for parents of persons with retardation and other disabilities.* Nashville, TN: Abingdon Press.

Perske, R. (1988). *Circles of friends: People with disabilities and their friends enrich the lives of one another.* Nashville, TN: Abingdon Press.

Reiss, S. & Aman, M. (1998). *International consensus handbook on psychotropic medication and developmental disabilities.* Columbus: Nisonger Center for Mental Retardation and Developmental Disabilities, The Ohio State University.

Wolfensberger, W. (1972). *Normalization: The principle of normalization in human services.* Toronto: National Institute on Mental Retardation.

Contributors

Alan Abeson, EdD
The Arc of the United States
500 East Border Street, Suite 300
Arlington, TX 76010

Hank Bersani, Jr., PhD
Oregon Health Sciences University
Child Development and Rehabilitation Center
P.O. Box 574
Portland, OR 97202-0574

David Braddock, PhD
Department of Disability and Human Development
University of Illinois at Chicago
1640 West Roosevelt Road
Chicago, IL 60608-6904

John Bricout, PhD
Masters Program
Rehabilitation Research and Training Center on Work Supports
Virginia Commonwealth University
1314 West Main Street
Box 842027
Richmond, VA 23284

Robert E. Cimera, PhD
Curriculum Instruction and Educational Psychology
Loyola University, Chicago
Mallinckrodt Campus
1041 Ridge Road
Wilmette, IL 60091

Deborah E. Cohen, PhD
Office for Prevention of Mental Retardation and Developmental Disabilities
Department of Human Services
222 S. Warren Street
CN 700, 4th Floor
Trenton, NJ 08625

Allen C. Crocker, MD
Developmental Evaluation Center
Children's Hospital
300 Longwood Avenue
Boston, MA 02115

Sharon Davis, PhD
Department of Research and Program Services
The Arc of the United States
500 East Border Street, Suite 300
Arlington, TX 76010

Gunnar Dybwad, PhD
390 Linden St.
Wellesley Hills, MA 02181

Raymond Gagne
2602 Derry Street
Harrisburg, PA 17111

Doug Guess, EdD
Department of Special Education
The University of Kansas
3001 Robert Dole Human Development Center
Lawrence, KS 66045

Michael J. Guralnick, PhD
Center on Human Development and Disability
University of Washington
Box 357920
Seattle, WA 98195-7920

Richard Hemp, MA
Department of Disability and Human Development
University of Illinois at Chicago
1640 West Roosevelt Road
Chicago, IL 60608-6904

Robert H. Horner, PhD
Specialized Training Program
1235 University Oregon
Eugene, OR 97403-1235

Craig H. Kennedy, PhD
Department of Special Education
Box 328, Peabody College
Vanderbilt University
Nashville, TN 37203

William E. Kiernan, PhD
Institute for Community Inclusion
Children's Hospital
300 Longwood Avenue
Boston, MA 02115

Jay Klein, MSW
Institute on Disability
University of New Hampshire
7 Leavitt Lane, Suite 101
Durham, NH 03824-3595

John Kregel, PhD
Rehabilitation Research and Training Center
  on Work Supports
Virginia Commonwealth University
1314 West Main Street
P.O. Box 842020
Richmond, VA 23284

Hugo W. Moser, MD
Neurogenetics Research Center
Kennedy Krieger Institute and Johns Hopkins
  University
707 North Broadway
Baltimore, MD 21205

Susan Parish, MSW
Department of Disability and Human Devel-
  opment
University of Illinois at Chicago
1640 West Roosevelt Road
Chicago, IL 60608-6904

James R. Patton, EdD
PRO-ED
8700 Shoal Creek Boulevard
Austin, TX 78757-6897

Robert Perske
159 Hollow Tree Ridge Road
Darien, CT 06820

Edward A. Polloway, EdD
Education and Human Development
Lynchburg College
1501 Lakeside Drive
Lynchburg, VA 24501

Siegfried M. Pueschel, MD, PhD, JD, MPH
Child Development Center
Rhode Island Hospital
593 Eddy Street
Providence, RI 02903

Steven Reiss, PhD
Nisonger Center
175 McCampbell Hall
Ohio State University
1581 Dodd Drive
Columbus, OH 43210-1296

Mary Ann Romski, PhD
Department of Communication
Georgia State University
Atlanta, GA 30303

Frank R. Rusch, PhD
National Center for Supercomputing Appli-
  cations
Education Division
University of Illinois at Urbana–Champaign
61 Children's Research Center
51 Gerty Drive
Champaign, IL 61820

Robert L. Schalock, PhD
Department of Psychology
Hastings College
Hastings, NE 68901

Rose A. Sevcik, PhD
Language Research Center
Department of Psychology
Georgia State University
Atlanta, GA 30303

J. David Smith, EdD
School of Education and Human Services
Longwood College
201 High Street
Farmville, VA 23909

Tom E. C. Smith, EdD
Department of Teacher Education
University of Arkansas at Little Rock
33rd and University
Little Rock, AR 72204-1099

Jeffrey L. Strully, EdD
Jay Nolan Community Services
8950 Lurline Avenue
Chatsworth, CA 91311

Travis Thompson, PhD
John F. Kennedy Center
Box 40, Peabody College
Vanderbilt University
Nashville, TN 37203

Ann P. Turnbull, EdD
Beach Center on Families and Disability
Life Span Institute
3111 Haworth Hall
University of Kansas
Lawrence, KS 66045

H. Rutherford Turnbull III, LLM
Beach Center on Families and Disability
Life Span Institute
3111 Haworth Hall
University of Kansas
Lawrence, KS 66045

Paul Wehman, PhD
Rehabilitation Research and Training Center
on Work Supports
Virginia Commonwealth University
1314 West Main Street
P.O. Box 842011
Richmond, VA 23284

Michael L. Wehmeyer, PhD
Beach Center on Families and Disabilities
Life Span Institute
3136 Haworth Hall
Univerisity of Kansas
Lawrence, KS 66045

Family Issues

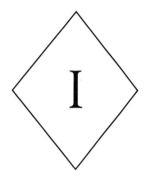

Family Support: Retrospective and Prospective

H. Rutherford Turnbull III and Ann P. Turnbull

I n this chapter, we review the several stages—the evolution—of family support, beginning 50 years ago and coming forward to the end of the millennium. We also link these retrospectives to the roles that families have been obliged or have chosen to play in their relationships with providers and policy makers (A. P. Turnbull & H. R. Turnbull, 1997).

We assert that, as policies about people with disabilities and their families have changed, so too have families' roles and expectations. For The Arc, the question, then, is not so much "Where have we been?" as "Where are we going and how do we secure the enviable lives to which we all aspire?" We answer that question, not in terms of specific policies, but in terms of a general policy and in terms of the roles and assumptions families should be able to play and make.

THE DISTANT PAST: THE ANCIENT COVENANT

To those who established The Arc in 1949, the term *family support* must have entailed mixed meanings. After all, the 1940s was a time when professionals still counseled families to institutionalize their children, and to do so sooner rather than later in the families' lives. It was a time when families who resisted that advice were regarded as noncompliant and in need of "treatment" themselves (Roos, 1985). The late 1940s was a time when involuntariness was regarded as a proper response to the needs of families, "the retarded," and society. What forms did involuntariness take? It took the form of involuntary commitment into state schools or hospitals when a family did not voluntarily admit their children to those facilities. And, of course, it took the form of compulsory sterilization of both those who were patently "retarded" and of those who, as parents, seemed to be on the cusp of having mental retardation (Barr, 1913; Ferguson, 1994).

If there is any overarching theme to the late 1940s, it is that the "ancient covenant" promised (!) that families would be "relieved" of the "burden" of caring for their children; the relief would come through institutionalization. The primary beneficiaries of the institution were not those who were put into them, not the people with mental retardation. Rather, the primary beneficiaries were the families, and their "support" was being relieved of caregiving duties. That is precisely the argument that the State of Alabama made as it resisted institutional reform in the case of *Wyatt v. Stickney* (1971). The ancient covenant was separatist in the most fundamental of senses: It separated families from their children and the children from society. And it was judgmental in the most Draconian of ways: It divided the family by segregating those with retardation.

Sad to say, the secondary beneficiaries were the professional cadre who operated the institutions. It was they who asserted that they alone were the most knowledgeable about mental retardation, about what was good for those affected by it and their families, and about how to support families.

It is important to understand the family-relief role of institutions and their professional cadre because the institution's and profession's roles shaped families' roles. The institutions reflected not only a (perverse) form of family support, but also a professional–family relationship. Simply put, the relationship was that families were expected to defer to professionals' judgment; the conventional wisdom was that the "professional (often, physician or psychologist) knows best."

What undergirded this kind of conventional wisdom, however, was more important than the wisdom itself. The underpinnings of professional dominance were the beliefs that parents were at fault; they alone or, if not they alone, at least they primarily were responsible for their children's having or not being able to thwart the effects of mental retardation. (In our Epilogue later in this book, we discuss the social Darwinism/eugenics movement.) The point, very simply, is that families were expected to surrender their children to the state's custody through institutionalization and to acquiesce to involuntary sterilization of their children (or at least to their placement in single-sex facilities).

The ancient covenant, then, was this: Families are a source of the "problem" of mental retardation; family support is determined by what professionals think is the "right" answer to the "problem" of mental retardation within the family; accordingly, family support consists of removing families from their roles as the caregivers or even procreators of "the retarded"; and institutions are the forms, the entities, that best support families. Information on how people with mental retardation and their families were regarded and dealt with during the early and mid-20th century is set out in other sources (Boggs, 1978; Brakel, Parry, & Weiner, 1985; Burgdorf, 1980; Ferguson, 1994; Kindred, Cohen, Penrod, & Shaffer, 1976; Roos, 1978; Scheerenberger, 1983).

THE RECENT PAST: THE ERA OF CONVERSION AND ADVOCACY

Beginning with The Arc's incorporation and extending through its early growth, family support entered still another phase. It is a phase characterized by conversion and advocacy. As in the ancient covenant phase, family support interacted with the roles that families chose or were obliged to play.

The term *conversion* refers to a change of posture, a change of public position regarding parents whose children have mental retardation. Symbolic of the conversion were various "comings out," various exits from the closets of shame derived from the stigma of mental retardation. President John F. Kennedy's mother bravely discussed her daughter, Rosemary (who has mental retardation), on national television. What marked Mrs. Kennedy's bravery was that she acted contrary to the traditional (one might say, conventional) wisdom of the past: At a time when public confession was not all the rage, she proclaimed what it means to be the mother of a person with mental retardation. The noted author and humanitarian Pearl Buck wrote about her own daughter; Dale Evans and Roy Rogers took off their cowgirl and cowboy costumes and appeared as "just" parents; and, increasingly, the private "problem" of mental retardation became a public matter.

Consistent with these types of conversion, members of The Arc and other parents affected by disability began to play other roles than "just" parents. They began to organize associations in which they could receive instrumental and emotional support; The Arc (Scheerenberger, 1983) and United Cerebral Palsy Associates (Goldenson, 1965) are the first examples of these organizations.

According to Woodhull Hay, first secretary of The Arc, there were seven reasons underlying parent efforts to form local groups (Hay, 1983, as cited in Scheerenberger, 1983, p. 229):

1. Evidence that institutions were limited in what they could do for children;

2. Increased awareness that regular public school programs were unsuited for such children;

3. The need to disseminate knowledge and information concerning mental retardation;

4. The need to challenge the validity of the finality in the words, "Nothing can be done for your child";

5. The desire of parents to learn what more could be done for these children and to pursue projects in their behalf;

6. The need to strengthen the growing conviction that the responsibility is social, i.e., money should be provided for building a fuller life for the mentally handicapped; and

7. The realization that it was not enough spiritually just to care for one's own child.

To this listing, one can readily add that parents were markedly concerned about poor institutional programs, the exclusion of mentally retarded children from public school programs, and professional mismanagement.

The Arc's incorporation marks the role of "organizer" that parents first undertook during the late 1940s and early 1950s, that they exercised throughout the 1960s as more and more disability-specific organizations were created, and that they execute even today (A. P. Turnbull & H. R. Turnbull, 1997).

In addition, parents increasingly organized programs for their children. These included special education classes and programs of recreation, employment (mostly sheltered), and residential living. Leading professionals acknowledge the pervasive impact of parent organizations in developing special education services:

> If I were to give credit to one group in this country for the advancements that have been made in the education of exceptional children, I would place the parent organizations and parent movement in the forefront as the leading force. (Kirk, 1984, p. 41)

In undertaking to secure an education for their children, these parents asserted that compulsory closeting of their children at home was supportive of neither the family nor their children. Their efforts signify the role that parents played as developers of services to supplement professionals' programs (or nonprograms) and to challenge professionals' dominance in policy and programs.

Family support, then, consisted of (a) organizational support of parents and participation by the parents, together with a concomitant obligation to contribute time, money, and energy to the organizations, and (b) direct services for the children with mental retardation, together with a similar obligation to help operate the services (A. P. Turnbull & H. R. Turnbull, 1997). One consequence of the mere existence of the organizations was that they sought more publicly funded services in all domains of their children's lives but principally in education, employment, and residential living.

Regarded in this light, family support consisted of advocacy by organizations on behalf of parents and their children. It was not so much that the organizations themselves stopped being "supports" in the instrumental and emotional ways, but rather that they added to these roles the new one of advocacy; they engaged in a deliberate conversion to advocacy.

There was something particularly problematic about these three roles—organizer, provider, and advocate. These roles underscored a singular and hard-to-take message about families and family support: Parents can make no assumptions about their lives or the lives of their children with mental retardation.

To be unable to make any assumptions! Think about what that means. To be unable to assume that you will maintain an intact family, that you can resist various kinds of compulsory interventions, that your children will be able to attend school, and that as you grow older your caretaking will be transferred to capable and caring caregivers.

Add to the parents' inability to make any assumptions the fact that they were also expected to play another role. That new role was to be the passive recipients of professional judgments. To acquiesce in what the professional cadre knew was "right" created dissonance for many parents.

Parents were expected, on the one hand, to organize, provide services, and advocate, and, on the other, to comply with professionals' advice (some of which was at the root of the very policies that families found abhorrent and that they advocated to reform). Parents were caught between Scylla and Charybdis: Either way they steered their lives, they most likely would find the course and destination to be inhospitable and hardly supportive. Either they would have to do it all themselves or they would be obliged to accept what professionals thought best and public funding offered.

In large part because the conditions in the institutions were unacceptable (Blatt & Kaplan, 1966; Goffman, 1961; Rothman, 1971; Wolfensberger, 1975) and unconstitutional (*Pennhurst State School and Hospital v. Halderman*, 1981; *Wyatt v. Stickney*, 1971; *Youngberg v. Romeo*, 1982) and their children's exclusion from or misclassification within school was patently unconstitutional (*Mills v. D.C. Board of Education*, 1972; *Pennsylvania Association for Retarded Citizens v. Commonwealth of Pennsylvania*, 1971), parents turned more and more in the direction of advocacy. They advocated against the institutions and for education and other services, provided on a nondiscriminatory basis. Their success—The Arc's—was magnificent.

Their efforts at deinstitutionalization took three forms: reform the institution (a strategy that proved fruitless, as the now 26-year-old *Wyatt* case evidences[1]), prevent people from being placed into institutions, and assure that people would be discharged from institutions and admitted to public schools. Their concurrent efforts at community services took complementary forms. In order for people with mental retardation to avoid the institutions, they must have a right to the following:

1. Free appropriate public education (originally codified in the Education for All Handicapped Children Act of 1975, now reauthorized as the Individuals with Disabilities Education Act [IDEA] of 1997)

2. Community-based services (now codified in the home and community-based programs authorized by Title XIX, Medicaid, of the Social Security Act)

3. Freedom from discrimination solely on the basis of disability (now codified by Sec. 504 of the Rehabilitation Act Amendments of 1975 and the Americans with Disabilities Act of 1990)

Parents' advocacy on behalf of their children's right to education contributed to their having to play another role. They became their children's "teachers." The

---

[1]The Wyatt litigation has been carried on for more than 25 years by the Judge David L. Bazelon Mental Health Law Center; the most recent decision in the case reiterated the rights that the court first enunciated in 1971 and found that, again, the state was in violation of those rights (*Wyatt v. Rogers*, Gv. Act. No. 3195-N, M.D. Ala., Dec. 15, 1997).

research community contributed evidence that family environment influences children's intelligence (Hunt, 1972; Zigler & Muenchow, 1992). A logical corollary of the research and theory was that parents should not only learn how to teach (raise) their children but also should be active in carrying out home-based educational programs for their children (Bricker & Bricker, 1976). Not surprisingly, given the research evidence and the commonsense nature of the ecological theory, family support came to consist of professionals teaching the parents and, in turn, the parents teaching their children (Karnes & Teska, 1980). Instead of relieving parents of some of their responsibilities, family support (parent as learner and teacher) paradoxically added to them.

One consequence of this development was that parents increasingly regarded themselves as "experts" on their children. Knowing a great deal about their children already and learning more about them through "follow-through" education programs, early intervention, and even Head Start programs, parents came to realize that they were competent to make decisions about their children. From this realization (but not from it alone) grew the public policy of parent participation in education decision making.

Codified into IDEA as the principle of parent participation (H. R. Turnbull & A. P. Turnbull, 1998), the role of parent as educational decision maker gave yet another meaning to the concept of family support: Family support means parents will (*must*, some would argue) be involved with professionals in all decision making regarding the education of students with disabilities. To "support" the family, then, meant that parents would be joint decision makers.

As the 1990s come to a close, the concept of family support and its relationship to parents' roles has taken on yet another meaning. Today, the focus is not only on the parents, but on the entire family. That new focus is a consequence of the family-systems research: Because each family is a "system" of interacting and interactive relationships (parental, marital, sibling, and extended family), family support must extend beyond the parents and include other members, too (A. P. Turnbull & H. R. Turnbull, 1997).

That extension—from parent to family—also is a consequence of the changing demographics of the family. There are many single-parent families; some families lack a parent, or one parent in intact families is not as active as the other in raising the children and being education decision makers; and more families are two-income families with "home alone" or "day care" children. As the demographics of the family changed, so did the expectations about family members' roles: The "parent" became the "family" in order to accommodate a new reality about families.

Moreover, it is not merely that the family as a system has become the focus of family support (displacing the singular focus on the parents), but also that families are expected to be collaborators with professionals—to make decisions not only about their own children (IDEA's original parent-participation principle) but also about the design of service systems and policies in general. To see how this all is so, it is appropriate to consider family support and family roles as they exist at the close of the 1990s.

THE PRESENT: FAMILY SUPPORT, A MULTIDIMENSIONAL CONCEPT

Family support today is both broadly and narrowly defined. Broadly defined, family support consists of the wide range of governmental and nongovernmental supports and services that assist families to obtain the types of lives they want and need. Within this wide range there exist the governmental programs that we describe later and, just as important, the informal supports that family, friends, and nongovernmental associations (such as The Arc) provide. Narrowly, it refers to state-sponsored cash transfers or voucherized programs. The two definitions and their implications for the future are important to consider.

"Assisting families to obtain the types of lives they want and need" covers a great deal of ground. First, it assumes that families, not only parents, are the proper focus of public policy. Second, it assumes that what is good for the family as a whole, as a system, is good for its individual members. Both assumptions reflect the increasing acceptance within public policy of the family systems approach.

Moreover, both reflect the maturation process that The Arc and similar advocacy organizations have experienced. From their original focus on instrumental and emotional support for parents and services for families' children with mental retardation, these organizations have become advocates for the entire family. The evidence of the two assumptions and the organizations' maturity can be found in numerous policies.

One of the earliest profamily policies is IDEA. As first enacted, IDEA provides that parents have a right to participate in educational decision making and to benefit from some of the related services that were necessary to help their children benefit from special education. Of the 22 related services that a student may receive under an Individualized Education Plan (IEP) or Individualized Family Services Plan (IFSP), 8 also provide for services to a parent or family member. IDEA's 1986 amendments authorized early intervention services for the child and family via the IFSP. Finally, IDEA authorizes the Parent Training and Information Centers. These provide training, information, and referral services for families; they also represent a reaction to professional dominance over parents in educational decision making and to the inadequacy of institutions of higher education and state departments of education in providing training and information to families.

The 1997 reauthorization of IDEA deliberately seeks to strengthen parents' participation in their children's education and to enhance their opportunities to participate in their children's education at school and at home. Among other things, it provides that parents are members of the teams that evaluate a student and decide on the student's program and placement (the nondiscriminatory evaluation team and the IEP team, respectively); their concerns must be taken into account when the team develops the student's IEP; a school must obtain their consent whenever it wants to evaluate or reevaluate the student; parents' consent to evaluation is not consent to placement into special education; and parents must constitute the majority of the membership of the state interagency coordinating council for early intervention and of the state special education advisory council. At both the microlevel (focusing on the student) and on the macrolevel (focusing on the school system), parents are regarded as collaborators with educators (professionals).

As important as IDEA is in expressing a policy of family support, it is by no means the only one. At the federal level, the children's Supplemental Security Income (SSI) program, a result of the antipoverty initiatives of the decade from the mid-1960s through the mid-1970s, has been an important source of family support. The program provides for a cash transfer to families who qualify because they meet federal poverty standards and have children who have severe disabilities. Despite Congress' shrinkage of the SSI program in 1996 (as part of welfare reform, the Personal Responsibilities and Work Opportunities Act of 1996), the SSI program still represents a federal commitment to family support. This is so because the families receive a cash transfer that they may spend as they choose. By putting expenditure power into families' hands, the SSI program helps them acquire the goods and services they need to live the kinds of lives they want to lead.

Another federal family support program is the Home and Community Based Services (HCBS) program authorized by the Medicaid (Title XIX) provisions of the Social Security Act. HCBS funds are available to families whose children (below and above the age of majority) have severe disabilities and are at risk of institutionalization. The purpose and effect of HCBS funding is to enable the family or adult person with a disability to purchase services that, in turn, make it possible for the family to maintain the person in the family's or person's own home and community. A decidedly anti-institutional program, the HCBS program itself is a form of family support.

Less obvious but still important federal family support programs are those related to child abuse and neglect, foster children, and adoption. Beginning with the failed effort to have the Supreme Court hold that Section 504 of the Rehabilitation Act Amendments of 1975 applies to the withholding or withdrawal of beneficial medical treatment for newborns with obvious disabilities (*Bowen v. American Hospital Association*, 1986), The Arc and other associations representing families and professionals launched a massive effort to secure medical treatment of the newborns and, at the same time, support for their families. Their efforts resulted in a consensus resolution on treatment of newborns with birth defects. That resolution was incorporated into the language and interpretative history of the Child Abuse Prevention and Treatment Act (CAPTA).

CAPTA provides that a state will receive federal funds for child abuse prevention and treatment if it agrees to establish a system for reporting unjustified withholding or withdrawal of medical treatment from newborns. The state system must address prevention and treatment, assuring that there will be some supports so families will receive services that will steer them away from maltreatment.

CAPTA has had another effect, albeit quite indirect. It has resulted in more newborns being "saved." That result, together with new life-prolonging technologies, has created a population that now justifies services. Infants and toddlers and their families now receive support under IDEA's early intervention authority.

Not all families with newborns or even older children with disabilities want to or can raise their children. With institutions now nearly unavailable to the families, foster care and adoption have become options for those families. For these families, then, family support consists of anti-institutional, pro-child policies, such as set out in the Adoption Assistance Program (Title IV-E, Social Security Act, Medicaid program). Moreover, the foster or adopting families themselves receive federal financial assistance to help them meet the disability-related costs of being parents. Finally, the Adoption and Safe Families Act of 1997 makes a state eligible for federal funds if it provides health care insurance to any child with special needs for whom there is an adoption agreement between the state and adopting parents. The act provides for family reunification services, themselves a type of family support. Family reunification services include family counseling, assistance to address domestic violence, temporary child care, and crisis nurseries. Accordingly, family support now includes maltreatment prevention and intervention programs and foster care and adoption services.

Another reliable indicator of family support is the extent to which the states themselves have enacted family support laws. Typically, these provide cash transfers or vouchers for families who meet income means tests and whose children meet severity-of-disability eligibility criteria. With 48 states having those programs as of 1996 (Braddock, Hemp, Parish, & Westrich, 1998), it is obvious that family support is as much a state concern as it is a federal one.

In all of these family support initiatives, there are several connecting themes. One relates to the nature of family support. It consists of cash (SSI and many state programs) and vouchers (state programs), both of which give families a degree of expenditure choice. Family support also consists of services delivered by professionals, but, in a departure from the traditional professionally dominated decision making regarding services, these services are now guided by the families' concerns, priorities, and resources, as stated by the families (such as in the early intervention IFSP provisions). The current model for these services, then, is one of family–professional collaboration, a model that intentionally redresses the imbalance of power between families (who were without much power) and professionals (who were replete with much power).

Another theme relates to the extent of family support. By extent, we do not mean the level of funding, which is inadequate. Instead, we refer to the breadth and variety of family support. To support families now seems to be an almost universal component of public policy. Programs in education (IDEA), child and family welfare (adoption and foster care), child protection (CAPTA), antipoverty (SSI), and disability intervention (state family support) now contain family support authorizations. That is remarkable testimony to a clear public policy in favor of family integrity and intactness.

A third theme has to do with the site or place for family support. In all of these programs, the place where the family is supported and where their children with disabilities receive support is a family home (biological, foster, or adoptive) and the community. The pro-institutional bias of the ancient covenant is a matter of history. The new covenant is pro-family and community based; it regards families as necessary and desirable, parent-ectomy and family-ectomy as undesirable, and home and community support as presumptively proper. You might well ask, "What more may be said about the new covenant?" And we should reply, "What are its policy and existential meanings for families? What will the future hold?"

THE FUTURE: THE NEW COVENANT

Before answering those questions, it may be helpful to review the past. The ancient covenant was that the state would "relieve" families of the "burden" of care; the form that this promise took was the institution. That promise regarded families as "the problem," as the cause of or contributors to their children's disabilities. Through the era of conversion and advocacy, a different form of family support emerged. In its early stages, its primary beneficiaries were children and adults with disabilities. Over time, its beneficiaries became those with disabilities and their families. With the identification of these beneficiaries, there came different roles that families played—organizers, providers, learners and teachers, recipients of professionals' expertise, advocates, co-decision makers, and, most recently, collaborators. And with these roles came new assumptions about families and their lives.

The basic assumption was that families and their lives are disability rooted. By disability rooted, we mean that disability is one of the most dominant forces in a family's life; it is to a very large degree the major determinant, if not (for some families) the sole determinant, of their lives. Few other traits—such as socioeconomic status (SES), race, culture, language, geography, citizenship, alienage, or family lineage—have such an impact on the family as disability; few others are so dispositive of what the family does. Of course we recognize that other factors than disability are powerful and may, for some families, be dispositive. A family's SES, race, culture, language, citizenship, or alienage does make a significant difference, and, for some families, it makes all the difference. The fact remains, however, that disability exerts a pervasive influence on nearly all families and a decisive influence on many. It is as though the child's disability disables the family. It is as though the fundamental fact about the family is this: Their roots are in disability and the support they receive should therefore be disability related.

What other assumptions accompany this basic one? One has to do with the kind of assumptions that families are able to make about themselves and their children with disabilities. During the ancient covenant era and well into the conversion and advocacy era, there was a time when families could make no assumptions, or at least they could make no assumptions except as they related to institutionalization and the roles they had to play as organization members, service developers, recipients of professionals' decision, teachers, advocates, and education decision makers.

Now, some families can assume that there will be myriad family supports available, namely, those we previously highlighted. Of course, not all families can assume that they will have access to all of these family support services; means testing (the SSI and state-law criteria), severity-of-disability criteria (the SSI and HCBS criteria), and need for service (the IDEA-related services criterion) will exclude some families. And those families who do qualify cannot assume that the services will be adequately funded.

Without gainsaying the obvious, which is that disability does profoundly affect a family, and without being unappreciative of the benefits that present family support programs confer on families, we do want to ask whether a different assumption should prevail and drive policy during the early decades of the new millennium. Remember, the present assumption is that some families will get some support because they, but not other nonqualifying families, are especially worthy. Thus, universal family support does not exist, nor does sufficiently funded family support.

But what if we were to reverse the assumption? What if we were to challenge the very premise that families are and should be disability rooted. What if we were to assume—what if we were to have the great expectation—that families would not be disability rooted? That they would not be permanently tethered to disability, that they would be able to shape their lives (to the extent anyone can shape one's life) without always having to account for disability? What if they could assume that their children would have friends and would belong in their neighborhood schools, that their children would experience transition from school to real work, living where they want to live rather than where they have to live? What if they did not face the nearly inevitable and always daunting prospect of waiting lists? What if they could assume their child or relative would have an enviable life?

Let us think about casting aside the old assumption of disability rootedness, of the chronic tether of disability. Let us instead conjure up a new image of the family. That new assumption would be that, in the next millennium, families would be no more affected by their children's disability than they are affected by the traits that their other children possess, by the musical gifts, mathematical genius, athleticism, or plain ordinariness of their other children. That assumption—that radical uprooting of the rootedness of disability within the family—would require a much more extensive and different type of family support than exists in these relatively halcyon days of 1999.

What kind of family support might be needed to uproot families' present disability rootedness? To answer that question, one must think about a different and far more extensive type of family support. That is itself an engaging prospect, for it impels us to think about the family's concerns, priorities, and resources, about its strengths, preferences, and needs. As we think about these matters, we are obliged (if we think clearly and open-mindedly) to answer this question: What would it take to make it possible for the family to be less "disabled," to be less disability rooted, less tied to the fact of disability?

To think about the type of family support is equally engaging. Given that families' concerns, priorities, and resources, their strengths, preferences, and needs, are idiosyncratic to each family, the type of support may include but not be limited to professional support; it could include informal support from unpaid friends, whether or not they are credentialed professionals. Family support then would consist of the family having the choice whether and to what degree to rely on professionals, nonprofessionals, or nobody to help them meet the challenge of disability across the entirety of their lives.

Given this approach to families, at least two implications emerge. One is that the goal of family support is to assist the family to achieve an enviable life. What is an enviable life? It is that which the particular family defines for itself, and it is therefore as variable as families themselves.

But we have an idea what it might mean for many families. As we have listened to families during the nearly 25 years of our work with each other and with families and as we ourselves have thought about these matters for our own family (we are the parents of a 31-year-old man, J.T., with mental retardation, autism, rapid cycling bipolarity, and obsessive–compulsive and challenging behaviors), we have reached a few conclusions about family support, quality of life, and enviable lives.

Perhaps the most important component of family support, of a so-called quality or enviable life, is what we call the "Cheers connection." We refer of course to the popular TV show "Cheers." The show took its title from a Boston bar, "Cheers, a place where everybody knows your name." The Cheers connection is just that: creating a life where nearly everybody knows who J.T. is and values him for himself. That life is built on connections, relationships, friendships, and commitments—the elements of what we call "reliable alliances" (A. P. Turnbull & H. R. Turnbull, 1997).

It is an exaggeration, but not much of one, for us to say that the greatest social security for J.T. is not a Social Security program, but his reliable allies. The safety net that we all need—the garment of family support that we all want to wear—is constructed from the warp and woof of human relationships. One challenge for the future is to find the ways, the language, the culture, that weaves a safety net of human relationships, for they are the strongest strands of family support. (For more thoughts on this matter, see our Epilogue in this book about public philosophy and rights.)

On a different level, the other conclusion about family support is that it must continue to be a policy priority. A nation that aspires to compassion, that subscribes to the family as the core unit of social organization, must retain and expand the family support programs it has already begun.

It should but will not go without saying that family support would have to be adequate, at least at some bare level. It would consist of a sufficiency of resources that the family could spend to meet its needs, as the family defines them and in the way the family judges it best to meet them. A well-funded family allowance, comparable to the cash transfers authorized by SSI and some state family support programs, would be the norm, not (as is the case today) a level that maintains a family at or just above the poverty level.

Unlike SSI and state family support laws, the new family support, the new allowance would be universal and available to all families (although the amount would vary according to a family's financial resources).

The new family support would not be limited according to the severity of the family member's disability. Mild mental retardation, profound mental disability, coexisting disabilities (retardation plus another)—each "severity" differs in some ways from the others, but each carries with it a degree of responsibility to the member with retardation. That is the chronicity of mental retardation, of disability.

Even the terms *severity* or *extent of need* are obsolete descriptors of persons with mental retardation. The reconceptualization of mental retardation by the American Association on Mental Retardation (AAMR) (Luckasson, 1992) should guide us in developing a new family support policy. AAMR jettisons the old "levels" or "degrees." What counts is the interaction of the person's capabilities (intelligence and adaptive skills) with the environments in which the person finds himself or herself (home, work, school, and community) and how the person can be supported to function in those environments. The emphasis is on the three-way nature of life as affected by mental retardation: capabilities, environments, and functioning with supports.

The AAMR approach has an instrumental value as far as family support goes. It teaches us that family support policy should be modeled along these lines: the family's capabilities, the family's environments, and the family's needed and preferred supports to enable it to have enviable life according to its criteria (and of course within the range of cost to the public fisc). Thus, family support would be comparable to the support that AAMR declares is the expectation, even the rightful claim, of persons with mental retardation.

The AAMR definition has more than an instrumental value, more than a policy-generation utility. It also points out that mental retardation is a condition that is, at its core, not defined so much by the degree of severity (the now-discarded mild, moderate, severe, and profound levels) as by the fact that capabilities and environment go hand in hand. Let us take that principle—that capabilities of the family go hand in hand with the family's environment—and move it into a wholly different realm of discussion.

The family's capabilities include those that it exercises to meet today's environment of challenges and opportunities. But they also include those that the family applies to the future, especially to the future time when, in the actuarially predictable course of things, the parents will predecease their child with mental retardation.

And there, in the contemplation of the future bereft of parents but full of the fact that the child with retardation survives them, the family comes face to face with the realization that their life must have some meaning, that their life as a "disabled" family must have significance.

Thus it is that many, if not most, families at some time or another, and almost always when the parents are at the edge of life, confront their existential angst, their own nagging inquiries about the meaning and consequence of their lives.

No family—however financially sound and however "mild" their member's disability—should have to come to the end of life and still ask the question that we all reluctantly ask (when we cannot avoid asking it): Have we done enough for our child with the disability, and who will care for our child after we die?

That double-barreled question is existential because it asserts that the meaning of our lives is disability rooted. And it expresses angst in the most obvious way: It reveals the profound concern that, after us, there is no one more fit to be the parent or caregiver for the survivor with a disability. How to relieve families when they face that question, when their lives are on the thin edge between the quick and the dead? And how to support them throughout their lives so that, as they live fully and eventually reach that edge, that "bourne"—that boundary—so poetically described in Hamlet's soliloquy, they will be comforted and strengthened? How to answer the existential question: What will be the consequence of my life?

The answer may lie as much in developing a life replete with reliable allies, a life characterized by a multitude of "Cheers connections," as in developing a public policy of universal family support. Both approaches—an approach that lies largely within the abilities of the family and its allies to create a place where everyone knows their child and an approach that takes what is now an exceptionalistic and limited policy and makes it universal and generous—promise to mitigate the effects of disability. Together, they may go a long way toward untethering families from the nearly dispositive and always significant fact of being disability rooted. That is a consummation devoutly to be wished in a new half century of The Arc.

REFERENCES

Adoption and Safe Families Act of 1997, 42 U.S.C. § 620 *et seq.* and § 670 *et seq.*

Americans with Disabilities Act of 1990, 42 U.S.C. § 12101 *et seq.*

Barr, M. W. (1913). *Mental defectives: Their history, treatment, and training.* Philadelphia: Blakiston.

Blatt, R., & Kaplan, F. (1966). *Christmas in purgatory.* Boston: Allyn & Bacon.

Boggs, E. (1978). Who is putting whose head in the sand? (Or in the clouds, as the case may be). In H. R. Turnbull & A. P. Turnbull (Eds.), *Parents speak out.* Columbus, OH: Merrill/Prentice-Hall.

Bowen v. American Hospital Association, 476 U.S. 610 (1986).

Braddock, D., Hemp, R., Parish, S., & Westrich, J. (1998). *The state of the states in developmental disabilities* (5th ed.). Washington, DC: American Association on Mental Retardation.

Brakel, S. J., Parry, J., & Weiner, B. A. (1985). *The mentally disabled and the law.* Chicago: American Bar Foundation.

Bricker, W. A., & Bricker, D. D. (1976). The Infant, Toddler, and Preschool Research and Intervention Project. In T. D. Tjossem (Ed.), *Intervention strategies for high risk infants and young children* (pp. 545–572). Baltimore: University Park Press.

Burgdorf, R. L. (1980). *The legal rights of handicapped persons.* Baltimore: Brookes.

Child Abuse Prevention and Treatment and Adoption Reform Act, 42 U.S.C. § 5106a.

Education for All Handicapped Children Act of 1975, 20 U.S.C. § 1400 *et seq.*

Ferguson, P. M. (1994). *Abandoned to their fate: Social policy and practice toward severely retarded people in America, 1820–1920.* Philadelphia: Temple University Press.

Goffman, E. (1961). *Asylums.* New York: Anchor Books.

Goldenson, L. H. (1965). *Remarks on the occasion of United Cerebral Palsy Associations' 15th anniversary.* Paper presented at the 15th annual meeting of the United Cerebral Palsy Associations, Los Angeles.

Hunt, J. (Ed.). (1972). *Human intelligence.* New Brunswick, NJ: Transaction Books.

Individuals with Disabilities Education Act Reauthorization of 1997, 20 U.S.C. § 1400 *et seq.*

Karnes, M. B., & Teska, J. A. (1980). Toward successful parent involvement in programs for handicapped children. In J. J. Gallagher (Ed.), *New directions for exceptional children: Parents and families of handicapped children* (Vol. 4, pp. 85–109). San Francisco: Jossey-Bass.

Kindred, M., Cohen, J., Penrod, D., & Shaffer, T. (Eds.). (1976). *The mentally retarded citizen and the law.* New York: The Free Press.

Kirk, S. A. (1984). Introspection and prophecy. In B. Blatt & R. J. Morris (Eds.), *Perspectives in special education: Personal orientations* (pp. 25–55). Glenview, IL: Scott, Foresman.

Luckasson, R. (Ed.). (1992). *Mental retardation: Definition, classification, and systems of support.* Washington, DC: American Association on Mental Retardation.

Mills v. D.C. Board of Education, 348 F. Supp. 866 (D.D.C. 1972).

Pennhurst State School and Hospital v. Halderman, 451 U.S. 1 (1981), 465 U.S. 89 (1984).

Pennsylvania Association for Retarded Children (PARC) v. Commonwealth of Pennsylvania, 334 F. Supp. 1257 (E.D. Pa. 1971), 343 F. Supp. 279 (E.D. Pa. 1972).

Personal Responsibilities and Work Opportunities Act of 1996, 110 Stat. 2105.

Rehabilitation Act Amendments of 1975, 29 U.S.C. § 701 *et seq.*

Roos, P. (1978). Parents of mentally retarded children—Misunderstood and mistreated. In H. R. Turnbull & A. P. Turnbull (Eds.), *Parents speak out.* Columbus, OH: Merrill.

Roos, P. (1985). Parents of mentally retarded children—Misunderstood and mistreated. In H. R. Turnbull and A. P. Turnbull (Eds.), *Parents speak out.* Columbus, OH: Merrill/Prentice-Hall.

Rothman, D. J. (1971). *The discovery of the asylum: Social order and disorder in the new republic.* Boston: Little, Brown.

Scheerenberger, R. C. (1983). *A history of mental retardation.* Baltimore: Brookes.

Social Security Act, Title XIX, Medicaid, codified at 42 U.S.C. § 1396(n)(b).

Turnbull, A. P., & Turnbull, H.R. (1997). *Families, professionals, and exceptionality: A special partnership.* Columbus, OH: Merrill/Prentice-Hall.

Turnbull, H. R., & Turnbull, A. P. (1998). *Free appropriate public education: Law and children with disabilities.* Denver, CO: Love.

Wolfensberger, W. (1975). *The origin and nature of our institutional models.* Syracuse, NY: Human Policy Press.

Wyatt v. Stickney, 325 F. Supp. 781 (M.D. Ala. 1971), 344 F. Supp. (M.D. Ala. 1972), aff'd. 503 F. 2d 1305 (5th Cir. 1974).

Youngberg v. Romeo, 457 U.S. 307 (1982).

Zigler, E., & Muenchow, S. (1992). *Head Start: The inside story of America's most successful educational experiment.* New York: Basic Books.

The Parent Movement in Mental Retardation

Alan Abeson and Sharon Davis

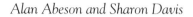

ORIGIN OF THE PARENT MOVEMENT

Prior to the organization of the first local parent groups in the United States in the 1930s and 1940s, families with children with mental retardation were alone. At that time, little was known about the condition or its causes and there were virtually no programs and activities in communities to assist in the development and care of these children and adults as well as to support their families. Today it is hard to imagine such a situation because of the extensive knowledge that now exists, the unending supply of information available, and, most significantly, the availability in many places of a wide array of programs for children and adults with mental retardation of all ages and their families.

Without question, today's opportunities are the direct result of the diligent and thoughtful work of the parents who, as they organized, gave birth to what became a national movement. While initially those parents focused primarily on obtaining or creating educational programs for their children, they simultaneously established a foundation for progress that continues to the present day. Some of those families, though, even then, formed groups to monitor and improve the institutions in which their children lived.

The creation of these groups has been described as an act of courage. It required parents "to bring their problem into the open and to challenge both the traditional image of mental defect and the rejection and discrimination practiced by society against them" (President's Committee on Mental Retardation [PCMR], 1977, p. 38). Specifically, they were challenged by the availability of few resources, as well as professional indifference, widespread ignorance, and powerful stigma directed against mentally deficient persons and to some degree themselves as well.

Aided by interested professionals, these isolated parent groups were invited to meet in Minneapolis in September 1950 to explore the organization of a national association. With 44 delegates representing 23 local organizations in 13 states, the National Association of Parents and Friends of Mentally Retarded Children, now The Arc of the United States, was born. With the founding of The Arc, an umbrella under which to organize, the parent movement grew rapidly. By 1975 approximately 218,000 members were organized in 1,700 state and local chapters.

The stated purposes of the new organization as written in The Arc's original constitution and bylaws were as follows (National Association of Parents and Friends of Mentally Retarded Children, 1950):

- To promote the general welfare of mentally retarded children of all ages everywhere;

- To further the advancement of all study, ameliorative and preventive research and therapy in the field of mental retardation;

- To develop a better understanding of the problem of mental retardation by the public and cooperate with all public, private and religious agencies, international, federal, state and local departments of education, health and institutions;

- To further the training and education of personnel for work in the field of mental retardation;

- To encourage the formation of parent groups, to advise and aid parents in the solution of their problems, and to coordinate the efforts and activities of these groups;

- To further the implementation of legislation in behalf of the mentally retarded;

- To serve as a clearinghouse for gathering and disseminating information regarding the mentally retarded, and to foster the development of integrated programs in their behalf; and

- To solicit and receive funds for the accomplishment of the above purposes.

Building on these purposes, one of the early priorities of the association was to change the public's perception of children with mental retardation. Another was to educate parents and the organization's leaders on the condition of mental retardation, as well as what was possible for people with the condition. A third major priority was to procure services for those children and adults who were denied education, work, day care, and preschool programs. Over time these priorities have evolved and now literally cover all aspects of life. The breadth of today's priorities are represented well by the current mission statement of The Arc of the United States:

The Arc of the United States works through education, research and advocacy to improve the quality of life for children and adults with mental retardation and their families and works to prevent both the causes and effects of mental retardation. (Board of Directors, The Arc, 1999)

CHANGING THE PUBLIC'S IMAGE OF CHILDREN AND ADULTS WITH MENTAL RETARDATION

From the beginning The Arc recognized the need to educate the public about mental retardation. Consequently, in 1954 a national campaign of information and appeal for children with mental retardation was begun. It sought to counter the ignorance of America as well as the negative image of "the mentally retarded individual as a destructive menace with a child's mind in a grown body" (PCMR, 1977). Using the slogan, "Retarded children *can* be helped," the campaign sought to present children as innocent beings who have the right to love and affection. Further, the message was that these children should not be discriminated against, because neither they nor their families could help the presence of mental retardation. With the emergence of this message and the association itself, a number of well-known people came forward to tell or write about children with mental retardation in their families. These included noted author Pearl Buck; actress Dale Rogers; Rose Kennedy, the mother of Rosemary and President John Kennedy; and Muriel Humphrey, wife of Senator and Vice President Hubert Humphrey and grandmother of Vicki. Although these portrayals were essentially of helpless children who elicited pity, many believe it was a first step in changing the public's image and understanding. If nothing more was communicated, at least the public began to become aware that mental retardation could occur in any family.

As the organization grew, the founders' children became adults who did not want to be viewed as "perpetual" children. Equally significant was the desire to do away with promoting images of pity because of the emergence of the critical concept that people with mental retardation are citizens like all other citizens, with rights defined and protected by law. Reflecting this logic, in 1973 the name of the organization was changed from the National Association for Retarded Children, the name adopted in 1951, to the National Association for Retarded Citizens. Additionally, in 1975 the board of directors banned the use of poster children. The image of an individual with mental retardation projected by the organization at that time was of a person impaired by the condition of mental retardation but having the basic human and civil rights of all citizens.

Today, The Arc is still striving for full acceptance of people with mental retardation. National media campaigns of recent years depict people with mental retardation as citizens and participants in their communities and often speaking for themselves. The association recognizes that children and adults with mental retardation are not yet receiving the respect to which they are entitled as human beings, that society generally remains ignorant about their capabilities, and that they can live fulfilling lives in the same communities and neighborhoods as all other people. Simply stated, The Arc's messages of today are that people with mental retardation are entitled to the same basic legal, civil, and human rights as other citizens, and that if they need supports, services, and protection to fully exercise their rights and responsibilities, they should have them.

Although all of society is not yet educated about people with mental retardation, progress has been achieved. Contributing significantly was the passage in 1975 of the Education for All Handicapped Children Act, which mandated the education of all children with mental retardation in the nation's public schools regardless of the severity of their disability. Because of that law, it can be posited that all children who began public school since 1975 have had the opportunity to learn and get to know children with mental retardation. Thus, it can be anticipated that in the future the entire population will have greater understanding and that, as a result, people with mental retardation will gain greater acceptance living, learning, working, and playing in communities across the country.

EDUCATING FAMILIES, LEGISLATORS, PROFESSIONALS, AND THE PUBLIC

Due to the paucity of responsible information about mental retardation available to families and the general public, the parent organization in the 1950s became the producer and disseminator of information. In fact, parents became the experts and provided information to other parents, policy makers, professionals, the media, and the general public.

Always a challenge faced by The Arc has been to eradicate myths associated with mental retardation. For example, The Arc was instrumental in defining mental retardation as a condition, not a disease, a critical distinction with massive implications for designing and delivering supports and services. Parents in the organization emphasized that learning could occur and thus there was a need for education and training to promote the growth of people with mental retardation. Today, because the "not in my back yard" syndrome is still encountered, particularly regarding residential arrangements, The Arc is continuing to work to dispel stereotypical notions about criminality, behavior, and property values.

Although The Arc today still serves as a clearinghouse for gathering and disseminating information regarding mental retardation, a key aspect of its mission, it is no longer the only organization filling this need. In fact, today if parents are even marginally aware of the information resources available, their challenge becomes sorting through it all to obtain what they need. The availability of federal funds in particular has led to the creation of numerous national and state organizations with the primary function of providing information to families in particular. Whereas in the beginning there was little professional literature, that situation is different today. As with parent organizations, numerous professional groups now exist, and all produce information. However, despite all of these resources, in communities across the nation, parents are often still the primary educators, reaching out to new families and providing them with direct attention and information.

ADVOCACY FOR SERVICES

The parent movement spearheaded by The Arc as the leading national disability family organization is considered the key force behind the development, expansion, and refinement of services and supports for people with mental retardation and their families (Braddock, Hemp, Parish, & Westrich, 1998). Parents helped create legislation and called on professionals to develop services needed by families. The advocacy efforts of parents are well documented in the priorities and positions taken by the national organization over the past nearly 50 years.

Education

In the 1950s, diagnostic evaluation and education were key concerns of families. In 1949, 24 states provided education to children classified as "educable," with IQs of 50 to 75, but no state mandated education for children with IQs below 50. The Arc's position was that the opportunity to learn is a universal right and that all children can learn, if not academic skills, then daily living and life-adjustments skills. This was stated in the organization's first position statement on education in 1953: "Every American child, including every retarded child, has the right to help, stimulation and guidance from skilled teachers provided by his community and state as part of a broadly conceived program of free public education" (National Association for Retarded Children, 1953).

In the early days of the parent movement, chapters of The Arc organized classes for children denied public education wherever space could be found—in church basements, vacant buildings, and abandoned one-room schoolhouses. They demonstrated that children with mental retardation could learn. By 1959, 49 states provided classes for children considered educable and 37 states provided classes for children considered "trainable" (IQs of 25 to 50). This still left children with the most severe disabilities unserved in many states, and no state served children classified as "dependent" retarded (IQs under 20). They were considered to be totally unable to learn, needing only custodial care (PCMR, 1977).

Part of the problem of states' providing adequate education for children with mental retardation was the lack of qualified teachers. New educational methods and approaches were necessary in order to individualize instruction for children who exhibited diverse learning styles, functional levels, and needs. In response, The Arc advocated for legislation and funding and in 1958, Public Law (P.L.) 85-926, To Encourage Expansion of Teaching in the Education of Mentally Retarded Children Through Grants to Institutions of Higher Learning and to State Education Agencies, was enacted (Weintraub, Abeson, Ballard, & LaVor, 1976). It was the first federal legislation passed that provided support for university training programs for leaders and teachers in special education for children with mental retardation. Most important, this law also established a federal role in dealing with people with mental retardation and their families in the United States.

The Arc continued to advocate for education for all children with mental retardation. Particularly influential were decisions made by several state chapters that, along with The Arc of the United States, brought successful right to education litigation in federal courts. Most notable was the case brought by The Arc of Pennsylvania (*Pennsylvania Association for Retarded Children v. Commonwealth of Pennsylvania*, 1971) that sustained the right of all children with mental retardation to a public education. A 1974 goal of the association called for mandatory education laws in each state based on the zero-reject concept, meaning that all children, regardless of the severity of their disability, were entitled to a free appropriate public education. In 1975 the advocacy begun by parents in the 1950s succeeded with the passage of P.L. 94-142, the Education for All Handicapped Children Act (now the Individuals with Disabilities Education Act, IDEA), which required all schools accepting federal funds under the act to educate all children with disabilities, and all truly meant all!

Now that children could get in the schoolhouse door, parents turned their attention to improving the quality of the education their children were receiving. They became concerned that segregated classes in which most children with mental retardation were placed simply were not helping children prepare for life outside the school. In 1978 The Arc developed a position paper on mainstreaming students with mental retardation in public schools. The paper discussed the pros and cons and called for a "national evaluation effort to assess the efficacy of mainstreaming" (National Association for Retarded Citizens, 1978).

By 1990 The Arc's position statement on education stated that each student with a disability belongs in an age-appropriate classroom with peers who are not disabled and has the right to receive individualized education that provides choices, meets the student's needs, and offers the necessary support (Association for Retarded Citizens of the United States, 1990). In 1992 the association began analyzing data published in the *Annual Report to Congress on the Implementation of the Individuals with Disabilities Education Act* to determine the extent to which children with mental retardation were being educated in regular classrooms with nondisabled peers. Family members and other advocates were shocked when The Arc's first annual report card on inclusion in education, 17 years after the law was enacted, documented that only 6.7% of students with mental retardation were placed in regular classrooms in school year 1989–1990 (Davis, 1992). In the ensuing years, although still disappointing, The Arc has noted a gradual increase in use of the regular classroom for these children with 10.25% in regular classes in the 1995–1996 school year.

It appears obvious that schools have interpreted the law in a manner that assumes segregated settings are appropriate placements for students with mental retardation. This is in spite of the fact that IDEA requires school districts to consider placing a child with disabilities in a regular classroom setting with the use of supplementary aids and services before exploring other more restrictive alternatives. Parents in The Arc believe that children with mental retardation who receive an appropriate education in integrated settings will be better prepared for adult life in the community. Furthermore, children without disabilities will learn to accept individual differences and appreciate the strengths and abilities of their classmates with disabilities.

The Arc continues to advocate for inclusion of children with mental retardation in regular classes, and by the Year 2000 The Arc's goal is that 50% will be included (The Arc, 1995b). Achieving this goal will be difficult, particularly because many educators remain resistant. Further, general problems that have emerged with school discipline, having little or nothing to do with children with mental retardation, have contributed to diminished emphasis on implementing inclusion for children with disabilities. In fact, to some degree, these problems have led to efforts to significantly amend IDEA that, if successful, could remove some of the basic protections built into the statute in 1975. The Arc's families recognize that, as difficult as it was to achieve these legislative guarantees, continued vigilance is necessary for their preservation.

Living Arrangements

When The Arc was founded, it supported parents' making decisions regarding living arrangements based on their children's needs. At that time, institutions were considered an integral part of a complete service system. Institutional committees were formed by many chapters of The Arc as a way to contribute amenities not provided by state government and also to provide a corps of volunteers.

By the late 1950s, parents concerned about conditions in institutions advocated for legislatively based reforms of institution practices. They worked steadily to improve the humane quality of institutions and to transform their missions from custody to training and from medically based approaches to the developmental model. The 1960s brought several exposes of intolerable conditions in institutions, and by the 1970s The Arc and its state chapters participated in a number of class action suits to improve institutional conditions, including eliminating the practice of using residents as unpaid laborers. In 1969 The Arc became a founding member of the Accreditation Council on Facilities for the Mentally Retarded. This organization, now the Council on Quality and Leadership in Supports for People with Disabilities, was established specifically to develop standards and serve as the accrediting body for residential and other services provided to people with mental retardation.

In 1974 the association's goals related to residential services called for improving existing residential services, including institutional programs. However, the focus was beginning to change, with the goal also calling for developing new, smaller community-based residential models as part of a continuum of services. By 1983 many families concluded that it was futile to continue trying to improve institutions. At The Arc's annual meeting that year, delegates passed a resolution calling for the phasing out of large institutions because of their lack of success in providing essential developmental opportunities needed by persons who are retarded. The call was for alternative community residential services. The Arc assumed some responsibility to help communities learn about optional residential opportunities and how to provide them.

The association also called for appropriately trained program staff and expressed concern that during the phase-out quality care should be provided to people still residing in institutions.

The Arc's 1989 position statement on residential living arrangements advocated for public policy providing full funding to support the development of community-based residential programs for people with mental retardation to grow, develop, and enjoy life. Also stated was that all people have a right to live in their local communities with nondisabled citizens and called for phasing out those services, activities, and environments that "inappropriately remove children and adults from their homes and neighborhoods, . . . would not be considered acceptable for persons within the same age range when they are not disabled and prevent or hinder normalized social support networks, family systems, peer relationships and friendships" (Association for Retarded Citizens of the United States, 1989).

By 1995, in the continuing evolution of The Arc's position, the organization expressed the belief that large congregate facilities (institutions) were not appropriate for anyone, regardless of the type or severity of a person's disabilities. All people with mental retardation, children and adults, have a right to live in their local communities with nondisabled citizens and be fully included. However, families should not be criticized for using institutional placements when this was the only option offered (The Arc, 1995a).

Even as The Arc's position was evolving, large state-operated institutions and psychiatric facilities serving people with mental retardation were closing and being downsized. From 1960 to 1997, 138 such institutions in 37 states closed. From a high of 228,500 children and adults who lived in institutions in 1967, only 57,236 lived in such settings in 1997. Conversely, the number of people living in various community alternatives outside their family's homes was increasing, and in 1997 individuals living in settings of 1 to 6 people numbered 194,968 (Prouty & Lakin, 1998).

Although rarely acknowledged, the downsizing of institutions brought recognition that families were the main caregivers of the family member with mental retardation. The reality was that most families raised their children at home, which led The Arc to recognize the value of in-home care in a 1983 position statement on family support. It stated that for most children with mental retardation, as for most normal children, growing up in a natural or adoptive family home is the most normal and least restrictive living arrangement. The Arc called for support services on an individualized and prescriptive basis to encourage and assist families to maintain their children at home. The Arc's current position calls for giving families control of the services they receive that promote inclusion in the community.

For more than 30 years, the federal Medicaid program, which has been the focus of intense advocacy by The Arc, has influenced institutions and community living arrangements. Medicaid, established in 1965, is a shared federal–state program that provides acute health care and long-term services and supports for people with mental retardation, most of whom qualify because of limited income. While it has been strongly supported by The Arc through the years, it has also been criticized for its "institutional" bias. For example, in 1996, 73% of total federal–state Intermediate Care Facilities for Persons with Mental Retardation (ICFs/MR) funding under Medicaid was used to operate public and private institutions (Braddock et al., 1998). For close to 20 years, families of The Arc have been calling for more Medicaid funds to be allocated to community services instead of institutions. In 1981 a major change in the Medicaid program was achieved with the creation of the optional Home and Community Based Services (HCBS) waiver, which allows states to use Medicaid funds for a wide array of community services and supports. States have gradually increased their use of the HCBS waiver until now all states participate in the program. Even with use of the waiver, most states have long waiting lists for individuals requesting waiver funding and community opportunities.

As indicated, there remains a great need for more community living opportunities for adults with mental retardation. They are needed most by people still living in institutions and by older adults living at home with older parents. Many of these parents struggle to care for themselves, let alone their adult child. Data gathered in Maryland in 1997 reveals that 40% of families on the waiting list needed services immediately. The caregivers were 60 years or older and in poor health, and their sons and daughters had significantly more behavior problems than others on the waiting list. Significant numbers of younger adults living at home, people who prior to the era of mandatory public education could have gone to institutions, are now also in need of places to live in usual communities. Further, their parents, unlike earlier generations, are aggressively seeking such options. The Arc collected information from the states indicating that approximately 70,000 people were on lists waiting for residential services in 1997 (Davis, 1997).

Documenting the severity of this problem led The Arc in late 1997 to create a national campaign, "A Key of Our Own/Unlock the Waiting List," to reduce and eliminate these waiting lists. Using the political clout of families to pursue public support, The Arc and many of its state chapters chose to tell the story of the people on the waiting list and their families to the media, who in turn would tell the story to the public. Putting a personal face on the crisis was how this tactic began to be described. With public understanding came political action, which by 1998 had already achieved commitments of close to a half billion dollars in New Jersey, New York, Maryland, and Massachusetts.

With new approaches to meeting the needs of people with mental retardation that center on creating supports and services rather than being assigned to a "slot" in a community agency, creative approaches to living in the community now know no limits. Fundamental to these approaches is recognizing and involving the individual with the disability in decision making about his or her life. Supporting this direction is The Arc's position on self-determination that says all people with mental retardation can express preferences and use those preferences to make choices. The Arc's position also expresses the belief that people with mental retardation must have community experiences, supports and accommodations, opportunities to advocate for themselves, and control over financial resources (The Arc, 1998a). Increasingly, these beliefs about self-determination are being demonstrated as individuals with their families are receiving vouchers from government to purchase the services and supports that they want to meet their needs as they define them.

Employment

Work has always been considered appropriate for the majority of people with mental retardation. Although many individuals may not be able to master academic programs, they can perform a variety of productive tasks. The parent movement began to address this issue when it became obvious that children who received education were leaving the schools with nothing to do. Parents began to advocate for development of vocational training and sheltered employment programs.

The vocational rehabilitation system was already in place in the 1950s, primarily serving people with physical disabilities. When it was directed to offer services to people with mental retardation as well as those with physical disabilities, some state vocational rehabilitation agencies were concerned that some people with mental retardation could not be considered employable in any setting, including sheltered workshops. In response, The Arc advocated for the development of training centers and sheltered workshops to serve individuals with mental retardation that would be the responsibility of the vocational rehabilitation system.

In 1965 The Arc of the United States created a program to encourage employers to hire job-ready workers with mental retardation by offering stipends to cover on-the-job training costs. Since then, this program has served more than 52,000 individuals with mental retardation, demonstrating that they are competent workers and can fulfill a wide array of jobs. Based on such experiences, over time many families and employers have slowly changed their perspective on employment of people with mental retardation.

The Arc's employment-related goals in 1974 called for increased employment of people with mental retardation, improved levels of employment, and expansions of vocational and prevocational training. At the same time, the goal called for continuing and expanding efforts to increase work opportunities in noncompetitive settings (e.g., sheltered workshops, work activity centers).

Over the next 10 years, family expectations continued to change. The Arc's 1984 position statement related to employment recognized that "regardless of the severity of the handicapping condition, all persons who are retarded should be provided the opportunity for work-related training." The position called for sheltered workshops to develop a wide variety of training and work opportunities to maximize work skills, pay, and placement in outside employment. The position also recognized the problems of low pay and productivity in workshops and called for wages commensurate with those paid for similar work performed by nondisabled workers and a study of disincentives to productivity.

The supported employment initiative began in the 1980s, making clear that even many people with significant mental retardation could enter and maintain competitive work. This contributed to strengthening family expectations regarding employment, and today The Arc's position statement on employment states that, "with appropriate education, training, technology and support, the vast majority of working-age people with mental retardation can be competitively employed" (1996, XI). People with mental retardation should have the opportunity to work based on their own preferences, interests, and strengths, to support themselves and to meet their own needs. The position further urges the conversion of traditional services to the provision of competitive employment in inclusive settings. This is the Arc's strongest stand to date regarding employability of people with mental retardation.

While supported employment has demonstrated the vocational potential of thousands of individuals with mental retardation, a network of sheltered workshop and day activity programs still exists, meaning many individuals still do not receive the benefits of supported employment. This is an issue that families will continue to address.

Another emerging issue is that of retirement from work of the person with mental retardation. As people with mental retardation are living longer, primarily due to better health, they are reaching the age at which people without disabilities retire from the workforce. The Arc's current position statement on employment advocates that people with mental retardation be provided access to pension plans as afforded other older citizens who have worked and retire. For workers in the competitive workforce, pensions are often available as they age. The majority of individuals with mental retardation, however, are still unemployed or participating in sheltered employment. How they occupy their daytime hours as they age is a concern that families must address in the future.

Recreation and Leisure

Not surprisingly, family concerns about recreation and leisure emerged after education, residential living, and employment were addressed by The Arc. For years, families were the source of recreation and leisure for people with mental retardation. As they grew, chapters of The Arc also began to offer recreational activities. Although siblings and other family members could participate, typically the outside community was excluded. Rarely did people with mental retardation venture into the community to participate in available programs and activities.

The association's first position statement addressing recreation was in 1972. The issue arose because federal funds were available to communities to support recreational activities, and few people with mental retardation were being included in tax-supported, public recreational facilities and programs. The position recognized that "recreational pursuits promote optimal physical health and provide a broad spectrum of educational and social learning experiences which assist persons to take their place in society as productive, well-adjusted adults" (National Association for Retarded Children, 1972). The position called for federally funded recreational projects to consider and provide for the special recreational needs of people with mental retardation, to eliminate architectural barriers, and to actively seek participation of people with mental retardation (in these special programs). Chapters were called on to monitor the delivery of recreational services in their communities.

The Arc's 1974 goal expanded on this position by stating that recreation leaders should have optimistic expectations about what people with mental retardation can do. The Arc also said that programs operated by chapters should demonstrate what can be done and involve the appropriate community agency at the earliest possible date. A wide spectrum of activities should be offered, as for all other people, and higher education should offer programs to train future recreation leaders about mental retardation.

By that time a number of chapters of The Arc were collaborating with Special Olympics International, Inc., in sponsoring Special Olympics sports programs. Founded in 1968, Special Olympics' mission is to provide children and adults with mental retardation year-round sports training and competition opportunities. Until 1990 only people with mental retardation were allowed to participate in the sports offerings. In that year Special Olympics initiated Unified Sports, a program including athletes with and without disabilities on the same sports teams. The aim is to provide athletes with disabilities the opportunity for meaningful training and competition with nondisabled teammates to assist integration into their communities.

The Arc's current position is that people with mental retardation should have opportunities to participate in the same recreational and leisure activities that are offered to all citizens. Inclusive recreational and leisure activities are an essential component of a quality life for people with mental retardation. Organizations providing segregated recreational and leisure activities are encouraged to develop inclusive options. Strategies should be developed to assist people to make the transition to inclusive recreation and leisure, including competitive sports (The Arc, 1998b). An example of one strategy is the current collaboration of The Arc and Special Olympics International to promote inclusive sports activities.

Many younger families in particular, having raised their children in an era where the expectation is inclusion rather than segregation, seek inclusive sports and recreational options for their family members. Because they know no other way, they will continue to drive the parent movement to promote inclusive recreational and leisure activities in the year 2000 and beyond.

FROM FUTILITY TO FULFILLMENT

The changes that have occurred since the formation of The Arc of the United States in 1950 were likely unimaginable to families of the past. Along with the availability of an amazing array of supports and services, a remarkable shift has occurred in expectations for people with mental retardation. Although they were once thought of as hopelessly dependent, it is now recognized that with education, support, and opportunity all people with mental retardation can live and enjoy life in usual neighborhoods in usual communities. Many can also be successfully employed, participate in volunteer and civic activities, and essentially live like all other Americans. Most remarkable about the continuous evolution of the paradigm of expectation has been the increasing recognition that people with mental retardation can make decisions about their own lives with help and support from families and friends when needed. As children and adults increasingly engage in self-determination about their own lives, their families can anticipate tensions similar to those experienced between all parents and children. The well-known temptation to ensure protection for family members with mental retardation is going to be severely tested.

Such tension is in and of itself symbolic of another historic shift that calls for children and adults to grow up, go to school, work, and play in usual communities. Although some large institutions still operate, it is clear that they will follow the now well-defined path of closing. The once popular group home for about six people that was the early mainstay of community residences is gradually giving way to wonderful options including supported houses and apartments, adult foster homes, and even people owning their own homes. Another innovation with much appeal is assisting families to maintain their family member with mental retardation by making in-home supports available to them.

Early in the history of the parent movement, families discovered that, even as they and their children with mental retardation had many similarities, they also had many differences. The simple reality that is always taught to professionals-to-be in mental retardation is that each person is an individual. That not-so-remarkable principle has often been overlooked in developing programs that in a sense assumed that all people with mental retardation "fit" into the same educational, vocational preparation, recreational, or living program. New recognition of individualism coupled with self-determination is leading to providing people with mental retardation, and their families and friends, with the opportunity to make decisions about the kind of services and supports they choose. The basis for this approach is that the people who are to receive the service and support, along with those who know them, are in the best position to know what is needed. They are the people who should plan, design, engage, and evaluate the services and supports received. In essence, no longer are people placed in program "slots"; rather, they determine their needs, locate the services and supports they design and use, and receive public funds to purchase them.

This new order featuring the community, self-determination, and individual choice will of course bring with it new challenges for the parent movement. First and foremost is the likelihood that it can no longer be referred to as the parent movement. No longer, for example, does The Arc of the United States refer to working *on behalf of* children and adults with mental retardation. Now the association's work is described as being done *with and for* people with mental retardation. Rightfully, with self-determination comes the opportunity, with and without support, for people with mental retardation to become a part of the movement.

Just as families with children and siblings with mental retardation who practice self-determination experience tension, so too will the future movement. Already, disagreements have occurred regarding the use of alternative, momentarily less offensive

terminology to describe people with mental retardation. Difficulties can also be anticipated due to the reality of the disability in enabling people with mental retardation
to deal with highly complex issues. Although support should always be available when
needed to help people understand complexity, there is a line, often not easily established, between being supportive and being coercive. Similarly, the easy tendency to
celebrate and reinforce inadequate participation and contributions by people with
mental retardation merely because they tried is inappropriate, condescending, and
ultimately exploitative of these people and must be avoided.

Today, many professionals working in the mental retardation community no
longer talk of a movement, but rather of "the industry." Given the estimate that
$22.78 billion of public money was spent in 1996 on people with mental retardation
and developmental disabilities (Braddock et al., 1998), it is easy to understand how
the effort can be described as an industry. It is big business that was essentially created
by parents. Increasingly at issue now is the role of parents in the operation of this business enterprise. Historically, after parents launched programs, they moved from operations to policy making and oversight as members of boards of directors. With the
growing size of these enterprises, coupled with the general satisfaction many families
enjoy with the programs in which their family members are served, their participation
is giving way to professionals. At risk is whether the voices of families and of people
with mental retardation will be heard in the future. It is known that although some
professionals within the field dismiss family views, others recognize their importance.

The strength of the advocacy conducted by the parent movement has always been
the parents telling their story. Adding to that asset today are people with mental retardation who also have compelling stories to share. Even if there were no other reason
to keep families actively involved, they and the field's professionals must recognize this
key ingredient in continuing to pursue and achieve positive change. As Wehman and
Kregel (1994) wrote, the "true power to change a human service system lies within the
consumers who receive the services" (p. 240). This is the principle that must guide
families, consumers, and the professionals the who serve them.

As rich as the landscape is for some people with mental retardation and their families in the United States, it is clearly uneven across the country. Frequently, it is
uneven within communities. Advocating to remove this bias remains a major national
need. Another equally important objective for continuing advocacy is accepting the
reality that people with mental retardation are by definition vulnerable. To level
opportunities across the country, to assure that the progress made to date is not lost,
and to continue to advance require perpetual vigilance. That is the future! People with
mental retardation will always be a part of humanity; they will always require supports
and services and protection from discrimination and exploitation. Equally true is that
there will likely always be needs to fulfill that are just emerging. All people with mental retardation of all ages, for example, are in need of accessible, affordable, and quality health care not yet available. All children with mental retardation are entitled to
an appropriate education, yet few are receiving it. All people with mental retardation
should be able to live in the community, a goal now far from being reached. And all

families should be able to age without fear or concern about the future of their loved ones after they pass away.

Fulfillment for some has been achieved, but not for all. The parent movement will continue, jointly with people with mental retardation and the professionals who serve them. Even as the 50th anniversary of The Arc of the United States is celebrated, when considered in the light of the future, it must be thought of as only "the first 50 years."

REFERENCES

The Arc. (1995a). *Where people live* (Position Statement). Arlington, TX: Author.

The Arc. (1995b). *Year 2000 Strategic Plan.* Arlington, TX: Author.

The Arc. (1996). *Employment* (Position Statement). Arlington, TX: Author.

The Arc. (1998a). *Self-determination* (Position Statement). Arlington, TX: Author.

The Arc. (1998b). *Inclusive recreation and leisure* (Position Statement). Arlington, TX: Author.

Association for Retarded Citizens of the United States. (1984). *Work and employment-related activities* (Position Statement). Arlington, TX: Author.

Association for Retarded Citizens of the United States. (1989). *Residential Living Arrangements* (Position Statement). Arlington, TX: Author.

Association for Retarded Citizens of the United States. (1990). *Education* (Position Statement). Arlington, TX: Author.

Board of Directors, The Arc. (1999). *Mission statement.* Arlington, TX: The Arc.

Braddock, D., Hemp, R., Parish, S., & Westrich, J. (1998). *The state of the states in developmental disabilities.* Washington, DC: American Association on Mental Retardation.

Davis, S. (1992). *1992 report card on inclusion in education of students with mental retardation.* Arlington, TX: The Arc.

Davis, S. (1997). *A status report to the nation on people with mental retardation waiting for community services.* Arlington, TX: The Arc.

Education for All Handicapped Children Act of 1975, 20 U.S.C. § 1400 *et seq.*

Individuals with Disabilities Education Act, 20 U.S.C. § 1400 *et seq.*

National Association for Retarded Children. (1953). *Education bill of rights for the retarded* (Position Paper). New York: Author.

National Association for Retarded Children. (1972). *Recreation* (Position Paper). Arlington, TX: Author.

National Association for Retarded Citizens. (1978). *Mainstreaming mentally retarded students in the public schools* (Position Paper). Arlington, TX: Author.

National Association of Parents and Friends of Retarded Children. (1950). *Constitution and bylaws.* Minneapolis: Author.

Pennsylvania Association for Retarded Children v. Commonwealth of Pennsylvania, 334 F. Supp. 1257 (E.D. Pa. 1971), 343 F. Supp. 279 (E.D. Pa. 1972).

President's Committee on Mental Retardation. (1977). *MR 76: Mental retardation past and present.* Washington, DC: Author.

Prouty, R., & Lakin, K. C. (Eds.). (1998). *Residential services for people with developmental disabilities: Status and trends through 1997.* Minneapolis: University of Minnesota, Research and Training Center on Community Living, Institute on Community Integration.

Wehman, P., & Kregel, J. (1994). Toward a national agenda for supported employment. *Journal of Vocational Reha-bilitation*, 4(4), 231–242.

Weintraub, F. J., Abeson, A., Ballard, J., & LaVor, M. (1976). *Public policy and the education of exceptional children*. Reston, VA: The Council for Exceptional Children.

Education Issues

Early Childhood Intervention: Evolution of a System

Michael J. Guralnick

The difficulties faced by parents of young children with general developmental delays seemed nearly overwhelming only 25 years ago. The general absence of a coherent, sensitive, and responsive system of early intervention services and supports for young children with developmental delays meant that few families during that period had the resources necessary to help manage the complex and often stressful circumstances they encountered (Gorham, Des Jardins, Page, Pettis, & Scheiber, 1975). Even the limited services that were available for young children with developmental delays were rarely organized and integrated in a meaningful way. In essence, the burden was placed on families to seek out knowledgeable professionals and to integrate the health, educational, and social services and supports that were required.

Kathryn Gorham (then Director of Community Relations for the Montgomery County [Maryland] Association for Retarded Citizens—now Montgomery County Arc) and her colleagues reflected the views of parents 25 years ago:

> The services available to handicapped [sic] children today are short in supply and low in quality or, worse, dehumanizing, as are most of our institutions. Since parents encounter a gulf of non-assistance as they look for services in their communities, it is inevitable that they will feel the message: Society does not view their children as worthy of investment; in fact, it disdains those with certain handicaps. The parent, in turn, feels devalued and often is as he proceeds about the business of looking for help for this child. (Gorham et al., 1975, pp. 154–155)

The shortage of well-trained professionals, particularly those trained within an interdisciplinary framework, created problems for families at every turn. The diagnostic and assessment process was often unsatisfactory, repetitive, and ambiguous, frequently resulting in multiple labels leading nowhere. Parents were hardly partners with professionals in this process, and had to become unusually assertive to have input in any form. Moreover, when communication between parents and professionals did occur, it often took the form of professionals communicating low expectations about the child's development and placing arbitrary limits on long-term independence. Thoughtful consideration of family strengths and needs was unusual. When early intervention services were available, they were inevitably provided in segregated settings, contributing further to the growing sense of isolation from the larger community experienced by many families and their children. Finally, there was limited appreciation of the broad developmental and ecological forces, including stressors, that influence the development of children, and of the fact that these forces act in a similar fashion irrespective of a child's disability. This emphasis on "difference" was a pervasive one, further reinforcing the social isolation of families and establishing a barrier to creative solutions to problems that may have emerged from the larger community of child development professionals.

Before any thoughtful system of early intervention services and supports can be established, it is essential to understand the stressors facing families that can adversely affect a child's development. In many respects, progress in developing an effective early intervention system during the past 25 years has paralleled recognition of these family-related stressors and their impact on child developmental outcomes. In this chapter, I attempt to characterize these stressors, evaluate their impact on the development of children with primarily general developmental (cognitive) delays, and examine the emergence and effectiveness of the contemporary early intervention system as a response to those stressors. In the final section, I discuss some of the work that remains to be accomplished in the field of early childhood intervention, addressing both the acquisition of new knowledge and the implementation of existing knowledge.

FRAMEWORK FOR EARLY INTERVENTION

Stressors Affecting Families

The potential stressors confronting families created by the presence of a young child with a developmental delay are now thoroughly appreciated. Although there are many ways to organize these stressors, four interrelated components can be identified (Guralnick, 1997c, 1998). First, families must seek out and make sense of an enormous amount of information. Resolving issues surrounding the diagnostic process, addressing their child's health concerns, struggling to identify capable professionals and programs, and sorting through and coordinating professionals' recommendations and therapeutic activities all constitute significant challenges for families. Information is needed at many levels, not the least of which is guidance with respect to the day-to-day parent–child questions and problems that arise as part of routine child-rearing experiences. For example, parents wish to understand what adjustments are needed when their child displays substantial unevenness in the various domains of development (e.g., unusually limited expressive language), how to manage attentional or behavioral difficulties, or how to interpret behaviors not observed in their child's siblings. Navigating through this "crisis of information" and searching for a coherent array of services and supports for their child can produce substantial levels of stress (Hanson & Hanline, 1990; Sontag & Schacht, 1994).

Second, interpersonal and family distress is often experienced. The diagnostic and assessment process is extraordinarily stressful and can easily challenge a family's coping resources (Turnbull et al., 1993). Moreover, the meaning and impact of a diagnosis of a child with a disability often differ between mothers and fathers, as does the process related to reevaluating child expectations and family functioning that often follows. This process and the differing perspectives within the family can result in interpersonal and family distress and may contribute as well to a pattern of increasing social isolation (e.g., Hodapp, Dykens, Evans, & Merighi, 1992). Furthermore, a shared stigma (Goffman, 1963) can arise, creating problems of self-esteem and a tendency of the family to withdraw from different aspects of their support system. Unquestionably, even in the absence of an early intervention system, many families adapt well to these circumstances, drawing upon personal and material resources. Nevertheless, unresolved interpersonal and family distress characterizes a substantial number of families of children with developmental delays.

Third, additional stress is placed on existing family resources. The need to alter usual family schedules and routines and the time and energy required to identify various therapeutic services and transport their child to these services complicates matters for busy families. A need for respite care or for assistance with siblings tends to increase as well. Parents may also delay returning to work to accommodate these additional responsibilities (Kelly & Booth, 1997). As a consequence of this lost income, as well as added financial responsibilities related to the care of their child (Birenbaum, Guyot, & Cohen, 1990), considerable stress on a family's resources is common.

Fourth, these three classes of stressors threaten the very essence of sound parenting—that is, the ability to maintain a sense of control, confidence, and mastery over the persistent and often surprising parenting challenges. This personal sense of loss can be devastating and may have widespread adverse effects on relationships with all family members.

Impact of Stressors

Having identified these four potential types of stressors, it is important to examine not only their impact on a child's development but also, and more important from the perspective of early intervention, the mechanisms through which these stressors operate to create adverse influences on child development. One approach is to consider stressors in the context of a developmental model of child development (Guralnick, 1998). As indicated in Figure 3.1, it is suggested that stressors exert their influence on child development by disturbing one or more of three cardinal *family interaction patterns*. Of course, stressors associated with a child's disability are not the only factors that influence family interaction patterns. As discussed in a later section, a number of *family characteristics* unrelated to a child's disability are also vital and can either mitigate or exacerbate those stressors linked to circumstances associated with a child's disability.

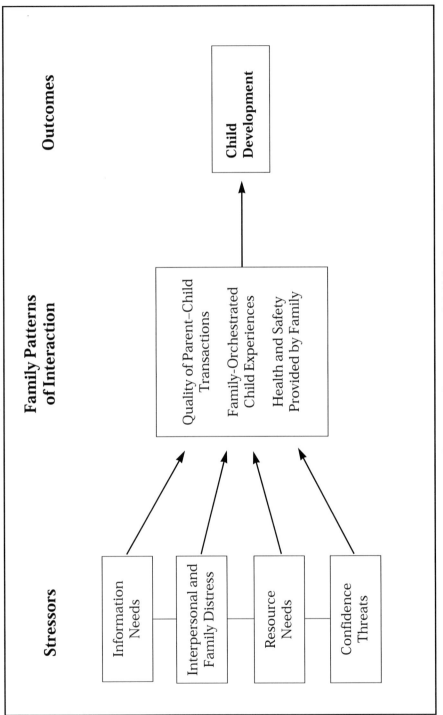

FIGURE 3.1. The relationships among stressors, family patterns of interaction, and child developmental outcomes.

Emphasized here, however, are the effects of stressors uniquely created by the presence of a child with a disability on family patterns of interaction.

First, stressors can operate to alter the quality of parent–child transactions. Of note, these proximal patterns of parent–child transactions have been carefully investigated, constructs have been defined, and associations with child developmental outcomes for all children have been well established. These relationship constructs include those related to ensuring contingent responding, establishing reciprocity, being nonintrusive and affectively warm, providing developmentally appropriate exchanges, and being discourse based (e.g., Baumrind, 1993; Clarke-Stewart, 1988; Wachs, 1992). However, any of the four types of stressors created by a child with a disability discussed above can create circumstances in which less than optimal parent–child transactions take place. Stressors related to information needs are perhaps most influential. For example, the absence of information with respect to how best to read their child's cues, how to interpret the child's inability to exhibit emotional expressions that bond child and parent together, or how to establish joint attention to foster receptive language can all contribute to a nonoptimal quality of parent–child transactions. Similarly, if interpersonal and family distress persists, parents are less likely to be able to build an ideal affective relationship with their child. Of course, sufficient financial and other resources must be available to allow families to devote the time and energy necessary to establish optimal family interaction patterns.

The second family pattern of interaction that can be affected by stressors consists of those experiences of the child occurring within the larger physical and social environment organized by their parents. These include such fundamental parenting activities as selecting appropriately stimulating toys and providing outside activities that consider their child's unique interests or special needs. It also includes introducing their child to adults in their own social network or efforts to arrange peer contacts for their child in order to encourage the development of a peer social network. Finding alternative care arrangements also constitutes an important aspect of these family interaction patterns as these choices, activities, and other family-orchestrated experiences are all associated with important child development outcomes (e.g., Bradley, Rock, Whiteside, Caldwell, & Brisby, 1991; Guralnick, in press; Ladd, Profilet, & Hart, 1992).

As in the case of the quality of parent–child transactions, stressors from various sources associated with a child's disability status can adversely affect family-orchestrated child experiences. For example, interpersonal and family distress can create a tendency toward social isolation, thereby limiting the child's experiences substantially. Similarly, the absence of adequate information about the most effective early intervention programs, combined early intervention and day care settings, or most advanced specialized therapeutic interventions can limit child developmental outcomes. This complex pattern of family-orchestrated child experiences is vital to optimal child outcomes, but can be influenced by stressors in quite subtle ways.

Third, parents are responsible for ensuring the health and safety of their child. Providing adequate nutrition, obtaining immunizations on schedule, and organizing a safe environment for play and physical growth are, of course, essential ingredients for optimal child outcomes (Gorman, 1995; Osofsky, 1995). Although related family circumstances such as poverty play a major role, as they do in other family interaction patterns, the presence of a child with a disability adds a new dimension that can further stress available resources. Proper nutrition is particularly susceptible to these stressors. Apart from financial demands, child health problems often create a need for information regarding dietary requirements or feeding techniques that is quite complex.

Accordingly, it appears that the four types of stressors discussed (information needs, interpersonal and family distress, resource needs, and confidence threats) exert their influence on child development by perturbing one or more of the three family patterns of interaction. When this occurs with sufficient magnitude, child developmental outcomes are likely to be compromised. In fact, it is now recognized that, in the absence of efforts to mitigate these stressors—that is, the absence of early intervention for children with developmental delays and their families—we can expect to see a gradual decline in children's intellectual development across the first 5 years of life (Guralnick, 1998; Guralnick & Bricker, 1987). These declines are of an order of magnitude of .5 to .75 standard deviation (8 to 12 IQ points). Of course, delays in development would still exist if these further declines did not occur. However, the continuing declines may well be attributable to nonoptimal family interaction patterns, and substantial benefits to children and families would result if these declines could be prevented or minimized through early intervention programs.

THE EARLY INTERVENTION SYSTEM

In the past 25 years, remarkable advances have occurred in the field of early intervention that have gradually produced an effective system of early intervention services and supports. At one level, advocates such as Gorham et al. (1975) and parent groups across the country successfully lobbied for legislation in support of early intervention. Unquestionably, most significant was Public Law (P.L.) 99-457, the Education of the Handicapped Act Amendments of 1986, encouraging a comprehensive program for infants and toddlers and virtually assuring services for preschool-age children. Support for programs for young children with disabilities was also found in other legislative developments, such as the maternal and child health program (Hutchins, 1994; Richmond & Ayoub, 1993). Paralleling these and other legislative changes was the emergence of interdisciplinary training programs, particularly for physicians and other health professionals; the development of model early intervention programs; the creation of dissemination networks; and similar activities (see Smith & McKenna, 1994). Additionally, dramatically increasing knowledge of the capacities of infants and toddlers, emerging developmental models emphasizing the importance of family patterns of interaction regulating child outcomes, and behavioral and neurobiological research emphasizing the disproportionate influence of the first few years of life and the plasticity of development during that period all converged to form a foundation for the creation of an effective early intervention system (see Guralnick, 1997a).

Over time, this system evolved in a manner that has progressively become more and more responsive to the stressors facing families. Three components of what now can be referred to as a true early intervention system can be identified (Guralnick, 1997c). First, most communities have established a series of *resource supports* that have facilitated an awareness of, access to, and the coordination of comprehensive services. In addition, supplemental supports in the form of financial assistance and respite care are also available. Together, these resource supports mitigate important stressors and therefore permit families to devote their attention and energies to more productive activities to create optimal family interaction patterns.

Second, most communities now have established a well-organized yet informal set of *social supports* for families, including parent-to-parent groups, family counseling services, and ways to help mobilize family, friend, and community networks as needed. These social supports constitute a powerful means of alleviating interpersonal and family distress. Parent-to-parent groups, in particular, are an important source of information for just about any topic, as these organizations have acquired a vast amount of knowledge based upon personal experiences of members with their own children and families, as well as experiences with professionals, programs, and policy makers.

Third, virtually all communities provide an array of *information and services*. Most prominent perhaps is the home- or center-based formal early intervention program available to children with developmental delays organized in a manner consistent with existing federal and state legislation. The total amount of time children and families participate in these formal programs varies with the child's age, usually only a few hours a week for infants and toddlers and a few hours a day for preschool-age children. But even for infants and toddlers, these programs provide an important "centering" function, serving as a meeting place for parents and children and as a place in which services are provided to the child, to the parent, or to the parent–child dyad. In fact, to the extent that these programs address family needs, they also encourage the development of social supports (Thompson et al., 1997).

Most formal programs also have a "curriculum," and the consistency with which such a curriculum is implemented and its organizing features appear to be the reasons why they are most beneficial (Shonkoff & Hauser-Cram, 1987). But parents also seek out relationships with professionals outside the formal early intervention program. This includes the child's primary care physician, and possibly specialists from other disciplines as well. It is in this context that additional health and safety issues are discussed, anticipatory guidance is provided, and supplemental child-focused individual therapies implemented. Clearly, the benefits of information and services provided through involvement with community professionals can mitigate a number of stressors. Together, however, it is the early intervention system composed of resource supports, social supports, and information and services that contributes to parents' growing confidence that they can retain control of and be effective in their caretaking role. In a real sense, parents' confidence grows with the recognition that, despite stressors associated with their child's disability, they are still able to engage in high-quality parent–child transactions, orchestrate their child's experiences so as to maximize developmental outcomes, and ensure the health and safety of their child.

When these community-based early intervention programs are in place, the decline in intellectual development observed for children with developmental delays during the first few years of life noted earlier is either prevented entirely or substantially reduced (Guralnick, 1998; Guralnick & Bricker, 1987). These well-documented findings reinforce the value of considering all children within a developmental–ecological framework, and validate the central role families must occupy in the early intervention system.

The accomplishments of the field of early intervention over the past quarter century, in what is generally referred to as the "first generation" of programs and related research, have indeed been remarkable. It is a system that we can all be proud of, as the evolution of early intervention programs has permanently altered our way of thinking about the forces that influence development for all children. Nevertheless, many issues remain to be addressed in the years ahead in order to build upon this important foundation. The remainder of this chapter is devoted to consideration of these future directions.

FUTURE DIRECTIONS IN EARLY INTERVENTION

In this section, I outline those early intervention issues that I see as most critical for the future. Two types of issues are considered. The first are those areas that require new knowledge gained through research or systems enhancements gained through program development. The second are those areas in which knowledge is available or systems already developed, but implementation has not occurred adequately. These issues range widely but, if considered in the context of the research, training, and practice enterprise of the early intervention system, can yield significant advances in the decades ahead. Specific issues to be addressed include children's social development, the inclusion of young children in the larger community (especially child care), the concept of specificity and individualizing interventions for children and families, the long-term effectiveness of early intervention, families facing unusual environmental stressors, ensuring family-centered programs, and the problem of quality in early intervention programs.

Knowledge and Systems Development

Social Development

Many aspects of early intervention programs, particularly the more didactic features, have emphasized children's primary disabilities. Figuring out how to promote cognitive and language development, particularly for children with general developmental delays, has been and continues to be a high priority for parents and professionals. However, this very understandable domain-specific interest has been accompanied by the relative neglect of more integrative aspects of early childhood development, particularly social development. Of special interest is the ability of children to establish productive relationships with their peers and to develop friendships. It is well recognized that the quality of one's later life is inextricably linked to interpersonal skills that develop in the peer context. Less recognized, however, is the importance of the early years in establishing a foundation for peer-related social competence, and that failure to do so places children on a nonoptimal developmental trajectory that is extremely difficult to alter at a later point.

Perhaps one reason for the relative neglect of children's social development is the expectation that improvements in cognitive and language development or the benefits obtained from many of the supports and services that are part of early intervention programs will promote social development as well. After all, there is every reason to believe that the three family patterns of interaction that have been linked to children's cognitive development (see Figure 3.1) are also relevant to children's social development (Patterson, Vaden, & Kupersmidt, 1991).

As reasonable as these expectations are, consistent findings have revealed that, despite participation in early intervention programs, young children with developmental delays display an unusual pattern of difficulties in the area of peer-related social development. Compared to children without delays, even when controlling for developmental level, young children with developmental delays exhibit lower levels of sustained socially interactive play; engage in higher levels of isolate play; display more negativity and discontent during play, especially during conflicts; have less success in gaining response to their social bids; are less directive; and exhibit an unusual and fragile developmental progression over the early childhood years (see Guralnick, 1999a; Guralnick & Neville, 1997). Of perhaps greatest concern is the very limited number of reciprocal friendships formed during this time (Buysse, 1993; Guralnick, 1992). The seriousness of these difficulties is underscored by the fact that socially competent interactions with peers require children to have the ability to formulate and carry out their interpersonal goals such as entering play, resolving conflicts, or maintaining play. It is these social skills that constitute the essence of independent decision making about important aspects of children's (and later adults') lives.

Why these unusual patterns exist is likely due to numerous factors, including child characteristics related to corresponding difficulties in information processing, attentional and planning processes, or expressive language. However, simply identifying these child-related cognitive and language characteristics in the absence of a conceptual framework linking it to peer-related social competence does little to advance our understanding of social development or help in the design of intervention programs.

Fortunately, recent theoretical and empirical advances have brought about a recognition that social development is an integrative domain involving a dynamic set of interacting processes. Foundation processes consist of a shared understanding of social rules or the event structure of play themes and the ability to regulate one's emotions during social play. Also important are social-cognitive processes related to the child's ability to properly attend to relevant cues in the social environment related to the child's interpersonal goals, interpret those cues appropriately, generate a positive array of responses to the situation, and, based on contextual information, evaluate and select a reasonable response. Finally, higher order processes that relate to sustaining and monitoring goal-oriented events over the sequence of exchanges are also critical.

To be sure, these integrative processes are affected by children's cognitive, communicative, and behavioral problems associated with their general developmental delays. For example, difficulties in working memory, particularly those related to play scripts (Bray, Fletcher, & Turner, 1997), can adversely affect key integrative processes underlying peer-related social competence. Beyond these more intrinsic child characteristics, experiential factors, particularly family interaction patterns, can also substantially influence these integrative peer-related social competence processes. For example, perhaps being preoccupied with other matters, such as devoting time to individual therapies, or due to difficulties in arranging play activities for their child, many parents of children with developmental delays find it difficult to foster the development of their child's peer social networks. The consequence of this is to limit experiences with peers that are necessary for trial-and-error exchanges that promote their child's peer-related social competence (Guralnick, 1997b). Moreover, many parents of children with delays, though highly valuing the development of children's social competence, tend to believe that their child's social skills with peers depend more on traits or enduring dispositional factors than on experiential processes and see only a relatively small role for adult facilitation. These beliefs and attributions are certain to dampen enthusiasm for directly addressing issues of social development. Finally, certain parent–child transaction patterns related to issues of control or emotion-regulating forms of play that are associated with peer-related social competence (e.g., physical play with father) often pose special problems for families of children with delays. These family-related patterns place many young children at an additional disadvantage with respect to developing peer-related social skills (see discussion by Guralnick & Neville, 1997).

Accordingly, to further enhance early intervention programs, future programs must bring to families comprehensive and validated approaches to promote children's peer-related social competence. Success has been hard to achieve in the limited work carried out so far, and it has tended to be narrowly focused and to not consider the important processes that appear to govern peer interactions. Clinical tools are needed that organize assessment and intervention within a social task or interpersonal goal framework. Child-focused interventions must be able to adapt to or enhance the processes that limit the full social development of children with delays. Success, however, will require a comprehensive approach closely involving families, including interventions to promote peer social networks, to develop reasonable attitude and belief systems regarding the causes and malleability of their child's social development, and to learn how to optimize parent–child transactions most relevant to peer competence. Such curricula and programs are now being developed and evaluated (Bruder,

1997; Guralnick & Neville, 1997), but will require close cooperation among researchers, practitioners, and families.

Inclusion in Community Life

The concept and practice of including children with and without disabilities in all aspects of community life has been one of the most important themes in the field of developmental disabilities in general and early intervention in particular (Guralnick, 1978, 1990). From an ideological perspective, experiences in inclusive settings during the early childhood years are capable of forming a foundation that fosters a sense of belonging to a common community, of encouraging respect for individual differences, and of ensuring equal access for all children and families. By establishing these values and principles at the outset, families come to expect to participate fully in all aspects of community activities. In fact, it is anticipated that well-designed, inclusive early education and early intervention programs will promote social integration–that is, positive peer relationships and even friendships between children with and without disabilities. From a developmental perspective, research has revealed many benefits of full participation in inclusive early childhood programs for children with delays, particularly increased levels of social interaction. Of equal importance, no adverse effects have been found for children with or without disabilities.

Parents of children with and without disabilities express strong support for the benefits of inclusive programs for young children, particularly promoting acceptance of children with disabilities (Bailey & Winton, 1987; Guralnick, 1994). Concerns are also evident, however. Some concerns relate to implementation issues to be discussed later, such as the availability of special services and trained personnel. Others relate to the consistent and certainly troublesome issue for parents regarding the possible social rejection of their children by their peers in inclusive programs. This is unquestionably a legitimate concern, as research has shown that children with developmental delays, even those with mild delays, find themselves socially separated in inclusive settings. Although frank rejection occurs on occasion, most often separation takes the form of exclusion. Moreover, social separation is most apparent for more demanding forms of relationships such as friendships.

How, then, is it possible to alter this social separation of children in inclusive early childhood settings in the future? After all, building social relationships and selecting friends are such highly idiosyncratic and personal matters that it is hard to imagine both the appropriateness of trying to change children's perspectives of social relationships or social partners as well as our ability to do so. In fact, to date, despite our best efforts to foster social integration and further encourage acceptance of individual differences in the context of inclusive programs during the preschool period, we have not been able to materially alter the level of social separation that exists (Guralnick, 1999b).

It appears that two powerful forces are operating that tend to press for social separation. First is the existence of the peer–social competence problems experienced by children with delays discussed in the previous section. This is clearly a significant barrier to productive social relationships. By developing effective intervention programs to address these peer interaction difficulties, we can expect to see improvements in social integration as well. However, the second force may be even more difficult to alter, as it relates to the expectations or perceptions of typically developing children and their families with regard to children with disabilities that they bring with them when entering preschool or child care programs. Unquestionably, major gains have occurred in the past 25 years in the general population with respect to positive parental attitudes toward people with disabilities, their acceptance of or even celebration of diversity, and their willingness to encourage specific experiences with children with disabilities. However, circumstances are still far from ideal, and many subtle as well as obvious negative messages are regularly communicated to and about people with disabilities within home and community settings (Stoneman, 1993). Moreover, these well-entrenched prior expectations are often reinforced by continuing experiences even when contact with children with disabilities occurs. As a consequence, meaningful participation in inclusive preschools is not likely to substantially alter a well-established pattern of behaviors.

What, then, can be done to alter these prior expectations in order to ensure a greater degree of inclusion during the early childhood years for children with disabilities? Public education efforts and targeted campaigns are likely to have only limited impact unless they occur on a massive scale—an unlikely prospect. But inclusive child care may provide the types of frequent and personal experiences so needed to modify long-standing attitudes and beliefs. In fact, child care, by beginning during infancy or the toddler years, has the potential to connect *families*, not only children. A clear challenge for the future, then, is to create a quality system of inclusive child care, one that considers the full spectrum of out-of-home child care placements, and one that creates as early as possible a sense of belonging to the community for all children and families. It is in these inclusive child care settings that community child care and early intervention can come together (Guralnick, in press; O'Brien, 1997). There are few opportunities in contemporary society in which it may be possible to bring about important changes in societal beliefs and attitudes about disabilities. The child care arena presents one such opportunity, one that we must capitalize on with thoughtful and creative support for the systematic development of programs that maximize inclusion.

Specificity

From both programmatic and cost-effectiveness perspectives, one of the most complex problems for the future is to ensure that early interventions are highly individualized and specific to families and children. As discussed earlier in the context of the developmental approach, families exhibit a range of needs due to stressors associated with a child with a disability. Matching services and supports in the context of the early intervention system to address these stressors has been achieved to a sufficient degree to produce the benefits that have been described.

Unfortunately, our knowledge is not yet adequate to individualize to the level needed to maximize our resources and child outcomes. Questions regarding the intensity of services, or the form they should take, or their comprehensiveness remain more dependent on local preferences than empirical findings. Absent as well are well-researched clinical tools that can evaluate the various potential stressors and, perhaps more important, directly assess the three family interaction patterns so closely linked to child outcomes (Figure 3.1). In that both stressors associated with a child's disability and stressors associated with family characteristics prior to the birth of their child (e.g., social supports, financial resources, culturally transmitted child rearing patterns) combine to influence the three patterns of family interaction, resources can be allocated most effectively if reliable and valid clinical instruments are available. Our ability, for example, to identify families where parent–child transaction patterns are not optimal, such as those adopting a performance orientation or an excessively directive style, would allow special programs to be developed and evaluated, and resources to be allocated in a more rational manner. Similarly, our ability to both conceptualize and assess the degree to which parents optimally adjust to their child's characteristics during parent–child transactions (e.g., properly balance directiveness, support, and warmth) is required for the design of highly specific and optimal early intervention programs (Roach, Barratt, Miller, & Leavitt, 1998). Of considerable concern is the unusual vulnerability of children with high-risk family characteristics (e.g., chronic poverty) combined with stressors related to a child's disability. Unfortunately, a substantial proportion of families of children with disabilities face these circumstances (Bowe, 1995). Accordingly, research and program development directed toward this notion of specificity may well constitute the primary challenge for the second generation of research in early intervention, with the potential to yield results that substantially enhance the effectiveness of the early intervention system (Guralnick, 1993, 1997a).

Long-Term Effects

A critical reason for investing extensive resources in early intervention is the expectation that long-term benefits will result. Short-term effects—that is, those occurring shortly after intervention has ended or evident during the first 5 years of life—are well documented, but demonstrating long-term effects for many groups of children with disabilities has been a more difficult task (e.g., Gibson & Harris, 1988). We do know from related research for risk populations where large-scale studies have been carried out that long-term effectiveness can be maximized through interventions that have high levels of comprehensiveness and intensity (Guralnick, 1998). Long-term benefits are particularly more likely to result if early intervention programs continue or even intensify services and supports across transition periods in the child's life (e.g., neonatal intensive care to home; birth-to-3 program to preschool program; preschool to kindergarten).

Consequently, a major task for the future is to gather knowledge regarding the pattern of early intervention program components most likely to yield long-term benefits. These comparative studies will not be easily accomplished as there are many practical and ethical concerns that must be addressed. As discussed in the previous section, specificity issues must be considered as well. However, by selectively adding program components to existing intervention programs, it should be possible to examine these important issues. In addition, long-term follow-up of children who have systematically received different arrays of intervention components expected to be related to long-term effectiveness must also be analyzed in the context of the post–early intervention environments they experience. This relationship between early intervention and later experiences has simply not received the attention it deserves. Accordingly, although this research agenda may appear to be overly ambitious, it does appear to represent fairly the complexity of the issues facing investigators. However, the knowledge gained is absolutely critical for both the future design of the components of the early intervention system and, of equal importance, for the significant public policy implications relating to the long-term benefits of early intervention.

Implementation

The issues for the future just discussed constitute a search for new knowledge or new program development that will ultimately enhance the early intervention system. But the fact remains that the knowledge, values, and approaches that have evolved in the past 25 years have not been fully incorporated into daily practice in far too many community programs. I discuss possible solutions to this problem shortly, but there does not appear to be any intrinsic difficulty translating research findings or programmatic advances into practice in the field of early intervention. Not only have model programs demonstrated their state-of-the art capabilities, but many diverse community programs have done so as well. Consequently, other barriers to implementation must be identified.

Lags in implementation exist in many areas. In this section, I discuss concerns related to implementation problems in family-centered programs, inclusion in preschool programs, and individualizing interventions. After identifying the nature of these implementation problems, I present some possible general solutions.

Family-Centered Programs

One of the major philosophical, conceptual, and practical advances in the field of intervention has been to place families at the center of the early intervention system (Guralnick, 1989). In essence, programs must be carefully designed to meet the overall needs of families and integrate intervention activities into the natural flow of family life as a means of maximizing child development (Bernheimer & Keogh, 1995; Gallimore, Weisner, Bernheimer, Guthrie, & Nihira, 1993). It has been in this context that the terms parent–professional partnerships and empowerment have been realized. Yet, despite considerable progress, continuing discrepancies remain between parental needs and the services and supports provided by the early intervention system, especially in relation to the formal intervention components (e.g., Filer & Mahoney, 1996; McBride & Peterson, 1997).

It is understandably a difficult transition for service providers to shift to a family-centered approach from a more child-oriented model. For experienced professionals, it may demand an entirely new way of thinking that often conflicts with long-established behavioral patterns. Professionals may not be comfortable with this new role, wondering whether they have the skills as they enter new domains related to family functioning. Moreover, the emphasis on family centeredness is often diluted when shifting from infant–toddler programs to preschool programs. Parents, too, must make adjustments and may need to be encouraged to adopt a more dominant, decision-making role and to recognize that child development unfolds and is maintained best when the total family and community ecology is considered.

In addition, successful family centeredness requires collaborating with other agencies to create an integrated system of resources and social supports. Yet this is particularly difficult, as this approach requires many service providers to thoroughly reconceptualize their own early intervention models. Clearly, despite the fact that the concept of family-centered services and supports is still evolving, the knowledge and tools are available to produce more widespread implementation than currently exists.

Inclusion in Preschool Programs

In a similar way, the availability of inclusive programs for children with a range of developmental delays is far from adequate. This observation is perhaps of most concern for preschool-age children as they participate in programs organized by the public education system. Despite repeated demonstrations in community programs that inclusive practices are both feasible and effective for preschool-age children, an unusually large number of communities have been unable, uninterested, or even resistant to adopting inclusive programs for young children. In part, this may be a result of "systems" resistance, as inclusive programs require new forms of administrative activities and thinking. However, the desire of parents of children with disabilities to press for inclusion is also tempered by persistent concerns about the need for well-trained personnel and the availability of specialized services (Guralnick, 1994). Consequently, some mechanisms must be found to address these systems-level and parental concerns in order to promote the implementation of inclusive early childhood programs.

Individualizing Interventions

There are few goals more important than individualizing interventions to accommodate to unique child needs and family characteristics. The fact is that successful individualizing implies an awareness of all the complex factors influencing child and family life and then selecting the most current intervention strategies in order to create a state-of-the-art program of services and supports. The goal of individualization for far too many children and families remains just that, however—a goal (e.g., Goodman, 1993).

One reason is that the demands on the early intervention system to individualize within a family-centered framework are increasing dramatically due to the large number of families with multiple risks (Hanson & Carta, 1995). These risk factors or nonoptimal family characteristics include poverty, mental health problems, limited intellectual abilities of parents, substance abuse, the absence of a support system, and intergenerationally transmitted inappropriate models of child development. Of note, fully one third of families of children with disabilities live at or below the poverty level (Bowe, 1995). As suggested earlier, these adverse family characteristics can also directly influence the three family interaction patterns governing child developmental outcomes. When life stressors due to family characteristics combine with the stressors associated with a child with a disability, the prospects for optimal family interaction patterns are dismally low (e.g., Bradley et al., 1994). Unfortunately, a strong association between stressors and the services and supports provided by the early intervention system has not been found (Gavidia-Payne & Stoneman, 1997).

Clearly, even if the rate of growth of multiple-risk families moderates, the challenge for individualization remains. At minimum, it will require the early intervention system to coordinate with an even larger array of agencies than currently exists in order to optimize services and supports. It may also force a consideration of new models of service, such as intensive intervention-oriented day care for children from multiple-risk families in a manner similar to that recommended for children without disabilities but with high family risks (Guralnick, in press).

Similarly, as our population becomes more diverse, knowledge about the unique beliefs, attitudes, child rearing practices, and expectations of culturally diverse families must be incorporated into each individualized plan in order to have any chance for a successful outcome. Evidence available from relationships between teachers and parents in ethnoculturally diverse early childhood settings suggests that much work needs to be done (Bernhard, Lefebvre, Kilbride, Chud, & Lange, 1998).

Admittedly, individualization is a seemingly never-ending process as more information becomes available through second-generation research on specificity issues. Yet, our inability to incorporate what we know (from both research and practice perspectives) into day-to-day curricula and interventions with children and families to permit high levels of individualization constitutes a severe challenge to meaningful implementation of quality programs. In the next section, I discuss some possible ways to address this particular problem, as well as those related to implementation in general.

Promoting Implementation in the Future

These and related implementation problems (e.g., transitions between birth-to-3 and preschool programs) are perhaps even more challenging to the field of early intervention than knowledge and program development issues. Unless new implementation approaches or models are found in the framework of the early intervention system, implementation will fall further and further behind as new information is made available through second-generation research. Suggestions are presented below with regard to a new approach to personnel preparation and strategies to enhance parent advocacy. Business as usual is not an acceptable alternative.

Consultant Specialists

One possibility for change is to reevaluate the training and skills required by certain key personnel. Consider the training of the early childhood educator, often the central person in program implementation. The training must, of course, include information and skills related to children's special needs and ways to conceptualize, organize, and develop family-centered relationships. However, to be compatible with the developmental framework, this specialized training must occur within a generalist tradition. Various blends of early childhood and disability-specific training have, of course, been created, and this process should be accelerated. Often this requires administrative restructuring of categorically organized training within university-based personnel preparation systems. In addition, similar (although certainly less extensive in many instances) training should be required for child development specialists or others who may be responsible for center-based day care. Whether these educators are the early interventionists of the birth-to-3 program, the early childhood (special) educators in the child's preschool program, or the child care specialists in the day care program, these individuals clearly play a pivotal role in the formal intervention program. As individuals with specialized knowledge of disability issues combined with generalist training, they often function as the child's service coordinator.

Through the increasing availability of generalist educators with specialized training, and by ensuring that the training occurs at the preservice level, it is likely that the comfort level of parents of children with disabilities will correspondingly increase. Parents should certainly be able to form partnerships with these generalists to implement family-centered programs, to contribute to the design of a state-of-the-art array of support and services, and to have increasing confidence that these programs can be effectively provided in an inclusive setting.

Yet, even through an active continuing education program, it is not reasonable to expect these generalists to have the sophisticated expertise needed to address the highly individualized needs of children with disabilities and their families. Consequently, it is imperative to ensure the availability of a well-trained (master's level at minimum) group of *consultant specialists*. These specialists (most already have or will obtain credentials for a generalist background) would be trained within a highly interdisciplinary framework and would be assigned to some organizational entity within the birth-to-3 system for infants and toddlers or the local education agency for preschool-age children. Their main responsibility would be to advise and consult with the generalist educational staff, helping to ensure implementation of state-of-the-art practices, with particular reference to the children with disabilities in the program. They would bring new information as it emerges to the attention of the generalist educator and work closely with other specialists to maximize the integrated and coordinated nature of the services and supports for individual children. Both technical assistance and advocacy roles can be envisioned. Through this process of ongoing professional exchange, knowledge would be enhanced for both the generalist and the consultant specialist. Despite the high level of expertise of these specialists with respect to disability issues, the parents' main contacts would remain with the generalist or service coordinator who essentially has primary responsibility for all children in the (hopefully inclusive) setting and would continue to work together with and to support and strengthen the family.

To ensure that the consultant specialist's knowledge continues to be current, links with local universities, required participation in continuing education programs, an awareness and examination of model programs that may develop addressing both knowledge and implementation issues, and perhaps involvement in a regional or national network that could be established devoted to ensuring that current knowledge and techniques are available to these specialists should all occur. Although the generalist will certainly participate in numerous continuing education activities, only a small proportion will likely involve disability issues. Accordingly, through advice, demonstration, and consultation, the consultant specialist will in essence be the conduit for expanding the knowledge and clinical skills related to children with disabilities for the generalist. It is this same consultant specialist who would play a similar role for designated staff in children's day care settings.

The benefits of such an approach would be to maximize the quality of inclusive practices both as part of the formal early intervention program and in the larger community system, help individualize intervention activities using the most current strategies and techniques, and continue to emphasize and reinforce the family's central role in this process. This approach also addresses concerns of both teachers and parents related to the availability of trained specialist personnel, particularly in inclusive settings. Of course, adequate resources must be available to assure that other well-trained specialists (e.g., physical therapists) are available to provide specialized therapeutic services. For the most part, this is an issue that requires advocacy backed by effectiveness data. Perhaps the involvement of a consultant specialist can help ensure cost-effective use of these specialists by integrating their therapeutic activities in the natural flow of the child's activities and thereby maximize their impact. A consultant model carried out in a larger and naturalistic context, rather than a specialist model involving a one-on-one didactic-like approach, makes considerable sense from an educational and developmental perspective in most instances and will likely be the model for the future (see Bailey, 1996).

Parent Advocacy

Finally, efforts to provide families with the motivation and techniques to be active advocates for their children should be expanded to address the implementation problem. One mechanism is for parent-to-parent groups, through their mentoring activities, to expand their formal ties to the early intervention system. As noted earlier, the difficulties in implementing family-centered programs, values, and principles can in part be traced to lack of a full appreciation of the implications of family centeredness by the families themselves. As such, expectations are either low or focus primarily or even exclusively on child-directed, often instructional activities. In other instances, professionals either do not understand or have difficulty altering their existing approaches to families. Not only would the implementation of a family-centered agenda be strengthened through family advocacy efforts, but parents would also ensure that the early intervention system would continue to be responsive to stressors across the entire early childhood period. As discussed earlier, long-term benefits of early intervention can be expected only if this type of continuity in the early intervention system is maintained over time, particularly across transition periods. Hopefully, expanded advocacy activities will extend beyond early childhood, encouraging a more family-centered agenda in general.

SUMMARY AND CONCLUSIONS

Over the course of the past 25 years, a comprehensive and well-organized early intervention system of services and supports has emerged. The system that has evolved can be well understood within a developmental framework as a thoughtful response to stressors facing families of young children with disabilities. When these systems components are available to families, evidence clearly indicates that important short-term benefits occur. Related evidence indicates the types of programs needed to achieve long-term impact.

Two major themes were identified that can serve as a guide for the future development of the early intervention system. First, areas requiring new knowledge or program development were discussed. Special emphasis was given to social development, inclusion in community life, specificity, and long-term effectiveness. In essence, these topics constitute the basis for an important agenda for second-generation research and program development in the next millennium. Second, problems in implementing existing knowledge and established practices were discussed focusing on the areas of family centeredness, inclusion of preschool-age children, and individualizing interventions for children and families. Although there are many ways to address implementation concerns, suggestions were made with respect to a model of personnel preparation emphasizing the role of a consultant specialist and the importance of expanding parent advocacy.

Taken together, the new millennium brings with it extraordinary opportunities to build upon the existing early intervention system. The complex issues to be faced can be matched only by the rapid advances in knowledge and program development likely to occur in the years ahead. How we conceptualize and manage this entire process will do much to determine the ultimate benefits obtained by children and families from participating in the early intervention system.

REFERENCES

Baily, D. (1996). Preparing early intervention professionals for the 21st century. In M. Brambring, H. Rauh, & A Beelman (Eds.), *Early childhood intervention* (pp. 488–503). Berlin: Walter de Gruyter.

Bailey, D. B., Jr., & Winton, P. J. (1987). Stability and change in parents' expectations about mainstreaming. *Topics in Early Childhood Special Education, 7*, 73–88.

Baumrind, D. (1993). The average expectable environment is not good enough: A response to Scarr. *Child Development, 64*, 1299–1317.

Bernhard, J. K., Lefebvre, M. L., Kilbride, K. M., Chud, G., & Lange, R. (1998). Troubled relationships in early childhood education: Parent-teacher interactions in ethnoculturally diverse child care settings. *Early Education and Development, 11*, 5–28.

Bernheimer, L. P., & Keogh, B. K. (1995). Weaving interventions into the fabric of everyday life: An approach to family assessment. *Topic in Early Childhood Special Education, 15*, 415–433.

Birenbaum, A., Guyot, D., & Cohen, H. J. (1990). Health care financing for severe developmental disabilities. *Monographs of the American Association on Mental Retardation, 14.*

Bowe, F. G. (1995). Population estimates: Birth-to-5 children with disabilities. *The Journal of Special Education, 20*, 461–471.

Bradley, R. H., Rock, S. L., Whiteside, L., Caldwell, B. M., & Brisby, J. (1991). Dimensions of parenting in families having children with disabilities. *Exceptionality, 2*, 41–61.

Bradley, R. H., Whiteside, L., Mundfrom, D. J., Casey, P. H., Kelleher, K. J., & Pope, S. K. (1994). Early indications of resilience and their relation to experiences in the home environments of low birthweight, premature children living in poverty. *Child Development, 65*, 346–360.

Bray, N. W., Fletcher, K. L., & Turner, L. A. (1997). Cognitive competencies and strategy use in individuals with mental retardation. In W. E. MacLean, Jr. (Ed.), *Ellis' handbook of mental deficiency, psychological theory and research* (3rd ed., pp. 197–217). Mahwah, NJ: Erlbaum.

Bruder, M. B. (1997). The effectiveness of specific educational/developmental curricula for children with established disabilities. In M. J. Guralnick (Ed.), *The effectiveness of early intervention* (pp. 523–548). Baltimore: Brookes.

Buysse, V. (1993). Friendships of preschoolers with disabilities in community-based child care settings. *Journal of Early Intervention, 17*, 380–395.

Clarke-Stewart, K. A. (1988). Parents' effects on children's development: A decade of progress? *Journal of Applied Developmental Psychology, 9*, 41–84.

Education of the Handicapped Act Amendments of 1986, 20 U.S.C. § 1400 *et seq.*

Filer, J. D., & Mahoney, G. J. (1996). Collaboration between families and early intervention service providers. *Infants and Young Children, 9*, 22–30.

Gallimore, R., Weisner, T. S., Bernheimer, L. P., Guthrie, D., & Nihira, K. (1993). Family responses to young children with developmental delays: Accommodation activity in ecological and cultural context. *American Journal on Mental Retardation, 98*, 185–206.

Gavidia-Payne, S., & Stoneman, Z. (1997). Family predictors of maternal and paternal involvement in programs for young children with disabilities. *Child Development, 68*, 701–717.

Gibson, D., & Harris, A. (1988). Aggregated early intervention effects for Down's syndrome persons: Patterning and longevity of benefits. *Journal of Mental Deficiency Research, 32*, 1–17.

Goffman, E. (1963). *Stigma.* Englewood Cliffs, NJ: Prentice-Hall.

Goodman, J. F. (1993). Curriculum issues in early intervention preschool programs. *Early Education and Development, 4*, 182–183.

Gorham, K. A., Des Jardins, C., Page, R., Pettis, E., & Scheiber, B. (1975). Effect on parents. In N. Hobbs (Ed.), *Issues in the classification of children* (Vol. 2, pp. 154–188). San Francisco: Jossey-Bass.

Gorman, K. S. (1995). Malnutrition and cognitive development: Evidence from experimental/quasi-experimental studies among the mild-to-moderately malnourished. *Journal of Nutrition, 125,* 2239S–2244S.

Guralnick, M. J. (Ed.). (1978). *Early intervention and the integration of handicapped and nonhandicapped children.* Baltimore: University Park Press.

Guralnick, M. J. (1989). Recent developments in early intervention efficacy research: Implications for family involvement in P.L. 99-457. *Topics in Early Childhood Special Education, 9*(3), 1–17.

Guralnick, M. J. (1990). Major accomplishments and future directions in early childhood mainstreaming. *Topics in Early Childhood Special Education, 10*(2), 1–17.

Guralnick, M. J. (1992). A hierarchical model for understanding children's peer-related social competence. In S. L. Odom, S. R. McConnell, & M. A. McEvoy (Eds.), *Social competence of young children with disabilities: Issues and strategies for intervention* (pp. 37–64). Baltimore: Brookes.

Guralnick, M. J. (1993). Second generation research on the effectiveness of early intervention. *Early Education and Development, 4,* 366–378.

Guralnick, M. J. (1994). Mothers' perceptions of the benefits and drawbacks of early childhood mainstreaming. *Journal of Early Intervention, 18,* 168–183.

Guralnick, M. J. (Ed.). (1997a). *The effectiveness of early intervention.* Baltimore: Brookes.

Guralnick, M. J. (1997b). The peer social networks of young boys with developmental delays. *American Journal on Mental Retardation, 101,* 595–612.

Guralnick, M. J. (1997c). Second generation research in the field of early intervention. In M. J. Guralnick (Ed.), *The effectiveness of early intervention* (pp. 3–22). Baltimore: Brookes.

Guralnick, M. J. (1998). The effectiveness of early intervention for vulnerable children: A developmental perspective. *American Journal on Mental Retardation, 102,* 319–345.

Guralnick, M. J. (1999a). Family and child influences on the peer-related social competence of young children with developmental delays. *Mental Retardation and Developmental Disabilities Research Reviews, 5,* 21–29.

Guralnick, M. J. (1999b). The nature and meaning of social integration for young children with mild developmental delays in inclusive settings. *Journal of Early Intervention, 22,* 70–86.

Guralnick, M. J. (in press). The early intervention system and out-of-home child care. In D. Cryer & T. Harms (Eds.), *Infants and toddlers in out-of-home care.* Baltimore: Brookes.

Guralnick, M. J., & Bricker, D. (1987). The effectiveness of early intervention for children with cognitive and general developmental delays. In M. J. Guralnick & F. C. Bennett (Eds.), *The effectiveness of early intervention for at-risk and handicapped children* (pp. 115–173). New York: Academic Press.

Guralnick, M. J., & Neville, B. (1997). Designing early intervention programs to promote children's social competence. In M. J. Guralnick (Ed.), *The effectiveness of early intervention* (pp. 579–610). Baltimore: Brookes.

Hanson, M. J., & Carta, J. J. (1995). Addressing the challenges of families with multiple risks. *Exceptional Children, 62,* 201–212.

Hanson, M. J., & Hanline, M. F. (1990). Parenting a child with a disability: A longitudinal study of parental stress and adaptation. *Journal of Early Intervention, 14,* 234–248.

Hodapp, R. M., Dykens, E. M., Evans, D. W., & Merighi, J. R. (1992). Maternal emotional reactions to young children with different types of handicaps. *Journal of Developmental and Behavioral Pediatrics, 13,* 118–123.

Hutchins, V. L. (1994). Maternal and Child Health Bureau: Roots. *Pediatrics, 94,* 695—699.

Kelly, J. F., & Booth, C. L. (1997). *Child care for infants at risk and with disabilities: Description and issues in the first 15 months.* Poster session presented at the annual meeting of the Society for Research in Child Development, Washington, DC.

Ladd, G. W., Profilet, S. M., & Hart, C. H. (1992). Parents' management of children's peer relations: Facilitating and supervising children's activities in the peer culture. In R. D. Parke & G. W. Ladd (Eds.), *Family–peer relationships: Modes of linkage* (pp. 215–253). Hillsdale, NJ: Erlbaum.

McBride, S. L., & Peterson, C. (1997). Home-based early intervention with families of children with disabilities: Who is doing what? *Topics in Early Childhood Special Education*, *17*, 209–233.

O'Brien, M. (1997). *Inclusive child care for infants and toddlers: Meeting individual and special needs*. Baltimore: Brookes.

Osofsky, J. D. (1995). The effects of violence exposure on young children. *American Psychologist*, *50*, 782–788.

Patterson, C. J., Vaden, N. A., & Kupersmidt, J. B. (1991). Family background, recent life events and peer rejection during childhood. *Journal of Social and Personal Relationships*, *8*, 347–361.

Richmond, J., & Ayoub, C. C. (1993). Evolution of early intervention philosophy. In D. M. Bryant & M. A. Graham (Eds.), *Implementing early intervention* (pp. 1–17). New York: Guilford.

Roach, M. A., Barratt, M. S., Miller, M. J., & Leavitt, L. A. (1998). The structure of mother–child play: Young children with Down syndrome and typically developing children. *Developmental Psychology*, *34*, 77–87.

Shonkoff, J. P., & Hauser-Cram, P. (1987). Early intervention for disabled infants and their families: A quantitative analysis. *Pediatrics*, *80*, 650–658.

Smith, B. J., & McKenna, P. (1994). Early intervention public policy: Past, present, and future. In L. J. Johnson, R. J. Gallagher, M. J. LaMontagne, J. B. Jordan, J. J. Gallagher, P. L. Hutinger, & M. B. Karnes (Eds.), *Meeting early intervention challenges* (pp. 251–264). Baltimore: Brookes.

Sontag, J. C., & Schacht, R. (1994). An ethnic comparison of parent participation and information needs in early intervention. *Exceptional Children*, *60*, 422–433.

Stoneman, Z. (1993). The effects of attitude on preschool integration. In C. A. Peck, S. L. Odom, & D. D. Bricker (Eds.), *Integrating young children with disabilities into community programs* (pp. 223–248). Baltimore: Brookes.

Thompson, L., Lobb, C., Elling, R., Herman, S., Jurkiewicz, T., & Hulleza, C. (1977). Pathways to family empowerment: Effects of family-centered delivery of early intervention services. *Exceptional Children*, *64*, 99–113.

Turnbull, A. P., Patterson, J. M., Behr, S. K., Murphy, D. L., Marquis, J. G., Blue-Banning, M. J. (Eds.). (1993). *Cognitive coping, families, and disability*. Baltimore: Brookes.

Wachs, T. D. (1992). *The nature of nurture*. Newbury Park, CA: Sage.

Transition and Youth with Mental Retardation: Past, Present, and Future

Robert E. Cimera and Frank R. Rusch

Over the past decade, the topic of transition has become of great interest to special educators. From early intervention to high school vocational programs, *transition* has become a buzzword—similar to *time on task*, *reflective inquiry*, and *inclusion*. However, to date few people have concisely answered the question, "What is transition?"

Some authors have emphasized that transition is the point between high school and employment (Will, 1984). Others have spoken of transition as a movement from high school to community adjustment (Halpern, 1985) or to adult life (Clark & Kolstoe, 1995). Although all of these perspectives involve transitions, they serve only as examples of what transitions are, not as definitions.

Very simply put, a transition is the point at which change occurs in somebody's life. Although the field of special education tends to focus mostly on the transitions experienced by high school–aged students with disabilities (e.g., school to work, independent living, community involvement), transitions begin at birth and persist continuously until death. In other words, each day of every student's life presents change, regardless of the student's IQ, abilities, or reported functioning level.

Consider your own life for a moment. Remember the tremendous changes that occurred in your life when you first entered elementary school? Trying to cope with unfamiliar surroundings, understand the rules, master the academic skills being taught by the teacher, and wondering if you were ever going to make friends—these are all points of transition. How about when you first started to date? The awkwardness of letting somebody know how you felt about him or her, learning the social nuances of dating behavior, experiencing the fear of being rejected—these are also examples of transitions. Other transitions include entering college, selecting a potential field of study, and learning the issues related to that field as you are doing now.

Transition is not something that occurs only with students with disabilities. We all experience changes in our lives, whether we want to or not. It is important to recognize that these changes enable us to move from one station in life (e.g., being single) to another (e.g., being married). How we prepare students, with and without disabilities, for these transitions often determines how successful they will be throughout the remainder of their lives.

The purpose of this chapter is to provide a general overview of transition as an emerging field of study, discuss salient issues currently being documented within the literature, and outline future trends related to the transitions faced by youth with mental retardation. By the end of this chapter, you should be able to identify the various transitions occurring in the lives of your students, but, more important, you should be able to prepare your students for the transitions that they will face when you are no longer with them. As with the field in general, the primary focus of this chapter involves postschool transitions (e.g., school to work); however, other transitions (e.g., reaching puberty) are no less important to the lives of your students.

IMPORTANCE OF SUCCESSFUL SCHOOL-TO-WORK TRANSITION

Prior to exploring the field of school-to-work transition, you must ask yourself a key question: "Why is a successful transition from school to work important for individuals with disabilities?" The answer may be found within your own life, although you might not realize it at first.

Think about your first part-time or summer job. In addition to hard work, this position offered you a wage that enabled you to buy desired possessions, and perhaps even save for a car or college tuition. In addition, the job gave you an opportunity to build your confidence, explore new interests, and make new friends. We often take for granted the importance that employment has in our lives. For students with disabilities, the importance of gainful employment cannot be overstated.

The benefits listed above, which accrue to everybody who is engaged in paid, meaningful work, take on a special significance for individuals with disabilities, who often have had little exposure to or opportunity to participate in extracurricular or other nonschool-related activities. Thus, for these individuals, exploring new interests and making new friends in a job setting combine to increase self-confidence and social skills in areas in which persons with disabilities are often deficient. In addition, students with disabilities gain many other rewards from being employed within the community. For instance, the workplace offers them a new and more effective "classroom" in which they can learn. Classrooms in schools are fabricated settings with arbitrary activities (e.g., worksheets, the importance of which often escapes students). Activities in workplaces, on the other hand, have a more obvious purpose—to make money for the hiring business. Further, successful completion of activities in the workplace has more tangible rewards than those in classrooms: If you do well in the classroom, you receive an A; if you do well in the workplace you earn money. In essence, workplaces are master teachers, the likes of which cannot be found in the school environment.

Successful transition from school to work for students with disabilities is also important on a much broader scale. Think of what would happen if everybody with a disability did not work. How would they live? How would they buy food or pay rent?

Most would have to rely on governmental programs such as Social Security Disability Insurance (SSDI) and subsidized housing.

When individuals with disabilities are gainfully employed, there is less need for taxpayers to fund subsidy programs. As a result, tax dollars otherwise spent on these areas can be saved or invested in other programs, such as education. Further, individuals with disabilities who are employed also pay taxes. By increasing the number of taxpayers and decreasing the number of people requiring public assistance, our nation's economy will grow and everybody will benefit.

In summary, transition from school to work does not benefit only students with disabilities. When students with disabilities learn the skills required to function successfully within the community and when schools furnish the services that these students need to accomplish their goals, everybody benefits—the students, their families, employers, co-workers, and society in general.

LEGISLATIVE DEVELOPMENT OF SCHOOL-TO-WORK TRANSITION

The development of school-to-work transition has a lengthy and diverse history. Its origin may even be traced back to medieval Europe, when parents sent their sons off to learn a trade from the local blacksmith or cobbler. In the United States, modern vocational training for individuals with disabilities did not get fully under way until the early 1900s.

World War I was just ending. Thanks to advances in medicine, thousands of American men were returning home alive. However, these medical advances came with a price. Whereas wounds that would have been fatal only years before were now treatable, limbs, sight, and mobility were often sacrificed. As a result, the United States was soon inundated with disabled veterans.

Realizing that the country could not support the thousands of individuals with disabilities resulting from the war, Congress passed a series of legislative measures designed to help these individuals support themselves. Among this legislation was the 1917 Smith-Hughes Act (P.L. 64-347), which provided rehabilitation and employment training services to veterans with disabilities. This act also provided funds for vocational programs in high schools across the country, including what you may know as home economics, agriculture, and shop classes. In 1920 the Smith-Hughes Act was extended by the Smith-Fess Act (P.L. 66-236), which authorized employment and rehabilitation training to civilians with disabilities.

Another flurry of disability legislation was passed by Congress following the United States's involvement in World War II. However, World War II presented another problem besides an inundation of disabled veterans. After the bombing of Pearl Harbor, the U.S. military needed to be rebuilt and modernized in a hurry. This required a large, skilled labor force. With most able-bodied men joining the armed forces, few were left to run the factories. This shortage of workers provided women and individuals with disabilities the opportunity to obtain jobs that otherwise would have been closed to them. To ensure proper preparation for this new area of job opportunity, the LaFollette Act (P.L. 77-113) was passed to provide vocational training to individuals with disabilities, including persons with mental retardation. This act was expanded in 1954 by the Vocational Rehabilitation Act Amendments (P.L. 83-565), which led to the creation of sheltered workshops and other employment-readiness programs.

Following World War II, the employment movement for people with disabilities gained additional momentum with the election of President John F. Kennedy. President Kennedy, having a sister with a disability, understood first-hand the need for vocational training programs. Consequently, the Vocational Education Act (P.L. 88-210) was passed by Congress in 1963. This act attempted to improve the vocational education system in the United States and created new programs for students with special needs, including those from lower socioeconomic backgrounds.

In an attempt to continue the late president's vision for employment opportunities for all individuals, Congress passed three other key pieces of disability-related legislation in the 1960s: the Vocational Rehabilitation Act Amendments of 1965 (P.L. 88-333), 1967 (P.L. 90-99), and 1968 (P.L. 90-391). These amendments authorized extended evaluations for potential vocational rehabilitation clients, eliminated the prerequisite for economic need to be eligible for vocational training, and expanded the definition of "handicapped" to include behavior disorders.

In the 1970s, additional landmark legislation was passed—the Rehabilitation Act of 1973 (P.L. 93-112), the Comprehensive Employment and Training Act of 1973 (P.L. 93-203), and the Education for All Handicapped Children Act of 1975 (P.L. 94-142; retitled the Individuals with Disabilities Education Act in 1990, P.L. 101-476). Among other things, the Rehabilitation Act of 1973 required that businesses receiving federal contracts initiate programs to hire, train, and promote persons with disabilities. Further, Section 504 of the Rehabilitation Act prevented discrimination against persons with disabilities based solely upon their disability.

The Comprehensive Employment Training Act (CETA) was designed to alleviate the high rates of unemployment experienced in the United States at the time. Specifically, CETA funded programs that helped train and find jobs for youth and adults without marketable skills. The Job Training Partnership Act (JTPA) of 1982 (P.L. 97-300) is an extension of CETA.

Finally, the Individuals with Disabilities Education Act (IDEA) addressed the issue of inequity between regular and special education students by ensuring that students with disabilities received a free and appropriate education (FAPE). Other stipulations included the development of an Individualized Education Program (IEP) for all special education students and the formulation of rights for students and their parents. Combined with CETA and the Rehabilitation Act, IDEA created an important foundation for contemporary special education as well as for the field of transition.

Transition programs and activities continued to grow throughout the 1980s. In 1984, for example, the Carl D. Perkins Vocational Education Act of 1985 extended the Vocational Education Act of 1963 by granting students with disabilities access to vocational education programs. This act also mandated that vocational goals and objectives be included in students' IEPs, thus forcing members of IEP teams to focus upon long-term vocational goals.

In 1990 transition services were officially defined in federal legislation. Thus, as part of its reauthorization, IDEA (P.L. 101-476) defined transition services as

> a coordinated set of activities for a student, designed within an outcome oriented process, which promotes movement from school to postschool activities, including postsecondary education, vocation training, integrated employment (including supported employment), continuing and adult education, adult services, independent living or community participation. The coordinated set of activities must: (a) be based on the individual student's needs; (b) take into account students' preferences and interests; and (c) include instruction, community experiences, the development of employment and other postschool adult living skills and functional vocational education. (34 C.F.R., § 300.18)

In addition to this definition, the reauthorization of IDEA required that transition be formally addressed in each student's IEP by the age of 16 or earlier, if appropriate. Specifically, the transition statement must include a listing of the services needed and the persons responsible for furnishing these services. Further, if the IEP team determines that a student does not need transition services, the IEP document must reflect and justify that decision.

IDEA was reauthorized again in 1997. Under this act (P.L. 105-17), the emphasis on long-term planning for transition from school to adult life continues with the requirement that transition be addressed by age 14, rather than 16 as mandated by the 1990 IDEA reauthorization. Further, the 1997 IDEA emphasizes the philosophy that IEPs should be driven by the student and his or her family, not by professional educators.

In summary, the legislative history of transition began in the early part of the 20th century, although at that time federal legislation addressed only the needs of disabled veterans. Shortly after World War II, however, legislative foci began to provide vocational training for individuals with developmental disabilities such as mental retardation. By the 1970s, legislation was addressing the issue of access to employment and education. Finally, in the 1990s, transition was defined and long-term planning for adult life was made a formal part of students' IEPs.

CURRENT ISSUES RELATED TO SCHOOL-TO-WORK TRANSITION

Several issues related to school-to-work transition are currently being debated within the special education literature. We briefly discuss some of these issues in this section.

Developing Student-Centered Transition Planning

Involving students in planning their own futures would appear to be commonsense. After all, who better than students themselves understand their hopes and dreams? Unfortunately, the emphasis on having students with disabilities attend their own IEP meetings is a relatively new one. And the concept of having students actively participate in, perhaps even coordinate, their own IEP meetings is even newer. Thanks to the passage of IDEA and the School-to-Work Opportunities Act, having students with disabilities actively participate in their IEPs is not only a fashionable policy, it is the law.

The benefits of having students actively involved in their educational planning are many and diverse. For example, students who aid in the development of their own goals tend to be more motivated to accomplish those goals. Students involved in the development of their IEPs often gain a greater sense of self-worth and confidence than students who are not actively involved in their educational planning. Further, other IEP members gain a greater understanding of the students' strengths, weaknesses, and desires than when students do not participate in their own educational planning.

Despite the many benefits of having students participate in developing their own IEPs, several barriers exist. For instance, participation is often limited by the student's capacity to make informed decisions. This is particularly true for students with severe cognitive disabilities or students who are very young. Active participation of students in their educational planning process may also be hampered by lack of motivation. This is frequently the problem when students have never been allowed to participate before or when they do not understand the purpose of the proceedings.

Cultivating Family Involvement

Much like student involvement in transition planning, active family participation in the development of IEPs also enhances the quality of educational planning. First, families possess insights into the behavior, abilities, and desires of their children that educators are often unable to obtain. Further, unlike educational professionals, families are intricately involved with their children's lives well after special education programming ends and, therefore, have a more permanent interest and commitment. For these reasons, recent legislation and educational policy have moved toward making family members equal members of the IEP process. However, despite this change in philosophy, barriers to cultivating family involvement still exist.

Specifically, families are often resistant to participating fully in educational planning because they lack an understanding of special education, especially the jargon used by special educators (e.g., IEPs, ITPs, LREs, LD, MR, FAPE). They also might not understand what is being expected of them, and perhaps view the special educator as the definite authority on what should be done with their children. Further, families are often going through transitions themselves, such as job changes, caring for elderly relatives and other children, and so on. The resulting stress, therefore, frequently inhibits their full participation in their children's education.

Educators can use numerous strategies to cultivate family involvement. For instance, by meeting with parents in neutral, nonthreatening locations (e.g., a coffee shop), family members and teachers can lay the groundwork for trusting relationships. Educators also need to learn how to listen actively to family members, allowing the family members to guide the discussion and to have a salient voice in the meeting. Further, teachers can encourage family members to actively participate in the education process by asking them to gather data or brainstorm ideas for potential solutions.

The most important point that special educators need to understand is that the concept of "family" is changing throughout America. Fifty years ago, single-parent households were nearly unheard of, let alone families with same-gender partners. To be effective, teachers must take into consideration the impact that these types of families might have on the education process and learn how to use the strengths these families offer. For instance, if a child comes from a cultural background that highly values an extended family, the transition process can be enriched by inviting members of the extended family (e.g., cousins, grandparents, neighbors, religious leaders) to IEP meetings.

Assessing Students and Their Progress

Educators cannot be effective without the ability to accurately assess their students' needs, abilities, and interests. In addition to guiding instruction, assessments evaluate a student's abilities and a teacher's effectiveness. In the area of transition, assessments are particularly important.

Transition-related assessments help determine a student's strengths, weaknesses, and interests. As such, they can offer important information to aid in future job development and in the selection of postsecondary education institutions and appropriate residential environments. Assessments can also identify possible accommodations and support systems.

Traditionally, assessments are thought to come in two varieties: formal and informal. Formal assessments involve standardized examinations, such as college entrance examinations and IQ tests. Simply put, formal assessments compare an individual student to an entire population of other students. For example, the results of an IQ test indicate how intelligent a student is compared to other students of the same age.

With informal assessments, on the other hand, specific information is gathered on a student that is subsequently compared to that individual student's goals and objectives. For instance, an interest inventory may be used to help students determine in what vocation they would be most successful. In this example, the skills and interests of the general population do not enter into the assessment. Other informal transition-related assessments include ecological inventories, vocational profiles, community-based work samples, interviews, portfolios, and observations.

For transition-related assessments to be useful, they must be diverse in nature. That is, they must gather information on a student in a number of different environments (e.g., classroom, playground, home), by a number of different individuals (e.g., regular educators, special education professionals, parents, the student), and across a broad time period. Finally, assessments are never complete. They are ongoing works in progress, constantly in need of being updated or reevaluated. As the student grows and changes, so too should the assessments used to help plan his or her future.

Facilitating Interdisciplinary and Agency Collaboration

For students to successfully transition from one stage of life (e.g., school) to another (e.g., work), they must be provided with support and resources. Because special educators are not experts in all areas of adult life, they need to call upon other professionals to help provide students with the supports and resources they require. For example, few special educators know about employment trends or are trained in job development. Vocational rehabilitation counselors and vocational technical educators are proficient in these areas, however, and therefore must be sought out. In other words, to be effective at facilitating transitions, special educators must be skilled collaborators.

The professionals with whom special educators must collaborate include more than vocational technical teachers and rehabilitation counselors. They also include, but are not limited to, regular educators, mental heath professionals, representatives from postsecondary or continuing education institutions, business leaders, representatives from government programs (e.g., Social Security, Medicare, food stamps, subsidized housing), and adult service providers (e.g., group homes, workshops, supported employment programs, semi-independent living facilities).

Collaborating with representatives from all these different fields and agencies is often difficult, given their diverse goals, expectations, and policies. For example, in special education programs, students with disabilities are entitled to certain services regardless of the cost to the school system. In contrast, in vocational rehabilitation programs, individuals with disabilities are not entitled to any services; further, the cost of services is frequently a major consideration when vocational rehabilitation counselors agree to program goals. Without an understanding of these differences between the various fields, effective interdisciplinary collaboration cannot transpire.

Briefly, effective collaborative relationships are based on five principles (Mattessich & Monsey, 1992):

1. *Identify mutual goals.* Even though all of the agencies listed above may have different perspectives, they all share the common goal of wanting to help individuals. Focusing upon this mutual goal could prevent many of the difficulties experienced by collaborators.

2. *Understand and work within each program's operating procedures.* Simply put, know how your teammates work. This includes understanding what rules gov-

ern their program and what personnel are responsible for certain aspects of the program operation.

3. *Share responsibility.* Nobody wants to be a part of a team if they always sit on the bench. To be effective, collaborators have to be actively involved in achieving the team's mutual goal.

4. *Share successes and failures.* The team wins together or loses together. If members of the team are blaming each other or taking all of the credit, a healthy collaborative relationship cannot develop.

5. *Share resources.* Sometimes agencies are reluctant to use their funds to finance an objective of the team (e.g., putting on a workshop for parents). In order for teams to be effective, they must share resources as equitably as possible. For instance, one agency might provide the funds for advertising a workshop, whereas others provide the staff needed to organize and conduct the workshop.

Collaboration in special education is no longer a philosophy or a best practice; it is the *only* practice. Special educators cannot hope to know everything about the world in which their students will live. Realizing this is the first step in linking students with disabilities with the supports and resources they will need to be successfully transitioned into the adult world.

Participating in Postsecondary Education

All too often, when people hear "student with a disability," thoughts of sheltered workshops, day programming, and residential services come to mind. However, what few people understand is that over 10% of college and university students have disabilities (National Center for Educational Statistics, 1993). Although these students typically have learning disabilities, sensory and physical impairments, or other health difficulties, students with all sorts of disabilities, including mental retardation, can benefit from postsecondary education.

Postsecondary education can be obtained through a variety of programs, not only colleges and universities. For example, trade schools teach skills ranging from welding to hair cutting. Further, community colleges, park district programs, and local clubs or groups may also be utilized by students with disabilities.

Effective participation in postsecondary education depends on three factors. First, there must be clear linkages between school-based programs and existing postsecondary options. That is, students and their parents need to know what options are available to them before the student leaves school. To accomplish this, representatives from postsecondary programs can be invited to attend IEP or Individual Transition Plan (ITP) meetings, or students could take tours of postsecondary programs.

Second, students must be empowered to advocate for the supports and accommodations that they require. Part of this empowerment involves informing students of their legal rights under the Americans with Disabilities Act of 1990 and Section 504 of the Rehabilitation Act and preparing them to be effective self-advocates.

Finally, professionals at postsecondary programs should be provided with information regarding a student's disabilities. This may range from training college professors in what to do in case a student has a seizure to making sure the university has the needed technology (books on tape or in Braille). Further, postsecondary teachers should be told of any teaching strategies that have been found to be effective with a given student in the past.

Promoting Social Inclusion

Prior to IDEA, most students with disabilities, especially those with severe disabilities, obtained their education in segregated settings. Gradually society's values began to evolve toward an emphasis on integrating students with disabilities in regular education classrooms. However, studies soon began to indicate that, even when students with disabilities were physically integrated, they often were not socially integrated. In other words, students with disabilities were not fully benefiting from the most important teachers in the classroom—their peers.

Students with disabilities spend more time with their peers than with their teachers and it is through their peers that they learn many valuable lessons. For example, peers model age-appropriate behaviors. They also explore topics typically not on the official school curricula (e.g., sex, fashion, drugs). Having students with disabilities interact with their peers is important because students tend to respect other students more than adults.

Facilitating social inclusion of students with disabilities is often more difficult than it sounds. For example, peers without disabilities may be reluctant to interact with students who appear different from themselves. Further, barriers between special and regular education may prevent opportunities for students with and without disabilities to interact. Despite these barriers, the social inclusion literature has documented several ways to promote and enhance social interactions between students with and without disabilities.

For instance, teaching students how to talk with others about their disability has been found to reduce fear and build social relationships. Teaching students social and dating skills has also been found to be beneficial. Further, teaching students with disabilities to self-monitor their social skills is also recommended.

However, changing students with disabilities is not the only way to facilitate social inclusion. For instance, it is often necessary to create opportunities for students with disabilities to interact with their peers. Methods of accomplishing this include, but are not limited to, having students with and without disabilities work together in groups, having students with and without disabilities eat lunch or have recess at the same time, and having students without disabilities serve as mentors to students with disabilities (or vice versa).

Facilitating social inclusion of students with disabilities is important because interaction with peers provides a valuable learning experience for all parties involved.

Further, the development of friendships is necessary to cultivate a high quality of life. Promoting social inclusion requires creativity and common sense. When trying to brainstorm ideas on how to create social integration, think first of how you meet people and then apply the same idea to your students.

CONCLUSION

While transitions from one stage of life to another can be challenging for any of us, the transition from school to work or postsecondary education and adult life can be especially daunting. For most young people, this means leaving the relative comfort of school and peers. Many even leave the protection and shelter of their families to venture into the "adult world," with its unique set of responsibilities and demands, to pursue postsecondary education or jobs. Add to these uneasy prospects a disability, and the looming transition often looks even more daunting.

After having been paid lip service in various educational, vocational, and political environments for many years, transition as a field of study was only formalized and defined with the reauthorization of IDEA in 1990 and again in 1997. However, although the law now mandates that transition be addressed by age 14, along with provisions for active student and family participation in the planning process, educators and others involved with long-range planning for students with disabilities are faced with the often complex task of implementing these laws and regulations.

In addition to a general overview of transition, including the legislative background, in this chapter we have focused on the most salient aspects of transition and transition planning, including student and family involvement, transition-related assessment, principles of collaboration, postsecondary education, and the importance of social inclusion of students with disabilities. As underscored in our projections for the future, although a lot has been accomplished in the area of transition from school to work for students with disabilities, the battle is not yet over. With expansion of the transition movement come questions related to who is responsible for various aspects of the process, what additional training is needed for educators to ensure successful lifelong transition of their students, and where to obtain funding.

REFERENCES

Americans with Disabilities Act of 1990, 42 U.S..C. § 12101 *et seq.*

Carl D. Perkins Vocational Education Act of 1985, 50 Stat. 759.

Clark, G. M., & Kolstoe, O. P. (1995). *Career development and transition education for adolescents with disabilities* (2nd ed.). Needham Heights, MA: Allyn & Bacon.

Education for All Handicapped Children of 1975, 20 U.S.C. § 1400 *et seq.*

Halpern, A. S. (1985). Transition: A look at the foundations. *Exceptional Children, 51*, 479–486.

Individuals with Disabilities Education Act of 1975, 20 U.S.C. § 1400 *et seq.*

Individuals with Disabilities Education Act Reauthorization of 1997, 20 U.S.C. § 1400 *et seq.*

Mattessich, P. W., & Monsey, B. R. (1992). *Collaboration: What makes it work.* St. Paul, MN: Amhert H. Wilder Foundation Publishing Center.

National Center for Educational Statistics. (1993). *Digest of educational statistics: The 1987 national postsecondary student aid study.* Washington, DC: U.S. Department of Education.

Rehabilitation Act of 1973, 29 U.S.C. § 701 *et seq.*

Smith-Fess Act (Vocational Rehabilitation of Persons Disabled in Industry Act of 1920), 41 Stat. 735.

Smith-Hughes Act (Vocational Education Act of 1917), 20 U.S.C. § 11 *et seq.*

Vocational Rehabilitation Act Amendments of 1954, 68 Stat. 652.

Vocational Rehabilitation Act Amendments of 1965, 79 Stat. 1282.

Vocational Rehabilitation Act Amendments of 1967, 81 Stat. 250.

Vocational Rehabilitation Act Amendments of 1968, 82 Stat. 298.

Will, M. (1984). *OSERS programming for the transition of youth with disabilities: Bridges from school to working life.* Washington, DC: Office of Special Education and Rehabilitative Services.

Educating Students with Mild Mental Retardation

James R. Patton, Edward A. Polloway, and Tom E. C. Smith

E xamining the connection of past, present, and future endeavors related to the education of students with mild retardation is well warranted as we approach a new millennium. However, we should not be misled by the belief that most of the issues that face the field of special education today or will face the field in the future are completely new. Patton, Blackbourn, and Fad (1996) noted that a recycling phenomenon can be seen if one looks back through the history of the field:

> If you read the historical literature, you will see that today's issues and problems are remarkably similar to those of long ago. Issues, problems, and ideas arise, flower, go to seed, and reappear when the conditions are again right for their growth. (p. 305)

Blatt (1987) cautioned that we also should not take our recent accomplishments too seriously and admonished us to not forget the historical legacies from which our field has evolved:

> The field suffers from "cultural amnesia" . . . the widespread belief that everything worthwhile has been invented during our lifetimes, and for the most part, has been invented within the last few years . . . we in this field have chosen to ignore or forget our rich history, traditions, and the wisdom accumulated through the decades. (p. 363)

Thus, a historical review of the condition of mild mental retardation confirms that it has been and continues to be a condition concerned with social competence. One of the earliest formal definitions of mental retardation highlighted the idea that a person's incomplete mental development contributed to a situation where "the individual is incapable of adapting himself to the normal environment of his fellows" (Tredgold, 1937, p. 4). Nearly all conceptualizations of mental retardation continue to focus on the problems of adaptation to one's environment as an important manifestation of this condition. Some professionals, such as Greenspan (1997), promote the notion of personal competence (conceptual intelligence, social intelligence, and practical intelligence) as the defining quality of mental retardation. Interestingly, today's emphasis on adult outcomes actually reconnects current educational efforts with the emphasis of earlier times on social competence.

Children and youth with mild mental retardation, along with those students with various sensory impairments, have received special education longer than students with most other disabilities. In the United States, special classes for students with mental retardation can be traced back to 1897. However, economic reasons for educating and employing students with mental retardation were recognized in Europe even earlier, as the following quote demonstrates:

> The proper care and instruction of these . . . children will no doubt be expensive; but whatever it may amount to, the cost of neglecting them is heavier still. They must be supported in idleness, if they are not taught to work. . . . A considerable proportion may be enabled to earn their own living, if placed under proper superintendence, and employed at work suited to their peculiar powers. (Pim, 1864)

Although it has been nearly two centuries since the first-documented attempts to instruct systematically individuals with mental retardation, it has only been since the beginning of the 1900s that the needs of individuals with more mild limitations have been recognized. It was not until the mid-1970s that special education became a federal mandate and a system to guarantee an appropriate education was put into place.

Beginning with Itard's work in the late 1700s and early 1800s, attention was focused on educating individuals with mental retardation. Itard, a French physician, attempted to educate Victor, a young boy with a number of severe delays (e.g., in language) found in the Aveyron forest in France in 1799 (Blatt, 1987). Although he worked with Victor for 5 years, Itard did not feel like he had been successful. However, regardless of his perceived success with Victor, Itard received a great deal of recognition for his efforts. The influence he had on other professionals of his time clearly distinguishes him as one of the most significant pioneers in the field of special education. His work was honored in a recent bicentennial celebration in the journal *Remedial and Special Education* (1998).

Several individuals followed the precedent established by Itard in their efforts to educate individuals with mental retardation. Edouard Séguin, Johann Guggenbuhl, Dorothea Dix, Samuel Howe, and Hervey Wilbur all worked to develop and implement educational programs during the early and middle 1800s. While the work of these individuals resulted in optimism, the late 1800s brought about a climate of pessimism, followed by a backlash in the early part of the 20th century (Beirne-Smith, Ittenbach, & Patton, 1998). Regardless of the uneven start in efforts to work with individuals who had mental retardation, the early efforts of these individuals laid the foundation for further developments that would positively impact individuals with disabilities.

The introduction of the mental test by Binet and Simon in 1905 provided a mechanism for making mild mental retardation a meaningful concept. Before then, it is safe to say that much of what occurred in the way of treatment, education, or services was directed to individuals who had a range of needs that were more extensive and pervasive; the archaic terms used to describe these individuals are imbecile and idiotic. Then, beginning in the early 20th century, a test was available for identifying students whose cognitive abilities (i.e., conceptual intelligence) would cause problems for them in academics. It became clear to many professionals that the primary concerns related to this educable group of students were manifest during the 6 hours that they were in school.

PAST

General Demographic Trends

Historically, mild mental retardation was the largest, or one of the two largest, areas of disability served in the field of special education. In the early 1930s, mild mental retardation was the largest category of students with disabilities provided services in the public schools (Dunn, 1973). Since the 1940s and prior to the advent of the learning disabilities category in the 1960s, the other high-incidence disability in the public schools was oral communication disabilities (i.e., speech and language disorders). The traditional assumptions of prevalence of mental retardation in the general population, and likewise of the school population, ranged from 2% to 3%.

The demographic pattern for traditional classes of students with mild mental retardation, typically referred to as EMR (educable mentally retarded) classes, painted a rather straightforward picture. Dunn's (1973) analysis was particularly apt. He described the population as being individuals from poverty backgrounds; with significant academic achievement difficulties, often with concomitant behavioral disorders (which may have led to their referral for special services); and frequently with a parent or sibling who also was mentally retarded. A large number of individuals from minority groups was included within the EMR population, and the population was largely male.

Paradigm Background

The predominant paradigm relative to individuals with mild retardation was a services-based view that emphasized segregation (Bradley & Knoff, 1995; Polloway, Smith, Patton, & Smith, 1996). Under this model, the assumption was that best practice for public school students with mild mental retardation required pull-out services, most often to special classes. However, in some locations, special schools that were populated only with students with disabilities were also initiated. This special class movement, as it has been referred to historically, was the dominant practice until rather recent times. These classes were often full-day, self-contained placements, although in more "progressive" situations and with the advent of the resource room, half-time placement in special education with the balance of the day in general education classes became another option.

A typical, traditional perspective on individuals with mild mental retardation was categorized as the "inverted U." Under the inverted-U concept, individuals were seen to benefit from integration to a certain extent (e.g., in art, music, physical education), but at some point in the segregation-to-integration continuum, the overall benefits of integration were considered to diminish as individuals were receiving more time in general education but less appropriate instruction. Under this analysis, the common assumption was that primary academic areas and vocational areas were best handled within special education placements.

This services-oriented system, while seemingly established on the reasonable goal of returning students to general education, typically meant a life sentence to special education that offered little contact with nondisabled peers or the promise of return to general education. Often, students even had lunch and recess at separate times from other students to ensure limited contact. The prevailing philosophy related to educational placement was that students with mild mental retardation should be placed with children who had similar learning problems (Ingram, 1960). During the heyday of the special class movement, few students with any type of mild disability actually exited special classes (Dunn, 1973).

The overriding point of the special services paradigm was that pull-out to special education was most beneficial because it would lead to enhanced achievement and preparation for postschool adjustment and provided settings in which students would be more comfortable. Furthermore, some researchers based support of this placement on their belief that many children with mild mental retardation were either rejected or totally isolated when they were placed in general classrooms (Kirk & Johnson, 1951). It was assumed that this commitment would best serve the long-term needs of individuals with mild mental retardation.

Assessment Practices

The assessment practices used with students with mental retardation were primarily clinical in nature. Psychologists, and often medical personnel, evaluated students suspected of having mental retardation and made the diagnosis (Kirk & Johnson, 1951). For most of this century, mental retardation was considered a clinical category of disabilities and was diagnosed by medical and psychological personnel primarily using intelligence tests. As a result, general and special education teachers had limited input into this diagnosis. Eventually, general education teachers began to play a primary role in the initial identification of students suspected of having mild mental retardation, as they were most often the ones to initiate a referral.

More complete and objective techniques for diagnosing mental retardation were sought in the 1920s. Doll (1924) noted that the prevailing measure of intelligence, the Binet Scale, was imperfect for use with individuals with mild mental retardation and that there was a need for the application of more uniform standards. He discussed the potential of using a "clinical syllabus" in its entirety as a way of obtaining a complete picture of the individual. The clinical syllabus covered 10 areas of inquiry, arranged under two main categories:

1. Study of the individual on the basis of previous history: family history, personal developmental history, social history, school history, and medical history

2. Study of the individual by direct examination: medical examination, neuropsychiatric examination, psychological examination, scholastic examination, and (if appropriate) industrial or vocational examination

Kolstoe (1976) described the typical system for identifying students with mental retardation that had emerged by the 1960s. Many school districts followed a hierarchical system composed of (1) school failure; (2) teacher nomination focused on motor, attention, and emotional behaviors; and (3) intelligence test score below a certain cutoff level (in the 1960s this technically was an IQ of 85).

In addition to the fact that emphasis in identification practices was primarily, or solely, on subaverage general intellectual functioning, limited amounts of time were available to diagnosticians. The following description, provided by Dunn (1973), captures the reality of the times:

1. The child was given an individual psychometric examination by a school psychologist or psychometrician. Typically, only one or two hours were available per pupil to administer and interpret a test battery and write up a report. Considering the shortage of such diagnosticians, the child was usually given only (a) an individual intelligence test such as the Stanford–Binet or one of the Wechsler scales and (b) an individual screening test of school achievement such as the Peabody Individual Achievement Test or the Wide Range Achievement Test.

2. The diagnostician may also have screened the pupil to rule out emotional disturbance as the major disability . . . .

3. The child may also have been referred to medical or paramedical people to rule out sensory deficits (vision and/or hearing losses) as the primary cause. (pp. 139–140)

The process described by Dunn varied across school systems. In certain schools during the 1960s and 1970s, a special education teacher, often the resource teacher, was given the responsibility of determining the academic achievement of students suspected of having mental retardation. The collection of adaptive behavior information, if done at all, was usually performed by the school social worker.

Prior to the implementation of the Education for All Handicapped Children Act of 1975 (EHA), the specific procedures for determining eligibility were characterized by great variability as well. In many schools, a case conference was convened after all the data had been gathered. A committee, composed of various professionals, discussed the results, determined whether the student met the designated eligibility criteria for special education, and made placement and program decisions. Far too often, however, as Dunn (1973) related, deviations occurred:

> Often, because of time considerations, system pressures, and manpower shortages, no such conference was convened. The director of special education, or one of his central office staff, simply placed the pupil in a special education program on the basis of his being declared eligible by a psychometrician. (p. 140)

Other than practices associated with identification and eligibility, little discussion of other types of assessment, such as program planning and progress monitoring, exists in the historical literature on mental retardation. One practice, diagnostic teaching, however, did grow in popularity during the 1960s and 1970s and received some attention in professional sources. This assessment technique was prescriptive in nature and related well to the clinical models from which it evolved. The sequence involves the following steps: (1) identify specific areas of behavior; (2) assess student to determine what behaviors currently are demonstrated; (3) identify specific behavioral objectives; (4) determine relative effectiveness of potential motivators and reinforcers; (5) note most effective modalities for working with the student; (6) obtain requisite materials for implementing the instructional program; (7) determine instructional strategies for teaching the behavioral objectives; and (8) evaluation of intervention—completed as a basis for further assessment. Many components of diagnostic teaching remain in vogue today.

Curricular and Instructional Practices

Historically, curricular and instructional practices in programs for individuals with mild mental retardation varied from theory to practice. In theory, the commitment was clearly to a functional orientation in curriculum and preparation for adulthood. Many professionals felt strongly that the four major objectives of education (self-realization, human relationships, economic efficiency, and civic responsibility), as specified by the Education Policies Commission (1938), were appropriate guidelines to use with students who had mild mental retardation as well.

Dunn (1973) identified four curricular approaches emphasized at different times from 1900 to the early 1970s in classes for students with mild mental retardation: (1) arts and crafts, (2) units of instruction with rudimentary academics, (3) mental health (i.e., "keep the students happy"), and (4) the occupational education approach. These orientations operated outside the flow of the general education curriculum, as they were housed in self-contained special education classrooms.

Other descriptions of curricular emphases can be found in the historical literature. Kirk and Johnson (1951) generated a list of eight purposes that should guide the curricular structure of programs for students with mild mental retardation. Kirk (1972) later noted that these eight purposes could be categorized into three broad areas: social competence (i.e., getting along with others), personal adequacy (i.e., ability to live with oneself in some sort of equilibrium), and occupational competence (i.e., ability to support oneself through productive activity). Four broad curricular areas, articulated by Dunn (1973), reflected the general orientation of curriculum during the 1970s: (1) basic readiness and practical academics development; (2) communication, oral language, and cognitive development; (3) socialization, family living, self-care, recreation, and personality development; and (4) prevocational and vocational development.

Unfortunately, however, in the 1970s and into the 1980s, curricular emphases often did not reflect the life adjustment commitment that many professionals were promoting. Frequently, special class programs represented little more than the watering down of the general education curriculum. Many programs could be characterized as not functional, and the limited, nonspecialized instruction provided in reading, math, and writing frequently was not effective. This demeanor of programs in mild mental retardation often led to the derisive comment that there were only two things wrong with special education: It is not special, and it is not education. The most apparent chastisement of these practices came with Dunn's (1968) article that called for an end to such special class programs for students with mild mental retardation who came from variant sociocultural backgrounds. The impact of Dunn's article cannot be overstated; it has commonly been rated as the seminal work in the field of special education (see Patton, Polloway, & Epstein, 1987).

Preparation for Adulthood/Transition

The title of this section may seem strange at first, especially as it applies to the past. The fact that, in the past, systematic transition planning and follow-through were not mandated should not be interpreted that transition-like activities did not occur. The previous section established the importance that many professionals gave to the preparation for adulthood and independent living. Unquestionably, students with mild mental retardation have made the transition from school to community ever since they have been in school. As a result, examining "transition" activities of the past is valid but must be understood in the context of the time.

Kolstoe (1970) suggested that the entire program for students with mild mental retardation should be focused on developing the necessary skills for independent living. Hungerford's (1943) Occupational Education curriculum and the emphasis on work–study programs, stemming from Kolstoe's earlier work (Kolstoe & Frey, 1965), typified the importance given to preparation for adulthood. Interestingly, the work of Hungerford and Kolstoe laid the foundation for the development of many of the contemporary life skills and vocational training curricula in evidence today.

As students progressed through school, a greater curricular emphasis was given to prevocational and vocational activities. Dunn (1973) remarked that, at the junior high school level, "the emphasis on academics should fall off considerably in favor of greater attention on such more practical skills as life adjustment, home management, and occupational education" (p. 174). Smith (1968) thought that at least half of the school day should be devoted to occupational instruction. By the time a student with mild mental retardation reached the senior high school level, it was suggested that a majority of time be given to vocational pursuits.

Many students with mild mental retardation participated in work–study programs that were set up in high schools. In this arrangement, the student spent half of the instructional day at a specific job in the community and the other half at school taking classes. In their often-cited book, *A High School Work Study Program for Mentally Subnormal Students*, Kolstoe and Frey (1965) described the job performance skills as well as the academic, personal, and social skills that are essential for meaningful outcomes.

In 1943 Congress passed the Barden–LaFollette Act that extended vocational rehabilitation services to individuals with mild mental retardation. Previously, services provided through vocational rehabilitation were sanctioned only for individuals with physical disabilities. The 1943 act made it possible for young adults with mild retardation to receive job training, placement, and other follow-up services after formal schooling was completed.

The value of supports in the everyday lives of individuals with mental retardation was advocated over 30 years ago. In his book, *The Cloak of Competence*, Edgerton (1967) highlighted the importance of benefactors in the lives of adults whom he followed up upon their exiting from an institutional setting in California. Benefactors were defined by Edgerton as "normal persons who help [former residents] with their many problems" (p. 172). His work clearly underscored the importance that other people play in assisting adults with mental retardation in dealing with the exigencies of everyday life.

Teacher Roles and Preparation

During the early part of the 20th century, no formal, systematic training of teachers of students with mental retardation existed. There were no special education teacher training programs or inservices for those who had been hired to work with this group of students. As the number of students with mild mental retardation began to reach significant numbers, schools were forced to hire "essentially untrained teachers, many of whom were told that they needed only to keep their pupils happy, busy, and out of trouble" (Dunn, 1973, p. 155).

Over the years, training programs in special education were created across the country. Most of these training programs were categorical in nature; that is, their intent was to prepare teachers to work with students with specific disabilities.

By the early 1970s, gallant efforts were under way to train large numbers of special education teachers. Fueled by substantial amounts of federal dollars, training programs were able to provide support to many prospective special educators.

PRESENT

Current Demographic Trends

The most recent two decades have set the tone for a significantly different population of students identified with mild mental retardation. The trend was first noted by MacMillan and Borthwick in 1980 when they identified a new group of students who were "patently more disabled" than their counterparts from earlier times. This trend, initially identified in California, became a national phenomenon throughout the 1980s. Polloway and Smith (1983, 1988) expanded on this concept and laid the foundation for subsequent research which analyzed the so-called "new EMRs" in the public schools.

The trend within this population has had some obvious impacts. Most apparently, the prevalence of the population has decreased significantly from earlier estimates of 2% to 3%. Recent federal data (U.S. Department of Education, 1997) indicate that the prevalence of children and youth ages 6 to 17 identified as mentally retarded was only 1.13% during the 1995–1996 school year. The change in number reflects a dramatic difference from data reported at the time of the implementation of EHA. Nevertheless, interstate variance in prevalence continues to be significant, with Alabama identifying 3.08% of its school population as having mental retardation while New Jersey serves only .29% percent and California .44%.

With the decreased prevalence has come a change in demographics. As a long-term response to the *Larry P. v. Riles* (1972) case in California, the absolute number of children from minority backgrounds has decreased significantly. Nevertheless, common findings indicate that an overrepresentation of minority children continues, with African American students 2.4 times more likely to be identified as mentally retarded than their non–African American peers (see Oswald, Best, & Singh, 1999). To some extent, these findings may be attributed in large part to the correlation between minority class status and social class in this country, with the presumption that lower social class brings with it elevated risks for mild mental retardation. Recently, MacMillan, Gresham, and Forness (1998) discussed at some length issues that continue to tie lower IQ to racial and social class differences and hence increase risks for mental retardation. Their analysis should be sought for further information. At the same time, it is instructive that Oswald and colleagues (1999) reported disproportionality even after correcting for demographic variables.

While the percentage of individuals with mild mental retardation has decreased, an assumption of higher numbers of male students seems to continue to be accurate. On the other hand, the frequency of behavior disorders (historically a biasing factor leading to referral and ultimately to labeling and placement) seems to be less significant in contemporary EMR programs.

Paradigm Considerations

The 1990s have brought a significant shift to a supports-based paradigm in discussions in the field of mental retardation. Although public school programs for students with mild mental retardation have been slower to respond to this paradigmatic shift, the influence is noteworthy. The publication in 1992 of the revised manual of the American Association on Mental Retardation (AAMR), *Mental Retardation: Definition, Classification, and Systems of Supports* (Luckasson, et al., 1992), has proven to be particularly influential in the current discussions of supports.

The supports paradigm is a powerful concept that extends the simple placement-based concept of inclusion. Specifically, through a supports model, inclusion thus would need to be seen as "supported education" in order to truly reflect the fact that individuals are not simply placed in general education classes but also provided appropriate supports in those settings. The supported education concept has been elaborated on elsewhere (e.g., Smith, Polloway, Patton, & Dowdy, 1998).

An intriguing paradox is that, although the trend toward inclusion has been a significant rhetorical one and the supports model has begun to gain favor, the placement of students with mental retardation in the public schools continues to reflect a significant emphasis on separate classes. For example, the U.S. Department of Education (1997) reported that, in the 1994–1995 school year, 57.7% of such students were in separate classes, whereas only 12.1% were taught full time in regular classes and 25.7% were served through resource room settings (with the remaining approximately 5% of individuals served through separate facilities, residential programs, or both). Although these data seem to suggest that inclusion is not a reality for many students with mild mental retardation, and in fact the data do represent a slight elevation in the placement figures for special classes from those of 10 years ago, certain provisos need to be considered. First, the number of students with mild mental retardation being served in the schools has been reduced significantly (as noted above). Therefore, it seems clear that those individuals who continue to be served are more likely to have more serious disabilities and perhaps then be deemed in need of more significant support services that are typically available in inclusive settings. Second, the most recent data are from the 1994–1995 school year, and thus the philosophical, sociopolitical, and educational trend toward inclusion may be reflected in data from more recent school years. At any rate, it is clear that separate classes have remained the placement of choice for many schools in their efforts to address the needs of students with mental retardation.

Assessment Practices

Assessment practices have changed somewhat in recent years. Whereas in the past students with mental retardation were traditionally identified via clinical testing by psychological or medical personnel, today identification and eligibility are determined by school-based teams composed of various members of the professional staff.

One aspect related to eligibility that has not changed is the preeminence of the intellectual functioning criterion in such determinations. Although definitionally adaptive behavior is supposed to be given the same weighting as intellectual functioning, in practice this requirement is not being implemented. Beirne-Smith et al. (1998) provided the following commentary: "Whatever the reason, adaptive behavior takes a back seat to intellectual functioning in the decision-making process. This undermines the value of determining typical behavior regimens and may be a disservice to many students at the margin of eligibility" (p. 87).

Recently, the State of Iowa developed technical assistance guidelines for assisting with the identification of students with mental retardation. The intent was to operationalize the criteria that were based on the definition used in Iowa. Initially, a number of innovative ideas were being considered. However, after a yearlong collaborative effort of a range of stakeholders, four criteria emerged: intellectual functioning, adaptive behavior, developmental period, and educational performance (Maurer, 1997). The resultant criteria and suggested ways to measure them were predictable; however, the fourth criterion did add a new element to the definitional picture.

Contemporary thinking has placed an increased emphasis on looking at students' strengths and areas of need. In addition, attention has been given to the need to have effective techniques for monitoring the educational progress of students. A call for the use of alternative forms of assessment (e.g., situational, curriculum-based, authentic, and outcome-based assessments) has been given (Norlander, 1995).

Perhaps one of the most problematic issues related to assessment for students with mild mental retardation is their required participation in all forms of "high-stakes" testing. As a result of the 1997 reauthorization of the Individuals with Disabilities Education Act (IDEA), students with disabilities are not to be excluded from such testing—a practice that has been very common in recent times.

Curricular and Instructional Practices

The inclusion movement has also influenced curricular and instructional practices. With the emphasis on greater involvement of students with mild disabilities in general education classrooms, curriculum and instruction often become a function of what is being taught in those classrooms. Thus, increasingly, the regular curriculum has become the program of choice for more students with mild mental retardation. Perusal of data on the preferences of general education teachers regarding modifications and adaptations for such students seems to indicate that preferred adaptations revolve around changes in instructional delivery systems and, in some cases, response modes (such as through testing), but not changes in the actual curriculum or the standards associated with the content (Polloway, Bursuck, Jayanthi, Epstein, & Nelson, 1996). To the extent that these observations are verified, it would appear that a specialized curriculum does not commonly await students with mild mental retardation when they are placed in such classes.

At the same time, it is noteworthy that some individuals have begun to explore ways in which inclusion and functional curricula can be accommodated jointly. For example, a position statement from the Division on Career Development and Transition of the Council for Exceptional Children (Clark, Field, Patton, Brolin, & Sitlington, 1994) described at some length a model for such an attempt. In addition, contemporary work in the area of life skills curricula (e.g., Patton, Cronin, & Wood, 1999) increasingly has indicated ways in which real-life topics can be integrated into existing curricula. Many of these recommendations can be implemented in a general education program, although evidence that this is happening to any great extent is limited.

The emergence of self-determination as a critical dimension that must be considered has had a major impact on students with mild mental retardation. Recent years have seen an explosion of writings on this topic, federal support for the projects, and the development of a number of curricula. The 1997 reauthorization of IDEA has strengthened the need for students to be able to exercise the skills associated with self-determination.

Preparation for Adulthood/Transitions

Historically, many students with mild mental retardation were in programs clearly characterized as functional and adult outcome oriented. However, in more recent times, more of these students were placed in inclusive settings where curricular emphases varied greatly. The curricula of those students who remained in special education settings typically maintained a functional orientation.

A discernible focus on supports has emerged. The idea that adults need and regularly use supports underscores the importance of implementing this concept with young adults with mild mental retardation. Attention had been focused on the need to develop natural supports that exist in one's environment.

In 1990, IDEA mandated that every student receiving special education services must have some type of transition planning activity in place by age 16. Recent changes to the law require that a statement of transition needs be determined and written into the IEP by age 14. These transition requirements can only enhance the set of activities designed to help these students move into new roles after school is over. Interestingly, prior to the transition mandates of IDEA, students with mild mental retardation probably had the best planning and preparation for adulthood of all groups of students in special education.

Even though the nature of their programs and various employment-related activities can be observed in the secondary programs of many students with mild mental retardation, the need to plan comprehensively for the transition to community is essential. The critical elements of good transition practice are reflected in the following list of guiding principles. Whereas these suggestions are recognized as essential by most professionals today, their actual implementation in school systems across the nation varies greatly.

- Transition efforts must start early.
- Transition planning must be comprehensive.
- Decisions must balance what is ideal with what is possible.
- Active and meaningful student participation is essential.
- Family involvement is crucial.
- Diversity issues must be considered.
- Supports are beneficial and used by everyone.
- Community-based experiences reap benefits.
- Interagency commitment, cooperation, and coordination is needed and must be improved.
- Timing is critical.
- Transition planning process should be considered a capacity-building activity.
- Transition needs must be ranked and acted upon based on a number of factors.
- Transition planning is needed by all students. (Patton & Dunn, 1998, pp. 14–19)

Another planning-related activity that has been used more with individuals with mental retardation than with other students is personal futures planning. Personal futures planning involves the identification of a "shared vision of the unique situation of a specific individual and a plan of action for moving toward that goal" (Bradley & Knoll, 1995, p. 15). Fundamentally, the transition planning process implemented in schools shares this goal; however, in practice, it often plays out differently as a mere compliance activity.

Teacher Roles and Preparation

Most of the training programs designed specifically for preparing teachers to work with students who have mental retardation are gone. Today, many special education preparation programs are generic in that they prepare teachers to work with students who have mild disabilities. The former training emphases of mild mental retardation, learning disabilities, and behavior disorders frequently have been joined together into one generic track. Whereas there used to be a separate course in methods, materials, and curriculum for each distinct disability area, there is now one generic course.

Many programs now require training, and therefore certification eligibility, in both general and special education. Graduates of many undergraduate programs leave with special education certification for Grades K–12 and general education certification for Grades K–6 or K–8. This is a beneficial trend, as it increases the chances that special education teachers will have more knowledge, skill development, and experiences in important areas such as reading. In the past, the only exposure some special education teachers received in a subject area like reading might be a session or two in a special education methods course.

Clearly the role of the special education teacher in today's schools has changed significantly. Even though some of the basic competencies related to behavior management, assessment, and instructional accommodations remain important, special education teachers today must be able to take their knowledge and skills to general education classroom settings, where they collaborate and sometimes co-teach with general education teachers.

A current area of training concern is the preservice preparation and inservice training required of paraeducators. Educational aides or assistants are frequently used nowadays in schools across the country. In addition to the many issues associated with their use, appropriate ways to train them have come to the forefront in recent years (see Pickett & Gerlach, 1997).

FUTURE

Considering the future poses both great freedom and debilitating limitations. On the one hand, who is to say that any future prognostication is wrong until that time when it is proven so? On the other hand, other than the earlier stated reality that many issues recycle, discussing the future comes with two major limitations. First, too many critical sociopolitical factors that greatly affect how we might educate students with mild mental retardation are unknown. Second, a distinction must be made between what one thinks might happen and what one might want to happen. Blatt (1987) offered the best caveat for a section on future trends like this one: "What follows is less a calculation of what will be than it is my understanding of what could be, of what should be" (p. 364).

Future Conceptual Trends

The projection of the future in terms of the field of mild mental retardation is fraught with problems. It would appear that the central issue is whether the contemporary concept of mild mental retardation itself will persevere. The AAMR (Luckasson et al., 1992) called for an end to the use of the term *mild* (as well as the other levels of retardation in the field of mental retardation), to be replaced by classification according to levels of supports (i.e., intermittent, limited, extensive, pervasive). However, recent data indicate that, at least in terms of research endeavors, the use of the levels of retardation within the 1983 AAMR system continues and the levels of supports model has been largely ignored (see Polloway, Smith, Chamberlain, Denning, & Smith, 1999). Polloway and associates (1999) found that less than 1% of research articles cited the 1992 AAMR system. In addition, research on the adoption of the new system by the respective state departments of education also indicates limited response to AAMR's 1992 definition and classification guidelines (Polloway, Denning, & Chamberlain, 1998). The American Psychological Association, for example, reacted so negatively to the definitional changes that the organization developed its own manual and definitional perspective (Jacobson & Mulick, 1996).

Thus, it appears that the concept of mild mental retardation will likely continue for the foreseeable future. However, the demographic trends, particularly in relation to identification patterns, do suggest that the number of individuals so identified will continue to decline, albeit probably at a less steep rate than has been the case between 1980 and 1995. Under the historical assumption that approximately .4% of the general population might be labeled as having moderate, severe, or profound retardation (as traditionally defined), an important data point to continue to investigate is the growing approximation of the total population with mental retardation to this figure of .4%. Currently, based on a prevalence figure of 1.13%, it would seem that approximately .7% of the school population might be seen as mildly mentally retarded but, as noted earlier, in some states that figure would be much lower.

Widespread reluctance to use the term mild mental retardation to label children continues to have an impact on practices in the schools. In the future, use of the mental retardation label for these higher functioning individuals will no doubt continue to be challenged. The use of some alternative terminology (e.g., general learning disabilities, educationally handicapped, adaptive deficiency) has been tried in the past and perhaps will bear fruit in the future. However, under the assumption that "a rose by any other name" holds sway, we will continue to identify and need to serve and support individuals with mild mental retardation.

Assessment Practices

Placement and assessment practices for students with mild mental retardation will likely continue to emphasize inclusion and less formal assessment procedures. Inclusion will probably continue to expand in the future. More and more states are changing special education certification to focus on supporting students in general classroom settings. Co-teaching, team teaching, and other collaborative instructional practices are being used as a framework for teacher training. The 1997 reauthorization of IDEA continues to emphasize placing students with disabilities in general education settings. Funding formulas in states and federal regulations support the provision of services in general classrooms.

Assessment procedures will also likely continue to deemphasize formal, norm-referenced testing and emphasize informal assessment procedures. The change in the AAMR definition of mental retardation continues to emphasize functional assessment of adaptive behavior and daily living skills (Luckasson et al., 1992). Although the use of psychologists to diagnose mental retardation using individual intelligence testing will likely continue in the future, the role of medical personnel will continue to decline as mental retardation is viewed more in the context of social implications rather than medical implications of the condition.

Curricular and Instructional Practices

The key issue in terms of curriculum and instruction is the resolution of the relevance of educational programming for students with mild mental retardation. In 1964 Cassidy and Stanton raised the core question of "effective for what?" in relation to the then-controversial efficacy studies of special classes. Essentially, the question these authors posed involved what it is that we wanted educational programs to be for individuals with mental retardation. In the new millennium, this question will be particularly apt as the social gains presumed to be stemming from inclusion will be evaluated against the academic and life skills accomplishments of students served in general education. It seems likely that the difficulties encountered by students with mild mental retardation in inclusive classrooms will create a more significant cry for substantial supports (e.g., collaborative teaching) for these individuals so that significant changes, not only in terms of instructional adaptations but also in curriculum content, will occur in order to ensure that these individuals are receiving appropriate educational programs.

Two trends may prove to have significant impacts on the successful inclusion of students with mild mental retardation in responsive general education classrooms. First, the more extensive use of technology promises to provide teachers with more opportunities to individualize instruction and, in theory, could provide students an opportunity for more curricular modifications and alternative curricular focus in the same class. Second, the emphasis on more authentic forms of assessment and learning may lead to more community-based educational opportunities for students in general. Past research supports the fact that community-based instruction is a critical variable for students with mental retardation and hence, to the extent that it is used in general education, it might provide students with mild mental retardation the best of both worlds.

Preparation for Adulthood/Transition

Many perplexing dilemmas await those who work with young adults with mild mental retardation in their attempts to prepare them for the challenges of adulthood. First, the continued increase of placing these students in inclusive school settings, albeit very desirable, will reduce the amount of time these students have in functional courses and in community-based experiences. Second, the workplace of the future will pose some new challenges. The more complex demands (i.e., skills needed) of the workplace will be problematic for this group. In addition, many of the jobs that have traditionally been available to, and a worthy source of fulfillment for, individuals with mild mental retardation will not be available. Third, there is a great chance that all of us, and given the employment scenario, particularly individuals with mild retardation, will have more leisure time. The implications for preparing students to use their leisure time in rewarding and useful ways are obvious. Fourth, the reality of the information age will hit this group hard. There is no question that a discernible distinction is occurring between the information "haves" and "have nots." Ways to ensure that this group is not part of the "have nots" are needed.

The importance of self-determination will continue to be felt. Empowering individuals to be in charge of their lives and make the key decisions in their lives is the goal of many professionals. Given that quality of life is what should drive all transition and person-centered planning, it would be advantageous if quality of life issues were based in individuals' feelings and not imposed on them by others. Wehmeyer (1998) noted that self-determination is the one element of the current transition movement that is likely to endure, particularly as funding ends and, to some extent, professional attention on various facets of the transition planning process abate.

Teacher Roles and Preparation

Special education teachers are likely to be more involved in working in inclusive settings in the near future. The 1997 IDEA reauthorization requires that special educators be more knowledgeable about the general education curriculum. This concern is particularly urgent given the emerging emphasis on state standards related to school accreditation and graduation requirements.

There is great opportunity for special education teachers to enhance their value to school systems. In addition to being expected to know about legal matters, behavior management, and accommodating the needs of students, special education teachers have the opportunity to demonstrate their curricular talents as well. With a continued interest in functionality and guided by the demands of adulthood, special education teachers can show how to integrate real-life topics into existing curricula.

FINAL THOUGHTS

The education of students with mild mental retardation has changed dramatically in recent years. The system has moved from one that primarily excludes this group of students to one that is attempting to include them in the general education programs with their nondisabled peers. It has moved from one that uses invalidated instructional methods to one that applies research-based methods and supports. Many changes have taken place; indeed, even the population has changed. Whereas students classified as having mental retardation at one point were the largest group of identified students in special education, the numbers have declined significantly over the past 20 years. Clearly over the years many things have changed in the field of educating students with mild mental retardation. Without question, the movement to include these students with their nondisabled peers has had a tremendous impact. The future of the education of students with mild mental retardation remains unclear.

REFERENCES

Beirne-Smith, M., Ittenbach, R. F., & Patton, J. R. (1998). *Mental retardation* (5th ed.). Upper Saddle, NJ: Prentice-Hall/Merrill.

Binet, A., & Simon, T. (1905). Methodes nouvelles pour le diagnostic du niveau intellectuel des anormaux. *Anneé Psychologique, 11*, 191–244.

Blatt, B. (1987). *The conquest of mental retardation.* Austin, TX: PRO-ED.

Bradley, V. J., & Knoff, J. (1995). Shifting paradigms in services to people with disabilities. In O. C. Karen & S. Greenspan (Eds.), *Community rehabilitation services for people with disabilities* (pp. 5–19). Boston: Butterworth-Heinemann.

Cassidy, V. M., & Stanton, J. E.

Clark, G. M., Field, S., Patton, J. R., Brolin, D. E., & Sitlington, P. L. (1994). Life skills instruction: A necessary component for all students with disabilities: A position statement of the Division on Career Development and Transition. *Career Development for Exceptional Individuals, 17*, 125–134.

Doll, E. A. (1924). Current problems in mental diagnosis. *Journal of Psycho-Asthenics, 29*, 298–308.

Dunn, L. M. (1968). Special education for the mildly retarded: Is much of it justifiable? *Exceptional Children, 35*, 5–22.

Dunn, L. M. (1973). Mental retardation. In L. M. Dunn (Ed.).

Edgerton, R. B. (1967). *The cloak of competence: Stigma in the lives of the mentally retarded.* Berkeley: University of California Press.

Education for All Handicapped Children Act of 1975, 20 U.S.C. § 1400 *et seq.*

Education Policies Commission. (1938). *The purposes of education in American democracy.* Washington, DC: National Education Association.

Greenspan, S. (1997). The role of intelligence in a broad model of personal competence. In D. P. Flanagan, J. O. Genshaft, & P. L. Harrison (Eds.), *Contemporary intellectual assessment: Theories, tests, and issues* (pp. 131–150). New York: Guilford.

Grossman, H. J. (1983). *Classification in mental retardation.* Washington, DC: American Association on Mental Deficiency.

Hungerford, R. H. (1948). Philosophy of occupational education. *Occupational Education.* New York: Department of Special Education, New York City Public Schools.

Individuals with Disabilities Education Act of 1990, 20 U.S.C. § 1400 *et seq.*

Individuals with Disabilities Education Act Reauthorization in 1997, 20 U.S.C. § 1400 *et seq.*

Ingram, C. P. (1960). *Education of the slow-learning child* (3rd ed.). New York: Ronald Press.

Jacobson, J. W., & Mulick, J. A. (1996). *Manual on diagnosis and professional practice in mental retardation.* Washington, DC: American Pychological Association.

Kirk, S. A. (1972). *Educating exceptional children* (2nd ed.). Boston: Houghton-Mifflin.

Kirk, S. A., & Johnson, G. O. (1951). *Educating the retarded child.* Boston: Houghton-Mifflin.

Kolstoe, O. P. (1970). *Teaching educable mentally retarded children.* New York: Holt, Rinehart and Winston.

Kolstoe, O. P. (1976). *Teaching educable mentally retarded children* (2nd ed.). New York: Holt, Rinehart and Winston.

Kolstoe, O. P., & Frey, R. M. (1965). *A high school work study program for the mentally subnormal students.* Carbondale, IL: Southern Illinois University Press.

Larry P. v. Riles, C-71-2270 (RFP, District Court of Northern California 1972).

Lukasson, R., Coulter, D., Polloway, E. A., Reiss, S., Schalock, R. L., Snell, M. E., Spitalnik, D. M., & Stark, J. A. (1992). *Mental retardation: Definition, classification, and systems of supports.* Washington, DC: American Association on Mental Retardation.

MacMillan, D. L., & Borthwock, S. (1980). The new mentally retarded population: Can they be mainstreamed? *Mental Retardation, 18,* 155–158.

MacMillan, D. L., Gresham, F. M., & Forness, S. (1988). *Remedial and Special Education.*

Mauer, S. (1997). Struggling with the definition issue: A state level perspective. *Education and Training in Mental Retardation and Developmental Disabilities, 32,* 191–193.

Norlander, K. A. (1995). Shifting paradigms in school environments: Special education and the role of the educator. In O. C. Karan & S. Greenspan (Ed.), *Community rehabilitation services for people with disabilities* (pp. 347–367). Boston: Butterworth-Heinemann.

Patton, J. R., & Dunn, C. (1998). *Transition from school to young adulthood: Basic concepts and recommended practices.* Austin, TX: PRO-ED.

Patton, J. R., Blackbourn, J. M., & Fad, K. S. (1996). *Exceptional individuals in focus* (6th ed.). Upper Saddle, NJ: Prentice-Hall/Merrill.

Patton, J. R., Cronin, M. E., & Wood, S. J. (1999). *Infusing real-life topics into existing curricula: Recommended procedures and instructional examples for the elementary, middle, and high school levels.* Austin, TX: PRO-ED.

Patton, J. R., Polloway, E. A., & Epstein, M. H. (1987). Are there seminal works in special education? *Remedial and Special Education.*

Pickett, A. L., & Gerlach, K. (Eds.). (1997). *Supervising paraeducators in school settings: A team approach.* Austin, TX: PRO-ED.

Pim, J. (1864, January 20). *On the necessity of a state provision for the education of the deaf and dumb, the blind and the imbecile.* Paper presented at the Statistical and Social Inquiry Society of Ireland.

Polloway, E. A., Bursuck, W. D., Jayanthi, M., Epstein, M. H., & Nelson, J. (1996). Treatment acceptability. *Intervention in School Clinic, 31,* 133–134.

Polloway, E. A., Denning, C., & Chamberlain, J. (1998). *An analysis of state regulations concerning definition and classification in mental retardation.* Manuscript in preparation.

Polloway, E.A., & Smith, J.D. (1983). Current status of the mild mental retardation construct: Identification, placement, and programs. In M. C. Wang, M. C. Reynolds, & H. J. Walberg (Eds.), *The handbook of special education: Research and practice* (pp. 7–22). Oxford, England: Pergamon Press.

Polloway, E. A., Smith, J. D., Patton, J. R., & Smith, T. E. C. (1996). Historic changes in mental retardation and developmental disabilities. *Education and Training in Mental Retardation and Developmental Disabilities, 31,* 3–12.

Polloway, E. A., Smith, J. D., Chamberlain, J., Denning, C., & Smith, T. E. C. (1999). Levels of deficit vs. levels of support in mental retardation classification. *Education and Training in Mental Retardation and Developmental Disabilities, 34.*

Smith, R. M. (1968). *Clinical teaching: Methods of instruction for the retarded.* New York: McGraw-Hill.

Smith, T. E. C., Polloway, E. A., Patton, J. R., & Dowdy, C. A. (1998). *Teaching students with special needs in inclusive settings* (2nd ed.). Needham Heights, MA: Allyn & Bacon.

Tredgold, A. F. (1937). *A textbook of mental deficiency*. Baltimore: Wood.

U.S. Department of Education. (1997). *Eighteenth annual report to Congress on the implementation of IDEA*. Washington, DC: Author.

Wehmeyer, M. (1998 October). *Transition in the 21st century and beyond: Self-determination and quality of life*. Keynote address at the 9th Bi-Annual DCDT Midwest Regional Conference.

Serving Persons with Severe and Profound Disabilities: A Work in Progress

Doug Guess

I n 1964 I started working in a state-operated institution for children and adolescents who experienced a wide range of cognitive and related physical and sensory impairments. Sandra was one of 20 teenagers living in one of the "wards" in which I served as a clinical psychologist. They all spent a large part of their day lying in two rows of white-painted iron beds, each with railings that were usually raised except for changing diapers and feeding. The ward staff were caring people who received minimal reimbursement for their work and who, like me, wondered what could be done for girls like Sandra. I often made extra visits to Sandra's ward to elicit a smile when I talked to her. Sandra could not talk, her limbs were severely contracted, and she had periodic respiratory problems that were common to residents who were rarely placed in the upright position. On another of my wards was Jennifer, a girl in her late teens with Down syndrome, who spent much of her day perched on the seat of a chair, often screaming. Jennifer also did not talk. And then there was Joel, who would always greet me by comparing our respective heights, and whose "progressive" neurological deterioration (tuberous sclerosis) never seemed to actually progress.

The institution employed one special education teacher who served only a handful of students, most of whom were considered to have mild or borderline mental retardation. Sandra, Jennifer, and Joel did not come close to qualifying for this class, along with the majority of the other 500 residents. In fact, other than brief episodes of physical or speech therapy, or infrequent placement (with qualifying criteria) in a vocational workshop, there were few systematic programs to teach our residents even basic self-care skills such as eating and dressing and toileting. Our institution was not the exception. The entire field of severe mental retardation needed an answer. What to do?

Partial support for the preparation of this chapter comes from D. Guess, J. Rues, and S. Roberts (co-investigators), "Longitudinal Assessment of Emerging Behavior State Patterns among Infants and Children with and Profound Disabilities." Research in Education of Individuals with Disabilities Program, U.S. Department of Education (Award # H023C30029, 1993–1998).

BEHAVIORISM: BEGINNING
THE FIRST CYCLE OF CHANGE

The 1960s experienced the emergence and very rapid expansion of behaviorism in the treatment of disabilities and related conditions, exemplified by clinical application of operant procedures to individuals with psychiatric disorders (Ullmann & Krasner, 1965), childhood schizophrenia (Lovaas, Berberich, Perloff, & Schaeffer, 1966), and milder degrees of mental retardation (Birnbrauer, Wolf, Kidder, & Tague, 1968). Extending the new technology to individuals with the most severe and profound disabilities was a potential answer for improving the lives of children like Sandra, and Jennifer, and Joel, and, significantly, a worthy challenge for proving the practical efficacy of the procedures—and the theoretical validity of Skinnerian behaviorism from which they were derived (Skinner, 1974). Thus, evolving over the next decade was a major commitment by professionals in higher education to the research and application of instructional procedures and approaches identified with the field of applied behavior analysis, extending to all areas of exceptionality and, eventually, the education of nondisabled students.

It is difficult to separate out the behaviorally derived instructional practices in the 1970s from other social and educational changes that affected in a significant way the lives of persons with severe cognitive and multiple disabilities. This includes major legislative mandates (e.g., the Education for All Handicapped Children Act of 1975 [EHA]; Public Law [P.L.] 94-142) and legal decisions that legitimized and required treatment and educational opportunities for all students, including those with the most severe and profound disabilities. Significant also was involvement in 1974 by the U.S. Bureau on Education of the Handicapped (now Office of Special Education and Rehabilitation Services) to help establish a new organization (now known as The Association for Persons with Severe Handicaps) that would serve and advocate for persons with severe and profound disabilities and their families. Early on, especially, this organization was pivotal in researching, developing, and disseminating (through books, a journal, and conference proceedings) instructional procedures that were consistent with applied behavior analysis. The application of this technology was derived from the assumptions that learning is best accomplished by teaching small steps of a larger skill (reductionism), using contingent reinforcers for correct responses to appropriate stimuli (discrimination), and doing so across different materials, persons, and settings (generalization). Reducing and then teaching small steps of a larger skill produced the emphasis on task analysis, recognized as a fundamental requirement for successfully teaching new skills to persons with a range of disabilities, and especially necessary for learners with severe and profound disabilities. Textbooks in the field included specific procedures and methods for task-analyzing developmental skills.

Other behavioral techniques, such as prompting, fading, scheduling reinforcers, and various feedback procedures for incorrect responding, were used (and still are) to help initiate or accelerate learning. Methods for reducing "unwanted" behavior were also used extensively, including the use of reinforcement-based techniques (e.g., differentially reinforcing other behavior) and contingent punishers. Importantly, the population of persons with severe and profound disabilities was used to confirm, at least in part, the validity of the applied behavior analysis procedures and the assumptions of human behavior and learning from which the procedures were derived. Individuals with the most pronounced cognitive disabilities provided a challenge to the efficacy of the procedures, as well as the validity of Skinnerian behaviorism on which they were based (Skinner, 1974). As such, persons advocating the use of applied behavior analysis procedures in clinical and educational interventions endorsed an empirically derived methodology that endeavored to emulate the physical sciences. That included, for example, insistence on identifying and measuring observable (dependent) behaviors, and then manipulating independent variables to demonstrate experimental control. The introduction of single-subject designs (Baer, Wolf, & Risley, 1968) provided the perfect scientific methodology for assessing outcome measures for the application of behavioral procedures to small subject populations. Later on, teachers were also encouraged to use these designs to evaluate and document educational efforts in their classrooms (see Tawney & Gast, 1984), an effort, in part, to help justify the personnel and financial costs for supporting students who were now beginning to enter public schools, although they were placed mostly in segregated classes.

The application and growing enthusiasm of behaviorism to the education and treatment of persons with severe and profound disabilities became more formally conceptualized through the "remedial approach," and its assumptions and perceptions of the learners who would benefit from this empirically based technology. The remedial approach required, first, that educators, service providers, and parents identify specific areas where a learner needed to acquire new skills (e.g., following instructions, dressing, using words) or to reduce those ("aberrant") behaviors that interfered with skill acquisition (e.g., stereotyped movements) or were potentially dangerous to the learner or those around him or her (e.g., aggression, self-injury). Attending adults (teachers, parents, service providers) assumed responsibility for selecting skills that would be targeted for remediation, using behaviorally based procedures with the requisite collection of observable data to assess outcomes.

Minimal consideration was given to the developmental level of the learner. The remedial approach was, in fact, a response to assumptions of the developmental approach that required a hierarchical ordering of training targets, and where instructional materials were selected according to the mental, and not chronological, age of the learner (e.g., teaching an adolescent student with profound disabilities to place rings on a peg, or point to colors). The "criterion of ultimate functioning" concept advanced by Brown, Nietupski, and Hamre-Nietupski (1976) provided convincing arguments for organizing instructional content around those skills that would be needed for living independently in community settings as an adult.

> The *criterion of ultimate functioning* refers to the ever changing, expanding, localized, and personalized cluster of factors that each person must possess in order to function as productively and independently as possible in socially, vocationally, and domestically integrated adult community environments. (Brown et al., 1976, p. 8)

This concept and the later concept of "partial participation" (Baumgart et al., 1982) provided rationale for basing instructional content on the acquisition of those functional skills needed for living in the community. The selection of skills for training, however, was still consistent with parameters of the remedial approach, except now the potential deficit areas were projected over a longer period of time for learners with severe and profound disabilities.

The remedial approach and its behaviorally based assumptions had a major impact on how we perceive persons with disabilities, and then provide for them based on these perceptions. Significant still today are methods for preparing Individualized Education Program (IEP) goals based on the content of P.L. 94-142 passed in 1975, at the height of the remedial approach movement. Specifications for the writing of IEP goals reflect, in spirit and content, requirements from the remedial approach to carefully define and then quantify instructional outcomes for students with disabilities (e.g., "Rachel will correctly sign the word 'toilet' on 75% of trials for 5 consecutive days").

Without question the behaviorally derived, remedial approach made significant and positive contributions to the education and treatment of learners with severe and profound disabilities. The instructional technology provided optimism that persons with even the most profound disabilities (like my friend Sandra) could be helped to lead a more engaging and productive life, with an emphasis on "quality." The effort to interject an empirically based method for assessing treatment and education outcomes was a similar improvement over previous conditions in this century, where little was done for this population of people, and there were few program outcomes to measure. Starting, however, even as early as the middle to late 1970s was a second cycle—one that began to question assumptions and practices associated with the more radical applications of the remedial approach to the treatment and education of persons with severe and profound disabilities.

The field did not suddenly jettison the behaviorally based practices and philosophies that accompanied the remedial approach. Educational practices were starting to change, however, and were accompanied by a more active social agenda by professional and parent advocates for individuals with severe and profound disabilities (e.g., the deinstitutionalization movement that started in the late 1970s, and the accompanying effort to provide education and related services for these children and youth in public schools).

DEVIATIONS FROM RADICAL BEHAVIORISM: THE SECOND CYCLE OF CHANGE

Starting in the late 1970s, several significant and interrelated changes emerged in educational and treatment practices for individuals with severe and profound disabilities, reflecting, in part, how we perceived and valued these children and adults. The first significant changes were in response to increasing questions on the very types of instructional procedures used by educators and, later, on the content of instruction.

Content Domains and Massed-Trial Presentations

The early application of behavioral technology to the education and treatment of learners with severe and profound disabilities mirrored the animal laboratory research that provided the empirical bases for Skinnerian behaviorism, even going back to Fuller's (1949) seminal investigation that used a sugar-water solution to "condition" arm raising in an individual described as a "vegetative organism." Fuller's application of operant conditioning procedures used massed-trial presentations to teach one specific skill in a person who, prior to training, did not respond to the stimulus event that set the occasion for the skill (arm raising) to be reinforced. This instructional format was adopted in a monumental way in the early education and treatment of learners with severe and profound disabilities. Textbooks were divided into content domains for self-help, communication, motor, and social skill areas that almost always required instructional procedures using massed-trial presentations. This is where trials for teaching a specific response were extensively repeated in training sessions, and usually in locations and instructional settings that were not natural to the behavior. Additional procedures were then required to get responses, once trained, to generalize to more natural contexts and settings. Getting trained skills to maintain over time was even more problematic to practitioners, and was seldom addressed adequately in the published research.

Refinements of the behavioral technology included the general case programming strategy described by Horner, Sprague, and Wilcox (1982) to address problems of response generalization, and a model presented by Guess et al. (1978) to provide an alternative approach to teaching single-content domains. General case programming was used by Horner et al. (1982) for teaching community activities (e.g., using vending machines and purchasing groceries) to learners with severe disabilities. This strategy used stimulus-control procedures to increase the probability that skills learned in one setting will be performed successfully with different stimuli or in settings different from those used in the original training.

A functional curriculum sequencing model (Guess et al., 1978) was an initial acknowledgment that, in natural contexts, individual skill domains are rarely displayed, or learned, in isolation. Accordingly, instructional environments and opportunities needed to better represent natural relationships between skills that occur in sequences or clusters; for example, learning to use appropriate signs (communication) is also a social interaction skill (engaging friends) that might be displayed during mealtime (self-help) instruction. Importantly, it was thought that each of these behaviors (signing, interacting socially, and feeding) would best be taught as interspersed trials in natural contexts, and not as discrete behaviors presented repetitively (massed trials). This approach also emphasized the need to insert instruction for critical skills (e.g., holding the head erect, communicating needs) across a variety of different and natural settings and opportunities. Basic instructional procedures (e.g., prompting, fading) were maintained in the functional curriculum sequencing model.

Aversive Procedures

In the 1980s a growing concern emerged about the excessive use of aversive procedures to reduce "unwanted" behavior among persons with disabilities, especially individuals with severe and profound disabilities who were in public school and other community settings. Up to this point in time, the use of punishers to reduce behavior was an accepted practice. Most textbooks included instruction on how to use punishment procedures in applied settings, along with related overcorrection and time-out procedures. A large number of published research articles (see Guess, Helmstetter, Turnbull, & Knowlton, 1986) presented the use of aversive procedures for reducing a variety of behaviors among persons with severe profound disabilities, including stereotypy, self-injury, aggression toward others and the environment, lack of compliance and on-task behavior, and other disruptive behaviors (e.g., grabbing tokens, attempting to leave a training room, pica). In several cases, punishers were also used for incorrect responses in learning tasks.

Table 6.1 presents some types of aversive stimuli reported in the published literature to reduce unwanted behavior among persons with disabilities. This table also lists stimuli used with political prisoners, as reported by Amnesty International in 1984. Motivations for applying the aversive stimuli are markedly different with respect to the two groups, and certainly the intensity of the aversive stimuli used on political prisoners is more severe. Nevertheless, there is a similarity of methods used with persons who are disabled and the treatment of political prisoners as reported by Amnesty International.

Since that time, of course, prominent parent and professional advocacy groups (e.g., The Arc, Association for Persons with Severe Handicaps, American Association on Mental Retardation) have issued resolutions that denounce the use of aversive stimuli to reduce or control unwanted behavior among persons with disabilities. Equally significant was the emergence of the positive behavioral support approach (Horner et al., 1990) to the treatment of challenging behavior. In great part, this approach was a response to the vacuum left when aversive procedures (pain-producing stimuli) were no longer acceptable for use with persons who had disabilities. Positive behavior support is a comprehensive, empirically derived technology that emphasizes development of skills in inclusive settings, and that provides strategies for identifying and assessing ecological factors and conditions that influence normalized living opportunities and choices in order to enhance present and future lifestyles with persons who have challenging behavior (Horner et al., 1990).

TABLE 6.1
Types of Aversive Stimuli Used with Persons
Who Have a Disability and with Political Prisoners

List 1	List 2
Population: Persons with a disability	**Population:** Political prisoners
Source: Professional journals	**Source:** *Torture in the Eighties.* *(1984).* London: Amnesty International Publications.
1. Electric shock	Electric shock
2. Slaps to hands, thighs, etc.	
3. Ice on cheeks, Chin, under chin	
4. Gums/teeth brushed with antiseptics	
5. Forced body movements	
6. White noise at 95db	
7. Forced exercise	Strenuous physical exercise
8. Contingent tickling	
9. Hair pulling	Hair pulling
10. Ammonia capsule under nose	
11. Pinching	
12. Water squirted in face	High-pressure water squirted in mouth
13. Forced to swallow vomitus	Forced to eat excrement
14. Lemon juice squirted in mouth	Hot pepper inserted in body orifices (mouth, nose, anus)
15. Placed in bathtub of cold water	Plunged into ice water
16. Verbal reprimand	Verbal abuse
17. Holding posture, physical restraint	Enforced standing

Choices and Preferences

The concern about the use of aversive procedures with persons having severe disabilities was paralleled by interest in the concept of choice and its application to these same individuals (Guess, Benson, & Siegel-Causey, 1985; Shevin & Klein, 1984; Zeph, 1984). The field to this point had experienced a history of direct instruction with considerable emphasis on compliant training as a prerequisite for successful instruction in related areas of adaptive behavior. The exercise of choice, expression of preferences, and opportunities for self-determination were not typically included in the curriculum content for preparing instructional personnel who served individuals with severe and profound disabilities. Choice, in fact, was not perceived as an option for these learners. Guess and Siegel-Causey (1985) referred to the prevailing "Let's-fix-it" (i.e., remedial) model of that time:

In the "Lets-fix-it" model instructional objectives are selected for the learners by caregivers, educators, and other service providers. The instructional format is highly structured, carefully controlled, and systematically implemented. Allowing the learner some exercise of choice over lesson content or instructional methodology is not consistent with the model. (p. 80)

Giving learners the opportunity for expressing choice and preferences is now widely accepted as an exemplary educational practice across school, community, and home settings, and serves as an important intervention strategy in the positive behavioral approach model (Dunlap et al., 1994; Horner et al., 1990).

INCLUSION OF LEARNERS IN PUBLIC SCHOOLS AND REGULAR CLASSROOMS: THE THIRD CYCLE OF CHANGE

The decade of the 1990s has further moved the field away from the radical behaviorism that first guided our journey to teach learners with severe and profound disabilities. Behaviorism is still strong in the field, and in many respects has continued to impact instructional procedures for learners with severe and profound disabilities. Certainly, the influences of behaviorism remain strong in many university programs that prepare teachers and other direct service personnel to work with these learners. Nevertheless, the inclusion movement has particularly dominated the field over the past decade, influencing how educational services are delivered to this population of learners, and raising questions of how best they should be taught.

As early as 1984, an edited book by Certo, Haring, and York presented rationale and arguments for including students with severe and profound disabilities in public school settings. Integration of these students into public school settings, with separate classrooms, soon emerged into *inclusion in regular classrooms* for at least part of the day. Sailor (1991) argued for restructuring public schools to unify school resources, including special education, in a manner that would better coalesce services for regular education students and those needing any specialized services. Under this plan, categorical programming would be drastically reduced, and replaced by a shared agenda that better accommodates the needs of all students, including those with severe and profound disabilities.

Inclusive education for students with severe and profound disabilities has redirected curriculum content (Stainback & Stainback, 1994) to better reflect the agenda of typical classroom instruction. This has required an emphasis on collaborative teaming, and the identification of educational goals that can be assimilated into existing classroom curricula. Collaborative teaming has replaced previous interdisciplinary, and even transdisciplinary, education models. Ryndak and Alper (1996) defined collaborative teaming for inclusive educational programs as "a STYLE of problem solving by a group of equal individuals who voluntarily (1) contribute their own knowledge and skills and (2) participate in shared decision making to accomplish one or more common and mutually agreed upon goals" (p. 84). The collaborative team includes all persons (teachers, therapists, parents, social workers, psychologists, etc.) who are directly or indirectly concerned with the educational programs for learners with severe and profound disabilities. Outcomes of the collaborative effort include adaptation of the curriculum and environment to best meet the learning style of learners with these significant disabilities, and to provide a context that expands and maintains their circle of friends (Downing, 1996). In part, the application of this effort is designed to embed instructional objectives within the regular classroom curriculum, and in a manner that also provides functional skill acquisition (Giangreco, Cloninger, & Iverson, 1993). Embedded instruction identifies areas in which the regular curriculum can be adapted to meet specific IEP goals for the learner with a disability.

Inclusion provides the opportunity for learners with severe and profound disabilities to observe and model important cognitive and social behaviors, and to do so in the context of ecologically enriched and complex environments provided in their neighborhood schools. Inclusion provides, in essence, the essential criteria from which human learning can best be experienced. It also offers, however, a challenge to educators that has not been met. At present there are too few teachers who can successfully integrate learners with significant disabilities into the regular education curriculum. Regular education teachers then become dependent on special educators (already in short supply) for this population of learners. Special education teachers are, themselves, highly dependent on the skills of paraprofessionals to carry out instruction in the typical classrooms. This latter problem is highlighted in a recent study (Giangreco, Edelman, Luiselli, & MacFarland, 1997) that found the close proximity of paraprofessionals to their students interfered with ownership and responsibility of regular educators, separated students from classmates, and, on occasion, interfered with instruction of other students. In too many instances, the instructional programs for learners in inclusive classes are separate from the regular curriculum activities, providing little more than one-to-one training in the larger classroom space.

These logistic problems and challenges must be resolved by regular and special educators who serve learners with severe and profound disabilities in inclusive settings. The challenge, however, extends beyond one of how to deliver the educational program in inclusive settings. The challenge also involves a reanalysis of our assumptions of how learning experiences should be provided for children and youth with severe and profound disabilities, and the organization of human resources to meet the next evolution of practices. Without a doubt, my friends with severe disabilities, Sandra and Jennifer and Joel, whom I knew early in my career, would be much better off today—some 30 years later. They would enjoy being accepted into our communities and schools, and having the opportunity to do things that were never available to them while living in a state institution. There are, nevertheless, other innovations that need to be incorporated into our mission that extends into the 21st century.

A NEW MISSION, A NEW APPROACH

Over the past several years, I have been searching for a new approach, a new theory, and new perspective to help me better understand the attributes and interconnections that define the parameters of severe and profound disability. I could no longer accept or work within a primarily behavioral framework for either understanding the complexities of severe and profound disability, or recommending the exclusive use of those instructional procedures and programs that have evolved from them. In the process I discovered the theory of nonlinearity and its multiple derivations, including what is popularly referred to as chaos science. I have also discovered that many of my colleagues in special education want nothing to do with a major paradigm shift in our field, or at least one that conflicts significantly with the assumptions of Skinnerian behaviorism. I understand. It is difficult to abandon, or even critically analyze, a worldview that has totally dominated the field of special education for the last three to four decades. In the remainder of this chapter, I wish to explore two, not totally related, areas that have promise for improving the lives of persons with significant disabilities in the next century: (1) the conceptual approach of nonlinearity (complexity) and (2) advances in technology. I want, especially, to discuss potential application of nonlinearity to early intervention with infants and young children who experience severe and profound disabilities, and then the extension of nonlinearity to the broader challenge of providing a more comprehensive and effective service delivery approach that connects across settings, and into their later years of age. Accelerating advances in technology offer almost limitless opportunities to enhance the lifestyle of persons with severe and profound disabilities. For this section, I have solicited the assistance of two colleagues working in this area—Chuck Spellman and Pamela Cress.

Nonlinear (Dynamic) Systems

I cannot fully present in this chapter what nonlinearity is, how it offers a new approach and optimism for better understanding the behavior of persons with severe and multiple disabilities, and the nature of the social and educational agencies that impact their lives. What I do hope to accomplish is to provide enough information that will excite readers to embark on their own journey to better understand and apply the basic tenets of a truly dynamic approach, and one that dominates the conceptual and applied endeavors of the physical and natural sciences.

Nonlinearity is an approach represented by systems theories, including chaos science and its variations (e.g., "dynamical" and "self-organizing" systems). The term *chaos* was popularized by Gleick (1987) to characterize the broader class of cross-disciplinary systems models and theories. It is a dynamic view of phenomena depicting in the behavior of systems a midpoint between strict determinism and total randomness. Chaos occurs when the condition of a system changes over time, although the term itself is a misnomer. Popular use associates the word chaos with complete randomness in the state of a system, without the possibility of prediction and control. Chaos science, however, is more complex, implying that "noise" (unexplained variance) in a system has a certain degree of pre-dictability. Nevertheless, total prediction for most complex phenomena can never be achieved, no matter how precise the measurements being used; this is explained in the phenomenon of sensitive dependence on initial conditions.

Sensitive Dependence on Initial Conditions

The phenomenon of sensitive dependence on initial conditions was earlier discovered by meteorologist Lorenz (Gleick, 1987), who demonstrated that only a tiny incremental change in a weather computer prediction program resulted in a radically different weather forecast. This term is also referred to as the "butterfly effect," to make an exaggerated point that the flapping of a butterfly's wings in China might set into play a chain of events that precipitates flooding in Lawrence, Kansas. Thelen (1990) used the sensitive dependence on initial conditions phenomenon to help explain individual differences in humans. She pointed out that, whereas major developmental progressions can be predicted, differences in individuals evolve from sensitive influences of a variety of unpredictable endogenous and exogenous factors during early infancy and childhood. Linear models are context bound and unidimensional. Individual differences, however, are better understood through the study of open systems (dynamical models) wherein predictable (constrained) influences interact in time with random influences. Accordingly, human variability may be demonstrated to arise from "the intricacies of ontogeny alone" (Thelen, 1990, p. 28). Chaos theory implies that there will be times when an open system will be highly variable and, thus, critically sensitive to perturbations (external influences). Chaos occurs in a system when small changes in the initial conditions produce large changes at a later time.

According to Thelen (1990), a careful examination of individual trajectories in a longitudinal design might capture the influence of critical events as identified from the endpoints of the trajectories during the period of initial sensitivity to these influences. Chaos science allows the search for influences during periods of sensitivity to initial changes in these component trajectories within open systems. It is this possibility that I think has direct application to altering the trajectories of conditions associated with profound and multiple disability in the next century. This is better understood by examining data from a longitudinal study being conducted by myself and colleagues at the University of Kansas wherein we have been measuring, across time, behavior state trajectories and later patterns of stability among 34 infants and young children with severe and multiple disabilities. Behavior state refers to varying degrees of alertness and responsiveness, ranging from deep sleep through crying and agitation.

Presented in Figure 6.1 are state data, across time, for a nondisabled infant (John) who was observed (2-week intervals) during the first year of life, and an infant (Natalie) with severe and multiple disabilities who was observed (monthly) over a 3-year period. The figure thus shows samples of early and then later state organization and stability. The data for Natalie are representative of other participants in our studies where behavior states eventually settle into patterns that are nonoptimal for learning and interacting with the environment, even though many of our participants show greater state variability than does Natalie during early weeks and months of life. Note particularly the high occurrences of the Awake–active state in the later observations of John, as compared with the prevalence of the Awake–alert and Stereotypy states in Natalie. Awake–active is the optimal state for interacting with the environment and represents the state that best characterizes adult waking hours.

Consistently, our ongoing and previous studies have shown that nonoptimal states (e.g., sleeping, drowse, excessive stereotypy) are common among infants, children, and youth with severe and multiple disabilities. Although Awake–alert (observant and "tuned in" to the immediate environment) is preferred over these nonoptimal states, it still does not provide an adequate opportunity for responding to, and physically interacting with, the environment. We find among infants and young children with severe and multiple disabilities similar paths of behavior state trajectories that stabilize in nonoptimal patterns of organization—patterns that persist across those years where important development and learning should occur. These nonoptimal state patterns include excessive Sleep and Awake–nonalert states (e.g., drowse, daze), and extensive time observed in the Stereotypy and Self-injurious (SIB) or Other (including crying/agitation) states. Our studies have shown, also, the expected complexity of early development among these infants and children, where severe medical and health-related conditions interact with cognitive, motor, and sensory impairments and delays to produce nonoptimal behavior state patterns. It is this very complexity, however, that is most important to early intervention based on the phenomenon of sensitivity to initial conditions. And this, I believe, offers for this population of children new opportunities for enhanced quality of life in the 21st century.

Als (1986) showed the benefits of very early intervention for infants born prematurely, starting in the neonatal intensive care unit. Very early intervention has not, however, been provided to most infants with identified severe and multiple disabilities. This is due, in part, to the magnitude of medical treatments required for these infants, accompanied by parents whose energies are consumed by coping with the realities of caring for infants with so many medical and health care needs. Paradoxically, this is also a time at which external influences (perturbations) might best provide those critical events that could significantly improve the developmental, and especially cognitive, trajectories for these infants—that is, produce behavior state patterns that are more similar to normally developing infants and young children.

I predict that in the next century extensive, interdisciplinary research will help identify those initial conditions that are critically sensitive to small perturbations and that, when activated, will produce positive changes in development at a later time, including behaviors associated with more adaptive state patterns. Behaviors most sensitive to initial conditions will be better known by observing the endpoints of their trajectories, and then tracing back to identify those critical events that potentially served to activate them. Importantly, the initial conditions will likely reflect complex, dynamic behaviors and conditions that are optimized in critical maturational time periods. What, for example, are sensitive initial behavioral and physical conditions

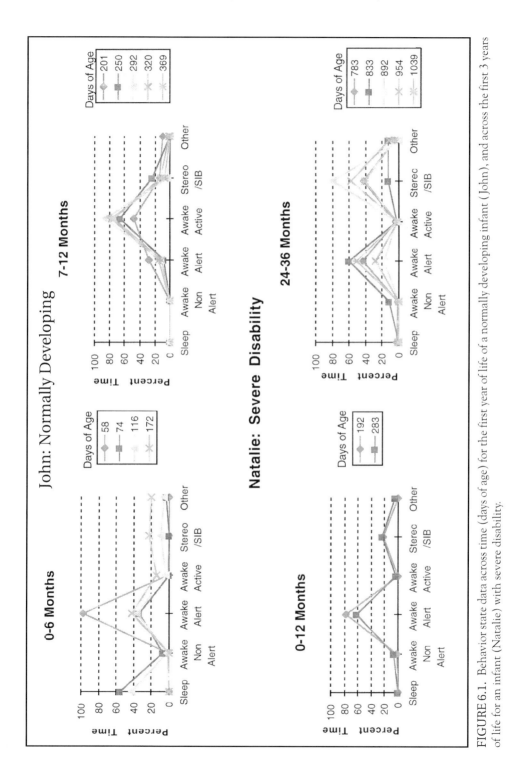

FIGURE 6.1. Behavior state data across time (days of age) for the first year of life of a normally developing infant (John), and across the first 3 years of life for an infant (Natalie) with severe disability.

that potentially contributed to the state pattern displayed by John (Figure 6.1) at 7 to 12 months, showing optimal time in the Awake-active state? Could some of these conditions have been activated upon to produce in Natalie state patterns that better approximate those observed in John? The computer technology that has been instrumental in discovering complex phenomena associated with chaos theory will be needed to identify and understand sensitivity to some of the initial conditions that can potentially impact the development of infants and young children who experience severe and profound disabilities. This will require a comprehensive, longitudinal database starting at their birth. In the subsequent section on technologies, I discuss new interventions, some of which have potential for this effort.

A better understanding of accelerated development based on sensitivity to initial conditions has potential for significantly improving early interventions among infants born with severe and profound disabilities. There will, of course, still be a significant need to provide, beyond the year 2000 complex, interrelated educational and community living services for this population. We know also that problems of service delivery have been commonplace for persons with severe and profound disabilities, and the families, caregivers, and professional personnel who have had responsibility for procuring and providing these services. This problem, I think, has partly resulted from the absence of a conceptual model that offers a better fit with the natural world, and that also has a firm scientific basis. Chaos science can address this conceptual model through the understanding of *fractal* patterns.

Fractal Geometry and Self-Similarity

Mathematician Benoit Mandelbrot (1990) used computer technology to discover fractal geometry, a visual representation of shapes that show the same degree of irregularity on all scales, and in which small identical patterns are embedded in larger identical patterns—that is, patterns within patterns. This is an important aspect of chaotic systems, and is referred to as *self-similarity* (Gleick, 1987). Fractal patterns, for example, range from short-term transient fluctuations in cotton prices that match the patterns of much larger pricing patterns across decades (Gleick, 1987), to nature where the fern and cauliflower have small branches and fronds that replicate the geometric pattern of the whole plant, and to our own physiology where the branching shape of blood vessels appears the same at larger or smaller scales. Marks-Tarlow (1995) described how the fractal metaphor can be used to better understand the psychological events that depict human nature. He discussed how individuals tend to resemble themselves in fundamental ways, independent of spatial, temporal, or situational scales of observation. Marks-Tarlow suggested that it is, indeed, this self-similarity that allows us to know ourselves across circumstances and time.

Koehler (1995) presented a theoretical approach for showing how fractals and path-dependent processes can be used for characterizing large-scale, emergency medical responses to major disasters in California. His theory and application model borrows from the *percolation fractal* presented earlier by Peitgen, Jurgens, and Saupe (1993): "When a structure changes from a collection of many disconnected parts into basically one big conglomeration, we say that percolation occurs" (Peitgen et al., 1993, p. 464). "Pores" are used by Peitgen et al. to represent the parts, or the critical components of the system that are potentially connected, and thus form self-similar clusters. The strength of the percolation fractal is determined by the probability that pores are connected with each other, and with similar pores in other clusters.

How might the percolation fractal metaphor be used to include in the next century the conceptual organization for educational and community living services for individuals with severe and profound disabilities? This question, I think, is particularly enticing given that services and programs for these individuals (as well as most persons with developmental disabilities) are often truncated. This is due, in part, to turf issues among professions and disciplines, a lack of consensus concerning what constitutes program quality, the absence of shared values on defining quality of life attributes, and generally inadequate communication between agencies and providers of services for persons with severe and profound disabilities. The percolation fractal is used here to illustrate a framework for organizing opportunities and services, with example pores that might constitute the essential ingredients to interconnect self-similar patterns within patterns.

Consider beyond the year 2000 a pattern (essential pores) of Shared Values, Services, and Opportunities for persons with severe and profound disabilities in our own society and culture, with smaller self-similar patterns within rural and urban communities, and still smaller self-similar patterns embedded in schools, workplaces, recreational programs, shopping facilities, and so on, within the community. Even smaller patterns of the same pores would occur in the home, or in other supported living arrangements.

The Shared Values represented in the fractal might include an acknowledgment of individual differences and the importance of identifying and appreciating positive attributes that accompany diversity, the role we all must take to support conditions and events that enhance the quality of our lives, and the safeguards needed to ensure that persons with severe and profound disabilities are protected from practices and policies that infringe upon their rights to optimal social and emotional development.

The Services pore would constitute a common denominator where learning, per se, is conceived as an intrinsically motivating attribute that is shared across instructional personnel, agencies, and settings; that is consistent across the life span of the learner; and, most of all, that is valued by the person with the disability. Earlier sections of this chapter reviewed how instructional strategies, concepts, and approaches for persons with severe and profound disabilities have changed across the last five decades. There is no reason to doubt that the instructional practices needed in many services will continue to evolve with, I think, a much larger application of principles and concepts for learning that are now starting to emerge from chaos theory (see Guess & Sailor, 1993; Robertson & Combs, 1995).

Opportunities include access of all persons with severe and profound disabilities to quality, early intervention, educational, and community living programs. A dedication to this quality should be equally represented at all levels, from national goals to school, and in-home learning and support services. A behavior support program, for example, would be considered successful only if positive outcomes were fully extended into a larger array of community settings that enhance and support one's quality of life.

The interconnection of Shared Values, Services, and Opportunities provides the basis for improving quality of life for persons with severe and profound disabilities. The major outcomes, however, would be the extent to which these same pores are consistent and self-similar across units of varying sizes such that, for example, Shared Values of persons with severe and profound disabilities are the same in the home, school, workplace, community, and our larger society. It is this result that is obtainable by efforts in the next century to realize the potential of the fractal metaphor. Further, the outcomes of achieving the benefits of the fractal, especially those related to Services and Opportunities, will be realized through the accelerating advances in technology. My colleagues Chuck Spellman and Pamela Cress, both researchers with the Lifespan Institute at the University of Kansas, prepared the following section on technology and its exciting potential for enhancing the lives of individuals with severe and profound disabilities in the next century.[1]

Technology

First, let's look just a few years into the future. Very soon we will have remote infrared signage technology available. This will allow "talking signs" that can be heard by an individual who is wearing a device that can translate the infrared signal to spoken words. This technology could have great impact on the lives of individuals who are unable to see signs or unable to read the signs but can understand spoken language. This technology will provide the information necessary for many people to move about in the community, within their work environments, and in public spaces such as shopping malls, libraries, and museums. Another example of "almost here" technology involves the miniaturization of talking bar code scanners so that one can scan signs and individual items in a grocery store; for example, one could locate the soup section, search the shelf for tomato soup, pick up an item, and be told the brand name, the number of ounces or servings contained, and the cost of the item. If one chose to purchase the product, it could be scanned again and the amount of the purchase would be deducted from the shopper's charge card. If there were not enough funds available

---

[1]The authors express appreciation to the following persons for their contributions to the technology section of this chapter: Susan Bashinski, Michael Byington, Kelly Flanagan, Ted Hasselbring, Jennifer Holvert, John Leslie, Jane Rhys, Charity Rowland, and Paul Tangen.

to make the purchase, the device could say "no" to the purchase. The possible applications of this technology are nearly endless.

Another technology that is currently being used on an experimental basis is a personal monitoring system that can be worn by an individual. These credit card–sized monitors can send information to a remote source to indicate changes in body functions such as blood pressure, respiration, heart rate, or seizure activity. These monitors also can contain microchips that store personal data on health histories and recommended treatments for specific health problems, as well as other relevant information about the individual. These monitors could allow individuals at risk for serious health problems a greater amount of independence without compromising the quality of support available in the event of a health emergency. In the future these devices could send information to a satellite, which in turn could signal implanted devices to release electrical stimulation, medication, hormones, and so on, to stimulate the body to respond to specific conditions.

A future generation of wireless pagers will offer an affordable option for providing regular prompts to individuals with memory deficits. Such devices will be inconspicuous and will provide visual and auditory prompts, or even electronically activated implanted devices, to wake up at a predetermined time, prepare food, take prescription medicines, go to the bus stop, continue working, or otherwise maintain the typical routines of the individual.

Moving slightly further into the future, the results of current research will lead to a direct brain interface for control of technology using cortically evoked potential. By using evoked potential or other "internal responses" that could be fed into a computer, an augmentative communication device, or an environmental control system, this technology would allow persons to have powered mobility; to talk, write, draw, and "paint" with the aid of a computer; operate power tools and telephones; and perform many vocational tasks that were previously not possible. With a combination of direct brain interface, "smart" cars, and global positioning devices, individuals with severe disabilities may be able to provide their own transportation in the future. By combining technology currently being developed by robotics engineers, direct brain interface technology, and smart devices, the potential for future assistive technology devices that can improve the quality of life of individuals with disabilities will be greatly enhanced.

To date most assistive technology is designed to "assist" individuals to overcome sensory or motor disabilities by altering how they receive information (input) or how responses are made (output). For instance, if a person is blind and cannot use printed words as an input system, he or she may use Braille or a screen reader to input visual stimuli. Individuals with very limited motor control might not be able to respond by typing on a keyboard, but can use a voice-activated computer or an eyegaze device to interface with a computer. The future will continue to offer many new assistive devices that will allow individuals to receive information and respond despite their sensory or motor limitations. For individuals who have sensory or motor disabilities, the next 25 years will provide an increasingly complex array of devices that will make it easier for them to live, learn, play, and work. Individuals with significant cognitive disabilities will profit less from advancements in assistive technology designed to assist individuals with sensory or motor disabilities.

Perhaps the greatest advances for individuals with the most severe disabilities will come from research to modify the cognitive processing abilities of individuals. Technology being developed now will ultimately allow for repairing, replacing, or reprogramming specific brain functions that will provide individuals with cognitive disabilities a greatly improved ability to learn, live, work, and play more independently. Biomedical technology that improves cognitive abilities will be developed as science strives to improve the lives of individuals with Alzheimer's disease, strokes, and traumatic brain damage, as well as other individuals with significantly impaired cognitive abilities. This research is the most challenging to imagine, yet we now routinely repair and replace joints, organs, lenses, and other body parts never believed possible in the past.

One could also assume that our technology for instruction will be greatly enhanced as the decades pass. We will have the capacity to routinely monitor brain wave patterns of persons with the most severe disabilities, whose behavioral states diminish their opportunities to learn, so that instruction can be delivered precisely when the individual is most ready to benefit from the exposure. Technology will also allow us to provide consistent consequences for emitted behaviors so that, at an early age, these individuals will be more likely to learn about cause and effect and may ultimately demonstrate a broader array of purposeful communicative and motor responses than is currently possible.

The technology of virtual reality and its future offspring will be a powerful tool for instruction. Learners who must be exposed to multiple exemplars of a task in order to respond appropriately will benefit from the ability of virtual reality to simulate an almost infinite number of possible variations of a task or event. No longer would an instructor need to travel with the student to many locations to learn the use of, say, vending machines, clothes washers and dryers, or automatic teller machines. One could program all the known versions of these machines into virtual reality–producing hardware and the instructor and student could remain in one location and still "sample the universe" of such machines. Simulation strategies will be used to teach vocational, recreational, and daily living tasks. Miniaturized multimedia technology will then follow the learner into the actual settings where these tasks occur so that the learner has a permanent reference to refer to as needed. Community-based instruction will thus be replaced with virtual reality training, with an occasional probe into the community-based setting to test the effects of the virtual reality training.

Clearly, there will be an explosion of new and exciting assistive technology devices in the next 25 years that have the potential for improving the lives of individuals with disabilities. Unfortunately, much of the new technology will not be used to benefit people with the most severe disabilities unless we develop better ways to disseminate information about technology, and unless systems change so that they exemplify the shared values, services, and opportunities that were discussed earlier.

Sandra, Jennifer, and Joel: The Past and Future

It is for me particularly pleasing to see in my own lifetime such a dramatic evolution in how we perceive, provide for, and value individuals with severe and profound disabilities. There is reasonable optimism to assume that these changes will accelerate even more in the next century. No longer will children like Sandra, Jennifer, and Joel be condemned to spending their lives in the sterility of an institutional environment where constant vigilance is often required to assure even a safe existence, let alone one that nurtures and teaches. Exciting new dynamic theories and approaches will continue to replace the mechanistic instructional methodologies of the past. Technology will provide the catalyst for improved opportunities for teaching and learning. Values that emphasize diversity of abilities, and yet the shared attributes of being human will continue to replace our earlier perceptions that persons with severe and profound disabilities are broken and need to be "fixed."

Serving persons with severe and profound disabilities is still a mission, and certainly one that is in progress. The turn of the century is a demarcation in time, but one that allows us to renew our commitment and complete the mission. I think Sandra and Jennifer and Joel would agree.

REFERENCES

Als, H. (1986). A synactive model of neonatal behavioral organization: Framework for the assessment of neurobehavioral development in the premature infant and for support of infants and parents in the neonatal intensive care environment. *Physical and Occupational Therapy in Pediatrics, 6*(3/4), 3–55.

Baer, D. M., Wolf, M. M., & Risley, T. R. (1968). Some current dimensions of applied behavior analysis. *Journal of Applied Behavior Analysis, 1*(1), 91–97.

Baumgart, D., Brown, L., Pumpian, I., Nisbet, J., Ford, A., Sweet, M., Messina, R., & Schroeder, J. (1982). Principle of partial participation and individualized adaptations in educational programs for severely handicapped students. *The Journal of the Association for the Severely Handicapped, 7*, 17–27.

Birnbrauer, J., Wolf, M., Kidder, J., & Tague, C. (1968). Classroom behavior of retarded pupils with token reinforcement. In H. Sloane & B. MacAulay (Eds.), *Operant procedures in remedial speech and language training* (pp. 19–39). Boston: Houghton Mifflin.

Brown, L., Nietupski, J., & Hamre-Nietupski, S. (1976). In M. Thomas (Ed.), *Hey, don't forget about me* (pp. 2–15). Reston, VA: Council for Exceptional Children.

Certo, N., Haring, N., & York, R. (1984). *Public school integration of severely handicapped students.* Baltimore: Brookes.

Downing, J. (1996). *Including students with severe and multiple disabilities in typical classrooms.* Baltimore: Brookes.

Dunlap, G., dePerczel, M., Clarke, S., Wilson, D., Wright, S., White, R., & Gomez, A. (1994). Choice making to promote behavior support for students exhibiting emotional and behavioral challenges. *Journal of Applied Behavior Analysis, 27*, 505–518.

Education for All Handicapped Children Act of 1975, 20 U.S.C. § 1400 *et seq.*

Fuller, P. R. (1949). Operant conditioning of a vegetative human organism. *American Journal of Psychology, 62*, 587–590.

Giangreco, M., Cloninger, C., & Iverson, V. (1993). *Choosing options and accommodations for children*. Baltimore: Brookes.

Giangreco, M., Edelman, S., Luiselli, T., & MacFarland, S. (1997). Helping or hovering? Effects of instructional assistant proximity on students with disabilities. *Exceptional Children, 63*, 329–342.

Gleick, J. (1987). *Chaos: Making a new science*. New York: Penguin Books.

Guess, D., Benson, H., & Siegel-Causey, E. (1985). Concepts and issues related to choice-making and autonomy among persons with severe disabilities. *Journal of The Association for Persons with Severe Handicaps, 10*(2), 79–86.

Guess, D., Helmstetter, E., Turnbull, R., & Knowlton, S. (1986). *The use of aversive procedures with persons who are disabled: An historical review and critical analysis*. Seattle, WA: The Association for Persons with Severe Handicaps.

Guess, D., Horner, R. D., Utley, B., Holvoet, J., Maxon, D., Tucker, D., & Warren, S. (1978). A functional curriculum sequencing model for teaching the severely handicapped. *American Association for the Education of the Severely and Profoundly Handicapped Review, 3*, 202–215.

Guess, D., & Sailor, W. (1993). Chaos theory and the study of human behavior: Implications for special education and developmental disabilities. *The Journal of Special Education, 29*(1), 16–34.

Guess, D., & Siegel-Causey, E. (1985). Behavioral control and education of severely handicapped students: Who's doing what to whom? and why? In D. Bricker & J. Filler (Eds.), *Serving the severely retarded: From research to practice* (pp. 230–244). Reston, VA: The Council for Exceptional Children.

Horner, R. L., Dunlap, G., Koegel, R. L., Carr, E. G., Sailor, W., Anderson, J., Albin, R. W., & O'Neill, R. E. (1990). Toward a technology of "nonaversive" behavioral support. *Journal of The Association for Persons with Severe Handicaps, 15*(3), 125–132.

Horner, R., Sprague, J., & Wilcox, B. (1982). General case programming for community activities. In B. Wilcox & T. Bellamy (Eds.), *Design of high school programs for severely handicapped students* (pp. 61–98). Baltimore: Brookes.

Koehler, G. (1995). Fractals and path-dependent processes: A theoretical approach for characterizing emergency medical responses to major disasters. In R. Robertson & A. Combs, (Eds.), *Chaos theory in psychology and the life sciences* (pp. 199–215). Hillsdale, NJ: Erlbaum.

Lovaas, O. I., Berberich, J. P., Perloff, B. F., & Schaeffer, B. (1966). Acquisition of imitative speech in schizophrenic children. *Science, 151*, 705–707.

Mandelbrot, B. (1990, September 15). Fractals—A geometry of nature. *New Scientist*, pp. 38–43.

Marks-Tarlow, T. (1995). The fractal geometry of human nature. In R. Robertson & A. Combs (Eds.), *Chaos theory in psychology and the life sciences* (pp. 275–283). Hillsdale, NJ: Erlbaum.

Peitgen, H., Jurgens, H., & Saupe, D. (1993). *Chaos and fractals*. New York: Springer-Verlag.

Robertson, R., & Combs, A. (Eds.). (1995). *Chaos theory in psychology and the life sciences* Hillsdale, NJ: Erlbaum.

Ryndak, D., & Alper, S. (1996). *Curriculum content for students with moderate and severe disabilities in inclusive settings*. Needham Heights, MA: Allyn & Bacon.

Sailor, W. (1991). Special education in the restructured school. *Remedial and Special Education, 12*(6), 8–22.

Shevin, M., & Klein, N. (1984). The importance of choice-making skills for students with severe disabilities. *Journal of The Association for Persons with Severe Handicaps, 9*(3), 159–166.

Skinner, B. F. (1974). *About behaviorism*. New York: Knopf.

Stainback, S., & Stainback, W. (1994). *Curriculum considerations in inclusive classrooms: Facilitating learning for all students*. Baltimore: Brookes.

Tawney,. J. W., & Gast, D. L. (1984). *Single subject research in special education*. Columbus, OH: Merrill.

Thelen, E. (1990). Dynamical systems and the generation of individual differences. In J. Colombo & J. Fagen (Eds.), *Individual differences in infancy* (pp. 19–43). Hillsdale, NJ: Erlbaum.

Torture in the eighties. (1984). London: Amnesty International Publications.

Ullmann, L. P., & Krasner, L. (Eds.). (1965). *Case studies in behavior modification.* New York: Holt, Rinehart and Winston.

Zeph, L. (1984, November). *The model of C.H.O.I.C.E.: A curriculum framework for incorporating choice-making into programs serving students with severe handicaps.* Paper presented at the 11th Annual Conference of The Association for Persons with Severe Handicaps, Chicago.

Employment and Residential Issues

Supported Employment in 2000: Changing the Locus of Control from Agency to Consumer

Paul Wehman, John Bricout, and John Kregel

W ithin less than a decade, the number of people participating in supported employment in the United States has increased from 9,800 to over 140,000 (Wehman, Revell, & Kregel, 1997). McGaughey, Kiernan, McNally, Gilmore, and Keith (1994) indicated that approximately 18% of all persons with developmental disabilities in adult day programs participate in some integrated employment. Many thousands more are working for the first time in countries all over the world. These are individuals who historically were confined to adult activity centers, sheltered workshops, nursing homes, and institutions, with unlikely competitive employment futures. The use of trained employment specialists, informed co-workers and mentors, and other technological supports, along with enlightened legislation, such as the Americans with Disabilities Act of 1990, have elevated the work possibilities for people with significant disabilities. Unfortunately, hundreds of thousands of people with disabilities still remain behind in segregated centers. Many more are on waiting lists for employment despite the fact that people with significant cognitive, physical, and behavioral challenges have shown their competence in the workplace.

These employment successes are not episodic or isolated, nor are they confined to any one region of the country or the world. As the time line in Table 7.1 indicates, the growth of supported employment as a real work option has emerged over the less attractive alternatives of segregation.

Despite the encouraging signs, the bulk of day program resources still go to maintain persons with significant disabilities in segregated work centers. Even though many people with disabilities and their families want real employment opportunities, the vast majority have been unable to sufficiently mobilize their communities to make this happen. Many reports indicate that people with disabilities want to work, ranging from anecdotal case studies to national survey analyses such as that reported by Louis Harris and Associates in 1994.

All players involved benefit from supported or competitive employment. The individual with a disability, often for the first time, has a real job, benefits, and dignity.

TABLE 7.1
Timeline of Supported Employment Growth and Emergence

1960–1970	1970–1980	1980–1990	1990–2000
Major domination of sheltered workshops, adult activity centers, and state institutions for mildly and severely disabled.	Placement into real work/competitive employment occurs at selected university centers on a research and demonstration basis.	National acceptance and growth of supported employment via several federal laws with funding.	Consumer empowerment philosophies and the Americans with Disabilities Act emerge as primary disability issues.
Well over 1 million persons in 5,000 segregated day programs in United States alone.	Focus on those with mental retardation only.	Expansion into *all* severe disabilities. All 50 states offer programs, with 3,000 programs offering SEP option.	Supported employment growth continues internationally. European Union of Supported Employment/World Association of SEP emerges as major force.
Emergence of applied behavior analysis as important training technology.	Emergence of the term *job coach*. Expanded use of term *normalization*. Increased deinstitutionalization.	Expanded use of job coach model. Growth is 10,000 to 100,000 persons (still leaves close to 1 million in day programs).	Efficacy of SEP challenged by well-entrenched adult day centers. Community business and natural supports given much greater emphasis.

Note. SEP = supported employment program.

The employer gets a good worker and receives specialized support to train and maintain the individual. The family sees the family member with a disability in a fully competent role in the workplace. Finally, taxpayers spend less money than they would to support the individual in a segregated day program year in and year out. The question remains: Why do the vast majority of individuals with mental and physical disabilities remain in segregated day programs?

The answer lies partially in the inability of advocates and people with disabilities to sufficiently marshal their collective efforts to increase work opportunities (Wehman & Kregel, 1995). The adult service systems in the world are deeply entrenched and have been for several decades (Albin, Rhodes, & Mank, 1994). To change this way of providing services, particularly in times of reduced funding and a serious fiscal crunch, is extremely difficult. Hence, there is an overwhelming necessity to market the positive attributes of supported employment for people with significant disabilities on a community level.

Unfortunately, we in the supported employment community, and even more broadly within the greater disability community, have not told our story well. We have not communicated the successes of this approach or the positive impact that work has on the lives of people who historically have been disenfranchised and written off as incompetent. As an interested society, we must get past the notion that people with severe disabilities are unable to work and do not want to work.

Our purpose in this chapter is to provide current information and data on the present status of supported employment in the United States. The emphasis is placed on quality outcomes and the design and evaluation of long-term job support mechanisms. We intend to closely address the issue of definitional aspects of natural supports in the literature, followed by a proposed taxonomy of work support literature.

QUALITY EMPLOYMENT OUTCOMES

Quality employment outcomes include competitive wages and good fringe benefits, including health insurance, long-term retention, flexibility in work schedule, and the opportunity to get on a career path. For most persons with truly significant disabilities, this level of employment outcome has not consistently occurred in rehabilitation programs around the world. Yet this is the avowed purpose of programs that embrace supported employment, transition from school to work, assistive technology, and other rehabilitation approaches.

Although supported employment programs have been able to generate employment outcomes for participants that are superior to those produced by segregated employment programs, in absolute terms (Rehabilitation Services Administration, 1995) many supported employment programs still yield employment outcomes that have fallen short of initial expectations. Lack of earnings and fringe benefits, integration in the workplace, employer attitudes, job retention, and job satisfaction remain issues of concern in supported employment program evaluation. Furthermore, the limited number of hours worked (with an average of 25 hours per week) is a stumbling block to greater prosperity.

The Rehabilitation Services Administration's data in 1995 indicated that 28% of persons in supported employment did not work at the minimum wage level of at least $4.50 per hour. This is based on 18,000 vocational rehabilitation closures, which is far below the overall national total of 140,000 persons in supported employment. Supported employment earnings have been reported to average $107 per week per client. Although this is a several hundred percent increase over wages earned prior to entering the program, annual wages in the range of $5,000 to $6,000 are certainly not consistent with the program's intent to enable individuals to pursue meaningful careers. In addition, such heavy reliance on part-time jobs means that many individuals with disabilities receive few fringe benefits such as health care or paid vacation. Table 7.2 summarizes the 1993 versus 1995 supported employment outcomes for people with disabilities in the United States.

TABLE 7.2
Supported Employment Outcomes in the
United States for Fiscal Years (FY) 1993 and 1995 (Preliminary Data)

Data Element	FY 1993	FY 1995
Number of participants in supported employment	105,381	139,812
Type of supported employment model	Individual placement: 79% Group placement: 21%	Individual placement: 77.4% Group placement: 22.6%
Mean average hourly wage	$4.53	$4.70
Mean average weekly wage	$107.10	$114.43
Mean average hours worked weekly	22.5	23.8
Number of supported employment providers	3,739	3,690
Primary disability	Mental retardation: 70.3% Mental illness: 19.3% Physical disability: 7.2% Other: 3.0%	Mental retardation: 61.5% Mental illness: 26.0% Physical disability: 9.6% Other: 3.1%
Level of mental retardation	Mild: 47.0% Moderate: 40.1% Severe/profound: 12.9%	Mild: 51.9% Moderate: 37.7% Severe/profound: 10.3%
The use of natural support is:	Increasing: 74% Staying the same: 7% Decreasing: 0% Don't know: 18.5%	**Not Available**
Natural supports are the predominant source of extended services:	Frequently: 3.7% Sometimes: 33.3% Rarely: 29.6% Don't know: 33.3%	**Not Available**

Note. Developed by W. Grant Revell at Virginia Commonwealth University Rehabilitation Research and Training Center. Data used by permission.

A commitment to employment opportunities implies that all individuals who can benefit from vocational rehabilitation should have equal access to quality employment programs that are equipped to respond to their preferences and needs. However, many excellent rehabilitation programs such as supported employment have the resources to serve only a small percentage of individuals who could benefit from the supports and services offered through local provider agencies. Persons with severe mental retardation, severe mental illness, cerebral palsy, or autism remain underrepresented in competitive employment programs in relation to their overall level of participation in adult day programs (Budde, Youngbauer, & Snyder, 1997; Snyder, O'Neil, Temple, & Crowell, 1996). Individuals who possess a specific disability, display severe inappropriate behaviors, or are merely viewed as too challenging or expensive to serve have been historically excluded from supported employment programs in many areas.

To be truly successful, rehabilitation programs must allow those persons with the greatest support needs to equally access and benefit from their services. Recently the President's Committee on Mental Retardation (1998) released 10 major principles to guide the development and reforms of employment policy. These excellent principles are listed in Table 7.3. However, administrative, programmatic, and attitudinal barriers have combined to limit or unnecessarily exclude certain groups of individuals from participation in vocational rehabilitation programs.

LONG-TERM SUPPORTS

Long-term support has been the key aspect of a supported employment approach. Ongoing development of long-term financial resources is essential to meet the needs

TABLE 7.3
Ten Principles To Guide Development and Reform of Employment Policy for Persons with Mental Retardation

1. People should be better off financially by working than they are if they are not working.
2. People should never be compelled to choose between working and having the medical services they need.
3. People should be assisted to be effective consumers of employment services through information on exemplary services, reasonable expectations for all agencies and the goals and outcomes of agencies in their communities.
4. People should be able to choose the agencies and people who provide employment support to them and to change agencies and support providers as they choose.
5. People should have access to skilled and motivated support providers to enable people who want to work to find and maintain satisfying employment.
6. Resources available for employment support should be sufficiently flexible to permit efficient and effective use in assigning people to locate, learn, and maintain work roles that are satisfying to them.
7. The number and variety of employment opportunities and employers should be continuously expanded.
8. There should be neither prohibitions nor disincentives within federal financing of services that restrict people's opportunities and choices to contribute to society through work.
9. There should be explicit recognition of employment services that model high standards of commitment, performance, and responsiveness to the needs and aspirations of workers.
10. Research development and application of existing and evolving technology should be promoted to enhance opportunities and productivity for workers with disabilities.

From *Closure Report*, by Rehabilitation Services Administration, 1995, Washington, DC: Author.

of people entering supported employment. Many vocational rehabilitation programs have successfully implemented cooperative agreements and leveraged extended service dollars from long-term funding agencies. These funds are predominantly from state agencies, social services, and mental health, mental retardation, and other developmental disability programs. As traditional providers of ongoing services, those agencies purchase extended employment supports with both new dollars and a redirection of funds normally used for day programs and sheltered work.

Ongoing supports, as defined in the amended regulations for the Federal Supported Employment Program (*Federal Register*, June 24, 1992, p. 28438), are those "needed to support and maintain an individual with severe handicaps in supported employment." They are the activities and relationships that help a person maintain a job in the community. Supports differ for each individual and vary widely in type and intensity for the duration of employment. Those provided through the services of a job coach or employment specialist may be job-specific or individual community supports.

Supports are one way to help people with disabilities become more independent and able to control the direction of their own lives. In recent years there has been a strong shift toward designing education and human service programs in such a way as to emphasize the role of supports in enhancing the success of persons with disabilities. No two people are the same, with or without disabilities. Every individual needs some level of help or assistance to succeed. There are some persons, for example, with very severe disabilities who need a great deal of support to succeed in school, work, home, and the community. The challenge is to collaborate with the person and together establish an array of supports to help him or her move forward.

Taking full advantage of all the support resources available to assist an individual with achieving his or her education, community living, or employment goals does not typically happen for persons with severe disabilities. Just because a support is available at the workplace or in the community does not necessarily mean that the person will automatically access it or benefit from its use. Often individuals do not know that potential supports are available, how to choose among the alternatives, or how to go about accessing a desired support. A critical factor in the use of a variety of supports is the role of the teacher who helps the individual with identifying, choosing, and accessing needed supports at whatever level of assistance he or she prefers.

Long-term funding is the unique feature of supported employment that makes it possible for people with severe disabilities to sustain employment over time. On- and off-site assistance and support continue indefinitely and differ significantly from services in day programs and other segregated models. For example, more traditional models move people through a continuum of program criteria in order to successfully transition them to competitive work. Unfortunately, independence from the service system is rarely achieved by people with severe disabilities when served through this approach.

The U.S. Congress recognized the value of supported employment in 1986 and identified this approach as a vocational outcome in the Rehabilitation Act Amendments (*Federal Register*, 1987). It authorized funding under Title I and Title VI (Part

C) for "time-limited post-employment services" leading to supported employment. The act includes "ongoing support services" as an essential element of supported employment and requires the availability of "extended services" before vocational rehabilitation funding can begin.

DEFINITION OF NATURAL SUPPORTS

One of the major mechanisms for extending services is through the use of what has been popularly termed *natural supports* (Nisbet & Hagner, 1988). Unfortunately, as Test and Wood (1996b) noted, natural supports has not been an easy concept to define or operationalize. Consequently, some important questions arise, such as these: What are natural supports? What are work supports? What is the relationship of natural supports to the implementation of supported employment?

To answer these questions, we turned to the recent literature on natural supports. Since Nisbet and Hagner (1988) first introduced the term natural support, this idea has been discussed and implemented to varying degrees (West, Kregel, Hernandez, & Hock, 1997). Paradoxically, this much-discussed, widely practiced concept has yet to be clearly and unambiguously defined. In fact, authors in the supported employment literature do not even appear to reach a consensus on two more basic issues: (1) What distinguishes natural supports from other workplace or work-related supports? This question is sometimes framed in terms of what the qualifier *natural* means. (2) What is the contribution of the job coach as paid service provider vis-à-vis the contribution of co-workers, supervisors, or employers to the integration of supported employees (Granger, Baron, & Robinson, 1997)? It can be seen that these two questions are related inasmuch as the job coach–initiated support strategies may be perceived of as less natural than those initiated by co-workers, supervisors, or employers.

The first issue, difficulty in limiting the scope of natural supports, has been recognized by authors in this field as confounding attempts to define the concept (Hagner, Butterworth, & Keith, 1995). Nonetheless, natural supports have been distinguished from other related strategies by some investigators (Storey & Garff, 1997), with one result being that several authors have elected to define their own natural support-like concepts, such as "internal supports," a term of more limited scope (Fabian & Luecking, 1991), and "typicalness," a term of more limited application (Mank, Cioffi, & Yovanoff, 1997).

The second issue, paid versus unpaid supports, appears to underlie the general approach to natural supports. For example, some writers appear to hold untested assumptions about how much the presence of a job coach facilitates, or hinders, the integration of workers with disabilities into a competitive workplace. At this point in time, the relative contribution of a job coach compared to co-workers, employer, or supervisor in the successful integration of a supported employee has *not* been empirically tested. However, Lee, Storey, Anderson, Goetz, and Zivolich (1997) conducted a study comparing job coach training to employer mentoring. Their findings suggested that mentors helped facilitate more social interaction than job coaches. Unfortunately, as Lee and her associates noted, they were unable to rule out differences in training methods and participant characteristics, and, perhaps more important, 1 year had passed between training and data collection (Lee et al., 1997). This yearlong lapse allows for the possibility that other factors may have confounded what is presumed to be a job coach training effect compared to an employer mentoring effect.

To examine how other writers have denoted natural supports, we looked at nine articles on natural supports. Table 7.4 provides a succinct overview of each of these papers. The type of study varied considerably among the seven empirical articles. Two of the studies were surveys (Unger, Parent, Gibson, Kane-Johnston, & Kregel, 1997; West et al., 1997). Three studies were qualitative, using staff notes and activities (Fabian, Edelman, & Leedy, 1993), case examples (Rogan, Hagner, & Murphy, 1993), or interviews (Hagner, Butterworth, & Keith, 1995). One study was observational, using repeated measures (Lee et al., 1997), and one employed archival data (Mank et al., 1997). The remaining two nonempirical articles were a conceptual piece (Fabian & Luecking, 1991) and a review article (Storey & Certo, 1996).

The discussions of natural supports in these articles vary a great deal in terms of how specific each author is about what constitutes natural supports. Probably the least specific definition is provided by Hagner, Butterworth, and Keith (1995) who simply list those who constitute natural supports: "an individual's network of family and friends, and an employee's employers and co-workers on the job" (p. 110). At the other end of the spectrum, Lee and associates (1997) specify not only whom and how, but also when natural supports are created: "Natural supports refers to the utilization of coworkers from the onset of placement to train and support workers with disabilities throughout their employment period. . . . supports and strategies that are inherent to a particular work environment such as coworkers, supervisors and managers. . . . [It] may involve continuing skills training, social skills training . . . advocacy . . . job modifications and adaptations" (p. 152). The obvious merits of this definition lie in its specificity about who, where, when, and, in several instances, how natural supports are to be effected.

In reviewing the articles, it becomes clear that no easily testable, measurable definition can be found. However, these different efforts do help us in understanding (a) who is involved with natural supports; (b) in what settings natural supports are found; and (c) what kinds of activities or features constitute natural supports.

The co-worker is the most commonly recurring figure in discussions of natural supports, appearing in almost every definition (Fabian, Edelman, & Leedy, 1993; Fabian & Luecking, 1991; Hagner et al., 1995; Lee et al., 1997; Mank et al., 1997; Rogan et al., 1993; West et al., 1997). In those instances in which the co-worker is not explicitly mentioned in conjunction with natural supports, the employer is mentioned (Storey & Certo, 1996; Unger et al., 1997). There is a high degree of consensus that natural supports involve those persons in the supported employee's work environment.

(*Text continues on page 125*)

TABLE 7.4
Current Definitions of Natural Supports (NS)

Source	Design	Definition of Concept
Fabian, Edelman, & Leedy (1993)	Qualitative data analysis of NS workplace demonstration project using staff notes and activities	"A natural support approach refers to enhancing or linking individuals to existing social supports in the work environment that are available either informally (from co-workers and peers on the job) or formally (from supervisors and company sponsored employment programs)" (p. 30)
		"Natural workplace support approaches require more intensive efforts up-front to link the employee to available supports since the approach does not rely on the continuing presence of the job coach" (p. 31).
Fabian & Luecking (1991)	Conceptual article	"Natural workplace supports include such examples as using co-workers as job trainers for the supported employee, promoting mentoring relationships between the supported employee and others in the environment, and using the environmental cues as a means of sustaining new behaviors by the supported employee" (p. 32).
Hagner, Butterworth, and Keith (1995)	Guided semi-structured interviews of 33 subjects on NS strategies and barriers to schools and vocational service agencies	"Natural sources of support include an individual's network of family and friends, and an employee's employers and co-workers on the job. Such natural supports may occur spontaneously or through human service facilitation or consultations" (p. 110).
Lee, Storey, Anderson, Goetz, & Zivolich (1997)	Observational study/ assessment of interactions on 30 workers in different training conditions (10 job coach; 10 manager–mentor; 10 coworker and manager)	"Natural Supports refers to the utilization of coworkers from the onset of placement to train and support workers with disabilities throughout their employment period. Basically, this approach utilizes supports and strategies that are inherent to the particular work environment such as coworkers, supervisors, and managers. Support may involve continuing skill training, social skills training, crisis intervention, advocacy, community skill training, validating instructional strategies, collecting subjective evaluations, collecting social comparison information, job modifications and adaptations" (p. 152).

(continues)

TABLE 7.4 *Continued*

Source	Design	Definition of Concept
Mank, Cioffi, & Yovanoff (1997)	Demographic data on 462 subjects in 13 vocational programs across eight states; data supplied by support persons	"The focus on natural supports emphasizes the participation of supervisors and co-workers in hiring, training and supervising supported employees. The concept of natural supports underscores an understanding of worksite culture that, in turn, dictates what is 'natural' or 'typical' for that particular situation" (p. 185).
Rogan, Hagner, & Murphy (1993)	Four case examples to illustrate provider strategies used to promote nonintrusive supports	"The term 'natural supports' has evolved to signify the involvement of work-site personnel and others in providing support to employees with disabilities. Natural supports may be described as any assistance, relationships, or interactions that allow a person to secure, maintain, and advance in a community job of his or her choosing in ways that correspond to the typical work routines and social actions of other employees and that enhance the individual's social relationships." (p. 275).
Storey & Certo (1996)	Review article	"Natural supports are people who are not disability service providers but who provide assistance, feedback, contact or companionship to enable people with disabilities to participate independently, or partially independently, in integrated employment settings or other community settings. Typically, individuals providing natural supports receive assistance and consultive support from disability service providers and provide natural supports with or without compensation [School and human service agency staff typically facilitate] natural support relationship(s). [Natural support people are usually] endemic to a job, a community environment, or community activity" (p. 63).
Unger, Parent, Gibson, Kane-Johnston, & Kregel (1997)	Survey of 36 individuals placed into supported employment by the VCU-RRTC Natural Supports Project; used community and workplace supports form	"Professional literature suggests that the role of the employment specialist when using natural supports is to serve as a consultant or facilitator to the employer by building on supports which exist in the workplace, as well as the expertise of the employer" (p. 111).

(continues)

TABLE 7.4 *Continued*

Source	Design	Definition of Concept
West, Kregel, Hernandez, & Hock (1997)	Survey of 385 supported employment provider agencies on use of NS in time-limited and extended services	(Cite from S. Rep. No. 357, 1992) "'Natural supports within the VR service context were intended to include: (a) individuals at the job site, such as employers, supervisors, or co-workers; (b) friends or family members in supportive roles; and (c) volunteers or members from work or the community.'"
		"The term natural supports refers to the resources inherent in community environments that can be used for habilitative and supportive purposes."
		"Recently, several writers in the field have further broadened the context to include other types of community and workplace resources, such as employee assistance programs, transportation providers, community service organizations, recreational and social associations, and governmental supports that are not limited to persons with disabilities such as subsidized housing, income tax assistance" (p. 175).

Note. VCU-RRTC = Virginia Commonwealth University Rehabilitation Research and Training Center.

When the job coach is considered, however, there is less consensus. According to several authors, the job coach or provider agency has an important role in developing and maintaining natural supports for the duration of employment (Brooke, Wehman, Inge, & Parent, 1995; Rogan et al., 1993; Storey & Certo, 1996; Unger et al., 1997; West et al., 1997). According to these authors, the role of the job coach with respect to natural supports is to facilitate natural supports. Although this does not imply that job coaches *are* natural supports, it does not allow them out from acting as such. Other authors, however, see job coaches as wholly exogenous to natural supports. Notably, Storey and Certo (1996) seem to exclude job coaches in their definition: "Natural supports are people who are not disability service providers" (p. 63). Occupying the middle ground on the issue of job coaches and unpaid natural supports, Fabian, Edelman, and Leedy (1993) seem to suggest that the job coach will fade out of the natural supports process in time: "Natural workplace support approaches require more intensive efforts up front to link the employee to available supports since the approach does not rely on the continuing presence of the job coach" (p. 31). To the extent that the concept of natural supports is extended beyond the workplace or worksite, other parties may be involved in natural supports as well, including friends, families, and community members (Hagner et al., 1995; West et al., 1997).

The setting of natural supports seems to occur, according to most authors, largely or exclusively in the workplace (Fabian, Edelman, & Leedy, 1993; Fabian & Luecking, 1991; Lee et al., 1997; Mank et al., 1997; Rogan et al., 1993). Some authors talk about natural supports in terms of being "inherent," "typical," or "endemic" to the workplace (Lee et al., 1997; Mank et al., 1997; Rogan et al., 1993; Storey & Certo, 1996; West et al., 1997). A different perspective seems to be articulated by authors who mention "promoted" or facilitated natural supports (Fabian, Edelman, & Leedy, 1993; Fabian & Luecking, 1991; Unger et al., 1997). A third possibility is that natural supports can be both "spontaneous" and "facilitated" (Hagner et al., 1995). Perhaps a better way of conceptualizing natural supports as they straddle the workplace and other locations is as a network reaching to and from the workplace, with the supported employee's job prospects, performance, and career progress at the center.

This leads us to the critical activities that constitute natural supports, such as social networks (Hagner et al., 1995; Rogan et al., 1993; Storey & Certo, 1996). In the community, natural supports may include such diverse elements as transportation, government subsidies and funding, and recreation and companionship (Storey & Certo, 1996; West et al., 1997). In the workplace, natural supports may also include static features such as "environmental cues," or processes such as skills training of various types, employee assistance programs, job modification, and adaptations (Fabian & Luecking, 1991; Lee et al., 1997; West et al., 1997). Considered as a whole, these articles still leave unanswered some fundamental questions. For example, what are the implications of our current understanding of natural supports for future research and practice? How are natural supports related to the larger topic of supported employment? These are some of the questions addressed in the next section.

WHAT THE RESEARCH LITERATURE TELLS US ABOUT NATURAL SUPPORTS

Test and Wood (1996a) reviewed procedural information and supports literature. Each of the 15 studies identified contained a specifically stated purpose. Of the studies, five involved case studies (Fabian, Edelman, & Leedy, 1993; Hagner & Farris, 1994; Rogan et al., 1993; Shafer, Tait, Keen, & Jesiolowski, 1989; West & Parent, 1995); two were surveys designed to describe the current status of natural supports (Hagner et al., 1995; Peterson, 1995); and two provided objective data on co-worker involvement (Rusch, Hughes, Johnson, & Minch, 1991; Rusch, Johnson, & Hughes, 1990). Test and Wood (1996a) provided a detailed table chronicling the design and results of each of the 15 studies conducted. *It is noteworthy that fewer than 100 total subjects were included in all of these studies.*

As noted earlier, very limited research has been designed to determine functional variables within supported employment as a whole; therefore, it is not surprising that none exist within the area of natural supports strategies. Unfortunately, the lack of this type of research leaves supported employment vulnerable to anyone who calls what he or she is doing "supported employment." In others words, if someone claims to be doing supported employment, then it must be supported employment. This same situation can be applied to natural supports strategies.

Additional research on natural supports strategies and related outcomes is clearly needed. Although many strategies have been suggested (e.g., Nisbet & Hagner, 1988; Rogan et al., 1993; Shafer et al., 1989), only one study was found that sought to investigate a specific strategy suggested by the literature, paid co-worker supports (Hood, Test, Spooner, & Steele, 1996). Research is needed to determine what strategies based on the concept of natural supports lead to improved consumer outcomes. Studies investigating procedures should include specific descriptions of subjects, replicable procedures, descriptions of research methodology, and specific intervention times.

One major study by West and colleagues (1997) reported findings from a survey of 385 supported employment provider agencies on their use of natural supports in time-limited and extended services. This study provided for a large-scale descriptive analysis of what practices community rehabilitation providers are following in natural supports. An overwhelming majority of 85% of all respondents reported that their agencies emphasize natural supports in the delivery of supported employment services and that these supports have generally been successful and useful for all individuals on their caseloads. Among the problems identified by the respondents were resistance to natural supports by employers and co-workers, as well as difficulty in locating natural supports at the job site.

Those agencies that emphasized natural supports reported that they have used co-workers or supervisors for initial training for an average of 41.5% of their consumers; for ongoing monitoring and support, this percentage increased to over half (56.3%) of their consumers. Natural supports appear to be used far less frequently in job development and placement, although the family-and-friends network is the typical avenue for early employment experiences for most persons starting out in the work world.

The findings of West and colleagues (1997) give clear and powerful support to the arguments we made earlier relating to the lack of a clear and concise definition of natural supports. When 85% of all programs indicate that they "emphasize the use of natural supports" in service delivery, the distinction between natural supports and job coaching is no longer meaningful. Most programs are using components from a number of different supported employment models in the design and delivery of services. Natural support strategies have become established as one of these components.

Provider agencies seem to agree about what constitutes a natural support. However, the natural supports that are being used by supported employment agencies appear to be limited in scope. When local programs describe their use of natural supports, they are almost always talking about the involvement of co-workers in the provision of job skill training or ongoing monitoring. Programs are far less likely to describe efforts at involving employer resources (i.e., employee assistance programs), family members or friends, consumer resources, or community resources (e.g., civic groups, professional organizations, churches) in the programs. In addition, most programs seem familiar with using natural support strategies during the training and follow-along stages of supported employment. Natural supports are used far less frequently during the consumer assessment, job development, and job placement phases of supported employment.

The findings of West et al.'s (1997) survey point to the potential impact of natural support methodologies on service access for these individuals. An encouraging finding is that better than 8 of 10 respondents indicated that they had found natural supports to be useful and relevant for all members of their caseload, including, presumably, those who are the most difficult to place, train, and maintain in employment. Among those reporting to the contrary, the primary reason was based not on the types of individuals served, but on *characteristics of the employment settings into which individuals were being placed*. Among the reported instances where natural supports did not "work" were such factors as fast-paced or high-stress jobs or environments, highly competitive businesses, and workplaces that were not particularly friendly to any worker, disabled or not.

Most programs feel that the use of natural supports has contributed to the overall success of their supported employment programs. However, about two thirds of the programs using natural supports indicate that they have experienced problems in the implementation of natural support strategies. These problems overwhelmingly fall into two areas. First, employers are unwilling to implement the natural support strategies recommended by the supported employment program and are "resisting" the notion that they should assume sole responsibility for the training, supervision, and support of the employee with a disability. Second, local programs are having a difficult time identifying staff members with the skills necessary to implement natural support strategies, as well as providing training to current staff members in the use of natural support techniques.

Taken in total, the perceptions of the respondents clearly illustrate the changing nature of supported employment service delivery. Natural supports have become so interwoven with all facets of supported employment implementation that it is no longer relevant to discuss the efficacy of natural supports versus the success of the job coach model of supported employment. It is no longer helpful to criticize natural support programs that place individuals into situations without providing sufficient support to enable the individual to retain employment for an extended period of time, or to chastise "job coach" programs that create unnecessary employer dependence on the presence and assistance of the job coach. Instead, it is now time to focus our energies on identifying those global program characteristics that contribute to a program's ability to generate high-quality, satisfying employment outcomes for individuals, regardless of the program's philosophical orientation.

At the level of the local supported employment program, there are no longer "pure" natural support programs or job coach programs. In reality, most local supported employment programs use a variety of different service delivery techniques. Far more important is the recognition that some supported employment programs are more successful than others in terms of their ability to generate high-quality employment outcomes for the consumer receiving services. Understanding the factors that contribute to individuals in one supported employment earning higher wages, retaining their jobs for a longer period of time, experiencing a larger degree of integration in their work setting, and expressing greater satisfaction with their job is a complex activity. It involves a close examination of the demographic and functional characteristics of the individual consumers, the characteristics of the service program, and the monetary and nonmonetary outcomes experienced by individual consumers.

TOWARD A TAXONOMY OF WORK SUPPORTS

Having established the importance of the relationship of extended services and natural supports to long-term quality employment outcomes, it is evident that there is a need for a classification and categorization system for organizing the myriad natural supports available to persons with disabilities. All too often, we have tended to approach the needs of workers with disabilities and of employers from mutually exclusive perspectives, in which the needs are identified without concomitantly acknowledging the availability of many potential work supports. We have rarely looked closely enough at the different types of work supports that are available to persons with disabilities in the workplace. In Table 7.5, we present four major categories of work supports and the subcategories within them. These categories include supports that are agency mediated, business mediated, government mediated, and family and community mediated.

These supports can be initiated, implemented, and evaluated in the business environment. However, they will be initiated usually from different starting points and with different entities mediating resources and services. We have conducted a rather extensive literature review as the basis for designing this taxonomy. What follows is a short literature review and discussion of each category of work supports.

Agency-Mediated Supports

Because most human services funding for rehabilitation flows through one common agency, an important starting point for examining workplace supports is the human service agency (or agencies) that provide supported employment services. One of the services provided by such agencies may be to coordinate services with other entities, be they employers, government agencies, or providers of specialized services such as mental health treatment, vocational rehabilitation, or education. Historically, the rehabilitation agency mediates the flow of supports. A number of different types of supports are mediated by agencies, as reported in the literature. These various types of supports are listed below.

Job Coach Support

The majority of the work support literature has focused on the job coach (individual placement) model of supported employment. This approach was initially presented by

TABLE 7.5
Taxonomy of Work Supports

Agency-Mediated Supports

Job coach assistance
  • Specialized training
  • Compensatory strategies
Compensatory strategies (e.g., memory
  aids)
Assistive technology
Counseling
Substance abuse services
Medical services
Specialized transportation
Vocational rehabilitation counselor

Government-Mediated Supports

Social Security Work Incentives
  • Plan for Achieving Self Support
  • Impairment Related Work Experience
Tax credits
  • Work Opportunity Tax Credit
  • Disabled Access Credit
  • Tax deduction to remove transportation
    and architectural barriers: Medicaid
    waiver

Business-Mediated Supports

Job restructuring
Workplace accommodations
  • Environmental modifications
  • Assistive technology
  • Task modification
  • Schedule modification
Co-worker mentoring
  • Job task training and support
  • Social support
Job creation
Employee Assistance Programs
Employment consultant (hired by
  business)

Family- and Community-Mediated Supports

Personal care attendant
Peer mentors
Family members as job developers
Friends and neighbors
Social support networks

Wehman (1981) and further articulated by Kregel and Wehman (1989). Since then, Bond (1998) and Becker and Drake (1994) have significantly built on this approach, focusing on persons with psychiatric disabilities. The process is the same, regardless of the population of consumers: to provide support services at the job site, rather than treatment-centered support at a clinic or elsewhere. Many researchers have written supporting the job coach or individual placement approach (e.g., Bond, Dietzen, McGrew, & Miller, 1995; Kregel, Wehman, & Banks, 1989; MacDonald-Wilson, Revell, Nguyen, & Peterson, 1991; Shafer, Banks, & Kregel, 1991; Sinnott-Oswald, Gliner, & Spenser, 1991; Wehman, Kregel, West, & Cifu, 1994; Wehman, Kreutzer, West, Sherron, Zasler et al., 1990). In fact, this model of supported employment appears to be the predominant practice of vocational service agencies in the field as well, and is viewed somewhat as a "gold standard" of services for many persons with severe disabilities (West et al., 1997).

The empirical research literature has demonstrated repeatedly that persons with severe mental retardation can work with job coach support (e.g., Parent, Kregel, Metzler, & Twardzik, 1992; Parent, Unger, Gibson, & Clements, 1994; Revell, Wehman, Kregel, West, & Rayfield, 1994; Test, Hinson, Solow, & Keul, 1993). Job coaches have provided equally effective support for persons with different disability labels, such as severe physical disabilities, traumatic brain injuries, or psychiatric disabilities (e.g., Danley, Rogers, MacDonald-Wilson, & Anthony, 1994; Inge, Wehman, Kregel, & Sherron-Targett, 1996; Wehman, Kreutzer, West, Sherron, Diambra et al., 1989; Wehman & Revell, 1996). Persons with different disabilities will require a somewhat different approach or emphasis on the part of the job coach (Fabian, Waterworth, & Ripke, 1993). For instance, persons with a psychiatric disability may need less skills instruction and supervision time than workers with a cognitive disability, but they may also need more advocacy and encounter greater stigma and isolation (Danley et al., 1994; Drake, Becker, Xie, & Anthony, 1995). Workers with different levels of disability may also require different support strategies. For example, there is empirical evidence to suggest that for workers with *mild* cognitive disabilities, social skills training is a powerful support for social interaction with co-workers (Park et al., 1991). However, other empirical evidence suggests that workers with *severe* cognitive disabilities may benefit more from a different modality, a "communications book" of pictures to stimulate conversations (Storey & Provost, 1996).

Compensatory Strategies

Compensatory strategies represent one avenue of support for overcoming the gap that sometimes occurs between worker abilities and environmental demands. Compensatory strategies are plans, behaviors, or materials that help workers with disabilities compensate for functional impairments. Certainly, others in addition to the agency alone can initiate compensatory strategies as supports. In fact, the person with the disability will usually be a driving force in selecting a compensatory strategy. The person with the disability will often help the agency or job coach identify what compensatory strategies or tasks make the best sense, given the situation and available resources.

Examples for workers with cognitive disabilities include memory aids or strategies, additional time to complete tasks, verbal rehearsals, checklists, and location markers (Adelman & Vogel, 1993; Briel, 1996). For persons with traumatic brain injury, compensatory strategies for cognitive remediation can be achieved using systematic task analysis (Giles & Shore, 1989; Kreutzer, Gordon, & Wehman, 1989; Kreutzer, Wehman, Morton, & Stonnington, 1988). The job coach conducts an intensive analysis of all job tasks until the constituent parts can be identified and listed sequentially. Compensatory strategies are then developed on the basis of the task analysis and the supported employee's abilities (Kreutzer et al., 1989; Kreutzer et al., 1988). Compensatory strategies can be developed that match the supported employee's presenting problems by integrating information from several sources in a graduated process of testing and modification (Briel, 1996). An evaluation of learning and memory abilities is conducted, followed by a situational working assessment and on-site job training feedback, with employee needs, preferences, and concerns an ongoing part of the process (Briel, 1996). Similar supports are possible using assistive technologies, which can aid the supported employee in his or her adaptation to the environment. These assistive technologies complement the supports provided by specialized professional services, such as mental health education and treatment, and other disability-specific services.

Assistive Technologies

One of the most influential definitions of assistive technologies is provided by a federal statute, the Technology-Related Assistance for Individuals with Disabilities Act of 1988 (P.L. 100-407) (Wallace, Flippo, Barcus, & Behrman, 1995). The act can be paraphrased as stating that, with respect to employment, assistive technologies are low- and high-technology devices, services, and adaptations that enable some persons with disabilities to participate in, contribute to, and interact in work life in much the same fashion as nondisabled co-workers. Although agency-mediated supports are the focus of this section, it is important to note that government, and more particularly the federal government, is a major funding source for assistive technologies (Parette & Van Biervliet, 1992). Supported employment provider agencies play a pivotal role in assistive technologies because job coaches have considerable input in the selection, procurement, implementation, and evaluation of assistive technologies used as work supports. Some illustrative examples of these work supports follow.

Assistive technologies can be of either low or high technology. Several examples from both will help make the picture of assistive technologies more clear. An example of a low-technology assistive technology is a support already alluded to briefly, a communications book. Such a book was used to help integrate workers with severe disabilities into a competitive workplace (Storey & Provost, 1996). This "device" consists of pictures bound together in a book or wallet and used to facilitate conversations with nondisabled co-workers. Two severely disabled workers using a communications book were able to increase their number of interactions with nondisabled co-workers in some circumstances (Storey & Provost, 1996). Recalling that services and adaptations are part of assistive technologies in addition to devices, another interesting example is found in the training of an adult with a brain injury to use bus transportation to and from work (Newbigging & Laskey, 1996). A combination of daily planning sessions and training on the bus resulted in the worker's being able to develop lasting bus riding skills (Newbigging & Laskey, 1996).

In the realm of high-technology devices, an 18-inch-long head pointer, together with an angled control panel and touch-sensitive screen, enables a worker with cerebral palsy to operate a copy machine as part of his job (Smith, 1992). Another copier innovation, an attached computer and voice synthesizer, allows a worker with a visual impairment to operate the equipment (Smith, 1992). A robotic device to assist workers with severe motor impairments to their upper and lower limbs has significantly reduced the amount of time per work unit that an assistant is needed, although at some loss of productivity (Birch et al., 1996). High-technology devices must sometimes be adapted to real-life situations that require a coordination of efforts between machine, supervisor, worker, and co-workers.

In fact, the effectiveness of high-technology devices may hinge more upon employer needs and worker preferences than the sophistication of the device (Lash & Licenziato, 1995). It is encouraging in this light to note that at least one study has found that job coaches can provide effective assessments of employment assistive technology needs (Behrman & Schepis, 1994). Apparently job coaches can serve as an effective link between worker and employer in identifying and implementing assistive technologies. Other specialists in addition to the job coach may be involved in the identification and implementation of assistive technologies; these include rehabilitation engineers, technology specialists, occupational therapists, and physical therapists, among others (Behrman & Schepis, 1994; Cooper, 1995; Leslie, 1995). However, the job coach is well situated to provide the necessary coordination between specialists and customers.

Specialized Agency Services

Supported employees also can benefit from multidisciplinary expertise in their adaptation to the competitive workplace. This holds true for disability-related functional impairments, as well as for the design and implementation of assistive technologies. Some combination of resources and coordination of efforts between the employment service provider and disability-related service provider is desirable (LaRocca, Kalb, & Gregg, 1996). Examples of specialized, disability-related service providers include psychological counseling (Roessler, 1988), substance abuse programs, medical programs, mental health programs (Rogers, Anthony, & Danley, 1989), taxi or shuttle transportation (Griffin, 1994), and developmental disabilities programs (McGaughey, Kiernan, McNally, & Gilmore, 1995). Vocational rehabilitation providers stand in the same relation to disability-related specialized services as do supported employment providers. It is possible for a supported employment provider to act as the specialized service provider for a vocational rehabilitation service. For the moment, however, supported employment programs and vocational rehabilitation services will be considered equally "vocational service" providers, with other providers lending their specialized expertise on the management and treatment of the disability in question.

A hypothetical example of the way vocational and specialized providers can influence the employment outcomes of workers with disabilities may bring these issues into sharper focus. Simon, a worker with a psychiatric disability, receives specialized services from mental health providers in accordance with his disability-related needs and his goals. Simon receives counseling and medication from a mental health provider to manage his illness. These treatments will help Simon achieve success in his employment goal. Simon has just landed his preferred job. Simon and his job coach have determined that co-worker aid is a critical work support for success in this job. The mental health services he receives will enable him to have successful social interactions with co-workers after he has received some additional social skill training from his job coach. The job coach is able to successfully complete social skills training with Simon because mental health treatments have increased Simon's receptivity.

As this example suggests, it is not only the supported employee who benefits from the efforts of the specialized service provider, but the job coach as well. When the specialized provider services are provided separately from vocational services, they are called *brokered services*. Particularly with respect to psychiatric disabilities, brokered services have been found to produce less effective employment outcomes and poorer customer service than integrated services (Drake et al., 1995). Ideally, integrated services are characterized by seamless customer-centered services and resources, together with cross-training and/or education of vocational and specialized service staff (Bybee, Mowbray, & McCrohan, 1995; Drake et al., 1995; Drake, McHugo, Becker, Anthony, & Clark, 1996). Several authors have suggested that the employer is also a critical rehabilitation resource (Flexer et al., 1994; Rhodes, Sandow, Taliaferro, & Mank, 1993). Positive employment outcomes have been attributed to employer collaboration in developing work supports (Rhodes et al., 1993), as well as to sustained relationships with employers (Cook, Razzano, Straiton, & Ross, 1994).

Business-Mediated Supports

Even though agencies have traditionally initiated the work support process, an ever-increasing number of professionals are concluding that employers should also be initiating work supports (Hanley-Maxwell & Millington, 1992; Harper, 1993; Sandow, Olson, & Yan, 1993; Test & Wood, 1996a). Businesses are a vital source of in-house work supports, including people (i.e., supervisors and co-workers), practices (i.e., flexible scheduling), policies (i.e., early return to work), and environmental supports (i.e., accessible work spaces) (Fabian & Luecking, 1991; Rhodes et al., 1993; Shoemaker, Robin, & Robin, 1992; Sowers, Kouwenhoven, Sousa, & Milliken, 1997). Businesses can also lead collaborations with human service providers (Rhodes et al., 1993). As Golden (1995) noted, businesses can tap into government-sponsored services such as those provided under the Job Training Partnership Act, federal employment-related funding such as the Disabled Access Tax Credit, and nonprofit funds such as those provided by the Association for Retarded Citizens' wage reimbursement program.

A wide variety of programs designed to meet the support needs of workers with disabilities have been sponsored by businesses. Businesses have entered into partnerships to hire and provide supports for workers with disabilities with public entities, nonprofit organizations, insurance companies, and other businesses (Akabas & Gates,

1993; Miano, Nalvern, & Hoff, 1996; Taylor, 1994; Tilson, Luecking, & West, 1996). Finally, businesses have also contracted with employment consultants and Employee Assistance Programs to provide work supports (Kiernan & McGaughey, 1992). In each of these instances, business is the mediator through which work support programs, practices, policies, and procedures for disabled workers are realized.

Workplace Accommodations

Accommodations such as assistive technologies, job modification, environmental modification, job restructuring, and schedule modification can often be achieved at a low cost. It is estimated that about 80% of accommodations cost between $100 and $500, while a full half of accommodations cost little or no money (Johnson, 1992). Moreover, the federal government offers businesses tax incentives to cover part of the cost of removing many barriers (Johnson, 1992). The cost of job creation, another accommodation possibility, could be justified by seasonal variations in product demand, the labor pool, or unmet company needs. At the same time, "free" accommodations, such as schedule modification or job restructuring, may contain a hidden cost in the burden or perceived inequity that they impose on co-workers, supervisors, and employers (Frierson, 1992). The need to have business personnel "buy in" to work supports and accommodations hints at why these individuals are themselves important work supports.

Co-Worker and Employer Supports

Co-worker support has been identified as critical to the work performance and job satisfaction of all employees, disabled and nondisabled alike (Curl, Hall, Chisholm, & Rule, 1992; Fabian & Luecking, 1991). An important dimension of co-worker support is social integration, which has been linked to both social support (important to job satisfaction) and mentoring (important to job performance) (Curl, Fraser, Cook, & Clemmons, 1996; Gaylord-Ross, Park, Johnston, & Lee, 1995; Storey & Provost, 1996). In addition to providing social support and mentoring, co-workers can provide formal training for workers with disabilities, and have done so successfully in a number of circumstances (Curl et al., 1996; Storey & Provost, 1996). Supervisors and employers provide training and mentoring support as part of their role, although in the case of workers with disabilities, they may provide more varied, extensive, or intensive training than for nondisabled workers. Supervisors or employers also provide work supports such as flexible scheduling, task modifications, job restructuring, and job sharing. Studies have indicated that employers do not object to providing additional task-related support for workers with disabilities (Adelman & Vogel, 1993). They do, however, object to providing additional support of a personal or emotional nature (Adelman & Vogel, 1993). Another source of supports is found in specialized in-house and contracted disability-related programs and policies.

Employer-Sponsored Programs and Policies

Return-to-work policies, disability case management, and rehabilitation have been identified as cost-saving procedures for employers, due to the high cost of disability claims and of replacement labor (Taylor, 1994). Disability management programs are one response to the high cost of worker disablement (Akabas & Gates, 1993). Such programs seek to identify and manage job-related stressors, along with workplace environmental limitations, in order to create a productive fit between the requirements of the job and the worker (Akabas, 1994; Akabas & Gates, 1993). Supervisory support, job accommodations, supportive policies, training, evaluation, and prevention are integral components of a successful disability management program (Akabas, 1994).

In addition to internal policies about family or medical leave, there are two federal statutes of importance to employers of workers with disabilities: the Americans with Disabilities Act of 1990 (ADA) and the Family and Medical Leave Act of 1993 (Akabas, 1994). The ADA has required an "early return to work policy" of employers (Shoemaker et al., 1992). It is not known to what degree employers have implemented, or even adopted, such a policy, although a 1992 study in Michigan found a minority of respondents had either adopted or implemented such a policy (Shoemaker et al., 1992).

However, several business-sponsored projects have successfully implemented the in-house hiring and support of workers with disabilities model (Miano et al., 1996; Rhodes et al., 1993). These projects used the supported employment and/or natural supports model (Miano et al., 1996; Rhodes et al., 1993). One corporation even sponsored a project team of professionals and employees who assessed the workplace environment for the special needs of a group of deaf workers (Berkay, 1993). The recommendations of this team resulted in a number of adaptations and accommodations and inspired the "Assessment Center Deaf Exercise Adaptation Model" (Berkay, 1993). The professionals in this team served as paid consultants for the corporation.

Businesses also use paid professionals with expertise in the issues affecting workers with disabilities in Employee Assistance Programs (Hanley-Maxwell & Millington, 1992). Employee Assistance Programs (EAPs) can be either in-house or contracted. These programs can be designed to serve the front-line supervisor and co-workers who have family members with a disability, in addition to the employee with a disability (Kiernan & McGaughey, 1992). Research indicates that EAPs provide effective supports to employees with disabilities (Kiernan & McGaughey, 1992). It is thought that the ADA will encourage the growth of employee supports for workers with disabilities, such as EAPs (Kiernan & McGaughey, 1992). Once again, as in the instance of the job audits, tax incentives, program funding, and workplace disability policies, federal statutes and initiatives loom large. Government is, in its own right, both a source and a mediator of work supports.

Government-Mediated Supports

Government-mediated supports are those policies and practices that enhance the likelihood that persons with disabilities will gain or maintain employment. Examples of government supports include selected Social Security policies, U.S. Department of Treasury tax policies, civil rights legislation, and other laws targeted specifically at the employment of persons with disabilities.

Consider, for example, the Targeted Job Tax Credit (TJTC), a law passed by Congress and administered by the U.S. Department of Treasury for the purpose of enticing employers to hire persons with disabilities. Zivolich and Weiner (1996) studied the effects of the TJTC and found it to be a useful support.

The Social Security Administration (SSA) has implemented a number of incentives to help support individuals with disabilities who want to work. For example, referral to state vocational rehabilitation services, trial work periods, continuing eligibility for Medicare, deduction of impairment-related work expenses from taxable earnings, and development of a Plan for Achieving Self Support (PASS) are all major elements of how the SSA tries to support individuals with disabilities. Because some of these incentives or supports have been difficult for many beneficiaries to access or understand (see Fagnoni, 1999), many of these supports have been underutilized.

Recently there has been another effort to greatly improve the viability of the PASS program. The Social Security Administration has provided a new set of guidelines to make PASS supports more viable:

- PASS evaluations and notices will differentiate between the feasibility of the goal and the viability of the plan. Goal feasibility will be assessed on the basis of reasonable expectations for an individual to perform the work. Plan viability will be assessed on the basis of the steps specified as necessary for goal attainment.

- As long as certain state or private vocational rehabilitation and employment professionals develop the PASS, PASS specialists will consider the occupational goal and plan to be feasible and viable, barring evidence to the contrary. If the specialist cannot approve a PASS, he or she will discuss it with the PASS authors, the customer, and professional.

- The upper limit on occupational goals is pegged at the first point on a career path (in the customer's chosen business, trade, or profession) at which the individual could produce earnings sufficient to meet his or her own living, work-related, and uncovered medical expenses. It is, therefore, not necessarily an "entry-level" limit.

- Funds set aside for installment payments, whether down payments or not, will be excluded as allowable expenses if they are related to and supportive of an approved occupational goal, provided that level of earnings does not obviate the need for continued exclusion.

- The role of the PASS specialist in PASS applications or reviews will be expanded in scope and in time (earlier involvement). Direct communication between the PASS specialist and the customer will be supported throughout the process.

Medicaid and Medicare reforms at the federal and state levels also have significant impact on health benefits and employment for persons with disabilities, as well as the way in which Medicaid funds are distributed. For example, in 1997, Congress amended the Medicaid statute to make long-term support funds available for Medicaid-eligible clients who were not previously institutionalized and who wish to enter supported employment. This is a major government support, which some have estimated will open the door for 150,000 new clients into supported employment (National Association of State Mental Retardation and Developmental Disabilities Directors, August 1997). The Home and Community Based (HCB) Waiver also can be seen as a major government support. For example, as of 1994, 49 states operated 80 HCB waiver programs for people with developmental disabilities (West, Revell, Kregel, & Bricout, 1999). In 1998 eight states operated HCB waiver programs for people with traumatic brain injuries (West et al., 1999).

As West et al. (1999) noted, in 1994, 135,000 individuals participated in MR/DD waiver programs, triple the number since 1990. State–federal outlays for these programs totaled $3.5 billion. Twice as many people with developmental disabilities participate in the HCB waiver program as reside in public institutions for persons with mental retardation. By 1995, the number of individuals participating in MR/DD HCB waiver programs exceeded the number served in intermediate care facilities for persons with mental retardation (ICFs/MR) of all types. States are continually increasing the number of services and supports they are offering in their programs, including supported employment.

The number of people participating in MR/DD HCB waiver programs likely will grow at an annual rate of 10% to 15% for the next 3 to 5 years (West et al., 1999). Perhaps the most wide-ranging government support can be found in the Americans with Disabilities Act, a law passed in 1990 that provides a host of civil rights and protections for persons with disabilities. For example, in Title I of the ADA, employment access is ensured through nondiscrimination protections in the workplace. This act was followed by a comprehensive set of regulations published exactly 1 year later (*Federal Register*, July 26, 1991). These regulations provide for accessibility, nondiscrimination, and greater entrance into workplaces, community facilities, use of public transportation, and telecommunications. As the law achieves successful implementation, there is an increasingly positive effect on young adults coming into a world that is less discriminatory against people with disabilities. This law is critical government-mediated social policy support necessary to enhance employment opportunity.

Under the ADA, employers are prohibited from discriminating against otherwise qualified individuals with disabilities during recruitment, hiring, evaluation, promotion, or any other facet of employment. Employers are further required to provide "reasonable accommodations" to enable individuals with disabilities to successfully perform their jobs, when accommodation can be provided without an employer sustaining an "undue hardship." Reasonable accommodations may include such things as restructuring jobs or work schedules, modifying equipment or providing assistive devices, providing an interpreter or reading aids, improving the overall accessibility of the worksite, or other action. Employers found to be in violation of the law face the same legal penalties as those found guilty of discrimination based on gender or race.

The Technology-Related Assistance Act

The Technology-Related Assistance for Individuals with Disabilities Act Amendments of 1994 (Tech Act) (P.L. 103-218) were signed into law on March 9, 1994. It was the successor to the original Tech Act of 1988. The 1994 Tech Act provides access to assistive technology services and devices for individuals with disabilities of all ages. The Tech Act has numerous specific purposes:

- To provide discretionary grants to states to assist them in developing and implementing a consumer-responsive, comprehensive, statewide program of technology-related assistance for individuals with disabilities of all ages.

- To fund programs of national significance related to assistive technology.

- To establish and expand alternative financing mechanisms to allow individuals with disabilities to purchase assistive technology devices and services.

With the passage and reauthorization of the Tech Act in 1994, Congress acknowledged the powerful role that assistive technology can play in maximizing the independence of individuals with disabilities. This law has the potential to open many new opportunities for individuals with disabilities and their families to receive appropriate assistive technology services. In particular, it opens up many new opportunities by being especially responsive to the needs of consumers.

The state grants program under Title I of the Tech Act was intended to be a catalyst for statewide systems change to increase access to appropriate assistive technology devices and services. These funds were to be used to support systems change and advocacy activities through fiscal year 1998. These funds increased the availability of, funding for, and access to assistive devices and services.

Family- and Community-Mediated Supports

In a consumer-driven system of human services, persons with disabilities should be serviced as true customers of supported employment. Brooke and her colleagues (1995) outlined a series of steps and strategies for consumers and families that help them take more power and responsibility for the supports they need. However, as evident in the following sections, the amount of literature in this area is scant.

Family Supports

Families play an important role in the quality of life, adjustment, and health outcomes of persons with disabilities (Kelley & Lambert, 1992). Families can provide informal care that ranges from general psychosocial support to job-related skills training (Prosser & Moss, 1996; Turner & Alston, 1994; Urbain, 1997). The ethnic group and culture to which the person with a disability belongs may have an impact on how strongly family influences consumer life choices and decisions, with some groups and cultures emphasizing independence more than others (Parette, 1997; Turner & Alston, 1994). Individual differences and context (i.e., employment) may also influence the degree of independence from family that a person with a disability displays (Mowbray, Bybee, Harris, & McCrohan, 1995). However, family continues to be an important mediator of various work supports (Killiam, Petranek, & Harding, 1996; Kutty, 1993; Parette, 1997; Prosser & Moss, 1996). For instance, family members have an important role to play in the selection and implementation of assistive technology devices and services (Parette, 1997). Parents have successfully managed a supported employment program for persons with severe disabilities (Killiam et al., 1996). Parents trained by professionals have also been involved in providing vocational services at community-based programs (Kutty, 1993). On the basis of experience from six projects nationwide, Urbain (1997), of the PACER organization in Minneapolis, has formulated a comprehensive approach for parental involvement in fostering natural supports in the supported employment process. She envisions parents as both facilitators and skills trainers. For instance, as facilitators, parents can use their unique access to interpersonal networks, including relatives, neighbors, friends, business contacts, and others, to provide the job developer with a broader range of employment possibilities (Urbain, 1997). Parents can also act as skills trainers by actively encouraging successful work-related behaviors at home, such as timeliness, task completion, and following instructions (Urbain, 1997).

It is not easy, however, to generalize about the relationship of family support to actual employment outcomes. In fact, the influence of family support on employment outcomes appears to be uneven. Some investigators have found positive associations of family support to favorable employment outcomes (see Kelley & Lambert, 1992; Siegel & Gaylord-Ross, 1991); others have reported negative associations of family support to favorable employment outcomes (e.g., Mowbray et al., 1995). Further research needs to take place that clearly specifies the degree of collaboration between family and supported employee, as well as specifying what constitutes "family support," before any conclusions can be drawn on the influence of different kinds of family support on employment outcomes. It has already been suggested that the interpersonal supports available to supported employees extend beyond family to include others with a stake in the employees' employment success. Disabled peers and other friends and acquaintances also mediate work supports for persons with disabilities.

Consumer, Friend, and Peer Support

One important force in enhancing the working potential and choices of persons with disabilities is found in the independent living movement. The independent living movement for persons with disabilities grew out of a desire to increase the autonomy and community participation of persons with disabilities (Asher, Asher, Hobbs, & Kelley, 1988). Independent living was intended to provide a barrier-free, self-directed environment and an alternative to institutionalization, medicalization, and dependence (Boland & Alonso, 1982; Budde & Bachelder, 1986). Independent living was first conceived of as a model for persons with severe physical disabilities, but came to serve persons with a wide range of disabilities, including many with mental retardation (Budde & Bachelder, 1986). Increasing the employability of persons with disabilities has always been one goal of independent living, within the broader goals of consumer decision-making control and community participation (Asher et al., 1988; Asher, Asher, Hobbs, & Kelley, 1991), or as it is sometimes called "total rehabilitation" (Boland & Alonso, 1982).

Personal attendants, also called personal care workers, are vital to successful independent living for many consumers (Atkins, Meyer, & Smith, 1982). Personal attendants make it possible for persons with disabilities to live in their own residences and work in the community (Budde & Bachelder, 1986). Attendants help consumers with domestic chores, personal hygiene and dress, cooking, and other daily living tasks (Asher et al., 1991; Budde & Bachelder, 1986). The services of the attendant can also be modified to include the role of advocate, advisor, or coach (Budde & Bachelder, 1986). Personal care decisions are an important domain for consumer self-direction. That is, in making personal care decisions and in directing their own personal care, persons with disabilities have the opportunity to exert choice and control in a critical area of their life, with direct consequences for employment, as well as overall quality of life (Asher et al., 1991). This consumer-driven approach is known as the consumer model of attendant care, in which the person with the disability is responsible for the decision-making and administrative tasks, including attendant recruitment, hiring, training, and management (Asher et al., 1988; 1991). At the other end of the spectrum, the agency model of attendent care locates all decisions and responsibilities in the agency (Asher et al., 1988; 1991). Both models are practiced to varying degrees in the community, allowing the consumer a continuum of choice making and control (Asher et al., 1988, 1991). A consumer focus suggests that the person with the disability have access to the attendant care model that permits him or her to have as much decision making and control as he or she wishes to have.

Consumers with psychiatric disabilities and their peers have contributed directly to their own work adjustment through the model of psychosocial rehabilitation. In the psychosocial rehabilitation model, consumers determine what their goals are for functioning in the community and how they will achieve them (Peterson, Patrick, &

Rissmeyer, 1990). This rehabilitation takes place in psychosocial "clubhouses," facilities in which consumer members and professional staff work together to create an environment that fosters the skills necessary to function successfully in the community (Barker, 1994; Peterson et al., 1990). Prevocational skills and even transitional employment may be offered through such clubhouses, in addition to community support and social relationships (Dougherty, 1994; Peterson et al., 1990).

In a related vein, mutual peer support and self-help in a joint consumer–professional employment project using a Self-Help Employment Center enhanced the vocational rehabilitation of a group of individuals with serious psychiatric disabilities (Kaufmann, 1995). Persons with disabilities have also successfully implemented and used a program of self-directed personal services while employing personal assistants and others (Asher et al., 1991). Friends as well as family may provide job leads or job networks through informal contacts (Wehman, Kregel, & Seyfarth, 1985). Community contacts and advocates can also provide job developers with critical referrals for persons with disabilities (Nietupski, Verstegen, Hamre-Nietupski, & Tanty, 1993). In one demonstration project, community members provided rehabilitation support of various kinds, including limited preemployment experience, to persons with psychiatric disabilities (Guay, 1994). On the job site, employees with disabilities may receive help from co-workers on the basis of perceived friendship, rather than as a collateral duty or shared obligation (Gaylord-Ross et al., 1995). Transportation is another work support that may be provided by friends as well as family (Parent et al., 1994).

Admittedly, persons with disabilities, their families, friends, and community may not always share the same perspective or have the same objectives. The focus in this discussion of family and community work supports is on each of these parties as facilitators of *consumer-centered* goals and objectives. As members of family groups, work organizations, and a broader community, persons with disabilities have to reconcile competing tugs toward dependence and independence, just as their nondisabled peers must. The work and career goals that they pursue are undertaken in a framework that requires both choice and compromise. What cannot, and must not, be compromised, however, is the ability of each consumer to realize an employment situation that he or she finds satisfying. The efforts of family, friends, peers with disabilities, and community together help realize the aspirations of the consumer, who is at the center of the process. The agency, the business, and the government each adds its distinctive contributions to the slate of possibilities, whose focus should always be the consumer.

KEY POINTS TO REMEMBER IN DESIGNING A SUPPORT SYSTEM: CONCLUDING REMARKS

The use of community and workplace supports in the provision of supported employment services represents the state of the art of what we know today about how best to support individuals with severe disabilities in the competitive jobs of their choice. Built on the knowledge and successes of the last decade, the development and utilization of a variety of innovative support technologies further enhance service delivery practices to better meet the needs of all persons who would like to work and receive assistance from supported employment. However, as the field of supported employment moves to this next level, several critical points must be kept in mind.

First, the utilization of community and workplace supports is not a panacea for correcting all of the shortcomings observed in supported employment implementation. It will not fix all of the inconsistencies in service delivery, the lack of funding resources, the shortages of skilled job coaches, the disincentives for conversion, the interagency "turf" issues, the large numbers of persons on waiting lists for services, or the poor quality outcomes reported for some supported employment participants (e.g., low wages, minimal integration, few hours, lack of career advancement). What it will do is place consumers in the driver's seat, allowing them to direct their careers and truly choose the type and amount of assistance they would like to receive to make them happen.

Second, the basic premises on which supported employment was established have not changed despite the expansion to include new service technologies. People with disabilities want to work in real jobs, and supported employment offers the means for achieving this goal. No support strategy or methodology, regardless of how good it sounds, should compromise the values on which this vocational model was based. Individuals have the right to be employed by community businesses where they can earn comparable wages, work side by side with their co-workers, receive worthwhile hours, and experience all the same benefits as other employees of the company. Most important, they should be able to choose these characteristics of their jobs and change their minds as their needs and preferences dictate.

Third, the reliance on community and workplace supports is not an all-or-nothing approach, but rather one of the supportive features of the existing supported employment model. The job coach is responsible for implementing all of the services characteristic of the consumer assessment; job development and job-site training; and ongoing, follow-along phases of supported employment. However, each individual needs different types of assistance, and the same individual will need varying levels of support at different times in the employment process. The type of support an individual receives to meet each of these needs and the way it is provided are decided by that person, using the systematic process outlined in this chapter. For example, an individual with extensive job-site training needs may choose to have a co-worker teach one task, the job coach teach another job duty, her parents arrange transportation, the rehabilitation counselor purchase uniforms, a friend assist with managing her paycheck, the cafeteria personnel help with taking lunch and breaks, the job coach accompany her for social events on the job and after work hours, the supervisor monitor work performance, and a Social Security consultant assist with writing a Plan for Achieving Self-Support (PASS).

Finally, with the advent of new and creative support technologies, the job coach's role is not eliminated but instead remains more than ever an essential element of the model. It is evident that community and workplace supports do not automatically meet the support needs of individuals with severe disabilities. People were not working before the establishment of supported employment and many more still are unemployed due to a lack of services. This situation does not mean that individuals cannot benefit from the assistance provided by different support resources, but only that some kind of help is needed in order to solicit that assistance in a meaningful way to meet particular support needs. The job coach is the one constant person who possesses the skills to be able to identify and develop support resources, assist with accessing their services, evaluate their effectiveness, and arrange alternative provisions as the need arises.

As important as the job coach is to the success of work supports, and as critical as the technologies and strategies of work supports are, these hinge on the active participation and even leadership of the consumer. Without the experience, ideas, and feedback of the person with a disability, adequate and appropriate work supports will not be developed and implemented. Moreover, the very notion of work "support" as something that enhances the employment success of a supported employee is meaningful only if it responds to the aspirations, abilities, and enthusiasms of the consumer, by whom success is measured. Again, the focus is on the consumer as the first and most basic mediator of work supports. The consumer focus is not a "new" focus; rather, it represents a salutory return to fundamental supported employment values and practices that put the success and interests of the person with the disability first.

REFERENCES

Adelman, P. B., & Vogel, S. A. (1993). Issues in the employment of adults with learning disabilities. *Learning Disability Quarterly, 16*, 219–232.

Akabas, S. H. (1994). Workplace responsiveness: Key employer characteristics in support of job maintenance for people with mental illness. *Psychosocial Rehabilitation Journal, 17*(3), 91–101.

Akabas, S. H., & Gates, L. B. (1993). *Stress and Disability Management Project: Final report.* New York: Columbia University, School of Social Work, Center for Social Policy and Practice in the Workplace.

Albin, J. M., Rhodes, L., & Mank, D. (1994). Realigning organizational culture, resources, and community roles: Changeover to community employment. *Journal of The Association for Persons with Severe Handicaps, 19*(2), 105–115.

Americans with Disabilities Act of 1990, 42 U.S.C. § 12101 *et seq.*

Asher, C. C., Asher, M. A., Hobbs, W. E., & Kelley, J. M. (1988). A preliminary investigation of the independent living movement in Pennsylvania. *Journal of Rehabilitation, 54*(2), 34–39.

Asher, C. C., Asher, M. A., Hobbs, W. E., & Kelley, J. M. (1991). On consumer self-direction of attendant care services: An empirical analysis of survey responses. *Evaluation and Program Planning, 14*(3), 131–139.

Atkins, B. J., Meyer, A. B., & Smith, N. K. (1982). Personal care attendants: Attitudes and factors contributing to job satisfaction. *Journal of Rehabilitation, 48*(3), 20–24.

Barker, L. T. (1994). Community-based models of employment for people with psychiatric disabilities. *Psychosocial Rehabilitation Journal, 17*(3), 212–218.

Becker, D. R., & Drake, R. E. (1994). Individual placement and support: A community mental health center approach in vocational rehabilitation. *Community Mental Health Journal, 30*, 193–206.

Behrman, M. M., & Schepis, M. M. (1994). Assistive technology assessment: A multiple case study review of three approaches with students with physical disabilities during the transition from school to work. *Journal of Vocational Rehabilitation, 4*, 202–210.

Berkay, P. J. (1993). The adaptation of assessment group exercises for deaf job applicants. *Journal of The American Deafness and Rehabilitation Association, 27*(1), 16–24.

Birch, G. E., Fengler, M., Gosine, R. G., Schroeder, K., Schroeder, M., & Johnson, D. L. (1996). An assessment methodology and its application to a robotic vocational assistive device. *Technology and Disability, 5*(2), 151–165.

Boland, J. M., & Alonso, G. (1982). A comparison: Independent living rehabilitation and vocational rehabilitation. *Journal of Rehabilitation, 48*(1), 56–59.

Bond, G. R. (1998). Principles of the individual placement and support model: Empirical support. *Psychiatric Rehabilitation Journal, 22*(1), 11–23.

Bond, G. R., Dietzen, L. L., McGrew, J. H., & Miller, L. D. (1995). Accelerating entry into supported employment for persons with severe psychiatric disabilities. *Rehabilitation Psychology, 40*, 91–111.

Briel, L. W. (1996). Promoting the effective use of compensatory strategies on the job for individuals with traumatic brain injury. *Journal of Vocational Rehabilitation, 7*(2), 151–158.

Brooke, V., Wehman, P., Inge, K., & Parent, W. (1995). Toward a customer-driven approach of supported employment. *Education and Training in Mental Retardation and Developmental Disability, 30*, 308–319.

Budde, J. F., & Bachelder, J. L. (1986). Independent living: The concept, model and methodology. *Journal of The Association for Persons with Severe Handicaps, 11*(4), 240–245.

Budde, J., Youngbauer, J., & Snyder, J. (1997). *Underserved consumers with mental retardation.* Lawrence: University of Kansas.

Bybee, D., Mowbray, C. T., & McCrohan, N. M. (1995). Towards zero exclusion in vocational services for persons with severe psychiatric disabilities: Prediction of service receipt in a hybrid vocational/casemanagement service program. *Psychosocial Rehabilitation Journal, 18*(4), 73–78.

Cook, J. A., Razzano, L. A., Straiton, D. M., & Ross, Y. (1994). Cultivation and maintenance of relationships with employers of people with psychiatric disabilities. *Psychosocial Rehabilitation Journal, 17*(3), 103–116.

Cooper, R. A. (1995). Forging a new future: A call for integrating people with disabilities into rehabilitation engineering. *Technology and Disability, 4*(2), 81–85.

Curl, R. M., Hall, S. M., Chisholm, L. A., & Rule, S. (1992). Coworkers as trainers for entry-level workers: A competitive employment model for individuals with developmental disabilities. *Rural Special Education Quarterly, 11*(1), 31–35.

Curl, R. M., Fraser, R. T., Cook, R. G., & Clemmons, D. (1996). Traumatic brain injury vocational rehabilitation: Preliminary findings for co-worker as trainer project. *Journal of Head Trauma Rehabilitation, 11*(1), 75–85.

Danley, K. S., Rogers, E. S., MacDonald-Wilson, K., & Anthony, W. (1994). Supported employment for adults with a psychiatric disability: Results of an innovative demonstration project. *Rehabilitation Psychology, 39*(4), 269–276.

Dougherty, S. J. (1994). The generalist role in clubhouse organizations. *Psychosocial Rehabilitation Journal, 18*(1), 95–108.

Drake, R. E., Becker, D. R., Xie, X., & Anthony, W. A. (1995). Barriers in the brokered model of supported employment for persons with psychiatric disabilities. *Journal of Vocational Rehabilitation, 5*(2), 141–149.

Drake, R. E., McHugo, G., Becker, D. R., Anthony, W. A., & Clark, R. E. (1996). The New Hampshire study of supported employment for people with severe mental illness. *Journal of Consulting and Clinical Psychology, 64*(2), 391–399.

Fabian, E. S., Edelman, A., & Leedy, M. (1993). Linking workers with severe disabilities to social supports in the workplace: Strategies for addressing barriers. *Journal of Rehabilitation, 59*(3), 29–34.

Fabian, E. S., & Luecking, R. G. (1991). Doing it the company way: Using the internal company supports in the workplace. *Journal of Rehabilitation Counseling, 22*(2), 32–35.

Fabian, E. S., Waterworth, A., & Ripke, B. (1993). Reasonable accommodations for workers with serious mental illness: Type, frequency, and associated outcomes. *Psychosocial Rehabilitation Journal, 17*(2), 163–172.

Fagnoni, C. M. (1999). *Social Security Disability: Multiple factors affect return to work.* Washington, DC: United States General Accounting Office.

Federal Register. (1987, August 14). Final regulations. Washington, DC: U.S. Government Printing Office.

Federal Register. (1991, July 26). Americans with Disabilities Act (ADA): Accessibility guidelines for buildings and facilities. Washington, DC: U.S. Government Printing Office.

Federal Register. (1992, June 24). 34 C.F.R. 363, 57 (122), 28432–28442. Washington, DC: U.S. Department of Education.

Flexer, R., Goebel, G., Baer, R., Simmons, T., Maryonyi, E., Shell, D., Steele, R., & Sabousky, R. (1994). Participant, employer, and rehabilitation resources in supported employment: A collaborative support. *Journal of Applied Rehabilitation Counseling, 25*(4), 9–15.

Frierson, J. G. (1992). An employer's dilemma: The ADA's provisions on reasonable accommodation and confidentiality. *Labor Law Journal, 43*(1), 309–312.

Gaylord-Ross, R., Park, H. S., Johnston, S., & Lee, M. (1995). Individual social skills training and co-worker training for supported employees with dual sensory impairments: Two case examples. *Behavior Modification, 19*(1), 78–94.

Giles, G., & Shore, M. (1989). A rapid method for teaching severely brain injured adults how to wash and dress. *Archives of Physical Medicine and Rehabilitation, 70,* 156–158.

Golden, T. P. (1995). *Employer incentives for hiring workers with disabilities: How job developers can consult with business to access supports for employees with disabilities.* St. Augustine, FL: Training Resource Network.

Granger, B., Baron, R., & Robinson, S. (1997). Findings from a national survey of job coaches and job developers about job accommodations arranged between employers and people with psychiatric disabilities. *Journal of Vocational Rehabilitation, 9,* 235–251.

Griffin, C. (1994). Organizational natural supports: The role of leadership in facilitating inclusion. *Journal of Vocational Rehabilitation, 4*(4), 296–307.

Guay, J. (1994). Involving citizens in the rehabilitation process. *Psychosocial Rehabilitation Journal, 18*(1), 145–150.

Hagner, D., Butterworth, J., & Keith, G. (1995). Strategies and barriers in facilitating natural supports for employment of adults with severe disabilities. *Journal of The Association for Persons with Severe Handicaps, 20,* 110–120.

Hagner, D., & Farris, S. (1994). *Inclusion support in the workplace, naturally.* Paper presented at the annual conference of The Association for Persons with Severe Handicaps, Atlanta, GA.

Hagner, D., Rogan, P., & Murphy, S. (1992). Facilitating natural supports in the workplace: Strategies for support consultants. *Journal of Rehabilitation, 58*(1), 29–34.

Hanly-Maxwell, C., & Millington, M. (1992). Enhancing independence in supported employment: Natural supports in business and industry. *Journal of Vocational Rehabilitation, 2*(4), 51–58.

Harper, J. (1993). Securing a role for people with disabilities in the work force. *Journal of Vocational Rehabilitation, 3*(4), 70–73.

Hood, E. L., Test, D. W., Spooner, F., & Steele, R. (1996). Paid co-worker support for individuals with severe multiple disabilities. *Education and Training in Mental Retardation and Developmental Disabilities, 31*(3), 251–265.

Inge, K. J., Wehman, P., Kregel, J., & Sherron-Targett, P. (1996). Vocational rehabilitation for persons with spinal cord injuries and other severe physical disabilities. *American Rehabilitation, 22*(4), 2–12.

Johnson, S. E. (1992). Creating a barrier-free work environment. *HR Focus, 69,* 15.

Kaufmann, C. L. (1995). The self-help employment center: Some outcomes from the first year. *Psychosocial Reha-*

bilitation Journal, 18(4), 145–162.

Kelley, S. D. M., & Lambert, S. S. (1992). Family support in rehabilitation: A review of research, 1980–1990. *Rehabilitation Counseling Bulletin, 36*(2), 98–119.

Kiernan, W. E., & McGaughey, M. (1992). Employee assistance: A support mechanism for the worker with a disability. *Journal of Rehabilitation, 58*(2), 56–63.

Killiam, S. G., Petranek, I., & Harding, G. (1996). Parents in charge of the system: Strategies for increasing supported employment opportunities for individuals with severe disabilities. *Journal of Vocational Rehabilitation, 6*(1), 41–45.

Kregel, J., & Wehman, P. (1989). Supported employment for persons with severe handicaps: Promises deferred. *Journal of The Association for Persons with Severe Handicaps, 14*(4), 293–303.

Kregel, J., Wehman, P., & Banks, P. (1989). The effects of consumer characteristics and type of employment model on individual outcomes in supported employment. *Journal of Applied Behavioral Analysis, 22*, 407–415.

Kreutzer, J. S., Gordon, W. A., & Wehman, P. (1989). Cognitive remediation following traumatic brain injury. *Rehabilitation Psychology, 34*, 117–130.

Kreutzer, J. S., Wehman, P., Morton, M. V., & Stonnington, H. (1988). Supported employment and compensatory strategies for enhancing vocational outcome following traumatic brain injury. *Brain Injury, 2*(3), 205–224.

Kutty, A. T. T. (1993). Parents associations for vocational training and employment of persons with mental retardation. *Indian Journal of Disability and Rehabilitation, 7*(1), 53–58.

LaRocca, N. G., Kalb, R. C., & Gregg, K. (1996). A program to facilitate retention of employment among persons with multiple sclerosis. *Work: A Journal of Prevention Assessment and Rehabilitation, 7*(1), 37–46.

Lash, M., & Licenziato, V. (1995). Career transitions for persons with severe physical disabilities: Integrating technological and psychosocial skills and accommodations. *Work, 5*(2), 85–98.

Lee, M., Storey, K., Anderson, J. L., Goetz, L., & Zivolich, Z. (1997). The effect of mentoring versus job coach instruction on integration in supported employment settings. *Journal of The Association of Persons with Severe Handicaps, 22*(3), 151–158.

Leslie, J. C. (1995). Worksite accommodation: Adaptation from a pragmatic perspective. *Technology and Disability, 4*(2), 131–135.

Louis Harris and Associates (1994). *Survey for the International Center for the Disabled. The ICD Survey II: Employing Disabled Americans.* Washington, DC: National Organization on Disability.

MacDonald-Wilson, K., Revell, G., Nguyen, N., & Peterson, M. (1991). Supported employment outcomes for people with psychiatric disabilities: A comparative analysis. *Journal of Vocational Rehabilitation, 1*(3), 30–44.

Mank, D. (1994). The underachievement of supported employment: A call for reinvestment. *Journal of Disability Policy Studies, 5*(2), 1–24.

Mank, D., Cioffi, A., & Yovanoff, P. (1997). Analysis of the typicalness of supported employment jobs, natural supports, and wage and integration outcomes. *Mental Retardation, 35*(3), 185–197.

McGaughey, M. J., Kiernan, W. E., McNally, L. C., & Gilmore, D. S. (1995). A peaceful coexistence? State MR/DD agency trends in integrated employment and facility-based services. *Mental Retardation, 33*(3), 170–180.

McGaughey, M. J., Kiernan, W. E., McNally, L. C., Gilmore, D. S., & Keith, G. R. (1994). *Beyond the workshop: National perspectives on integrated employment.* Boston: Boston Children's Hospital, Institute for Community Inclusion.

Miano, M. N., Nalvern, E. B., & Hoff, D. (1996). The Pachysandra Project: A public–private initiative in supported employment at the Prudential Insurance Company of America. *Journal of Vocational Rehabilitation, 6*(1), 107–118.

Mowbray, C. T., Bybee, D., Harris, S. N., & McCrohan, N. (1995). Predictors of work status and future work orientation in people with a psychiatric disability. *Psychiatric Rehabilitation Journal, 19*(2), 17–29.

National Association of State Mental Retardation and Developmental Disabilities Directors. (1997). *Summer newsletter.* Alexandria, VA: Author.

Newbigging, E. D., & Laskey, J. W. (1996). Therapy methodology. Riding the bus: Teaching an adult with a brain injury to use a transit system to travel independently to and from work. *Brain Injury, 10*(7), 543–550.

Nietupski, J., Verstegen, D., Hamre-Nietupski, S., & Tanty, S. (1993). Leveraging community support in approaching employers: The referral model of job development. *Journal of Vocational Rehabilitation, 3*(4), 38–45.

Nisbet, J., & Hagner, D. (1988). Natural supports in the workplace: A reexamination of supported employment. *Journal of The Association for Persons with Severe Handicaps, 13,* 260–267.

Parent, W. D., Kregel, J., Metzler, H. M. D., & Twardzik, G. (1992). Social integration in the workplace: An analysis of interaction activities of workers with mental retardation and their co-workers. *Education and Training in Mental Retardation, 27*(1), 28–38.

Parent, W., Unger, D., Gibson, K., & Clements, C. (1994). The role of job coach: Orchestrating community and workplace supports. *American Rehabilitation, 20*(3), 2–11.

Parette, H. P. (1997). Assistive technology devices and services. *Education and Training in Mental Retardation and Developmental Disabilities, 32*(4), 267–280.

Parette, H. P., & Van Biervliet, A. (1992). Tentative findings of a study of the technology needs and patterns of persons with mental retardation. *Journal of Intellectual Disability Research, 36*(1), 7–22.

Park, H., Simon, M., Tappe, P., Wozniak, T., Johnson, B., & Gaylord-Ross, R. (1991). Effects of a coworker advocacy program and social skills training on the social interaction of employees with mild disabilities. *Journal of Vocational Rehabilitation, 1*(4), 73–90.

Peterson, C. L., Patrick, S. L., & Rissmeyer, D. J. (1990). Social work's contribution to psychosocial rehabilitation. *Social Work, 35,* 468–472.

Peterson, M. (1995). Ongoing employment supports for persons with disabilities: An exploratory study. *Journal of Rehabilitation, 61*(2), 58–67.

President's Committee on Mental Retardation. (1998). Natural Conference Forum, Washington, DC.

Prosser, H., & Moss, S. (1996). Informal care networks of older workers with an intellectual disability. *Journal of Applied Research in Intellectual Disabilities, 9*(1), 17–30.

Rehabilitation Services Administration (1995) Closure report. Washington, DC: Author.

Revell, W. G., Wehman, P., Kregel, J., West, M., & Rayfield, R. (1994). Supported employment for persons with severe disabilities: Positive trends in wages, models and funding. *Education and Training in Mental Retardation and Developmental Disabilities, 29*(4), 256–264.

Rhodes, L., Sandow, D., Taliaferro, W., & Mank, D. (1993). *Final report: The Community Employment Development Project, April, 1993.* Eugene, OR: University of Oregon, Specialized Training Program.

Roessler, R. T. (1988). A conceptual basis for return to work interventions. *Rehabilitation Counseling Bulletin, 32,* 98–107.

Rogan, P., Hagner, D., & Murphy, S. (1993). Natural supports: Reconceptualizing job coach roles. *Journal of The Association for Persons with Severe Handicaps, 18*(4), 275–281.

Rogers, E. S., Anthony, W. A., & Danley, K. S. (1989). The impact of collaboration on system and client outcomes. *Rehabilitation Counseling Bulletin, 33*(2), 100–109.

Rusch, F. R., Hughes, C., Johnson, J., & Minch, K. (1991). A descriptive analysis of coworker involvement in supported employment. *Mental Retardation, 2,* 207–212.

Rusch, F. R., Johnson, J., & Hughes, C. (1990). Analysis of coworker involvement in relation to level of disability versus placement approach among supported employees. *Journal of The Association for Persons with Severe Handicaps, 15,* 32–39.

Sandow, D., Olson, D., & Yan, X. Y. (1993). The evolution of support in the workplace. *Journal of Vocational Rehabilitation, 3*(4), 30–37.

Shafer, M. S., Banks, P. D., & Kregel, J. (1991). Employment retention and career movement among individuals with mental retardation working in supported employment. *Mental Retardation, 29*(2), 103–110.

Shafer, M. S., Tait, K., Keen, R., & Jesiolowski, C. (1989). Supported competitive employment: Using coworkers to assist follow-along efforts. *Journal of Rehabilitation, 55*, 68–75.

Shoemaker, R. J., Robin, S. S., & Robin, H. S. (1992). Reaction to disability through organization policy: Early return to work policy. *Journal of Rehabilitation, 58*, 18–24.

Siegel, S., & Gaylord-Ross, R. (1991). Factors associated with employment success among youths with learning disabilities. *Journal of Learning Disabilities, 24*(1), 40–47.

Sinnott-Oswald, M., Gliner, J. A., & Spenser, K. C. (1991). Supported and sheltered employment: Quality of life issues among workers with disabilities. *Education and Training in Mental Retardation, 9*, 388–397.

Smith, B. (1992). Technology gives workers greater freedom in the office. *HR Focus, 69*, 12–13.

Snyder, J., O'Neil, T., Temple, L., & Crowell, R. (1996). *Psychiatric disabilities: Concerns, problem solutions.* Boston: Boston University.

Sowers, P. C., Kouwenhoven, K., Sousa, F., & Milliken, K. (1997). *Community-based employment for people with the most severe disabilities: New perspectives and strategies.* Durham: University of New Hampshire, Institute on Disability.

Storey, K., & Certo, N. J. (1996). Natural supports for increasing integration in the workplace for people with disabilities: A review of the literature and guidelines for implementation. *Rehabilitation Counseling Bulletin, 40*(1), 62–76.

Storey, K., & Garff, J. T. (1997). The cumulative effect of natural support strategies and social skills instruction on the integration of a worker in supported employment. *Journal of Vocational Rehabilitation, 9*, 143–152.

Storey, K., & Provost, O. N. (1996). The effect of communication skills instruction on the integration of workers with severe disabilities in supported employment settings. *Education and Training in Mental Retardation and Developmental Disabilities, 31*(2), 123–141.

Taylor, M. C. (1994, October). *Managing disability, recovery and reemployment.* Paper presented at the Eighth Annual National Disability Management Conference, Northwestern National Life, Minneapolis.

Technology-Related Assistance for Individuals with Disabilities Amendments of 1994, 29 U.S.C. §2201 *et seq.*

Test, D. W., Hinson, K. B., Solow, J., & Keul, P. (1993, March). Job satisfaction of persons in supported employment. *Education and Training in Mental Retardation, 28*(1), 38–46.

Test, D. W., & Wood, W. M. (1996a). Natural supports in the workplace: The jury is still out. *Journal of The Association for Persons with Severe Handicaps, 21*(4), 155–173.

Test , D. W., & Wood, W. M. (1996b). Some additional thoughts about supported employment using natural supports. *Journal of The Association for Persons with Severe Handicaps, 21*(4), 189–193.

Tilson, G. P., Luecking, R., & West, L. L. (1996). The employer partnership in transition for youth with disabilities. *Journal for Vocational Special Needs Education, 18*(3), 88–92.

Turner, W. L., & Alston, R. J. (1994). The role of the family in psychosocial adaptation to physical disabilities for African Americans. *Journal of the National Medical Association, 86*, 915–921.

Unger, D., Parent, W., Gibson, K., Kane-Johnston, K., & Kregel, J. (1997). An analysis of the activities of employment specialists in a natural supports approach to supported employment. In P. Wehman, J. Kregel, & M. West (Eds.), *Supported employment research: Expanding competitive employment opportunities for persons with significant disabilities* (pp. 110–127). Richmond: Virginia Commonwealth University, Rehabilitation Research and Training Center on Supported Employment.

Urbain, C. (1997). *Supported employment using a natural supports approach: A handbook for parents.* Minneapolis: PACER Center.

Wallace, J. F., Flippo, K. F., Barcus, J. M., & Behrman, M. (1995). Legislative foundation of assistive technology policy in the United States. In K. F. Filippo, K. J. Inge, & J. M. Barcus (Eds.), *Assistive technology: A resource for school, work and community* (pp. 3–22). Baltimore: Brookes.

Wehman, P. (1981). *Competitive employment*. Baltimore: Brookes.

Wehman, P., & Kregel, J. (1985). A supported work approach to competitive employment of individuals with moderate and severe handicaps. *Journal of The Association for Persons with Severe Handicaps, 10*(1), 3–11.

Wehman, P., & Kregel, J. (1995). Supported employment: At the crossroads. *Journal of The Association for Persons with Severe Handicaps, 20*(4), 286–299.

Wehman, P., Kregel, J., & Seyfarth, J. (1985). Employment outlook for young adults with mental retardation. *Rehabilitation Counseling Bulletin, 29*(2), 90–99.

Wehman, P., Kregel, J., West, M., & Cifu, D. (1994). Return to work for patients with traumatic brain injury: Analysis of costs. *American Journal of Physical Medicine and Rehabilitation, 73*(4), 280–281.

Wehman, P., Kreutzer, J., Sale, P., Morton, M., Diambra, J., & West, M. (1989). Cognitive impairment and remediation: Implications for employment following traumatic brain injury. *Journal of Head Trauma Rehabilitation, 4*(3), 66–75.

Wehman, P., Kreutzer, J., West, M., Sherron, P., Diambra, J., Fry, R., Groah, C., Sale, P., & Killiam, S. (1989). Employment outcomes of persons following traumatic brain injury: Pre-injury, post-injury, and supported employment. *Brain Injury, 3*(12), 397–412.

Wehman, P., Kreutzer, J., West, M., Sherron, P., Zasler, N., Groah, C., Stonnington, H., Burns, C., & Sale, P. (1990). Return to work for persons with traumatic brain injury: A supported employment approach. *Archives of Physical Medicine and Rehabilitation, 71*, 1047–1052.

Wehman, P., & Revell, W. G. (1996). Supported employment from 1989 to 1993: A national program that works. *Focus on Autism and Other Developmental Disabilities, 11*(4), 235–242.

Wehman, P., Revell, W. G., & Kregel, J. (1997). Supported employment: A decade of rapid growth and impact. In P. Wehman, J. Kregel, & M. West (Eds.), *Supported employment research: Expanding competitive employment opportunities for persons with significant disabilities*. Richmond: Virginia Commonwealth University, Rehabilitation Research and Training Center.

West, M., Kregel, J., Hernandez, A., & Hock, T. (1997). Everybody's doing it: A national study of the use of natural supports in supported employment. *Focus on Autism and Other Developmental Disabilities, 12*(3), 175–181, 192.

West, M. D., & Parent, W. S. (1995). Community and workplace supports for individuals with severe mental illness in supported employment. *Psychosocial Rehabilitation Journal, 18*(4), 13–24.

West, M., Revell, G., Kregel, J., & Bricout, J. (1999). The Medicaid Home and Community-based Waiver and supported employment. *American Journal on Mental Retardation, 104*(1), 78–87.

Zivolich, S., & Weiner, S. (1996). The impact of jobs tax credit on employment opportunities for persons with disabilities. *Journal of Vocational Rehabilitation, 6*(3), 303–310.

Where We Are Now: Perspectives on Employment of Persons with Mental Retardation

William E. Kiernan

Employment is an avenue to economic independence, a route to social identification, and a source for personal networking for most adults in U.S. society. In our adult years, we define ourselves by our careers, support our lifestyles through our wages, and develop our friendships through our place of work. Unfortunately, for many persons with mental retardation, employment and the associated benefits of employment have not been a realistic option. In this chapter, I review the status of employment, consider some of the emerging approaches to enhancing employment of persons with mental retardation, and present some of the future opportunities to employment for persons with mental retardation.

STATUS OF EMPLOYMENT

In the early 1950s the concept of employment for persons with mental retardation did not receive a great deal of consideration. It was felt that there was a need for a highly structured and somewhat protective setting where persons with mental retardation could work at their own pace, produce on routine and repetitive tasks, and be reimbursed based on their individual level of productivity. The development of sheltered workshops, while advancing the concept of employment for persons with mental retardation, did not afford the individual worker an opportunity to become economically self-sufficient (Whitehead & Marrone, 1986). Given the very nature of the sheltered workshop, co-workers were all individuals who had a disability; thus, the chances for developing peer networks involving persons other than those with disabilities was unlikely.

The emergence of the sheltered workshop as an employment option for persons with mental retardation was embraced by many of the local Associations for Retarded Citizens (then called Associations for Retarded Children). The number of sheltered workshops grew rapidly in the 1950s and 1960s, with placement in a sheltered workshop felt by many to be the most logical and desirable outcome for persons with mental retardation. Industry began to access this labor resource through subcontracts for production with sheltered workshops. For many persons with mental retardation, employment in a sheltered workshop was considered as the end goal rather than a transitional goal (Whitehead, 1981).

For a few, the concept of movement from the sheltered workshop to a "real" job was felt to be a possible sequence. The focus of the training in the sheltered workshop was on the development of work-based skills (following simple instructions, being able to appropriately complete the sequenced steps in a multistep task, and demonstrating an ability to attend to a work task for extended periods of time). Once these skills were mastered, the individual would be considered a candidate for a real job. Movement from the sheltered setting was limited, however, due in part to the lack of expectation on the part of professionals that persons with mental retardation could work in a real work setting and in part from the concerns of parents about the individual's potential loss of benefits or social isolation in the competitive workplace.

In the early 1970s it became apparent that there was little movement of persons with mental retardation from the sheltered setting to a real job. Whereas the concept of step-by-step training progressing from prevocational through skills training made some sense in theory, in actuality the skills that were developed in the sheltered workshop had little relevance to the tasks preformed in a real work setting. Additionally, the transfer of skills learned in a sheltered setting to the real work setting was minimal for individuals with mental retardation. Recognizing that persons with mental retardation can work, that skills learned in one setting are seldom generalized to another, and that the economy was shifting from a manufacturing to a service industry, a number of researchers began to raise questions about the efficacy of the sheltered workshop approach to employment supports and employment training (Boles, Bellamy, Horner, & Mank, 1984; Wehman, 1981).

At about this same time, the first model demonstration programs utilizing a place-and-train approach (as opposed to a pretraining and placement model) emerged. The concepts of supported employment were based on what was known about how persons with disabilities learn, how the economy was changing, and a recognition of the benefits of a more inclusive work setting for persons with mental retardation. Supported employment called for the placement of the individual into a real job by completing a job analysis of the job tasks and providing training for the individual in an actual workplace (Kiernan & Stark, 1986). Supported employment over the past decade has provided employment opportunities to more than 200,000 persons with disabilities nationally (Mank, 1994; McGaughey, Kiernan, McNally, Gilmore, & Keith, 1994; Wehman & Kregel, 1995). As an outgrowth of these initial demonstrations, many of the community rehabilitation programs soon developed supported employment options for persons served in their sheltered workshop and rehabilitation training programs. Although the initial intent of supported employment was to assist those individuals with more severe disabilities in entering employment, to date most of the persons served through supported employment are persons with less significant disabilities (Kiernan & Schalock, 1997; Mank, 1994; Wehman & Kregel, 1995).

The accomplishments since the mid-1980s in supported employment have been significant, yet there continue to be many concerns about the nature of the population served, the extent of the support required, the role of the employment training specialist (or job coach), and the nature of the jobs realized through supported employment (Kiernan & Schalock, 1997; Mank, 1994). The adoption of supported employment has brought to the forefront the recognition that employment is a realistic option for persons with mental retardation. The original intent of supported employment—that is, to provide employment opportunities for individuals with severe disabilities—has been somewhat compromised in that most of those served in the current supported employment programs are persons who have less severe disabilities. Several have raised concerns about the need to maintain a focus on serving those individuals with more severe disabilities in supported employment programs (McGaughey et al., 1994; Wehman & Kregel, 1995). A growing concern also revolves around the nature of the jobs accessed and the structure of the supports provided through supported employment. The vast majority of persons entering real work settings, through either supported or competitive employment, enter jobs in the food services or cleaning areas. Many of these positions are of a part-time nature and seldom offer wages above the minimum wage or provide benefits such as health care coverage or paid vacations (Temelini & Fesko, 1996). The entry into these jobs, while not atypical for most new workers in general, is often viewed as the final placement rather than the beginning of an employment history for the supported employee. Career growth and development is not a topic of discussion for persons with mental retardation. Rather, there is an assumption that persons with mental retardation are best suited for entry-level employment, will remain in these placements for extended periods of time (if not for their entire employment history), and will have little motivation to advance in employment.

The nature of the supports provided and the source of the supports offered through supported employment programs have also come under examination and debate in recent years. The introduction of on-site supports has been noted by many as a key strategy to the success of individuals with mental retardation in the workplace. In many instances the need for additional training is essential, yet there are concerns as to the reliance for this training upon the services of an outside trainer rather than the use of those supports that exist within the workplace, the natural supports of the job (Hagner & Dileo, 1993; Nisbet, 1992). Paralleling this concern is the growing recognition of the need to incorporate the individual not only into the production but into the social and cultural aspects of the workplace. Success in the workplace is measured not exclusively by the level of productivity of the individual worker, but also by the level of satisfaction and the inclusion of the employee in the nonwork aspects of the job (Kiernan & Schalock, 1997).

There is a growing recognition of the need to look at the inclusion of the person with mental retardation in the production and social aspects of the workplace (Chadsey & Shelden, 1998). There is an expanding body of research that is supporting the utilization of naturally occurring supports (co-workers as trainers and support resources, employer-based training services, and other social supports) in the training and assimilation of the worker with mental retardation into employment (Mank, 1994). These data support the concept that employers and co-workers are willing and able (often with some assistance from a job coach) to assume a leadership role in training and supporting the worker with mental retardation on the job. These studies serve also to support a redesign of the relationship between employers and community rehabilitation professionals, as well as the employees with mental retardation and co-workers.

The technology and the approaches to supporting persons with mental retardation in integrated employment are available. The struggle is not one of *how* but rather *when* programs and services will focus on employment as the goal for persons with mental retardation. Although significant accomplishments in increasing both the awareness of and the actual number of persons with mental retardation entering employment have been realized, there continues to be a strong reliance on utilization of sheltered employment programs nationally. Data on the rates of employment of persons with disabilities in real work settings and the number of persons continuing to enter segregated employment settings reinforce the need for systemic changes and a continuing focus on facilitating the entry into real jobs for persons with mental retardation nationally (Gilmore & Butterworth, 1996; Ma & Gilmore, 1997; McGaughey et al., 1994).

EMERGING APPROACHES TO ENHANCING EMPLOYMENT

Over the past two decades a number of factors have influenced the employment of individuals with mental retardation and other developmental disabilities. Some of these relate to the evolution of the American workforce, whereas others reflect changes in the systems that support individuals with mental retardation.

The Changing Workplace

A current unemployment rate averaging 4%, with some areas of the country reporting less than 1%, would imply that there is a growing need for workers in all sectors. In fact, many employers are considering workers who in the past would not have been regarded part of the labor pool. Companies are offering supports to workers in the form of more flexible work schedules, home employment, nontraditional benefits plans, shared job options, and supports for workers who may need personal or family assistance. In a few instances employers have developed expanded human resource services offering case management, child care, and housing assistance (Kiernan, Marrone, & Butterworth, 1999). Although these are the exceptions, it would seem that, given the current shortage of employees, the opportunities to increase the employment for persons with mental retardation should be significant. Unfortunately, the rate of unemployment or "not in the labor force" for persons with mental retardation hovers around 70% (Louis Harris and Associates, 1995; McGaughey et al., 1994).

Employers, while asking for assistance, are having difficulty in making the connection between the untapped labor resource of persons with mental retardation and their company needs. The need for a more direct link between employers and the public rehabilitation system (including community rehabilitation programs) is essential. Participation in business associations (the Chamber of Commerce, Associated Industries, and local trade associations) will increase visibility but, unless there is more aggressive marketing and outreach, such participation is unlikely to lead to real jobs for persons with mental retardation. Community rehabilitation providers must understand employer needs, assist in responding to those needs, and link the labor resources available through these programs to the job duties in the company. The development of a strong employer relationship will serve to open the doors to jobs, but the actual matching of the individual skills to the specific job needs in a company is the essential element of an effective job placement strategy.

At the federal level, the passage of the Americans with Disabilities Act of 1990 (ADA) served to substantially increase the awareness of the need for employers to recognize persons with disabilities as potential and qualified employees. This legislation in many ways has served to increase both awareness of and concerns regarding the employment of persons with disabilities. The initial response by many companies was not "How can we open the doors of opportunity?" but "How can we establish the avenues of compliance to the law?" Concerns about litigation have given way to strategies of expanding the intent of the ADA to real job opportunities. Several studies have documented changes in larger employers regarding the employment and support of workers with disabilities (Blanck & Marti, 1997). The ADA has served as a lever or opener, and the next step is for the translation of that opportunity into real jobs for persons with mental retardation.

The changing workforce, the increased emphasis on equality and opportunity, and the recognition that there is a need for a closer working relationship between employers and those charged with facilitating the entry into work of the nontraditional worker are all elements that in the coming years will create more jobs for persons with mental retardation. There are also some systemic changes that are and will be occurring that will also facilitate increased employment opportunities.

Changes in the System

Concerns of family members, consumers, and many professionals revolve around the loss of currently provided health and cash assistance, apprehension about the types of jobs offered, the level of wages paid, and the potential instability of jobs in the open market, which are all reported as significant barriers to the employment of individuals with mental retardation and other developmental disabilities (Fallavollita, 1997). Other concerns reflect issues of inadequate transportation, the needs for a highly customized set of job duties, and apprehension about loss of friends made in the current sheltered or nonwork setting. Each of these barriers has merit in some way and contributes to the significant apprehension expressed by consumers, family members, and others regarding employment.

Several strategies have been proposed, and some implemented, that would begin to address these concerns. The changes in the Social Security Supplemental Security Income (SSI) program through work incentives have provided a more rational approach for dealing with the movement from public benefits to real jobs (National Academy of Social Insurance, 1996). These work incentives have opened the doors to retaining cash benefits when wage payments are low, as well as providing an opportunity to maintain health care benefits when employer-sponsored benefits are either unavailable or inadequate. These same work incentives are not currently available for those individuals on Social Security Disability Insurance (SSDI); however, legislation has been proposed to modify the SSDI policies to allow for a more gradual reduction in cash benefits and a way to remain on health care benefits in those instances where such benefits are unavailable or inadequate in the workplace.

The SSI work incentives have been in place for a number of years yet are poorly utilized. There is a need not only for the establishment of more effective marketing of these incentives but for a change in the basic tenets of Social Security, with a stronger focus on employment as a realistic and desirable goal for persons with disabilities. Current application processes for SSA benefits require extensive documentation of incapacity, with no reference to eventual return or entry into employment by a potential SSA applicant. It is thus with the mindset of complete dependence that the individual with a disability approaches the SSA application process. Once on the rolls, there is little incentive to exit given the historic difficulty in gaining initial eligibility status. Exit from the SSA rolls must be made easier and more desirable and can be accomplished through the development of easy on–easy off policies, a commitment by SSA to encourage entry into employment and the development of demonstration programs that will show that return or entry into a job can lead to greater economics gain and security for the individual. The current perception among many is that there is less gain and greater risk to the individual who enters or considers entering employment, given the perceived loss of benefits.

Changes proposed in SSA and the growing awareness that this system can be used to enhance employment will significantly address the concerns of consumers and family members when considering employment. Flexibility in benefits reductions as a result of earned income, continuation of medical coverage, and easy return to benefits given job changes will address a long-standing barrier to employment.

In addition to the changes in SSA through work incentives for the individual, some systemic changes that have occurred over the past 5 years may have a positive impact upon the employment of persons with mental retardation. For most state Mental Retardation and Developmental Disabilities agencies, the provision of day and employment services is through a network of community-based rehabilitation providers. These typically not-for-profit programs contract with the public agency and provide services often on an ongoing basis to persons with mental retardation. Through a system of complicated reimbursement policies and practices, the federal government partially reimburses states for the costs associated with maintaining individuals in community settings through the Home and Community Based Waiver program. This system of reimbursement was designed to prevent institutionalization, with the states receiving a portion of their expenses for serving persons who have been or may be at risk of institutionalization, in community-based programs rather than institutions. Initially, employment supports were not considered as a reimbursable expense by the Health Care Financing Administration (HCFA) of the U.S. Department of Health and Human Services. However, a few years ago HCFA regulations were expanded to include supported employment as a covered service for individuals who are covered by the state waiver program.

With the strong focus in many states on maximizing federal reimbursement, the change in regulations relating to reimbursement of supported employment services has the potential for greatly increasing the interest by state agencies in expecting that those individuals served in the current community rehabilitation system should be served in supported employment. The opportunity to share expenses for supported employment should encourage states to begin to stipulate that supported employment is the desired outcome for individuals served in day and segregated employment.

The changes in reimbursement for supported employment, while offering promise for increasing opportunities for employment for more persons with mental retardation entering employment, do not address the concerns of a fragmented system of services at the state and local levels. Current services often respond to needs in one life area (work, community living, recreation, or health), with little coordination across all major life areas. Often the services offered in one area are in conflict with those offered in another. If an individual enters employment on a schedule other than the traditional Monday thru Friday, 9 to 5, there is often great confusion and, typically, reluctance on the part of the community living staff to support this type of employment. Recreational services continue to be organized in small specialized groups, with infrequent utilization of the local recreational services and options in the community. The inflexibility of the current system to accommodate to differences in work schedule, preferences in recreational activities, or individual choice have often limited the employment options for persons with mental retardation. More creative options such as home ownership and shared apartments, as well as flexible and individually designed supports, have begun to address the rigidity of the typical community services. Programs and approaches focusing on person-centered panning, personal networks, and community inclusion will provide for the development of services and supports that reflect individual preferences and interests rather than availability of current services and program slots for persons with mental retardation.

Service integration within employment and training programs likewise has been identified as a major concern. This has been a front burner issue in Congress and at the state level for the past few years. Several reports have noted the need to integrate the various employment and training programs (Fallavollita, 1997). The recently passed Workforce Investment Act of 1998 legislatively brings together many of the employment and training programs of the federal government, encourages a more integrated approach to employment and job placement at the state and local levels, and calls for the establishment of a single employment service (One Stop Career Centers) at the community level. The One Stop Career Center design seeks to respond to the fractured employment programs of the current system. While there is some apprehension regarding the movement toward a more generic employment and training system, with advocates fearing that persons with mental retardation will again be unserved, there is growing recognition among many of both the capacity and the interest of persons with mental retardation to work. This awareness and the changing expectation on the part of consumers, family members, and others can serve to advocate for assuring that individuals with mental retardation are served through the One Stop Career Centers.

The advantages to a more integrated employment and training system would seem to outweigh the disadvantages from the perspective of a more comprehensive system of job identification and placement. The concerns about the possibility of "creaming," where individuals with severe disabilities are not served by a more generic system because either the system does not have the capacity or such services are perceived as too costly, are real and must be addressed through both legislation and regulation. The assurance that any One Stop system must respond to the needs of all job seekers has to be a core part of any reform of the employment and training system at the federal and state levels (Connolly, Kiernan, & Marrone, 1997).

In response to the interest in development of a more integrated approach to services, several federal initiatives have been developed. Both the Social Security Administration and the Department of Education's Rehabilitation Services Administration have just begun to support projects that would encourage states to link services and supports together and to develop a more integrated approach to supporting persons with disabilities. These demonstration approaches are designed to facilitate new ways in which a state can combine resources and develop systems that will respond to individual interests and preferences of persons with disabilities. These projects, while in their developmental stages, can be viewed as an initial step in establishing a single point of entry and a single service delivery system.

In addition to the interest in systemic changes, there is also a growing movement to support greater consumer control through the use of vouchers. The intent of the voucher system of service delivery is to offer control over the allocation of resources by the consumer. The control of resources is one of a number of elements that are being identified as interest in consumer-designed and -controlled service emerges. Although there have been several versions of vouchers or individual payment systems, there is a growing interest in developing individual-controlled and -managed accounts where the individual with a disability will be in full control over the allocation of money (Callahan & Mank, 1998). The Social Security Administration's proposed ticket system is a legislative initiative in which consumers will have an ability to control resources and select service providers and support resources that will meet their individual interests. The concept of vouchers, though not new, is an area that many consumers and families feel can have a considerable impact on the redesign of services locally and nationally.

CHANGES IN APPROACH: EMERGING PRACTICES LEADING TO INNOVATION IN EMPLOYMENT

As noted in the initial portion of this chapter, the emphasis on employment for persons with mental retardation has been a major focus only for the past three decades. Initially, efforts were placed on development of segregated training centers, specifically sheltered workshops and craft centers. This was followed by a recognition of the advantages to placement and training through the on-site supports of a job coach or employment training specialist, with the development of supported employment. Concerns about placement and inclusion in the workplace led to a more recent interest in the development of strategies that would access naturally occurring supports for persons with mental retardation and other developmental disabilities at work.

Natural supports reflect those services, supports, and resources that are typically available in the workplace. In some instances a natural support may be the utilization of a co-worker as a trainer, whereas in others it may be a shared ride to work, a simple modification in job tasks, a change in the work environment, or the development of a mentor–mentee relationship at work. Initially, some felt that the adoption of natural supports would mean that there is no need for the presence of a job coach in the workplace, giving rise to concerns that the worker with a disability would not be adequately supported in learning the work tasks. Some even implied that the intent of natural supports was to reduce costs by abandoning the worker with a disability too early in the employment placement and supports process. More recently, as the concept of natural supports has taken hold, realization is that the emphasis of natural supports is not to save money (though in some instances that may be the case) but to foster inclusion and involvement of workers with and without disabilities in getting the job done, developing social networks, and creating a supportive work of culture for all workers.

Coupled with the interest in accessing naturally occurring supports is the interest in developing personal networks for persons with mental retardation. Planning approaches focusing on circles of support, person-centered planning, and whole life planning are recognizing the importance of a wide range of persons in the identification of opportunities, the development of support systems, and the attainment of individual goals for persons with mental retardation (Butterworth et al., 1993). The significance of personal networks has been reinforced by research reporting that their use is the most effective strategy in finding work for persons with disabilities (Temelini & Fesko, 1996). The development of personal networks is an emerging approach, which has been used in some instances to increase job opportunities and identify community resources that can support individuals with mental retardation.

Strategies linking personal networks with natural supports are showing greater promise for job success for persons with mental retardation. Studies are showing a higher level of satisfaction for the individual with a disability and co-workers, with greater earnings and increased length of employment when personal networks and typical supports are used both to access the job and to develop skills on the job (Mank, 1994; Temelini & Fesko, 1996). Not necessarily a solution to the high rate of unemployment, the use of natural supports and personal networks can certainly play a role in increasing the access to and retention of employment for persons with mental retardation.

The development of personal networks is a process that begins in early years and is enhanced by the inclusion of students with disabilities in the typical classroom setting. In the early school years, students with and without disabilities can learn together, develop social relationships, and realize each others' skills and abilities (McGregor & Vogelsberg, 1998). This same interaction in later school years can lead to more cooperative planning about adult years and involve students with and without disabilities in the identification of interests and preferences. The changes in the transition planning process, with the need to begin transition planning at age 14, have led to a greater awareness of the role that educators and students can and must play in the movement from school to work. The emphasis on service learning and the recognition that education is intimately tied to employment confirm the central role that schools must play in the preparation for adult life.

Along with growing interest in the development of networks and the use of natural supports, a parallel expansion has occurred in the use of an ecological approach to matching individual interests to the workplace. The ecological approach to employment matches the interests of the individual with the requirements and job needs of the employer. This approach to job matching has had success in developing a better fit between the interests of the individual and the needs of the employer. There is a growing awareness of the need to match the individual's interests and preferences to both the job tasks and the culture of the workplace. Such an approach recognizes the importance of the social and interpersonal relationships in the workplace, as well as the production requirements (Kiernan & Schalock, 1997). This expanded ecological approach allows for a greater opportunity to identify networks and social support resources in the workplace and to integrate the preferences and interests of the individual to the social and production expectations of the job.

Much concern has been raised not only about the high rate of unemployment but also about the nature of the jobs that are being accessed. Many of the jobs identified for persons with disabilities are in low-wage, nonbenefited service industries. Few of these jobs provide opportunities for career growth and advancement. There is an underlying assumption that individuals with mental retardation who are placed in such jobs will remain indefinitely, be pleased with such work, and not become bored with routine repetitive tasks. This perception may in some ways be an outgrowth of the concepts of the sheltered workshops, where routine and repetitive tasks were the staple, or from the initial outreach efforts in which employers were told that persons with mental retardation would never get bored, always be at work on time, and demand little in the area of job growth. Within the current work culture, job change and career development are essential parts of a person's job history. There is no reason why they should not also be a part of the course of employment for persons with mental retardation.

Concerns about the difficulty in getting a job may serve to discourage consumers, family members, and professionals to consider job change. The current service delivery system has a tendency to view job change for persons with mental retardation as a sign of failure rather than career growth. Often services are "closed" once the individual is employed, so the supports that may facilitate job change are no longer available and the initial job coaching that might make the difference in success on another job is not available. If we are to consider that persons with mental retardation are to have the same opportunities as persons without disabilities, then job coaching and the support for job change must be available. The concept of closing a case, as in the public Vocational Rehabilitation system, and of the use of the sheltered workshop as a safety net when job change occurs are two concepts that must be changed. Permanent eligibility for and availability of supports, not at the time of job termination but in the planning process for accessing jobs or changing jobs, must be developed. Career growth is an essential element of reaching the goal of economic independence, is a form of recognition of the employee's own growth and development, and is an avenue of expanding one's social support network.

Finally, in any discussion of emerging trends in employment of persons with mental retardation, it is essential to consider concepts of self-employment or joint ownership. Although considerable concerns about the option of self-employment have been raised, self-employment may offer an additional avenue to an effective match between individual interests and actual job tasks. Some initial data are showing that, although self-employment in general does have some risk, this level of risk (business failure) is much less than what has been reported in the popular literature (Aley, 1993). Other studies have reported that, for some individuals with disabilities, self-employment is a viable option (Arnold & Seekins, 1994). For persons with mental retardation, the concerns about ability to make good business decisions are often raised. As in the case of both person-centered planning and social network development, there are opportunities for others to assist the individual with mental retardation who is interested in self-employment to have the necessary supports to address issues of decision making, budgeting, and other potentially difficult areas.

The option of self-employment should not be a primary focus for persons with mental retardation, but rather one possible way of viewing persons with mental retardation as bringing skills and abilities rather than limitations and incapacity. In some instances persons with mental retardation may be aligned with a co-owner who might handle the development of the business side while the individual with mental retardation might be more actively involved in the production side of a small, jointly held self-employment operation.

FUTURE EMPLOYMENT OPPORTUNITIES: DREAMS CAN COME TRUE

This final section reflects some of the dreams I see for the 21st century for persons with mental retardation. Some of these dreams will require a change in perspectives and others the adoption of new approaches to accessing and supporting individuals with mental retardation in employment. Some of the key changes include the following:

- *The change in exception:* Employment is a viable and necessary goal and should be included as an outcome in all transition plans. Rather than not being included in the workforce statistics by the Department of Labor, persons with mental retardation should be reported as in the unemployed and part of the group of job seekers who would benefit from the generic employment and training services and supports. The safe harbor of sheltered employment must be turned around to indicate that sheltered workshops and sheltered employment settings do not contribute to the independence, productivity, and integration of individuals with mental retardation. Networking and personal networks must be developed in early years, thus fostering continuous opportunities for inclusion of persons with mental retardation in all major life activities.

- *Change in performance indicators:* The expectation among states that purchase services for persons with mental retardation must reflect changes in how services are provided from the standpoint of who directs the service, how services and supports are directed, and where such supports are offered. Performance contracting with integrated employment for all serving as the desired outcome is an effective strategy for changing the community rehabilitation provider system and increasing the number of individuals with mental retardation who enter employment.

- *Changes in funding and support:* Flexible funding designs, including vouchers, cash payments directly to nontraditional support resources (employment services, head hunter organizations, One Stop Career Centers, personal networks, and employer supports), and the development of informal networks of support, will lead to more effective job placement, community inclusion, and ongoing supports for persons with mental retardation.

- *Changes in employment strategies:* Effective partnerships between persons with mental retardation and co-workers, employers and persons with mental retardation, employers and community provider networks, and persons with mental retardation and community providers are all necessary. These partnerships must be viewed as mutually beneficial and not one-sided as they have been in the past. Partnerships lead to positive outcomes for each of the partners and thus all partnerships must look at each of the stakeholders as an equal contributor and equal beneficiary.

There are some approaches that ought to be adopted that will lead to more effective employment opportunities in the 21st century for persons with mental retardation. These strategies for adoption are no different from those that have been recognized for persons without mental retardation and include the following:

- The adoption of a lifelong learning strategy where there is a recognition that learning is continuous and occurs over a lifetime and not only during the formal academic years.

- The adoption of a career development strategy where the first job ought to lead to the second and the second to the third, each providing greater economic independence and greater recognition by co-workers of contributions made.

- The adoption of inclusive designs in workplace supports where persons with disabilities support persons without disabilities, and vice versa, when networks and co-worker supports are available to all persons.

- The adoption of the universal application where any modifications within the workplace, such as job accommodations, job modifications, and technology, have a positive influence on all employees, and where technology, external supports, and other resources have a direct benefit for all employees, not only those with disabilities.

In conclusion, this chapter has tried to reflect some of the historic perspectives on employment, some of the current activities regarding employment, and some of the future potential for persons with mental retardation in the 21st century. Although the economy is booming and persons with mental retardation are showing some gain in the world of employment, we have a long way to go. I am optimistic that, given continued recognition of persons with mental retardation as contributing members to society, the reality of the 21st century will be one of greater employment opportunities for persons with mental retardation in jobs that are not merely entry-level jobs, but that offer benefits, security, and a chance to be a contributing member of a workforce and a social culture within the workplace.

REFERENCES

Aley, J. (1993). Debunking the failure of fallacy. *Fortune, 128*(5), 21.

Americans with Disabilities Act of 1990, 42 U.S.C. § 12101 *et seq.*

Arnold, N., & Seekins, T. (1994). Self-employment as a vocational rehabilitation closure. *Journal of Disability Policy Studies, 5*(2), 66–67.

Blanck, P. D., & Marti, M. W. (1997). Attitudes, behavior and the employment provisions of the Americans with Disabilities Act. *Villanove Law Review, 24*(2), 345–406.

Boles, S. M., Bellamy, G. T., Horner, R. H., & Mank, D. M. (1984). Specialized training program: The structured employment model. In S. Paine, G. T. Bellamy, & B. Wilcox (Eds.), *Human services that work: From innovation to standard practice* (pp. 181–208). Baltimore: Brookes.

Butterworth, J., Hagner, D., Heikkinen, B., Faris, S., DeMello, S., & McDonough, K. (1993). *Whole life planning: A guide for organizers and facilitators.* Boston: Children's Hospital Institute for Community Inclusion.

Callahan, M., & Mank, D. (1998). Choice and control of employment for people with disabilities. In T. Nerney & D. Shumway (Eds.), *The importance of income* (pp. 15–33). Durham, NH: Institute on Disability.

Chadsey, J. G., & Shelden, D. L. (1998). *Promoting social relationships and integration for supported employees in work settings.* Champaign-Urbana, IL: Transition Research Institute.

Connolly, P., Kiernan, W. E., & Marrone, J. (1997). *An analysis of the One Stop Career Center system as it relates to persons with disabilities.* Boston: Institute for Community Inclusion.

Fallavollita, B. (1997). *Social Security: Disability programs lag in promoting return to work.* Washington: General Accounting Office.

Gilmore, D. S., & Butterworth, J. (1996). *Trends in supported employment: The experiences of ninety four community rehabilitation providers between 1986 to 1991.* Boston: Institute for Community Inclusion.

Hagner, D., & Dileo, D. (1993). *Working together: Workplace culture, supported employment, and persons with disabilities.* Cambridge, MA: Brookline Books.

Kiernan, W. E., Marrone, J., & Butterworth, J. (1999). *Beyond demographics: Strategic response to a changing workforce.* Boston: Institute for Community Inclusion.

Kiernan, W. E., Schalock, R. L. (1997). *Integrated employment: Current status and future directions.* Washington, DC: American Association on Mental Retardation.

Kiernan, W. E., & Stark, J. A. (Eds.). (1996). *Pathways to employment for adults with developmental disabilities.* Baltimore: Brookes.

Louis Harris and Associates. (1995). *National Organization on Disability/Harris survey on employment of people with disabilities.* New York: Author.

Ma, V., & Gilmore, D. S. (1997). *National day and employment service trends to MR/DD agencies.* Boston: Institute for Community Inclusion.

Mank, D. (1994). The underachievement of supported employment: A call for reinvestment. *Journal of Disability Policy Studies, 5*(2), 1–24.

McGaughey, M. J., Kiernan, W. E., McNally, L. C., Gilmore, D. S., & Keith, G. R. (1994). Beyond the workshop: National trends in integrated and segregated day and employment services. *Journal of The Association for Persons with Severe Disabilities, 20,* 270–285.

McGregor, G., & Vogelsberg, R. T. (1998). *Inclusive schooling practices: Pedagogical and research foundations.* Missoula, MT: Consortium on Inclusive Schooling Practices.

National Academy of Social Insurance. (1996). *Balancing security and opportunity: The challenge of disability income policy.* Washington, DC: Author.

Nisbet, J. (1992). *Natural supports in school, at work, and in the community for people with severe disabilities.* Baltimore: Brookes.

Temelini, D., & Fesko, S. (1996). *Shared responsibility: Job search practices from the consumer and staff perspective.* Boston: Institute for Community Inclusion.

Wehman, P. (1981). *Competitive employment: New horizons for severely disabled individuals.* Baltimore: Brookes.

Wehman, P., & Kregel, J. (1995). At the crossroads: Supported employment ten years later. *Journal of The Association for Persons with Severe Disabilities, 20,* 286–299.

Whitehead, C. (1981). *Final report: Training and employment services for handicapped individuals.* Washington, DC: Department of Health and Human Services.

Whitehead, C. W., & Marrone, J. (1986). Time-limited evaluation and training. in W. E. Kiernan & J. A. Stark (Eds.), *Pathways to employment for adults with developmental disabilities* (pp. 163–176). Baltimore: Brookes.

Workforce Investment Act of 1998, 20 U.S.C. § 9276.

From Unit D to the Community: A Dream to Fulfill

Jay Klein and Jeffrey L. Strully

 BILL'S STORY

Bill was born to a loving and caring family in 1932. Sadly, his mother died during his birth, leaving Bill in the care of his father, grandmother, and two older siblings. Like all young children, Bill loved to explore, but walking was difficult because he could not see and was unsteady on his feet. He often fell, sometimes resulting in serious injuries. By the age of 5, Bill was beginning to dress and feed himself with a great deal of assistance and had not yet learned to speak or use the toilet. His frequent violent seizures, challenging behavior, and trouble moving about on his own made it difficult for his family to care for him.

When his grandmother's health began to fail, there was no one to care for Bill while his father worked. Unlike the other children in the family, he did not go to school, and there were no services available to support the family to take care of him or to enable him to be educated at home. When Bill was 5 years old, the family doctor, the pastor from the family's church, and Bill's aunts, uncles, and grandparents advised his father to send Bill to live at the state institution 50 miles away. Reluctantly, Bill's dad took him there.

For the next 45 years, Bill remained in the institution. He shared a ward with 20 to 40 other boys, and later men, with disabilities. As a child, Bill was energetic and liked to be on the move, and his adventures often led to injury. Since there were not enough staff to accompany Bill on his explorations, he was tied to a chair or to his bed for up to 20 hours each day. This practice continued into his adulthood. Having never learned to speak, Bill shouted loudly if he needed assistance, or was hungry, bored, frustrated, or lonely. He began to hit his head against the wall and to slap himself almost constantly. Eventually, Bill was forced to wear a helmet to keep him from hurting himself.

Over the years, there were a few caring staff people who taught Bill some sign language and helped him learn to better feed and dress himself. Occasionally someone would even take Bill to the pool, which he loved. Aside from the considerations and actions of a handful of people, Bill's life was devoid of any kindness or compassion. Early in 1983, at the age of 51, Bill left the institution and moved into his own home in the community. With careful planning, he received the assistance he needed and became part of his community. He established relationships with his neighbors, was recognized as a citizen in his small town, became a volunteer for various community organizations, and voted in the local elections.

The story of Bill, until he reached the age of 51, is a tragic example of how people with developmental and other disabilities have been forced to live throughout our country's history. From generation to generation, abuse, neglect, isolation, loneliness, and poverty have endured as common threads in the lives of people with disabilities. Individuals who looked, moved, learned, or communicated in ways that differed greatly from the majority were feared, misunderstood, mistreated, or ignored. Fortunately, services and supports for people like Bill have undergone a tremendous transformation over the past five decades.

This chapter explores the principles and practices that have dramatically shaped the lives of people with disabilities in the United States from colonial times to the present. Beginning with the deplorable living conditions in institutions from their inception in the 1700s, the chapter describes the changes over time in societal attitudes toward people with disabilities, the concurrent evolution of the service system, and the influence of history on current perspectives and approaches to service delivery. A new set of principles and practices for the future is then proposed that could move the service delivery system from congregate care to community, and thus change the course of experiences for thousands of people over the next 50 years. These principles and practices are based on people's rights and needs, including the right to have a voice, rich personal relationships, and control over personal supports and assistance, as well as the need for supports that are flexible, individualized, and offered within communities that value all of their citizens. Finally, the chapter calls for a strong commitment to change if society is to acknowledge and learn from past injustices and embrace the rights of people with disabilities to lead full lives in the community as contributing citizens, homeowners, neighbors, and friends.

PRINCIPLES AND PRACTICES OF THE PAST: DEHUMANIZATION AND EXCLUSION

My family was talked into putting me away as a child. I would never have gotten out alive had I not been a fighter.

Cassie J., Pennsylvania state "school" survivor (*Testimony*, 1995, p. 4)

Since the founding of this country, attitudes toward people with disabilities have been less than positive. People who were "different" were perceived by various generations as deviant, dangerous, helpless, objects of pity, or gifts from God. Disabilities have been misunderstood, feared, and thought to be passed from generation to generation.

During the settlement of the original American colonies in the early 1600s, some people with disabilities were bought and sold as slaves at auction. Others resided in towns that were expected to provide for citizens who were poor or elderly, or had disabilities. Occasionally this obligation was met by paying parents or relatives to care for their own family members with disabilities. However, later in the century the societal view of people with disabilities began to shift from "those who needed care" to people who were "inferior and without rights or dignity." During the summer of 1692, in the town of Salem, Massachusetts, over 200 people were accused of practicing witchcraft; 20 were put to death as a result of these charges. Given the feelings of many citizens toward people who were different, it is quite likely that some of the accused and condemned were people with disabilities (Scheerenberger, 1983).

From 1700 through the mid-1800s, people with mental, physical, or emotional disabilities were sent to almshouses, where conditions were filthy, treatment was often inhumane, and care was strictly custodial. From the mid-1800s to the early 1900s, there was a wide range of opinions and theories, but little consensus, about the capacity of people with disabilities to be educated or trained. As towns grew into cities and farmers became workers during the Industrial Era, most people were sent to live and be educated in large state-operated and funded institutions. Some felt that, with adequate training and instruction, people with disabilities could return to their home communities (Scheerenberger, 1983). However, the vast majority of institutions had no formal discharge program. The primary function of the institution, while providing varying degrees of training and instruction, was to serve as a warehouse or asylum for people with disabilities. Institutions were seen as places where vulnerable people could be kept safe and sheltered from the community, while protecting society from the "unpleasantness," even "danger," of being forced to include its deviant members. Parents of institutionalized children and adults were reassured that the professionals knew best how to care for their sons and daughters, and were often discouraged from being overly involved in decisions regarding their care and treatment.

According to Scheerenberger (1983), the science of eugenics was widely accepted during this era as a means of reducing and ultimately eliminating human beings who were considered genetically inferior. This led to widespread sterilization of individuals who were thought of as undesirable, such as "the feebleminded, paupers, criminaloids, epileptics, the insane, the constitutionally weak, those predisposed to certain diseases, the congenitally deformed, and those having defective sense organs" (p. 154).

From 1907 to 1958, 30 states reported that a total of 31,038 individuals with mental retardation were sterilized. Because people with disabilities were looked upon as eternal children, remaining chaste and innocent throughout their lives, there was little opportunity for them to develop intimate relationships, to fall in love, and to marry. The majority of places where children and young people lived and spent their time prevented typical learning through observation of role models such as parents or other couples who were romantically involved. As teenagers grew up, they were discouraged from expressing their feelings or acting on crushes, or were intensely ridiculed by the institution's workers. Intimate contact and sexual experiences for people with disabilities consisted primarily of assault and abuse by individuals who were physically or socially more powerful. Even between two adults, a mutual and consenting relationship was nearly impossible. In fact, 39 states passed laws that prohibited marriage between people with disabilities (Scheerenberger, 1983).

From 1920 to 1940, a number of positive legislative changes occurred that significantly benefited people with disabilities. These included the passage of the Smith-Fess Act of 1920, which provided services to veterans with physical disabilities such as vocational rehabilitation, job training, and prostheses; the Social Security Act of 1935, which provided federal grants for vocational rehabilitation and for "needy" persons who were blind; and the Fair Labor Standards Act of 1938, which created special provisions governing the employment of people with mental and physical disabilities in sheltered workshops and similar work settings. Despite this progress, conditions within institutions continued to decline. Abuse and neglect were rampant. Residents were subjected to physical, sexual, and emotional mistreatment; barbaric "punishment" that included prolonged periods of isolation, withholding of food, and physical beatings; and a humiliating lack of privacy for even the most private activities (Blatt, 1966).

During the 1960s and 1970s, media attention on the horrific living conditions for people with disabilities in institutions ignited public outrage. Powerful reform efforts by parents, lawmakers, and advocates for people with disabilities resulted. Lawsuits over the injustices suffered by people with disabilities at the hands of institutions ignited the birth of a movement to replace state-run institutions with community-based services. One outcome was the establishment of regional agencies to provide services for people as they moved from institutions. A second outcome was the establishment of the Independent Living movement, which advocated for the equal inclusion and participation of people with disabilities in all facets of society. These changes in attitudes, practices, and policies of the United States toward its citizens with disabilities were reflected in the term *Normalization* promoted by Wolfensberger (1977). Normalization was defined as "the utilization of culturally valued means in order to establish and/or maintain personal behaviors, experiences, and characteristics that are culturally normative or valued" (p. 28).

Despite the transition from institutions to community-based services, the majority of people with disabilities continued to live in places that kept them excluded from ordinary life. Residential options or "programs" included congregate settings, such as nursing homes, intermediate care facilities (ICFs), group homes, psychiatric facilities, or adult foster care. These limited choices were nearly always owned and controlled by agencies and inseparable from funding sources. Additionally, these options typically had stringent entrance criteria and long waiting lists.

During the 1970s, residential options and services were created on the basis of the "continuum of services" theory. According to this theory, individuals with disabilities would live in a place considered to be the least restrictive setting possible. The acquisition of new skills or the reduction of problematic behavior (presumably as a result of the training and instruction received in each setting) enabled people to move into a less restrictive setting. In theory, individuals progressed through the continuum, stopping at each level and receiving more training and skill development until they were ready for the next least restrictive setting.

When people enrolled in a residential services program, rules and regulations dictated how and with whom their time was spent. Recreational, vocational, and social activities were restricted to group situations, which included only other people with disabilities. Individuals who staffed the residences earned low wages, worked exhausting schedules, and were often inexperienced and untrained. The people who lived in these residences were treated like children by individuals often decades younger than they were, and abuse and neglect were not uncommon. In short, although these new community-based options were an improvement over the institutions, life for people with disabilities was a far cry from the standards for living conditions that most Americans would consider even minimally satisfactory.

As service providers realized the flaws and dehumanizing characteristics of available programs, they attempted to be more responsive to what they believed people with disabilities needed. New models were introduced; those that seemed to work for a few people were considered effective, and were subsequently standardized so that agencies could dispense the models to the people who relied on them for services. Ultimately, people with disabilities were still thought of in terms of their differences, deficits, and vulnerabilities, and the focus remained on fixing and protecting, rather than providing assistance and listening.

PRINCIPLES AND PRACTICES OF THE PRESENT: CONGREGATION AND EXTERNAL CONTROL

I sit on a man's back choking him, and making him carry me, and yet assure myself that I am very sorry for him and wish to ease his lot by any means possible except getting off his back.

Leo Tolstoy (cited in Schumacher, 1973, p. 17)

LISA'S STORY

Lisa lives on Unit D in a large institution in a large western state. She has spent most of her teenage years in a locked unit within a locked building. Having been moved from one institution to another, Lisa doesn't know many of the staff people who work on her unit. She doesn't like most of the people with whom she lives. Lisa is angry. To prevent her from hurting herself, Lisa wears a helmet. Arm and wrist restraints are used to prevent her from pinching and scratching, and leg restraints keep her from attacking staff and other people on her unit. Lisa takes an assortment of tranquilizers to control her behavior.

After months of planning and assistance from a team of people who know Lisa, she will soon move into her own place in the community. She will live close to her family, and will receive the assistance she needs, from people whom she likes and trusts, to begin to live a rich, full life. As Lisa embarks on her journey toward a desirable future, her story has really just begun.

Today, many individuals, their families, and those who provide them with assistance are working diligently to include people with disabilities in community life. In the community, people with disabilities become valued neighbors, friends, spouses, taxpayers, parents, homeowners, voters, co-workers, and students. People can now exercise choice about where and with whom they live and spend their time; engage in meaningful work; demonstrate competency in many areas; and enjoy intimate relationships with others. It was through these efforts to assist people with disabilities to have a full life that the concept of "supported living" emerged. Supported living involves housing that is (a) chosen by the individual with a disability and shared with others at the person's discretion, and (b) is not owned by the agency or service provider. Supported living also assures that people are members of their community and that a personalized support plan is created with each person and that this plan is flexible enough to change with his or her changing needs and abilities (Braddock, Hemp, Bachelder, & Fujiura, 1995; Braddock, Hemp, Parish, & Westrich, 1998).

At present, many service providers would contend that they subscribe to the concept of supported living. In reality, however, only a fraction of people with disabilities have real choices and decision-making power in their lives. Although the number of people living in large institutions decreased by 67% between 1967 and 1994 (from 194,650 to approximately 63,250), residential services for most people continue to reflect principles and practices of the past, such as congregation and external control. Of the 394,284 people who live in out-of-home placements, less than 8.8% (about 45,000 people) actually receive supported living services. In other words, the vast majority of individuals (91.2%) live in places that are owned and controlled by someone else (Braddock & Hemp, 1996; Braddock et al., 1995; Braddock et al., 1998). Often, housing and assistance are offered as a package deal in which a given level or type of assistance is available only if the person lives in a particular setting, usually with individuals who have similar assistance needs. Funding sources compensate agencies for delivering both housing and assistance as one service, making it more difficult to tailor support to any one individual.

In recent years, people with disabilities have euphemistically been referred to as "consumers" or "customers." Perhaps it would be more accurate to say that people have been consumed by the service system. Because people with disabilities have limited access to and control over the resources necessary to choose how, where, and by whom their assistance will be delivered, they cannot realistically be considered consumers.

The continuum of services approach advanced in the 1970s maintains a stronghold today. Many providers still believe that people with disabilities need to learn more skills and competencies, or to reduce behavior thought to be problematic, in order to move toward more independent living; and that with appropriate assistance and intervention, people with disabilities can be "fixed," "rehabilitated," or "made acceptable" to the community. Within the concept of a continuum of services is the assumption that people must earn their way to freedom or a good life (Wieck & Strully, 1987).

For the many individuals with disabilities who rely on long-term support to live in their own homes, maintain jobs, and participate in community life, the introduction of managed care has had a profound impact. Managed care emerged in the early 1990s in an attempt to reign in the skyrocketing costs of medical services. Over the past few years, managed care has grown from coordinating health-related services and short-term medical care to including long-term care services. While proponents of managed care argue that it may be the key to controlling costs and ensuring access to quality services, its opponents maintain that it shifts local control and decision making to large, distant, and impersonal corporations. Additionally, people with very different health care needs (people with various disabilities and elderly people, for example) are being grouped together for the convenience of those who allocate funding and services, making the delivery of adequate, personalized, and appropriate services to some individuals extremely difficult.

The notion of homeownership for people with disabilities only recently has gained acceptance. Many individuals around the country have now found it possible to circumvent the traditional hurdles to homeownership, such as developing a credit history, saving money for a down payment, and demonstrating a stable source of income. Relative to income, many people have negotiated with lenders to include funds from public assistance. These new opportunities are the result of efforts by a handful of people with disabilities, their families, and advocates. While homeownership is not the answer for everyone, it is one way for people to gain greater control over their lives, and to be seen as valued citizens, neighbors, and taxpayers.

Despite the imperfections of the present service delivery system, the belief that people must be assisted to live in their own homes, rather than in large institutions, has taken a strong foothold. Individuals with even the most complex assistance needs are moving out on their own, holding down jobs, developing relationships, having children, and making decisions that impact their lives. Increasingly, assistance is being tailored to meet individual needs and is delivered in people's homes, at their jobs, and in the community.

PRINCIPLES AND PRACTICES OF THE FUTURE: COMMUNITY LIVING FOR ALL

Home is the place where, when you go there, they have to take you in.

Robert Frost (1939 p. 53)

Over the past 50 years, people with disabilities and those working on their behalf have conquered daunting legal, attitudinal, and societal barriers to community living. The recent past has provided compelling examples of people with disabilities living in their own homes and receiving the assistance they need to live as valued members of their communities. Family members, policy makers, individuals with disabilities, and service providers are working hard to listen to people with disabilities, to accompany them on their personal journeys, and to learn how to assist them in their efforts toward a rich and rewarding life. From their experiences it has become evident that, if a desirable future is a matter of course for every person with a disability, we must begin by assisting people to choose and control their homes and supports.

In an ideal world, communities would embrace and include all of their members, regardless of disability or differences. Individuals who require more assistance than others to fully belong, participate, learn, work, recreate, and have meaningful relationships would rely on their communities, their families, and friends for that assistance, rather than on agencies or service providers. Fifty years ago, it would have been impossible to envision such a world; today, this goal is realistic and attainable if (a) people with disabilities and their families guide the process; (b) friends, service providers, and others become competent listeners and are willing to let go of old assumptions and habits; and (c) energy and resources are directed at implementing worthwhile goals, as well as a new set of fundamental principles and associated practices. What follows are nine principles and practices for the future that will move us toward an ideal world where all people with disabilities are members of our communities and neighborhoods.

People Will Have a Voice

The first fundamental principle is that of free expression, a most basic human right. For far too long, people who do not use common language that the majority of us understand have not had an opportunity to exercise this right. In the future, a top priority is to ensure that every person with a disability has an effective means of communicating his or her desires, needs, feelings, and thoughts.

People with disabilities and those who assist them need to learn to use all available means to increase our ability to communicate with and understand each other. The first step in listening to someone is finding a common language. This may include the use of assistive technology, facilitated communication, and other alternatives to the spoken word.

For people who are still struggling to find their voices, or who do not have typical life experiences on which to base their decisions, we ought to start with the basic notion that everyone wants to live in and control a place that is their own. Because people, with or without disabilities, do not choose to live in institutions or homes that are controlled by someone else, it must be assumed that people who cannot express their desires would not choose this lifestyle either. In the future, placement in institutions such as nursing homes or group homes will not be acceptable options.

People Will Have Control over Their Personal Assistance

A second fundamental principle is that, in order to provide the most effective assistance to people with disabilities in the future, we need to ensure that they receive the assistance they need and have control over that assistance. This includes helping people to design and plan for assistance based on their individual needs and desires; recruit, interview, hire, train, manage, compensate fairly, and schedule the individuals who will assist them; and solicit assistance from unpaid individuals in their communities and neighborhoods.

Historically, we have relied on system solutions to concerns and problems. This tactic has left a wealth of potential resources untapped. A key to future success will be to request assistance from everyone who is willing and able to help. Often the simplest solutions are overlooked. For example, a stay-at-home mother who lives next door may be quite willing to stop by or call once a day to help a person take medicine or change positions. This type of arrangement has two benefits: first, it eliminates the need for scheduling another paid contact, and second, it creates an opportunity for a relationship to develop between neighbors.

It is not necessary for experts and professionals to determine what people with disabilities need. Those individuals who are closest to the person with a disability are in the best position to help the person achieve a life that is considered desirable. This does not mean that professional assistance is unnecessary. It does mean that experts will be called upon for consultation, training, and advice on areas related to living in the community.

In the future, assistance will be provided by individuals who are willing to take the time to get to know the person they are supporting. This includes knowing who is important in the person's life, what the person's most significant dreams are, learning about the person's history, and understanding what an ideal living situation looks like from the person's perspective. Whether people who provide assistance are paid or unpaid, a feeling of genuine equality and personal connection must be established.

Learning is more likely to happen in situations where assistance is based on the person's changing schedule, interests, and needs, not on a program's. Individuals must receive assistance where, when, how, and with whom it is needed. Flexibility must be maintained to increase, decrease, or change the amount and type of assistance a person receives as his or her needs and desires change.

Personal Relationships Will Be Promoted and Supported

The third principle for the future concerns personal relationships. People do not need or want to be congregated or segregated based on their disabilities. Friendships need to be encouraged to develop and grow based on common interests and mutual fondness. People must be assisted to spend time in places and to engage in activities that offer the greatest chance for relationships to begin. If individuals want to share their living space, they must decide with whom they will live based on the relationships they develop, rather than on their disabilities.

If people are to have full, rich lives in the future, they need to have the kinds of experiences that lead to romance, love, and intimacy. The children of present and future generations will have role models for intimate relationships, beginning with their parents, and typical interactions with friends of both genders. These factors give weight to the expectation that people with disabilities will have a future that includes love, marriage, and parenting experiences. As people with disabilities enter into relationships, become sexually active, or decide to become parents, we have a responsibility to provide the assistance and education that will give them the greatest chance of success and happiness.

Resources Will Be Flexible

A fourth fundamental principle for the future pertains to the flexibility of available funds and other resources. People with disabilities and their families must have access to, and control over, subsidies, benefits, and financing options. This flexibility and control will allow people to purchase and design the services they need from agencies, service providers, or individuals. Services must be available "à la carte." "Package deals" that force people to live in a certain building in order to receive the assistance they need will not be an option. This flexibility must not be limited to the person's home, but should also allow people to purchase appropriate assistance in the workplace, the classroom, and the community; as parents; and as homeowners.

Asset limitations placed on recipients of public benefits have kept the vast majority of people with disabilities in poverty. These limits need to be relaxed or eliminated to allow people to raise their standard of living above the poverty level by accumulating cash in savings, earning competitive wages, purchasing homes, obtaining quality education, developing credit histories, investing money, and traveling. By earning money, becoming consumers, contributing to their local economies, and saving and investing money, people with disabilities will gain status and become less vulnerable.

One of the ways that people can develop their assets is through the establishment of Individual Development Accounts (IDAs). The Personal Responsibility and Work Opportunity Reconciliation Act of 1996 permitted states to use federal funds to establish IDAs. These "matched" savings accounts, established in the name of an individual, can be initiated as early as birth. IDAs are similar to Individual Retirement Accounts (IRAs), but can serve a broader range of purposes. These include homeownership, education, training, and small business development.

Housing Will Be Affordable

A fifth fundamental principle for the future concerns affordable, safe, and decent housing. Our communities have a responsibility to provide housing that is safe, accessible, desirable, and affordable for all its citizens. In 1997, 67.6 million families and individuals owned their own homes in the United States. Homeownership can provide new opportunities for people to become empowered by contributing to their local economy. Federal subsidies in the form of vouchers need to have the flexibility to be used as rental or mortgage subsidies. Individuals must be free to use these vouchers in locations of their choosing.

Individuals who have low incomes can obtain loans from their local banks, hire members of their community to do repair work on their new homes, and pay property taxes which contribute to the purchase of local services enjoyed by other community members. Homeowners experience a feeling of greater safety, security, and belonging in their communities.

Realtors, mortgage lenders, and people with disabilities need to work together to create greater opportunities for home purchase. Not every person with a disability will hold the mortgage to a home. However, every person must sign his or her own lease, own the furnishings and decorations in the home, and control what happens within its walls (Klein, 1994).

Services Will Meet the Needs of Individuals

A sixth fundamental principle for the future involves the design and delivery of services. Living situations that put people with disabilities at risk of being lonely, isolated, poor, victimized, or without medical and health assistance can never again be acceptable. Although controlling the high cost of health care is a priority for the future, viable solutions cannot be reached by limiting the services that people with disabilities receive. Health care and long-term support must not limit opportunities for people with disabilities; rather, they must ensure that all individuals live in homes that they control and receive the assistance they need, regardless of the type or severity of their disability or medical needs. People with disabilities, their families, and those working on their behalf must remain knowledgeable and actively involved in policy and planning issues that will affect future generations.

Equally important are the issues of unmet needs and waiting lists for services. In the future, people must not be placed on waiting lists for adequate, personalized, and appropriate services. The majority of available dollars must be allocated for people, rather than buildings, administrative costs, service systems, or "expert" consultants. Supporting people to live in their own homes is invariably less costly than supporting institutional structures and settings.

As the first wave of students who have been fully included in their schools, communities, and families reach adulthood, they will not settle for yesterday's thinking. These young people will have a stronger voice and will expect inclusion, choices, and high-quality services as a minimum acceptable standard. Group home living, segregated recreational activities, and sheltered workshop programs will not be accepted by the next generation.

If the service system is to continue to play a role in the lives of people with disabilities, it must become an entity that offers an array of effective, useful, and affordable services based on market needs. This can be achieved if small, locally managed agencies are encouraged and supported to deliver high-quality assistance that is tailored to individuals, and if people with disabilities and their families have the power to collaborate with the service system to create policies and influence practices affecting their lives.

Learning Will Occur Naturally

The seventh principle states that, if adults with disabilities are to be included in everyday life, they must have a greater opportunity to learn in typical ways (i.e., in the classroom, from their parents and peers, and from role models). In the future, everyday experiences will allow learning to occur naturally. Financial planning will be gained through paying bills, having a bank account, and budgeting; interpersonal skills will be developed as people spend time with others in social situations; knowledge will be gained and opinions formed through reading, conversing with others, having real-life experiences by taking lessons, and adult education including classes at universities, colleges, and technical schools; and relationships will be developed based on what is learned from parents and mentors.

In the future, education and training ought to focus on gaining skills, building capacity by enhancing talents and gifts, and developing and broadening interests. The focus must remain on discovering what people can and want to do, providing assistance for things people cannot do, and creating opportunities for learning to occur in typical settings. Employment opportunities must be expanded beyond low-paying, unskilled food service and janitorial positions. Public benefits need to be structured to allow individuals to pursue employment opportunities without fear of losing income for personal assistance and health care.

Assistive Technology Will Be Available and Affordable

The eighth principle states that, as we step into the 21st century, technology is a necessary form of assistance for many people with disabilities. The increasing availability and affordability of power chairs and lifts will make it easier for people with disabilities to move about. Computers, automation, and other forms of technology will make it possible for many people to communicate, live on their own, maintain jobs, and participate in their communities.

A voice-activated computer can be programmed to dial the phone in case of emergency, a lighted doorbell or telephone can be used by a person who does not hear, a trained dog can open and close doors or retrieve items, a roll-in shower or power lift can make bathing an independent task, and textured floor and wall surfaces can assist a person who does not see to move about more easily in his or her home. The Internet can assist people to locate and research available resources; to gain knowledge and information about a wealth of topics; and to exchange information, using a variety of mediums, with people throughout the world.

Communities Will Be Strengthened To Support the Needs of All Citizens

According to the ninth and final principle for the future, the focus must shift from the shortcomings of communities or their individual members to recognizing the capacities and gifts of each person and the richness of resources that results when such gifts are considered collectively. The needs of people with disabilities must not be added to the list of items needing money and attention, such as rising crime, increasing drug use, parental apathy, unemployment, a lack of local control, and other modern social ills. When all of a community's people are valued equally for their unique talents and contributions, and supported equally in their struggles, then no single member is viewed as more or less valuable than the next. When the competencies of all individuals are pooled, they complement and build upon one another to create far greater possibilities than if each person stood alone.

Communities must organize, choose leaders, identify common goals, and use resources to build on the capacity of all their citizens rather than focus on individual problems and needs. For example, the Community Reinvestment Act of 1977 (CRA) requires financial institutions to invest in the communities in which they are located. In the future, investment will be accomplished by providing resources to assist individuals to make investments and accumulate savings to be used for homeownership, education, and small business development.

COMMITMENT TO CHANGE: NOT JUST A PASSING TREND

If the future for people with disabilities is to be positive, fulfilling, meaningful, and rich in relationships, then the nine principles and associated practices discussed in this chapter must be more than merely a passing trend or experiment. It is not possible to look responsibly toward the future without keeping the past firmly in mind. Bill, Lisa, and countless others before and after them lost the opportunity to live meaningful, respected, and fulfilling lives. As we approach the future, there are still many individuals among us who have survived years of torment, loneliness, abandonment, and confinement in places that none of us would choose to live. In order for us to assist the next generation to realize their dreams and have a full life, we must listen very hard to what people are saying and honor those dreams.

REFERENCES

Blatt, B. (1966). *Christmas in purgatory: A photographic essay on mental retardation.* Boston: Allyn & Bacon.

Braddock, D. & Hemp, R. (1996). Medicaid spending reductions and developmental disabilities. *Journal of Disability Policy Studies, 7*(1), 10–13.

Braddock, D., Hemp, R., Bachelder, L., & Fujiura, G. (1995). *The state of states in developmental disabilities* (4th ed.). Washington, DC: American Association on Mental Retardation.

Braddock, D., Hemp, R., Parish, S., & Westrich, J. (1998). *The state of states in developmental disabilities* (4th ed.). Washington, DC: Association on Mental Retardation.

Community Reinvestment Act of 1977, 12 U.S.C. § 2901 *et seq.*

Frost, R. (1939). *Collected poems of Robert Frost.* New York: Henry Holt.

Klein, J. (1994). Supportive living: Not just another "rung" on the continuum. *TASH Newsletter, 20*(7), 16–18.

Personal Responsibility and Work Opportunity Reconciliation Act of 1996, 42 U.S.C. § 1305, 110 Stat. 2105.

Scheerenberger, R. C. (1983). *A history of mental retardation.* Baltimore: Brookes.

Schumacher, E. (1973). *Small is beautiful: Economics as if people mattered. The problem of unemployment in India.* New York: Harper and Row.

Testimony. (1995). Rochester, NY: Free Hand Press.

Wieck, C., & Strully, J. (1987). What's wrong with the continuum: A metaphorical analysis. In L. H. Meyer, C. A. Peck, & L. Brown. (Eds.), *Critical issues in the lives of people with severe disabilities* (pp. 229–234). Baltimore: Brookes.

Wolfensberger, W. (1977). The normalization principle, and some major implications to architectural–environment design. In M. Bednar (Ed.), *Barrier free environments.* Stroudsburg, PA: Dowden, Hutchenson and Russ.

Issues in Psychology

Positive Behavior Supports

Robert H. Horner

Positive behavior support involves the assessment and reengineering of environments so people with problem behaviors experience reductions in their problem behaviors and increased social, personal, and professional quality in their lives. Positive behavior support is not a new technology; in fact, it builds directly from a long experimental history (Bijou & Baer, 1961; Bijou, Peterson, & Ault, 1968) and a rich conceptual analysis of the variables influencing human behavior (Catania, 1992; Koegel, Koegel, & Dunlap, 1996; Neef, 1994). Positive behavior support is the application of behavior analysis to the intensely social problems created by behaviors such as self-injury, aggression, property destruction, pica, defiance, and disruption. It is an approach that blends values about the rights of people with disabilities with a practical science about how learning and behavior change occur. The excitement about positive behavior support lies in the promise it holds for addressing the very real and difficult challenges posed by problem behaviors.

Problem behaviors continue to be a major cause of isolation and exclusion for people with disabilities (Koegel et al., 1996; Lehr & Brown, 1996; National Institute of Health, 1989; Reichle, 1990). Without effective support, children and adults with disabilities who perform problem behaviors can expect exclusion from regular educational settings, community environments, and employment opportunities; increased medical risks; isolation from social relationships; and exposure to highly intrusive forms of treatment (Horner, Diemer, & Brazeau, 1992; Knitzer, 1993; Sailor & Skrtic, 1995). Families are challenged by young children with intense self-injury and aggression (Koegel & Koegel, 1995; Turnbull & Ruef, 1997). Schools facing fiscal and professional pressure are questioning whether they have the ability to educate children

This chapter was supported in whole or in part by the Department of Health and Human Services, Grant No. 90DD0439/01. However, the opinions expressed herein do not necessarily reflect the position or policy of the Department of Health and Human Services, and no official endorsement by the department should be inferred.

with problem behaviors. It is in this context of intense need that the technology of positive behavior support has emerged.

The purposes of this chapter are to define the current status of positive behavior support and to provide a vision for where this technology will lead. As we look forward, existing excitement about recent advances is tempered by serious concern over the extent to which these advances will be allowed to touch the lives of children and adults across the country. At this point we have better science than practice, better understanding than policy, better vision than reality.

The signature feature of positive behavior support has been a committed focus on fixing environments, not people. Building behavioral competence in children and adults with disabilities is essential, but not enough. We also must design schools, homes, and communities that effectively prevent problem behaviors. Effective environments make problem behaviors irrelevant, inefficient, and ineffective. The technology of positive behavior support is a technology that emphasizes the fact that a child with disabilities is part of his or her surrounding environment. Effective behavior support includes modifying environments, as well as teaching new skills and controlling consequences.

Take the example of Leslie, a 10-year-old with moderate intellectual disabilities, limited verbal communication, and a history of intense self-biting. Self-biting is a dangerous, disruptive behavior that holds the potential of serious harm for Leslie, frustration for her teacher, and reduced educational options for her classmates. One approach to this challenge is to remove Leslie from her social peers and isolate her in a special location where she must learn appropriate behaviors to earn her way back to her class. An alternative is available through positive behavior support. The alternative begins not with technology but with a social commitment to the importance of Leslie's inclusion with her peers; that is, a recognition of the contributions she brings to her class. The alternative further accepts that, with extra supports, Leslie's classroom probably can be transformed into an environment where self-biting is irrelevant, inefficient, and ineffective. If done well, this transformation benefits Leslie's peers and her teacher, as well as results in reduced self-biting. The science of behavior analysis tells us that this process begins by better understanding Leslie's behavior, and how she uses her behavior to interact with the people around her. By learning where, when, and why Leslie engages in self-biting, and where, when, and why she *does not* engage in self-biting, her teachers and family move from worrying about how to change Leslie, to thinking about how to change the classroom.

In Leslie's case, the effort to understand her self-biting resulted in identification of three situations that reliably produced self-biting: (1) asking Leslie to do a task she had failed at previously, (2) asking her to speak in front of the whole class, and (3) asking her to do long (15-minute) periods of work without recognition. This information was used to redesign her day to make self-biting irrelevant, inefficient, and ineffective. Self-biting became irrelevant by redesigning her curriculum so she worked on exactly the same instructional goals she had before, but did so with materials that better fit her abilities. The aversive curricular features were minimized, and the need for self-biting (at least some self-biting) became irrelevant. She also was not asked to speak in front of the whole class, but did work (and spoke) more within small groups of peers. Self-biting became inefficient by teaching Leslie signals for "help" (to make a task easier) and "break" (to get away from frustrating situations), which became efficient strategies for avoiding aversive and frustrating situations. It was far easier to signal the teacher to escape than to engage in intense bouts of self-biting. These signals were taught as a regular part of her curriculum, and became central to later curricular additions. Leslie also was taught how to recruit teacher attention for the work she had done. It would be unacceptably demanding to expect the teacher to remember to pay extra attention to Leslie, and in truth, Leslie was not interested in teacher attention all the time, only when she wanted it. A far more effective system was to teach Leslie how to monitor her own progress, as well as a signal that she could use to let the teacher (or teaching assistant) know that she had done well, and was interested in some recognition for her efforts. These new signals proved far more efficient ways of avoiding aversive tasks and gaining needed attention than self-biting.

Leslie's self-biting was made ineffective by not allowing self-biting to result in escape from tasks or access to teacher attention. Because self-biting could not be ignored completely, the process was to physically block self-biting and redirect Leslie to the appropriate signal for (a) getting help, (b) asking for a break, or (c) getting extended attention. This was done by a teaching assistant. Leslie was not allowed to move away from tasks, or to receive teacher attention without using the appropriate signals.

Together, these procedures resulted in change from a situation where self-biting occurred 5 to 15 times per day with high levels of disruption, and increasing tissue damage to Leslie's hand, to a situation where self-biting occurred less than once per week, and that instance was usually very mild. Of equal importance, the reduction in self-biting was associated with increased positive contact with peers, increased academic performance, and a girl who no longer appeared tense and distressed. The changes required extra teacher assistant time, but minimal changes by the classroom teacher and no reduction in the quality of education experienced by Leslie's fellow students.

This is an example about more than behavior change. It is about a technology of behavior support that applies basic laws of behavior analysis to produce broad change in the living, learning, work, and leisure options available to people who perform problem behaviors. It is a technology that demands functional change in problem behaviors, but holds that behavior change in the context of barren life is an unacceptable goal. This technology of positive behavior support emphasizes four central messages that shape a vision for the future:

1. Behavior support should reduce problem behaviors *and* affect how a person lives.

2. Functional assessment is the foundation for understanding patterns of problem behavior.

3. Behavior support should be comprehensive in structure and scope.

4. The unit of behavioral intervention must be expanded if we are to build the capacity of our schools and communities to deliver behavior support efficiently.

These messages guide the remaining structure of this chapter.

BEHAVIOR SUPPORT SHOULD REDUCE PROBLEM BEHAVIOR *AND* AFFECT HOW A PERSON LIVES

Among the most important changes to occur over the past 15 years has been an expansion in the outcomes expected from behavior support (Durand, 1990; Evans & Meyer, 1985; Horner et al., 1990). Behavior change is a necessary outcome of any behavior support effort. Since the mid-1980s, however, there has been an increasing expectation that, if problem behaviors are reduced, there should be a broader impact on the child's life. Behavior change that leaves a child in an isolated, restricted life is a hollow accomplishment (Risley, 1996). The expectation now is that behavior support also affects the activities a child performs (e.g., the family can go out to eat), the people with whom the child spends time (e.g., a range of peers, and a range of relationships that shape his or her social development), the extent to which personal choice (self-determination) is available, and the extent to which the child is learning skills that will make him or her less dependent on paid supporters (Lehr & Brown, 1996).

This change is of extreme importance because the outcomes we use to define "success" shape the content of a technology. There often is a temptation to contrast positive behavior support with conventional behavior management. I find this effort of minimal value. There is no difference in the theory or science between positive behavior support and behavior modification. These are the same technology with different names. If any difference exists, it is in the acceptance of much larger outcomes, and the need to construct and deliver the global technology that will deliver these outcomes. Exciting demonstrations have been reported in which the lives of people with very extreme histories of problem behavior have changed as their problem behaviors were reduced (Berkman & Meyer, 1988; Carr et al., 1994; Durand, 1997; Horner et al., 1996; Lucyshyn, Olson, & Horner, 1995). These examples, however, are too few. They suggest that the expectations are doable, but they stand in significant contrast to the day-to-day experience of teachers, families, and support personnel (Ruef, 1997). The future of positive behavior support rests directly on whether the approach can be demonstrated to produce practical change in severe problem behaviors *and* transform that change into constructive effects on what people do, where they go, with whom they spend time, to what extent their life reflects their personal choices, and what level of personal independence they achieve. This standard should shape both the research being done and the multiple outcomes used to assess all behavioral support. A science often is shaped by the outcomes used to measure success. In the area of behavior support, the outcomes have expanded, and the resulting science is beginning to adapt.

FUNCTIONAL ASSESSMENT IS THE FOUNDATION FOR UNDERSTANDING PATTERNS OF PROBLEM BEHAVIOR

Functional assessment is the process of identifying events that reliably predict and maintain problem behaviors. The purpose of functional assessment information is to improve the effectiveness and efficiency of behavior support. At one level, functional assessment is a respectful process of trying to understand when, where, and why a child engages in problem behaviors. It is respectful in the sense that the process adopts the perspective of the person with problem behaviors. The assumption is not that these individuals are defective or broken, but that they are experiencing the world around them in a very different way from their peers. Events that others see as neutral or rewarding may seem very aversive. Events that others find commonplace may be intensely positive. Assuming that problem behavior "makes sense" from the perspective of the child with disabilities frames the challenge of assessment as one of first understanding that perspective. This is a very different approach from the traditional model of diagnosis and placement.

The importance of functional assessment for behavior support is hard to overstate. The past 30 years of applied behavior analysis document that antecedent and contingent events associated with specific behaviors affect the likelihood that those behaviors will occur in the future. If the goal is to identify the features of a classroom, home, or workplace that will reduce problem behaviors, then critical information is needed about the events that reliably predict (set the occasion for) and follow (maintain) problem behaviors. Consider what information might be important to you if you were trying to respond to your 9-year-old son's pattern of pulling other people's hair. It may help you to know what it was about some people that increased the likelihood they would get their hair pulled, and to know if hair pulling were more likely if it resulted in your son's getting attention, versus the termination of an activity, versus the increased speed with which a meal is delivered. This knowledge would change your ability to avoid some dangerous situations, to predict and adapt to others, to identify new communication skills that may replace hair pulling, and to identify ways to reduce the payoff (reinforcement) currently available for hair pulling. Not only is it clear that the information from a functional assessment would be of tremendous value in designing effective support, but it is scary to think about the support that might be developed without this information. If consideration were not given to the consequences maintaining problem behavior, a strategy may be implemented that had been very effective in reducing the hair pulling of some other person but may actually *increase* hair pulling when applied to your son.

Functional assessment is important. The products of a functional assessment are (a) operational definitions of the problem behavior(s); (b) identification of the events that reliably predict when the problem behaviors *will and will not* occur; (c) identification of the events that maintain the problem behavior (the function or reinforcer); and (d) direct observation data supporting these hypotheses. When we begin a functional assessment, we typically make a daily schedule for the person (this often requires different schedules for weekends, or different schedules for different school agendas) and identify both what daily routines are most common and which of these routines are most likely to be associated with problem behaviors. This overall assessment of the routines that "work" and those that "do not work" is then used in structured interviews to gather more detailed information. There are many fine descriptions of the procedures for conducting functional assessment (Axelrod, 1987; Carr, 1977; Carr et al., 1994; Durand, 1990; Iwata, Dorsey, Slifer, Bauman, & Richman 1982, 1994; Mace & Roberts, 1993; O'Neill et al., 1997; Repp, Felce & Barton, 1988; Repp & Horner, 1999; Touchette, MacDonald, & Langar, 1985; Wacker, Steege, Northup, Reimers, et al., 1990; Wacker, Steege, Northup, Sasso, et al., 1990). They differ in the forms and steps employed, but the key outcomes remain consistent. In each case information is gathered to build a hypothesis about when, where, and why problem behaviors keep happening, and this hypothesis is tested (or verified) through direct observation. The different tools for conducting a functional assessment can be divided into three main classes: interviews, descriptive observations, and functional analyses.

Functional assessment interviews now exist in a range of forms, levels of detail, and structure (Horner & Carr, 1997; Kern, Dunlap, Clarke, & Childs, 1994; Repp & Horner, 1999). Initially interviews were conducted with the family member, teacher, or support person who knew the individual best. Recently, functional assessment interviews have been developed for use with the person with disabilities (Reed, Thomas, Sprague, & Horner, 1997). Functional assessment interviews often focus on the history of the problem behavior, as well as the current events that appear to predict and maintain the problem behavior. The tremendous advantage of the interview approach is that it allows an efficient strategy for assessing the potential impact of a very large number of antecedents and consequences across a huge number of situations. Keep in mind that it is as important to know where and when problem behaviors do not occur as it is to know when they do occur. As such, the interviews can guide us quickly to those conditions most likely to be controlling problem behavior, and to produce a hypothesis about the context, behavior(s), and consequences associated with the behavior(s) of concern.

The major disadvantage of interviews is that they reflect the subjective perception of the person(s) interviewed. These perceptions may or may not be accurate. The time saved conducting interviews may be time wasted if the information is inaccurate. There is sufficient evidence of inaccurate interview information to require that the hypotheses developed from interviews be validated through some form of direct observation or systematic functional analysis (Iwata & Fisher, 1997).

Descriptive observations involve direct data collection about the occurrence of problem behaviors, and their antecedents and consequences (Bijou et al., 1968; Doss & Reichle, 1989; O'Neill et al., 1997; Touchette et al., 1985). An observer uses a data sheet, and actually watches what the child does and the events preceding and following the child's behavior as it naturally occurs. This information is examined to identify patterns. If interviews have been conducted earlier, the observed pattern is compared with the interview hypothesis. The interviews may also have guided the selection of where and when observations would occur. The end result of direct observations, however, is a hypothesis about the problem behavior that can be used in the design of behavioral support. Direct observations often are used to verify hypotheses developed through interviews.

The most rigorous approach to functional assessment is a *functional analysis*. In a functional analysis direct observation is combined with systematic manipulations of events in an experimental format to define exactly what controls problem behavior. Information is provided about conditions where the problem behaviors occur and do not occur, and the specific consequences that are functionally related to continued occurrence of the problem behavior(s). As an example, consider Danny, a second-grade student with disabilities who had developed a pattern of whining and complaining about headaches and pains. His teacher was initially concerned and then increasingly frustrated by his lack of participation in class, and the high level of his complaining. His complaining had further escalated into a pattern of food refusal, and he had lost a medically dangerous amount of weight. Interview information indicated that whining occurred across a wide range of conditions. Direct observation also indicated that a lot of whining was occurring, but it was unclear why. A functional analysis was conducted to compare and contrast several possible functions of whining. In one condition, Danny worked one-on-one with a teacher doing his work. If he whined the teacher took the materials away for 30 seconds. If whining was maintained by escape from work, we would have expected to see an increase in whining under this condition. In another condition, Danny was allowed to play, but many of his favorite toys were up out of reach. If he whined he would receive his toy. This would test if whining was maintained by access to toys. In yet another condition, Danny was given simple work to do, and the teacher was present but did not attend to Danny unless he whined. This would test to see if teacher attention maintained whining.

When the behavior specialist for the school placed Danny in these conditions, it became clear that only when whining produced attention did it become high frequency. Danny's whining was not maintained by avoiding work or getting objects. His whining was maintained by the sincere attention (or frustrated attention) of his teacher (and other important adults). This information was exceptionally helpful in designing a program of support in which Danny learned more appropriate ways of recruiting teacher attention, and whining was placed on extinction. Not only did Danny's whining decrease, but the teacher's perception of his contribution to the class and his academic gains improved. He began eating again, and his weight was within medical norms within 2 months. Whines continued to occur from time to time, especially when he really was sick, but not at a level that jeopardized his placement in the class (Gorham & Todd, 1998).

Functional assessment can be done any number of ways. The goal is always to identify the antecedents and consequences that control problem behaviors, and use that information to improve the quality of the behavior support plan. Interviews have proven useful and efficient, but need to be used in conjunction with either direct observation or functional analysis. Direct observation procedures have the advantage of being simple and accurate, but may not sample the full range of conditions in which problem behaviors occur. Functional analysis is the most rigorous approach to gathering information, but it requires substantial skill to design the manipulations, and requires the setup of situations that produce problem behaviors. This can be a major concern if intense problem behaviors (aggression) are being considered. Together, however, the three approaches to gathering assessment information provide a powerful array of options from which to select (Repp & Horner, 1999).

The future of behavior support will include functional assessment. The challenges for the future lie in how to make the process efficient, accurate, and usable. I see the largest challenge in the area of usability. Moving from functional assessment information to functional plans of support remains poorly defined. A major danger exists that assessments will be done, but not influence the plan of support. As school psychologists, teachers, families, and specialists struggle with how to gather functional assessment information, tremendous care must be taken to include training and systems that define how to *use* the functional assessment information in the design of effective environments.

Another major concern lies in the design of assessment tools that address more complex patterns of problem behavior. Behaviors maintained by multiple functions (e.g., attention *and* escape) or behaviors maintained by physiological consequences (automatic reinforcement) are far more complex to assess and change. There remain too many situations where children with intense, and complex, problem behaviors present challenges that outstrip assessment techniques. Rigorous research into the basic mechanisms responsible for these behaviors will be needed, in addition to adaptations of current functional assessment tools, before the technology is able to respond across the range of behavioral challenges faced by families and teachers.

BEHAVIOR SUPPORT SHOULD BE COMPREHENSIVE IN STRUCTURE AND SCOPE

Because behavior support is about lifestyle change as well as behavior change, there must be an expansion in the structure and scope of interventions. This will involve the simultaneous application of multiple procedures across the full range of times, behaviors, and contexts needed to generate real change in a child's life. Interventions conducted in the context of careful research studies often must emphasize narrow analysis of behavior in highly controlled contexts. Only with this level of intense analysis can we tease out the basic mechanisms responsible for patterns of behavior. In the classroom, home, or community, however, the question is less one of basic mechanisms and more one of getting important changes to occur. The technology of positive behavior support is an applied technology. It exists only because of the detailed research that produced key procedures, but the day-to-day application of positive behavior support requires the application of multiple procedures. This more "comprehensive" approach is guided by five central features.

1. *Comprehensive interventions address all problem behaviors performed by the focus individual.* Problem behaviors create physical risks, social barriers, and educational obstacles. An effective plan of behavior support has limited impact if it addresses some problem behaviors and leaves others unaltered. A comprehensive plan of behavior support addresses all the behaviors that form serious barriers for the child.

2. *Comprehensive interventions are applied across all appropriate times of the day.* Positive behavior support must do more than demonstrate change in the behavior of a child in a short, narrow context. If behavior support is to have broad impact, it must be relevant across the full range of routines, times of day, and conditions that the child (and her family and teacher) encounters. This is an extremely important criterion. Many procedures can have dramatic effects, but only with intense effort that cannot be sustained throughout the day. Behavior support that is designed to change the living options of a child will focus both assessment and support across the full range of conditions where problem behaviors are functional barriers.

3. *Comprehensive interventions are driven by a functional assessment.* Comprehensive behavior support will be guided by the functional assessment results. The fundamental purpose of doing a functional assessment in clinical contexts is to improve the effectiveness and efficiency of behavior support. There is now a wide and compelling literature documenting that if behavior support is consistent with functional assessment, the effectiveness of the intervention increases (Carr et al., in press; Carr et al., 1994; Didden, Duker, & Korzilius, 1997). Comprehensive positive behavior support involves taking the time to assess the broad plan for a person's future and the specific environmental events that control his or her problem behavior. The hypotheses that arise from this process should define the central features of any plan of support.

4. *Comprehensive interventions blend multiple procedures.* Comprehensive positive behavior support often includes the simultaneous application of many different intervention strategies. A classroom may be changed in terms of the physical layout, daily schedule, curriculum focus, curriculum materials, and so forth, to prevent problem behaviors. A child may receive direct instruction on communication skills, academic skills, and so on, that make problem behaviors irrelevant or inefficient (Lee, Sugai, & Horner, in press). In addition, specific procedures may be applied to increase the reinforcers available for appropriate behaviors, eliminate (or minimize) the reinforcers available for problem behaviors, and in some instances apply punishers contingent upon problem behaviors. The picture is even more complex given that all these procedures may be implemented to address attention-maintained problem behaviors and a

companion set of procedures may be implemented to address escape-maintained problem behaviors. The point is not that all behavior support must now become incomprehensibly complex, but rather that our traditional focus on finding one strategy to eliminate problem behaviors now seems inadequate. Comprehensive support will involve the simultaneous use of multiple procedures. One reason this is both possible and desirable is that all implemented procedures must be guided by the common messages from the functional assessment. Where in the past there was valid concern that multiple procedures had the potential of conflicting with each other, the current model requires that all procedures be consistent with the functional assessment hypothesis. The functional assessment serves to ensure that multiple procedures will be more likely to enhance rather than negate each other.

The application of multiple procedures also provides the opportunity for the cumulative introduction of support procedures across time. A common assumption is that behavior support is a linear process: A plan of support will be developed, support will be designed and implemented, and behavior will change. In most cases of serious behavior support, however, the process of support is dynamic and can occur across an extended time period. The importance of the initial assessment and support plan cannot be overvalued, but initial gains often create new support needs. For example, a child who experiences behavior change, and can now go into the community, is faced with new challenges in the community that were previously unidentified. These new challenges set the stage for ongoing assessment, and ongoing evolution of behavior support. The process of multielement interventions includes recognition that all elements are not implemented at one point in time, but can be added in response to behavior change, context change, and new assessment information.

5. *Comprehensive interventions "fit" the context.* Comprehensive positive behavior support must work for all people in the context where support occurs. If support in a classroom is of benefit to the child with disabilities, but hinders effective education for other children, or transforms the jobs of the staff into a set of intolerable demands, then the support either will not be implemented at all, or will be abandoned as soon as the basic behavioral crisis is past.

The new challenge is that behavior support must result in broad, durable impact. This challenge has changed the perception of what support procedures must look like. Behavior support must be doable: It must (a) be consistent with values of those who will implement the procedures, (b) be consistent with the skills of the people who will implement the procedures, (c) be consistent with the resources available to the people who will implement the procedures, and (d) be matched by administrative support. To date, we have focused on identifying procedures that produce real change in behavior. There remains much to learn about how to change behavior, but the wonderful advances of the past 50 years will be of little value if we do not attend to the key variables that affect implementation. Behavior support is less likely to be implemented if the family or staff who must implement it consider the intervention (a) to be too cruel or dehumanizing, (b) unlikely to be effective, (c) to include procedures they do not know how to perform (e.g., direct instruction), (d) to require time and equipment they do not have, or (e) to place them at risk of reprimand or abandonment by their supervisors.

Comprehensive positive behavior support builds from a functional assessment, and incorporates the most advanced procedures available, but also recognizes that support must "work" for everyone in the setting. There is seldom only one strategy for supporting a person with problem behaviors. As such, the goal in support planning is not to find the one, technically perfect intervention, but to identify a plan of support that is both technically sound *and* a good "fit" with the values, skills, and resources of people within the particular setting. To do this typically involves thoughtful involvement of the teachers, family, and staff in the functional assessment and design of the support (Albin, Lucyshyn, Horner, & Flannery, 1996).

THE "UNIT" OF BEHAVIORAL INTERVENTION MUST BE EXPANDED

The fourth message for the future of positive behavior support is that we must expand the unit of analysis to include social systems. This does not mean abandoning the important attention given to understanding the behaviors of individuals, but adding an emphasis on the application of the technology within larger systems.

As a general approach, positive behavior support emerged from the early framework of applied behavior analysis (Bandura, 1969; Bijou et al., 1968; Blackham & Siberman, 1971; Catania, 1992; Millenson & Leslie, 1979; Rachlin, 1976) and incorporates more recent conceptual and methodological advances (Carr, 1988, 1994; Dunlap & Fox, 1996; Durand, 1990; Iwata et al., 1982, 1994; Koegel et al., 1996; Lalli, Mace, Wohn, & Livezey, 1995; Mace, 1994; Michael, 1988, 1993; O'Neill et al., 1997). Too often, however, the impact of these gains has had a limited impact on the procedures applied throughout our schools, homes, and communities. One reason for the limited impact is that the detailed attention to individuals has not been combined with attention to the organizational systems needed to implement the technology on a broad scale.

Figure 10.1 provides one vision for increasing the impact of positive behavior support. The level of impact defined on the vertical axis refers to the number and range of people who use and benefit from the technology. The level of analysis depicted on the horizontal axis traces areas of current and future focus for positive behavior support. Early emphasis on understanding *individual problem behaviors* led to important understanding about basic behavioral mechanisms (reinforcement, extinction, punishment, generalization) but had limited clinical impact. These basic mechanisms were used to define specific *intervention strategies* (e.g., response cost, time-out) that proved of tremendous value in some conditions, but of limited value in others. The

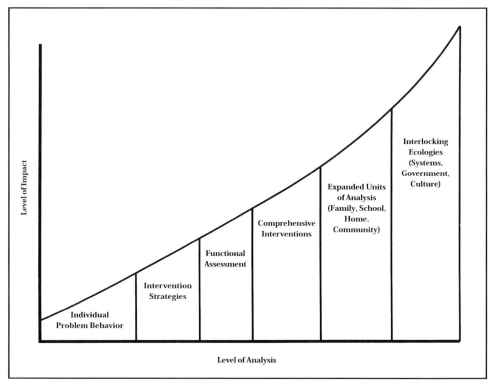

FIGURE 10.1. Expanding positive behavior support for maximum impact.

more recent attention on *functional assessment* procedures has helped to identify where and when specific behavioral strategies will be effective, and the emerging emphasis on *comprehensive interventions* will further expand the array of conditions and settings where positive behavior support is used. Each of these developments has expanded the level of impact of positive behavior support technology.

For the next level of impact to occur, however, we must include application of positive behavior support across larger groups. Biglan (1995) argued persuasively that behavior analysis may be applied across "communities" as the unit of analysis to address social problems such as teen pregnancy and underage smoking. Sugai and Horner (in press) provide a model that applies positive behavior support with the entire school serving as the unit of intervention. They suggest that when principles of behavior analysis are applied across the entire student body, effects can be achieved that not only benefit all students in the school, but improve the capacity of a school to work with the small number of children who need intense, individualized support. A recent, descriptive analysis in which positive behavior support was implemented schoolwide documented a 47% annual reduction in the number of office discipline referrals in one 530-student middle school (Grades 6, 7, and 8) (Taylor-Greene et al.,

1997). These efforts are consistent with recommendations that positive behavior support procedures be applied for preventive effects as well as a remedy for severe problem behaviors (Walker, Colvin, & Ramsey, 1995; Walker et al., 1996). The basic message for the future is that positive behavior support is more than a technology of reducing the behavior of disruptive individuals. It is a technology for engineering environments where people are productive and safe.

SUMMARY

Problem behavior is an issue of intense concern for anyone interested in the future of people with mental retardation in the 21st century. The impact of problem behaviors on the lives of children and adults with mental retardation has been intense and debilitating. Positive behavior support is a technology that has emerged from a long history of research and practice. It is grounded in the values that have long guided The Arc, but blends these values with a strong science. Recent developments in positive behavior support are encouraging. We are better prepared to respond to problem behaviors than we have ever been before. The challenges we face in the near future are to deliver current technical developments to schools and communities, to make the existing technology more accessible and usable by families and teachers, to extend the technology so it addresses more intense and complex problem behaviors, and to expand the unit of intervention to include broader support systems such as schools, families, and workplaces. These challenges frame a constructive, if humbling, scope of work for the next several decades. The success with which these challenges are met will be reflected in the lives of people with mental retardation throughout the 21st century.

REFERENCES

Albin, R. W., Lucyshyn, J. M., Horner, R. H., & Flannery, K. B. (1996). Contextual fit for behavior support plans: A model of "goodness of fit." In L. K. Koegel, R. L. Koegel, & G. Dunlap (Eds.), *Positive behavioral support* (pp. 81–98). Baltimore: Brookes.

Axelrod, S. (1987). Functional and structural analysis of behavior: Approaches leading to reduced use of punishment procedures. *Research in Developmental Disabilities, 8,* 165–178.

Bandura, A. (1969). *Principles of behavior modification.* New York: Holt, Rinehart & Winston.

Berkman, K. A., & Meyer, L. H. (1988). Alternative strategies and multiple outcomes in the remediation of severe self-injury: Going "all out" nonaversively. *Journal of The Association for Persons with Severe Handicaps, 13,* 76–86.

Biglan, A. (1995). Translating what we know about the context of antisocial behavior into a lower prevalence of such behavior. *Journal of Applied Behavior Analysis, 28,* 479–492.

Bijou, S., & Baer, D. M. (1961). *Child development: Vol. 1. A systematic and empirical theory.* New York: Appleton-Century-Crofts.

Bijou, S. W., Peterson, R. F., & Ault, M. H. (1968). A method to integrate descriptive and experimental field studies at the level of data and empirical concepts. *Journal of Applied Behavior Analysis, 1,* 175–191.

Blackham, G. J., & Siberman, A. (1971). *Modification of child behavior.* Belmont, CA: Wadsworth.

Carr, E. G. (1977). The motivation of self-injurious behavior: A review of some hypotheses. *Psychological Bulletin, 84,* 800–816.

Carr, E. G. (1988). Functional equivalence as a mechanism of response generalization. In R. Horner, R. L. Koegel, & G. Dunlap (Eds.), *Generalization and maintenance: Lifestyle changes in applied settings* (pp. 221–241). Baltimore: Brookes.

Carr, E. G. (1994). Emerging themes in the functional analysis of problem behavior. *Journal of Applied Behavior Analysis, 27,* 393–399.

Carr, E. G., Horner, R. H., Turnbull, A., Marquis, J., Magito-McLaughlin, D., McAtee, M., Smith, C. E., Anderson-Ryan, K. A., Ruef, M. B., & Doolabh, A. (in press). *Positive behavior support as an approach for dealing with problem behavior in people with developmental disabilities: A research synthesis.* AAMR Monograph.

Carr, E. G., Levin, L., McConnachie, G., Carlson, J. I., Kemp, D. C., & Smith, C. E. (1994). *Communication-based intervention for problem behavior: A user's guide for producing positive change.* Baltimore: Brookes.

Catania, A. C. (1992). *Learning* (3rd ed.). Englewood Cliffs, NJ: Prentice-Hall.

Didden, R., Duker, P. C., & Korzilius, H. (1997). Meta-analytic study on treatment effectiveness for problem behaviors with individuals who have mental retardation. *American Journal on Mental Retardation, 101,* 387–399.

Doss, S., & Reichle, J. (1989). Establishing communicative alternatives to the emission of socially motivated excess behavior: A review. *Journal of Applied Behavior Analysis, 24,* 387–397.

Dunlap, G., & Fox, L. (1996). Early intervention and serious problem behaviors: A comprehensive approach. In L. K. Koegel, R. L. Koegel, & G. Dunlap (Eds.), *Positive behavioral support: Including people with difficult behavior in the community* (pp. 31–50). Baltimore: Brookes.

Durand, V. M. (1990). *Severe behavior problems: A functional communication training approach.* New York: Guilford Press.

Durand, V. M. (1997, September). *Longterm effects of positive behavior support.* Paper presented at the Research and Training Center Conference on Positive Behavior Support, Santa Barbara, CA.

Evans, I. M., & Meyer, L. H. (1985). *An educative approach to behavior problems: A practical decision model for interventions with severely handicapped learners.* Baltimore: Brookes.

Gorham, G., & Todd, A. W. (1998). *Applying function-based behavior support to teach self-management skills to a second grader.* Manuscript in preparation.

Horner, R. H., & Carr, E. G. (1997). Behavioral support for students with severe disabilities: Functional assessment and comprehensive intervention. *Journal of Special Education, 31*(1), 84–104.

Horner, R. H., Close, D. W., Fredericks, H. D., O'Neill, R. E., Albin, R. W., Sprague, J. R., Kennedy, C. H., Flannery, K. B., & Tuesday-Heathfield, L. (1996). Supported living for people with severe problem behaviors: A demonstration. In D. H. Lehr & F. Brown (Eds.), *People with disablities who challenge the system* (pp. 209–240). Baltimore: Brookes.

Horner, R. H., Diemer, S. M., & Brazeau, K. C. (1992). Educational support for students with severe problem behaviors in Oregon: A descriptive analysis from the 1987–88 school year. *Journal of The Association for Persons with Severe Handicaps, 17*(3), 154–169.

Horner, R. H., Dunlap, G., Koegel, R. L., Carr, E. G., Sailor, W., Anderson, J., Albin, R. W., & O'Neill, R. E. (1990). Toward a technology of "nonaversive" behavioral support. *Journal of The Association for Persons with Severe Handicaps, 15*(3), 125–132.

Iwata, B. A., Dorsey, M. F., Slifer, K. J., Bauman, K. E., & Richman, G. S. (1982). Toward a functional analysis of self-injury. *Analysis and Intervention in Developmental Disabilities, 2,* 3–20.

Iwata, B. A., Dorsey, M. F., Slifer, K. J., Bauman, K. E., & Richman, G. S. (1994). Toward a functional analysis of self-injury. *Journal of Applied Behavior Analysis, 27,* 197–209.

Iwata, B. A., & Fisher, W. W. (1997). *Current research on the assessment and treatment of severe behavior disorders.* Symposium presented at the Association for Behavior Analysis Annual Convention, Chicago.

Kern, L., Dunlap, G., Clarke, S., & Childs, K. E. (1994). Student-assisted functional assessment interview. *Diagnostique*, 19, 29–39.

Knitzer, J. (1993). Children's mental health policy: Challenging the future. *Emotional and Behavioral Disorders*, 1(1), 8–16.

Koegel, R. L., & Koegel, L. K. (1995). *Teaching children with autism*. Baltimore: Brookes.

Koegel, L. K., Koegel, R. L., & Dunlap, G. (Eds.). (1996). *Positive behavioral support: Including people with difficult behavior in the community*. Baltimore: Brookes.

Lalli, J. S., Mace, F. C., Wohn, T., & Livezey, K. (1995). Identification and modification of a response-class hierarchy. *Journal of Applied Behavior Analysis*, 28, 551–560.

Lee, Y., Sugai, G. M., & Horner, R. H. (in press). Using an instructional intervention to reduce off-task and problem behaviors of elementary school students with academic and behavioral deficits. *Journal of Positive Behavior Interventions*.

Lehr, D. H., & Brown, F. (Eds.). (1996). *People with disabilities who challenge the system* (pp. 209–240). Baltimore: Brookes.

Lucyshyn, J. M., Olson, D., & Horner, R. H. (1995). Building an ecology of support: A case study of one young woman with severe problem behaviors living in the community. *Journal of The Association for Persons with Severe Handicaps*, 20, 16–30.

Mace, F. C. (1994). The significance and future of functional analysis methodologies. *Journal of Applied Behavior Analysis*, 27, 385–392.

Mace, F. C., & Roberts, M. (1993). Factors affecting selection of behavioral intervention. In J. Reichle & D. Wacker (Eds.), *Communicative alternatives to challenging behavior: Integrating functional assessment and intervention strategies* (pp. 113–133). Baltimore: Brookes.

Michael, J. L. (1988). Establishing operations and the mand. *The Analysis of Verbal Behavior*, 6, 3–9.

Michael, J. L. (1993). Establishing operations. *The Behavior Analyst*, 16, 191–206.

Millenson, J. R., & Leslie, J. C. (1979). *Principles of behavior analysis* (2nd ed.). New York: Macmillan.

National Institute of Health. (1989, September). *Treatment of destructive behaviors*. Abstract presented at National Institute of Health Consensus Development Conference, Rockville, MD.

Neff, N. (Ed.). (1994). Functional assessment [Special issue]. *Journal of Applied Behavior Analysis*, 27(2).

O'Neill, R. E., Horner, R. H., Albin, R. W., Sprague, J. R., Storey, K., & Newton, J. S. (1997). *Functional assessment for problem behavior: A practical handbook* (2nd ed.). Pacific Grove, CA: Brooks/Cole.

Rachlin, H. (1976). *Behavior and learning*. San Francisco: W. H. Freeman.

Reed, H., Thomas, E., Sprague, J. R., & Horner, R. H. (1997). Student guided functional assessment interview: An analysis of student and teacher agreement. *Journal of Behavioral Education*, 7(1), 33–49.

Reichle, J. (1990). *National working conference on positive approaches to the management of excess behavior: Final report and recommendations*. Minneapolis: Institute on Community Integration, University of Minnesota.

Repp, A. C., Felce, D., & Barton, L. E. (1988). Basing the treatment of stereotypic and self-injurious behaviors on hypotheses of their causes. *Journal of Applied Behavior Analysis*, 21, 281–289.

Repp, A., & Horner, R. H. (Eds.). (1999). *Functional analysis of problem behavior: From effective assessment to effective support*. Pacific Grove, CA: Brooks/Cole.

Risley, T. (1996). Get a life! In L. K. Koegel, R. L. Koegel, & G. Dunlap (Eds.), *Positive behavioral support* (pp. 425–437). Baltimore: Brookes.

Ruef, M. (1997). *The perspectives of six stakeholder groups on the challenging behavior of individuals with mental retardation and/or autism*. Unpublished doctoral dissertation, University of Kansas, Lawrence.

Sailor, W., & Skrtic, T. (1995). American education in the post modern era. In J. L. Paul, H. Roselli, & D. Evans (Eds.), *Integrating school restructuring and special education reform* (pp. 418–432). Ft. Worth, TX: Harcourt Brace College.

Sugai, G. M., & Horner, R. H. (in press). Discipline and behavioral support: Preferred processes and practices. *Effective School Practices.*

Taylor-Greene, S., Brown, D., Nelson, L., Longton, J., Gassman, T., Cohen, J., Swartz, J., Horner, R. H., Sugai, G., & Hall, S. (1997). School-wide behavioral support: Starting the year off right. *Journal of Behavioral Education, 7*(1), 99–112.

Touchette, P. E., MacDonald, R. F., & Langer, S. N. (1985). A scatter plot for identifying stimulus control of problem behavior. *Journal of Applied Behavior Analysis, 18,* 343–351.

Turnbull, A. P., & Ruef, M. B. (1997). Family perspectives on inclusive lifestyle issues for individuals with problem behavior. *Exceptional Children, 63*(2), 211–227.

Wacker, D., Steege, M., Northup, J., Reimers, T., Berg, W., & Sasso, G. (1990). Use of functional analysis and acceptability measures to assess and treat severe behavior problems: Ana outpatient model. In A. C. Repp & N. N. Singh (Eds.), *Perspectives on the use of nonaversive and aversive interventions for persons with developmental disabilities* (pp. 349–359). Sycamore, IL: Sycamore Publishing.

Wacker, D. P., Steege, M., Northup, J., Sasso, G., Berg, W., Reimers, T., Cooper, L., Cigrand, K., & Donn, L. (1990). A component analysis of functional communication training across three topographies of severe behavior problems. *Journal of Applied Behavior Analysis, 23*(4), 417–429.

Walker, H., Colvin, G., & Ramsey, E. (1995). *Antisocial behavior in public schools: Strategies and best practices.* Pacific Grove, CA: Brooks/Cole.

Walker, H. M., Horner, R. H., Sugai, G., Bullis, M., Sprague, J. R., Bricker, D., & Kaufman, M. J. (1996). Integrated approaches to preventing antisocial behavior patterns among school-age children and youth. *Journal of Emotional and Behavioral Disorders, 4*(4), 194–209.

Psychopharmacology and Mental Retardation

Steven Reiss

I n this chapter, I provide an overview of the use of psychotropic medicines for the treatment of psychiatric and behavioral disorders in people with mental retardation and developmental disabilities (MR/DD). I address issues of concern, the types of medications commonly used, and issues of best practices. A more detailed discussion of this information can be found in Reiss and Aman's (1998) co-edited book, *Psychotropic Medications and Developmental Disabilities: The International Consensus Handbook*. Our discussion begins with a summary of the major concerns that have influenced practice and how the field has come together to address these concerns in a constructive manner.

COMMON CONCERNS

Many concerns have been expressed about the use of psychotropic medicines with people with MR/DD. Surveys of use have shown that 30% to 50% of the adults in U.S. institutions, and 25% to 40% of those in the community, take psychotropic medications on a daily basis (Rinck, 1988). Many professionals feel that psychotropic medications have been overused, sometimes given for the convenience of caregivers rather than as treatment for a specific condition. Others feel that, instead of trying to reduce the absolute amount of drugs that are used, we should try to reduce the inappropriate use of medications. People with this opinion have expressed concern that drugs are often given with no formal diagnosis or specific target behavior. Further, the drugs are sometimes prescribed indefinitely, with no specified endpoint to treatment.

The use of psychotropic medications has its risks, variously called adverse reactions or side effects. Adverse reactions to medication are a particular concern with people who have MR/DD. Many people with MR/DD are nonverbal and cannot easily alert caregivers concerning possible adverse effects. Particularly in children, the drugs may interfere with learning, making acquisition of basic skills and knowledge even more difficult. Further, the drugs may cause life-threatening interactions, toxicity, or other unfortunate consequences. Because many prescribers are unaware of the special issues posed by patients with MR/DD, they are not as careful as they need to be in compensating for the patients' diminished abilities to report or observe adverse effects, exposing this population to increased risks compared with the population in general.

Another concern is the shortage of physicians trained to prescribe psychotropic medications for people with MR/DD. The diagnosis of mental health disorders in this population requires special expertise because patients may be nonverbal and unable to report symptoms, symptoms may be expressed differently because of the patients' limited experience, or symptoms may be masked by developmental delay (Reiss, 1994). Few physicians, however, are trained to work with this population because physicians are trained in either mental retardation (pediatrics) or mental illness (psychiatry), but not in both. Because there is little interdisciplinary training between pediatrics and psychiatry, our medical schools produce few physicians trained to serve the needs of people who have a "dual diagnosis" (both mental retardation and mental illness).

Some experts have expressed concerns about the need for scientific research to evaluate the safety and efficacy of psychotropic medications when prescribed for people with MR/DD. The use of these drugs is often based on extrapolation of knowledge regarding effects with people who do not have intellectual disability. This is a questionable basis for practice, because psychopathology sometimes is expressed differently in people with intellectual disability. Moreover, evidence from studies on children and adolescents suggests that psychotropics interact with the developing brain in ways not seen in adults (Vitiello & Jensen, 1995). Because intellectual disability affects brain development, it is possible that psychotropics have different effects in people with intellectual disability than in the general population.

Further, some people with MR/DD show a number of disorders, such as autism and fragile X syndrome, which have associated behavioral conditions. Typically, these associated conditions, as well as dual diagnosis symptoms generally, are treated with drugs based on the effects of those drugs in the general adult population. Effective dosage levels often vary between people with MR/DD and adults with average intelligence, and sometimes drugs interact with developmental disorders to produce unusual or different effects. We need more scientific research evaluating the specific effects of various agents on the conditions seen in the population with MR/DD, and we need a vastly expanded effort to develop or find new medications to treat self-injurious behavior, autistic behavior, and other behavior associated with certain MR/DD conditions.

A consensus process on psychopharmacology and intellectual disability was started in 1992 on the initiative of Steven Reiss and Michael Aman, both professors of psychology and psychiatry at The Ohio State University Nisonger Center. The Arc of the United States became an early co-sponsor, and Arc psychologist Sharon Davis joined the organizing committee. By 1995 twelve organizations had endorsed the international conference that was held as part of the consensus process, including the U.S. Administration on Developmental Disabilities, American Association on Mental Retardation, American Psychiatric Association, and American Psychological

Association. Partial funding for the conference was provided by the National Institute of Mental Health.

In this chapter, we summarize some of the main results of the consensus process, called The Nisonger UAP–The Arc Consensus Process on Psychopharmacology. Reiss and Aman (1997) already have provided a detailed statement of the methods, and Reiss and Aman's (1998) edited volume, mentioned earlier, provided a full statement of the results.

HISTORY

By definition, psychoactive drugs produce behavioral, emotional, or cognitive effects. Clinical psychopharmacology is the use of such drugs to treat mental and behavioral disorders. This treatment approach is associated with the neuroscience model of mental disorders. Emphasis is given to understanding drug effects in terms of genetics, brain structure and biochemistry, and the functioning of the central nervous system. Most psychoactive medicines exert their clinical effects on one or more neurotransmitters, the substances responsible for the transmission of impulses from one nerve cell to another, or on the receptors for neurotransmitters. Future progress in understanding these substances, in identifying related substances and processes, and in understanding how the genetic code affects these substances, all may lead to improved drugs.

It was only in the last 50 years that psychopharmacology became an important area of scientific research. In 1949 John Cade, an Australian psychiatrist, discovered that lithium introduced a lethargic state in animals. He thus summarized its potential benefits in agitated states in mental disorders. His initial patients showed remarkable effects—patients who had been agitated became more manageable and appropriate. However, the unwanted side effects, particularly those affecting the renal and thyroid system, limited use to acute interventions. Twenty years later, the toxicity of lithium was understood, thus allowing lithium to be a long-term treatment for agitated manic episodes.

In 1950 Charpontier synthesized chlorpromazine (phenothiazine) at the Rhone Poulene Laboratories in France. His attempt was to deliver a drug that would serve as an adjunct sedative to anesthesia. Delay, Deniker, and Harl (1952) tried the drug in 38 patients who had acute psychosis and discovered that, in excited states, psychotic agitation, aggressiveness, and delusions improved. Chlorpromazine was subsequently introduced into the United States where American psychiatrists, through clinical trials, found similar benefits. This was the catalysis for other medications being introduced through pharmacology research, including haloperidol in 1958 by Paul Janssen.

These early discoveries led to the development of new drugs, and to research based on the effects of older drugs such as reserpine, which was known in India in 1755. The introduction of reserpine into western medicine by Swiss scientists in the 1950s eventually stimulated interest on the role of the neurotransmitter serotonin in schizophrenia and depression. The enthusiasm surrounding the use of these drugs encouraged the testing of other agents, establishing psychopharmacology as one of the two major treatment approaches to dual diagnosis.

The early tranquilizer drugs, especially chlorpromazine (Thorazine), became widely used with people with mental retardation, particularly those living in institutions. From about 1960 to about 1985, people with MR/DD who showed extreme agitation generally were diagnosed as having schizophrenia, a psychosis, or atypical psychosis. The most commonly used antipsychotic drug treatment during this period was Thorazine (Baumeister, Sevin, & King, 1998). Especially in the 1960s and 1970s, advocates for people with MR/DD became concerned that antipsychotic medication was being used as *chemical restraint*, in which the aim is to sedate a patient for the benefit of caregivers, as opposed to treatment of a specific disorder.

The American Association on Mental Retardation (AAMR; formerly AAMD), the Accreditation Council on Services for People with Disabilities, the American Psychiatric Association, and other organizations formed various committees that set guidelines intended to end the practice of chemical restraint and encourage appropriate use of medications. On May 5, 1971, the Accreditation Council issued the following standards for care of people residing in institutions: "Chemical restraint shall not be used excessively, as punishment, for the convenience of staff, as a substitute for a treatment program, or in quantities that interfere with a resident's habilitation program" (cited in Kalachnik et al., 1998). In 1972 a similar conclusion was reached by United States District Court Judge Frank Johnson in *Wyatt v. Stickney*.

After more than a quarter century of contentious litigation, the Nisonger–The Arc International Consensus Process brought together diverse elements of the field to develop a new set of guidelines. An unusual aspect of this effort was the full participation of psychiatrists and other experts—this was the most extensive effort to date for self-regulation. Whereas past guidelines called for minimal use of psychotropic medicines, these guidelines sought to maximize appropriate uses and minimize inappropriate uses. Under the leadership of John Kalachnik and Bannett Leventhal, a detailed statement of appropriate and inappropriate practices was developed.

ADVERSE EFFECTS

Adverse drug reactions are noxious, unintended events associated with medications (Wilson, Lott, & Tsai, 1998). Usually these can be managed by monitoring effects of drugs and adjusting dosages or by changing to alternate agents. The probability of adverse side effects varies considerably depending on the specific class of medication, dosage, and individual. Adverse reactions common to many psychoactive agents include *anticholinergic effects* (e.g., blurred vision, constipation, dry mouth, urinary hesitance), *extrapyramidal symptoms* (restlessness to the point of not being able to sit still, bizarre postures, lack of movement, spasms, tics, facial grimacing, "to-and-fro" rhythmic movements), and *sedation* (daytime drowsiness). *Tardive dyskinesia* (sucking and smacking of lips, lateral jaw movements, tongue thrusting, rolling movements of shoulders or limbs, excessive salivation) is a complex of adverse extrapyramidal symptoms that occurs after prolonged use of antipsychotic drugs. This condition may persist throughout a patient's lifetime. Other possible adverse effects include *blood abnormalities* (aplastic anemia, agranulocytosis, leukocytosis, eosinophilia, thrombocytopenia), *cardiovascular effects* (e.g., dysrythmias, hypotension, hypertension), *cholestasis* (slowing of bile through the liver), *confusion, dermatological reactions, dizziness, falls, jitteriness, learning impairment, tics, tremors, urinary dysfunctions* (enuresis, incontinence, nephrogenic diabetes inspidius), *seizures,* and *sleep disturbance. Death* is rare but some cases have been documented resulting from overdose, toxic reactions, or interactions.

Adverse reactions may go unnoticed if patients cannot alert caregivers or if they misunderstand the signs indicating an adverse reaction. Anytime a person is taking more than one medicine, attention must be paid to possible interactions. In most cases, when a psychoactive drug enters the bloodstream, most of it binds to plasma proteins and has no clinical effect. Instead, clinical effects are caused by the relatively small amount of unbound drug (free fraction) in the bloodstream. If a second drug that binds to the same plasma proteins is given, competition for binding sites may cause a large increase in the free fraction of the first drug, resulting in other adverse effects.

Drug interaction also can occur as a consequence of changed rates of metabolism (Somni et al., 1998). If Drug A induces or inhibits the enzymes that metabolize Drug B, the peak amount of Drug B available at a site of action may be increased or decreased, altering Drug B's usual clinical effects. Other causes of interactions include additive or antagonistic effects, as when two drugs that each lower blood pressure produce an excessive decrease when given together, or absorption effects, as when the action of one medication increases or decreases the rate of absorption by the gastrointestinal tract of a second. Drug interactions can be minimized or controlled through proper planning of dosages, administration times, or routes, and by choice of medication preparation. However, careful monitoring of drug effects is always needed.

MAJOR DRUG CLASSES

The following sections cover some of the major groups of psychotropic drugs used with people with MR/DD.

Antipsychotics

The antipsychotic drug class, also called *neuroleptics* or *major tranquilizers*, has been the most widely used class of psychotropic medications with people with MR/DD. These drugs are indicated for schizophrenia and other psychotic conditions. They reduce the intensity of the core symptoms of psychosis, including thought disorder (loose associations, conceptual disorganization), hallucination, delusion, and withdrawal.

These symptoms are not cured, however, and the drugs may be needed for periods of years. Individual variation in response to these medications is considerable. Most people who respond positively do so within the first 6 weeks of treatment. Relapse rates within 1 to 2 years are significant, with some authorities citing rates as high as 50% even when the medicines are continued (Schatzberg, Cole, & DeBattista, 1997).

The antipsychotics also are used in the treatment of aggression or irritability with psychotic features, as well as in various movement disorders, such as the tics seen in Tourette syndrome and the stereotypies seen in autism. They are widely used for the treatment of self-injurious behavior, although many authorities feel they are overused for this purpose and recommend instead trials of antidepressants (Reiss & Aman, 1998).

The *typical* (or first-generation) antipsychotics are phenothiazines, butyrophe-none, thioxanthene, and dihydroindolone. *Atypical* (or second-generation) antipsy-chotics include dibenzodiazepine, thienobenzodiazepine, benzisocazole (risperidone), and phenolindole (sertindole). The main advantage of most second-generation drugs is fewer side effects. The drug names of commonly prescribed antipsychotics include the typical agents Haldol, Mellari, Navane, and Thorazine as well as the atypical agents Clozaril and Risperdal. All of the antipsychotic medications in use today are dopamine antagonists, which seems to be an important mechanism responsible for their antipsychotic effects.

The side effect profiles of these medications can be divided into two categories, nonneurologic and neurologic. The nonneurologic side effects are thought to be more frequent with high-potency drugs. The more common side effects in this category include low blood pressure (often associated with dizziness upon standing), sexual side effects (anorgasmia or reduced libido), weight gain and anticholinergic side effects (dry mouth, blurred vision, constipation, urinary retention), and drowsiness. Less common side effects are blood cell problems, skin problems, liver problems, heart problems, and endocrine problems (breast enlargement, menstrual period changes, galactorrhea).

Neurologic side effects include medication-induced Parkinsonism (muscle stiff-ness, rigidity, stooped posture, drooling, shuffling gait, and pill-rolling–like tremor), medication-induced acute dystonia (slow sustained muscle spasms or contractions, usually involving the neck, jaw, eyes, and arms), medication-induced tardive dyskine-sia (abnormal, involuntary, and irregular muscle movements in the head, limbs, and trunk), and neuroleptic malignant syndrome (rigidity, fever, agitation, confusion, blood pressure and pulse changes, with abnormal laboratory findings).

Antidepressants

Antidepressents have been used with people with MR/DD since they were first intro-duced in 1957 (Sovner et al., 1998). By 1970 these drugs had fallen out of favor for use with patients with MR/DD, but renewed interest was stimulated by the introduction of the selective serotonin reuptake inhibitors (SSRIs). Additionally, use has grown as a result of reports that people with MR/DD are vulnerable to the full spectrum of depressive disorders, obsessive–compulsive disorders, and impulse control disorders such as trichotillomania (see Reiss, 1994).

Antidepressant drug classes include the tricyclics and related compounds, monoamine oxidase inhibitors (MAOIs), selective SSRIs, and atypical agents. Early MAOIs interact with tyramine, a substance found in certain foods and beverages (e.g., cheese, salami, fruits, beer), to cause life-threatening hypertensive reactions. Newer reversible MAOIs (e.g., moclobemide, brofaromine) have fewer side effects and no dietary restrictions. The tricyclic and heterocyclic compounds (e.g., amitriptyline, clomipramine, imipramine), which are fairly effective against depression but can cause cardiovascular complications (particularly dysrhythmias), are being superseded by the SSRIs (e.g., fluoxetine, sertraline), which also are highly effective but do not cause anticholinergic or cardiovascular side effects and are significantly safer in overdose. The atypical antidepressants (e.g., trazodone, buproprion, venlafaxine, nefazodone), so called because their chemical structures differ from those of other antidepressant drugs, offer action against depressive symptoms similar to that of the tricyclics, but with fewer significant side effects.

All of these classes of agents have their uses, since individual patients may respond better to one than to another. Trade names of frequently prescribed antidepressants include Parnate (MAOI); Tofranil, Norpramin, Anafranil, Elavil, and Pamelor (tri- and heterocyclics); Prozac, Zoloft, and Paxil (SSRIs); and Desyrel, Wellbutrin, Effexor, and Serzone (atypicals).

Antidepressants affect dopamine, norepinephrine, and serotonin. Effects are mediated through blockade of presynaptic neurotransmitter reuptake, direct agonist or antagonist activity, or inhibition of neurotransmitter degradation.

The cyclic compounds and SSRIs have an established role in managing major depressive disorder. However, the evidence is based mostly on extrapolation from the general population. Few well-controlled studies have been reported in the treatment of depression in people with MR/DD. Generally, the various antidepressant medications appear to be about equally effective. The question of depression in childhood is relatively recent, and there is disagreement on how to treat it.

Antidepressants are used to treat a range of behavioral and psychiatric conditions in addition to depression. Clomipramine (Anafranil) and fluvoxamine (Luvox) are both indicated for the treatment of obsessive–compulsive disorder, although cognitive-behavior therapy offers the possibility of a cure. They are used to treat ritualistic behavior, but there is controversy regarding the extent to which such ritualistic behaviors are symptoms of obsessive–compulsive disorder. The SSRIs also are used to treat enuresis, but evidence of effectiveness with patients with MR/DD is limited. Other indications in the general population for which limited evidence is available for people with MR/DD are panic disorder, eating disorder, attention-deficit hyperactivity disorder (ADHD), and, to a lesser extent, aggression.

Anxiolytics and Sedatives

Anxiolytics and sedatives are commonly prescribed in the management of anxiety or anxiety disorders. At low doses these drugs have antianxiety properties; at higher doses they sedate and induce sleep. Many anxiolytics have anticonvulsant properties. The benzodiazepines (e.g., diazepam, lorazepam, and alprazolam), which were introduced in the early 1960s, are the most widely prescribed anxiolytics because they are effective and fairly safe in overdose. However, they cause physical dependency. Their most common side effect is daytime drowsiness. The trade names of commonly used benzodiazepines include Valium, Ativan, and Xanax.

In 1987 Buspirone became the first nonbenzodiazepine anxiolytic to be introduced in the United States in 25 years. Used in short-term treatment of generalized anxiety disorder, it offers clinical effectiveness comparable to the benzodiazepines, and the advantage of fewer withdrawal symptoms when it is discontinued.

Beta-blockers (e.g., propranol) and alpha-2 agonists (e.g., clonidine) also are used as antianxiety agents on the theory that certain symptoms of anxiety suggest involvement of the beta-adrenergic arm of the sympathetic nervous system. These drugs also may calm anxiety-induced aggression. Inderal has been the most widely used beta-blocker for this indication, but newer, more selective agents are beginning to replace it.

Sedative drugs are used to treat insomnia or to induce sleep quickly in extremely agitated patients. Phenobarbital was widely used for sedation prior to 1965, but its current use is mostly for the treatment of epilepsy. The use of the drug with people with MR/DD is controversial because of concern about side effects. Trazodone, a serotonergic tricyclic, is gaining favor for bedtime sedation.

Little scientific research has been reported to evaluate the safety and efficacy of anxiolytics with people with MR/DD (Werry, 1998). However, most adverse effects are dose related and duration dependent; they more commonly occur with high-potency, short-acting benzodiazepines. Buspirone may have a role in the management of aggression and anxiety in people with MR/DD. The drugs are most widely prescribed to treat generalized anxiety conditions.

Stimulants

In 1937 amphetamines were reported to reduce disruptive behavior and hyperactivity and to improve academic performance in school children (Bradley, 1937; Molitch & Eccles, 1937). Today, these drugs are used by as many as 3% of school-aged children in the treatment of ADHD. They also are used to treat ADHD in people with MR/DD, although few studies have been reported with this population (Arnold, Gadow, Pearson, & Varley, 1998). Upwards of 70% of the children treated show improvement in attention span, disruptive behavior, and academic performance. Chronic use is required over a period of years, but the drugs are considered relatively safe. In clinical doses, these medicines do not cause physical dependency in children who take them for ADHD. Stimulants also are used in adults for the treatment of ADHD and of obesity. The trade names of commonly prescribed stimulants include Dexedrine, Ritalin, and Cylert.

Mood Stabilizers

The use of lithium salts in the treatment of mania was introduced by Cade in 1949, but it was not until the 1970s that a technology for controlling toxic effects was available to support widespread clinical use. Lithium is the first-line treatment for bipolar disorder, but anticonvulsant drugs, especially carbamazepine and valproic acid, are preferred in the treatment of rapid cycling conditions and for patients who are children. Carbamazepine or valproate also are used for patients who are impulsive or show episodic, uncontrolled outbursts of violent rage. Verapamil, a calcium channel–blocking agent, also has been found useful in the treatment of bipolar disorder. Lithium, carbamazine, and valproate have an antiaggressive effect apart from their effects on specific psychiatric syndromes (Poindexter et al, 1998). Trade names include Eskalith and Lithane and, for anticonvulsants, Tegretol, Depakene, and Depakote.

Opiate Blockers

Based mostly on the work on Sandman and his associates, naltrexone, an opiate blocker, has been evaluated for the treatment of self-injurious behavior. According to a review conducted by Sandman and colleagues (1998), the rate of positive response in studies that directly observed behavior was between 35% and 70% for individuals tested. One recent study showed no positive responders (Willemsen-Swinkels, Buitelaar, & Nijhof, 1995), although the failure to find benefit may have been a consequence of inadequate observation. Despite these concerns, a risk–benefit analysis supports a trial of naltrexone in many cases of severe self-injury (Sandman et al., 1998), although additional research is needed to establish efficacy.

Treatment of Substance Abuse

Psychoactive drugs are used in the treatment of substance abuse in several ways. They are used to treat comorbid psychological conditions, such as anxiety or depression. They also are used to counteract the effects of intoxification, to manage withdrawal symptoms, and to help prevent reuse through sensitization. Success is heavily dependent on the patient's cooperation and motivation. Psychopharmacological treatments are best used as part of an overall psychological treatment program aimed at behavior modification and the resolution of associated psychological issues.

The benzodiazepines, which are anxiolytics, are used in the management of alcohol withdrawal symptoms and of panic reactions induced by hallucinogens. Disulfiram (Antabuse) is used to sensitize a person to alcohol, so that consumption produces nausea and other reactions aimed at conditioning aversion to drinking during long-term treatment. This approach is often not successful because of frequent lapses in patient compliance. Naltrexone and methadone are used to prevent euphoric reactions to heroin. Methadone produces cross-tolerance with heroin but is a more manageable and safer drug. Nicotine chewing gum or topical patches have been used in the treatment of smoking. (Nicotine also is used to treat adult ADHD and Tourette disorder.)

Almost no research has been reported on the safety and efficacy of psychoactive drugs in treating substance abuse of people with MR/DD. Substance abuse may be rarely diagnosed in this population (Reiss, 1994), or when it is diagnosed, people may not come to the attention of MR/DD services.

Vitamin and Dietary Treatments

Over the years, a number of vitamin and dietary treatments have been suggested for diverse effects, such as raising IQs, treating ADHD, or preventing severe effects of autism. However, none of these treatments have been supported by scientific evidence (Singh, Ellis, Mattila, Mulick, & Poling, 1998). There is little evidence for the efficacy of megavitamins, folic acid, vitamin B6, or other dietary treatments with people with MR/DD (Singh et al., 1998).

BEST PRACTICES

Best practices in using psychotropic medicines in people with MR/DD require informed consent, clinical expertise, consulting with various teams and disciplines, and systematic monitoring of effects (Davis et al., 1998).

Informed Consent

Except in an emergency, written informed consent must be obtained from the individual or guardian before the use of any psychotropic medication. Additionally, the information should be presented orally and in layperson's terms in a manner that ensures effective communication. Informed consent should be renewed at least every 6 months.

Clinical Expertise

Drug use should be based on a comprehensive assessment of the person's problem behavior. When possible, this should include a formal psychiatric diagnosis. The diagnosis should be based on clinical interviews, observations, a reading of the case history, interviews with family and staff, and the results of relevant laboratory tests and psychological rating scales. When a psychiatric diagnosis cannot be established, a target behavior should be indicated. Written treatment goals should be made. Physicians who make diagnostic and treatment decisions should take into account research and clinical literatures on dual diagnosis.

Multidisciplinary Care Plan

By themselves, psychoactive drugs do not cure mental illnesses. They lessen symptoms of mental illness, but the symptoms often reappear after medication is withdrawn. Some patients do not respond at all, and many still show significant (although improved) symptomatology even while on medication. Psychoactive drugs do not solve the life problems that give rise to stress, anxiety, depression, and other signs of mental illnesses. Often they are best used to manage symptoms while patients undergo other therapies, counseling, or training.

Psychotropic medication should be used within the context of a coordinated, multidisciplinary care plan designed to improve the person's quality of life (Kalachnik et al., 1998). Psychotropic medication alone is not a care plan; the person also must be taught skills or given therapy to bring about improvement in quality of life. Physicians, psychologists, educators, social workers, nurses, and other professionals involved with the person should work together to coordinate efforts and develop a formal, written plan.

Monitoring for Effects

The patient should be monitored for treatment benefit and possible adverse effects. Standardized rating scales should be used to as great an extent as possible, because these remind people to check for all important symptoms and behavior changes on a periodic basis. Examples of standardized scales include the *Reiss Screen for Maladaptive Behavior* (Reiss, 1988) and the *Aberrant Behavior Checklist* (Aman & Singh, 1986). The total scores on these instruments are sensitive measures of severity of most behavioral or psychiatric conditions.

NEED FOR RESEARCH

Controlled research studies are needed to evaluate the safety and efficacy of psychotropic medications with people with MR/DD and to develop new and more effective medications. Until recently, much of the available evidence was poorly controlled, so that we still lack basic scientific information, even on older agents such as the traditional neuroleptic drugs. There have been few studies that have looked at issues of substance, such as dose effects, short-term drug effects, and long-term drug effects. Many studies, especially those conducted prior to the late 1980s, failed to take psychiatric diagnosis into account.

REFERENCES

Aman, M. G., & Singh, M. N. (1986). *Aberrant Behavior Checklist manual*. East Aurora, NY: Slosson Educational Publications.

Arnold, L. E., Gadow, K. D., Pearson, D. A., & Varley, C. K. (1998). Stimulants. In S. Reiss & M. G. Aman (Eds.), *Psychotropic medications and developmental disabilities: The international consensus handbook* (pp. 229–258). Columbus: The Ohio State University.

Baumeister, A., Sevin, J. A., & King, B. H. (1998). Neuroleptic medications. In S. Reiss & M. G. Aman (Eds.), *Psychotropic medications and developmental disabilities: The international consensus handbook* (pp. 133–150). Columbus: The Ohio State University.

Bradley, C. (1937). The behavior of children receiving benzedrine. *American Journal of Psychiatry, 94*, 577–585.

Davis, S., Wehmeyer, M. L., Board, J. P., Jr., Fox, S., Maher, F., & Roberts, B. (1998). Interdisciplinary teams. In S. Reiss & M. G. Aman (Eds.), *Psychotropic medications and developmental disabilities: The international consensus handbook*. Columbus: The Ohio State University.

Delay, J., Deniker, P., & Harl, J. (1952). Utilization therapeutique psychiatrique d'une phenothiazine d'action centrale elective. *Annals of Medical Psychology (Paris), 110*, 112–117.

Kalachnik, J. E., Leventhal, B. L., James, D. H., Sovner, R. L., Kastner, T. A., Walsh, K., Weisblatt, S. A., & Klitzke, M. G. (1998). Guidelines for the use of psychotropic medication. In S. Reiss & M. G. Aman (Eds.), *Psychotropic medications and developmental disabilities: The international consensus handbook* (pp. 45–72). Columbus: The Ohio State University.

Molitch, M., & Eccles, A. K. (1937). The effect of benzedrine sulfate on the intelligence scores of children. *American Journal of Psychiatry, 94*, 587–590.

Poindexter, A. R., Cain, N., Clarke, D. J., Cook, E. H., Jr., Corbett, J. A., & Levitas, A. (1998). Mood stabilizers. In S. Reiss & M. G. Aman (Eds.), *Psychotropic medications and developmental disabilities: The international consensus handbook* (pp. 215–228). Columbus: The Ohio State University.

Reiss, S. (1988). *The Reiss Screen for Maladaptive Behavior*. Worthington, OH: IDS Publishing.

Reiss, S. (1994). *Handbook of challenging behavior*. Worthington, OH: IDS Publishing.

Reiss, S., & Aman, M. G. (1997). The international consensus process on psychopharmacology and intellectual disability. *Journal of Intellectual Disability Research, 41*, 448–455.

Reiss, S., & Aman, M.G. (1998). *Psychotropic medications and developmental disabilities: The international consensus handbook*. Columbus: The Ohio State University.

Rinck, C. (1998). Epidemiology and psychoactive medication. In S. Reiss & M. G. Aman (Eds.), *Psychotropic medications and developmental disabilities: The international consensus handbook* (pp. 31–44). Columbus: The Ohio State University.

Sandman, C. A., Thompson, T., Barrett, R. P., Verhoeven, W. M. A., McCubbin, J. A., Schroeder, S. R., & Hetrick, W. P. (1998). Opiate blockers. In S. Reiss & M. G. Aman (Eds.), *Psychotropic medications and developmental disabilities: The international consensus handbook* (pp. 291–302). Columbus: The Ohio State University.

Schatzberg, A. F., Cole, J. O., & DeBattista, C. (1997). *Manual of clinical psychopharmacology*. Washington, DC: American Psychiatric Press.

Singh, N. N., Ellis, C. R., Mattila, M. J., Mulick, J. A., & Poling, A. (1998). Vitamin, mineral, and dietary treatments. In S. Reiss & M. G. Aman (Eds.), *Psychotropic medications and developmental disabilities: The international consensus handbook* (pp. 311–320). Columbus: The Ohio State University.

Somni, R. W., Benefield, W. H., Jr., Curtis, J. L., Lott, R. A., Saklad, J., & Wilson, J. (1998). Drug interactions with psychotropic medications. In S. Reiss & M. G. Aman (Eds.), *Psychotropic medications and developmental disabilities: The international consensus handbook* (pp. 115–132). Columbus: The Ohio State University.

Sovner, R., Pary, R. J., Dosen, A., Geyde, A., Barrera, F. J., Cantwell, D. P., & Huessy, H. R. (1998). Antidepressants. In S. Reiss & M. G. Aman (Eds.), *Psychotropic medications and developmental disabilities: The international consensus handbook* (pp. 179–200). Columbus: The Ohio State University.

Vitiello, B., & Jensen, P. S. (1995). Developmental perspectives in pediatric psychopharmacology. *Psychopharmacology Bulletin, 31*, 75–81.

Werry, J. S. (1998). Anxiolytics and sedatives. In S. Reiss & M. G. Aman (Eds.), *Psychotropic medications and developmental disabilities: The international consensus handbook* (pp. 201–214). Columbus: The Ohio State University.

Willemsen-Swinkles, S. H., Buitelaar, J. K., & Nijhof, G. H. (1995). Failure of naltrexone hydrochloride to reduce self-injurious and autistic behavior in mentally retarded adults. *Achieves of General Psychiatry, 52*, 766–773.

Wilson, J. G., Lott, R. S., & Tsai, L. (1998). Side effects: Recognition and management. In S. Reiss & M. G. Aman (Eds.), *Psychotropic medications and developmental disabilities: The international consensus handbook* (pp. 95–114). Columbus: The Ohio State University.

Health Conditions Contributing to Problem Behavior Among People with Mental Retardation and Developmental Disabilities

Craig H. Kennedy and Travis Thompson

P eople with mental retardation and related developmental disabilities experience health problems more frequently than their same-age peers who do not have developmental delays (Kerr, 1997; van Schrojenstein et al., 1997). Among the more common difficulties are gastrointestinal disorders, ear infections, eating disorders, and sleep problems. Some of these adverse health conditions are directly related to congenital developmental abnormalities (e.g., gastric reflux disease in Cornelia de Lange syndrome and immune disorders in autism), whereas others may be iatragenic, resulting from treatments received for another condition. Many of the psychotropic medications (e.g., neuroleptics or tricyclic antidepressants) that are commonly administered to people with mental retardation for behavior problems cause constipation and nasal congestion as side effects, which can lead to extreme discomfort or intestinal obstructions, or make the individual prone to sinus and ear infections. In many public institutions, substantial numbers of individuals with mental retardation routinely receive laxatives for chronic constipation problems, or are treated prophylactically with antihistamines and antibiotics for sinus and ear infections.

Other people in the general population who experience gastrointestinal problems consume many millions of dollars worth of prescription and over-the-counter medications (e.g., antacids, histamine blockers, laxatives) to relieve discomfort. Similarly, self-medication for cold and allergy symptoms occurs in the general population to the tune of tens of millions of dollars per year. It seems surprising, therefore, that so little attention has been paid to these commonly associated health conditions in mental retardation. There are several reasons for the neglect of this issue: (a) Many people with mental retardation are unable to report their symptoms, and therefore go unnoticed until the symptoms are severe; (b) signs of physical illness are often expressed as behavior problems among people with mental retardation, and caregivers and health professionals may assume the behavior problem is occurring for some other reason (e.g., a psychiatric problem) and treat it accordingly, and often incorrectly; and

(c) until recently, biological and behavioral aspects of the individual's well-being were seen as independent and unrelated spheres, so that health professionals have dealt with one set of issues, and habilitative or educational personnel have concerned themselves with psychological or behavioral issues. Although we would prefer to think otherwise, the common belief persists that people with mental retardation do not experience discomfort the same way as other people, and therefore there is less cause for concern.

The social and psychological interpretation of health conditions has been the topic of considerable theoretical analysis (Sontag, 1978). If disability is seen as "illness," to use Sontag's term, then the co-occurrence of other health problems (e.g., ear infections, sleep disorders, constipation) would be an expected part of the inherent condition, and not seen as requiring special attention. Reiss, Levitan, and Szysko (1982) empirically and theoretically examined the phenomenon of "diagnostic overshadowing," the tendency to underdiagnose psychiatric problems among people with mental retardation. The presence of mental retardation tends to lead mental health professionals to overlook the possibility of an underlying psychiatric disorder. In the case of other health conditions, the same phenomenon seems to occur. Because the person has mental retardation, some professionals may tend to scrutinize less carefully the possibility that the person's behavior problem is due to an earache or gastrointestinal pain; instead, they see a person who is "acting out" (i.e., being oppositional or defiant). In light of the prevalence of these associated health problems, which we discuss later, we believe far more care should be given to these issues by educational, habilitative, and health care professionals.

AN EMERGING UNDERSTANDING OF THE CAUSES OF PROBLEM BEHAVIOR

Twenty years ago the reasons why behavior problems occurred were rarely identified. Instead, interventions were developed without regard to the causes of the behavior. The result was a poor understanding of the ontogeny of problem behavior and desultory intervention effects. Recently, the emergence of functional assessments to identify the causes of problem behavior has led to successful outcomes in approximately 70% of cases (see Horner's Chapter 10 in this volume). What functional assessment techniques have allowed is the identification of why a person is behaving inappropriately. The most typical causes of problem behavior include obtaining attention from others, accessing otherwise unobtainable objects or activities, and escaping from instructional or other demand situations (Derby et al., 1992). For example, a child may hit her head during difficult instructional tasks to escape instruction or at home to gain attention from her parents (Carr & Durand, 1985). Interestingly, the reinforcers identified in successful functional assessments are almost all social in nature (i.e., to obtain reinforcement, another person is required).

From the success of functional assessments, an emerging understanding of health issues has arisen. As researchers began assessing problem behavior over extended periods of time to understand its social or environmental causes, some cases revealed intermittent increases in problem behavior that could not be explained by social or environmental events alone. On further investigation, health issues—not readily identified in psychological assessments—are often involved in the cause of problem behavior (Carr & Smith, 1995; Cataldo & Harris, 1982; Peine, Darvish, Blakelock, Osborne, & Jenson, 1995). In some cases these increases were *episodic*; in other cases they were *cyclical*. An example of episodic health factors is the effect of sleep deprivation in increasing problem behavior (Kennedy & Itkonen, 1993; Symons, Davis, & Thompson, in press). That is, when a person with disabilities sleeps poorly, the result is often an increase in problem behavior the next day. An example of a cyclic health factor affecting problem behavior is painful menses (Carr, Reeve, & Magito-McLaughlin, 1996; Pyles & Bailey, 1990). Often when a woman with a disability has an uncomfortable menses, increases in aggression or self-injury coincide with the onset of menstruation.

Prior to the development of functional assessment techniques that facilitated the identification of health variables affecting problem behavior, biological influences on behavior were often unidentified. As a result, behavioral interventions often neglected health factors as a contributing variable in the cause of problem behavior. However, with an increased interest in the *biobehavioral analysis of problem behavior*, the neglect of health issues as influential events is changing. That is particularly apropos because health factors that may contribute to problem behaviors occur at the same or higher rates in people with developmental disabilities than in other populations (Kerr, 1997; van Schrojenstein et al., 1997).

Health issues can have substantive effects on the occurrence and intensity of problem behaviors, which, if left unidentified, may result in behavioral interventions that only partially decrease problem behavior. The effects of adverse health conditions on a person's quality of life, then, are multiple. First, the person with disabilities is experiencing a medical problem that is not being treated. This can lead both to physical discomfort for the individual and increases in the probability of additional complications occurring as a result of the untreated health issue. Second, if a health issue is involved in the cause of problem behavior, but is left untreated, problem behaviors will continue to occur. That pattern of problem behavior may become less predictable, as is the case with episodic health factors, or remain at levels that persist despite behavioral interventions (e.g., as a result of chronic constipation). The continued occurrence of problem behavior can place the individual at greater risk for physical injury, as well as increase the possibility of a more restrictive educational or residential placement. As a whole, it is becoming increasingly clear that adverse health concerns cannot remain outside the purview of behavioral assessment and intervention. However, understanding the theoretical role of health issues in the cause of problem behavior, determining ways to effectively identify these factors, and developing multicomponent interventions requires several changes in how the assessment of problem behavior occurs, and in the interventions that result from this process.

THEORETICAL RELATIONSHIPS BETWEEN ADVERSE HEALTH CONDITIONS AND PROBLEM BEHAVIOR

Antihistamine medications designed to reduce common cold symptoms also produce drowsy feelings, which may make it difficult to remain alert during a less than scintillating lecture. The cold symptoms, combined with the drowsiness caused by the antihistamine, reduce the control the lecturer's remarks have over the listener's attention. A parent who has a headache may feel irritable when his 5-year-old child is playing loudly nearby, but on another occasion may be amused with the child's stream of comments about the building she is constructing out of blocks. The parent may say, "Don't make so much noise!" instead of "That's a really neat castle you made with your blocks." Such experiences of discomfort (e.g., headache, drowsiness, nasal congestion, dysmenorrhea) change the value of external stimulation, reducing the value of positive stimuli and exaggerating the significance of unpleasant or aversive stimuli. These *establishing operations* are similar to being tired due to lack of sleep (Kennedy & Meyer, 1998). Establishing operations function like a rheostat that regulates the set point at which an external event becomes aversive or pleasant (Michael, 1982).

Adverse health conditions operate precisely that way. They determine the set point at which a given external event becomes sufficiently aversive that the person who is experiencing discomfort reacts to the external cue. In response to a spouse's request to climb up on the ladder and replace the broken light fixture, the husband who slept poorly the night before may say, "I'll do it later. Right now I'm going to lie down and take a nap." That is a socially acceptable avoidance response to what is normally a reasonable request, even though sleep deprivation has made that request especially unpleasant. People with mental retardation, autism, and related developmental disabilities often lack sufficient communication skills to respond in socially acceptable ways under such circumstances. As a result, when confronted with a difficult, overly demanding or frightening situation, it is not uncommon for some people with mental retardation to strike out at the person making the request or to injure themselves. If the individual is otherwise healthy, his or her tolerance for such requests may be high. However, when an individual with a significant developmental delay is also experiencing pain (e.g., menstrual cramps), even a minimally aversive demand becomes intolerable and leads to aggression (Carr et al., 1996; Pyles & Bailey, 1990). The following are typical examples of health conditions that lead to behavior problems, which were initially misinterpreted by caregivers, teachers, and parents.

MARK'S STORY

A 27-year-old man with severe mental retardation, Mark, who had Bassen-Komzweig syndrome, resided in a public residential setting. He was referred for evaluation because of his chronic ingestion of items of clothing, self-injury, and aggression against others. Mark received buspirone for his behavior problems. It was reported that Mark had frequent rumination and vomiting, for which he received a histamine blocker. On examination it was discovered that he had a hiatal hernia. He was nonverbal and had no communication system to indicate his desire to terminate an activity. Bassen-Kornsweig syndrome is associated with chronic intestinal malabsorption, including cholestatic liver disease and Crohn's disease. Deterioration of the intestinal lining in Crohn's disease can cause unpredictable intestinal hemorrhaging, and individuals with this disease experience frequent nausea, intestinal cramping, and diarrhea. After observing Mark, reviewing his records, and interviewing staff who worked with him, it seemed clear that his pica was associated with bouts of intestinal gassiness and signs of abdominal pain. It appeared that his pica was an attempt to reduce the gastrointestinal discomfort caused by Crohn's disease. In the absence of a communication system, his aggression and self-injury appeared to be responses to demand situations when he was in pain. When this man's pain became sufficient, he struck out against others when demands were made on him, since he had no way of requesting that the demand be delayed or terminated. In addition, Mark managed his own pain by consuming bulky materials that filled his intestinal tract, thereby reducing cramping.

CINDY'S STORY

Cindy was diagnosed at the age of 3 with Rett syndrome. She lives with her parents and attends a neighborhood high school. Over the last several years, her teachers have reported increasingly frequent "bad days." Typically, Cindy is a pleasure to teach and interact with, but on her bad days she screams loudly and repeatedly bites her hands. When she was in elementary school, her teachers rarely reported sustained instances of screaming and biting; however, when she entered high school, her teachers said that she had significant problems at least twice per week. Previous behavioral assessments identified instructional situations as associated with her problem behavior. Communication and preference-based interventions had helped reduce her problem behavior, but on some days her teachers indicated that screaming and self-biting seemed out of control. Cindy's parents reported that she had become increasingly listless when she went to bed and was often awake when her alarm sounded in the morning. Her pediatrician, who is familiar with Rett syndrome, suggested that Cindy receive a sleep disorder assessment. The results of the sleep assessment suggested that

Cindy was sleeping only a few hours per night and may have had some nights with little or no sleep, a pattern that is not unusual for young women with Rett syndrome. Cindy's teachers and parents began keeping sleep records for her at night and found a relation between nights of poor sleep and increases in her screaming and biting the next day at school.

JAMES'S STORY

James, a 9-year-old boy in a public school classroom for students with severe disabilities, was referred because of his severe self-injury. He was extremely self-injurious and was held on his teacher's or aide's lap most of the time, restraining his arms so he would not strike his face with his fists. He had a bruise on one cheek from repeatedly hitting his face. He had no spoken communication, but had a history of using iconic communication cards. He was taught to request preferred items or activities by selecting, then pointing to a pictorial communication card kept in a fanny pack around his waist. Initially, familiar foods and beverages were used, but soon preferred activities were introduced. James learned to use 15 communication cards over 16 sessions, including a card to request a break from instruction. His self-injury dropped to near zero after 8 sessions and had begun to decrease during normal classroom activities as well. His self-injury began to return episodically, unrelated to teaching activities. During these episodes he engaged in frequent self-injury from which he could not be distracted. During two such periods, he had nothing to eat or drink for at least the previous 24 hours, according to school staff and his mother.

Figure 12.1 shows the relation between James's self-injurious behavior (SIB) and episodes of constipation. During the first 5 days of the intervention project, baseline measures of self-injury in his classroom were recorded without communication intervention or medication. At the vertical black line, functional communication training was initiated in daily intervention sessions (black boxes) for the next 16 school days. Observations in his classroom, where the communication interventions were not being conducted, were also made, to test for generalization (open circles) of intervention effects. Gray areas indicate periods during which the student consumed less than one quarter of his breakfast and lunch while at school, which corresponded to periods of constipation. Three to 5 days following the onset of periods of low food consumption (and constipation), self-injury increased during generalization observations in the classroom (when no functional communication intervention was being conducted) as indicated by large circles. Self-injury also increased during functional communication training sessions on the last two constipation episodes. Thus, while functional communication training clearly reduced his self-injury, it was not able to overcome the effects of constipation with resulting pain, nausea, and associated

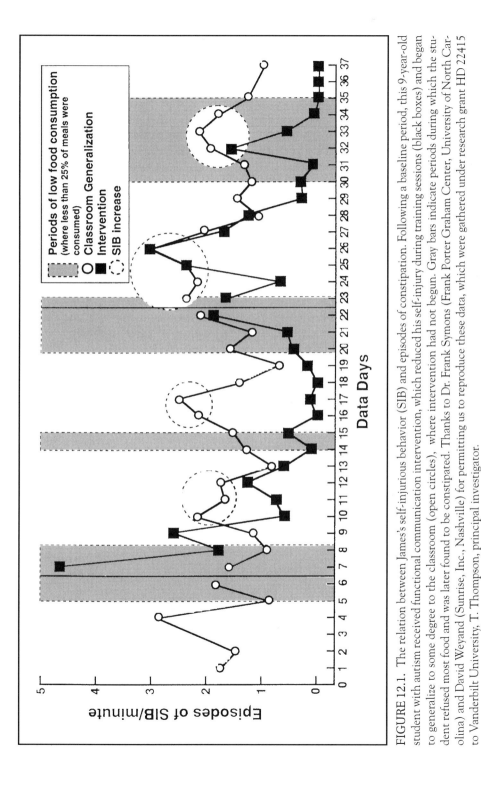

FIGURE 12.1. The relation between James's self-injurious behavior (SIB) and episodes of constipation. Following a baseline period, this 9-year-old student with autism received functional communication intervention, which reduced his self-injury during training sessions (black boxes) and began to generalize to some degree to the classroom (open circles), where intervention had not begun. Gray bars indicate periods during which the student refused most food and was later found to be constipated. Thanks to Dr. Frank Symons (Frank Porter Graham Center, University of North Carolina) and David Weyand (Sunrise, Inc., Nashville) for permitting us to reproduce these data, which were gathered under research grant HD 22415 to Vanderbilt University, T. Thompson, principal investigator.

discomfort. James was seen by a pediatrician who found him to have a bowel obstruction that required colonic irrigation and treatment with antibiotics.

Need for an Interdisciplinary Approach

The cases described previously make it very clear that the solution to problems such as these requires a fully integrated interdisciplinary approach. Given these observations and case histories, it is clear that a range of individuals need to be involved in any assessment of problem behavior. Unfortunately, such interdisciplinary assessments are rare. The net effect is that either the causes of problem behavior remain unidentified or the information that is known is not shared with support providers across settings. The result often is continuing behavior problems that may increase in severity over time or across settings. This is particularly important for people with problem behaviors and health concerns. It is unlikely that any one professional involved in assessing the cause(s) of chronic problem behavior will have the expertise in the variety of areas noted above. Because of these interdisciplinary assessment needs, increasing attention is needed to better integrate professional efforts in complex cases involving problem behavior (Hodapp & Dykens, 1994).

Because medical, genetic, and environmental variables can often combine to cause problem behavior, an assessment from only one disciplinary perspective may not suffice in identifying why problem behavior is occurring, and how to intervene to reduce its occurrence. Knowledge of genetic and congenital syndromes and their common features is an essential starting point—knowledge that is often beyond the purview of school personnel. Medical specialists in ear, nose, and throat diseases, and gastrointestinal disorders are also essential members of a team. Also, because people with developmental disabilities are the most medicated group of individuals (Singh, Ellis, & Weschler, 1997) specialists with expertise in psychotropic medications, as well as professionals experienced in functional assessment and diagnosis, are needed. In addition, communication, educational, and habilitative professional expertise in functional support services are required. Finally, a case manager whose job it is to integrate the various treatment and service components is essential.

HEALTH CONDITIONS AND THEIR CONSEQUENCES FOR PROBLEM BEHAVIOR

Twenty years ago teachers were often taught that health conditions were not associated with problem behavior. Educators and other support providers were told that the causes of problem behavior were environmentally based, and that physiological variables were unlikely to be related to problem behavior. Although well intentioned, this may have been a case of "not seeing the forest for the trees." Our understanding of the interrelations between health conditions and problem behavior, although far from complete, suggests the importance of biological events in the cause and maintenance of at least some cases of problem behavior. In the section that follows, a selective review of several health conditions that have been empirically linked to the occurrence of problem behavior will be provided to illustrate the need for increased interdisciplinary assessment and biobehavioral approaches to functional assessment. In particular, we will focus on how sleep deprivation, gastrointestinal problems, eating disorders, and chronic infections can influence the occurrence of problem behaviors.

Sleep Deprivation

People with mental retardation and developmental disabilities exhibit more sleep problems than any other identifiable group of individuals. Overall, prevalence rates have suggested that 34% of these individuals have sleep problems, which contrasts substantially with the prevalence rate of 12% in the general population (Clements, Wing, & Dunn, 1986). In fact, with some genetically based traits, for example Rett syndrome, sleep problems can affect as many as 57% of individuals.

Sleep problems take many different forms, but all produce sleep deprivation. Humans have five different levels of sleep: Four levels can be generally referred to as slow-wave sleep, with the fifth often referred to as rapid eye movement (REM) sleep. Sleep problems can generally be categorized as reductions in overall amounts of slow-wave and REM sleep or the selective decrease in either slow-wave or REM sleep (Lask, 1997). The former can be viewed as obtaining too little sleep (e.g., receiving only 4 hours of sleep a night); the latter forms of sleep deprivation are caused by disruptions such as sleep apnea (slow-wave sleep) or enuresis (REM sleep).

Teachers and family members have often suspected a link between sleep disruption and problem behaviors. Recent research has begun to establish a more formal link. Kennedy and Itkonen (1993) and Symons et al. (in press) have documented correlations between increased self-injury or aggression and decreased levels of sleep. In general, these studies show that nights of decreased or disrupted sleep were associated with increased behavior problems the next day. Follow-up studies have recently demonstrated that problem behaviors negatively reinforced by escape from demands can substantially increase following sleep problems (Horner, Day, & Day, 1997; Kennedy & Meyer, 1996; O'Reilly, 1995). Basic research seems to support these findings, and suggests that sleep problems can make negative reinforcers more invidious and may reduce the value of positive reinforcers (Kennedy, Meyer, Werts, & Cushing, in press). As a collection, research clearly indicates a causal link between sleep deprivation and increased problem behaviors.

Sleep problems can arise from a number of sources, both behavioral and physiological. Perhaps the most frequent cause of sleep deprivation is a person going to bed too early or too late in the evening (Durand, 1997). Going to bed too late and having to rise for school or work the following morning is an obvious source of abbreviated sleep. However, requiring that a person go to sleep early in the evening can also produce sleep disruptions, such as prolonged night wakings, as well as resistance to sleep-related routines. As Durand (1997) suggested, behavioral interventions relating to bedtime routines are often the interventions of choice to reestablish typical sleep routines. Figure 12.2 illustrates how sleep deprivation and sleep routines can affect problem behavior. Anita was a 19-year-old woman with moderate disabilities. She liked to watch late-night movies during the week, which often resulted in her sleeping 4 or fewer hours the night before school (shaded areas). The result was that when Anita was sleep deprived, she engaged in much higher levels of problem behavior (closed circles). A program was developed that had her go to bed each night at a designated time and wake up the next day in time to prepare for school (through a differential reinforcement intervention). With the program in place, Anita's sleep problems were eliminated and fewer problem behaviors were observed.

Unfortunately, other sleep problems may have a more pronounced physiological component that requires medical intervention along with behavioral support. For example, there appears to be a subgroup of people with autism who have elevated levels of the neurotransmitter serotonin and who sleep very little (Rapin & Katzman, 1998). Basic neuroscience has shown that increasing levels of serotonin results in a dramatic reduction or elimination of sleep (see Jouvet, 1969). If serotonin is involved in disrupted sleep for some people with autism, such a finding might require pharmacological, as well as behavioral, interventions to (re)establish typical sleep patterns. Other genetically based disabilities, such as Rett or Angelman syndromes, may also have physiological bases for disrupted sleep that could require a multidisciplinary approach to intervention. Although in the last decade data have emerged that link sleep deprivation to increases in problem behavior, a great deal of work remains to be done to better understand the etiology of sleep disruptions and how to effectively treat them.

Gastrointestinal Factors

Millions of Americans take antacids, histamine blockers, and other over-the-counter remedies to relieve discomfort of heartburn or acid indigestion, what physicians often call dyspepsia. In reality, heartburn happens when stomach contents wash up into the esophagus and irritate the last inch or so of the esophagus where it joins with the stomach. In the general population, 36% of people in a European and American sample experienced heartburn at least once a month, and 7% experienced daily acid indigestion.

Chronic heartburn is the classic symptom of a more serious underlying condition, gastroesophageal reflux disease (GERD). GERD results from chronic exposure of the esophagus to stomach contents, with resulting irritation and tissue damage in the esophagus, which is called esophagitis (inflammation of the esophagus). Esophagitis is estimated to occur in 2% to 10% of people complaining of heartburn. The reasons for GERD are complex, but they begin with stomach contents, which are very acidic, with pH values as low as 1.5. The lower the pH value, the more acidic the solution. For comparison, the pH of battery acid approaches zero, lemon juice is 2, and apple juice is 3.8 (Peterson, Skinner, & Strong, 1995). Most people suffering from GERD are

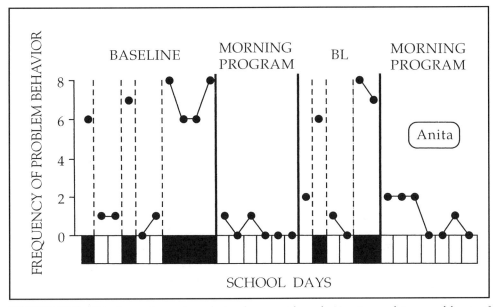

FIGURE 12.2. This figure shows the relation between sleep deprivation and increased bouts of problem behavior. Anita, a 19-year-old woman with moderate disabilities often stayed up late at night. On school days when she had slept less than 4 hours the night before (shaded areas), she was more likely to engage in problem behavior (closed circles). An evening routine was established that facilitated her going to bed and awakening for school at reasonable times of the day. From "Effects of Setting Events on the Problem Behavior of Students with Severe Disabilities," by C. H. Kennedy and T. Itkonen, 1993, p. 324. Copyright 1993 by Society for the Experimental Analysis of Behavior. Reprinted with permission.

very sensitive to stomach pH values in the 1 to 2 range. Other ingredients in stomach contents, such as pepsin, trypsin, and bile, worsen the corrosive effects of the acidic stomach contents on the tissues lining the esophagus of the affected person.

Until recently relatively little was known about the prevalence of GERD among people with developmental disabilities, though it has been recognized for many years that people with specific disabilities, such as Cornelia de Lange syndrome, have frequent problems with reflux disease (Lachman, Funamura, & Szalay, 1981; Rosenbach, Zahavi, & Dinari, 1992). In the most comprehensive investigation to date, Bohmer (1996) studied 1,687 people with developmental disabilities retrospectively, and 1,607 prospectively for presence of GERD, as well as other factors associated with reflux disease. Bohmer found that 6% of the institutionalized population of people with mental retardation had endoscopically documentable GERD with severe esophagitis. Bohmer compared predisposing factors to GERD among groups of people with mental retardation in the Netherlands and Belgium, as well as examining any behavioral covariates. People who were nonambulatory; who had scoliosis, cerebral palsy, or frequent constipation; or who received anticonvulsant drugs were at highest risk for developing

GERD. From 13% to 19% displayed self-injury and 13% to 33% exhibited aggression, which were believed to be associated with the gastric reflux disease.

Individuals with Cornelia de Lange syndrome not only suffer from the discomfort associated with reflux disease, but also exhibit twisting of the neck to one side, eyes averting upward, and curving and twisting of the trunk in a backward paroxysm, which is called the Sandifer complex (Sommer, 1993). These body contortions are often misunderstood by professionals who may not be aware of the ubiquity of reflux disease in de Lange syndrome, and are unaware of the connection between reflux disease and the Sandifer complex. Instead it is often assumed that the body twisting is an indication of either a tic disorder or neuroleptic-induced Tardive dyskinesia. This involuntary spasm-like postural response resulting from the esophageal pain is also often associated with self-stimulation and severe self-injury.

Bohmer et al. (1997) also found that 5% to 50% of individuals residing in institutions for people with mental retardation in the Netherlands were infected with Helicobacter pylori (H.Pylori), the bacterium that is a causal agent in gastric and doudenal ulcers and plays a role in stomach cancer. H.Pylori is a bacterium (germ) that lives in the inner lining of the stomach. H.Pylori produces products that attack the lining of the stomach. Once the infection is present, it persists for many years, if not for life, if left untreated. Proujansky, Shaffer, Vinton, and Bachrach (1994) reported increased incidence of symptomatic H.Pylori infection in children with neurological impairments. Although the percentages were low in Bohmer et al.'s study of youngsters, 83% of 51-year-olds were infected with H.Pylori, and the likelihood of being infected is more common in males than females.

The reasons GERD is more common among people with mental retardation is unclear. Among contributing factors are abnormalities in the development of the esophageal-gastric sphincter which regulates pressure necessary for stomach contents to be expelled into the esophagus. Specific dietary factors, such as fatty and spicy foods, carbonated beverages, coffee, and cigarette smoking all exacerbate GERD symptoms. Obesity and eating large meals before bedtime aggravate the condition. Certain medications that affect gastric sphincter flaccidity also seem to contribute to GERD.

Among the most common treatments for GERD have been dietary adjustments, symptomatic treatment with antacids, and in recent years prophylactic treatment with histamine (H_2) receptor antagonists such as famotidine (Pepcid), cimetidine (Tagamet), and ranitidine (Zantac). More recent studies used omeprazole (Prilosec), a socalled acid (proton) pump inhibitor that produced prolonged suppression of stomach acid production and doubled the effectiveness of cimetidine alone (Bohmer et al., 1997). Studies with other clinical populations indicate that the combination of omeprazole and clarithromycin (Baxin) are effective in treating H.Pylori infection, often reversing gastric ulcers.

Extreme GERD associated with esophageal strictures causes malnutrition due to reduced food intake, which is secondary to the severe pain induced during swallowing, called dysphagia. When prolonged, GERD has produced esophageal strictures;

esophageal dilation is usually performed after examining the esophagus with a gastro-scope. Gastroscopy is necessary to clearly see what is causing the problem and to exclude serious conditions such as cancer. Most strictures are treated with tapered rub-ber tubes that are passed gently down the throat and through the stricture. A series of dilators of gradually larger sizes are used to enlarge the narrowed area. In the most extreme cases, or where precancerous tissue is apparent, fundoplication surgery is per-formed.

Figure 12.3 shows the relation between meals and bouts of self-injury by a 29-year-old man with profound mental retardation and autism over a 1-month baseline obser-vational period. His self-injury was severe, causing hyperplasia of both hands, abra-sions on his face and head, loss of one thumb, and retinal detachment. The pattern of meal-related increases in self-injury led to endoscopic examination and confirmation of two esophageal strictures and a hiatal hernia. This individual was first treated with antacids before and after meals, and subsequently underwent esophageal dilation,

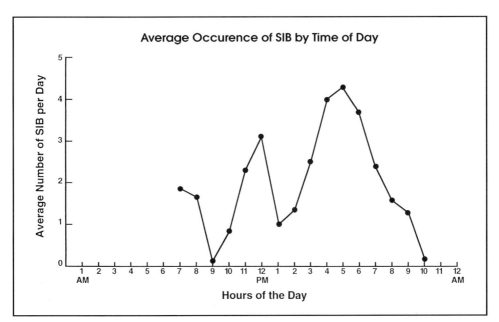

FIGURE 12.3. This figure shows self-injurious behavior (SIB) by a 29-year-old man who had dis-played unremitting hand and head hitting for many years, resulting in considerable tissue damage. He had received numerous medication and behavioral treatments over many years, most ineffective. As baseline observational data revealed, he had meal-related bouts of self-injury. These were dimin-ished when treated with antacids, and subsequently esophageal dilation. In addition, this individual benefited from functional communication training and instruction in practical skills geared to his daily living environment. Thanks to Tom Chamberlain (Fairbault Regional Center, Fairbault, MN) and Mary Piggott (InterMountain's Center for Human Development, Prescott, AZ).

which markedly reduced meal-related self-injury. Concurrently, he benefited from skills acquisition training and functional communication training, which further reduced his need to self-injure.

Eating Disorders

Eating disorders are common among people with developmental disabilities. One of the most striking is the voracious appetite seen in Prader Willi syndrome (PWS). PWS is a disability caused by deletion or inactivation of genes in the q11–13 region of chromosome 15 (Thompson, Butler, MacLean, & Joseph, 1996). People with PWS have a severe sense of being insatiably hungry. Though they are on average relatively intellectually capable (average IQ of 65), they display tantrums and aggression arising from problems associated with controlling their food intake, which often lead to placement in restrictive settings.

People with PWS never feel as though they have had enough to eat. As a result some individuals have eaten to the point that their stomachs have ruptured. Parents inevitably become involved with struggles with their children with PWS in an effort to control their food intake, and a rich lore has arisen among caregivers about "do's and don'ts" in dealing with food among people with PWS (see the *Gathered View,* the Prader Willi Syndrome Association Newsletter). One of the most commonly held views is that food should never be used as a reward in working with individuals with PWS, on the assumption that they will become obsessed and so preoccupied with access to food that they will pay little attention to the immediate learning tasks or work activities involved. While the reasons for this common perception are very understandable, we have found that it is an erroneous assumption.

Among the other striking features of individuals with PWS is their compulsive insistence on following predictable routines. They are very intolerant of changes in routine, often displaying tantrums and aggression upon any deviation from an agreed upon or expected schedule of activities. Recent studies of substantial samples of people with PWS have shown that as many as 60% to 70% of individuals with PWS meet most of the diagnostic criteria for obsessive–compulsive disorder (Dykens & Kasari, 1997), with these symptoms emerging as early as 2 or 3 years of age (Dimitropolous, Thompson, & Butler, 1998). We have found that people with PWS respond well to food as a reinforcer in learning situations as long as the conditions under which the food will be available are very clear from the outset, and there is no room for negotiating about access to food (e.g., Joseph, Overmier, & Thompson, 1997). Many support providers have difficulty being sufficiently consistent, which leads to problems in dealing with individuals who have PWS. For them, it is easier to avoid problems by precluding food from learning or daily living activities. However, using access to low-calorie, low-fat, healthful foods (e.g., natural fruit or yogurt) contingent on exercise, for example, can work very effectively if done consistently with no deviation in routine. By capitalizing on the predisposition toward regularity of routines, one can create a highly motivating activity schedule that is also behaviorally effective.

Otitis Media/Recurrent Chronic Infections

Kids get sick and act poorly. An advanced degree is not necessary to make this observation; however, the interrelation between some types of recurrent illnesses and problem behavior has largely remained within the realms of "clinical lore" and personal observations. Only recently have researchers made a clear link between some types of recurrent illnesses and increases in problem behavior. In particular, data have recently emerged about the interrelations between otitis media, a painful middle-ear infection, and problem behavior. From a theoretical perspective, some painful infections may alter the value of reinforcers present in a person's environment (i.e., they act as establishing operations). For example, a painful ear infection may reduce the value of rewards or food as positive reinforcers and increase the invidiousness of stimuli, such as requests for information or the need to complete specific tasks, that otherwise are tolerable to a person. When a person is healthy, the rewards are effective positive reinforcers and typical demands are relatively neutral events. However, when the person becomes sick, rewards become neutral and demanding situations may become aversive.

When such events are imposed upon a person, they create the potential for problem behavior to occur. In fact, this appears to be what happens. Researchers for a number of years have postulated that middle-ear infections may be related to increases in problem behavior (Carr, 1977; de Lissovoy, 1963, 1964). For example, it is often possible to trace the ontogeny of chronic head banging by a person with disabilities to the onset of recurrent bouts of otitis media. Although the specific causal interrelations between head banging and otitis media are still speculative, researchers have hypothesized that head banging originates because it reduces the pain associated with middle-ear infections (i.e., it is negatively reinforced), but that, over time and recurrent infections, the person learns to use head banging for a range of behavioral functions that are linked to the environment (e.g., escaping from demands or gaining attention).

While the exact mechanism linking otitis media and problem behavior is still under investigation, the association between the two events is becoming increasingly clear. For instance, O'Reilly (1997) studied a child with developmental disabilities and recurrent otitis media over the course of several months. Using structured observations, O'Reilly demonstrated that low rates of problem behavior occurred when the child did not have otitis media, but when the child's ear(s) became infected, rates of problem behavior increased dramatically. In fact, this general relationship tends to occur whether or not the child has a developmental disability, suggesting a more general biobehavioral process (de Lissovoy, 1964).

Interventions relating to problem behavior and otitis media are, as with other health issues, multidisciplinary in nature. If the otitis media and associated problem behavior are of recent origin, the elimination of the infection and prevention of repeat infections may be the primary focus of intervention (Liston, 1992). However, if a history of recurrent otitis media is present in conjunction with chronic problem behavior, focusing on eliminating the infection may be only a first step. Once the infections are under control, then an analysis of the functions of problem behavior across environments and development of positive behavior supports may be required to effectively reduce problem behavior.

Although otitis media has been the focus of most research on problem behavior and recurrent or chronic infections, a number of other illnesses may also warrant careful study. For example, the common cold, sore throats, sinus infections, and urinary tract infections—among many other viral or bacterial illnesses—may be associated with increases in problem behavior. Adequately documenting possible interrelations with problem behavior for each of these types of potentially chronic infections, as well as studying the biobehavioral mechanisms that affect problem behavior, is required. A primary concern at this time is the development of diagnostic strategies to easily identify infections in people with developmental disabilities who may not be able to effectively communicate via verbal behavior. It may be reasonable to suggest, from an epidemiological perspective, that infectious diseases contributing to problem behavior are currently underestimated and that closer scrutiny of possible interrelations may begin to reveal the full extent of these potential biobehavioral causes of problem behavior.

SUMMARY AND FUTURE DIRECTIONS

An appreciation of the interdependence between biomedical substrates and behavior is beginning to emerge in the assessment and intervention of problem behavior for people with mental retardation and developmental disabilities. This nascent understanding of biobehavioral issues is largely due to recent innovations in assessing the environmental causes of problem behavior. What these improved assessment strategies have revealed, however, is not only the environmental causes of problem behavior, but also instances in which an environmental account of problem behavior is incomplete. Importantly, it is becoming clearer that a substantive percentage of problem behavior cases that were previously thought to be primarily environmentally based also have physiological dimensions that need attention for an effective intervention to be developed. Currently, researchers are facing practical as well as theoretical challenges in understanding health issues as they relate to problem behavior, or other behaviors of interest.

In regard to practical issues involved in improving the field's understanding of biobehavioral issues impacting problem behavior, we note the following topics as important for improving current practices.

1. As the foundation of improving assessment and intervention practices relating to biobehavioral analyses, a greater interdisciplinary focus will be required. Medical and educational personnel have long been involved in the lives of people with disabilities, but these groups have largely worked independently of each other. In part this is because of the different foci that medical and educational practitioners have in regard to people with disabilities—physicians and nurses focus on physiological issues, whereas

teachers and psychologists focus on behavior and learning. However, by its nature, biobehavioral issues relating to problem behavior incorporate these varied areas of expertise. Strategies for forging greater collaboration among the medical and educational communities, such as facilitating the role of nurse practitioners in public schools and increasing the integration of personnel preparation for medical and educational practitioners, may serve as starting points.

2. An underlying issue regarding health concerns and problem behavior is the extent to which biological issues have not been adequately assessed and diagnosed in the past. Although assessment strategies have routinely called for the assessment of "medical issues" prior to psychological assessment, in both practice and research this recommendation has not been effectively followed. In part the field's current limitations in assessing health issues are due to the fact that psychologists and educators are often the individuals who conducted assessments of problem behavior (and who are not explicitly trained in medical issues). It may also be due to the limitations of people with severe disabilities in communicating, or to professionals' limitations in understanding, possible health complaints. Improved methods of assessing possible biobehavioral interactions is an important area for further development.

3. With improved assessment practices, the development of strategies to effectively integrate interventions focusing on physiological variables and environmentally based tactics will be required. Current approaches to positive behavioral support may need to be more interdisciplinary not only in assessment, but also in the development of interventions and the monitoring of behavioral outcomes. If the interplay between biological and behavioral variables is as dynamic as our current understanding of their interrelations suggests, interventions will require the involvement of more than educational personnel to be successful.

4. Continued research innovations will assist in the development of the previous three recommendations. The majority of research on biobehavioral issues and problem behavior has, at best, treated biological influences as epiphenomena. Often, only when environmentally based assessments prove inconclusive are further investigations of biobehavioral issues instigated. However, this relationship, perhaps by the weight of empirical evidence, is beginning to change. An improved understanding of the complex interrelations between biology and psychology will require increased research attention that specifically targets these issues as interdependent variables.

In regard to theoretical issues involved in improving the field's understanding of health concerns impacting problem behavior, the following issues may be relevant to future research and development efforts.

1. The functional relations that emerge from biobehavioral analyses seem to entail a dynamic interaction between biomedical conditions and behavior. In many cases what may result from combining variables may be greater than the sum of the parts. It could be argued that future research on biobehavioral issues will focus on the interaction effects that are produced by linking physiology and behavior. However, unlike

previous conceptualizations of interaction effects, these complex functional relations may need to be viewed as important experimental effects in and of themselves, and not by-products of improperly designed experiments. Such a perspective would suggest that increased sophistication in designing research investigations will be required to adequately analyze the kinetic structures inherent in biobehavioral functions.

2. How are the interrelations between biology and behavior going to be conceptualized? At present neither psychological nor medical theories appear adequate to incorporate this range of variables being investigated. A complete accounting of biology and behavior may require a synthesis of theoretical disciplines. Currently, behavior analysis is demonstratively the most effective system in accounting for behavior–environment relations—the hallmark of research, to date, relating to the problem behavior of people with disabilities. However, because of its environmental focus, behavior analysis only broadly incorporates biological variables into an overall accounting of psychological phenomena (e.g., via establishing operations). What may be needed is a link between behavior analysts and researchers who focus on the physiological causes of behavior to provide the necessary consilience. If this proposition is accurate, then future research on biobehavioral issues may occasion an increased integration of basic neuroscience and behavior analysis. Such a collaboration appears to be able to account for biological and behavioral phenomena without the need for additional extraneous and untested variables (e.g., mentalistic theories).

3. A final theoretical issue that may be of interest to researchers studying biobehavioral issues is the role of *private events*. Often the physiological events under study in a biobehavioral analysis occur within a person, but are functionally related to changes in his or her behavior. Such stimuli appear to fall within the operant framework of private events (e.g., Thompson, 1998). However, current conceptualizations of problem behavior have not explicated a clear role for private events in determining behavior. Perhaps one reason for this is the issue of measurement. Because private events, by their nature, occur inside an individual, their identification, measurement, and manipulation provide for a number of logistical difficulties. However, work in behavioral pharmacology may provide both conceptual and tactical guidance to researchers interested in biobehavioral issues and problem behavior.

As researchers and practitioners continue to work toward a better understanding of health conditions impacting problem behavior, an increased integration between medicine and education appears inevitable. Such an integration should have numerous practical benefits for people with disabilities and others in their lives. However, it is interesting to speculate that the practical benefits that arise from biobehavioral analyses for people with disabilities may extend to the population in general. Research, for example, that improves our basic and applied understanding of eating disorders or sleep deprivation, should apply to any individual, regardless of his or her "label," who is experiencing the particular condition. In addition, the integration of medical and educational knowledge should occasion theoretical discussions on issues that may not have previously been considered by researchers in problem behavior and developmental disabilities (e.g., the role of private events in the cause of behavior). The focus on health conditions and problem behavior is beginning to bear tangible fruit. Perhaps, the biobehavioral analysis of problem behavior is beginning to emerge from its long dormant state as a promising area for future development, into an exciting area of basic and applied research that spans conventional disciplinary boundaries. If this is indeed the case, then people with and without disabilities stand to benefit substantially from the findings that may result from this exciting area of research.

REFERENCES

Bohmer, C. J. M. (1996). *Gastro-oesophageal reflux disease in intellectually disabled individuals*. Amsterdam: VU University Press.

Bohmer, C. J., Niezen-de Boer, M. C., Klinkenberc-Knol, E. C., Tuynman, H. A., Voskuil, J. H., Deville, W. L., & Meuwissen, S. G. (1997). Gastroesophageal reflux disease in intellectually disabled individuals: Leads for diagnosis and the effect of omeprazole therapy. *American Journal of Gastroenterology, 92*, 1475–1479.

Carr, E. G. (1977). The motivation of self-injurious behavior: A review of some hypotheses. *Psychological Bulletin, 84*, 800–816.

Carr, E. G., & Durand, V. M. (1985). Reducing behavior problems through functional communication training. *Journal of Applied Behavior Analysis, 18*, 111–126.

Carr, E. G., Reeve, C. E., & Magito-McLaughlin, D. (1996). Contextual influences on problem behavior in people with developmental disabilities. In L. K. Koegel, R. L. Koegel, & G. Dunlap (Eds.), *Positive behavioral support: Including people with difficult behavior in the community* (pp. 403–424). Baltimore: Brookes.

Carr, E. G., & Smith, C. E. (1995). Biological setting events for self-injury. *Mental Retardation and Developmental Disabilities Reviews, 1*, 94–98.

Cataldo, M. F., & Harris, J. (1982). The biological basis of self-injury in the mentally retarded. *Analysis and Intervention in Developmental Disabilities, 7*, 21–39.

Clements, J., Wing, L., & Dunn, G. (1986). Sleep problems in handicapped children: A preliminary study. *Journal of Child Psychology and Psychiatry, 21*, 399–407.

de Lissovoy, V. (1963). Head banging in early childhood: A suggested cause. *Journal of Genetic Psychology, 102*, 109–114.

de Lissovoy, V. (1964). Head banging in early childhood: Review of empirical studies. *Pediatric Digest, 6*, 49–55.

Derby, K. M., Wacker, D. P., Sasso, G. M., Steege, M., Northup, J., Cigrand, K., & Asmus, J. (1992). Brief functional assessment techniques to evaluate aberrant behavior in an outpatient setting: A summary of 79 cases. *Journal of Applied Behavior Analysis, 25*, 713–722.

Dimitropolous, A., Thompson, T., & Butler, M. (1998, March). *Temperament and compulsive behavior in children with Prader Willi syndrome*. Paper presented at the 31st Gatlinburg Conference on Research and Theory in Mental Retardation and Developmental Disabilities, Charleston, SC.

Durand, V. M. (1997). *Sleep better! A practical guide for dealing with sleep problems*. Baltimore: Brookes.

Dykens, E. M., & Kasari, C. (1997). Maladaptive behavior in children with Prader-Willi syndrome, Down syndrome, and nonspecific mental retardation. *American Journal of Mental Retardation, 102*, 228–237.

Hodapp, R. M., & Dykens, E. M. (1994). Mental retardation's two cultures of behavioral research. *American Journal on Mental Retardation, 98*, 675–687.

Horner, R. H., Day, H. M., & Day, J. R. (1997). Using neutralizing routines to reduce problem behaviors. *Journal of Applied Behavior Analysis, 30*, 601–614.

Joseph, B., Overmier, J. B., & Thompson, T. (1997). Food- and nonfood-related differential outcomes in equivalence learning by adults with Prader Willi syndrome. *American Journal on Mental Retardation, 101*, 374–386.

Jouvet, M. (1969). Biogenic amines and the states of sleep. *Science, 163*, 32–41.

Kennedy, C. H., & Itkonen, T. (1993). Effects of setting events on the problem behavior of students with severe disabilities. *Journal of Applied Behavior Analysis, 26*, 321–327.

Kennedy, C. H., & Meyer, K. A. (1996). Sleep deprivation, allergy symptoms, and negatively reinforced problem behavior. *Journal of Applied Behavior Analysis, 29*, 133–135.

Kennedy, C. H., & Meyer, K. A. (1998). Establishing operations and the motivation of problem behavior. In J. Luselli & M. Cameron (Eds.), *Antecedent control: Innovative approaches to behavioral support*. Baltimore: Brookes.

Kennedy, C. H., Meyer, K. A., Werts, M. G., & Cushing, L. S. (in press). Effects of sleep deprivation on free-operant avoidance responding. *Journal of the Experimental Analysis of Behavior*.

Kerr, M. P. (1997). Primary health care for people with an intellectual disability. *Journal of Intellectual Disability Research, 41*, 363–364.

Lachman, R., Funamura, J., & Szalay, G. (1981). Gastrointestinal abnormalities in the Cornelia de Lange syndrome. *Mount Sinai Journal of Medicine, 48*, 236–240.

Lask, B. (1997). Sleep disorders. *Journal of the American Academy of Child and Adolescent Psychiatry, 36*, 1161.

Liston, T. E. (1992). Prevention of recurrent otitis media. *Journal of Pediatric Infectious Diseases, 11*, 897–899.

Michael, J. L. (1982). Distinguishing between discriminative and motivational functions of stimuli. *Journal of the Experimental Analysis of Behavior, 37*, 149–155.

O'Reilly, M. F. (1995). Functional analysis and treatment of escape-maintained aggression correlated with sleep deprivation. *Journal of Applied Behavior Analysis, 28*, 225–226.

O'Reilly, M. F. (1997). Functional analysis of episodic self-injury correlated with recurrent otitis media. *Journal of Applied Behavior Analysis, 30*, 165–167.

Peine, H. A., Darvish, R., Blakelock, H., Osborne, J. G., & Jenson, W. R. (1995). Medical problems, maladaptive behaviors, and the developmentally disabled. *Behavioral Interventions, 10*, 149–159.

Peterson, W. H., Skinner, J. T., & Strong, F. M. (1995). *Elements of food biochemistry*. Englewood Cliffs, NJ: Prentice-Hall.

Proujansky, R., Shaffer, S. E., Vinton, N. E., & Bachrach, S. J. (1994). Symptomatic Helicobacter pylori infection in young patients with severe neurologic impairment. *Journal of Pediatrics, 125*(5 Pt. 1), 750–752.

Pyles, D. A. M., & Bailey, J. S. (1990). Diagnosing severe behavior problems. In A. C. Repp & N. N. Singh (Eds.), *Perspectives on the use of nonaversive and aversive interventions for persons with developmental disabilities* (pp. 381–401). Sycamore, IL: Sycamore Publishing.

Rapin, I., & Katzman, R. (1998). Neurobiology of autism. *Annals of Neurology, 43*, 7–14.

Reiss, S., Levitan, G. W., & Szysko, J. (1982). Emotional disturbance and mental retardation: Diagnostic overshadowing. *American Journal on Mental Deficiency, 86*, 567–574.

Rosenbach, Y., Zahavi, I., & Dinari, G. (1992). Gastroesophageal dysfunction in Brachmann–de Lange syndrome. *American Journal of Medical Genetics, 42*, 379–380.

Singh, N. N., Ellis, C. R., & Weschler, H. (1997). Psychopharmacoepidemiology of mental retardation. *Journal of Child and Adolescent Psychopharmacology, 7*, 255–266.

Somrner, A. (1993). Occurrence of the Sandifer complex in the Brachmann–de Lange syndrome. *American Journal of Medical Genetics, 47*, 1026–1028.

Sontag, S. (1978). *Illness as metaphor*. New York: Farrar, Straus and Giroux.

Symons, F. J., Davis, M. L., & Thompson, T. (in press). Self-injurious behavior and sleep disturbance in adults with developmental disabilities. *Research in Developmental Disabilities*.

Thompson, T. (1998, May). *Forces beyond our control: Behavioral and neurochemical mechanisms in self injury.* Academy on Mental Retardation Career Scientist Award Acceptance Address, San Diego, CA.

Thompson, T., Butler, M. G., MacLean, W. E., & Joseph, B. (1996). Prader Willi syndrome: Genetics and behavior. *Peabody Journal of Education, 7,* 187–212.

van Schrojenstein , E. L., Lantman-de Valk, H. M., Metsemakers, J. F., Soomers-Turlings, M. J., Haveman, M. J., & Crebolder, H. F. (1997). People with intellectual disability in general practice: Case definition and case finding. *Journal of Intellectual Disability Research, 41,* 373–379.

Issues in Medicine and Health

Genetics and Gene Therapies

Hugo W. Moser

Mental retardation in the 21st century will differ profoundly from the 20th. In respect to genetics we will know the cause of all of the thousands of genetically determined disorders that may be associated with mental retardation. Therapies will become available for a substantial proportion. In addition to gene replacement therapy, a variety of other approaches will also be found. Strategies for prevention will be improved and become available throughout the world. The artificial distinction between nature and nurture will finally be laid to rest. Nevertheless, challenges will continue to abound, and the wisdom and outreach of The Arc of the United States will be needed sorely. In the specific domain of genetics, these challenges include the following.

1. Identification of the gene abnormality that causes a specific disorder is the beginning rather than the end. In most instances, the mechanisms through which gene abnormalities damage the nervous system and cause mental retardation are not understood. Down syndrome, in which the gene abnormality has been known for nearly half a century, is an example of this. Continued research is needed to define these mechanisms, and solutions are likely in view of the astounding recent advances in genetics, neuroscience, and neuroimaging. Once the disability-causing mechanisms are defined, specific therapies can be developed.

2. Replacement of defective genes is a major task. "Vectors" that carry the gene to the appropriate cell, and do so safely and for long periods of time, are still far from perfected (Kay, Liu, & Hoogebrugge, 1997), and the genetic research community recognizes the harm that has been done by premature promises (Verma & Somia, 1997). Nevertheless, it is likely that these problems will be overcome relatively early in the 21st century. In addition, a variety of promising approaches other than gene replacement, which may prove safer and less expensive, will become available.

3. Therapies are expensive. While in the aggregate the genetic disorders associated with mental retardation make up a substantial number, this aggregate comprises thousands of distinct disorders. Many of these disorders are infrequent, yet each represents

a challenge in respect to the understanding of the disease mechanism and the development of therapeutic agents. Although some common features exist that permit some economy of scale, the development of a diagnostic assay and of therapeutic agents for a disorder that affects a few hundred persons may be as challenging and expensive as finding a cure for breast cancer. Although it is not reasonable to exclude the frequency of a condition as a criterion for resource assignment, the 1983 Orphan Drug Act and the efforts of groups such as the National Organization of Rare Disorders have "leveled the playing field" somewhat by providing some financial incentives for attention to rare disorders. National and international efforts, in which The Arc can play a major role, will continue to be needed in the 21st century.

4. Although identification of causative genes and the potential of early interventions provide exciting new opportunities for the prevention of mental retardation, ethical issues abound. I anticipate that in the 21st century it will become possible to identify all persons who are at risk of having children affected with a genetic disorder associated with mental retardation. This capacity provides enormous potential for the prevention of mental retardation. My own experience with one disorder (X-linked adrenoleukodystrophy), in which this capacity has been achieved during the last 5 years, has made me aware of the challenge of implementing this capacity constructively. I am pleased that The Arc has already taken a leadership role in resolving these issues by launching an education program on genetics issues in mental retardation, which addresses the issues of genetic screening, gene therapy, and the Human Genome Project.

THE CAUSES OF MENTAL RETARDATION

I anticipate that in the 21st century, it will be possible to identify the cause of mental retardation in every person. Determination of the causes of mental retardation has been my personal interest since 1963. Prior to that time my training and experience had been in medicine, neurology, and biochemistry, without significant exposure to mental retardation. This changed radically with my appointment in that year as director of research at the Walter E. Fernald State School (for persons with mental retardation) in Waltham, Massachusetts. In part this appointment was a consequence of the Mental Retardation Facilities and Community Mental Health Centers Construction Act of 1963 (P.L. 88-164), under which the Kennedy administration created a national program of University Affiliated Centers for Persons with Mental Retardation (later changed to Developmental Disabilities) and Centers for Research on Mental Retardation and Developmental Disabilities. This led to an affiliation agreement between the State School and the Massachusetts General Hospital and Harvard Medical School, and the creation of the Eunice Kennedy Shriver Center, directed by my mentor Dr. Raymond D. Adams. My experiences at the state school soon alerted me to the role of behavioral science, mainly through contacts with Dr. Murray Sidman. In addition, there was the fortunate and fortuitous circumstance that Dr. Gunnar Dybwad had joined Brandeis University, only 15 minutes away from the State School. Dr. Dybwad taught me more about mental retardation than anyone else. His advocacy for persons with mental retardation and his immense role in the successful development of community placements is recognized and honored worldwide.

The "Two Group" Approach to Mental Retardation

My experiences in the State School, combined with my background in the biological sciences, led me to value the concept of the "two group" approach to mental retardation emphasized by Zigler (1967) (see Table 13.1). The larger "physiological" group includes individuals with IQs of 50 to 70 and represents a group in which there is no demonstrable brain pathology and sociocultural and environmental factors play a major role. The smaller "pathological" group includes individuals with IQs of 50 or below and in whom various biochemical or brain structure abnormalities are present. It is obvious that this is a "broad-brush" distinction. There are many persons with organic pathology, such as partially treated phenylketonuria, whose IQs are in the 50 to 70 range. Under the modification of the definition of mental retardation adopted by the American Association on Mental Retardation in 1992, many persons in the physiological category are no longer assigned to the mental retardation category. Although I welcome the fact that the 1992 definition removes the stigma that the mental retardation designation may impose, I believe that the earlier definition (which includes most persons with an IQ more than two standard deviations below the mean) should be retained for epidemiological and etiological studies.

TABLE 13.1
Two Groups of Individuals with Mental Retardation

Characteristic	Group I (Physiological, Subcultural, Culturo-familial, Familial)	Group II (Organic Pathological)
Estimated incidence	20–30 per 1,000	3 per 1,000
Most frequent IQ score	50–70	Less than 50
Most common age of ascertainment	During school years	Preschool
Apparent age of prevalence	Apparently diminishes after school years	No change
Demonstrable brain abnormality	No	Yes
Relationship to socioeconomic status	More common among socio-economically deprived or disrupted families	None or slight

Note. From "Mental Retardation," by H. W. Moser in *The Horizons of Health* (p. 143), by H. Wechsler and G. F. Cahill (Eds.), 1977, Cambridge, MA: Harvard University Press. Copyright 1977 by the President and Fellows of Harvard College. Reprinted with permission.

Earlier Data About Etiology of Mental Retardation

Etiological surveys of mental retardation are hampered by the fact that few meet the requirement of detailed individual etiological analysis in a population that is representative of the general population. Most surveys of large populations do not include the detailed investigations needed for accurate diagnosis, whereas most surveys that do provide these details do not deal with a representative population. The surveys that meet both these requirements most effectively are those of Hagberg and Kyllerman (1983). Table 13.2 summarizes their key results. It shows that genetic abnormalities are the most common cause of severe mental retardation (IQ <50), whereas in the mild mental retardation group (IQ 50–70), the cause of mental retardation was "untraceable" in 55%. The untraceable group includes persons with metabolic or structural brain defects that were not detectable by currently used techniques, as well as persons in whom the mental retardation is attributable to sociocultural or environmental factors. Because sociocultural conditions in Sweden are generally favorable, it is likely that these factors play a more important role in many other countries. Table 13.3 presents an analysis of the relative frequency of various genetic conditions associated with mental retardation (Moser, 1995).

Technological Advances That Promise Definition of All Causes of Mental Retardation

The following technological advances have been achieved during the last decades of the 20th century, and are surely to be enhanced in the 21st.

1. *Refined biochemical and enzymatic assays* which permit precise diagnosis of more than 200 genetic disorders associated with mental retardation. In almost all instances, these techniques are noninvasive since they can be applied to samples of urine or small amounts of blood. One example, the "Guthrie blood spots," which are collected on filter paper, has had a major effect on public health through newborn screening programs for conditions such as phenylketonuria and hypothyroidism. The Arc, aided by the foresight of Gunnar Dybwad, played a significant role in the initiation of these screening programs.

2. *Advances in neuroimaging.* Magnetic resonance imaging can provide a detailed and quantifiable image of brain structure, again in a noninvasive manner, and without exposure to radiation. Even more exciting and astounding is the neuroimaging of human brain function (Posner & Raichle, 1998). These techniques permit delineation of the location, timing, and interaction of processes involved in reading, hearing, cognitive processes, and learning.

3. *Advances in neuroscience.* The systems required for nerve impulse transmission and nerve cell interaction have been defined. The nerve cell impulse is carried by a single axon; in addition, each nerve cell has multiple other processes referred to as dendrites, which have small excrescences referred to as spines, through which a nerve

TABLE 13.2
Causes of Mental Retardation (MR) in Sweden

Cause	Severe MR		Mild MR	
Genetic	46		15	
Chromosomal		(29)		(4)
Mutant Genes		(5)		(1)
Multiple Anomaly Syndromes		(12)		(10)
Prenatal Acquired	8		8	
Alcohol		(0)		(8)
Infection		(7)		(0)
Other		(1)		(0)
Perinatal	15		18	
Postnatal	11		2	
Psychosis	1		2	
Untraceable	18		55	

Note. Adapted from "Mild Mental Retardation in Swedish School Children," by B. Hagberg, G. Hagberg, A. Lewerth, and U. Lindberg, *Acta Pediatrica Scandinavica, 70,* p. 446.

cell interacts with other nerve cells. Recently developed electron-microscope techniques permit the visualization of these spines. One nerve cell may have as many as 10,000 spines. Interaction between nerve cells and the process of learning involves a mechanism referred to as long-term potentiation. Technically, the term is used to describe the "long-term enhancement in synaptic strength after a brief high-frequency stimulation" (Teyler & DiScenna, 1984). It is of overriding importance to the field of mental retardation since it forms the basis of memory and learning (Harum & Johnston, 1998; Singer, 1995). Synapses in networks that fire together repeatedly "learn" to have a lower threshold for firing and therefore are more likely to be activated. Long-term potentiation is the basis of neuronal plasticity. During infancy and childhood, dendritic spines and nerve cell synapses are "pruned": Connections that are not used are disassembled while those that are used are retained and expanded. This is one of the mechanisms through which experience and early stimulation can alter brain structure, and thus is highly relevant to mental retardation associated with environmental deprivation. Dendritic abnormalities have been demonstrated in many of the disorders associated with severe mental retardation, such as Down syndrome, Rett syndrome (Armstrong, 1997), and the fragile-X syndrome. In these syndromes, specific genetic defects may limit stimulation-induced synaptic plasticity.

4. Last, but clearly not least, the *U.S. Human Genome Project* (F. G. D. Collins, 1995), which is part of an international effort to develop genetic and physical maps and determine the DNA sequence of the human genome by the year 2005. While this massive effort is in progress, it has already led to the identification of genes relevant to

(*Text continues on page 242*)

TABLE 13.3
Genetic Disorders Associated with Mental Retardation with an Estimated Incidence in Excess of 1:100,000

Diagnosis	Category	Genetics	Incid Gen/1000	Incid Spe/1000	MR Fre	MR Sev	Gene Map	Gen Clon	Therapy
Down syndrome	chromosomal	chromosomal	1.30		4	2-4	21		
Klinefelter syndrome	chromosomal	chromosomal	0.8	1.7 male	1	1			
Fragile X	triplet repeat	triplet repeat	0.60	0.80 male	4	3	Xq27		
Chromosome X, triplo-X	chromosomal		0.4		2	2			
Neurofibromatosis	malformation	autos dom	0.33		2	2	17q11.2	yes	
Hypothyroidism congenital	thyroid	various	0.25		4	4		yes	yes
Acyl-CoA dehydrogenese def medium chain	fatty acid	autos rec	0.17		2	1		yes	yes
Duchenna muscular dystrophy	metabolic	X-rec	0.15	0.3 male	2	2	Xp21.2	yes	
Edwards syndrome, trisomy 15	chromosomal		0.15		4	4	18		
Patau syndrome, trisomy 13	chromosomal		0.125		4	4	13		
Tuberous sclerosis	malformation	autos dom	0.1		2	2	9q33-q34		
Williams syndrome	malformation	uncertain	0.1		4	2	4q33-qter		
Hartnup disease	amino acid	autos rec	0.068		1	1		yes	
Phenylketonuria	amino acid	autos rec	0.067		4	4	12q22-q24.2	yes	yes
Prader-Willi syndrome	chromosomal		0.067		3	3	15q11-q12		
Kallman syndrome	malformation	X-rec?	0.06	0.1 male	1	1	Xq22.32		
Cri du chat syndrome	chromosomal		0.05		4	4			
Myotonic dystrophy	triplet repeat	autos dom	0.05		2	2	19q13.2-q13.3	yes	
Adrenoleukodystrophy	peroxisomal	X-rec	0.04		2	2	Xq28	yes	?yes
Ceroid lipofuscinosis	lipidosis	autos rec	0.04		4	4	16q22	yes	
Sanfilippo syndrome	mucoploysaccharidosis	autos rec	0.04		4	4	12q14		
Zellweger syndrome + neonatal ALD + infantila Refaum	peroxisomal	autos rec	0.04		4	4			
Rett syndrome	uncertain	?x-dom	0.033	0.066 female	4	4			

Diagnosis	Category	Genetics	Incid Gen/1000	Incid Spe/1000	MR Fre	MR Sev	Gene Map	Gen Clon	Therapy
Biotinidase deficiency	vitamin	autos rec	0.03		4	4			yes
Ornithine transcarbamylase deficiency	amino acid	X-dom	0.03		4	3	Xp21.1	yes	?yes
Rubinstein-Tayt broad thumb-Hallux	malformation		0.03		4	4	16p13.3		no
De Lange syndrome	malformation		0.025		4	4			
Metachromatic leukodystrophy	lysosomal	autos rec	0.025		3	3	22q13.31 qter	yes	?yes
Smith Lemli Opitz	sterol	autos rec	0.025		4	4			
Ataxia telangiectasia	immunodeficiency	autos rec	0.02		1	1	11q22-q23		
Gaucher disease	lysosomal	autos rec	0.02	1.6 (Jewish)	1	1	1q21-31	yes	yes
Chromosome 13, monosomy 13	chromosomal		0.017		4	4	13		
Galactosemia	carbohydrate	autos rec	0.017		4	3	9p13	yes	yes
Carbamyl phosphate synthetase defic	amino acid	autos rec	0.01		4	4			?yes
Hunter syndrome	mucoploysaccharidosis	X-rec	0.01		3	3	Xq27.3-28	yes	?yes
Hurler syndrome	mucoploysaccharidosis	autos rec	0.01		4	3	22pter-11	yes	yes

Abbreviations: autos = autosomal; rec = recessive; dom = dominant; incid = incidence; gen = general; spe = special; clon = cloned; fre = frequency; sec = severity. The numbers in the MR fre and MR sev columns indicate degrees of involvement with 1 the least and 4 the most. From "A Role for Gene Therapy in Mental Retardation," by H. W. Moser, 1995, *Mental Retardation and Developmental Disabilities Research Reviews, 1,* p. 6. Copyright 1995 by Wiley-Liss, a division of John Wiley & Sons. Reprinted with permission.

mental retardation by facilitation of the technique of positional cloning (F. S. Collins, 1995) (see Figure 13.1). These disorders include Huntington's disease and the fragile-X syndrome. Upon the completion of the Human Genome Project, this is likely to be extended to all genetic disorders associated with mental retardation.

Examples of Recent Advances

The Smith-Lemli-Opitz syndrome is a disorder that causes mental retardation associated with multiple anomalies, including small head size, characteristic facial appearance, limb abnormalities, endocrine disturbances, cataracts, and heart and kidney

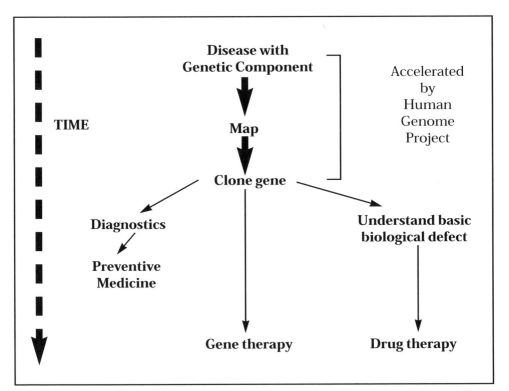

FIGURE 13.1. Progress in molecular medicine. The time needed to clone a disease gene has been rapidly shrinking, based on maps and technologies emanating from the Human Genome Project. Improved diagnostic capabilities often result relatively quickly from gene discovery. In some instances, this allows powerful preventive medicine strategies to be initiated (e.g., colonoscopy for individuals at high risk for colon cancer). The timetable for development of effective gene therapies is much less predictable. From "Positional Cloning Moves from Perditional to Traditional," by F. S. Collins, 1995, *Nature Genetics*, 9, p. 349. Copyright 1995 by *Nature Genetics*. Reprinted with permission.

malformations. Its incidence is 1:20,000 to 1:40,000. The mode of inheritance is autosomal recessive. In 1994 Tint and colleagues showed that it is caused by a defect in cholesterol metabolism. The defect involves the last step in the synthesis of cholesterol, and leads to a deficiency of cholesterol and the accumulation of its precursor 7-dehydrocholesterol, which differs from cholesterol only in that it has a double bond in the 7 position of the molecule. The usual analytical techniques do not separate cholesterol from this precursor, so that cholesterol measurements that had been performed many times in the past did not detect this abnormality. It was only through the use of recently developed chromatographic techniques that this key alteration was identified. Even though 7-dehydrocholesterol closely resembles cholesterol, the slight structural difference has profound biological effects and leads to major abnormalities in the brain and multiple organs. Noninvasive diagnostic tests are now readily available, the carrier state can be identified, and prenatal diagnosis is possible. The oral administration of cholesterol to patients with Smith-Lemli-Opitz syndrome has beneficial effects (Irons et al., 1997), counter to the valid current advice that most people should reduce their cholesterol intake. Until 1994 the Smith-Lemli-Opitz syndrome was a mysterious disorder that could not be treated or prevented. Unequivocal diagnosis and prevention through genetic counseling are now readily available. While postnatal therapy with cholesterol is of some benefit, it cannot reverse the organ malformations that occur prenatally, and additional research is needed to develop a fully effective therapy.

A totally unexpected finding has been that a dozen human neurogenetic disorders are caused by the expansion of repeated sequences of three nucleotides (Paulson & Fishbeck, 1997). Several of these disorders, namely the fragile-X syndrome, myotonic dystrophy, Huntington disease, and the spinocerebellar ataxias, are relevant to mental retardation. The effect is dominant, only one of the two alleles of the gene are needed to produce the full pathology, and the degree of pathology is proportional to the length of the expanded repeat unit. In eight of these disorders the triple repeat consists of the sequence CAG, which codes for the amino acid glutamine and creates a protein that contains an abnormally large number of glutamine residues. The mechanism through which the excess of CAG repeats leads to the neurologic deficit in the fragile-X syndrome is beginning to be defined. Their accumulation leads to the failure of formation of a protein, now referred to as FMRP (fragile-X mental retardation protein) (Eberhart, Malter, Feng, & Warren, 1996). The physiological role of FMRP is not yet understood. It is located in the nucleus of the cell and involved in the export of mRNA particles from the nucleus. More complete understanding of its role may make it possible to develop means to administer FMRP or to find other ways to substitute for its function.

THERAPY OF GENETIC DISORDERS ASSOCIATED WITH MENTAL RETARDATION

In a survey that I presented in 1992, I identified 65 genetically determined metabolic disorders in which various forms of therapy are available (Moser, 1992). The strategies include the reduction of substances to which the patient is genetically vulnerable (phenylketonuria), replacement of missing metabolites (hypothyroidism), the removal of toxic substances (copper in Wilson disease), enzyme replacement (Gaucher disease), and organ transplants (bone marrow transplantation for mucopolysaccharidoses, and certain leukodystrophies). Some of these measures, such as the dietary therapy of phenylketonuria and thyroid hormone replacement therapy for hypothyroidism, are highly successful. New therapies continue to evolve, such as creatine therapy for Guanidinoacetate methyltransferase deficiency (Stockler et al., 1994). The latter disorder is of particular interest and has implications for the future. Patients with this disorder show developmental delay, hypotonia, and ataxia. Magnetic resonance imaging and spectroscopy studies were performed as part of a systematic investigation to determine etiology. It was a surprise when magnetic resonance spectroscopy studies of the brain revealed an absence of creatine, one of the key substances in intermediary metabolism, and crucially important in the energy production cycles. The striking finding in this neuroimaging study then led to metabolic and genetic investigations which defined the enzymatic defect, and proved that it was a genetically determined disorder. Oral administration of creatine, a substance that is readily available and inexpensive, caused significant neurological and cognitive improvement in a 22-month-old boy.

This experience and others, such as the improvement following removal of copper in adolescents or adults with Wilson disease, indicate that the nervous system is capable of considerable restoration of function when there is precise knowledge of the pathogenetic mechanism and a therapy that corrects the key abnormality. Since the capacity to identify specific disorders and their disease mechanisms is increasing rapidly, it is certain that additional therapies of this type will be developed in the 21st century. It is my hope that therapies of this type will become available for up to half of the metabolic disorders associated with mental retardation.

GENE THERAPY

Gene therapy has attracted hope and excitement, which at this time exceeds reality and has caused the scientific community to express a cautionary note (Verma & Somia, 1997). Table 13.4 lists the approved gene therapy trials that are under way currently in the United States (Anderson, 1998). Only a very limited number are relevant to mental retardation. These consist of three protocols for Gaucher disease, two for Canavan disease, and one each for ornithine transcarbamylase deficiency and the Hunter syndrome. This paucity is attributable to the relative inaccessibility of the nervous system, and the fact that the disorders associated with mental retardation are relatively infrequent and do not command the same degree of attention as cancer and AIDS. The strong representation of cystic fibrosis is due to the importance of the problem, the accessibility of the main site of pathology (the lungs), and the efforts of an active advocacy group.

TABLE 13.4
Disease Targets and Gene Therapy Protocols

	Number	Percentage of Total
(a) Types of gene therapy clinical protocols *		
Therapy	200	(86%)
Marker	30	(13%)
Non-theraputic**	2	(1%)
Total	232	(100%)
(b) Disease targets for therapeutic gene therapy clinical protocols		
Cancer	138	(69%)
Genetic diseases	33	(16.5%)
Cystic fibrosis	16	
Other***	17	
AIDS	23	(11.5%)
Other****	6	(3%)
Total	200	(100%)

*Roughly 60% of all protocols use retroviral vectors, 20% use nonviral delivery systems, 10% use adenoviral vectors, and the remainder use other viral vectors.

**A "non-therapeutic" protocol means a non-therapeutic portion of a non-gene-therapy clinical protocol.

***These 17 include 12 other monogenic diseases.

****The five "other" are: peripheral artery disease, rheumatoid arthritis, arterial restenosis, cubital tunnel syndrome, and coronary artery disease.

From "Human Gene Therapy," by W. F. Anderson, 1996, *Nature, 392*(Suppl.), p. 28. Copyright 1998 by Macmillan Magazines Limited. Reproduced with permission.

A serious limiting factor for gene therapy is the lack of effective vectors, the vehicles into which the desired gene is incorporated and targeted to the desired cells. Table 13.5 lists the vectors that are currently in use. Most are viruses. The retroviruses are used in 60% of current protocols. They have the advantage of being safe, but the disadvantage of being able to introduce the gene only into cells that are dividing. Human nerve cells no longer divide at the age at which gene therapy might be considered. Adenovirus is an efficient transfer vehicle, but may be toxic to the host and cause an immunological response that destroys the cells carrying the desired gene. The more recently introduced adeno-associated virus is promising since it is an efficient transfer agent and it is safe, but is limited by the fact that it can incorporate only small genes. The nonviral agents have a very low capacity to transfer genes to the nucleus. Work is in progress throughout the world to develop safe and effective vectors that will yield long-lasting incorporation of the gene into the appropriate tissues and cells. It is likely that these goals will be achieved some time in the 21st century.

TABLE 13.5
Gene Transfer Vehicles

Vector	Advantages	Disadvantages
Viral		
Retrovirus	Integration into host DNA All viral genes removed Relatively safe	Semi-random integration Transduction required cell division Relatively low titer
Adenovirus	Higher titer Efficient transduction of non-dividing cells *in vitro* and *in vivo*	Toxicity Immunological response Prior exposure
Adeno-associated virus	All viral genes removed Safe Transduction of nondividing cells Stable expression	Small genome limits size of foreign DNA Labor-intensive production Status of genome not fully elucidated
Nonviral		
Liposomes	Absence of viral components Lack of previous immune recognition	Inefficient gene transfer into the nucleus Lack of perisistence of DNA Lack of tissue targeting

Note. From "Gene Therapy," by M. A. Kay, D. Liu, and A. Hoogebrugge, 1997, *Proceedings of the National Academy of Sciences USA, 94,* p. 12745. Copyright 1997 by the National Academy of Sciences. Reproduced with permission.

Gene therapy for disorders that affect the nervous system is hampered further by the inaccessibility of this tissue (Karpati, Lochmüller, Nalbantoglu, & Durham, 1996), and the appropriate hesitancy to inject materials directly into the nervous system. In the future it will become possible to bypass these limitations in several ways. For some disorders, such as the urea cycle disorders, the nervous system pathology is a consequence of impaired liver function, so that gene therapy targeted to the liver may also correct the nervous system defect. This approach has been successful in an animal model of ornithine transcarbamylase deficiency (Xuehai et al., 1997), and is now undergoing phase 1 human trial. Ex-vivo gene therapy directed toward bone marrow cells, a procedure in which the desired gene is introduced into bone marrow cells by incubating them outside the body, and then reintroducing them into the patient, shows promise for those nervous system disorders that benefit from bone marrow transplantation (certain of the mucopolysaccharidoses and leukodystrophies). An exciting potential exists for a procedure in which the gene is introduced into nervous system progenitor cells. In studies of animal models of human disease, these cells have shown remarkable properties. When injected into the cerebrospinal fluid of young animals, they have seeded into many parts of the nervous system and matured into a variety of cell types, such as neurons and myelin-producing cells, and thus correct the gene defects in many parts of the nervous system (Snyder & Flax, 1995). Stereotactic techniques are being developed for the safe injection of genes into specific brain regions, such as the striatum of patients with Parkinson disease (Rayman et al., 1997). A study is now in progress at Yale University in which patients with Canavan disease, a fatal demyelinating disease due to a genetically determined deficiency of the enzyme aspartoacylase, have received injections into the brain ventricles of a vector containing the normal gene. Magnetic resonance spectroscopy studies suggest that this treatment alleviated some of the biochemical abnormalities in the brain. In conclusion, while gene therapy for nervous system disorders is still severely limited, it is likely that substantial progress will be achieved in the early part of the 21st century.

PREVENTION OF GENETIC DISORDERS ASSOCIATED WITH SEVERE MENTAL RETARDATION

Prevention is subdivided into two categories. In primary prevention the disorder that is associated with mental retardation is prevented. When primary prevention is not possible, the aim becomes to prevent the ill effects of the disorder, in this instance the mental retardation that may be associated with it. Primary prevention starts with genetic counseling and includes the identification of persons at risk (carriers) for a particular disorder, who can then make a variety of reproductive choices. Examples of secondary prevention are the neonatal screening programs for phenylketonuria and hypothyroidism that are now conducted in many parts of the world; when combined with promptly instituted therapy, these are among the most important public health advances achieved during the 20th century. New techniques are being developed. The technique of Tandem Mass Spectrometry shows particular promise (Millington, Kodo, Norwood, & Roe, 1990). At present this technique permits screening for 32 metabolic disorders in Guthrie blood spot. While this involves a large initial investment, it can identify a large group of disorders, including those that are rare, without additional cost. It is anticipated that early in the 21st century, most newborn children will be screened for all metabolic disorders that cause mental retardation.

REFLECTIONS ON THE FUTURE

The advances in genetics and neuroscience that are taking place now and will continue during the early part of the next century will lead to exciting opportunities and challenges.

1. *Expanded screening of newborns for genetically determined metabolic disorders.* From the Human Genome Project in the early part of the 21st century, we will learn the genetic basis of all or nearly all of the thousands of genetically determined disorders associated with mental retardation. Diagnosis will be based on a variety of noninvasive techniques that utilize biochemical and DNA-based assays that will permit screening of all persons for a large number of disorders. Because therapies are most apt to be successful when offered early, it will be most desirable to apply these multiple screens to the present mass newborn screening programs that utilize the Guthrie blood spots. In that a large number of conditions can be identified, positive results, some of uncertain significance and in need of further follow-up, will be detected. The interpretation of results will require quality control and the availability in regional laboratories of qualified personnel who can interpret the findings. Equally important is the development of channels of communication and education. Notification of an ambiguous or positive result causes a great deal of concern and anxiety, and networks must be established to allay these concerns and provide counseling.

2. *Improved primary prevention.* Primary prevention requires the identification of persons at risk of bearing children with genetic disorders associated with mental retardation. Traditional methods for identification of carriers and persons at-risk and genetic counseling already exist. In the 21st century it is likely that carriers for all genetic disorders will be identified. Problems to be faced include the enhanced need for counseling and education, preservation of confidentiality, and issues relating to health and life insurance and job security for the carrier. Review of reproductive options is crucial. Greater availability of preimplantation diagnosis is highly desirable, as are the development of a greater range of in utero therapies.

3. *Improved therapy.* It is likely that therapies of genetic disorders associated with mental retardation will be improved. Examples of dietary pharmacological and transplant therapies have already been given and will be enhanced by the advances in gene therapy. There will be increased emphasis on early and presymptomatic diagnosis, since therapies are much more likely to be effective at the early stages. The great variety of these disorders, individually rare but substantial in number in the aggregate, heightens the cost of providing these therapies. These financial concerns raise the specter of health rationing for persons with rare and disabling disorders. A combination of approaches will be needed to combat these concerns. These include the following:

1. Public information and education.

2. Careful evaluation of effectiveness. Such evaluations are particularly difficult for disorders that are severely disabling and rare. Evaluations require carefully designed multicenter trials.

3. Enhancement of current programs to provide financial incentives for companies that develop and provide therapies for "orphan diseases."

In conclusion, I approach the 21st century with hope and excitement, but also with concern and fear that we may fail to achieve what can be done. Contrary to expectations when I first entered this field in 1963, it will become possible to prevent and treat a large proportion of the conditions that are associated with severe mental retardation. To achieve this we must reorient our thinking and expectations. There is great need for enhancement of networks of communication and counseling, changes in public policy, assignment of additional resources to service programs, and maintenance of research efforts.

REFERENCES

American Association on Mental Retardation. (1992). *Mental retardation, classification and systems of supports* (9th ed.). Washington, DC: Author

Anderson, W. F. (1998). Human gene therapy. *Nature, 392* (Suppl. 30), 25–30.

Armstrong, D. D. (1997). Review of Rett syndrome. *Journal of Neuropathology and Experimental Neurology, 56,* 843–849.

Collins, F. G. D. (1995). A new five-year plan for the U.S. Genome Project. *Science, 262,* 43–46.

Collins, F. S. (1995). Positional cloning moves from perditional to traditional. *Nature Genetics, 9,* 347–350.

Eberhart, D. E., Malter, H. E., Feng, Y., & Warren, S. T. (1996). The Fragile-X mental retardation protein is a ribonucleoprotein containing both nuclear localization and nuclear export signals. *Human Molecular Genetics, 5,* 1083–1091.

Hagberg, B., Hagberg, G., Lewerth, A., & Lindberg, U. (1981). Mild mental retardation in Swedish school children. *Acta Paediatrica Scandinavica, 70,* 445–452.

Hagberg, B., & Kyllerman, M. (1983). Epidemiology of mental retardation—A Swedish survey. *Brain Development, 5,* 441–449.

Harum, K. H., & Johnston, M. V. (1998). Developmental neurobiology: New concepts in learning, memory and neuronal development. *Mental Retardation and Developmental Disabilities Research Reviews, 4,* 20–25.

Irons, M., Elias, E. R., Abuelo, D., Bull, M. J., Greene, C. L., Johnson, V. P., Keppen, L., Schanen, C., Tint, G. S., & Salen, G. (1997). Treatment of Smith-Lemli-Opitz syndrome: Results of a multicenter trial. *American Journal of Medical Genetics, 68,* 311–314.

Karpati, G., Lochmüller, H., Nalbantoglu, J., & Durham, H. (1996). The principles of gene therapy for the nervous system. *Trends in Neuroscience, 19,* 49–54.

Kay, M. A., Liu, D., & Hoogebrugge, A. (1997). Gene therapy. *Proceedings of the National Academy of Sciences USA, 94,* 12744–12746.

Mental Retardation Facilities and Community Mental Health Centers Construction Act of 1963, Title 45 C.F.R. part 1388.

Millington, D. S., Kodo, N., Norwood, D. L., & Roe, C. R. (1990). Tandem mass spectrometry: A new method for acylcarnitine profiling with potential for neonatal screening for inborn errors of metabolism. *Journal of Inherited Metabolic Diseases, 13,* 321–324.

Moser, H. W. (1977). Mental retardation. In H. Wechsler & G. F. Cahill (Eds.), *The horizons of health* (pp. 141–160). Cambridge, MA: Harvard University Press.

Moser, H. W. (1992). Therapy of genetically determined metabolic disorders. In Y. Fukuyama, Y. Suzuki, S. Kamoshita, & P. Casaer (Eds.), *Fetal and perinatal neurology* (pp. 93–107). Basel, Switzerland: AG Karger.

Moser, H. W. (1995). A role for gene therapy in mental retardation. *Mental Retardation and Developmental Disabilities Research Reviews, 1,* 4–6.

Paulson, H. L., & Fishbeck, K. H. (1997). Trinucleotide repeats in neurogenetic disorders. *Annual Review in Neuroscience, 19,* 79–107.

Posner, M. I., & Raichle, M. E. (1998). The neuroimaging of human brain function. *Proceedings of the National Academy of Science USA, 95,* 763–764.

Raymon, H. K., Gage, F. H., & Thode, S. (1997). Application of ex vivo gene therapy for Parkinson disease. *Experimental Neurology, 144,* 82–91.

Singer, W. (1995). Development and plasticity of cortical processing architectures. *Science, 270,* 758–764.

Snyder, E. Y., & Flax, J. D. (1995). Transplantation of neural progenitor and stem-like cells as a strategy for gene therapy and repairs neurodegenerative disease. *Mental Retardation and Developmental Disabilities Research Reviews, 1,* 27–38.

Stockler, S., Holzbach, U., Hanefeld, F., Marquardt, I., Helms, G., Requart, M., Hanicke, W., & Frahm, J. (1994). Creatine deficiency in the brain: A new, treatable inborn error of metabolism. *Pediatric Research, 36,* 409–413.

Teyler, T. J., & DiScenna, P. (1984). Long-term potentiation as a candidate mnemonic device. *Brain Research Reviews, 7,* 15–28.

Tint, G. S., Irons, M., Elias, E. R., Batta, A. K., Frieden, R., Chen, T. S., & Salen, G. (1994). Defective cholesterol biosynthesis associated with the Smith-Lemli-Optiz syndrome. *New England Journal of Medicine, 330,* 107–113.

Verma, I. M., & Somia, N. (1997). Gene therapy: Promises, problems, and prospects. *Nature, 389,* 239–242.

Xuehai, Y., Robinson, M. B., Pabin, C., Quinn, T., Jawad, A., Wilson, J. M., & Batshaw, M. L. (1997). Adenovirus-mediated in vivo gene transfer rapidly protects ornithine transcarbamylase-deficient mice from ammonium challenge. *Pediatric Research, 41,* 527–534.

Zigler, E. (1967). Familial mental retardation: A continuing dilemma. *Science, 155,* 292–298.

Health Promotion and Disability Prevention: The Case for Personal Responsibility and Independence

Deborah E. Cohen

HEALTH AND WELLNESS COME OF AGE

The late 20th century may be characterized as the "era of personal health consciousness." During the past several decades, an increasing number of people have become concerned with their health status, engaging in better dietary practices, getting regular exercise, giving up tobacco products, and moderating alcohol intake. The plethora of athletic sportswear and vitamin and health food stores that have sprouted up in shopping malls symbolizes the transition from a "health craze" of the 1960s to a "standard of living" in the closing years of this century. What is most notable with respect to the new standard of living is that health and wellness are not the exclusive domain of the allied health community. It is the individual and the choices that are available and made that are of paramount importance.

One of the clearest testaments to institutionalizing the transition from craze to standard of living is found in *Healthy People 2000* (U.S. Department of Health and Human Services [USDHHS], 1990). This document delineated health objectives for the nation for the final decade of this century. It also provided the name for the new standard of living: "health promotion and disease prevention."

As *Healthy People 2000* was nearing publication, a major omission was identified. National health objectives for persons with disabilities had been excluded. Perhaps highlighted by this omission, a major shift in attitudes began to emerge: Persons with disabilities were not sick. Rather, there was the beginning of a consciousness that persons with disabilities may have physical or intellectual attributes that made them more vulnerable to risk factors that, in turn, result in "poor health." The acknowledgment that persons with disabilities were healthy, but potentially more vulnerable to becoming ill, aging more rapidly, or acquiring additional limitations or disabilities, provided the impetus for substituting "disability" for "disease" in what is now a campaign for health promotion and disability prevention for persons with disabilities.

Several events occurred in the last decade that have influenced the acceptance of health promotion and disability prevention. First, the Centers for Disease Control and Prevention (CDC), with encouragement from the National Council on Disabilities (NCD), established the Disabilities Prevention Program (CDC-DPP) in 1988. The CDC-DPP provided funds to states to establish Offices for Disability Prevention. The state offices were responsible for increasing public awareness of ways in which disabilities could be prevented and for establishing or improving surveillance systems on disabilities (particularly those concerned with developmental disabilities or as results of injuries). The CDC-DPP originally funded 9 state offices; this number was expanded to 29 over a 6-year period. During this time, the state Offices for Disability Prevention began to focus on prevention of secondary conditions among persons with disabilities as well.

Second, in 1990, as the national health objectives were being published, advocacy organizations quickly mobilized to ensure that additional documents addressing persons with disabilities were produced to supplement our nation's health objectives. One of these, *Health Promotion and Disability Prevention for People with Disabilities: A Companion to Healthy People 2000* (American Association of University Affiliated Programs for Persons with Developmental Disabilities [AAUAP], 1995), addressed the concerns of persons with developmental disabilities. The Arc was one of the organizations that participated in producing the document.

Third, working with the CDC-DPP and others, the Institute of Medicine (IOM) published a major document in 1991. *Disability in America: Toward a National Agenda for Prevention* (IOM, Pope & Tarlov, 1991) defined disability as the result of a process that included physical, social, and environmental elements, stating, *"Disability is the expression of a physical or mental limitation in a social context—the gap between a person's capabilities and the demands of the environment"* (IOM et al., 1991, p. 1). This definition reflects a profound statement of a shift in attitudes. The individual with a disability is no longer to be blamed for his or her "shortcomings." The context in which the individual lives, works, and plays must be taken into account as well. This document is also notable for the fact that it addressed the need for improvement in both primary prevention efforts and in prevention of secondary conditions in persons with disabilities.

Fourth, following the publication of *Disability in America*, the CDC, in partnership with the NCD and the Minority Health Professions Foundation (MHPF), sponsored a national conference in 1991 on the Prevention of Primary and Secondary Disabilities: Building Partnerships Toward Health—Reducing the Risks of Disability and published the proceedings (USDHHS, 1993). Using *Disability in America* as the basis for discussion, the conference addressed a broad range of issues for prevention of both primary and secondary conditions, including quality of life, education, work, home and community living, surveillance and data needs, and advocacy.

Fifth, in 1997 the CDC-DPP was transformed into the Office on Disability and Health (ODH). The intent of ODH is to instill the value of health and wellness for persons with disabilities into the public health sector. The state Offices for Disability Prevention were no longer supported. They have been replaced by Offices for Disability Prevention in 14 states. These offices are focusing on establishing the systems and programs needed to ensure health and wellness for persons with disabilities.

Finally, during the past decade, major advocacy organizations have become concerned with promoting health and wellness among the persons they represent. The Arc and sister organizations recognized the importance of balancing efforts to prevent mental retardation while encouraging good lifestyle practices among their constituents. To this end, the boards of directors of both The Arc and the American Association on Mental Retardation (AAMR) expanded the role of Prevention Committees, which focused primarily on primary prevention, to include health promotion and disabilities prevention as well.

At the most fundamental level, health promotion and disability prevention pertain to quality of life for all citizens. Healthy lifestyles—exercise; nutrition; good hygiene practices; intellectual stimulation; participation in home, work, and play; and routine physical and dental checkups—are all choices that we make, irrespective of whether we have a disability. For persons with disabilities, these choices may be more difficult, not only because of limitations, but due to environmental and behavioral barriers as well.

This chapter presents a brief overview of the paradigm that has been used to describe the disabling process. A model for assessing risk factors is then presented (adapted from Spitalnik & Cohen, 1995). Finally, an inclusive model for encouraging personal responsibility and independence is presented.

THE DISABLING PROCESS

Disability is a term commonly used to describe physical or mental limitations that may compromise the extent or the ease with which an individual may participate fully in all segments of community life (Spitalnik & Cohen, 1995). Disabilities may result from a broad range of causes, including genetics, adverse prenatal effects, illnesses, injury, and the process of growing older. Whether it occurs in childhood or later in life, disability is a social phenomenon and cannot be described independently of social context.

The terms *disability, handicap,* and *impairment* are often used interchangeably in everyday life and as figures of speech. In fact, these discrete terms refer to different stages within the disabling process. A conceptual model for describing the progression from a pathological condition to disability has been put forth by Nagi and the World Health Organization (IOM et al., 1991). Figure 14.1 illustrates this model.

One strength of this model lies in its ability to distinguish between disease or illness (pathology), loss of anatomical or behavioral functioning (impairment), functional limitations (restrictions in performance or requirements for assistance or supports), and disability (IOM et al., 1991). Disability in this model is a social construct that may reflect self-perception, attitudes of others, or social barriers. Quality of life is influenced by both the underlying impairment and the societal attitudes, barriers, and supports (Spitalnik & Cohen, 1995).

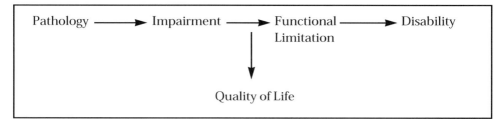

FIGURE 14.1. The Disabling Process. *Note.* From *Disability in America: Toward a National Agenda for Prevention,* by Institute of Medicine, A. M. Pope & A. R. Tarlov (Eds.), 1991, Washington, DC: National Academy Press.

A second strength of the model lies in its assumption that the disabling process may not be linear, despite its graphic display, and is not static. Opportunities for intervention through health promotion activities and personal responsibility are available. These interventions may have the benefits of slowing, halting, or even reversing the movement from one stage to the next. The goal of limiting the progression to disability is to maintain the highest level quality of life. As a result, the types of health promotion activities and ways in which they take place are very much influenced by the individual's social context.

RISK FACTORS AND PREVENTION OF SECONDARY CONDITIONS

Persons with disabilities are not only susceptible to those chronic conditions that are typical of the general population, but also may be at risk of developing conditions that result from their primary disability. Secondary conditions are those that are related to an individual's primary disability that may result in further deterioration in health status, functional capacity, and quality of life (IOM et al., 1991). The effects of secondary conditions are similar for people with developmental disabilities as for those who are disabled later in life (e.g., from injury, chronic diseases, or aging), independent of age of onset of the primary disability. Secondary conditions directly affect the opportunities for individuals to be independent, to participate in all facets of community and social life, and to enjoy a high standard of living .

Secondary conditions may be classified into two categories: progressive and causal (USDHHS, 1993). Progressive conditions are those secondary conditions that may occur as a direct result of the primary condition. For example, precocious aging in people with Down syndrome is a direct result of this chromosomal disorder. Causally related conditions are those that may occur as an indirect result of the primary condition. For example, people who are nonambulatory and use wheelchairs may be prone to decubiti ulcers (pressure sores) due to spending long periods of time in the same position. Similarly, inadequate or improper positioning of a person with cerebral palsy may create or exacerbate contractions, which may diminish mobility of the fine motor coordination involved in many of the activities of daily living (Spitalnik & Cohen, 1995).

The conceptual model for describing the progression from pathological condition to disability illustrated in Figure 14.1 applies to both primary and secondary conditions. The presence of a pathological secondary condition alone does not mean that a secondary disability must occur. This model suggests that a secondary condition follows a trajectory similar to the primary disabling condition and that, without prevention or intervention, may result in further deterioration and disability.

Risk factors are those personal and environmental characteristics that make an individual more susceptible to acquiring a secondary condition. Risk factors can be classified into three categories: biological factors, environmental factors, and lifestyle and behavioral factors (IOM et al., 1991; USDHHS, 1993).

To a significant degree, preventing the pathology of the biological factor from moving along the continuum toward disability (see Figure 14.1) is dependent upon both the environmental and the lifestyle and behavioral risk factors. Each of the three risk factors involves complex variables that interact with one another. To be effective, prevention of secondary conditions must address these interactions.

Biological Factors are those that develop within the body as part of one's basic biological and organic makeup. They include genetic and other inborn or inherited characteristics, as well as the metabolic aspects of maturation, growth, and aging, and the interactions of the varied and complex systems of the body. Often, the pathological course of the secondary conditions can be addressed to prevent a more serious secondary disability. Figure 14.2 illustrates specific secondary conditions that are associated with four types of developmental disabilities.

Interventions can be implemented that will slow, and may even prevent, biological risk factors that result in secondary conditions. Interventions are dependent upon good health care, the individual, and those with whom he or she interacts. For example, hypothyroidism in Down syndrome can be controlled by medication. This means that individuals must have access to good health care for monitoring the functioning of the thyroid and for medication prescriptions. It also means that the individual must assume responsibility for complying with the medication regimen (lifestyle/behavioral factor). Similarly, decubiti ulcers (biological factor) can be prevented in individuals whose disability results in their being nonambulatory or having to sit for long periods of time by educating them on positioning and weight shifting, as well as ensuring that the type of wheelchair they use is appropriate (environmental factor).

Environmental Factors are health-related risks that exist outside the person and over which the individual appears to have little or no control. They may be either physical risks, primarily the product of the built (i.e., human-made) environment, or social risks reflecting attitudes, assumptions, preferences, and prejudices in society. Environmental risk factors include a broad range of issues. Work circumstances, lack

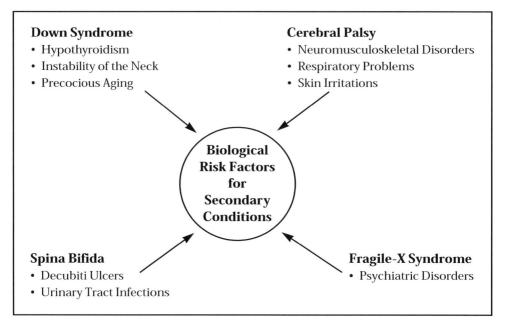

FIGURE 14.2. Biological risk factors for secondary conditions.

of access to community recreational facilities, or lack of education about home safety may all contribute to environmental risks.

The prevention of biologically related secondary conditions is integrally related to access to ongoing primary health care and health care management. The difficulties in accessing high-quality, appropriate, continuous, community-based health care for persons with disabilities have been well documented (Garrard, 1983; Spitalnik & Like, 1987; USDHHS, 1993; AAUAP, 1995). Difficulties in obtaining health care are often beyond the control of the individual and thus can be considered an environmental risk factor. Figure 14.3 illustrates the interaction between environmental risk factors and biological risk factors in the context of health care.

Prevention and intervention for the secondary conditions associated with the environmental risk factors shown in Figure 14.3 are examples of the ways in which facets of health care may contribute to poor health outcomes. Environmental risk factors arise in most all situations. For example, if an individual with a disability is employed in a site in which environmental contaminants are present, but the place of employment does not educate about exposure or follow federal protection standards, the employee may develop secondary conditions or the exposures may give rise to new primary disabilities. In this case, the lack of precautions and education are equally as important as access to health care.

Lifestyle and Behavioral Factors consist of personal decisions and habits that affect one's health and over which the individual has considerable control (USDHHS, 1993).

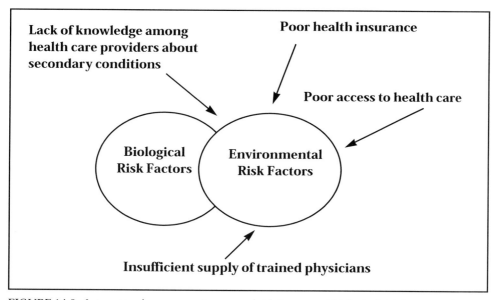

FIGURE 14.3. Interaction between environmental risk factors and biological risk factors in the context of health care.

The degree to which secondary conditions can be prevented from moving along the continuum is dependent upon lifestyle and behavioral risk factors. Many persons with disabilities can be supported or assisted in participating in or assuming responsibility for some aspects of their own personal health and wellness habits. Figure 14.4 illustrates the role of lifestyle and behavioral risk factors.

The capabilities and commitment of persons with disabilities, independently or with support and assistance, to engage in a healthy lifestyle can greatly influence the pathological movement of secondary conditions across the continuum. Compliance with health-related recommendations, including the correct use of medication when appropriate, good nutrition, exercise, and the use of assistive technology in a manner that supports good body mechanics, can influence outcomes and contribute to quality of life. The nature of the support options available to persons with disabilities can also contribute greatly to healthy lifestyle and behavioral practices or can function as risks in these areas.

Lifestyle and behavioral risk factors can also serve as the primary cause of secondary conditions. As more persons with developmental disabilities are included in community life, they are also being introduced to society's more harmful practices. For example, the lack of inclusion of persons with developmental disabilities in family life education may result in engaging in unsafe sexual practices or adolescent pregnancy. Likewise, exclusion from drug and alcohol education programs may give rise to habitual use of these substances.

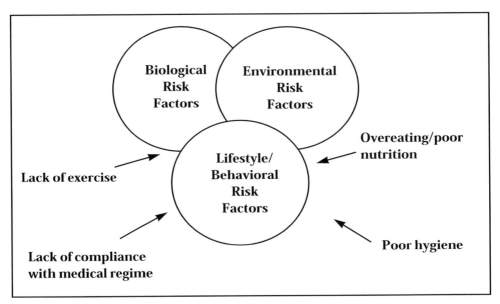

FIGURE 14.4. Role of lifestyle and behavioral risk factors.

QUALITY OF LIFE

The association between quality of life and prevention of secondary conditions is a close one. For persons with developmental disabilities, secondary conditions can seriously threaten independence. Each of the risk factors can operate independently of one another, but it is far more common for there to be interaction or reaction among the three variables. It is therefore of great importance to view the risk factors as precursors to the disabling process, which in turn influences the individual's quality of life (see Figure 14.5).

Although health care plays a great role in addressing the prevention of secondary conditions, which in turn affect quality of life, this is not the whole story. Approaches to preventing secondary conditions must be holistic. The equation must include the role and influences of other environmental variables, the degree to which support and assistance is needed, and the extent to which the individual invests in health and wellness activities.

PERSONAL RESPONSIBILITY, INDEPENDENCE, AND QUALITY OF LIFE

Early onset of disability characterizes developmental disabilities and often has dramatic implications for the nature of the disability. Having an impairment that origi-

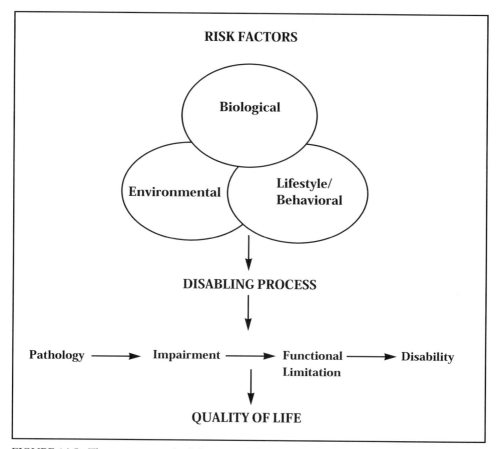

FIGURE 14.5. The interaction of risk factors and disabling process that affects quality of life.

nates at birth or in childhood means that the person with a developmental disability "grows up disabled," altering the life trajectory in many ways. The child may lack the skills for achieving developmentally and chronologically appropriate tasks or the cognitive skills needed for play or learning (Spitalnik & Cohen, 1995). However, the degree to which the life trajectory of a child with developmental disabilities deviates from the "usual" track can be moderated by the extent to which the individual is educated and supported by families, health care professionals, and educators, and, as an adult, by employers, to assume personal responsibility.

We often associate health promotion and disability or disease prevention as being the province of the health care community. Yet, the beneficial effects of healthy lifestyles accrue to the individual and are generally entirely dependent upon the individual's commitment to maintaining the lifestyle. The family needs to serve as the child's "health case manager" while the child is young. As children grow older, families need to be educating their children to assume responsibility, with support if needed, to carry through on their health care needs. In addition, health care providers also need to be educated about the best health care practices for persons with developmental disabilities in order to ensure high-quality health services and to prevent secondary conditions from arising. The Arc's Women's Health Care Project, developed by the Arc of New Jersey, is a good example of an educational program for health care providers.

The difficulties inherent in navigating the health care world have been well documented elsewhere and will not be reiterated here. However, it is important to note that health promotion incorporates the expertise of the health care community, but health care is only one variable in the equation.

Educating persons with developmental disabilities about health promotion and wellness needs to begin early in life, as for children without disabilities. Although it may take longer to teach children with developmental disabilities about bathing, dental hygiene, home safety, good nutrition, and regular sleeping patterns, most families do engage in these practices with their child. This early education will go far to ensure that the child with a developmental disability grows into an adult who continues to engage in health and wellness practices.

Although many infants and toddlers and their families have enjoyed the benefits of early intervention programs, these services are often provided in segregated facilities. Child care facilities provide the opportunity for children with developmental disabilities to learn and play in natural environments with their peers. The 1997 reauthorization of the Individuals with Disabilities Education Act mandates that state early intervention programs shift from program-based services to providing services in natural environments. Families can educate child care providers, early educators, and others about their child's special needs while ensuring that their children are assimilated into play groups and all activities. For example, the State of Texas has adapted its early intervention services to natural environments. Early interventionists provide services at the child's home or in child care settings. Both families and child care staff are taught to carry out the therapeutic services in natural environments.

School systems play a large role in reinforcing health promotion and independence among children and adolescents, but rarely are children with special needs included in these educational programs. Inclusive education is greater than merely sitting in an academic classroom with other children. It is also ensuring that all programs and educational opportunities are accessible and welcoming. For example, states in which family life education is mandated routinely exclude children with developmental disabilities from these classes, despite the legislative mandate. Few examples of inclusion are currently available. However, the educational program to prevent fetal alcohol syndrome, developed by the Arc's Self-Advocates, incorporates some aspects of family life education into the curriculum. This resource could be expanded and adapted for use by school systems. In another exciting Arc venture, The Arc of Warren County, New Jersey, recently received a grant from the state to develop a program to educate adolescents with developmental disabilities about preventing pregnancy.

It is the rare school system indeed that encourages children with developmental disabilities to participate in extracurricular activities, by soliciting their participation in trying out for sports teams or the school play. These activities have as much to do with being part of the school's culture as they do with building the individual's self-esteem and personal confidence. Exclusion from activities outside the classroom results in continued emphasis on the "differences" between persons with disabilities and those without. Exclusion may have the unintended consequences of exacerbating secondary conditions or even causing them. Loneliness, depression, and other emotional problems may be indicative of feelings of exclusion on the part of the child with a disability.

As the children grow older, families of children with developmental disabilities must learn a particularly difficult lesson in order to foster independence and self-reliance: They must allow their children to take risks. This often translates to "letting go," meaning that young adults with developmental disabilities must become equipped to handle life's challenges appropriately. Often, young persons with developmental disabilities have only a vague notion of human sexuality and appropriate social behavior. Families, health care providers, and schools must ensure that, by adolescence, young persons with developmental disabilities understand the physiological changes that are taking place, and that they are educated about sexuality and their own biological urges, about parenting, and about alcohol and tobacco (Institute on Community Integration, 1994).

Equally important, families, health care providers, schools, and community and recreational organizations all contribute to the adolescent's self-esteem and psychological health. Talking directly with adolescents with developmental disabilities about their mental health and encouraging them to participate in school and community activities can help alleviate isolation, loneliness, and depression (Institute on Community Integration, 1994).

Educating children with disabilities about resources in their communities as well as appropriate community behavior must also begin early so that, by the time they reach adulthood, these young adults are prepared to navigate the world beyond their front porches. The community, too, must be educated about opening their doors to welcome children and adults with disabilities. Religious institutions can take the lead in demonstrating acceptance of families and individuals with developmental disabilities, as well as educating the congregation about the assets and abilities of these members. Further, persons with developmental disabilities need to experience their own spirituality. Participation in communal religion and celebrations of holy rites can reinforce the sense of belonging and of achieving milestones, thus contributing to emotional well-being.

For example, the Elizabeth Monroe Boggs Center, the University Affiliated Program (UAP) of the University of Medicine and Dentistry of New Jersey, has a well-established ministry program. Clergy, who are staff members of the UAP, work with religious organizations to educate congregations about their members with developmental disabilities and to assist community clergy to train members to celebrate holy rituals. This has resulted in numerous persons with developmental disabilities participating in First Communions or celebrating their Bar or Bat Mitzvahs.

Recreational and social facilities, such as the YMCA, YWCA, Boys and Girls Clubs, gymnasiums, sports leagues, and other community organizations, also need to open their doors to persons with developmental disabilities. For example, The Arc has a grant from Special Olympics that focuses on developing inclusive sports programs. Further, it is often assumed that, once young adults with developmental disabilities have left high school, the only further education they need is associated with work. Adults with developmental disabilities can participate in adult education in community colleges to keep themselves stimulated and a part of their community.

Employment, too, can be an important influence on health promotion and disability prevention for persons with developmental disabilities. Access to work benefits, including health insurance and pension plans, is important. However, access to more subtle employment-related activities can benefit the worker with the developmental disability while educating colleagues about his or her capabilities. For example, many large corporations have on-site athletic and recreational facilities, as well as health-related lunchtime educational programs (e.g., Johnson & Johnson's Live for Life program). Employees with disabilities should be encouraged by management to take advantage of these opportunities. In addition, many corporations encourage their employees to participate in community volunteer activities. Workers with developmental disabilities can join their colleagues in these community efforts as well.

Figure 14.6 provides a schematic view of the various roles that families, the health care community, educational institutions, community and social organizations, and employment can play in encouraging individuals with developmental disabilities to engage in health promotion activities.

"Managing one's health is a key to becoming self-sufficient, maintaining independence, and enjoying full participation in society" (USDHHS, 1994, p. 3). While educating persons with mental retardation and other developmental disabilities to assume responsibility for their own health and safety is a difficult, perhaps even daunting, challenge, the payoff for many of these individuals can be great. Understanding the need to maintain good hygiene practices, learning their medication routines, and participating in school, community, and employment activities can result in the prevention of secondary conditions, which, in turn, greatly influence quality of life. While many persons with developmental disabilities may require assistance, support, and advocacy from others throughout their lifetimes to maintain healthy lifestyles, the capacity of many individuals with developmental disabilities to assume responsibility has yet to be established.

Further, although examples of health promotion efforts have been presented in this chapter, established programs and educational efforts for promoting healthy lifestyles and preventing secondary conditions are few and far between. The challenge to us all is to develop, implement, and evaluate programs that support families in their efforts to address the health promotion needs of their children with developmental disabilities throughout the life cycle. In this way, persons with developmental disabilities can become more self-reliant and independent in their personal health promotion and disability prevention habits and behaviors.

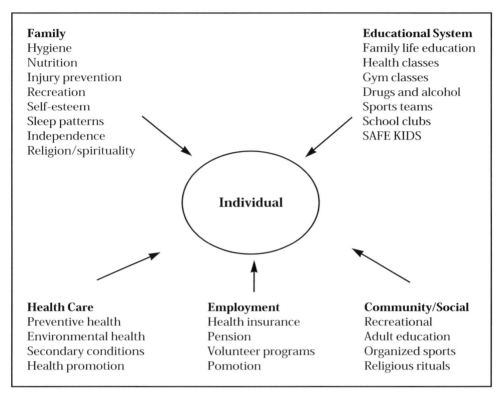

Family
Hygiene
Nutrition
Injury prevention
Recreation
Self-esteem
Sleep patterns
Independence
Religion/spirituality

Educational System
Family life education
Health classes
Gym classes
Drugs and alcohol
Sports teams
School clubs
SAFE KIDS

Individual

Health Care
Preventive health
Environmental health
Secondary conditions
Health promotion

Employment
Health insurance
Pension
Volunteer programs
Pomotion

Community/Social
Recreational
Adult education
Organized sports
Religious rituals

FIGURE 14.6. Model for individual health promotion.

REFERENCES

American Association of University Affiliated Programs for Persons with Developmental Disabilities. (1995). *Health promotion and disability prevention for people with disabilities: A companion to healthy people 2000.* Washington, DC: Author.

Garrard, S. D. (1983). Community health issues. In J. L. Matson & J. A. Mulick (Eds.), *Handbook of mental retardation.* New York: Pergamon Press.

Individuals with Disabilities Education Act Reauthorization of 1997, 20 U.S.C. § 1400 *et seq.*

Institute on Community Integration (1994, Fall). *IMPACT, 7*(2).

Institute of Medicine, Pope, A. M. & Tarlov, A. R. (Eds.). (1991). *Disability in America: Toward a national agenda for prevention.* Washington, DC: National Academy Press.

Spitalnik, D. M., & Cohen, D. E. (1995). Primary and secondary disabilities: An introduction. In *Health promotion and disability prevention for people with disabilities: A companion to healthy people 2000.* Washington, DC: American Association of University Affiliated Programs for Persons with Developmental Disabilties.

Spitalnik, D. M., & Like, R. C. (1987). *The provision of primary health care to adults with chronic disabilities.* Proposal to the Robert Wood Johnson Foundation, New Brunswick.

U.S. Department of Health and Human Services. (1990). *Healthy People 2000.* Washington, DC: Author.

U.S. Department of Health and Human Services. (1993). *Proceedings of a national conference on the prevention of primary and secondary disabilities.* Washington, DC: Author.

U.S. Department of Health and Human Services. (1994). *Preventing secondary conditions associated with spina bifida or cerebral palsy: Proceedings and recommendations of a symposium.* Washington, DC: Author.

Community-Based and Managed Health Care

Allen C. Crocker

WHERE HAVE WE BEEN? (THE 20TH CENTURY)

Systematic concern with medical care for persons who have mental retardation can be said to have started around 1970. A handful of articles appeared in the 1960s (including some notable ones by George Tarjan—Tarjan, 1966; Tarjan, Brooke, Eyman, Suyeyasu, & Miller, 1968; Tarjan, Eyman, & Miller, 1969), but the history of policy considerations in the field is really one of the last 30 years.

In the early period, pediatric teaching was occupied with issues of causation and pathology, following on the pioneering discoveries in infectious disease, Rh sensitization, chromosomal variation, and inborn errors of metabolism. Hospital-based studies gathered important scientific information about specific developmental dilemmas, but care of children with serious disorders at home was scattered and was otherwise dominated by the chronic residential facility model (where medically related habilitative elements were characteristically limited). Outreach to children with mental retardation was greatly assisted by the activities of President John F. Kennedy's administration, including the establishment of a network of University Affiliated Facilities (later called University Affiliated Programs). Gradually a group of children's hospitals and departments of pediatrics came to put a premium on providing care for children with serious special needs. Developmental pediatrics, and a general interest in children with developmental disabilities, became a significant force by the early 1970s.

During that time adult health care groups and forums still gave little formal attention to the field. Obviously a great deal of dedicated individual care was going on in communities and in special settings, but educational backup was sparse. At the peak the roughly 165 state residential facilities ("state schools") had an aggregate population of almost 200,000 residents. Initially this was a mixed group regarding age and severity of disability. The corner turned in the late 1960s, and as institutional discharges began,

Preparation of this material was supported in part by the U.S. Department of Health and Human Services, Maternal and Child Health Bureau (Project MCJ-259150A) and Administration on Developmental Disabilities (Project 90DN003202).

there was a gradual shift toward the remaining residents being those who were older and of more complex developmental and health care needs (Nelson & Crocker, 1978). Medical staffs at the state schools had limited academic or community support. The long series of class action suits that began then frequently focused on specified health care inadequacies as a central complaint, and the beginning of a small revolution was at hand.

Two phenomena occurred. One was a major reinforcement of state school medical staffs, often through contracts with hospitals, medical schools, or private agencies. The other was a marshaling of medical inquiry and resources for persons in the community with mental retardation who either were dischargees or had been there all along. Our understanding of care requirements improved greatly in the 1970s and 1980s.

One characteristic that is important to acknowledge (and, actually, is quite predictable) is that usage levels for medical care vary substantially among a group of people with mental retardation. This has been described by several authors. Cole (1987) postulated a "Level I, low-consuming group," with a need for 1 to 3 medical encounters per year, constituting about 45% of the clients from the Department of Mental Retardation in Massachusetts; a "Level II, intermediate group," occasionally requiring medical specialty consultants as well (40% of the total); and a "Level III, high-consuming group" (15%), needing ongoing monitoring and access to tertiary care. Obviously most of the persons at Level I and some at Level II can be reasonably accommodated by the generic community medical system. In a regional survey by Minihan and Dean (1990), nearly half of the medical conditions among the 330 clients they studied could be appropriately cared for by usual primary care physicians. Many of the rest needed more specialized attention.

In a population with serious developmental disabilities, there are a number of regular and important challenges in medical care. At the Wrentham State School (Wrentham, Massachusetts) those were, in order of prevalence, seizures, mobility problems and physical disability, deafness, obesity, chronic respiratory disease, ocular problems, and severe dental or periodontal disease (Nelson & Crocker, 1978). For individuals with mental retardation living in the community, Minihan and Dean (1990) noted, in order, neurologic, ophthalmologic, dermatologic, psychiatric, and orthopedic difficulties. In an interesting review of 27 persons discharged from a New York institution and then residing in supervised community living accommodations, McDonald (1985) noted 200 primary physician contacts in a year (some for annual physical examinations), 57 acute care visits, 5 emergencies, and 10 elective surgical procedures. The most common topical areas of concern involved ophthalmology, ear–nose–throat, orthopedic, neurology, audiology, and psychiatry. In a Pennsylvania study, adults with mental retardation living with their families had an average of 5.9 medical visits per year, compared to 3.0 for the general population. Those in community living arrangements had 14.8 visits, more often because of agency patterns of monitoring and response than a higher level of illness (Nowell, Baker, & Conroy, 1989).

As consciousness has been raised regarding the need for more devoted medical care for adults who have serious developmental disabilities, there has been a slow gain in knowledge about systems. An extensive symposium was held in 1986 that attempted to establish some basic principles (Crocker, 1987). A textbook that includes adult care became available in 1989 (Rubin & Crocker, 1989), and a number were published on mental health concerns (Menolascino & Stark, 1984; Szymanski & Tanguay, 1980). A valuable monthly newsletter is distributed by Kastner ("Exceptional Health Care," 45 Park Place South, Morristown, NJ 07960-9886). Major presentations in this area are given at the annual meetings of the American Association on Mental Retardation, especially in the Medicine Division. In a series of important articles from the Developmental Disabilities Center at the Morristown Memorial Hospital by Ziring and colleagues (see, e.g., Ziring et al., 1988), many of the lessons of community care for involved adults have been elucidated. The University Affiliated Programs (mentioned above) in diverse settings have now led the way to improved care of adults as well.

Two of the most critical elements that have come into the health care scene for persons with mental retardation and related disabilities in the past two decades are the emergence of a value system and the derivation of standards of care. Regarding children a large debt is owed to the federal Maternal and Child Health Bureau, The American Academy of Pediatrics, and, above all, to then Surgeon General C. Everett Koop for promoting the thoughtful enumeration of the values that should characterize the provision of care for children generally, and particularly those with disabilities and chronic illness. Some components featured were that such care must be comprehensive, developmentally oriented, continuous, integrated, nondiscriminatory, and payment ensured. Much was captured in the simple phrase that care should be "family-centered, community-based, and coordinated" (Brewer, McPherson, Magrab, & Hutchins, 1989).

Once the tabulation of fundamental values had been carried out, it was possible to proceed with conversion of those to operational principles, or standards. Useful material that catalyzes good health care can be found in federal Title XIX guidelines or various accrediting manuals, but these often deal with minimal levels of service acceptable. An example of an ideal scheme, on the other hand, is that produced by New England SERVE as *Enhancing Quality: Standards and Indicators of Quality Care for Children with Special Health Care Needs* (Epstein et al., 1989). In this pioneering effort, desired behaviors and characteristics are considered for health care teams, facilities, health departments, and the social setting. This kind of orientation is appropriate to ensure best supports for the health care needs of children with mental retardation.

There has been no *Enhancing Quality* equivalent for adult care planning, but hospitals, community health programs, vendors, mental retardation departments, and other settings where adults are followed could reflect on the design. "Family-centered, community-based, and coordinated" care can translate to goals that are personalized, inclusive, and coordinated. Some of the class action suits mentioned previously, in relation to content about medical care in institutions, led to speculation about societal expectations. One such configuration of treatment rights is presented here.[1]

A Declaration of Health Care Rights for the Adult with Developmental Disability

I. A thoughtful consideration of etiology for the person's developmental disorder shall have been made or be made, recorded in defensible and available form, shared with the family and the medical providers, and updated if new technology suggests a potential value therefrom.

II. A problem-oriented continuing care record shall be established and maintained, being viewed as a central and valued component of the person's life accouterments. This record shall be handy, portable, legible, and interesting.

III. Provision of primary care shall be based in a location that is proximate, be stable and accessible, and be graced by love.

IV. Referral for specialty care shall be generated by the quest for accuracy, and draw on quality, dedicated resources.

V. Signs of worsening cortical disorder, experienced in the domains of cognition, language, mobility, sensory function, or structure, shall be viewed with alarm, and explanations and intervention sought.

VI. Common secondary conditions that diminish health, such as aspiration, bladder infection, bowel problems, poor nutrition, periodontal disease, seizures, and sleep disturbances, shall be foreseen and treated considerately.

VII. Preventive care approaches shall be invoked for avoidable or detectable health defections, such as untoward cardiovascular, gynecologic, or infectious ailments.

VIII. Medications that alter mood or behavior shall be considered double-edged swords, justifying particular caution in prescription and watchfulness.

IX. Habilitative, rehabilitative, and assistive therapies and technologies shall be richly provided, for the goals of joy, action, and extension.

X. The person, family members, and/or their surrogates shall share in all decision making, with extraordinary attention shown to display options, risks, and benefits.

---

[1]From "A Declaration of Health Care Rights for the Adult with a Developmental Disability," by A. C. Crocker, 1992, in *Proceedings of Conference on Health Care for Youth and Adults with Disabilities: Policies and Partnerships* (p. 44), by E. M. Eklund (Ed.), Silver Springs, MD: American Association of University Affiliated Programs.

XI. Care shall be coordinated across facilities and agencies, and along with this financial counseling provided regarding assistance for reimbursing the costs of care.

XII. Supportive health care services shall be maximally unobtrusive, shall celebrate the presence of wellness, and also look to buttressing the state of personal happiness.

These are some of the stirrings that the new investment in medical care produced in the last decades of the 20th century. We began also to learn about new roles for various health care personnel, consumer partnerships, and formulas for referral and financial support—but more on this later.

WHERE ARE WE NOW? (TRANSITION TIME)

In the last years of the 20th century, the United States became increasingly distressed by economic and equity issues that troubled health care delivery for citizens generally, and not merely those with disabilities. The era of free-choice, indemnity-insured procurement of medical care, also characterized by availability of a vastly increased selection of modern studies and interventions, had led to cumulative costs that were forbidding (13% to 14% of the gross national product was going for health support). We as a nation appeared to be unable to establish a rational, single-payer system that would reach all citizens and yet promise some cost control. Hence, it was inevitable that multiple efforts would proceed on the theme of "managed" care and that this would, of course, affect the world of persons with disabilities as well.

Managed care, a design for marketing medical care services, involves some structured features for service engagement and maintenance that could be expected to generate predictable and somewhat reduced ("controlled") costs. This conception could be invoked by existing agencies and companies as their new method, or could be merchandised by freshly formed firms. Begun as small consumer-oriented experiments more than 30 years ago, managed care organizations have surged in the past decade. They are rapidly becoming the predominant form of health care delivery in the United States, enrolling well over half of the citizens in a number of states.

Some helpful expectations in the managed care environment run parallel to the intention for reduced individual and societal expenditure, and these are pertinent to the interests of persons with disabilities. Included are goals for access (often in a "one-stop" model), continuity, a commitment to prevention of secondary conditions, availability of care coordination, and enhanced monitoring of quality and outcomes. Varying degrees of realizations of these ambitions have been achieved, and also of the hope that there would be more nearly universal enrollment in coverage. A "new paradigm" is often hailed regarding the transition from traditional care to managed care, involving now a continuum, integration, teams, consumer participation, prevention, and accountability (Spink, 1997).

The ultimate characteristics defining the practice of managed care are that (a) customers receive services from within a fixed network of providers, owned or contracted by the company, and this includes out- and in-patient care, pharmacy, home care, and so on; (b) there is a "gatekeeper" (generally the primary care physician, but can be a nurse, social worker, or case manager) who reviews and approves all services and referrals; and (c) the systems are "capitated," meaning that consumers have joined and paid one prior fee, and the company guarantees yearlong coverage for this previously determined cohort of members. These actions are carried out in Health Maintenance Organizations or HMOs (Staff Models, Group Models, or Independent Practice Associations) or by Preferred Provider Organizations or PPOs (groups of doctors or hospitals who give special fees).

For persons with developmental disabilities, the plunge toward managed care has particularly involved the utilization of Medicaid funds to purchase HMO coverage. Medicaid has become increasingly the most accessible and most used source of health benefits for persons with disabilities. Braddock (1996) noted that for 1992, 1.30 million Medicaid recipients had developmental disabilities, 1.04 million of whom were receiving health care therefrom. Some of these individuals tended to be high users of heath care services. Overall, persons with disabilities represent 15% of Medicaid enrollment but 37% of medical care costs (Kastner, Walsh, & Criscione, 1997). Although Medicaid is a federal–state partnership, the states have major involvement and retain a significant control over the utilization. As Medicaid enrollments have grown, state governments have felt pressed to seek cost containment for the health care of these citizens (in a fashion resembling companies providing benefits for employees). Utilizing Medicaid monies for enrollment in various managed care programs has been an attractive prospect to secure savings. With the assistance of several key federal provisions (e.g., Medicaid sections 1915b and 1115 waivers), state departments could mandate transfer of clients to managed care plans in HMOs (or in innovative designs, such as utilizing specifically listed primary care physicians in the community).

This process has been moving rapidly. By mid-1996, 21 states were actively involved in enrolling Medicaid recipients with disabilities in managed care, constituting a mean of 28% of that population (Landon, Tobias, & Epstein, 1998). C. Tobias (personal communication, 1998) estimated that in 1998 more than half of all persons with Medicaid participated in managed care programs.

There are a number of theoretical and real advantages to be considered in a Medicaid managed care milieu for persons with developmental disabilities, as mentioned earlier. An insinuation of stability exists, with a dependable "medical home" and an orientation to consumer satisfaction. Add-on's and out-of-pocket expenses are usually eliminated or minor. Some specialty services may be more accessible, and the commitment to community-based services is desirable. There are troubling potential disadvantages as well. Although there is a well-identified primary care provider, many components of choice, including that one, are limited. There is an understandable apprehension that the uniqueness of mental retardation or other developmental disabilities will not be given expert or fully empathetic reception, and that referral to key specialists may be considered less essential and thus denied. The atmosphere of cost control may discourage availability of some support services, or press for service substitution.

Care coordination is assuredly a hypothetical capacity of a managed care organization, and synchronous with Title XIX (Medicaid) goals. It refers to increasing the effectiveness of services by expediting linkages within the organization and beyond it, seeking completeness but avoiding duplication, and building for best communication and understanding. Such efforts are common in Social/Health Maintenance Organizations, but rare in conventional models. The Developmental Consultation Services program of Harvard Pilgrim Health Care is an example of a unique commitment by an HMO to clients with developmental disabilities for service and care coordination (Pangburn, 1999). Criscione, Walsh, and Kastner (1995) have shown the usefulness of care coordination regarding hospital utilization. Another product of coordination can be the identification of model waivers (such as Katie Beckett) that assist in procuring a broader service package (see discussion in Kastner et al., 1997).

The measurement of quality of services in the managed care world has particular requirements for enrollees who have developmental disabilities. Clinical outcome indicators, functional health status measures, satisfaction surveys, and input from advisory committees need to have true relevance (Kastner et al., 1997). State and federal oversight processes are also becoming involved. The challenge for state Medicaid agencies to assess the quality of the care they have purchased will be an interesting force in the managed care market (Landon et al., 1998).

The situation for managed care coverage of children with disabilities has many similar elements to those mentioned previously for adults. Studies and statistics in this area are commonly expressed in terms of children with "special health care needs," a characterization that includes those with disabilities but also those with chronic illness or other sustained higher health care needs. It has been noted that children and youth comprise the population moving most quickly into managed care, especially through public sector arrangements. In 1996, 36% of the children with special health care needs discharged from children's hospitals were assisted by Medicaid. About a million children with disabilities were receiving Supplementary Security Income (SSI), and hence were eligible for Medicaid (Alliance for Health Reform, 1997). The majority are now, or will be soon, in a managed care program.

There are design attributes of managed care that can be salutory for children with disabilities. The savings for families can be considerable, compared to traditional fee-for-service systems. Multiple aspects of care may be at one site, and may be coordinated. Usually there is less need to use emergency rooms and hospitals (Perrin et al., 1997). On the other hand, covert incentives within the plan may diminish access to more expensive services, and moving to managed care may disrupt long-standing service arrangements. Perrin et al. (1997) reflected that ultimate evaluations of managed care will need to study child health outcomes, family impact, and a complex of expenditure questions.

New England SERVE (1997) did a preliminary assessment in 1995–1996 of responses to the use of managed care for children with special health care needs, and this can provide some insights regarding the experience. In reporting on overall satisfaction, 57% of a sample of 368 families responded that their child received appropriate, quality services through their health plan. Over three fourths were very satisfied with well-child care, and high numbers were satisfied with the primary care provider's knowledge of their child's special needs and with the available pediatric specialty care providers. Favorable reports were given regarding building access, waiting times to schedule primary care appointments, and times for specialty referral. Areas that seriously troubled families were the availability of occupational therapy, speech therapy, and psychological services. Most notably they were concerned about the provision of mental health services. They wished for access to care coordination and for help in communicating with school teams and in learning about new knowledge in the field of their child's disability.

WHERE MUST WE GO? (THE 21ST CENTURY)

Many Programs Later, We Know the Issues

As noted earlier in this chapter, the descriptions have become available of programs and experiences relating to the delivery of medical care for adults with mental retardation and developmental disabilities. A critically valuable review, almost a meta-analysis, was provided by Hayden and DePaepe (1991), summarizing 47 reports of care arrangements. There is much methodological heterogeneity in the reports. The study involves small and large populations; institutional, transitional, and community settings; and life largely before managed care systems. Intriguingly, the human elements are surprisingly comparable with those in today's challenges. The needs identified, the barriers reflected upon, and the commitments undertaken appear very current, and have much to tell us for our present deliberations. Hayden and DePaepe came to realize that four categories of services were necessary to sustain health and personal stability in the community: (1) accessible direct medical services (primary and emergency care, specialty physicians with continuity, community-based health centers), (2) other health care components (clinical therapies, nursing care, medical equipment), (3) additional support services (case management, interagency coordination, health care coordination), and (4) family and community supports (health aides, home modifications, respite care, trained direct care staff, transitional homes). They recognized a useful cluster of health-related outcome measures that we should retain: hospitalization and illness rates, medication changes, performance of regular physical examinations, care provider satisfaction, overall health and nutritional status, identification of undiagnosed conditions, and meeting unmet service needs. This, then, is the legacy.

Pulcini and Howard (1997) provided a conceptual framework for consideration of the dynamics of new plans, including managed care. They wrote, "Traditional fee-for-service systems have been largely replaced with systems that incorporate some form of managed care" (p. 209). Utilizing Donabedian's model for assessing programs, they view structure leading to process, which in turn creates outcome. In this conception, structure has three domains. The first is *access,* which requires us to consider location, compatibility, integration, and penetration. The second is *comprehensiveness,* which asks examination of levels of care, scope, health promotion, health care coordination, and personnel training. The third is *financing,* which asks about revenue mixes, supplementary funding, and design of capitation. Pulcini and Howard increased the value of their exposition by noting the frequent special contributions (especially in new programs) of specific highly committed persons, and the importance of good interrelations with state agencies. Ongoing data collection and quality measurement are also a responsibility of a plan. They point out the reality on occasion of trade-offs, such as comprehensiveness versus cost, or access versus normalization. The authors applied these analytic elements to care plans in Illinois, New Jersey, and California.

A single program report of particular teaching value is the one by Master et al. (1996) that describes the Community Medical Alliance (CMA) in Boston. This is a courageous experiment in capitated care that enrolls only persons with serious disability (or HIV infection). Individuals with developmental disabilities are given very personal, often home-based, coordinated management by experienced nurse practitioners and physicians. Persons join voluntarily, particularly from independent living centers. There is high satisfaction, little use of hospitals, and feasibility by risk adjustment of rates. The program uses decubitus ulcer experience as a quality improvement measure, with gratifying results. Some of the same kind of optimistic planning is involved in another project in Boston called Pediatric Alliance for Coordinated Care (PACC), with Robert Wood Johnson Foundation support in the early period. There the care of a group of children with serious disabilities is facilitated in six selected pediatric office or clinic settings by experienced pediatric nurse practitioners, who provide service coordination, keep records of work, visit homes, and assist in the hospital when needed. CMA and PACC are examples of dedicated programming to bring effective care for individuals in the high-consuming group mentioned previously, persons who are often in jeopardy in traditional systems.

Improved Facilitation

Physician Education

As provision of medical care for adults who have mental retardation has become more visible and defended, much discussion has occurred regarding practitioner expertise (Birenbaum, 1995). Clearly the medical disorders are fundamentally similar to those in the general population, but the mode of presentation can be quite special and the schema for the best management requires acknowledgment of communication, compliance, and cultural differences. Work with co-morbidities and unusual syndromes may cause uncertainty, and developmental service team relationships are not part of usual practice.

It is often noted that pediatricians are more at home with patients who have developmental disabilities, and, in fact, Brown (1987) supported some older extension of pediatricians here. Kastner (1991) commented that this should occur at least for young adults. Limits on this area are obvious. Minihan and colleagues' papers speak supportively of the primary care services being provided in Massachusetts (Minihan & Dean, 1990) and Maine (Minihan, Dean, & Lyons, 1993) by internists and family or general practitioners. It would seem unquestionable that in the long run and for the major distribution we will need a steady graduation of family practice physicians who can be informed stewards for community patients with mental retardation. A leading effort in this regard has been carried out by a team collaboration in New Brunswick, New Jersey, involving the University Affiliated Program of New Jersey (The Boggs Center), Department of Family Medicine, University of Medicine and Dentistry of New Jersey/Robert Wood Johnson Medical School, and the Family Practice Center at St. Peter's Medical Center (Spitalnik, 1996). There the residents in family practice have a mentored clinic responsibility for patients with retardation, with favorable feedback. A follow-up survey after graduation reported that 68% of the trainees are seeing patients with retardation in their practice. A study by Goodenough and Hole-Goodenough (1997) queried all 403 family practice residency programs in the United States, and learned that 32% (of the respondents) are having didactic training in mental retardation and 24% are receiving scheduled clinical sessions. Enthusiasm is described as moderate; the ultimate promise is favorable.

Information and Referral Systems

Limited investment has gone to date into the establishment of databases regarding service availability for persons with disabilities, and toward computerized information systems that use them. About a dozen exist around the country, mostly at a state level, but some for cities or counties (R. W. Bass, personal communication, 1998). It is generally agreed that the original data collecting is quite workable; maintaining the information in updated condition is very difficult. A lively project was begun in 1987 by New England INDEX. Its physician register quickly became popular, with contacts for appropriate primary care doctors by far the most frequent requests (psychiatry and neurology next). INDEX has now moved on to have a base of over 30 agencies (local Arc chapters, independent living centers, consumer groups, state bureaus), called the Massachusetts Network of Information Providers. It answers questions on programs, agencies, physicians, consultants, and multilingual facilities, receiving over 800 calls a month (Bass, 1997). It is believed that this is an area of endeavor that substantially assists access to services, including medical care.

Special Insurance Endeavors

An extraordinary event one occasionally experiences in the developing field of improved human services is the joy of welcoming a special new component into the armamentarium of supports. Such a happening was the passage in August 1997 of the state Children's Health Insurance Program (or CHIP), authorized under Title XXI of the Social Security Act, as the largest coverage advance since the enactment of Medicaid. Senator Edward M. Kennedy's leadership has been inestimable. This act was designed to reduce the numbers of the deeply troubling cohort of uninsured children in the United States (both disabled and otherwise) whose families are in economic stress but above the level of Medicaid. The provisions involve a shared federal–state design, with much state determination, and around $4 billion of federal aid annually (Committee on Child Health Financing, 1998). Previously about 20% of children with disability or chronic illness were uninsured. In some states (e.g., Massachusetts), the formula now potentially exists for no child to be without some form of meaningful health insurance. It is estimated that 5.8 million children may be eligible for CHIP nationwide, but some concerns exist that it may be difficult to achieve enrollment of more than 60% of that number, in part because of structural problems (Ullman, Bruen, & Holahan, 1998). There is an active outreach strategy component of the act, but there are practical aspects to reaching all relevant families (who may be limited by illiteracy, unawareness, transportation difficulties, paperwork avoidance, no interpreters, restrictive enrollment hours, etc.). Hence, although we have moved a giant step closer to an important coverage goal, achievement of the details is still complicated.

Enhanced State Departmental Functions

The relevant department in each state's government (Mental Retardation, Developmental Disabilities, or other local terms) has a tactical and moral charge to furnish life-ameliorating supports for persons with mental retardation. Commitment regarding activities in the area of health care waned two decades or so ago, correlating with a negative reaction to supposed intrusion of the "medical model" in developmental services. Currently a more holistic design accepts health care and health promotion as part of the coordinated effort, and even in some leadership role. Significant components of modern (and future) departmental programs include the following:

- Improved information and data systems that will allow review of epidemiologic issues, resource use in care assignments, and patterns and circumstances of mortality

- Strong guidance in effective charting of health concerns in Individualized Service Plans (ISPs) or related documents, with accurate annual update, and reinforcement of material in the "portable medical record" for use in health care visits

- Practical assistance in the conduct of primary medical care contacts, such as involvement of Service Coordinators and/or Area Office nurses in medical visits and follow-through, and assuring appropriated physician reimbursement capacity via Medical Assistance funds (e.g., Medicare and Medicaid)

- Leadership in providing services relating to good nutrition, fitness, and wellness, in both day and residential programs

- Monitoring of enrollment in Medicaid managed care, with verification of sound benefits and customer satisfaction

It is widely agreed that collaboration by the department with community health care providers, especially in care coordination activities, is critically valuable. Some of the work listed above or its supervision could be contracted with university or private units.

Shaping Up

Beyond the elements discussed previously, a number of other adult service system improvements are in the "work in progress" category. Many of them were considered in the Garrard Symposium on Community Health Care Services, and appear in the "Basic Issues" report from that time (Crocker, Yankauer, & Conference Steering Committee, 1987). Acceptance of this emerging field suggests that there should be a *health care network* within a state or region, where there could be forums on service availability, evolution in the delivery system, lessons about reimbursement, and areas of special need. Within this formulation, administrators, program people, consumers, and clinicians could talk together, avoid isolation, and enhance coordination. The potential identification of *resource centers* is also germane, for referral studies, information, assistive technology support, and so forth. Such facilities (in University Affiliated Programs, hospitals, state residential facilities, or private institutes) could also offer in-service training and outreach consultation. *Health services research* can be carried out within a resource center, a provider organization, a university, or the state department; there could be discussion of prevention of secondary conditions, possible protocols for care in various settings, codification of health care outcomes, and decisions on evaluative methods. *Standards of care* can emerge from provider organizations, University Affiliated Programs, or state department task forces. Individual administrative areas (state, city) should consider formation of a permanent *coordinating council* for health matters involving persons with mental retardation, with representatives from agencies, consumer groups, payers, and care providers. There should be a clear mandate for monitoring functions, with a legislative or high official origin, and possible direct liaison to the governor's office. This could be a venue for quality control, introduction of resource materials, planning, and changes in system design. Work with children's services can share in many of these same operations, in addition to ongoing involvement with health departments, Title V assistance, pediatric standards groups, and school districts.

CONCLUSION

An outline has been presented that describes increasingly accountable designs for community services, particularly within the rubric of enrollment in the state mental retardation agency. Physicians have better orientation, the knowledge base is improved, paperwork and coordination have more attention, and there are beginnings of materials for care standards and outcomes measurement. But we are not at a satisfying level. In the present managed care setting (primary physician in the community or HMO), persons with mental retardation somehow remain strangers. They are generally considered to be expensive clients. There is not enough time to maximize preventive or rehabilitative efforts. Awkward negotiation may be required for referral approval, and if one goes outside the system the reimbursement is inadequate to engage the premier specialists. At present new governmental regulations seem to be continually required to keep firms on line and nondiscriminatory. There is uncertainty about organizational continuity in many of the programs, including some that are part of the seemingly inevitable shift to for-profit status.

There is further unrest here. Access to quality health care remains in our ethos as a natural right (although not literally an entitlement), yet many individuals are still left out of present coverage, or tumble out of it. The problems of people being underinsured or uninsured have not been eliminated (although some groups are buttressed). The only way to produce equitable, stable, and adaptable coverage is by universal health insurance. A single payer can then assure full access, transferability, and non-contentious referral. In a review written almost a decade ago about anticipated health care delivery characteristics for *Mental Retardation in the Year 2000*, Crocker (1992b) predicted that a full national health insurance system would replace continual readjustment of Medicaid coverage (p. 174), and "it seems not too much to hope that this will be secured by the year 2000" (p. 179). When the moment for decisions came, our nation seemed uncertain about the feasibility of a single universal system, and hence the prophesy crashed. There is now another opportunity to move toward fairness, strength, and fulfillment in medical care systems for persons with mental retardation.

REFERENCES

Alliance for Health Reform. (1997). *Managed care and vulnerable Americans: Children with special health care needs.* Washington, DC: Author

Bass, R. W. (1997). Progress report: Massachusetts Network of Information Providers. Waltham, MA: Eunice Kennedy Shriver Center.

Birenbaum, A. (1995). Managed care and the future of primary care for adults with mental retardation. *Mental Retardation, 33,* 334–337.

Braddock, D. (1996). Medicaid and persons with developmental disabilities. *Mental Retardation, 34,* 331.

Brewer, E. J., McPherson, M., Magrab, P. R., & Hutchins, V. L. (1989). Family-centered, community-based, coordinated care for children with special health care needs. *Pediatrics, 83,* 1055–1060.

Brown, G. W. (1987). Pediatricians and people with developmental disabilities. *American Journal of Diseases of Children, 141*, 729.

Cole, R. F. (1987). Community-based prepaid medical care for adults with mental retardation: Proposal for a pilot project. *Mental Retardation, 25*, 233–235.

Committee on Child Health Financing. (1998). Implementation principles and strategies for Title XXI (State Children's Health Insurance Program). *Pediatrics 101*, 944–948.

Criscione, T., Walsh, K. K., & Kastner, T. A. (1995). An evaluation of care coordination in controlling inpatient hospital utilization of people with developmental disabilities. *Mental Retardation, 33*, 364–373.

Crocker, A. C. (Ed.). (1987). Symposium on community health care services for adults with mental retardation. *Mental Retardation, 25*, 189–242.

Crocker, A. C. (1992a). A declaration of health care rights for the adult with a developmental disability. In E. M. Eklund (Ed.), *Proceedings of Conference on Health Care for Youth and Adults with Disabilities: Policies and Partnerships* (p. 44). Silver Springs, MD: American Association of University Affiliated Programs.

Crocker, A. C. (1992b). Expansion of the health-care delivery system. In L. Rowitz (Ed.), *Mental retardation in the year 2000* (pp. 153–183). New York: Springer-Verlag.

Crocker, A. C., Yankauer. A., & Conference Steering Committee. (1987). Basic issues. *Mental Retardation, 25*, 227–232.

Epstein, S. G., Taylor, A. B., Halberg, A. S., Gardner, J. D., Walker, D. K., & Crocker, A. C. (1989). *Enhancing quality: Standards and indicators of quality care for children with special health care needs.* Boston: New England SERVE.

Goodenough, G. K., & Hole-Goodenough, J. (1997). Training for primary care of mentally handicapped patients in U.S. family practice residencies. *Journal of the American Board of Family Practice, 10*, 333–336.

Hayden, M. F., & DePaepe, P. A. (1991). Medical conditions, level of care needs, and health-related outcomes of persons with mental retardation: A review. *Journal of the Association of Persons with Severe Handicaps, 16*, 188–206.

Kastner, T. A. (1991). Who cares for the young adult with mental retardation? *Journal of Developmental and Behavioral Pediatrics, 12*, 196–198.

Kastner, T. A., Walsh, K. K., & Criscione, T. (1997). Overview and implications of Medicaid managed care for people with developmental disabilities. *Mental Retardation, 35*, 257–269.

Landon, B. E., Tobias, C., & Epstein, A. M. (1998). Quality management by state Medicaid agencies converting to managed care: Plans and current practice. *Journal of the American Medical Association, 279*, 211–216.

Master, R., Dreyfuss, T., Connors, S., Tobias, C., Zhou, Z., & Kronick, R. (1996). The Community Medical Alliance: An integrated system of care in Greater Boston for people with severe disability and AIDS. *Managed Care Quarterly, 4*, 26–37.

McDonald, E. P. (1985). Medical needs of severely developmentally disabled persons residing in the community. *American Journal of Mental Deficiency, 90*, 171–176.

Menolascino, F. J., & Stark, J. A. (1984). *Handbook of mental illness in the mentally retarded.* New York: Plenum Press.

Minihan, P. M., & Dean, D. H. (1990). Meeting the needs for health services of persons with mental retardation living in the community. *American Journal of Public Health, 80*, 1043–1048.

Minihan, P. M., Dean, D. H., & Lyons, C. M. (1993). Managing the care of patients with mental retardation: A survey of physicians. *Mental Retardation, 31*, 239–246.

Nelson, R. P., & Crocker, A. C. (1978). The medical care of mentally retarded persons in public residential facilities. *New England Journal of Medicine, 299*, 1039–1044.

New England SERVE. (1997). *Assessing the quality of managed care for children with special health care needs.* Boston: Author.

Nowell, N., Baker, D., & Conroy, J. (1989). *The provision of community medical care in Philadelphia and northwestern Pennsylvania for people who live in community living arrangements and with their families.* Philadelphia: Philadelphia Coordinated Health Care.

Pangburn, D. A. (1999). Referral processes. In M. D. Levine, M. B. Carey, & A. C. Crocker (Eds.), *Developmental-behavioral pediatrics* (3rd ed., pp. 851–856). Philadelphia: Saunders.

Perrin, J. M., Kuhlthau, K., Walker, D. K., Stein, R. E. K., Newacheck, P. W., & Gortmaker, G. L. (1997). Monitoring health care for children with chronic conditions in a managed care environment. *Maternal and Child Health Journal, 1,* 15–23.

Pulcini, J., & Howard, A. M. (1997). Framework for analyzing health care models serving adults with mental retardation and other developmental disabilities. *Mental Retardation, 35,* 209–217.

Rubin, I. L., & Crocker, A. C. (1989). *Developmental disabilities: Delivery of medical care for children and adults.* Philadelphia: Lea & Febiger.

Spink, J. E. (1997). *The managed care handbook: A resource guide for consumers, families, and advocates.* Waltham, MA: Eunice Kennedy Shriver Center.

Spitalnik, D. M. (1996). *Training family physicians in developmental disabilities: A research and training project.* Piscataway: University Affiliated Program of New Jersey.

Szymanski, L. S., & Tanguay, P. E. (Eds.). (1980). *Emotional disorders of mentally retarded persons: Assessment, treatment, and consultation.* Baltimore: University Park Press.

Tarjan, G. (1966). Cinderella and the prince: Mental retardation and community psychiatry. *American Journal of Psychiatry, 122,* 1057–1059.

Tarjan, G., Brooke, C. E., Eyman, R. K., Suyeyasu, A., & Miller, C. R. (1968). Mortality and cause of death in a hospital for the mentally retarded. *American Journal of Public Health, 58,* 1891–1900.

Tarjan, G., Eyman, R. K., & Miller, C. R. (1969). Natural history of mental retardation in a state hospital. *American Journal of Diseases of Children, 117,* 609–620.

Ullman, F., Bruen, B., & Holahan, J. (1998). *The State Children's Health Insurance Program: A look at the numbers.* Washington, DC: The Urban Institute.

Ziring, P. R., Kastner, T. A., Friedman, D. L., Pond, W. S., Barnett, M. L., Sonnenberg, E. M., & Strassburger, K. (1998). Provision of health care for persons with developmental disabilities living in the community. *Journal of the American Medical Association, 260,* 1439–1444.

Toward a Brighter Future for Persons with Down Syndrome

Siegfried M. Pueschel

HISTORICAL PERSPECTIVE

Although chromosomal aberrations including Down syndrome probably have been with mankind since the dawn of early civilization, the first description of a child who presumably had Down syndrome was provided by Esquirol in 1838. Shortly thereafter, in 1846, Séguin described a child with features suggestive of Down syndrome, a condition he called "furfuraceous idiocy." In 1866 Duncan gave an account of a girl "with a small round head, Chinese looking eyes, projecting a large tongue who only knew a few words." During the same year, Down (1866) published his historic paper reporting some of the features of this syndrome that today bears his name. Down deserves credit for describing some of the classical features of this condition and thus distinguishing these children from others with mental retardation, in particular those with cretinism.

Many scientists of the mid-19th century, including Down, were undoubtedly influenced by Darwin's (1859) book, *The Origin of the Species.* In keeping with Darwin's theory of evolution, Down believed that the condition we now call Down syndrome was a reversion to a primitive racial type. Because of the oriental appearance noted in the affected children, Down coined the term "mongolism" and inappropriately called this condition "mongolian idiocy." Of course, today we know that the racial implications are incorrect. Although terminology such as mongoloid and mongolism are generally not used today, there are still "old timers" who adhere to such terms. To call a child with Down syndrome "a mongoloid idiot" is not only demeaning to the child but also an incorrect description of the person, who, though having a mental handicap, is first and foremost a human being who is capable of learning and functioning in society.

After Down's report, only a few articles were published in the last decades of the 19th century. In 1876 Fraser and Mitchell described patients with this disorder using the term "Kalmuck idiocy." Fraser and Mitchell provided the first scientific report on Down syndrome at a meeting in Edinburgh in 1875 when they presented observations on 62 persons with Down syndrome. In 1877 Ireland included individuals with Down syndrome as a "special type" in his book *Idiocy and Imbecility*. A decade later Shuttleworth (1886) called children with Down syndrome "unfinished."

In the beginning of this century, numerous authors described additional details of abnormal phenotypic findings in persons with Down syndrome and scientists attempted to find the cause of Down syndrome. In the mid-1950s progress in the method of visualizing chromosomes allowed more accurate studies on human chromosomes, leading to Lejeune's discovery in 1958 that children with Down syndrome had one extra chromosome 21 (Lejeune, Gautier, & Turpin, 1959).

ACCOMPLISHMENTS DURING THE PAST DECADES

During the past few decades, much has been learned about the chromosomal abnormality, genetic concerns, biochemical aberrations, various medical problems, and educational and psychological issues relating to Down syndrome. A multitude of publications on these subjects has permeated the medical literature. When Pueschel and Steinberg (1980) conducted an intensive literature search, they compiled more than 6,000 articles relating to various aspects of Down syndrome. It is estimated that an even larger number of publications appeared in print during the 1980s and 1990s. This enormous information explosion in recent years is in part a reflection of the progress that has been made in the biochemical, psychological, educational, and other areas pertaining to Down syndrome.

Providing Optimal Medical Care

It is well known that previously persons with Down syndrome were frequently not afforded adequate medical care. They were often deprived of all but the most elementary medical services. In the past, children with Down syndrome often were institutionalized, and medical problems including infections, congenital heart disease, endocrine disorders, sensory impairments, and musculoskeletal problems were rarely identified and treated properly. Moreover, early intervention and educational and recreational services were most often nonexistent. Fortunately, there have been major improvements in both the health care and in the provision of educational services for individuals with Down syndrome during the past decades. We have become cognizant of numerous medical concerns and have learned to manage them more appropriately. Over the years, professionals have developed guidelines for optimal medical care in order to improve the quality of life of people with Down syndrome (Pueschel et al., 1995). A summary of these guidelines will be provided in the following sections.

Counseling of Parents

After the birth of a child with Down syndrome, it is of utmost importance that the parents of the newborn child be approached by professionals with tact, compassion, and truthfulness. The initial counseling will have a vital influence of the parents' subsequent adjustment. If the parents are told that the infant with Down syndrome is first and foremost a human being, then they will also see positive attributes in their child and their distress will be lessened (Pueschel & Murphy, 1976).

Soon after the clinical diagnosis has been made, professionals should explain to both parents the meaning of Down syndrome, as well as discuss developmental expectations for the child, the results of the chromosomal analysis, and other related issues. In addition, other parents who have an older child with Down syndrome can also be helpful to the new parents since they are living proof that families can survive such a crisis.

The infant with Down syndrome should undergo a thorough physical and neurological examination soon after birth. A number of congenital anomalies frequently observed in infants with Down syndrome require immediate attention. Some of them may be life threatening and need to be corrected at once, whereas others may become apparent during subsequent days and weeks.

Gastrointestinal Anomalies

Numerous anomalies of the gastrointestinal tract have been reported in infants with Down syndrome, including tracheoesophageal fistula and atresia, duodenal atresia, annular pancreas, aganglionic megacolon (Hirschsprung disease), imperforate anus, and others. Most of these anomalies require immediate surgical intervention in order to allow nutrients and fluids to be absorbed through the intestinal tract. No form of treatment should be withheld from any child with Down syndrome that would be given unhesitatingly to a child without this chromosomal disorder.

Congenital Heart Disease

Because of the high prevalence of congenital heart disease in children with Down syndrome (40% to 50%), it is important to identify children with these defects early. Because some of the infants with congenital heart disease may develop heart failure or early pulmonary artery hypertension, or may thrive poorly, it is recommended that newborn infants with Down syndrome be examined by a pediatric cardiologist and that an electrocardiogram and echocardiogram be obtained during the neonatal period. If an infant with Down syndrome has been diagnosed to have congenital heart disease, the child should be provided with appropriate medical management, such as administration of digitalis and diuretics if indicated, and surgical repair of the cardiac defect at an optimal time in the child's life.

Congenital Cataracts

About 3% of children with Down syndrome have congenital cataracts, which are usually very dense and require prompt extraction soon after birth in order to prevent blindness. Subsequently, appropriate correction with glasses or contact lenses will assure adequate vision.

Nutrition Counseling

During early infancy, feeding problems and poor weight gain may be observed in those infants who have severe congenital heart disease or other significant medical problems. Once the congenital heart defect is surgically repaired or the prevailing medical condition has been treated appropriately, children with Down syndrome usually thrive well.

Referral to an Early Intervention Program

Most children with Down syndrome will benefit from enrollment in an early intervention program. In these programs, children with Down syndrome are followed by a developmental specialist who is knowledgeable in providing appropriate stimulation in areas of gross and fine motor, cognitive, language, and social developments. Environmental enrichment and early intervention approaches should be individualized.

Regular Child Care

As for all children, the child with Down syndrome should be examined at specific time intervals to monitor the child's growth and development and overall health. During these well-child checkups, the pediatrician or family physician should discuss with the parents developmental concerns and provide further nutritional counseling. Regular child care should include immunizations and other preventive measures.

Ear and Hearing Examinations

Because of the high frequency of ear infections and fluid accumulation in the middle ears of children with Down syndrome, often resulting in hearing impairment, it is recommended that the physician examine the child's ears at regular intervals. If there is an indication of middle ear involvement or if there is a suspected hearing impairment, the child should have a formal hearing examination including tympanometry and audiogram. Should the latter examination be difficult to carry out in a very young child, an auditory evoked potential study may be indicated. If a hearing deficit is identified, appropriate treatment is of paramount importance since a hearing impairment may affect both the psychological and language developments of a child. If has been well documented that even a mild conductive hearing deficit may lead to a reduced rate of language development and secondary interpersonal problems. Therefore, regular ear examinations and audiological evaluations should be performed.

Opthalmological Examination

The young child with Down syndrome should undergo an eye examination by a pediatric ophthalmologist during the first year of life since many children with Down syndrome have ocular disorders, including blepharitis, strabismus, nystagmus, and refractive errors. It has been reported that about 30% to 40% of children with Down syndrome are myopic and another 20% to 45% are hyperopic. Normal visual acuity is important for any child; however, if the child is mentally retarded, as many children with Down syndrome are, and additional sensory handicap may further limit the child's overall functioning and prevent the child from participating in significant learning processes. Therefore, children with Down syndrome should be examined regularly by an ophthalmologist.

Dental Care

Like all children, youngsters with Down syndrome should practice proper dental hygiene and should have at least semiannual dental examinations. Although dental caries does not occur more frequently in children with Down syndrome than in other children periodontal disease has been reported to be more prevalent. Therefore, appropriate dental hygiene, flouride treatments, good dietary habits, and appropriate dental care are important to prevent dental problems.

Thyroid Disorders

Whereas hyperthyroidism in children with Down syndrome is rare, the vast majority of individuals with thyroid disorders have hypothyroidism. The prevalence of thyroid disorders has been estimated to be between 15% and 20% in persons with Down syndrome. It is recommended that thyroid function tests, including thyroid stimulating hormone, thyroxine, and others if indicated, be carried out at yearly intervals, without waiting for clinical signs of thyroid disorders. If a person with Down syndrome is found to have hypothyroidism, prompt treatment should be instituted, because if thyroid dysfunction is not recognized, it may compromise the child's central nervous system function. Optimal thyroid function will help normal learning processes to take place.

Radiologic Examination of the Cervical Spine

Because atlantoaxial instability has been observed at a higher frequency in individuals with Down syndrome, X-ray examination of the cervical spine should be considered at about 3 years of age and again before entering competitive sports activities, in particular Special Olympics sports events. Some professionals also recommend another X-ray examination during adolescence. Radiologic evaluations reveal that the majority of children with Down syndrome (about 85%) have normal cervical spine X-rays, about 13% have asymptomatic atlantoaxial instability, and 1% to 2% have symptomatic atlantoaxial instability (Pueschel & Scola, 1987). It is usually recommended that individuals with asymptomatic atlantoaxial instability not engage in certain sports activities that potentially could injure the neck. Individuals with symptomatic atlantoaxial instability will often require an operative procedure to stabilize their cervical spine.

Both atlantoaxial and atlantooccipital instability in individuals with Down syndrome should be identified as early as possible because of their relatively high prevalence and their potential for remediation. A delay in recognizing these conditions may result in irreversible spinal cord damage.

Other Orthopedic Problems

There is a higher prevalence of hip dislocation and patella subluxation in children and adolescents with Down syndrome. Therefore, during routine physical examination, attention should be paid to those as well as other orthopedic problems, such as foot disorders and scoliosis. Appropriate management should be provided for children with these disorders.

Airway Obstructive Disease and Sleep Apnea

Sleep apnea due to upper airway obstruction occurs more often in children and adolescents with Down syndrome than in other children. The upper airway may be obstructed by a narrow hypopharynx, large tonsils and adenoids, increased fat tissue in the pharynx of obese individuals, and glossoptosis. Children with sleep apnea usually snore while sleeping and have episodes during which they do not breathe well. Sleep apnea may result in reduced oxygen supply to the brain and other organs. Children who are diagnosed to have upper airway obstruction can often be treated successfully by tonsillectomy and adenoidectomy, uvulopalatopharyngoplasty, and continuous positive airway pressure. In rare circumstances tracheostomy may be required.

Bacterial Infections

During early childhood, children with Down syndrome may have frequent ear infections. Also sinusitis has been reported to occur at higher prevalence in children with Down syndrome. Respiratory infections, particularly in children with congenital heart disease, are more often observed. Skin infections, primarily at the thighs, lower abdomen, and perigenital area, are commonly noted in adolescents who are overweight. The increased prevalence of infectious disorders in individuals with Down syndrome may be in part due to their immunological deficiencies, including T-cell and B-cell dysfunction. Whenever bacterial infections are encountered, appropriate antimicrobial treatment should be forthcoming.

Behavior and Psychiatric Disorders

Pervasive developmental disorders and attention-deficit/hyperactivity disorders have been reported in children with Down syndrome. In addition, some children exhibit conduct disorders and oppositional behaviors. Also, psychiatric disorders are observed more often in persons with Down syndrome. In particular, major depressions have been noted in young adults with this chromosomal disorder. Behavior management and behavior modification strategies should be provided to children with behavior problems, and specific treatment with medications and counseling should be offered to individuals with psychiatric conditions.

Accelerated Aging Process and Increased Prevalence of Dementia

Adults with Down syndrome have been found to have an accelerated aging process. Many reports in the literature indicate a high prevalence of dementia and Alzheimer's disease in adults with Down syndrome (e.g., Lai, 1992). Although the neuro-histopathology in persons with Down syndrome is nearly identical to that found in patients with Alzheimer's disease who do not have this chromosomal abnormality, the underlying neurologic process may be different in persons with Down syndrome. It has been reported that 15% to 25% of elderly persons with Down syndrome will develop symptoms of dementia.

Other Considerations

There are numerous clinical conditions observed in persons with Down syndrome, as described above, which should be taken into account in the course of their medical care and clinical management. In addition, there are other important aspects in the life of an individual with Down syndrome, such as developmental concerns in cognitive, motor, social, and language areas; educational strategies; vocational and recreational opportunities; sexual and maturational factors; and continued support to parents. If provided with optimal medical services, fostering the well-being in all areas of human functioning, the quality of life of individuals with Down syndrome can be enhanced significantly and their contribution to society will be substantial.

Advances in Genetics

Since Lejeune et al. (1959) discovered that Down syndrome is caused by trisomy 21, much progress has been made in the field of cytogenetics. In particular, in the early 1970s, new staining methods allowed identification of specific bands on chromosomes.

It has been suggested that it is not the entire chromosome 21 that produces the phenotype in Down syndrome but only a small section of the long arm of chromosome

21, the so-called "Down syndrome region." In recent years, however, it has become apparent that other genes on chromosome 21 may also contribute to the phenotype (Korenberg et al., 1990).

During the past decades, molecular genetic studies have contributed to a better understanding of the imbalance of the extra chromosome material in people with Down syndrome and made possible the molecular definition of regions responsible for specific phenotypic features of Down syndrome. Long-range restriction maps of the long arm of chromosome 21 have become available that utilize somatic cell hybrids, irradiation reduction hybrids, Southern blot hybridization, and pulsed field gel electrophoresis, which in turn have resulted in the placement of over 60 unique DNA markers on the long arm of chromosome 21. Thus, enormous progress has been made in the area of cytogenetics and more recently in molecular genetics in Down syndrome.

Educating Children with Down Syndrome

When children with Down syndrome enter school, we often wonder what they will get out of their educational experience. We hope that school will provide the kind of stimulating and enriching experiences that make the world appear to be an interesting place to explore. Learning situations should provide children with Down syndrome a feeling of personal identity, self-respect, and enjoyment. Inclusive education should also give children an opportunity to engage in sharing relationships with others and should prepare them to contribute productively to society in the future. In integrated settings, schools should provide a foundation for life by encouraging the development of basic academic skills, physical abilities, self-help skills, and social as well as language competence. If the school approaches education in terms of humanizing the teaching process, if it views each student as a person with individual integrity, if it exposes the student to forces that will contribute to self-fulfillment in the broader sense, then the individual with Down syndrome will be given the opportunity to develop optimally in the educational setting.

Whereas for many people with Down syndrome, formal education will be completed once they leave high school, usually at age 21 years, some youngsters with Down syndrome may want to continue to study in a postsecondary educational program. Those programs could be offered in a variety of settings, including trade schools, vocational technical schools, community colleges, and specialized training in business and industry.

Once it has been decided that the individual with Down syndrome will engage in postsecondary educational activities, one needs to determine whether the program can meet the student's academic, social, and emotional needs. Through effective planning, development of appropriate support, and a shared commitment, postsecondary educational programs can provide people with Down syndrome opportunities to pursue their dreams and goals.

Engaging in Meaningful Employment

During the transition from school to the world of work, job development issues need to be addressed. Identifying the person's strengths, determining which people are available to assist with these efforts, and deciding the strategies to be used are central to finding a job for a person with Down syndrome (Wehman, Parent, Unger, & Gibson, 1997).

Unforunately, many individuals with Down syndrome are still employed in sheltered workshops. This may be due in part to the unavailability of jobs in the community. In other circumstances some persons with Down syndrome may be so severely handicapped that they will not be able to participate in a community employment setting. One should realize, however, that workshops often provide stereotypic, monotonous, and boring environments. In addition, workers have very little or no interaction with nonhandicapped employees. Although some individuals may need the support and supervision available in sheltered workshops, such settings must be viewed as limiting the opportunities for people with Down syndrome. More positive benefits will accrue from supported employment in the community (Wehman et al., 1997).

Living Options

After leaving school, some persons with Down syndrome decide to move out of the parental home and live independently. Others may feel secure and comfortable in the parental home environment. In other situations, parents may not want to "cut the umbilical cord" and instead keep the youngster at home, assuming that he or she will not be able to manage in a semiindependent or independent living arrangement.

Those who wish to move out of the parental home should be prepared properly for living in a group home or apartment. Thorough training, including role playing, can reduce the likelihood of some undesirable outcomes. It has been demonstrated that many adults with mental retardation, including those with Down syndrome, are capable of living in the community. Of importance is the availability of ongoing training and support specifically matched to the individual's skills and needs. The combination of formal support from the semiindependent living program and of informal assistance from family, friends, and benefactors, as well as active involvement of consumers themselves, appears to be related to a positive adjustment.

In addition to a place to live, persons with Down syndrome need food, clothing, affection, and a feeling of being worthwhile and needed by others. They will have to learn the social, self-care, and domestic skills that will help them to become more independent. They also will need support services such as health care and, if indicated, occupational and physical therapy, as well as involvement in vocational activities as briefly described above. An ideal service system must be able to accommodate a great many social, emotional, and physical needs of each individual served.

Involvement in Recreational Activities

Successful mastery of recreational skills can build the self-esteem and self-confidence of a person with Down syndrome. Interacting with people in leisure activities can enlarge a person's social network, promote friendships, and encourage the development of social relationships in general. Involvement in physical activities, such as skiing, jogging, swimming, and basketball, can enhance fine and gross motor skills, agility, muscle strength, and cardiovascular endurance. Also, various artistic activities, including drawing, painting, acting, dancing, and learning to play a musical instrument, can encourage persons with Down syndrome to express their talents and creativity.

Special Olympics is an important recreational activity, in that it provides consistent training in sports competition so essential to the physical, mental, and social developments of young people with Down syndrome. The benefits from such training and competition usually go beyond the important outcomes of learning functional sports skills to include stimulating self-confidence and promoting acceptance by society.

Thus, if we provide young people with Down syndrome with appropriate recreational opportunities; if we continue to build upon their strengths, abilities, and contributions; and if we cultivate the development of community groups that are truly inclusive, people with Down syndrome will prosper in the area of recreation and sports that formally appeared out of their reach. Such positive outcomes then can contribute greatly to a young person's overall quality of life (Heyne, Schleien, & Rynders, 1997).

Social Skills, Relationships, and Sexuality

Social–sexual skill training should be available for every person with Down syndrome starting at adolescence and throughout adulthood. Social–sexual skill training is especially important for young people with Down syndrome who often do not have the opportunities to acquire this awareness through typical channels of socialization as do other children. Effective social–sexual behavior involves the intricate application of motor, cognitive, and affective skills that are carefully displayed according to the circumstances, environment, and person.

Like other individuals who do not have this chromosomal disorder, youngsters with Down syndrome need sex education. Sex education should dwell on the teaching of facts not only about body parts and the act of intercourse, but about important human relationships, which include personal feelings and desires as well as attitudes and values. It is important that persons with Down syndrome learn appropriate social behaviors and how to avoid socially unacceptable behaviors. A curriculum that both meets individual needs and provides an active learning experience is vital to a successful sex education program for young people with Down syndrome.

In the future more persons with Down syndrome may desire sexual satisfaction and may indicate a biological need for sexual contact and stimulation. Whereas some individuals with Down syndrome may enjoy sexual togetherness as a rewarding human relationship, others may become lifelong friends without any sexual element. Either type of relationship can provide freedom from loneliness and give new meaning to life (Edwards, 1988).

Sexual activity and marriage are sometimes feared aspects of social skill training. Sex, sexuality, and sexual activity, however, are important facets of social skill training. To neglect the teaching of appropriate social–sexual facts is to deny people with Down syndrome a large measure of their personal rights. The expression of sexual needs and the self-control important in sexual expression are critical to the development of self-concept and self-esteem in people with Down syndrome (Edwards, 1988).

Because people with Down syndrome will live in the community, it is essential to address issues relating to prevention of sexual exploitation and sexual abuse. As persons become more independent, they may be exposed to risks and dangers that are lurking in the community, and therefore sexual exploitation is a possibility. Hence, self-reliance in an ongoing training program should be stressed, with emphasis on protection against vulnerability to sexual exploitation.

LOOKING INTO THE FUTURE

Although much progress has been made in both biomedicine and the behavioral sciences relating to Down syndrome during the past decades, we still lack a basic understanding of central nervous system functions and we do not have appropriate tools available that could bring about primary prevention of trisomy 21. Moreover, our knowledge is quite limited with regard to the effects of certain genes at chromosome 21 and ways to counteract the overproduction of certain gene products. Also, no effective medical treatment is available at the present time to improve significantly the cognitive function of persons with Down syndrome.

Future research on Down syndrome should focus on the causative mechanism resulting in aneuploidy. Further progress will have to be made with maping and sequencing of human chromosome 21; specific cognitive deficits that distinguish people with Down syndrome from those with other forms of mental retardation need to be elicited; and pharmacological and other forms of therapy need to be developed that will ameliorate or prevent mental retardation and Alzheimer's disease (Epstein, 1997).

Genetic Investigations

It is assumed that, at the present pace of research activity, the genetic code of the entire chromosome 21 will be obtained within the next few years. It will be important to identify those genes that play a role in metabolic pathways involved in the cognitive development of persons with Down syndrome and those directly involved in central nervous system function.

Through identification of DNA sequences on chromosome 21 and their correlation with phenotypic features observed during detailed examinations, it may be feasible in the future to elucidate the pathogenesis of Down syndrome and to discover which particular genes are responsible for which aspect of the phenotype. Ultimately, this should lead to prevention or amelioration of symptoms, novel treatment approaches, or both.

If future research efforts lead to identification of the intricate mechanism by which a human chromosome can be "inactivated" as one of the chromosomes in the female, perhaps the same or a similar mechanism may lend itself to inactivate the extra chromosome 21 in the person with Down syndrome in the future. Some research activities will use animal models, in particular the partial trisomy 16 mouse, which may assist in deriving at a better understanding of the effect of gene products and how to counteract them.

Central Nervous System Research

Concerning central nervous system dysfunction in persons with Down syndrome, the underpinnings of the neurophysiological, neurochemical, and neuroanatomical alterations will need to be elucidated. Further work will need to be pursued on early identification of atypical cognitive development using event-related brain potential in order to shed light on development of cerebral inhibitory processes in individuals with Down syndrome (Karrer & Karrer Hill, 1997).

Because the major consequences of Down syndrome are impairments in learning and memory, investigative work, particularly involving the hippocampus, cerebellum, and prefrontal cortex, should be pursued. Refinement of position emission tomography scanning and functional magnetic resonance imaging technology may result in information on cognitive functions, learning processes, language acquisition, and memory in people with Down syndrome.

Moreover, further research on enhancement of cognitive function should involve medications that target cholinergic and glutaminergic neurotransmissions, both of which play an important role in learning and memory. Pharmacologic agents that increase the brain's responsiveness to activity-dependent synaptic plasticity may be of therapeutic benefit to children with Down syndrome (Capone, 1997). It will be important to identify specific medications that are both safe and efficacious.

Important new research findings should also be forthcoming in the psychoeducational arena. Novel studies should be pursued that focus on maximizing developmental and learning processes of infants with Down syndrome in early intervention programs. Also, investigations that probe the learning capabilities and cognitive processes of children with Down syndrome should ultimately lead to optimal learning strategies in an inclusive educational environment. New creative approaches should produce educational settings that will not only enhance learning processes but also foster the social needs of the child with Down syndrome.

Behavioral and Psychiatric Concerns

Because numerous reports have indicated a high prevalence of psychiatric disorders and behavior problems in persons with Down syndrome, future studies will have to address whether it is feasible to prevent, at least in part, certain behavioral and psychiatric conditions in individuals with Down syndrome. To attain appropriate mental health in persons with Down syndrome, their parents need initial counseling and positive guidance so that they can adjust better and provide a family atmosphere to foster optimal physical and mental well-being of the child. It will be important for individuals with Down syndrome to live in a nurturing environment that promotes self-confidence and self-esteem and avoids undue stressful situations. Persons with Down syndrome can be involved in numerous activities that will result in a well-adjusted lifestyle and should ultimately lead to optimal mental health.

Preventing and Treating Patients with Alzheimer's Disease

Another area of investigation should involve a search for prevention and treatment of Alzheimer's disease, which is known to occur at a high prevalence in aging people with Down syndrome. Because nearly all persons with Down syndrome over the age of 35 to 40 years have the characteristic neuropathological findings of Alzheimer's disease and because the life expectancy of people with Down syndrome has increased substantially over the past few decades, it is paramount that investigative work in the area of accelerated aging and Alzheimer's disease be pursued vigorously. Studies should focus on the increased lipid peroxidation observed in people with Down syndrome and how it can be reduced or eliminated, as well as the oxygen metabolism and antioxidant functioning in persons with Down syndrome.

Also, molecular genetic studies should elucidate the gene products that may contribute to the formation of the neuropathology in people with Alzheimer's disease. Furthermore, the effect of newly developed medications for treatment of persons with Alzheimer's disease needs to be evaluated.

Prenatal Diagnostic Considerations

An important area of discussion relates to the prenatal diagnosis of Down syndrome and its ramifications. Some professionals favor selective abortions is a fetus has been identified with Down syndrome. They claim that such action will benefit the family and society, and reduce the financial burden of raising and educating such an individual. Although many of the prenatal diagnostic procedures have significantly contributed to the advances in human genetics and some have been hailed as major breakthroughs, one has to question whether the identification and subsequent abortion of genetically defective fetuses indeed constitutes "real progress." Whereas prenatal diagnosis has certain potential beneficial uses, these justifiable uses should not be overshadowed by the use of the procedures strictly as an exercise of selective abortion. To determine that a fetus with Down syndrome should be aborted is to make a social judgment about the place of individuals with developmental disabilities in society. Many parents consider human life precious and reject the assumption of a life's lack of worth and value as justification for its termination. The assumption of the presence of mental retardation in the fetus with Down syndrome is not a justification for aborting that fetus.

Concerning Discrimination

In the past, discrimination against children with handicapping conditions, including those with Down syndrome, has been common. Yet, discrimination against any individual with a disability regardless of the nature or severity of the disability is morally and legally indefensible. A person with mental retardation such as Down syndrome has the same inherent rights as other human beings, with those rights protected to the maximum degree.

The withdrawing of medical treatment from infants because they are handicapped, which was common practice previously, is an important civil rights issue. Moreover, the withholding of treatment on the basis of the best interests of society and the family is discriminating.

Children with Down syndrome should be valued as human beings with equal rights. If one believes that human life is infinite in value, then one must believe that the sanctity of life is bound to be unaffected by either mental or physical defects.

CONCLUSION

Beyond the myriad of future research possibilities mentioned in this chapter, many more investigations need to be carried out to increase the knowledge in this field which, in turn, will improve the quality of life for persons with Down syndrome. Such investigations not only will shed light on many unknown biological aspects, but also should help individuals with Down syndrome cognitively, educationally, and socially so that they can develop optimally and reach their fullest potential. Once they do so, they can contribute to society and perform tasks that previously were never expected of them.

Moreover, people with Down syndrome can teach society that using quality as a measure of relationships brings a dimension that quantity cannot match. In my view the value of people with Down syndrome is intrinsically rooted in their very humanity and in their uniqueness as human beings which allows them to reach a point of significant fulfillment.

It is imperative that we as parents, professionals, and friends of people with Down syndrome affirm the absolute fullness of their humanity and the absolute worth and sanctity of their lives. We have to fight for the dignity and self-respect of all people with Down syndrome. We have to assure that people with Down syndrome be offered a status that observes their rights and privileges as citizens in a democratic society and in a real sense preserves their human dignity.

REFERENCES

Capone, G. (1997, November). National Down Syndrome Society's 1997 International Down Syndrome Research Conference on Cognition and Behavior, Amelia Island Plantation, FL.

Darwin, C. (1859). *The origin of the species.* London: Murray.

Down, J. L. (1866). Observations on an ethnic classification of idiots. *London Hospital Clinical Lectures and Reports, 3,* 259–262.

Duncan, P. M. (1866). *A manual for the classification, training, and education of the feeble-minded, imbecile and idiotic.* London: Longmans, Green.

Edwards, J. (1988). Sexuality, marriage, and parenting for persons with Down syndrome. In S. M. Pueschel (Ed.), *The young persons with Down syndrome: Transition from adolescence to adulthood* (pp. 173–186). Baltimore: Brookes.

Epstein, C. (1997, November). National Down Syndrome Society's 1997 International Down Syndrome Research Conference on Cognition and Behavior, Amelia Island Plantation, FL.

Esquirol, J. E. D. (1838). *Des maladies mentales considerés sous les rapports medical, hygiénque et médico-légal* (2 vols.). Paris: Bailiére.

Fraser, J., & Mitchell, A. (1876). Kalmuck idiocy: Report of a case with autopsy with notes on 62 cases by A. Mitchell. *Journal of Mental Science, 22,* 169–179.

Heyne, L. A., Schleien, S. J., & Rynders, J. E. (1997). Promoting quality of life through recreation participation. In S. M. Pueschel & M. Sustrova (Eds.), *Adolescence with Down syndrome* (pp. 317–340). Baltimore: Brookes.

Ireland, W. W. (1877). *Idiocy and imbecility.* London: Churchill.

Karrer, R., & Karrar Hill, J. (1997, November). *Neural and behavioral indices of attention and cognition in infants with Down syndrome.* Paper presented at the National Down Syndrome Society's 1997 International Down Syndrome Research Conference on Cognition and Behavior, Amelia Island Plantation, FL.

Korenberg, J. R., Kawashima, H., Pulst, S. M., Ikeuchi, T., Ogasawara, N., Yamamoto, K., Schonberg, S. A., West, R., Allen, L., Magenis, E., Ikawa, K., Taniguchi, N., & Epstein, C. J. (1990). Molecular definition of a region of chromosome 21 that causes features of the Down syndrome phenotype. *American Journal of Human Genetics, 47,* 236–246.

Lai, F. (1992). Alzheimer disease. In S. M. Pueschel & J. K. Pueschel (Eds.), *Biomedical concerns in persons with Down syndrome* (pp. 175–196). Baltimore: Brookes.

Lejeune, J., Gautier, M., & Turpin, R. (1959). Études des chromosomes somatiques de neuf enfants mongoliens [Study of somatic chromosomes of nine mongoloid children]. *Comptes Rendus Hebdomadaires des Seances de L'Academie des Sciences* (Paris), 248, 602–603.

Pueschel, S. M., Anneren, G., Durlach, R., Flores, J., Sustrova, M., & Verma, I. C. (1995). Guidelines for optimal medical care of persons with Down syndrome. *Acta Paediatrica, 84,* 823–827.

Pueschel, S. M., & Murphy, A. (1976). Assessment of counseling practices at the birth of a child with Down's syndrome. *American Journal of Mental Deficiency, 81,* 325–330.

Pueschel, S. M., & Scola, F. (1987). Atlanto-axial instability in idividuals with Down syndrome: Epidemiologic, radiographic, and clinical studies. *Pediatrics, 80,* 555–560.

Pueschel, S. M., & Steinberg, L. (1980). *Down syndrome: A comprehensive bibliography.* New York: Garland STPM Press.

Séguin, E. (1846). *Le traitement moral, l'hygiène et l'éducation des idiots.* Paris: J. B. Baillière.

Shuttleworth, G. E. (1886). Clinical lectures on idiocy and imbecility. *British Medical Journal, 1,* 183–185.

Wehman, P., Parent, W. S., Unger, D. D., & Gibson, K. E. (1997). Supported employment: Providing work in the community. In S. M. Pueschel & M. Sustrova (Eds.), *Adolescence with Down syndrome* (pp. 245–266). Baltimore: Brookes.

Life Span Issues

VI

Communication, Assistive Technology, and Mental Retardation

Mary Ann Romski and Rose A. Sevcik

> At 19 years of age, FG used his SAL [System for Augmenting Language, a
> speech-output communication device] to talk with his grandmother on a weekend
> visit, and she told his mother that it was the "first time" she has ever communicated
> with her grandson. She reminded her daughter that other family members
> had always been present to interpret FG's communications for her.
>
> Romski & Sevcik, 1996, p. 148

The ability to communicate permits a person to express basic wants and
needs, thoughts, and feelings, as well as to interact independently with others. Our communications also provide a window into our inner selves and often are the
basis by which others perceive us. The majority of children and adults with mental
retardation learn to communicate through speech either spontaneously or more typically with the aid of language intervention during the developmental period (Rosenberg & Abbeduto, 1993). Some children and adults with mental retardation, however,
encounter significant difficulty developing communication skills. Such difficulty during childhood results in an inability to express oneself, to maintain social contact with
family, to develop friendships, and to function successfully in school. As the individual
moves into adulthood, an inability to communicate continues to compromise his or her
ability to participate in society, from accessing more advanced education and employment to engaging in leisure activities and personal relationships.

For the most part, individuals who experience a considerable level of difficulty
communicating are those with the most significant degrees of mental retardation.

This chapter is dedicated to the pioneers of the field of communication and language intervention for persons with mental retardation: Richard L. Schiefelbusch and his colleagues, Lyle L. Lloyd, James E. McLean,
Jon F. Miller, and David E. Yoder. Their dedication to supporting the communication abilities of children
and adults with mental retardation has provided a strong foundation for the field. The preparation of this
chapter was supported by NICHD-06016, a Research Enhancement Grant from Georgia State University,
and the Department of Communication, Georgia State University.

They may also exhibit accompanying disabilities that include, but are not limited to, seizure disorders, cerebral palsy, sensory impairments, or maladaptive behaviors (Romski & Sevcik, 1991). They range in age from very young children just beginning their development to adults with a broad range of life-span experiences, including a history of institutionalization. They all can and now do benefit from language and communication intervention focusing on the development and use of functional communication skills, although the precise areas of concentration vary with age and experience.

This chapter takes the reader on a journey through the relationship between communication disorders and significant mental retardation in the 20th century. First, we provide a historical perspective on the early research and practice developments that set the stage for the present. Second, we highlight key advances made in approximately 40 years of communication research and practice with individuals with significant mental retardation, including the recent use of assistive technology devices and services. Finally, we look ahead to the opportunities and challenges that face us as we move into the 21st century.

HISTORICAL PERSPECTIVES

Prior to the 1960s, a child who was diagnosed with significant mental retardation received little or no attention from research or practice in communication disorders because it was thought that the child with mental retardation could not learn and thus would make few gains in speech development (Berry & Eisenson, 1956; Lillywhite & Bradley, 1969; Sheehan, Martyn, & Kilburn, 1968). Sparked by President John F. Kennedy's national initiative, the 1960s brought the emergence of the scientific study of mental retardation, including communication disorders. Communication disorders and significant mental retardation has approximately a 40-year history. In fact, it was not until 1969 that the American Association on Mental Retardation established a special interest group and then a division in 1972 devoted to speech–language pathology and audiology and later communication disorders (David Yoder, August 10, 1998, personal communication). Over this relatively brief period, broad changes in social policy played an important role in expanding and changing the delivery of communication services to children and adults with mental retardation. The earlier literature was clearly focused on the needs of individuals who were institutionalized from birth or early childhood (Calculator & Dollaghan, 1982; Romski, Sevcik, & Pate, 1988). In our own professional and educational experiences over the past 25 years, for example, we have both worked with adults who were institutionalized from early childhood and children who were excluded from public school services.

Three key pieces of federal legislation directed toward improving the lives of children and adults with a range of disabilities have tackled issues related to education, assistive technology devices and services, and, most recently, civil rights. First, in 1975, the original passage of the Education for All Handicapped Children Act (EHA) (Public Law [P.L.] 94-142) guaranteed all children from 5 to 21 years of age, regardless of their disability, the right to a free and appropriate public education, including related services (such as speech and language services) that they needed to obtain that education. This law has been reauthorized three times since its initial passage. In the latest reauthorization, the Individuals with Disabilities Education Act, in 1997, assistive technology has a new section (Section 300.308) that requires, on a case-by-case basis, the use of school-purchased assistive technology devices in a child's home or in other settings if the child's IEP team determines that the child needs access to those devices in order to receive a free and appropriate public education. Second, in 1988 the Technology-Related Assistance Act for Individuals with Disabilities (P.L. 100-407) highlighted the role that assistive technology devices and services can play in ensuring that all people with disabilities are able to participate fully in society. An assistive technology device is any item, piece of equipment, or product system, whether commercially off the shelf, modified, or customized, that is used to increase, maintain, or improve functional capabilities of individuals with disabilities. Included are augmentative and alternative communication (AAC) devices that permit individuals who do not speak to communicate independently. Under this act, funding was provided to states through the National Institute for Disability and Rehabilitation Research (NIDRR) for the development of consumer-driven assistive technology programs whose goal was the comprehensive incorporation of assistive technology devices and services into extant public and private service delivery systems (e.g., education, rehabilitation). In 1990, landmark legislation, the Americans with Disabilities Act (P.L. 101-336), guaranteed the basic civil rights of persons with disabilities and addressed the use of supports and accommodations (including AAC devices and services) to counter the employment and educational access challenges they have experienced.

The impact of these three fundamental pieces of federal legislation is that children and adults with significant mental retardation and severe spoken communication disabilities now have a guaranteed legal right to be included in society and to be provided with the supports needed to accomplish this goal. A fundamental support for the successful implementation of any and all of this legislation is communication skills. Without the ability to communicate, education, employment, inclusion, and self-determination clearly are compromised. These laws have placed demands on communication disorders specialists to develop approaches to both assess and intervene with children and adults who previously had been excluded from speech–language services since, unfortunately, in many cases they had been considered "too retarded" to benefit from communication and language intervention.

ADVANCES FROM RESEARCH AND PRACTICE

The social climate generated by these laws has resulted in the conduct of substantial research and the development of recommended service delivery practices for children and adults with mental retardation. With the establishment of the Mental Retardation Research Centers (MRRCs) in the 1960s (Begab, 1984) came exciting research findings in the area of language and communication that have formed a strong foundation upon which communication intervention is implemented (e.g., McLean, Yoder, & Schiefelbusch, 1972; Miller & Chapman, 1984). In the 1970s, Schiefelbusch and his colleagues at the University of Kansas's MRRC hosted an ongoing series of national conferences on specific topics; each culminated in an edited volume. These conferences served as national think tanks bringing together researchers and practitioners to focus on critical issues about communication and mental retardation (for detailed reviews, see Schiefelbusch, 1978a, 1978b, 1980; Schiefelbusch & Bricker, 1981; Schiefelbusch & Lloyd, 1974; Schiefelbusch & Pickar, 1984). From our perspective, the scholarly energy generated by these volumes fueled innovative approaches to language assessment and intervention for children and adults with mental retardation (e.g., McLean & Snyder-McLean, 1978). These advances can be underscored within three broad areas: philosophy about communication and service delivery, language and communication assessment issues, and language and communication intervention strategies.

A Philosophy About Communication and Service Delivery

Perhaps the most important conceptual development for mental retardation that has emerged in the field of communication disorders is a differentiation among the terms speech, language, and communication. This differentiation has permitted an expanded view of an individual's communication strengths and weaknesses. In this context, speech is the narrowest of terms and refers to an output mode for language and communication. Thus, if a person does not speak, it does not mean that he or she does not have language or cannot communicate. Language, in turn, is an arbitrary symbolic code for expressing information. Communication is defined broadly as "any act by which one person gives to or receives from another person information about that person's needs, desires, perceptions, knowledge, or affective states" (National Joint Committee on the Communication Needs of Persons with Severe Disabilities, 1992, p. 2). The modes by which children and adults with mental retardation can communicate range along a representational continuum from symbolic (e.g., spoken words, manual signs, arbitrary visual–graphic symbols, printed words) to iconic (e.g., actual objects, photographs, line drawings, pictographic visual–graphic symbols) and to nonsymbolic (e.g., signals such as crying or physical movement) (Siegel-Causey & Guess, 1989; see Sevcik, Romski, & Wilkinson, 1991, for a discussion of visual–graphic representational systems). Such a continuum of modes provides a broad range of choices by which a person may communicate. Some children and adults with severe spoken communication disabilities who have no conventional way to communicate also may express their communicative wants and needs in socially unacceptable ways, such as through aggressive or destructive means (e.g., Donnellan, Mirenda, Mesaros, & Fassbender, 1984; Doss & Reichle, 1991). These aggressive, self-stimulatory, and perseverative behaviors can now be assessed and replaced with conventionally accepted forms of communication (see Mirenda, 1997, for a review).

The critical distinction among speech, language, and communication opened the way for the emergence of an inclusive philosophy: *all children and adults can communicate.* The National Joint Committee (1992) published a set of 12 communication rights that all persons, regardless of the degree or severity of their disabilities, must be afforded. These rights, listed in Table 17.1, provide a clear and specific perspective upon which current and future communication service delivery systems, including assessment and intervention, must be built.

Such a philosophical perspective about communication has also resulted in a major shift in how communication services are delivered. "Pull-out" therapy approaches that provided one-on-one therapy outside of the communication setting of use exclu-

TABLE 17.1
Communication Bill of Rights

1. The right to request desired objects, actions, events, and persons, and to express personal preferences, or feelings.
2. The right to be offered choices and alternatives.
3. The right to reject or refuse undesired objects, events, or actions, including the right to decline or reject all proffered choices.
4. The right to request, and be given, attention from and interaction with another person.
5. The right to request feedback or information about a state, an object, a person, or an event of interest.
6. The right to active treatment and intervention efforts to enable people with severe disabilities to communicate messages in whatever modes and as effectively and efficiently as their specific abilities will allow.
7. The right to have communication acts acknowledged and responded to, even when the intent of these acts cannot be fulfilled by the responder.
8. The right to have access at all times to any needed augmentative and alternative communication devices and other assistive devices, and to have those devices in good working order.
9. The right to environmental contexts, interactions, and opportunities that expect and encourage persons with disabilities to participate as full communicative partners with other people, including peers.
10. The right to be informed about the people, things, and events in one's immediate environment.
11. The right to be communicated with in a manner that recognizes and acknowledges the inherent dignity of the person being addressed, including the right to be part of communication exchanges about individuals that are conducted in his or her presence.
12. The right to be communicated with in ways that are meaningful, understandable, and culturally and linguistically appropriate.

Note. From "Guidelines for Meeting the Communication Needs of Persons with Severe Disabilities," by the National Joint Committee for the Communication Needs of Persons with Severe Disabilities, 1992, *ASHA*, 34(Suppl. 7), pp. 1–8. Copyright 1992 by American Speech-Language-Hearing Association. Reproduced with permission.

sively have failed for children and adults with significant mental retardation because they do not facilitate communicative use during daily activities at home, at school, and in the community. Today a broad-based communication assessment and intervention plan is the norm, implemented in all contexts of the child's or adult's daily life and coordinated by a collaborative team of people (i.e., families, the child or adult him- or herself, and a range of professionals representing disciplines including, but not limited to, speech–language pathologists, general and special educators, and physical and occupational therapists) who can manage the many and varied components of the plan.

Language and Communication Assessments

Communication disorders assessment for persons with significant mental retardation has been a particularly challenging area because traditional standardized assessment tools have not been found to be useful. Not surprisingly, standardized speech–language assessment batteries (as well as standardized psychological tests) are difficult to employ with some children and adults with mental retardation because of the severity of their oral language impairments. Often the children or adults are unable to obtain basal scores on measures or their scores are so far below those of their chronological-age peers that converting a raw score into a standard score is not possible or meaningful. Some of the factors that affect assessment outcomes include unfamiliar examiners and unfamiliar testing environments, the lack of a communication output mode, difficulty understanding the requirements of the task, test stimuli that are too complex (e.g., line drawings), and stimuli that are configured in a difficult manner (e.g., 2×2 display). We highlight developments in three areas related to assessment: the diagnosis of hearing loss, communication intervention prerequisites, and discrepancy criteria between language age and mental age.

Diagnosis of Hearing Loss

In the field of communication disorders, ruling out that an individual's communication difficulties are the result of a hearing loss is crucial to the delivery of appropriate communication services. One particular difficulty the field faced early on was how to assess the hearing acuity of an individual with mental retardation who did not respond to traditional audiometric testing methods. In 1969 Fulton and Lloyd developed innovative behavioral protocols that permitted audiologists, in most cases for the first time, to assess the hearing acuity of individuals with mental retardation, particularly those who had been considered difficult to assess. If a child or adult was determined to have a diagnosed hearing loss, then the speech–language assessment and treatment he or she received was required to account for that hearing loss (Berger, 1972). Such behavioral assessment protocols are now common practice, and new sophisticated audiometric techniques (i.e., brainstem evoked potentials, otoacoustic emissions) increasingly are becoming available.

Communication Intervention Prerequisites

Another assessment issue that the field of communication disorders has confronted is the question about whether some cognitive prerequisite skills (e.g., object permanence) had to be demonstrated by the child or adult prior to initiating communication intervention. Even after the passage of EHA, children and adults with severe mental retardation were frequently excluded from speech and language treatments because their assessed levels of intelligence and their sensorimotor development were not commensurate with the cognitive and sensorimotor skills that the extant literature had linked to the emergence of first words in young typically developing children (Romski & Sevcik, 1988; Sheehan et al., 1968). Thus, they were not ready for communication intervention. Although one may argue that some basic cognitive skills are essential for language to develop, the interactions between the domains of cognition and language are certainly complex (for reviews, see Rice, 1983; Rice & Kemper, 1984). Given the impact that language itself can exert on cognitive development, the absence of a functional communication mode may place a child or an adult at both developmental and assessment disadvantages.

Research with children and adults with significant mental retardation has demonstrated that sensorimotor prerequisite skills are not essential to the development of communication skills (Reichle & Yoder, 1985; Romski, Sevcik, & Pate, 1988). Thus, investigators have argued against excluding children and adults from communication and language intervention based solely on the lack of prerequisite sensorimotor skills (Kangas & Lloyd, 1988; Reichle & Karlan, 1985; Romski & Sevcik, 1988). This approach has opened the door for all children and adults to receive speech–language services.

Discrepancies Between Mental Age and Language Age

Other children with mental retardation have been excluded from speech–language services because little or no discrepancy was found between their mental ages (MA) and their language ages (LA), as measured by standardized intelligence and language measures. The rationale for excluding such children from services was that, since cognition was the base from which language emerged, children with these profiles could not advance their language and communication skills beyond their intellectual skills. They could not benefit from speech–language intervention services. In fact, research studies have demonstrated that children with Down syndrome evidence a specific language impairment in addition to their tested intellectual skills (Miller & Chapman, 1984). This exclusionary criterion has been questioned given the critical role that language plays in all development, and children and adults are not being excluded based on this argument (ASHA, 1989).

Language and Communication Intervention Strategies

The greatest development over the past four decades has been in language and communication intervention approaches (Warren, 1990). Psycholinguistic research combined with behavioral instructional procedures provided the early foundation for communication curricula for persons with significant mental retardation (McLean & Snyder-McLean, 1978; Miller & Yoder, 1972). This emphasis was followed by an increased interest on teaching lexical and pragmatic skills, on measuring generalization, and on the creation of more naturalistic intervention approaches (McLean & Snyder-McLean, 1988; Warren & Rogers-Warren, 1985; Warren & Yoder, 1997). The majority of this work has focused on spoken communication intervention approaches. There are, however, some children and adults with mental retardation who fail to develop speech even after extensive spoken language intervention efforts.

Some two decades ago, Schiefelbusch (1980) edited *Nonspeech Language and Communication: Analysis and Intervention*, which marked the first synthesis of a newly emerging area of investigation focused on the development of language and communication through alternative means for children and adults with significant mental retardation. Early investigations, employing manual signs and visual–graphic symbols, focused on demonstrating the feasibility of employing AAC with children and adults with mental retardation (e.g., Carrier, 1974; Deich & Hodges, 1977). In general, these investigations found that, when children and adults were provided with AAC systems, they learned to communicate expressively using the skills they explicitly had been taught. Since that time, AAC has matured into an integral component of language and communication intervention programs for children and adults with mental retardation who encounter significant difficulty learning to speak (e.g., Beukelman & Mirenda, 1998; Mirenda & Iacono, 1990; Reichle, York, & Sigafoos, 1991; Romski, Lloyd, & Sevcik, 1988; Romski & Sevcik, 1988, 1997). AAC can be employed on a temporary basis until speech develops or as a permanent means to communicate (Romski & Sevcik, 1997). It encompasses all forms of communication, from simple gestures, manual signs, and picture communication boards to American Sign Language and sophisticated computer-based devices that can "speak" in phrases and sentences for its users.

There are currently many choices about modes of communication, from manual signs and communication boards to speech-output communication devices. For example, Romski and Sevcik (1996) reported that adolescents with moderate to severe mental retardation (with a mean chronological age of 12 years, 8 months at the initiation of the study) who had previously been unsuccessful with other speech–language interventions were able to learn and use a speech-output communication device with arbitrary visual–graphic symbols to communicate with adults and peers in home, school, and community settings. Choosing an appropriate communication mode is only the beginning of the intervention process, which then must be focused on the long-term development of functional language and communication skills via, if necessary, the alternative mode. Research has focused on approaches for teaching communicative functions, such as requesting, protesting, and commenting via manual signs or visual–graphic symbols; the locale and format of instruction; the integration of technology into instruction; and the role of receptive spoken language skills in instruction (Romski & Sevcik, 1997). The development of language and communication skills, regardless of the mode, also sets the stage for the development of literacy skills. Although literacy is an extremely important area of emphasis, it is only in its infancy for children and adults with significant mental retardation (Koppenhaver, Pierce, & Yoder, 1995).

ANTICIPATING THE 21ST CENTURY

During the last four decades, we have witnessed changes in philosophy about communication service delivery, assessment strategies, and the development of innovative treatment approaches for children and adults with significant mental retardation. The 21st century is nearly upon us, and we envision communication at the heart and soul of many of the issues that the field of mental retardation will be confronting. Perhaps the most clear demonstration of what we want to accomplish for every child and adult comes in an example from our own work:

> As one of our participants was independently ordering lunch with his SAL at a local fast-food restaurant, the manager remarked to us, "If your children can use computers, they must be pretty smart." He went on to say that he would seriously consider hiring them to work at his store in the future. (Romski & Sevcik, 1996, p. 148)

In this example, the child was using technology and functioned as an independent communicator. His skills, coupled with the technology he used, changed the perception of this communication partner and facilitated the child's acceptance and long-term inclusion in society. This is a powerful outcome that should be available to all children and adults with significant mental retardation. To ensure such broad outcomes for all children and adults with significant mental retardation, growth is essential in the following areas: self-determination, treatment efficacy, and assistive technology.

Communication, Self-Determination, and Inclusion

The past few years have seen an increased emphasis on the issue of self-determination and individuals with significant disabilities. Wehmeyer (1996, 1998) has argued that individuals must have adequate opportunities, including supports and accommodations, to be the causal agent in their lives, to make choices, and to learn self-determination skills so that they can maximize their active participation in their lives and communities. AAC technology is an essential accommodation and the ability to communicate with familiar and unfamiliar partners is an essential support for self-determination efforts to come to fruition.

A firm recognition of the communication potential of persons with significant mental retardation is essential for all practicing professionals in the field of communication disorders. Typically, the area of mental retardation is only one small part of the scope of educational training in communication disorders. We must work to ensure that appropriate information related to communication and mental retardation is included in preservice and inservice education for speech–language pathologists. Philosophically, daily in educational and rehabilitative agencies across the United States, there are debates concerning how important communication is for children and adults with significant mental retardation. As this chapter highlights, communication is critical to self-determination. At the policy level, we must be ever vigilant so that the laws we have fought so long and hard to establish are not weakened or overturned if we are to ensure that individuals with significant mental retardation are embedded within the mainstream of our society.

Efficacy and Communication Intervention Research

These philosophical and policy issues must go hand in hand with continued advances in research and practice. The current national emphasis on managed care challenges our accountability for the communication services we deliver to persons with significant mental retardation. Although our field has progressed substantially since the notions of "feasibility" studies, the issue of communication treatment efficacy is one that must continue to be given serious consideration if we are to be accountable to the people we study and serve. Clearly, for individuals with significant mental retardation, measuring change is easier said than done. In our experience, change is multidimensional. There are specific changes, such as the development and expansion of vocabulary in comprehension and production, that occur and serve as a foundation for broader, more global, developments, such as using appropriate vocabulary to communicate with unfamiliar partners. How do we, then, link these specific changes, in a cause–effect fashion, to broader changes in how a child or adult is perceived by familiar and unfamiliar partners or to, for example, obtaining employment when the individual completes his or her educational experience? How do we faithfully document changes over time? The development of measurement tools can be a difficult task. These are some of the questions we must confront in the 21st century (Sevcik, Romski, & Adamson, 1999).

We must also safeguard against the use of unreliable treatments. For example, during the 1990s, an extremely controversial intervention, facilitated communication (FC), has attracted a substantial amount of clinical and research attention. FC is defined as

> a method, or group of methods, for providing assistance to a nonverbal person in typing letters, words, phrases, or sentences using a typewriter, computer keyboard,

or alphabet facsimile. It involves a manual prompting procedure, with the intent of supporting a person's hand sufficiently to make it more feasible to strike the keys he or she wishes to strike, without influencing key selection. (Jacobson, Mulick, & Schwartz, 1995)

Initial observations suggested that FC may facilitate literacy skills for the individuals who were using it (e.g., Biklin, 1993). While these clinical observations were striking, it was unclear how independently authored the individuals' facilitated communications were. Results of a strong cluster of quantitative research studies found that the facilitator was actually producing the messages and not the learner (see Jacobson et al., 1995, for a review). If the goal for communication intervention is functional communicative competence, then this intervention does not facilitate the individual's communicative competence in the community and is not likely to be a viable intervention.

As we acquire greater knowledge about efficacious treatments, we also will be able to address the underlying mechanisms that permit individuals to communicate. In turn, understanding these mechanisms will permit us to develop superior effective language interventions for children and adults with significant mental retardation.

AAC and Assistive Technology

One striking characteristic of the AAC field today is the rapid development of new technologies (Beukelman & Mirenda, 1998). Changes in the types of communication devices that are available occur so frequently that it can be difficult to keep abreast of every device on the market today. While AAC and assistive technology (AT) in general have developed as a field, people with mental retardation have not always been included in the mainstream of that development (Wehmeyer, 1995). Well into the 1980s, the prevailing philosophy was that children and adults with significant mental retardation would not benefit "enough" from the use of speech-output communication devices to justify the initial fiscal outlay for the purchase of a device (Turner, 1986). Research with individuals with significant mental retardation has shown that this is an incorrect assumption (Beukelman & Mirenda, 1998; Romski & Sevcik, 1996). In the early 1980s, The Arc created a bioengineering initiative to evaluate available AT in terms of its applicability to the needs of children and adults with mental retardation and to develop new devices to address the unmet needs of individuals with mental retardation (Mineo, 1985). This type of effort drew attention, within the mental retardation community, to a striking need for exemplary demonstration projects, like Project FACTT (Sevcik et al.,1995), focusing on successful programs about AT and individuals with significant mental retardation.

Currently, a number of technological advances in AAC and AT access have opened up new possibilities for people with significant mental retardation. Recent additions to the AAC device market are able to provide a range of capabilities within one device that may enable a child or adult to use one piece of equipment for a more extended period of time. Technological advances such as the speed of computer-based communication and speech recognition technology have the potential to further facilitate the inclusion of individuals with significant mental retardation into society.

SUMMARY AND CONCLUSIONS

In summary, substantial growth has occurred in the field of language and communication intervention with persons with significant mental retardation over the second half of the 20th century. The acquisition of communication skills can be the key to unlocking the world for every child and adult with significant mental retardation (Mirenda & Iacono, 1990; Romski & Sevcik, 1996). Its use can change the quality of a child's or adult's life by enhancing communication in inclusive settings, in transitions from school to work, in family interactions, and in the perceptions and attitudes of others toward children and adults who do not speak (Romski & Sevcik, 1996). The field's focus has moved away from an assessment of who can use what type of device and a concentration on the technology alone toward effective interventions and their implementation and use, along with broader issues of self-determination and social policy. Innovative behavioral research is answering questions that influence social policy decisions, but there is still a substantial amount of uncharted territory that must be studied in the future.

In conclusion, we look to the 21st century with cautious optimism. Children and adults with significant mental retardation and severe spoken communication disabilities have indeed demonstrated communication achievements far beyond the early clinical expectations afforded them. Essential research and resultant recommended practices continue to expand our views about the communication abilities of individuals with significant mental retardation and severe spoken communication disabilities who require supports and accommodations to communicate. Our hope for the 21st century is that our knowledge base will serve to facilitate the full and meaningful inclusion of all children and adults with significant mental retardation and severe spoken communication disabilities into society.

REFERENCES

American Speech-Language-Hearing Association. (1989). Issues in determining eligibility for language intervention. *ASHA, 31*, 113–118.

Americans with Disabilities Act of 1990, 42 U.S.C. § 12101 *et seq.*

Begab, M. (1984). Guest editorial: Mental retardation research centers. *American Journal of Mental Deficiency, 88*, 461–464.

Berger, S. (1972). A clinical program for developing multimodal language responses with atypical deaf children. In J. McLean, D. Yoder, & R. L. Schiefelbusch (Eds.), *Language intervention with the retarded: Developing strategies* (pp. 212–236). Baltimore: University Park Press.

Berry, M. F., & Eisenson, J. (1956). *Speech disorders: Principles and practices of therapy.* New York: Appleton-Century-Crofts.

Beukelman, D. R., & Mirenda, P. (1998). *Augmentative and alternative communication.* Baltimore: Brookes.

Biklin, D. (1993). *Communication unbound: How facilitated communication is challenging traditional views of autism and ability/disability.* New York: Teachers College Press.

Calculator, S., & Dollaghan, C. (1982). The use of communication boards in a residential setting: An evaluation. *Journal of Speech and Hearing Disorders, 47,* 281–287.

Carrier, J. (1974). Nonspeech noun usage training with severely and profoundly retarded children. *Journal of Speech and Hearing Research, 17,* 510–517.

Deich, R., & Hodges, P. (1977). *Language without speech.* New York: Brunner/Mazel.

Donnellan, A., Mirenda, P., Mesaros, R., & Fassbender, L. (1984). Analyzing the communicative functions of aberrant behavior. *Journal of The Association for Persons with Severe Handicaps, 9,* 141–150.

Doss, S., & Reichle, J. (1991). Replacing excess behavior with an initial communicative repertoire. In J. Reichle, J. York, & J. Sigafoss (Eds.), *Implementing augmentative and alternative communication: Strategies for learners with severe disabilities* (pp. 215–238). Baltimore: Brookes.

Education for All Handicapped Children Act of 1975, 20 U.S.C. § 1400 *et seq.*

Fulton, R., & Lloyd, L. L. (1969). *Audiometry for the retarded with implications for the difficult-to-test.* Baltimore: Williams & Wilkins.

Jacobson, J. W., Mulick, J. A., & Schwartz, A. A. (1995). A history of facilitated communication. *American Psychologist, 50,* 750–765.

Kangas, K., & Lloyd, L. (1988). Early cognitive skill prerequisites to augmentative and alternative communication use: What are we waiting for? *Augmentative and Alternative Communication, 4,* 211–221.

Koppenhaver, D., Pierce, P., & Yoder, D. (1995). AAC, FC, and the ABCs: Issues and relationships. *American Journal of Speech-Language Pathology, 4,* 5–14.

Lillywhite, H., & Bradley, D. (1969). *Communication problems in mental retardation: Diagnosis and management.* New York: Harper & Row.

McLean, J., & Snyder-McLean, L. (1978). *A transactional approach to early language training.* Columbus, OH: Merrill.

McLean, J., & Snyder-McLean, L. (1988). Applications of pragmatics to severely mentally retarded children and youth. In R. L. Schiefelbusch & L. L. Lloyd (Eds.), *Language perspectives: Acquisitions, retardation and intervention* (pp. 255–288). Austin, TX: PRO-ED.

McLean, J., Yoder, D., & Schiefelbusch, R. (1972). *Language intervention with the retarded: Developing strategies.* Baltimore: University Park Press.

Miller, J. & Chapman, R. (1984). Disorders of communication: Investigating the development of language of mentally retarded children. *American Journal of Mental Deficiency, 88,* 536–545.

Miller, J., & Yoder, D. (1972). A syntax teaching program. In J. McLean, D. Yoder, & R. L. Schiefelbusch (Eds.), *Language intervention with the retarded: Developing strategies* (pp. 191–211). Baltimore: University Park Press.

Mineo, B. (1985). Technology for the future: A report from the ARC Bioengineering Program. *Exceptional Parent, 15,* 11–15.

Mirenda, P. (1997). Supporting individuals with challenging behavior through functional communication training and AAC: Research review. *Augmentative and Alternative Communication, 13,* 207–225.

Mirenda, P., & Iacono, T. (1990). Communication options for persons with severe and profound disabilities: State of the art and future directions. *Journal of The Association for Persons with Severe Handicaps, 15,* 3–21.

National Joint Committee for the Communication Needs of Persons with Severe Disabilities. (1992, March). Guidelines for meeting the communication needs of persons with severe disabilities. *ASHA, 34* (Supp. 7), 1–8.

Reichle, J., & Karlan, G. (1985). The selection of an augmentative system in communication intervention: A critique of decision rules. *JASH, 10,* 146–156.

Reichle, J., & Yoder, D. (1985). Communication board use in severely handicapped learners. *Language, Speech, and Hearing Services in Schools, 16,* 146–157.

Reichle, J., York, J., & Sigafoos, J. (1991). *Implementing augmentative and alternative communication: Strategies for learners with severe disabilities.* Baltimore: Brookes.

Rice, M. (1983). Contemporary accounts of the cognition/language relationship: Implications for language clinicians. *Journal of Speech and Hearing Disorders, 48,* 347–359.

Rice, M., & Kemper, S. (1984). *Child language and cognition.* Baltimore: University Park Press.

Romski, M. A., Lloyd, L. L., & Sevcik, R. A. (1988). Augmentative and alternative communication issues. In R. L. Schiefelbusch & L. L. Lloyd (Eds.), *Language perspectives: Acquisition, retardation and intervention* (2nd ed., pp. 343–366). Austin, TX: PRO-ED.

Romski, M. A., & Sevcik, R. A. (1988). Augmentative and alternative communication systems: Considerations for individuals with severe intellectual disabilities. *Augmentative and Alternative Communication, 4,* 83–93.

Romski, M. A., & Sevcik, R. A. (1991). Patterns of language learning by instruction: Evidence from nonspeaking persons with mental retardation. In N. Krasnegor, D. Rumbaugh, R. Schiefelbusch, & M. Studdert-Kennedy (Eds.), *Biobehavioral foundations of language development* (pp. 429–445). Hillsdale, NJ: Erlbaum.

Romski, M. A., & Sevcik, R. A. (1996). *Breaking the speech barrier: Language development through augmented means.* Baltimore: Brookes.

Romski, M. A., & Sevcik, R. A. (1997). Augmentative and alternative communication for children with developmental disabilities. *Mental Retardation and Developmental Disabilities Research Reviews, 3,* 363–368.

Romski, M. A., Sevcik, R. A., & Pate, J. L. (1988). The establishment of symbolic communication in persons with mental retardation. *Journal of Speech and Hearing Disorders, 53,* 94–107.

Rosenberg, S., & Abbeduto, L. (1993). *Language and communication in mental retardation: Development, processes, and intervention.* Hillsdale, NJ: Erlbaum.

Schiefelbusch, R. L. (1978a). *The bases of language intervention.* Baltimore: University Park Press.

Schiefelbusch, R. L. (1978b). *Language intervention strategies.* Baltimore: University Park Press.

Schiefelbusch, R. L. (1980). *Nonspeech language and communication: Analysis and intervention.* Baltimore: University Park Press.

Schiefelbusch, R. L., & Bricker, D. (1981). *Early language: Acquisition and intervention.* Baltimore: University Park Press.

Schiefelbusch, R. L., & Lloyd, L. L. (1974). *Language perspectives: Acquisition, retardation, and intervention.* Baltimore: University Park Press.

Schiefelbusch, R. L., & Pickar, J. (1984). *The acquisition of communicative competence.* Baltimore: University Park Press.

Sevcik, R. A., Romski, M. A., & Adamson, L. B. (1999). Measuring AAC interventions for individuals with severe developmental disabilities. *Augmentative and Alternative Communication, 15,* 38–44.

Sevcik, R. A., Romski, M. A., Collier, V., Rayfield, C., Nelson, B., Walton-Bowe, A., Jordon, D., Howell, M., & Ross, J. (1995). Project FACTT: Meeting the communication needs of children with severe developmental disabilities. *Technology and Disability, 4,* 233–241.

Sevcik, R. A., Romski, M. A., & Wilkinson, K. (1991). Roles of graphic symbols in the language acquisition process for persons with severe cognitive disabilities. *Augmentative and Alternative Communication, 7,* 161–170.

Sheehan, J., Martyn, M., & Kilburn, K. (1968). Speech disorders in retardation. *American Journal of Mental Deficiency, 73,* 251–256.

Siegel-Causey, E., & Guess, D. (1989). *Enhancing nonsymbolic communication interactions among learners with severe disabilities.* Baltimore: Brookes.

Technology-Related Assistance for Individuals with Disabilities Act of 1988, 29 U.S.C. § 2201 *et seq.*

Turner, G. (1986). Funding VOCAs for the lower cognitive functioning. *Closing the Gap, 5,* 26.

Warren, S. (1990). Early communication and language intervention: Challenges for the 1990s and beyond. In A. P. Kaiser & D. Gray (Eds.), *Enhancing children's communication: Research foundations for intervention* (pp. 375–396). Baltimore: Brookes.

Warren, S., & Rogers-Warren, A. (1985). *Teaching functional language.* Austin, TX: PRO-ED.

Warren, S., & Yoder, P. (1997). Communication, language, and mental retardation. In W. McLean (Ed.), *Ellis' handbook of mental deficiency, psychological theory and research* (pp. 379–403). Mahwah, NJ: Erlbaum.

Wehmeyer, M. L. (1995). The use of assistive technology by people with mental retardation and barriers to this outcome: A pilot study. *Technology and Disability, 4,* 195–204.

Wehmeyer, M. L. (1996). Self-determination for youth with significant disabilities: From theory to practice. In L. E. Powers, G. H. Singer, & J. Sowers (Eds.), *On the road to autonomy: Promoting self-competence in children and youth with disabilities* (pp. 115–134). Baltimore: Brookes.

Wehmeyer, M. L. (1998). Self-determination and individuals with significant disabilities: Examining meanings and misinterpretations. *JASH, 23,* 5–16.

Riding the Third Wave: Self-Determination and Self-Advocacy in the 21st Century

Michael L. Wehmeyer, Hank Bersani, Jr., and Raymond Gagne

In the last quarter of the 20th century, there has been increased attention to the importance of self-determination and self-advocacy in the lives of people with mental retardation. Bersani (1996) characterized this as the third wave of the disability movement: the self-advocacy movement. Like other contributions to this book, this chapter examines where we have been and where we are now, and provides our opinion as to where we need to go in the future. Unlike other chapters, however, we provide two voices to describe this history and vision. The first is the voice of professionals and advocates who have worked to achieve self-determination for people with mental retardation and to promote self-advocacy. The second voice is the voice of experience—a look at the past, present, and future of self-advocacy and self-determination through the life of someone who experiences a significant disability and whose life experiences better define and describe the importance of self-advocacy and self-determination than any historical literature review. These voices will be interchanged throughout the chapter. In his autobiography, Ray Gagne (1994) characterized the phases in his life in which he either lived in an institution for people with mental retardation or lived in the community as times of power or no power. Such headings capture the true sense of the 20th century for most people with mental retardation as well: It is a century of movement from a lack of power to increased opportunities for control and self-determination. The headings in this chapter mirror the imagery of power as ways to portray the historical and current status in this area.

Ray Gagne's contributions to this chapter are excerpts from "A Self-Made Man," by R. Gagne, in *Creating Individual Supports for People with Developmental Disabilities* (pp. 327–334) by V. J. Bradley, J. W. Ashbaugh, and B. C. Blaney (Eds.), 1994, Baltimore: Paul H. Brookes. Copyright 1994 by Paul H. Brookes. Reprinted with permission.

POWERLESS LIVES

At the dawn of the 20th century, the field of mental retardation was essentially a medical discipline in which medical professionals held all the cards and all the power. Bersani (1996) describes this as the *First Wave* of the disability movement, one of professionalism. Professionals were not interested in the rights of people whom they called "clients," "retardates," or "the mentally deficient." Indeed, far from a focus on humanity and human rights, in the late part of the 19th century and the early part of the 20th century, people with mental retardation were often viewed as menaces and linked with crime, poverty, promiscuity, and the decline of civilization. They were seen by professionals and society as subhuman (a "vegetable") or as objects to be feared or dreaded.

Goddard (1912) summarized his study of the Kallikak family as such:

> We find on the good side of the family prominent people in all walks of life and nearly all of the 496 descendants owners of land or proprietors. On the bad side we find paupers, criminals, prostitutes, drunkards, and examples of all forms of social pest with which modern society is burdened. From this we conclude that feeble-mindedness is largely responsible for these social sores. (p. 116)

Goddard concluded that what needed to be done about "feeble-mindedness" was a program of segregation and sterilization. He stopped short of recommending eugenics, recommending instead further study of the mechanisms of heredity. By 1926 Goddard had dropped his hesitation to the implementation of eugenics, which he defined as a science and equated with race betterment, recommending a program of segregation and sterilization to control the spread of feeble-mindedness and concluding that

> feeble-mindedness is sufficiently prevalent to arouse the interest and attract the attention of all thotful [sic] people who are interested in social welfare; that it is mostly hereditary; that it underlies all our social problems; that because of these facts it is worth the attention of our most thotful [sic] statesmen and social leaders; that much of the time and money and energy now devoted to other things may be more wisely spent in investigating the problem of feeble-mindedness; and that since feeble-mindedness is in all probability transmitted in accordance with the Mendelian Law of heredity, the way is open for eugenic procedure which shall mean much for the future welfare of the race. (Goddard, 1926, pp. 589–590)

Although not all professionals shared Goddard's enthusiasm for eugenics, there was fundamentally no opportunity for people with mental retardation to exert control in their lives. The leaders and decision makers in the field were physicians and, to a lesser degree, humanitarians. At the height of the First Wave, professionals defined the issues and created the then new discipline of mental retardation as separate from the fields of medicine, psychology, and education. They made decisions on their own, or in consultation with each other. Parents and the general public assumed that the professionals, because of their education and social status, knew what was best. Emphasis was on diagnosis and, particularly with the growing popularity of intelligence testing, in determining who would benefit from treatment and who would not. A person labeled with mental retardation was stripped of basic civil rights, from education to the opportunity to enlist in the military service.

As the country approached the midpoint of the 20th century, a *Second Wave* emerged in the disability movement: the parent movement. After World War II, advances in science and medicine changed the way disability was perceived and greatly increased the life span of people with disabilities. Influenced by the large number of veterans disabled in World War II, which spurred an emphasis on rehabilitation and training, and successes in developing vaccines for diseases like polio, giving hope to greater cures for disabling conditions, the earlier stereotypes of disability were replaced with more humane, though still in many ways debilitating, stereotypes. People with disabilities were viewed as objects to be fixed, cured, rehabilitated, and simultaneously pitied. People with disabilities became viewed as "victims" worthy of charity. Shapiro (1993) described this phenomenon when discussing the emergence of the poster child as a fund-raising tool:

> The poster child is a surefire tug at our hearts. The children picked to represent charity fund-raising drives are brave, determined, and inspirations, the most innocent victims of the cruelest whims of life and health. Yet they smile through their unlucky fates . . . no other symbol of disability is more beloved by Americans than the cute and courageous poster child. (p. 12)

Within this stereotype, people with mental retardation were viewed as "holy innocents" (special messengers, children of God, etc.), and thus incapable of sin and not responsible for their own actions. Based at least partially on the prevalent use of mental age calculated from intelligence scores, people with mental retardation came to be perceived as "eternal children." Although no longer feared and blamed for all social ills, people with mental retardation were perceived as children, to be protected, pitied, and cared for.

Concurrent to the economic boom post–World War II, there was the now infamous baby boom. The dramatic increase in the U.S. birthrate meant not only that more babies were being born, but also that more children with disabilities were being born. The changing attitudes toward disability described above led more and more families, particularly families of children with mental retardation and families of children with cerebral palsy, to band together and form their own groups. At first, the goal of these organizations was simply for members to support one another. Later, as these organizations matured, parents began to advocate for themselves and their children. Out of this emerged the parent movement, including organizations like The Arc and the United Cerebral Palsy Associations. Slowly, professionals joined in the parent rebellion and recognized the importance of parents in the decision-making process. This movement gained political clout, and during the 1950s through 1970s radically and unalterably changed the face of the disability movement. This was a period of rapid growth in services and legislative protection. It was also a critical step in the emergence of self-determination and self-advocacy. Early in the Second Wave, parents and family members told professionals that they were the consumers of services and they spoke for their sons or daughters. As these sons and daughters aged and the movement matured, so too did this emphasis change. Parents and family members, along with professionals, began to recognize that people with mental retardation could, in fact, speak for themselves. The *Third Wave* of the disability movement, the self-advocacy movement, emerged during the 1970s and 1980s.

Several factors contributed to the emergence of this Third Wave. In the early 1940s the field of personality psychology began to form as a means to better explain and predict human behavior. One of the central questions to this young discipline was the question of determinism—that is, to what degree human behavior is determined by internal versus external forces. To describe circumstances under which human behavior was conceptualized to be internally determined, theorists coopted a term from political science—self-determination. The earliest conceptualizations of self-determination within the personality literature used the term as it related to the determination of one's own fate or course of action without compulsion. For example, in his early text titled *Foundations for a Science of Personality,* Angyal (1941) proposed that an essential feature of a living organism is its autonomy, where autonomous means self-governing or governed from inside. According to Angyal, an organism "lives in a world in which things happen according to laws which are heteronomous (e.g., governed from outside) from the point of view of the organism" (p. 33). Angyal stated that "organisms are subjected to the laws of the physical world, as is any other object of nature, with the exception that it can oppose self-determination to external determination" (p. 33).

As it was, however, issues of self-determination were not discussed in relationship to the right of people with mental retardation to govern their own lives until the early 1970s. In 1972 Wolf Wolfensberger's classic text on the principles of normalization was published. In that text Bengt Nirje (1972) authored a chapter titled "The Right to Self-Determination," and in the opening paragraph stated,

> One major facet of the normalization principle is to create conditions through which a handicapped person experiences the normal respect to which any human being is entitled. Thus the choices, wishes, desires, and aspirations of a handicapped person have to be taken into consideration as much as possible in actions affecting him. To assert oneself with one's family, friends, neighbors, co-workers, other people, or vis-à-vis an agency is difficult for many persons. It is especially difficult for someone who has a disability or is otherwise perceived as devalued. But in the end, even the impaired person has to manage as a distinct individual, and thus has his identity defined to himself and to others through the circumstances and conditions of his existence. Thus, the road to self-determination is both difficult and all important for a person who is impaired. (p. 177)

Although the language referring to people with disabilities dates Nirje's quote, his concepts remain relevant today. His is a call for self-determination or self-governance for people with mental retardation. Nirje (1972) identified making choices, asserting oneself, self-management, self-knowledge, decision making, self-advocacy, self-efficacy, self-regulation, autonomy, and independence (albeit often not using those terms) as important to promoting self-determination. His is a call for a wide range of actions that enable people to control their lives and their destinies.

Obviously, the perceptions of people with mental retardation as eternal children or holy innocents were antithetical to people with disabilities as self-determined, self-sufficient, and competent human beings. Adults with "the mind of a 3-year-old" are not expected to hold a job, make decisions, or live independently. Holy innocents are not expected to learn about sexuality and human relationships. Recipients of pity and charity are to be helped and not accepted as colleagues, friends, or neighbors. Gunnar Dybwad pointed this out as early as 1961, stating,

> The community at large and public officials in the states have heard so much of the mentally retarded as having the mentality of children—of well-meaning but so misleading labels as "eternal children" or "the unfinished child"—that there remains considerable hesitancy to recognize the retarded as adults, let alone as adults capable of sustained productive effort. (p. 159)

In short, the way in which people with disabilities were perceived needed to change before Nirje's call for self-determination could be realized. Blatt and Kaplan's (1966) expose of the conditions of institutions in the United States, *Christmas in Purgatory*, starkly illustrated how far we had to go to achieve Nirje's vision. The last two decades of the 20th century proved to be a time during which old stereotypes and perceptions were slowly replaced by perceptions of people with mental retardation as competent and worthy of respect and dignity. These changes occurred largely as a result of the rapid growth and implementation of the normalization principle, the emergence and growth of the Independent Living Movement, increased civil rights protections for people with disabilities, and the emergence and maturation of the self-advocacy movement.

RAYMOND GAGNE'S STORY: THE INSTITUTION

My name is Raymond J. Gagne. This is my story about my life and why self-advocacy and self-determination are important to me. I was born on January 10, 1945. I am a person with cerebral palsy.

I lived with my mother, grandmother, uncle, two brothers, and a sister in a large house in Attleboro, Massachusetts. My mother felt there was something wrong with me. She took me to many doctors and hospitals to see if they knew how to help me. They told my mother I would never walk.

When I lived at home, I used to sit in a rocking chair next to a yellow window. I would sit there for hours watching people and cars go by. When my family went out, they put me in my baby carriage and usually included me in the activities. My brothers and sister went to school. At the time, there was no school for me. I stayed home with my grandmother, who took care of me. She had her hands full. I could not walk, talk, feed myself, or dress myself. She had to carry me upstairs each time I had to go to the bathroom. I crawled on the floor to get around.

When I was 8, my mother told me I was going away. She put my name on my clothes and packed my new suitcase. I remember the night before I left. I was bathed and my fingernails and toenails were cut. On February 19, 1953, two ladies picked my mother and me up for the drive to a state school. I didn't know where we were going. My mother had just told me I was going away and that I would be better off.

After arriving at the state school, I was put in Building 7. An orderly brought me to a ward. He put me in a bed and took all my clothes off. He put a johnny on me. My mother left, and I didn't see her any more that day. I was scared because I didn't know where I was or why I was there. I had arrived early in the afternoon. The rest of the day and night I was in bed. The bed was different from mine at home. The ward itself was drab. The windows were high with white shades. There were no curtains or decorations on the wall, not even a clock or calendars. There was a radio. The first song I heard was "Pretend You're Happy When You're Blue." It made me sad to hear it. I cried for 3 days.

Later, I was moved to Building 15. They put me on the floor. The other patients stepped all over me. I cried all day because I wanted to go back home. That evening they gave me a group bath with five other boys. The bathtub looked like a bird bath. There were water sprayers all around the inside of the bath. I was put to bed after the bath. At midnight, the attendants woke everybody up to go to the bathroom. I hated that, but I went. Every morning we would wake up at 6:00 a.m. An attendant would help me put on the clothes he had laid out the night before. I didn't have any say about what I wore. What they put on, I wore. Sometimes they wouldn't put underwear on me.

The first time I had a visitor was a month after being left at the state school. My mother came to visit me. I cried all the time she was there. I told her I wanted to go home. During this visit, she asked me about taking me home for a 1-day visit. When the visit was over and they got ready to take me back, I acted up. I hit and bit my mother. I also hid underneath the bed so she couldn't get me. She finally returned me to the state school.

As I look back on my childhood, I realize that I have been on my own since I was 8 years old. Some people would disagree and say that I was taken care of for many years. However, I felt as though I had no love or understanding from anyone.

That spring, I went to the dentist for the first time ever. The dentist pulled out eight teeth. He did not use any Novocain or any pain killers. I tried to be brave and not cry.

On Sunday afternoons in the summer, I used to spend the day lying on the floor of the ward waiting for company. No one ever came. Once I waited a full day for my mother to come and pick me up. I had to wait on a bench all day because the attendants didn't know when my mother was coming. During my visit, my grandmother fell down the steps and had to be hospitalized. A few days after I returned to the state school, my grandmother died. I wasn't told until Christmas day, 5 months later.

Looking back, I feel my strength and stubbornness helped me to survive these years of my life when I had so little control. Once I went to Building 5 and saw that people had more freedom there. I asked the staff if I could move to this building. In the new building, I could go to bed at 9:30. I never actually had my own personal bed. It made me think that, even in prison, you at least have your own cell. At the state school, I didn't have any living space of my own.

The staff who worked at the state institution were insensitive and cruel. There was one attendant who would take me to a back room and beat me up. Other times, he would hit me right in front of everybody. Another attendant hit the residents on the head with his keys.

The staff never seemed to prepare me for living outside the institution. They didn't seem to think I would make it on my own. I never had support, role models, or mentors to guide me in growing up. Very few of the staff ever assisted me in developing my identity, creativity, or self-esteem.

When I was 19, I started to work in a workshop. I worked in the workshop for 1 year. We put nails in boxes and then sealed the boxes. I got paid $30 a week. This was the first real money I had to call my own. Within a year I was promoted to the position of supervisor. I learned good work habits such as being on time, doing good work, responsibility, and getting along with others. Although I learned some good things at the workshop, many basic skills were never taught. These included budgeting skills, personal grooming skills, and most any other skills that a person needs to live outside an institution.

When I was in the institution, sometimes I went home for a visit. I didn't want to go back so I would act up. I didn't know it, but even then I was advocating for myself. At that time, there were no self-advocacy groups like there are now. I wish there had been, so someone could speak up for me. There I was, only eight years old. It is very important that people learn to speak up for themselves.

Scheerenberger (1987) suggested that no single categorical principle has had a greater impact on services for people with mental retardation than normalization. In conjunction with the independent living movement, whose influence was felt most heavily by people with physical and sensory impairments, the normalization principle paved the way for self-determination. Nirje (1969) explained that the normalization principle had its basis in "Scandinavian experiences from the field" and emerged, in essence, from a Swedish law on mental retardation that was passed July 1, 1968. In its original conceptualization, the normalization principle provided guidance for creating services that "let the mentally retarded obtain an existence as close to the normal as possible" (Nirje, p. 363). Nirje stated, "As I see it, the normalization principle means making available to the mentally retarded patterns and conditions of everyday life which are as close as possible to the norms and patterns of the mainstream of society" (p. 363). Nirje (1969) identified eight "facets and implications of the normalization principle":

1. Normalization means a normal rhythm of day.

2. Normalization implies a normal routine of life.

3. Normalization means to experience the normal rhythm of the year.

4. Normalization means the opportunity to undergo normal developmental experiences of the life cycle.

5. Normalization means that the choices, wishes and desires [of the mentally retarded themselves] have to be taken into consideration as nearly as possible, and respected.

6. Normalization also means living in a bisexual world.

7. Normalization means normal economic standards [for the mentally retarded].

8. Normalization means that the standards of the physical facility should be the same as those regularly applied in society to the same kind of facilities for ordinary citizens.

Scheerenberger (1987) noted that, "at this stage in its development, the normalization principle basically reflected a lifestyle, one diametrically opposed to many prevailing institutional practices" (p. 117), as was aptly illustrated by Blatt and Kaplan (1966). In fact, the ideas forwarded by Nirje in 1969 remain, to a significant extent, the philosophical basis upon which exemplary services are based almost 30 years after their original presentation.

Nirje expanded on these ideas. A "normal rhythm of the day" means that people with disabilities should go about their day in much the same way as most people do: getting out of bed, getting dressed, eating under normal circumstances within typical settings (e.g., families), going to bed at times comparable with peers, and having opportunities for personal time and relaxation. A "normal routine of life" means that people with disabilities should live in one place, work or attend school in another, and have leisure activities in various places. A "normal rhythm of the year" means that people with disabilities should experience holidays and family days of personal significance, including vacations.

Much of the emphasis in the normalization principle relates to the importance for people with disabilities to experience the rich stimulation of being involved in one's community, in living with family members, of experiencing friendships. The normalization principle stresses that contact with people without disabilities, and people from both genders, is critically important across all age ranges. The importance of economic self-sufficiency is also highlighted. Finally, it is evident that self-determination is critical to the normalization principle, as Nirje went on to describe in subsequent writings (Nirje, 1972). At a time when most services to people with disabilities viewed them as patients, when public education was not available, and when public opinion viewed them as charity cases and eternal children, Nirje stressed the importance of choice, and the need to respect the preferences and dreams of people with mental retardation. In a later paper on the normalization principle, Nirje (1972) stated, "Normalization also means that normal understanding and respect should be given to the silent wishes or expressed self-determination" of persons with mental retardation (p. 176).

Self-advocacy as a movement has its roots within these same early activities. In the United States, the origins of the self-advocacy movement are usually attributed to a small group of people with mental retardation in Salem, Oregon, who are credited with formulating the phrase "We are people first" (Edwards, 1982). However, the roots of that movement lie in Sweden in the late 1960s and 1970s. Beginning in 1965 in Sweden, Nirje (1969) described the use of social clubs called "flamslattsklubben" to promote training in Sweden for "the adolescent retardate." This training was embedded within Nirje's development of the normalization principle. Within only a few years, reports on the training for the social groups included instruction in parliamentary procedure (Nirje, 1969).

From those humble beginnings, the self-advocacy movement gained ground rapidly. Within 5 years of the formation of the Oregon self-advocacy group, there were 1,000 members in Oregon alone, with sister groups in 3 states and requests from 42 states for assistance in starting similar organizations (Edwards, 1982). The first self-advocacy conference took place in October 1974 in Otter Crest, Oregon. Edwards described one moment from that historic meeting: "The earth moved just a bit when Valerie Schaaf, first president of People First, stepped onto the podium and spoke clearly into the microphone: 'This, the first People First convention, is officially called to order!'" (p. 10)

The history of this movement, from Oregon, to Nebraska, to New York, to Tennessee is a rich and exciting history (see Dybwad & Bersani, 1996, for a comprehensive look at the movement). It is, in essence, the history of a people who had been powerless finding their voice and demanding control over their lives . . . self-determination. The power of this movement is elegantly captured in Ray Gagne's description of his life after the institution—his self-described "life of power."

RAY GAGNE'S STORY: AFTER THE INSITUTION

The day I moved from the institution to an apartment that I shared with two other men, some staff told me I would be back in a month. They may still be waiting for me to come back. I lived in an apartment for 3 years on my SSI income and the income from my job at the institution's workshop. The institution did not have professionals coming to help make the move easier. To be honest, I only saw my social worker a week before I moved. If I had a question, I had to call the halfway house.

After I had shared an apartment for 3 years, the staff asked me to move into a halfway house to help five men move out on their own. While I was working in the halfway house, I met an employee named John. After he was hired, we broke all the rules in the book. One night he allowed beer into the house. Another night he took my friend and me to a bar. The bartender refused to serve me because he thought I was drunk. John paid the bill and walked out. This was one of the first times that I felt I was important.

That same year I went on a vacation to Washington, D.C., by myself. This was the first time I had ever done this.

One day I asked John where I could get a different job. John referred me to a state vocational rehabilitation agency. They wanted me to go to a workshop that I did not want to attend. Even John and I had a fight over this. Within that year, I finally agreed to go to the workshop. It was boring. After 4 months I quit. They told me either I stayed at the workshop or I could stay at home and do nothing. I stayed home.

During that fall I moved to my own apartment after a counselor at a camp for people with cerebral palsy told me she thought I could. I did well in living alone for 3 years. After living alone for 3 years, I decided to move near the city where my sister lived. While there I began to volunteer with a local chapter of the United Cerebral Palsy. While there I learned about Section 504 of the Rehabilitation Act and helped found an advocacy group named the Massachusetts Coalition of Citizens with Disabilities. I learned the skills of leadership, advocacy, consumer organization and assertiveness by watching people, participating in group meetings, and asking questions.

After 4 years, I moved twice more. I continued to learn new skills and became more involved in self-advocacy and consumer advocacy. I moved to New Bedford, Massachusetts. I was interviewed by the ARC directors and was hired as a public information coordinator. Unlike the staff at the institution, the human service professionals I met at this job treated me with respect. They gave me a chance to contribute my input and feedback, and believed in many of my ideas. My colleagues also adapted the working environment to help me communicate with them. After several years I became the staff liaison to a self-advocacy group of adults with mental retardation. I worked at this job for 6 years.

When I moved to New Bedford, I wanted to open a checking account. I went over to the bank and I gave the $10 to open the account and asked them if there would be a problem. They said no. But, when I went back a couple of days later, they said they couldn't understand my signature. I thought about this and I realized that I had a checking account before I moved, and that had worked fine. The next morning, I put on a suit and tie and went down to the main branch. I asked to see the bank president. They told me he was at a meeting. I told them I would wait. I waited for about two minutes and he came out. He brought me into a room and asked me what the problem was. I told him. I also brought my canceled checks and showed him that I had an account before. He apologized, and I got my checking account.

Through my job I met many people who have become friends. I began to get involved in national issues. In 1988, I was selected to be the National Chairperson of the Self-Advocacy Advisory Committee for the National Association of Retarded Citizens (now The Arc). I helped coordinate a successful voting rights campaign and assisted in promoting self-advocacy initiatives. I also lectured on these issues at Harvard University.

After 6 years, I decided to look for another job. I was hired as a training specialist in Harrisburg, Pennsylvania. My duties include providing self-advocacy and social skills training to over 200 people at residences for people with mental retardation. My colleagues at my present job treat me well and have made adaptations so I can do a better job.

LIVES OF EMERGING CONTROL: THE 1990s

There has been considerable progress in promoting self-determination and self-advocacy, particularly in the 1990s. Federal policy related to disability has increasingly emphasized the importance of self-determination. For example, in the 1992 reauthorization of the Rehabilitation Act, the findings of Congress [Section 2 (29 U.S.C. 701)] were as follows:

1) millions of Americans have one or more physical or mental disability and the number of Americans with disabilities is increasing;

2) individuals with disabilities constitute one of the most disadvantaged groups in society;

3) disability is a natural part of the human experience and in no way diminishes the right of individuals to:

a) live independently;

b) enjoy self-determination;

c) make choices;

d) contribute to society;

e) pursue meaningful careers; and

f) enjoy full inclusion and integration in the economic, political, social, cultural and educational mainstream of American society;

and

6) the goals of the nation properly include the goal of providing individuals with disabilities the tools necessary to:

  a) make informed choices and decisions; and

  b) achieve equality of opportunity, full inclusion and integration into society, employment, independent living and economic and social self-sufficiency, for such individuals.

The significant change reflected in this conceptualization is that disability is no longer seen as aberrant, outside the norm, or pathological, but instead as a part of being human. Within this conceptualization, all human abilities and experiences exist on a continuum, and disability is a part of, not outside, that continuum. Whereas Nirje's call to self-determination came before such a conceptualization of disability was in place, the demands of people with disabilities today for more control and choice come at a time when changing stereotypes of disability, coupled with progress in education, rehabilitation, and legislative protections, ensure that people with disabilities, including the most significant disabilities, can with adequate support work competitively, live independently, and become contributing members of the community.

Two major national initiatives have focused attention on self-determination in the disability services community. The earliest was the U.S. Department of Education, Office of Special Education's self-determination initiative, which funded, from 1990 to 1996, 26 model demonstration and five assessment development projects to promote self-determination for youth with disabilities (Ward, 1996; Ward & Kohler, 1996). These projects and other education-related efforts have resulted in numerous frameworks within which the term self-determination has been defined (Abery, 1993; Brown & Gothelf, 1996; Field, 1996; Field & Hoffman, 1994; Mithaug, 1996; Powers et al., 1996; Sands & Wehmeyer, 1996; Wehmeyer, 1997; Wehmeyer, Agran, & Hughes, 1998), and in a larger number of efforts to promote self-determination that, implicitly, define self-determination by the types of activities and interventions introduced and implemented (Agran, 1997; Carter-Ludi & Martin, 1995; Martin & Marshall, 1996; Serna & Lau-Smith, 1995; Van Reusen, Bos, Schumaker, & Deshler, 1994).

The second major initiative has been the Robert Wood Johnson funded self-determination projects (Nerney & Shumway, 1996; O'Brien, 1997). The intent of this initiative was to provide state agencies that have authority over developmental disability systems to implement changes in state policy and enact system change reforms based on the principles of self-determination. Projects funded under this initiative must engage in activities such as implementing individual budgets to be spent based on decisions made by people with disabilities and their families or helping service providing agencies retrain employees to enable self-directed service brokerage. These ongoing projects address political or collective self-determination, focusing attention on systemic and overarching changes and reforms to support and enable individual control and choice.

As a result of these initiatives, schools and service providers across the country have begun to examine how what they do impacts self-determination and to put into place mechanisms to promote self-determination.

The self-advocacy movement has also come of age in the current decade. There are now in excess of 700 self-advocacy groups across the country, not to mention hundreds more across the world, and a relatively new national organization of self-advocates, Self-Advocates Becoming Empowered, is providing direction for the movement as a whole. The People First convention held in Anchorage, Alaska, in April 1998 was the fourth international conference bringing together self-advocates from around the continent, with previous conferences in Tennessee, Virginia, Oklahoma, and Toronto, Canada. These gatherings draw as many as 1,500 people to network, learn, and celebrate self-advocacy. In two states, self-advocacy organizations have been the lead plaintiffs in class action lawsuits that eventually closed state-run institutions for people with mental retardation. People first language has become widely adopted by professionals and advocates alike, and locally and nationally self-advocates spearhead efforts to change organizational names and labels. For example, in 1991 the Association for Retarded Citizens of the United States (ARC-US) changed its name to The Arc of the United States (with lowercase letters to indicate that the name is no longer an acronym). This name change had support from professionals and families alike, but was particularly important to and advocated by people with mental retardation.

Self-advocacy groups have impacted areas other than language. Many self-advocates actively campaign against congregate settings, such as nursing homes, and advocate for social justice. Advocating Change Together, in Minnesota, has launched a campaign to raise funds to place headstones on the graves of people with mental retardation who had died while living in a Minnesota institution, both in respect for those powerless people and as a statement of social justice. In addition, self-advocacy groups have become the training ground for leaders, enabling people with mental retardation to assume leadership positions. Self-advocates now sit on visible boards and committees, including the board of directors for organizations like The Arc, the American Association on Mental Retardation, and TASH, as well as serving on the President's Committee on Mental Retardation and the President's Committee on the Employment of Persons with Disabilities.

LIVES OF POWER AND CONTROL: THE 21ST CENTURY

The Self-Advocacy Movement

It is clear as we move toward the 21st century that people with mental retardation and other disabilities will be more in control of their own lives as individuals and that, as a group, people with disabilities will be much more influential in the planning, operating and monitoring of the services they use. However, self-advocacy (as a social or civil rights movement) will need to resolve several issues. These issues were premature at the end of the 20th century, but given the success of the movement to this point, a second generation of issues now emerges for the future.

Assuming the Mantle of Power

What does it mean to be "powerful" as a self-advocate or as a self-advocacy organization? Many advocates are uncomfortable discussing the concept of their power. However, as there is a growing appreciation on the part of parents and professionals of the importance of self-advocacy and self-determination, so too is there growing interest from all quarters in self-advocates and their organizations, and this interest presents challenges to the self-advocacy movement. Self-advocacy groups and group members are now regularly approached to participate in grant applications, sit on boards of directors, and speak on panels. These requests will likely outstrip the movement's ability to respond before too long. Leaders will have to be selective in their alliances and examine their relationships to professional or parent organizations carefully. It is a fine line between receiving the kind of support that a fledgling organization needs to become established to the overbearing "support" that might be used to keep a radical element "in its place." Self-advocates and self-advocacy groups will need to thoughtfully consider requests from various associations, other advocates, and service providers while balancing the reality that progress will likely occur through equal partnerships and collaborations with these stakeholders. By definition, the increasing power of self-advocates challenges the power of these other groups. The need in the 21st century will be to define opportunities for collaboration and to occasionally agree to disagree, rather than create hostile opposition that will prevent true collaboration.

Group Identity

Who is a self-advocate? There are at least two issues related to this question that present challenges to the movement. First, does the term apply only to people with mental retardation, or can someone with a developmental disability other than a cognitive impairment also be considered a self-advocate? Historically, the terms self-advocacy and self-advocate have referred to entities organized by people with mental retardation or to members of such organizations. There are other self-help organizations organized and run by people with disabilities, but the term self-advocacy has typically referred to the mental retardation–linked organizations. That said, there are many people with cerebral palsy and other disabilities who are exemplary advocates and, in some quarters, they too are known as self-advocates. However, some of these advocates say that they find the term offensive because it makes them sound like they have mental retardation. Certainly, no one needs to be assigned a label they find offensive, but this concern seems to needlessly heighten the between-group differences. Just as progress will likely stem from meaningful collaborations with parent and professional organizations, so too will progress in the self-advocacy movement in the next century likely rely on collaborations with other disability self-help organizations. Issues of the stigma associated with the term mental retardation are real and will not likely go away soon, but there is a very real need to address the underlying stereotypes and beliefs that lead to such stigma, even among and between people with disabilities and organizations that serve them.

Second, in some places the term self-advocate has become just the latest euphemism or politically correct term for referring to a person with mental retardation. People say that they saw a self-advocate down at the mall, or that they provide support for three self-advocates. In many of these cases, quite frankly, the individuals being described have shown no real advocacy efforts. Clearly there is some benefit to expecting individuals to, in some way, earn their stripes before calling them self-advocates. Just as not all minority group members are civil rights activists, not all people with disabilities are self-advocates.

The Long-Term Role for People Who Are Not Disabled

Sometimes called the temporarily able bodied by disability activists, many nondisabled activists (present company included!) have become less secure in their roles as the movement matures. (Indeed, it is with some trepidation and the recognition that we cannot speak for or to the self-advocacy movement, that we address future issues!) The issue of the role of people without disabilities in the self-advocacy movement is difficult. It is perhaps most difficult on the front lines—the role of the adviser to the group. It seems evident to us that in far too many circumstances, the group acts based primarily on the will of the adviser. The potential conflicts between advisers who are employed by agencies that, in turn, provide services to the group members are real and, perhaps, unavoidable. Many self-advocacy groups have established guidelines and deal with potential threats to the groups' power effectively, whereas others remain powerless to initiate needed changes because of the power balance between the group and the adviser and support agency.

As with other social movements (Bersani, 1998), there is some value to groups to clearly identify themselves. Even if they seek social integration, there may be a role for "formative segregation," that is, conducting group-only events in order to form a self-identity. As Bersani (in press) pointed out,

> Those of us who consider ourselves allies of the movement may be tempted to feel that we have earned the right to be involved in the future because we have been supportive in the past. However, part of being supportive is knowing when to stand back. Ultimately, we must realize that the decision is not ours to make. We may not agree with the decisions that self-advocates make, but we must respect them or belie our beliefs.

Leadership as the Legacy of the Self-Advocacy Movement

There is an ongoing need in virtually any volunteer, social, or civil rights movement for the continued development of leaders who can replace current leaders in the organization. This is as true for The Arc as it is for the NAACP, Civitans, or Disabled People's International, and it is no different for the self-advocacy movement. Without concentrated focus on the development of new leaders for self-advocacy groups at all levels, the movement will flounder. The formation of Self-Advocates Becoming Empowered was an important step in the process of ensuring ongoing leadership, and there are already efforts coming from self-advocates, like the work of Tia Nellis at the Universtiy of Illinois at Chicago, to develop leadership development models, materials, and supports. With a maturing base of leaders, the movement can both prosper and begin to address the issues that challenge them in the coming century.

Self-Determination

As we previously noted, there have been two major initiatives that have, in some sense, programmatized self-determination in the disability arena. These initiatives, one launched by the U.S. Department of Education in the early 1990s and the other by funding from the Robert Wood Johnson Foundation in the mid-1990s, have taken self-determination from a psychological or political construct to a set of actions that attempt to enable people with mental retardation to achieve greater independence and control. When examined within the context of the entire 20th century, it seems evident that these initiatives are, genuinely, in their infancy. As a field of service providers, be it educators or adult service providers, we have a half-century–long history of wielding power "on behalf" of people with mental retardation, but only a half-decade history of trying to enable people with mental retardation to take control over their own lives.

There is a compelling need to link these two initiatives, which addressed this issue from different ends of the spectrum in several ways: who is served (students vs. adults) and focus of the intervention (individual vs. corporate or political self-determination). A number of false dichotomies continue to plague our capacity to effectively enable people to assume control over their lives. One such dichotomy is the skills versus opportunity debate. This is reminiscent of the nature–nurture debate in psychology and will likely be resolved in the same manner. Napoleon Bonaparte stated that ability is of little account without opportunity. Thus, an overemphasis on skills development and the individual seems destined to fail if there are no opportunities for people to exercise choice and control. Additionally, an overdue focus on skills development in some sense emphasizes that the "problem" is with the person, not the system. On the other hand, opportunity is wasted without capacity. There are a great many adults with mental retardation who simply did not have the experiences that lead them to be able to take control over their lives even if they are given the chance. One aspect of "supports" for all people, disabled or not, is enhancing capacity.

We need to better listen to self-advocates when debating what is or is not self-determination. On its Web page, Self-Advocates Becoming Empowered defined self-determination as

> speaking up for our rights and responsibilities and empowering ourselves to stand up for what we believe in. This means being able to choose where we work, live, and our friends; to educate ourselves and others; to work as a team to obtain common goals; and to develop the skills that enable us to fight for our beliefs, to advocate for our needs, and to obtain the level of independence that we desire.

This definition recognizes that skills and opportunities are equally important. There is a need to begin to take a life-span approach to self-determination by better understanding the role of families and schools in the development of a personal self-determination and by implementing models and strategies, like personal budgeting and person-centered planning, that lead to enhanced opportunities for adults to take control over their lives.

It is important to continue to emphasize that there is a reciprocal nature to providing opportunities to take control over one's life (be it chairing an educational planning meeting, deciding one's own educational goals, or choosing one's own service provider) and the increased capacity to take control. That is, we must never confuse the importance of developing and enhancing skills with the need to move ahead and turn over power and control to people with disabilities. A skills development approach is not equivalent to a flow-through model in which a person is not allowed to take control until he or she has a prerequisite set of skills. Instead, it is through the interaction of capacity building, opportunities to exercise choice and control, and providing supports that the goal of enabling people to achieve self-determination is accomplished.

The challenges for the next century are real and many. How does one provide brokerage services that do not fall victim to the old perils of case management? How does a teacher enable students to become self-directed learners? The programmatization of self-determination introduces many threats to the continued focus on this issue. Already too many schools think that promoting self-determination means merely that a student serves as a chairperson (often in a token role) in a planning meeting. Likewise, some adult service providers think that conducting a person-centered planning meeting to which the individual is invited constitutes a self-determination program. And, almost predictably, we have heard professionals and others proclaim that self-determination is not for such and such a student because he could not lead his meeting, or such and such a person because she cannot make independent medical decisions.

What we need to emphasize as we head into the next century is that self-determination is about *control over one's life and one's destiny*. All people have the right to such control, have the right to an education that supports their capacity to take greater control, and deserve the supports necessary to enable them to assume greater control. There is much we do not know about how to make that a reality, but we do know that it is the right direction in which to head and, as a field, must remain diligent and stay the course. It does seem almost inevitable to us, given the strength of the self-advocacy and self-determination movement in the last third of the 20th century, that the 21st century will witness increased power and control for people with disabilities, so perhaps the charge most appropriate for the field was one proclaimed, appropriately, by Burton Blatt. Commenting on his landmark work *Christmas in Purgatory* (Blatt & Kaplan, 1966) and referring to the reception this book, which pictorially documented the deplorable conditions of institutions for people with mental retardation in the United States, received among some professionals in the field, Blatt noted,

> In spite of those who protest this presentation, there will be no turning back. Once seeds are sown, one only has to wait for the crop to harvest. It has been said that, when the bellman is dead, the wind will toll the bell. So hurry, wind! Or revive yourselves, noble bellringers. (Blatt, 1971, p. 360)

REFERENCES

Abery, B. (1993). A conceptual framework for enhancing self-determination. In M. Hayden & B. Abery (Eds.), *Challenges for a service system in transition: Ensuring quality community experiences for persons with developmental disabilities* (pp. 345–380). Baltimore: Brookes.

Agran, M. (1997). *Student-directed learning: Teaching self-determination skills.* Pacific Grove, CA: Brooks/Cole.

Angyal, A. (1941). *Foundations for a science of personality.* Cambridge, MA: Harvard University Press.

Bersani, H. (1996). Leadership in developmental disabilities: Where we've been, where we are, and where we are going. In G. Dybwad & H. Bersani (Eds.), *New voices: Self-advocacy by people with disabilities* (pp. 258–269). Cambridge, MA: Brookline Books.

Bersani, H. (1998). From social clubs to social movement: Landmarks in the development of the international self-advocacy movement. In L. Ward (Ed.), *Innovations in advocacy and empowerment for people with intellectual disabilities.* Lancaster, England: Lisieux Hall.

Bersani, H. (in press). *The social evolution of self-advocacy, past present and future.*

Blatt, B., & Kaplan, F. (1966). *Christmas in purgatory.* New York: Allyn & Bacon.

Blatt, B. (1971). Purgatory. *Changing patterns in residential services for the mentally retarded* (pp. 347–360). Washington, DC: President's Committee on Mental Retardation.

Brown, F., & Gothelf, C. R. (1996). Self-determination for all individuals. In D. H. Lehr & F. Brown (Eds.), *People with disabilities who challenge the system* (pp. 335–353). Baltimore: Brookes.

Carter-Ludi, D., & Martin, L. (1995). The road to personal freedom: Self-determination. *Intervention in School and Clinic, 30,* 164–169.

Dybwad, G. (1961). *Challenges in mental retardation.* New York: Columbia University Press.

Dybwad, G., & Bersani, H. (1996). *New voices: Self-advocacy by people with disabilities.* Cambridge, MA: Brookline Books.

Edwards, J. (1982). *We are people first; Our handicaps are secondary.* Portland, OR: Ednick.

Field, S. (1996). Self-determination instructional strategies for youth with learning disabilities. *Journal of Learning Disabilities, 29,* 40–52.

Field, S., & Hoffman, A. (1994). Development of a model for self-determination. *Career Development for Exceptional Individuals, 16,* 159–169.

Gagne, R. (1994). A self-made man. In V. J. Bradley, J. W. Ashbaugh, & B. C. Blaney (Eds.), *Creating individual supports for people with developmental disabilities* (pp. 327–334). Baltimore: Brookes.

Goddard, H. H. (1912). *The Kallikak family: A study in the heredity of feeble-mindedness.* New York: Macmillan.

Goddard, H. H. (1926). *Feeble-mindedness: Its causes and consequences.* New York: Macmillan.

Martin, J. E., & Marshall, L. H. (1996). ChoiceMaker: Infusing self-determination instruction into the IEP and transition process. In D. J. Sands & M. L. Wehmeyer (Eds.), *Self-determination across the life span: Independence and choice for people with disabilities* (pp. 215–236). Baltimore: Brookes.

Mithaug, D. (1996). *Equal opportunity theory.* Thousand Oaks, CA: Sage.

Nerney, T., & Shumway, D. (1996). *Beyond managed care: Self-determination for people with disabilities.* Durham: University of New Hampshire.

Nirje, B. (1969). The normalization principle and its human management implications. In R. B. Kugel & W. Wolfensberger (Eds.), *Changing residential patterns for the mentally retarded* (pp. 363–376). Washington, DC: President's Committee on Mental Retardation.

Nirje, B. (1972). The right to self-determination. In W. Wolfensberger (Ed.), *Normalization: The principle of normalization* (pp. 176–200). Toronto: National Institute on Mental Retardation.

O'Brien, J. (1997). *Implementing self-determination initiatives: Some notes on complex change.* Lithonia, GA: Responsive Systems Associates.

Powers, L. E., Sowers, J., Turner, A., Nesbitt, M., Knowles, E., & Ellison, R. (1996). Take Charge: A model for promoting self-determination among adolescents with challenges. In L. E. Powers, G. H. S. Singer, & J. Sowers (Eds.), *On the road to autonomy: Promoting self-competence in children and youth with disabilities* (pp. 291–322). Baltimore: Brookes.

Sands, D. J., & Wehmeyer, M. L. (1996). *Self-determination across the life span: Independence and choice for people with disabilities.* Baltimore: Brookes.

Serna, L. A., & Lau-Smith, J. (1995). Learning with a PURPOSE: Self-determination skills for students who are at risk for school and community failure. *Intervention in School and Clinic, 30,* 142–146.

Scheerenberger, R. C. (1987). *A history of mental retardation: A quarter century of promise.* Baltimore: Brookes.

Shapiro, J. (1993). *No pity: People with disabilities forging a new civil rights movement.* New York: Times Books.

Van Reusen, A. K., Bos, C. S., Schumaker, J. B., & Deshler, D. D. (1994). *The self-advocacy strategy for education and transition planning.* Lawrence, KS: Edge Enterprises.

Ward, M. J. (1996). Coming of age in the age of self-determination: A historical and personal perspective. In D. J. Sands & M. L. Wehmeyer (Eds.), *Self-determination across the life span: Independence and choice for people with disabilities* (pp. 1–16). Baltimore: Brookes.

Ward, M. J., & Kohler, P. D. (1996). Promoting self-determination for individuals with disabilities: Content and process. In L. E. Powers, G. H. S. Singer, & J. Sowers (Eds.), *On the road to autonomy: Promoting self-competence in children and youth with disabilities* (pp. 275–290). Baltimore: Brookes.

Wehmeyer, M. L. (1997). Self-determination as an educational outcome: A definitional framework and implications for intervention. *Journal of Developmental and Physical Disabilities, 9,* 175–209.

Wehmeyer, M. L., Agran, M., & Hughes, C. (1998). *Teaching self-determination to youth with disabilities: Basic skills for successful transition.* Baltimore: Brookes.

Three Decades of Quality of Life

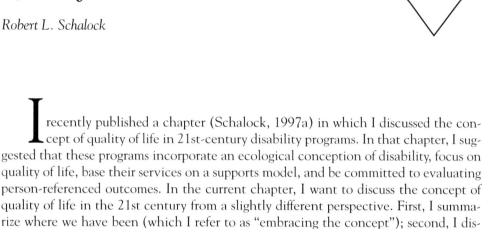

Robert L. Schalock

I recently published a chapter (Schalock, 1997a) in which I discussed the concept of quality of life in 21st-century disability programs. In that chapter, I suggested that these programs incorporate an ecological conception of disability, focus on quality of life, base their services on a supports model, and be committed to evaluating person-referenced outcomes. In the current chapter, I want to discuss the concept of quality of life in the 21st century from a slightly different perspective. First, I summarize where we have been (which I refer to as "embracing the concept"); second, I discuss where we are now ("clarifying the concept"); third, I project where I think we are going with the concept as we embark on the 21st century ("pursuing the concept"); and finally, I offer 10 guidelines to assist our efforts.

I suggest at the outset of our consideration of three decades of quality of life that the importance of the concept of quality of life to persons with mental retardation is reflected well in the following three statements:

1. The concept of quality of life is a social construct that is impacting program development and service delivery in the areas of education (Halpern, 1993; Snell & Vogtle, 1997), health care (Coulter, 1997; Renwick, Brown, & Nagler, 1996), mental retardation (Brown, 1997; Schalock, 1996b, 1997b), and mental health (Lehman, Rachuba, & Postrado, 1995).

2. The concept of quality of life is being used as the criterion for assessing the effectiveness of services to people with disabilities (Felce & Perry, 1996; Gardner, Nudler, & Chapman, 1997; Perry & Felce, 1995; Rapley & Hopgood, 1997; Schalock, 1995b).

3. The pursuit of quality is apparent at three levels of today's human service programs: persons who desire a life of quality (Ward & Keith, 1996; Whitney-Thomas, 1997), providers who want to deliver a quality product (Albin-Dean & Mank, 1997), and evaluators (policy makers, funders, and consumers) who want quality outcomes (Gardner & Nudler, 1997; Schalock, 1999).

How did we get to where we are in reference to the concept of quality of life, and where are we going as we embark on the 21st century? In the following three sections of this chapter, I suggest that we got here by embracing during the decade of the 1980s the concept of quality of life; during the current decade we have attempted to clarify the concept; and I predict that during the next decade the concept will be pursued even more intensely by individuals advocating for a life of quality, service and support providers focusing on ways to produce quality products, and evaluators analyzing quality outcomes.

EMBRACING THE CONCEPT (THE 1980s)

During the 1980s the field of mental retardation and closely related disabilities embraced the concept of quality of life as both a sensitizing notion and an overarching principle for service delivery. Why? Because the concept captured the changing vision of persons with disabilities, provided a common language for persons across disciplines and functional statuses, and was consistent with the larger "quality revolution."

Captured the Changing Vision

Over the last two decades, there has been a significant change in the way we view persons with disabilities. This transformed vision of what constitutes the life possibilities of persons with mental retardation is reflected in terms that are familiar to the reader: self-determination, strengths and capabilities, the importance of normalized and typical environments, the provision of individualized support systems, equity, and enhanced adaptive behavior and role status. As a term and concept, quality of life became during the 1980s a *social construct* that captured this changing vision and thus became the vehicle through which consumer-referenced equity, empowerment, and increased life satisfaction could be achieved. It was also consistent with the individualization and person-centered focus that was rapidly emerging in the field. The assumption of most was that if adequate and appropriate supports were available, the person's quality of life would be enhanced significantly.

Provided a Common Language

Anyone who was involved in the field of mental retardation remembers that during the 1980s the field was expanding and trying to adjust to the major upheavals caused by normalization, deinstitutionalization, and mainstreaming. As important as these movements were, they were more process than outcome oriented, and thus failed to provide a clearly articulated goal for the persons involved. The concept of quality of life became attractive as a universal principle that provided a common goal across environments and people. Thus, the statement, "to enhance one's quality of life," became our goal. This *sensitizing notion* went beyond the processes of systems change, to the outcomes of those processes. The desire for a life of quality was characteristic of everyone, and thus a common language was born.

A second aspect of a common language was that the quality of life concept fit the increasing need for accountability in rehabilitation programs. Increasingly, programs were being asked to evaluate their efficiency and effectiveness, and the notion that one's quality of life could be enhanced became a mantra for many who were looking for a way to evaluate program outcomes across a vast array of persons and services. Thus, the quality of life concept became both a common goal for all programs and hence a common language for those concerned about evaluating their outcomes (Schalock, 1995b).

Was Consistent with the Quality Revolution

The quality revolution, with its emphasis on quality products and quality outcomes, was emerging rapidly during the 1980s. One of the main products of this revolution was a "new way of thinking," which was guided largely in the mental retardation field by the concept of quality of life, which became the *unifying theme* around which programmatic changes and "the new way of thinking" were organized. This new way of thinking stressed person-centered planning, the supports model, quality enhancement techniques, and person-referenced quality outcomes (Schalock, 1999). More specifically, this new way of thinking based on the unifying theme of quality of life allowed

- Service providers to reorganize resources around individuals rather than rearranging people in program slots (Albin-Dean & Mank, 1997; Albrecht, 1993; Edgerton, 1996; Gardner & Nudler, 1997; Schalock, 1994).

- Consumers and service providers to embrace the supports paradigm (Schalock, 1995a).

- Program evaluation to shift its focus to person-referenced outcomes that could be used to improve organizational efficiency and enhance person-referenced services and supports (Clifford & Sherman, 1983; Mathison, 1991; Schalock, 1995b; Torres, 1992).

- Management styles to focus on learning organizations (Senge, 1990), reengineered corporations (Hammer & Champy, 1993), entrepreneurship (Osborne & Gaebler, 1992), and continuous (quality) improvement (Albin-Dean & Mank, 1997).

Thus, by the end of the 1980s we had embraced the concept of quality of life for at least the three reasons just mentioned. However, embracing a concept and fully understanding it are two different things. Before considering the decade of the 1990s, during which we have made significant progress in understanding and applying the concept, it is important to mention two additional phenomena regarding the concept of quality of life that were evident by the end of the 1980s decade. These two phenomena became significant catalysts to the work that was to be done during the 1990s. First, the concept of quality of life was being used in at least three different ways:

- As a *sensitizing notion* that was giving us a sense of reference and guidance from the individual's perspective, focusing on the person and the individual's environment

- As a *social construct* that was an overriding principle to improve and enhance a person's perceived quality of life

- As a *unifying theme* that provided a systematic or organizing framework to focus on the multidimensionality of the concept

Second, there were a number of quality of life principles upon which the field was beginning to agree. These 11 principles, which are summarized in Table 19.1, were based on considerable discussion and input from all stakeholders (Goode, 1990; Schalock, 1990).

CLARIFYING THE CONCEPT (THE 1990s)

During the 1980s the field of mental retardation embraced a concept that was neither well defined (hence the presence of over 100 definitions of quality of life) nor completely understood. Thus, the 1990s decade began with investigators and advocates attempting to answer a number of questions about the conceptualization and measurement of quality of life. Chief among these questions were (Raphael, 1996; Schalock, 1996b) the following:

- *Conceptual Issues*—How should we refer to the term quality of life? Is quality of life a single, unitary entity, or a multidimensional, interactive concept? How is it best to conceptualize indicators of quality of life? Is quality of life the same for all individuals?

- *Measurement Issues*—What should be measured? How do we measure quality of life? What psychometric standards need to be considered? How do we overcome measurement challenges?

As we near the end of this decade, these questions are beginning to be answered, thanks largely to a number of significant conceptual shifts regarding how we view and assess quality of life. In this section, I discuss five of these shifts: (1) the multidimensional nature of quality of life, (2) satisfaction as the primary measure of quality of life, (3) the hierarchical nature of quality of life, (4) the use of multivariate research

TABLE 19.1
Fundamental Quality of Life Principles (1980s Decade)

Quality of Life . . .

1. For persons with disabilities is composed of those same factors and relationships that are important to persons without disabilities.
2. Is experienced when a person's basic needs are met and when he or she has the same opportunity as anyone else to pursue and achieve goals in the major settings of home, community, and work.
3. Factors vary over the life span of a person.
4. Is related to a person's and group's cultural and ethnic heritage.
5. Is based on a set of values that emphasize consumer and family strengths.
6. Is determined by the congruence of public policy and behavior.
7. Is a concept that can be consensually validated by a wide range of persons representing a variety of viewpoints of consumers and their families, advocates, professionals, and providers.
8. Study requires an in-depth knowledge of people and their perspectives.
9. Measurement requires multiple methodologies.
10. Has both objective and subjective components, but it is primarily the subjective view of the individual that determines the quality of life he or she experiences.
11. Variables should occupy a prominent role in overall program evaluation.

designs to study important correlates of quality of life, and (5) the use of multiple methods to assess one's perceived quality of life.

Multidimensional Nature

There is increasing agreement that quality of life is a multidimensional concept that precludes reducing it to a single "thing" of which the person may have considerable, some, or none. Current and ongoing research in this area has identified *eight core quality of life dimensions* (Schalock, 1996c): emotional well-being, interpersonal relationships, material well-being, personal development, physical well-being, self-determination, social inclusion, and rights. Although the number and configuration of these core dimensions vary slightly among investigators, the summary presented in Table 19.2 indicates quite clearly the generality of these dimensions. The core dimensions listed in Table 19.2 are based on the work of Cummins (1996, 1997a), Felce (1997), Felce and Perry (1996, 1997b), Hughes and Hwang (1996), and Schalock (1996c). Similar listings can be found in Heal, Khoju, Rusch, and Harnisch (in press), Parmenter and Donelly (1997), Renwick and Brown (1996), and Stark and Goldsbury (1990).

TABLE 19.2
Core Quality of Life Dimensions (1990s Decade)

Schalock (1996c)	Felce (1997)	Cummins (1997)	Hughes & Hwang (1996)
Emotional Well-Being	X	X	X
Interpersonal Relations	X (Social)	X (Intimacy)	X
Material Well-Being	X	X	X
Personal Development	X (Productive)	X (Productivity)	X
Physical Well-Being	X	X	X
Self-Determination	X (Productive)	X (Productive)	X
Social Inclusion	X (Social)	X	X
Rights	X (Civic)	X (Savety)	X (Civic Responsibility)

Focus on Satisfaction

Increasingly, we are seeing that a person's measured level of satisfaction is the most commonly used dependent measure in evaluating the person's perceived quality of life. One might well ask, "Why this emphasis on satisfaction?" Actually, there are a number of reasons, including the following:

- It is a commonly used aggregate measure of individual life domains (Andrews, 1974; Campbell, Converse, & Rogers, 1976).

- It demonstrates a traitlike stability over time (Diener, 1984; Edgerton, 1990, 1996; Heal, Borthwick-Duffy, & Saunders, 1996).

- There is an extensive body of research on the level of satisfaction across populations and service delivery recipients (Cummins, 1997b; Halpern, 1993; Harner & Heal, 1993; Heal & Chadsey-Rusch, 1985; Heal, Rubin, & Park, 1995; Schalock & Faulkner, 1997).

- It allows one to assess the relative importance of individual quality of life dimensions and thereby assign value to the respective dimensions (Campbell et al., 1976; Cummins, 1996; Flanagan, 1978, 1982; Felce & Perry, 1996, 1997b; Schalock, Bontham, & Marchant, in press).

Thus, the major advantages of using satisfaction as a common indicator of one's perceived quality of life are its usefulness in comparing population samples; providing a common language that can be shared by consumers, providers, policy makers, regulators, and researchers; assessing consumer needs; and evaluating organizational outputs. Its major disadvantages include its limited utility for smaller group comparisons that might provide only a global measure of perceived well-being, and its discrepancy with current multidimensional theories of quality of life (Cummins, 1996). For these

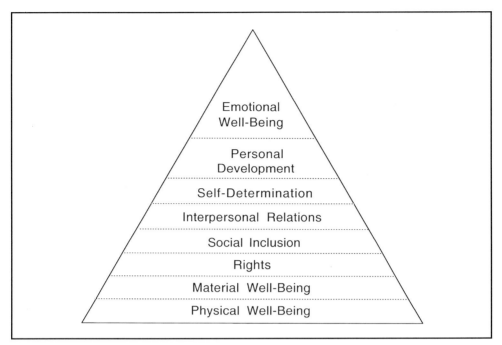

FIGURE 19.1. Hierarchial nature of core quality of life dimensions.

reasons, other dependent measures of one's quality of life are needed, and these are described in a later section of this chapter.

Hierarchical Nature

There is good agreement in the quality of life literature about three things: First, quality of life, by its very nature, is subjective; second, the various core dimensions are valued by persons differently; and third, the value attached to each core dimension varies across one's life. These three points of agreement indicate strongly that the concept of quality of life must be viewed from a hierarchical perspective. A model that allows one to integrate these three factors is presented in Figure 19.1, which is based on the work of Elorriaga, Garcia, Martinez, and Unamunzaga (in press), Flanagan (1978), Maslow (1954), and Verdugo (in press). The model depicts a hypothetical, hierarchical arrangement of the various core quality of life dimensions listed in Table 19.2.

Multivariate Research Design

One of the biggest stumbling blocks overcome during the decade of the 1990s has been shifting our mindset regarding the research and statistical design used to study the quality of life concept. Specifically, we have seen a significant shift from a "between" to a "multivariate/within" approach. Historically, the study of quality of life was approached from a between-groups (or between-conditions) perspective; hence, investigators sought to find factors such as social economic status and large demographic population descriptors that could discriminate between those persons or countries with a higher and those with a lower quality of life. This "between" mentality spilled over to our early work on quality of life in subtle ways, as reflected in the attitude expressed by some that "we need to have different measures or quality of life indices for those who are higher functioning and for those who are either nonverbal or lower functioning.

Shifting to a multivariate research design has a number of heuristic and practical advantages. First, it allows one to focus more on the correlates and predictors of a life of quality rather than comparing quality of life scores or status. More specifically, one can use multivariate research designs to determine the relationship among a number of measured predictor variables and one's perceived quality of life. This approach has been one that I have used to evaluate the relative contribution to one's assessed quality of life of a number of personal characteristics, objective life conditions, and provider characteristics. Across a number of studies (e.g., Schalock et al., in press; Schalock & Faulkner, 1997; Schalock, Lemanowicz, Conroy, & Feinstein, 1994), personal factors (e.g., health status and adaptive behavior level), environmental variables (e.g., perceived social support, current residence, earnings, home type, and integrated activities), and provider characteristics (e.g., worker stress and job satisfaction) have been shown to be significant predictors of persons' assessed quality of life. Second, once these significant predictors are identified, programmatic changes can be made to enhance a person's quality of life through techniques such as personal development and wellness training, quality enhancement techniques, and quality management techniques (Schalock, 1994; Schalock & Faulkner, 1997). Third, multivariate research designs help us understand better the complexity of the concept of quality of life and the role that a number of contextual variables play in the perception of a life of quality. Finally, these designs shift the focus of our thinking and intervention from personal to environmental factors as major sources of quality of life enhancement.

Quality of Life Assessment

One of the most significant changes during the current decade has been the shift toward outcome-based evaluation and person-referenced outcomes. This emerging focus on person-referenced outcomes reflects not only the subjective and personal nature of one's perceived quality of life, but also the quality revolution that we are currently experiencing; consumer empowerment with the associated expectations that human service programs will result in an improved quality of life for service recipients; the increased need for program outcome data that evaluate the effectiveness and efficiency of intervention and rehabilitation programs; the supports paradigm, which is based on the premise that providing needed and relevant supports will enhance one's quality of life; and the pragmatic evaluation paradigm, which emphasizes the practical, problem-solving orientation to program evaluation.

The quality of life assessment approach discussed in this section of the chapter is based on three assumptions that the author has gleaned from the current literature on quality of life conceptualization and measurement: (1) quality of life is composed of the eight core dimensions presented in Table 19.2 and Figure 19.1; (2) the focus of quality of life assessment should be on person-referenced outcomes; and (3) assessment strategies should use either personal appraisal or functional assessment measures reflecting one or more of the eight core dimensions. A model that incorporates these three assumptions is presented in Figure 19.2. As shown in the model, each of the eight core dimensions is defined operationally in terms of a number of specific indicators, which include attitudinal, behavioral, or performance factors representing one or more aspect of each core dimension. The following criteria should guide one's selection of specific indicators (Anastasi, 1982; Schalock, 1995b): The indicator is valued by the person, multiple indicators are used, the indicator is measurable with demonstrated reliability and validity, the indicator is connected logically to the service or support received, and the indicator is evaluated longitudinally. Exemplary quality of life indicators are listed in Table 19.3.

The indicators listed in Table 19.3 can be measured using either the personal appraisal or the functional assessment strategies described next. The reader should also note that the *personal appraisal* strategy should be equated to the historical notion of *subjective indicators*, whereas the *functional assessment* strategy should be equated to the historical notion of *objective indicators*.

Personal Appraisal

The personal appraisal strategy addresses the subjective nature of quality of life, typically asking the person how satisfied he or she is with the various aspects of his or her life. For example, this is the approach we have used in the *Quality of Life Questionnaire* (Schalock & Keith, 1993), wherein we asked questions such as, "How satisfied are you with your current home or living situation?" and "How satisfied are you with the skills and experience you have gained or are gaining from your job?" Although the person's responses are subjective, his or her responses need to be measured in psychometrically acceptable ways. Thus, a 3- to 5-point Likert scale can be used to indicate the level of expressed satisfaction. The advantages to this approach to measurement are that it encompasses the most common dependent measure used currently in quality of life assessments, it allows one to measure those factors that historically have been considered to be major subjective indicators of a life of quality, and it allows one to quantify the level of expressed satisfaction.

(Text continues on page 344)

TABLE 19.3
Quality of Life Indicators

Dimension	Exemplary Indicators	
Emotional Well-Being	Safety	Freedom from stress
	Spirituality	Self-concept
	Happiness	Contentment
Interpersonal Relations	Intimacy	Interactions
	Affection	Friendships
	Family	Supports
Material Well-Being	Ownership	Employment
	Financial	Possessions
	Security	Socio-economic status
	Food	Shelter
Personal Development	Education	Personal competence
	Skills	Purposeful activity
	Fulfillment	Advancement
Physical Well-Being	Health	Health care
	Nutrition	Health insurance
	Recreation	Leisure
	Mobility	Activities of daily living
Self-Determination	Autonomy	Personal control
	Choices	Self-direction
	Decisions	Personal goals/values
Social Inclusion	Acceptance	Community activities
	Status	Roles
	Supports	Volunteer activities
	Work environment	Residential environment
Rights	Privacy	Due process
	Voting	Ownership
	Access	Civic responsibilities

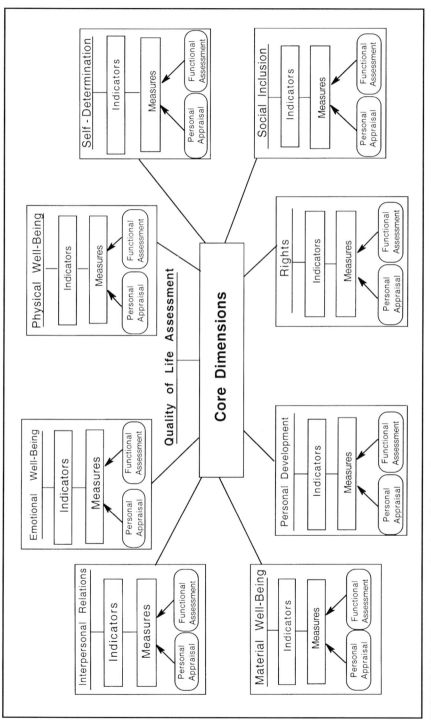

FIGURE 19.2. Measurement of quality of life core dimensions.

Functional Assessment

The most typical formats used in functional assessment include rating scales, participant observation, and questionnaires (Schalock, 1996c). Each attempts to document
a person's functioning across one or more core quality of life dimensions and the
respective indicator. To accomplish this, most instruments employ some form of an
ordinal rating scale to yield a profile of the individual's functioning. For example, one
might ask (or observe), "How frequently do you use health care facilities?" or "How
many civic or community clubs do you belong to?" The advantages of functional
assessments are that they are more objective and performance based, allow for the
evaluation of outcomes across groups, and thus provide important feedback to service
providers, funders, and regulators as to how they can change or improve their services
to enhance the recipients' perceived quality of life.

As mentioned previously, historically the subjective indicators used to assess one's
quality of life were different from the objective ones. The advantage of using the
approach to quality of life assessment depicted in Figure 19.2 is that one need not
use different indicators for subjective versus objective measurement; rather, the core
dimensions remain constant, and what varies is whether one uses a personal appraisal
or a functional assessment approach to assess the respective indicators. Thus, all assessment is focused clearly on the eight core dimensions of quality of life.

It is apparent that some of the domains are more amenable to personal appraisal,
and others to functional assessment. For example, personal appraisal might best be
used for the core dimensions of emotional well-being, self-determination, rights, and
interpersonal relations, whereas functional assessment might better be used for the
core dimensions of material well-being, personal development, physical well-being,
and social inclusion. Hence, there is a definite need to use multiple measures of one's
perceived quality of life.

Despite the conceptual breakthrough regarding the assessment of quality of life
just described, to date no single instrument implements fully the assessment model
depicted in Figure 19.2. The interested reader is referred to Cummins (1997a) and
Schalock (1996c) for reviews of the most commonly used instruments and advancements in the area of quality of life assessment.

PURSUING QUALITY (THE 2000s)

The discerning reader will have noticed that quality of life has yet to be defined in this
chapter. And that is by design, because one needs to understand fully the concept in
order to define it. And that may well explain why one can find over 100 definitions of
quality of life in the literature today. Over the years I have consistently referred to
quality of life as "a concept that reflects a person's desired conditions of living"
(Schalock, 1994, p. 121). Given the five significant changes that have occurred during the 1990s, I am now ready to modify slightly my definition:

Quality of life is a concept that reflects a person's desired conditions of living related to eight core dimensions of one's life: emotional well-being, interpersonal relationships, material well-being, personal development, physical well-being, self-determination, social inclusion, and rights.

With this definition clearly in mind, I suggest that the concept of quality of life will be pursued in the first decade of the 21st century from the following three perspectives: individuals pursuing a life of quality, service and support providers producing quality products, and evaluators (policy makers, funders, and consumers) analyzing quality outcomes.

Individuals Pursuing a Life of Quality

I anticipate that there will be at least three major thrusts by persons pursuing a life of quality. First, we will continue to see strong advocacy for increased opportunities to participate in the mainstream of life, associated with increased inclusion, equity, and choices. Related efforts will involve advocating for increased individual supports within regular environments; inclusion in major activities such as decision making, person-centered planning, and participatory action research (Whitney-Thomas, 1997); and incorporating the concept of quality of life in international and national disability policies (Goode, 1997a, 1997b). With these increased opportunities and involvement, more positive personal appraisals and functional assessments—that is, an enhanced perceived quality of life—should result.

Second, consumers will work jointly with researchers in determining the relative importance or value of the core dimensions depicted in Figure 19.1. Referring to Figure 19.1, for children and youth, for example, the most important dimensions may well be personal development, self-determination, interpersonal relationships, and social inclusion (Schalock, 1996a; Stark & Goldsbury, 1990); for adults, the hierarchy as shown in Figure 19.1 may well reflect the ordering of many peoples' valued dimensions; and for the elderly, physical well-being, interpersonal relationships, and emotional well-being may be the most important dimensions (Schalock, DeVries, & Lebsack, in press). The net result of these efforts should be the development of relevant quality of life outcome categories across the life span.

Third, consumers will increasingly become involved in assessing their own quality of life. For example, we (Schalock et al., in press) have recently shown that consumers are excellent surveyors and can assess other consumers' quality of life with highly acceptable reliability and validity.

Service Providers Producing Quality Products

The first decade of the 21st century will see service providers responding to the challenges posed by implementing quality enhancement techniques that focus on what program personnel and services or supports can do to enhance a person's perceived quality of life. As we move into the 21st century, I predict that these techniques will be either environmentally or program based.

Environmentally Based Enhancement Techniques

The implementation of two concepts related to environmentally based quality enhancement techniques will characterize the first decade of the 21st century. One is the belief that an enhanced quality of life is the result of a good match between a person's wants and needs and his or her fulfillment (Cummins, 1996; Michalos, 1985; Murrell & Norris, 1983; Schalock, Keith, Hoffman, & Karan, 1989); the second is a corollary that it is possible to assess the match between persons and their environments (Schalock & Jensen, 1986). The importance of these two concepts is supported by data suggesting that reducing the discrepancy between a person and his or her environment increases the person's assessed quality of life (Schalock et al., 1989).

Page constraints limit a thorough discussion of these environmentally based enhancement techniques. However, the following two examples will indicate how two such techniques might well be used in the 21st century. One technique involves the assessment of particular environmental characteristics as reflected in the Program Analysis of Service System (PASS 3) (Felce & Perry, 1997a; Wolfensberger & Glenn, 1975). This technique allows one to evaluate the following aspects to rehabilitation-oriented environments: physical integration, social integration, age-appropriate interpretations and structures, culture-appropriate interpretations and structures, model coherency, developmental growth orientation, and quality of setting. The second technique involves the design of environments that are user friendly and meet the following criteria (Ferguson, 1997): opportunity for involvement (e.g., food preparation); easy access to the outdoor environment; modifications to stairs, water taps, and door knobs; safety (e.g., handrails, safety glass, nonslip walking surfaces); convenience (e.g., orientation aids such as color coding or universal pictographs); accessibility; sensory stimulation (windows, less formal furniture); prosthetics (personal computers, specialized assistive devices, high technological environments); and opportunity for choice and control (e.g., lights, temperature, privacy, personal space, personal territory).

Program-Based Enhancement Techniques

Once the core dimensions of quality of life are assessed, then it is possible to implement a number of program-based (quality) enhancement techniques that will result in an enhanced perceived quality of life for the person. Examples include the following:

- *Emotional Well-Being*—increased safety, stable and predictable environments, positive feedback

- *Interpersonal Relations*—foster friendships, encourage intimacy, support families

- *Material Well-Being*—ownership, possessions, employment

- *Personal Development*—education and functional rehabilitation, augmentative technology

- *Physical Well-Being*—health care, mobility, wellness, nutrition

- *Self-Determination*—choices, personal control, decisions, personal goals

- *Social Inclusion*—community role, community integration, volunteerism

- *Rights*—privacy, voting, due process, civic responsibilities

In addition to pursuing these quality enhancement techniques, service providers will also need to evaluate the impact of these strategies. Thus, during the first decade of the 21st century, service providers will need also to pursue the quality outcomes discussed in the next section. In this process, they will need to evaluate where they are, where they want to be, and what organizational changes will be required to increase both person-referenced outcomes and program-referenced outputs.

Evaluators Analyzing Quality Outcomes

Human service organizations throughout the world are currently being challenged to provide quality services that result in quality outcomes. This is a challenging task because of two powerful, potentially conflicting forces: person-centered values and economically based restructured services. The focus on person-centered values stems from the quality of life movement; the human rights and self-advocacy movements' emphasis on equity, inclusion, empowerment, respect, and community living and work options; numerous public laws that stress opportunities and desired person-referenced outcomes related to independence, productivity, community integration, and satisfaction; and research demonstrating that persons can be more independent, productive, community integrated, and satisfied when quality of life concepts are the basis of individual services and supports. Conversely, the focus on restructured services stems from economic restraints, an increased need for accountability, and the movement toward a market economy in health care and rehabilitation services.

How can service providers adapt to these two potentially conflicting forces and still focus on valued, person-referenced outcomes? A heuristic model for doing so is presented in Figure 19.3. The model has three components: standards, focus, and critical performance indicators.

- *Standards* reflect the current emphasis on efficiency and value. Efficiency standards are based on the economic principles involved in increasing the net value of goods and services available to society; value standards reflect what is considered as good, important, or of value to the person.

- *Focus* represents the current accountability emphasis on programmatic outputs and person-referenced outcomes. In the model, *outputs* reflect the results of organizational processes, and *outcomes* represent the impact of services and supports on the person.

- *Critical performance indicators* for the organization ("outputs") include responsiveness, consumer satisfaction, quality improvements, staff competencies, normalized environments, user-friendly environments, placement rates, unit costs, recidivism, bed days, and waiting lists; for the person ("outcomes"), critical performance indicators include activities of daily living, self-direction, functional skills, community living and employment status, and indicators of home ownership, decision making, self-esteem, social relations, and education, health, and wellness.

The reader may ask at this point a very basic question: "How might this model be used to analyze quality outcomes within the current environment that stresses person-referenced outcomes *and* program-referenced efficiency measures? I would suggest through the use of one or more of the following types of outcome-based evaluation analyses that are described in more detail elsewhere (Schalock, 1995b; Schalock, 1999). Each analysis summarized below is related to a respective cell in the model shown in Figure 19.3.

- *Efficiency outputs* can be determined by using either allocation efficiency analysis or benefit–cost analysis that evaluates whether the program used its allocation well, whether the program's benefits outweigh the costs, or both.

- *Efficiency outcomes* can be determined through impact analysis that determines whether the program made a difference compared to either no program or an alternative program.

- *Value outputs* can be determined through effectiveness that determines whether the service or support in question meets its stated goals and objectives.

- *Value outcomes* can be determined through participant analysis such as that described in reference to the quality of life assessment model presented in Figure 19.2.

The primary challenge to service providers and evaluators alike is to reach a balance in their evaluation efforts among the four types of analyses summarized above, and to recognize that different constituents will emphasize their respective desired analysis. Funders, for example, will most likely focus on efficiency outputs, whereas advocacy groups will stress the importance of evaluating value and efficiency outcomes. Those emphasizing public policy might well stress efficiency outcomes and value outputs. A second challenge for each of us will be to reach a reasonable balance between accountability demands and available evaluative resources so that we can use the resulting outcome data to do the following:

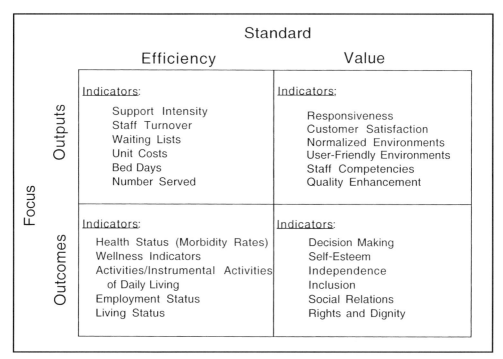

		Standard	
		Efficiency	Value
Focus	**Outputs**	Indicators: Support Intensity Staff Turnover Waiting Lists Unit Costs Bed Days Number Served	Indicators: Responsiveness Customer Satisfaction Normalized Environments User-Friendly Environments Staff Competencies Quality Enhancement
	Outcomes	Indicators: Health Status (Morbidity Rates) Wellness Indicators Activities/Instrumental Activities of Daily Living Employment Status Living Status	Indicators: Decision Making Self-Esteem Independence Inclusion Social Relations Rights and Dignity

FIGURE 19.3. Outcome-focused evaluation model.

- Determine whether functional limitations have been reduced and the person's adaptive behavior and role status enhanced

- Provide feedback to decision makers about the effectiveness and efficiency of the respective services or supports provided

- Provide the basis for program changes and improvements

- Target those areas where increased resources can be applied to improve the match between persons and environments

- Show a commitment to consumers that we are serious about program evaluation, and that we are willing to involve them in the evaluation activities

21ST CENTURY GUIDELINES

As we embark on the 21st century and undoubtedly continue to pursue both the concept of quality of life and an enhanced life of quality for persons with mental retardation, what guidelines might assist our efforts? I propose 10 guidelines that need to be understood within the context of the three decades of quality of life just discussed. As a quick summary of those decades, remember that during the 1980s we embraced the concept of quality of life as a sensitizing notion, social construct, and unifying theme; during the 1990s we came to a better understanding of the conceptualization and measurement of quality of life; and during the first decade of the 21st century I predict we will see individuals pursuing a life of quality, service providers producing quality products, and evaluators analyzing quality outcomes. Thus, in addition to reaffirming the 10 fundamental quality of life principles summarized in Table 19.1, I offer the 10 guidelines summarized in Table 19.4 for our work during the ensuing decade.

In conclusion, the first decade of the 21st century will be an exciting and active time as we jointly "pursue quality." This pursuit will involve individuals desiring and advocating for a life of quality, service and support providers producing quality products, and evaluators analyzing quality outcomes. However, despite the optimism expressed in the above predictions and guidelines, we should never forget that the first decade of the 21st century will probably continue to reflect the value clashes that we

TABLE 19.4
21st Century Quality of Life Guidelines

1. Consider that quality of life for persons with mental retardation is composed of those same core dimensions that are valued by all of a nation's citizenry.
2. Base public policies and service delivery principles on the concept of quality of life and the enhancement of a life of quality for all people.
3. Realize that the value ascribed to the various core quality of life dimensions will probably vary over the life span of the person, but, regardless of age, an enhanced quality of life is experienced when a person's basic needs are met and when he or she has the same opportunities as anyone else to pursue and achieve goals in the major life domains and settings.
4. Focus evaluation activities on both consumer outcomes and system performance.
5. Stress that continuous quality improvement is a fundamental aspect of an organization's culture.
6. Have evaluation activities play a complementary and supportive role that is consistent with the changing concept of disability as resulting from the interaction of the person and his or her environment.
7. Identify the significant predictors of a life of quality and evaluate the impact of targeting resources to maximize their positive effect(s).
8. Assist consumers, policy makers, funders, service providers, and advocates to understand the multidimensionality of the concept of quality of life (Figure 19.1) and its assessment (Figure 19.2).
9. Use multivariate statistical and research designs to determine the effectiveness and efficiency of quality of life–focused education and rehabilitation programs (Figure 19.3).
10. Integrate subjective and objective quality of life indicators into a unified concept of the core dimensions of quality of life, realizing that some aspects of each core dimension can be evaluated best via personal appraisal strategies, other aspects through objective functional assessments (Figure 19.2).

have experienced during the current decade. Thus, considerable hard work, advocacy, and risk lie ahead.

The last two decades have seen considerable progress in understanding the significant role and impact that the concept of quality of life has played in the lives of persons with mental retardation and the systems that interact with those lives. Indeed, the concept of quality of life has extended beyond the person and has now impacted an entire service delivery system because of its power as a social construct, unifying notion, and integrating concept. But what about the fourth decade? Will the concept of quality of life still be the same as it is today and predicted to be tomorrow? Only time will tell. What is certain is that, because of this concept, the lives and hopes of people with mental retardation will never be the same. And that is a lot to ask of any concept.

REFERENCES

Albin-Dean, J. M., & Mank, D. M. (1997). Continuous improvement and quality of life: Lessons from organizational management. In R. L. Schalock (Ed.), *Quality of life: Vol. 2. Application to persons with disabilities* (pp. 165–179). Washington, DC: American Association on Mental Retardation.

Albrecht, K. (1993). *The only thing that matters: Bringing the power of the customer into the center of your business.* New York: Harper Business.

Anastasi, A. (1982). *Psychological testing* (5th ed.). New York: Collier Macmillan.

Andrews, F. M. (1974). Social indicators of perceived quality of life. *Social Indicators Research, 1,* 279–299.

Brown, R. I. (Ed.). (1997). *Quality of life for people with disabilities: Models, research and practice.* Cheltenham, UK: Stanley Thornes.

Campbell, A., Converse, P. E., & Rogers, W. L. (1976). *The quality of American life: Perceptions, evaluation, and satisfaction.* New York: Russell Sage Foundation.

Clifford, D. L., & Sherman, P. (1983). Internal evaluation: Integrating program evaluation and management. In A. J. Love (Ed.), *Developing effective internal evaluation: New directions for program evaluation* (No. 20). San Francisco: Jossey-Bass.

Coulter, D. L. (1997). Health-related application of quality of life. In R. L. Schalock (Ed.), *Quality of life: Vol. 2. Application to persons with disabilities* (pp. 95–104). Washington, DC: American Association on Mental Retardation.

Cummins, R. A. (1996). The domains of life satisfaction: An attempt to order chaos. *Social Indicators Research, 38,* 303–328.

Cummins, R. A. (1997a). Assessing quality of life. In R. I. Brown (Ed.), *Quality of life for people with disabilities: Models, research and practice* (pp. 116–150). Cheltenham, UK: Stanley Thornes.

Cummins, R. A. (1997b). Self-rated quality of life scales for people with an intellectual disability: A review. *Journal of Applied Research in Intellectual Disabilities, 10,* 199–216.

Diener, E. (1984). Subjective well-being. *Psychological Bulletin, 95,* 542–575.

Edgerton, R. B. (1990). Quality of life from a longitudinal research perspective. In R. L. Schalock (Ed.), *Quality of life: Perspectives and issues* (pp. 149–160). Washington, DC: American Association on Mental Retardation.

Edgerton, R. B. (1996). A longitudinal–ethnographic research perspective on quality of life. In R. L. Schalock (Ed.), *Quality of life: Vol. 1. Conceptualization and measurement* (pp. 83–90). Washington, DC: American Association on Mental Retardation.

Elorriaga, J., Garcia, L., Martinez, J., & Unamunzaga, E. (in press). Quality of life of persons with mental retardation in Spain. In K. D. Keith & R. L. Schalock (Eds.), *Cross-cultural perspectives on quality of life*. Washington, DC: American Association on Mental Retardation.

Felce, D. (1997). Defining and applying the concept of quality of life. *Journal of Intellectual Disability Research*, *41*(2), 126–135.

Felce, D., & Perry, J. (1996). Assessment of quality of life. In R. L. Schalock (Ed.), *Quality of life: Vol. 1. Conceptualization and measurement* (pp. 63–72). Washington, DC: American Association on Mental Retardation.

Felce, D., & Perry, J. (1997a). A PASS 3 evaluation of community residences in Wales. *Mental Retardation, 35*(3), 170–176.

Felce, D., & Perry, J. (1997b). Quality of life: The scope of the term and its breadth of measurement. In R. I. Brown (Ed.), *Quality of life for people with disabilities: Models, research and practice* (pp. 56–70). Cheltenham, UK: Stanley Thornes.

Ferguson, R. V. (1997). Environmental design and quality of life. In R. I. Brown (Ed.), *Quality of life for people with disabilities: Models, research and practice* (pp. 56–70). Cheltenham, UK: Stanley Thornes.

Flanagan, J. C. (1978). A research approach to improving quality of life. *American Psychologist, 33*, 138–147.

Flanagan, J. C. (1982). Measurement of quality of life: Current state of the art. *Archives of Physical Medicine and Rehabilitation, 63*, 56–59.

Gardner, J. F., & Nudler, S. (1997). Beyond compliance to responsiveness: Accreditation reconsidered. In R. L. Schalock (Ed.), *Quality of life: Vol. 2. Application to persons with disabilities* (pp. 135–148). Washington, DC: American Association on Mental Retardation.

Gardner, J. F., Nudler, S., & Chapman, M. S. (1997). Personal outcomes as measures of quality. *Mental Retardation, 35*(4), 295–305.

Goode, D. A. (1990). Thinking about and discussing quality of life. In R. L. Schalock (Ed.), *Quality of life: Perspectives and issues* (pp. 41–58). Washington, DC: American Association on Mental Retardation.

Goode, D. A. (1997a). Assessing the quality of life of adults with profound disabilities. In R. I. Brown (Ed.), *Quality of life for people with disabilities: Models, research and practice* (pp. 56–70). Cheltenham, UK: Stanley Thornes.

Goode, D. A. (1997b). Quality of life as international disability policy: Implications for international research. In R. L. Schalock (Ed.), *Quality of life: Vol. 2. Applications to persons with disabilities* (pp. 211–222). Washington, DC: American Association on Mental Retardation.

Halpern, A. S. (1993). Quality of life as a conceptual framework for evaluating transition outcomes. *Exceptional Children, 59*, 486–498.

Hammer, M., & Champy, J. (1993). Reengineering the corporation: A manifesto for business revolution. New York: HarperCollins.

Harner, C. J., & Heal, L. W. (1993). The Multifaceted Lifestyle Questionnaire (MLSS): Psychometric properties of an interview schedule for assessing personal satisfaction of adults with limited intelligence. *Research in Developmental Disabilities, 14*, 221–236.

Heal, L. W., Borthwick-Duffy, S. A., & Saunders, R. R. (1996). Assessment of quality of life. In J. W. Jacobson and J. A. Mulick (Eds.), *Manual of diagnosis and professional practice in mental retardation* (pp. 199–209). Washington, DC: American Psychological Association.

Heal, L. W., & Chadsey-Rusch, J. (1985). The Lifestyle Satisfaction Scale (LSS): Assessing individual's satisfaction with residence, community setting, and associated services. *Applied Research in Mental Retardation, 6*, 475–490.

Heal, L. W., Khoju, M. R., Rusch, F. R., & Harnisch, D. L. (in press). Predicting quality of life of students who have left special education high school programs. *Special Education*.

Heal, L. W., Rubin, S. S., & Park, W. (1995). *Lifestyle Satisfaction Scale*. Champaign-Urbana: Transition Research Institute, University of Illinois.

Hughes, C., & Hwang, B. (1996). Attempts to conceptualize and measure quality of life. In R. L. Schalock (Ed.), *Quality of life: Vol. 1. Conceptualization and measurement* (pp. 51–62). Washington, DC: American Association on Mental Retardation.

Lehman, A. F., Rachuba, L. T., & Postrado, L. T. (1995). Demographic influences on quality of life among persons with chronic mental illness. *Evaluation and Program Planning, 18*(2), 155–164.

Maslow, A. H. (1954). *Motivation and personality.* New York: Harper & Row.

Mathison, S. (1991). What do we know about internal evaluation? *Evaluation and Program Planning, 14,* 159–165.

Michalos, A. C. (1985). Multiple discrepancy theory (MDT). *Social Indicators Research, 16,* 347–413.

Murrell, S. A., & Norris, F. H. (1983). Quality of life as the criterion for need assessment and community psychology. *Journal of Community Psychology, 11,* 88–97.

Osborne, D., & Gaebler, T. (1992). *Reinventing government: How the entrepreneurial spirit is transforming the public sector.* Reading, MA: Addison-Wesley.

Parmenter, T., & Donelly, M. (1997). An analysis of the dimensions of quality of life. In R. I. Brown (Ed.), *Quality of life for people with disabilities: Models, research and practice* (pp. 91–114). Cheltenham, UK: Stanley Thornes.

Perry, J., & Felce, D. (1995). Objective assessments of quality of life: How much do they agree with each other? *Journal of Community and Applied Social Psychology, 5,* 1–19.

Raphael, D. (1996). Defining quality of life: Debates concerning its measurement. In R. Renwick, I. Brown, & M. Nagler (Eds.), *Quality of life in health promotion and rehabilitation: Conceptual approaches, issues, and applications* (pp. 146–165). Thousand Oaks, CA: Sage.

Rapley, M., & Hopgood, L. (1997). Quality of life in a community-based service in rural Australia. *Journal of Intellectual & Developmental Disabilities, 22*(2), 125–141.

Renwick, R., & Brown, I. (1996). The Centre for Health Promotion's conceptual approach to quality of life. In R. Renwick, I. Brown, & M. Nagler (Eds.), *Quality of life in health promotion and rehabilitation: Conceptual approaches, issues, and applications* (pp. 75–86). Thousand Oaks, CA: Sage.

Renwick, R., Brown, I., & Nagler, M. (Eds.). (1996). *Quality of life in health promotion and rehabilitation: Conceptual approaches, issues, and applications.* Thousand Oaks, CA: Sage.

Schalock, R. L. (Ed.). (1990). *Quality of life: Perspectives and issues.* Washington, DC: American Association on Mental Retardation.

Schalock, R. L. (1994). Quality of life, quality enhancement, and quality assurance: Implications for program planning and evaluation in the field of mental retardation and developmental disabilities. *Evaluation and Program Planning, 17,* 121–131.

Schalock, R. L. (1995a). The assessment of natural supports in community rehabilitation services. In O. C. Karan & S. Greenspan (Eds.), *Community rehabilitation services for people with disabilities* (pp. 184–203). Newton, MA: Butterworth-Heinemann.

Schalock, R. L. (1995b). *Outcome-based evaluation.* New York: Plenum Press.

Schalock, R. L. (1996a). The quality of children's lives. In A. H. Fine & N. M. Fine (Eds.), *Therapeutic recreation for exceptional children: Let me in, I want to play* (2nd ed.), pp. 83–94. Springfield, IL: Thomas.

Schalock, R. L. (Ed.). (1996b). *Quality of life: Vol. 1. Conceptualization and measurement.* Washington, DC: American Association on Mental Retardation.

Schalock, R. L. (1996c). Reconsidering the conceptualization and measurement of quality of life. In R. L. Schalock (Ed.), *Quality of life: Vol. 1. Conceptualization and measurement.* Washington, DC: American Association on Mental Retardation.

Schalock, R. L. (1997a). The concept of quality of life in 21st century disability programs. In R. I. Brown (Ed.), *Quality of life for people with disabilities: Models, research and practice* (pp. 327–340). Cheltenham, UK: Stanley Thornes.

Schalock, R. L. (1997b). *Quality of life: Vol. 2. Application to persons with disabilities.* Washington, DC: American Association on Mental Retardation.

Schalock, R. L. (1999). A quest for quality: Achieving organizational outputs and personal outcomes. In J. Gardner & S. Nudler (Eds.), *Quality performance in human services* (pp. 55–80). Baltimore: Brookes.

Schalock, R. L., Bontham, G., & Marchant, C. (in press). Consumer based quality of life assessment: A path model of perceived satisfaction. *Evaluation and Program Planning.*

Schalock, R. L., DeVries, D., & Lebsack, J. (in press). Rights, quality measures, and program changes. In S. S. Herr & G. Weber (Eds.), *Aging, rights and quality of life of older persons with developmental disabilities.* Baltimore: Brookes.

Schalock, R. L., & Faulkner, E. H. (1997). Cross-validation of a contextual model of quality of life. *European Journal on Mental Disability, 4*(1), 18–27.

Schalock, R. L., & Jensen, M. (1986). Assessing the goodness-of-fit between persons and their environments. *Journal of The Association for Persons with Severe Handicaps, 11*(2), 103–109.

Schalock, R. L., & Keith, K. D. (1993). *Quality of Life Questionnaire.* Worthington, OH: IDS Publishing.

Schalock, R. L., Keith, K. D., Hoffman, K., & Karan, O. C. (1989). Quality of life: Its measurement and use. *Mental Retardation, 27*(1), 25–31.

Schalock, R. L., Lemanowicz, J. A., Conroy, J. W., & Feinstein, C. S. (1994). A multivariate investigative study of the correlates of quality of life. *Journal on Developmental Disabilities, 3*(2), 59–73.

Senge, P. (1990). *The fifth discipline: The art and practice of the learning organization.* New York: Doubleday/Currency.

Snell, M. E., & Vogtle, L. K. (1997). Facilitating relationships of children with mental retardation in schools. In R. L. Schalock (Ed.), *Quality of life: Vol. 2. Application to persons with disabilities* (pp. 43–62). Washington, DC: American Association on Mental Retardation.

Stark, J. A., & Goldsbury, T. (1990). Quality of life from childhood to adulthood. In R. L. Schalock (Ed.), *Quality of life: Perspectives and issues* (pp. 71–84). Washington, DC: American Association on Mental Retardation.

Torres, R. T. (1992). Improving the quality of internal evaluation: The evaluator as consultant–mediator. *Evaluation and Program Planning, 14,* 189–198.

Verdugo, M. A. (in press). Quality of life for persons with mental retardation and developmental disabilities in Spain: The present zeitgeist. In K. D. Keith & R. L. Schalock (Eds.), *Cross-cultural perspectives on quality of life.* Washington, DC: American Association on Mental Retardation.

Ward, N., & Keith, K. D. (1996). Self-advocacy: Foundations for a life of quality. In R. L. Schalock (Ed.), *Quality of Life: Vol. 1. Conceptualization and measurement* (pp. 5–10). Washington, DC: American Association on Mental Retardation.

Whitney-Thomas, J. (1997). Participatory action research as an approach to enhancing quality of life for individuals with disabilities. In R. L. Schalock (Ed.), *Quality of life: Vol. 2. Application to persons with disabilities* (pp. 181–198). Washington, DC: American Association on Mental Retardation.

Wolfensberger, W., & Glenn, L. (1975). *Program Analysis of Service Systems: Handbook and manual* (3rd ed.). Toronto: National Institute on Mental Retardation.

Policy Issues

Transforming Service Delivery Systems in the States

David Braddock, Richard Hemp, and Susan Parish

S ervice delivery systems in the states for people with mental retardation and developmental disabilities (MR/DD) have undergone an enormous transformation during the life of The Arc, particularly in the past two decades. In this chapter, we identify and describe many of these demographic, fiscal, and programmatic changes, using the 50 states and the District of Columbia as the central focus of our analysis and discussion. The chapter draws extensively from the University of Illinois at Chicago's fifth edition of *The State of the States in Developmental Disabilities* (Braddock, Hemp, Parish, & Westrich, 1998), which is distributed by the research monographs and books publication program of the American Association on Mental Retardation. The present chapter is organized into five parts, each summarizing relevant trends in the states. The first four components address out-of-home residential placements, state-operated institutions, privately operated residential facilities for 16 or more persons, and community services and supports. The fifth and concluding section of the chapter discusses demographic, economic, and political trends influencing the expansion of community mental retardation services in the 21st century.

OUT-OF-HOME RESIDENTIAL PLACEMENTS

The transformation of the nation's residential care system is reflected in the growing percentage of individuals being served in smaller, more individualized community settings. In 1977 only 14% of the 290,220 persons with developmental disabilities residing in out-of-home residential settings lived in settings for 15 or fewer individuals, and only 7% (20,409 persons) resided in settings for 6 or fewer individuals. In contrast, by

This chapter is adapted from *The State of the States in Developmental Disabilities* (5th ed., Chapter 2), by D. Braddock, R. Hemp, S. Parish, and J. Westrich, 1998. Washington, DC: American Association on Mental Retardation. Copyright 1998 by David Braddock. Adapted with permission.

1996, 65% of the 394,284 persons in out-of-home placements were residing in settings for 15 or fewer persons. Fifty-one percent of this total, or 199,890 individuals, resided in settings for 6 or fewer persons. The growth in utilization of the smaller settings was quite rapid during recent years. The number of persons in settings for 6 or fewer individuals increased by 55% from 1992 to 1996, from 129,377 to 199,890.

There is great diversity among the states, however. In 1996, 13 states provided 70% or more of their residential services in settings for 6 or fewer persons. These states were Alaska, Arizona, California, Colorado, Hawaii, Maryland, Michigan, New Hampshire, New Mexico, Vermont, Washington, West Virginia, and Wyoming. In contrast, more than 50% of all persons living in out-of-home residential placements in 1996 in Georgia, Illinois, Kentucky, Louisiana, Mississippi, New Jersey, Oklahoma, Tennessee, Texas, and Virginia were served in congregate settings for 16 or more persons. Table 20.1 presents state-by-state data with respect to the proportion of persons living in settings for 6 or fewer persons, for 7 to 15 persons, or for 16 or more persons.

Total public spending for MR/DD residential and community services in the United States (excluding nursing homes) has grown from $3.457 billion in 1977 to $22.780 billion in 1996. In real economic terms (adjusted for inflation), this was a growth rate of 167%. During the 1992–1996 period, MR/DD spending continued its rapid upward momentum, advancing from $17.3 billion to $22.8 billion. Adjusted for inflation, the 1992–1996 growth rate was 18% over the 5-year period. This compared to growth rates of 27% for 1988–1992; 28% for 1984–1988; 15% for 1980–1984; and 20% for 1977–1980.

The increase in total spending for MR/DD services in the nation is wholly attributable to the dramatic expansion of funds allocated for community services activities. During 1992–1996, inflation-adjusted spending for community services advanced 41%, while adjusted spending for large congregate care services (state-operated institutions and privately operated residential facilities for 16 or more persons) decreased by 12%. There was, however, considerable variation among the states with regard to community services resource commitments. Growth in spending during 1992–1996, for example, ranged from 163% in New Mexico to 1% in the District of Columbia. And, despite the 12% decline nationally in large congregate care spending, 10 states increased spending for these settings during 1992–1996.

STATE-OPERATED INSTITUTIONS

An *institution* was defined in this study to include state-operated facilities for 16 or more persons, including state-operated institutions, developmental centers, training centers, state schools, and designated MR/DD units in state psychiatric hospitals. Inflation-adjusted spending for state-operated institutions declined 15% between 1977 and 1996. During this 20-year period, the number of people living in state-operated institutions was reduced by 60%, falling from 149,892 to 59,726 (Figure 20.1). Average daily costs in real economic terms advanced dramatically, however, from $45 in 1977 to $258 in

TABLE 20.1
Persons Served by Size of Residential Settings: Fiscal Year 1996

Rank	State	1–6 Settings Number	%	7–15 Settings Number	%	16+ Settings Number	%	Total
1	Hawaii	1,435	93	7	1	105	7	1,547
2	Vermont	810	92	0	0	68	8	878
3	Alaska	1,392	89	110	7	59	4	1,561
4	Michigan	9,895	89	0	0	1,231	11	11,126
5	New Hampshire	1,441	87	90	5	132	8	1,663
6	Colorado	3,785	85	300	7	352	8	4,437
7	Arizona	2,269	85	43	2	356	13	2,668
8	Wyoming	956	79	75	6	178	15	1,209
9	New Mexico	2,167	78	181	7	435	16	2,783
10	Washington	7,640	75	400	4	2,212	22	10,252
11	Maryland	4,075	74	0	0	1,413	26	5,488
12	West Virginia	2,668	73	686	19	303	8	3,657
13	California	35,056	71	2,854	6	11,608	23	49,518
14	Nebraska	2,320	67	9	0	1,126	33	3,455
15	Oregon	2,822	66	600	14	836	20	4,258
16	Maine	1,882	66	567	20	395	14	2,844
17	Connecticut	4,206	66	442	7	1,716	27	6,364
18	Rhode Island	1,009	66	337	22	184	12	1,530
19	Minnesota	8,086	66	1,683	14	2,535	21	12,304
20	Nevada	505	64	27	3	254	32	786
21	Wisconsin	9,058	64	914	7	4,172	30	14,144
22	Idaho	1,662	61	540	20	517	19	2,719
23	Kansas	2,202	58	269	7	1,316	35	3,787
24	Massachusetts	6,466	56	1,459	13	3,603	31	11,528
25	Pennsylvania	10,496	56	728	4	7,662	41	18,886
26	North Carolina	4,060	54	334	4	3,180	42	7,574
27	Utah	1,253	52	122	5	1,025	43	2,400
28	Delaware	465	52	21	2	413	46	899
29	Montana	839	50	501	30	326	20	1,666
30	North Dakota	1,023	50	647	31	393	19	2,063
31	South Dakota	986	46	684	32	487	23	2,157
32	South Carolina	2,167	44	1,089	22	1,724	35	4,980
33	Arkansas	2,493	42	978	17	2,447	41	5,918
34	Florida	4,743	42	2,701	24	3,968	35	11,412
35	New Jersey	4,644	41	533	5	6,039	54	11,216
36	Virginia	2,642	40	562	9	3,322	51	6,526
37	Iowa	2,619	38	1,401	21	2,819	41	6,839
38	Ohio	6,563	37	3,082	18	7,976	45	17,621
39	Louisiana	2,892	36	763	10	4,419	55	8,074
40	Missouri	2,944	34	1,427	17	4,215	49	8,586
41	New York	13,446	34	17,180	43	9,311	23	39,937
42	Texas	5,891	34	953	5	10,700	61	17,544
43	Georgia	1,805	31	7	0	3,968	69	5,780
44	Illinois	6,167	31	2,399	12	11,663	58	20,229
45	Indiana	2,978	30	2,767	28	4,313	43	10,058
46	Oklahoma	1,574	29	230	4	3,580	67	5,384
47	Dist. of Columbia	328	28	790	68	37	3	1,155
48	Kentucky	992	28	276	8	2,284	64	3,552
49	Alabama	694	19	1,431	38	1,617	43	3,742
50	Tennessee	981	17	1,773	31	3,008	52	5,762
51	Mississippi	399	10	255	7	3,165	83	3,819
	United States	199,890	51	55,227	14	139,167	35	394,284

Note. From *The State of the States in Developmental Disabilities* (5th ed., Chap. 2), by D. Braddock, R. Hemp, S. Parish, and J. Westrich, 1998, Washington, DC: American Association on Mental Retardation. Copyright 1998 by David Braddock. Used with permission.

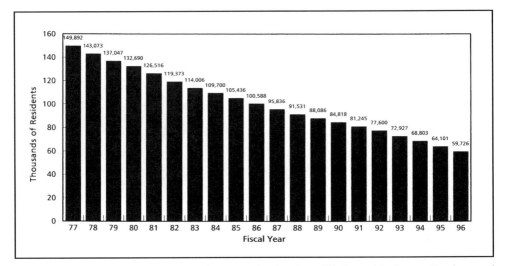

FIGURE 20.1. Residents in state-operated institutions. *Note.* From *The State of the States in Developmental Disabilities* (5th ed., Chap. 2), by D. Braddock, R. Hemp, S. Parish, and J. Westrich, 1998, Washington, DC: American Association on Mental Retardation. Copyright 1998 by David Braddock. Used with permission.

1996. Improved staffing ratios accounted for some of the cost-per-resident increases. Ratios grew from 1.6:1 in 1983 to 2.23:1 in 1996, an increase of 46%. The complement of professional staff in state institutions also increased significantly over the past 20 years, and staff wage levels in institutions grew as well (Braddock & Mitchell, 1992).

The number of residents in state institutions declined 23% during 1992–1996, from 77,600 in 1992 to 59,726 in 1996. The average annual decline during 1992-1996 was slightly higher than the rate of decline experienced for the preceding 25 years. The state institution census peaked at 194,650 in 1967 (Lakin, 1979) and diminished by between 3% and 5% per year through 1992. The rate of decline then increased to 6% annually during 1992–1996. All states except Arkansas and Nevada reduced their institutional census during 1992–1996.

Seven states now have no institutions—Alaska, District of Columbia, New Hampshire, New Mexico, Rhode Island, Vermont, and West Virginia—and 14 other states have fewer than 400 individuals each residing in institutional settings—Arizona, Colorado, Delaware, Hawaii, Idaho, Maine, Michigan, Minnesota, Montana, Nevada, North Dakota, South Dakota, Utah, and Wyoming. A number of these states have been or are currently involved in class action litigation requiring community placement of institutional residents.

Costs of Care

On a nationwide basis, average daily costs in state-operated institutions, in nominal dollars, advanced from $210 to $258 during 1992–1996. In real economic terms, this was an increase of 10% over the 5-year period. The increase in inflation-adjusted average daily costs during the 1988–1992 period was 19%. Although the rate of growth in costs per resident slowed during the 1992–1996 period, it still significantly exceeded the rate of inflation. Figure 20.2 displays, in real economic terms, the growth of average daily costs across the past two decades. During the 1977–1996 period, this increase was 132%.

The states exhibited great variation in average daily costs in 1996. Rates ranged from over $400 per day in Alaska, Idaho, Maine, Massachusetts, Michigan, Minnesota, New Mexico, Oregon, and West Virginia downward to $165 to $225 per day in Arizona, Arkansas, Florida, Illinois, Louisiana, Mississippi, Nebraska, New Jersey, South Carolina, South Dakota, Texas, and Virginia. In 1996 average daily costs exceeded $300 in 14 states. The most rapid rates of growth (50% or more) in inflation-adjusted average daily costs during 1992–1996 occurred in Tennessee, New Mexico, and Mississippi.

Closure of Public Institutions

The trend toward closing public institutions gained momentum during the recession of the early 1980s and has continued. In a 1984 national survey, Braddock and Heller (1985) identified 24 closures in 12 states. Our 1988 national study identified 44 closures in 20 states, and our 1992 study identified 94 scheduled or completed institutional closures in 29 states. The most recent study update identified 113 closures in 36 states by the year 2000 (Braddock et al., 1998).

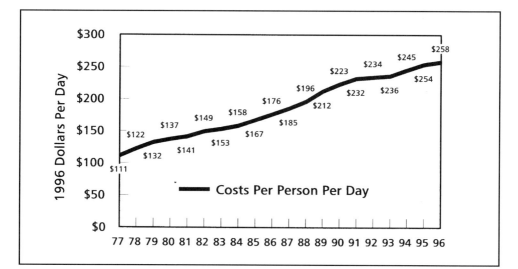

FIGURE 20.2. Daily costs per resident in state-operated institutions. *Note.* From *The State of the States in Developmental Disabilities* (5th ed., Chap. 2), by D. Braddock, R. Hemp, S. Parish, and J. Westrich, 1998, Washington, DC: American Association on Mental Retardation. Copyright 1998 by David Braddock. Used with permission.

In 1991 New Hampshire closed the Laconia State School and became the first state to eliminate state-operated institutions for people with mental retardation. About a year later, the District of Columbia closed Forest Haven, an institution that since 1925 had served persons with mental retardation who were residents of the District. Vermont and Rhode Island closed their remaining institutions in 1993 and 1994, respectively, and New Mexico and Alaska closed all public institutional facilities in 1997. West Virginia closed, and Hawaii proposed to close, their remaining institutions in 1998. During 1992–1996, 12 states without previous closure experience announced plans to close, or did close, facilities. These states included Alabama, Alaska, Georgia, Hawaii, Indiana, Maine, Oklahoma, South Carolina, South Dakota, Texas, Vermont, and Washington. New York, which in 1992 announced the closure of all its state institutions by 2000, has since rescinded its closure plans for several facilities. Missouri was the only state to open a new public institution during the 1992–1996 period.

LARGE PRIVATELY OPERATED RESIDENTIAL FACILITIES AND NURSING HOMES

Large privately operated residential facilities in this study referred to privately operated residential facilities serving 16 or more persons with developmental disabilities in the same location. This includes state-funded facilities (not state-operated facilities) whether or not the facilities were certified as intermediate care facilities for people with mental retardation (ICFs/MR). The total population of privately operated facilities for 16 or more people (excluding nursing homes) declined 11% from 46,168 in 1992 to 41,003 in 1996. There was an 8% decline in the number of persons residing in ICF/MR-certified private facilities for 16 or more persons (decrease of 2,631 individuals) and a decline of 20% (2,534 individuals) residing in private settings not certified as ICFs/MR.

Private residential settings for 16 or more individuals were provided in 39 states during 1992–1996. Despite the overall 11% decline in population in this sector during 1992–1996, financial support for these settings grew 3% in inflation-adjusted terms during the 5-year period. However, between 1995 and 1996 inflation-adjusted spending declined by 5%.

The number of persons residing in *nursing homes* nationally declined by 13%, from 44,291 in 1992 to 38,438 in 1996. Population declines were reported by 30 states. The five leading states in terms of percent decline in nursing home population were Colorado (75%), Iowa (59%), and DC, Michigan, and Wyoming (48%). The five leading states in terms of reducing the absolute number of nursing home residents were Michigan (1,069), Pennsylvania (920), Ohio (827), Iowa (758), and Alabama (610). These five states represented 71% of the total national reduction in nursing home residents with mental retardation and related conditions.

Eighteen states increased the number of nursing home residents with developmental disabilities by 1,740 people. Six of these states increased the number of residents by more than 100: Mississippi (328), Tennessee (271), Minnesota (229), New York (173), Georgia (120), and New Jersey (101). Kansas remained the only state that reported no residents with mental retardation and related conditions living in nursing homes. Arizona, Florida, Colorado, and South Carolina reported the lowest per capita utilization of nursing homes, at 2 to 3 per 100,000 of state population. Arkansas, Mississippi, and Oklahoma reported the highest utilization rates at 39 to 40 per 100,000 of the state population.

COMMUNITY SERVICES AND SUPPORTS

The growing proportion of residential placements in smaller, more individualized community settings is dramatically reflected in the financing of these services over time. Total spending for community services, defined in terms of residential services for 15 or fewer persons and related day programs, services, and supports, advanced from $9.9 billion in 1992 to $15.5 billion in 1996. This was an increase of 41% in inflation-adjusted terms, or 9% per year. During 1988–1992, real community spending growth totaled 50%; during 1984–1988, growth was 63%, and during 1980–1984, the growth rate was 52%. For the past 20 years, the rate of resource expansion for financing community services in the United States has been remarkably strong, even though the growth has not been uniformly distributed across all states and communities.

The steady 20-year growth of inflation-adjusted community spending is illustrated in Figure 20.3 (top chart). Congregate spending increased modestly from 1977 to 1991, and then declined during 1992–1996. In 1989, the volume of public funds deployed to support persons with mental retardation and developmental disabilities in community settings *first exceeded* the amount of funds allocated for institutions and other congregate settings for 16 or more persons. In 1996, 68% of total MR/DD funding was being used to support individuals in community settings for 15 or fewer persons. The remainder supported residents in state-operated institutions and privately operated facilities for 16 or more persons.

A second, contrasting graphic is presented in the bottom chart of Figure 20.3, in which community services are redefined to refer to settings for 6 or fewer persons. This redefinition has a profound effect on the analysis of the pattern of financial support across the 20-year period. By reclassifying facilities that serve 7 to 15 persons into the large congregate care category, it becomes clear that the nation has a significant distance to travel before the allocation of financial resources reflects the values of small, truly family-scale services and supports. *If present trends continue, by the year 2002 we can expect roughly the same percentage of total public resources expended nationwide in 1996 in settings for 15 or fewer persons (68%) to be expended in residential programs serving 6 or fewer persons.*

Public spending for family support, supported living, personal assistance, and supported employment is collectively represented by the white portions of the bars in Figure 20.3. Termed "individual and family support," this spending comprised 10.3% of total resources for community services in 1996. However, extreme variation in state commitments to individual and family support programs was noted, ranging from less than 1% of total spending for MRJDD services in DC, Alabama, and Mississippi, to more than 25% of total MR/DD spending in Alaska, New Mexico, Oklahoma, and Washington.

Sources of Revenue

State government general revenues continue to provide the majority of funds used nationally to finance community services and supports. State funds, including state supplementation of federal Supplemental Security Income (SSI) payments, comprised 53% of total community services revenues of $15.5 billion in 1996. However, due primarily to the rapid expansion of federal funding available to the states through the Medicaid Home and Community Based Services (HCBS) Waiver, there was a decline in state funds as a portion of total community spending from 62% in 1992. As shown in Figure 20.4, federal HCBS Waiver funds and associated federal income maintenance represented over 55% of federal funding for community services in 1996, and nearly one quarter of all community services funding available in the United States.

Funds for ICF/MR settings supporting 15 or fewer persons in community residential facilities grew modestly during 1992–1996. In 1996 43,357 persons were supported in public and private ICF/MR settings for 15 or fewer persons at a federal reimbursement level of $1.6 billion. The comparable figures for 1992 were 40,611 persons and $1.3 billion in federal reimbursements. Federal ICF/MR reimbursements to settings for 15 or fewer individuals grew 13% in inflation-adjusted terms during 1992–1996, but they declined 10% between 1995 and 1996 as states converted ICFs/MR placements to the HCBS Waiver. Fifty-eight percent of total federal ICF/MR reimbursements of $5.724 billion in 1996 supported residents in state-operated institutions.

The HCBS Waiver

The HCBS Waiver grew from $1.2 million in federal reimbursements in 1982 to $833 million in 1992, and this rapid rate of growth has continued. In 1996 federal HCBS Waiver reimbursements totaled $2.757 billion and supported 184,983 participants (Braddock et al., 1998). The types of services financed by the Waiver include case management, homemaker assistance, home health care, personal care, residential habilitation, day habilitation, respite care, transportation, supported employment, adapted equipment, home modification, and occupational, speech, physical, and behavioral therapy.

In 1996, adjusting for the size of state general populations, Vermont and Rhode Island had the largest HCBS Waiver programs, followed by Wyoming, New Hampshire,

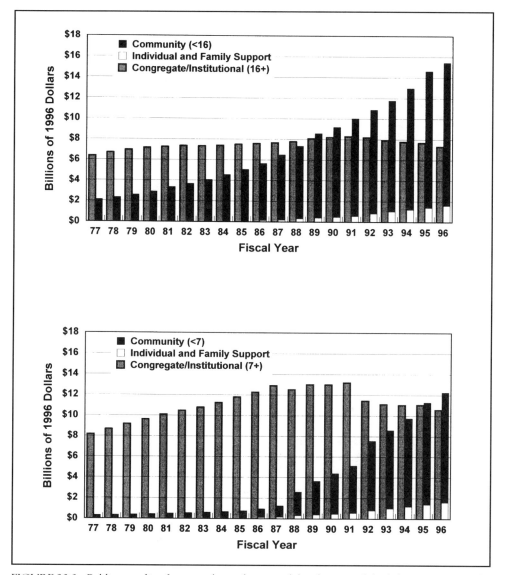

FIGURE 20.3. Public spending for mental retardation and developmental disabilities services in the United States. "Community" spending includes public funding (federal, state, local) for residential services for 15 persons or fewer (top chart) or 6 persons or fewer (bottom chart), and other day and support services. "Congregate/institutional" spending includes public funding for residences such as group homes and public or private institutions for 16 persons or more (top chart) or 7 persons or more (bottom chart). "Individual and family support" in both charts includes spending for family support, supported living/personal assistance, and supported employment. Nursing home spending is excluded in both charts. *Note*. From *The State of the States in Developmental Disabilities* (5th ed., Chap. 2), by D. Braddock, R. Hemp, S. Parish, and J. Westrich, 1998, Washington, DC: American Association on Mental Retardation. Copyright 1998 by David Braddock. Used with permission.

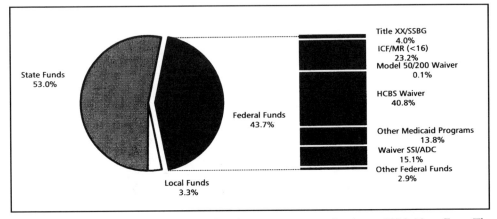

FIGURE 20.4. Community services spending by revenue source: fiscal year 1996. *Note.* From *The State of the States in Developmental Disabilities* (5th ed., Chap. 2), by D. Braddock, R. Hemp, S. Parish, and J. Westrich, 1998, Washington, DC: American Association on Mental Retardation. Copyright 1998 by David Braddock. Used with permission.

South Dakota, New York, North Dakota, Minnesota, Maine, and Arizona. In terms of total participants served, the largest HCBS Waiver programs in 1996 were, predictably, in the populous states of California, New York, Florida, Massachusetts, and Pennsylvania. Table 20.2 presents data on individuals participating in HCBS Waiver-funded services along with reimbursement levels, years in effect, and spending rank (adjusted for state general population).

Over the past decade, the HCBS Waiver has far surpassed Title XX/Social Services Block Grant (SSBG) and the ICF/MR program as the major source of federal funding for community services. The HCBS Waiver was established in all 50 states by 1996 (see "years in effect" column in Table 20.2). Federal Waiver revenues increased by an average of 32% per year in real economic terms during 1992–1996. In 1996 the Model 50/200 Waiver program provided Medicaid coverage in six states for 820 medically fragile children living at home, at a cost of $13.9 million nationally. Connecticut, Iowa, and Ohio have absorbed their Model Waivers into their larger HCBS Waiver programs.

The funding level for ICF/MR-financed community services for 15 or fewer individuals increased by 4% annually in inflation-adjusted terms across the 1992–1996 period. However, as previously noted, ICF/MR funding in these settings declined 10% between 1995 and 1996. Eighteen states converted ICF/MR settings to the HCBS Waiver during 1992–1996, and reduced community ICF/MR residents by a total of 3,867 people during this period. The largest conversions in terms of participant numbers were in Massachusetts, Michigan, New York, and Rhode Island. The total number of persons served in ICFs/MR for 15 or fewer persons actually grew by 2,746 persons on a national basis, a 7% increase. Twenty-five states expanded the number of

TABLE 20.2
Medicaid Home and Community Based Services Waiver Spending: Fiscal Year 1996

Rank	State	Participants	Years in Effect	Federal Spending	Per Capita
1	Vermont	1,101	14	$27,584,284	$47.01
2	Rhode Island	1,924	13	$42,031,186	$42.41
3	Wyoming	864	6	$17,538,328	$36.52
4	New Hampshire	2,005	13	$38,434,156	$33.27
5	South Dakota	1,371	14	$22,498,434	$30.78
6	New York	27,442	5	$558,962,129	$30.73
7	North Dakota	1,771	13	$19,623,967	$30.54
8	Minnesota	5,422	12	$116,264,551	$25.08
9	Maine	1,053	13	$30,946,435	$24.94
10	Arizona	5,753	8	$104,168,321	$23.86
11	Connecticut	2,832	9	$69,990,000	$21.39
12	New Mexico	1,553	12	$34,988,990	$20.56
13	Massachusetts	8,027	12	$122,600,000	$20.16
14	Colorado	3,874	13	$66,816,402	$17.65
15	Oklahoma	2,125	11	$55,249,088	$16.80
16	Nebraska	1,834	9	$27,107,780	$16.47
17	Kansas	3,146	13	$42,268,636	$16.46
18	Montana	855	15	$14,393,063	$16.45
19	West Virginia	1,359	13	$27,556,000	$15.10
20	Utah	2,128	9	$29,015,574	$14.66
21	Wisconsin	4,753	13	$73,200,000	$14.24
22	Oregon	2,601	15	$44,236,993	$13.93
23	Pennsylvania	6,015	13	$163,181,586	$13.53
24	Maryland	3,397	13	$64,106,432	$12.68
25	Washington	4,570	13	$55,224,008	$10.06
26	New Jersey	5,280	13	$77,484,000	$9.72
27	Michigan	5,118	9	$88,365,032	$9.22
28	Alabama	3,624	14	$39,212,900	$9.19
29	Tennessee	2,721	10	$43,981,292	$8.32
30	Delaware	343	12	$5,756,407	$7.98
31	Lousiana	2,100	10	$30,536,652	$7.03
32	Iowa	2,434	4	$19,804,019	$6.96
33	Hawaii	600	13	$7,007,500	$5.93
34	South Carolina	2,096	5	$21,147,330	$5.74
35	Alaska	190	3	$3,372,600	$5.58
36	Kentucky	1,000	13	$21,036,000	$5.44
37	California	29,133	12	$169,888,000	$5.36
38	Idaho	415	13	$6,218,333	$5.28
39	North Carolina	3,073	13	$36,827,242	$5.07
40	Ohio	2,536	6	$55,637,706	$4.99
41	Georgia	1,619	7	$34,336,186	$4.72
42	Missouri	3,957	8	$23,183,268	$4.34
43	Florida	9,014	13	$57,139,210	$4.00
44	Arkansas	459	7	$9,958,728	$3.99
45	Virginia	1,575	6	$25,769,587	$3.88
46	Indiana	1,073	7	$20,126,600	$3.46
47	Illinois	5,267	13	$36,800,000	$3.11
48	Texas	3,164	11	$52,588,628	$2.77
49	Nevada	373	14	$2,320,096	$1.48
50	Mississippi	44	1	$141,825	$0.05
51	Dist. of Columbia	0	0	$0	$0.00
	United States	184,983	15	$2,756,625,484	$10.44

Note. From *The State of the States in Developmental Disabilities* (5th ed., Chap. 2), by D. Braddock, R. Hemp, S. Parish, and J. Westrich, 1998, Washington, DC: American Association on Mental Retardation. Copyright 1998 by David Braddock. Used with permission.

people in ICFs/MR for 15 or fewer persons over the 4 years. The six leading states in this expansion were Texas, California, Louisiana, Michigan, North Carolina, and Ohio. Texas alone accounted for 70% of the total nationwide increase.

Local Funding

Total county, township, and municipal government resources allocated for community services grew from $538.4 million in 1992 to $670.0 million in 1996. This was an inflation-adjusted growth rate of 12% over the total 4-year period. Twenty-four percent of these local government resources were used as state matching funds for the Medicaid HCBS Waiver or the ICF/MR program. The remaining funds supported county government-operated group homes, day programs, or other community supports.

Local government funding of community services represented only about 4% of community services resources nationally. However, these funds were major revenue components in several states, most notably in Ohio and Iowa, where county funding comprised 41% and 39%, respectively, of total community spending. In Nebraska, Texas, Kansas, Virginia, Wisconsin, and Missouri, municipal or county government resources contributed between 4% and 24% of total community services spending in 1996. One half of all local funding supporting community services in the United States was attributable to the State of Ohio.

Emergence of Individual and Family Support

Family Support

Family support consists of any community-based service administered or financed by the state MR/DD agency providing for family vouchers, direct cash payments to families, reimbursement to families, or direct payments to service providers that the state agency identified as family support. Examples of family support programs include cash subsidy payments, respite care, family counseling, architectural adaptation of the home, in-home training, sibling support programs, education and behavior management services, and the purchase of specialized equipment. In some states, even though a formal family support program initiative was not in place, the state agency reported that a variety of discretionary family support activities were being carried out by local providers with state funds. Family support emerged as an important priority for MR/DD state agencies in the early 1980s (Agosta & Bradley, 1985; Fujiura, Garza, & Braddock, 1990; Heller, 1997). Michigan's establishment of a cash subsidy program was a particularly notable development (Fujiura et al., 1990; Herman, 1991; Meyers & Marcenko, 1989).

Family support data were collected in the present study in three specific categories: cash subsidy payments, respite care, and other family support. Total expenditures for the three categories of family support advanced from $282 million in 1992 to $525 million in 1996. Family support spending in 1996 constituted 2.3% of total MR/DD resources, compared to 1.6% in 1992 (Hemp, Braddock, Lakin, & Smith, 1994). The total number of families supported grew substantially, from 174,441 in 1992 to 280,535 in 1996. Per capita spending for family support ranged from less than $0.50 per capita in 16 states (based on general population) to more than $3.00 per capita in 10 states: Vermont ($10.20), Montana ($8.20), Massachusetts ($5.62), North Dakota ($5.18), Alaska ($4.90), California ($4.15), New Hampshire ($3.94), North Carolina ($3.79), Wyoming ($3.75), and Kansas ($3.37). The average for the United States was $1.99 per capita. Forty-nine states reported a family support initiative in either cash subsidy, respite care, or other family support activity. Mississippi and the District of Columbia reported discontinuing family support programs in 1996. All other states funded some form of family support that year.

In 1996, 20 states reported cash subsidy payments, up from 17 states in 1992. Total cash payments to families increased to $43 million in 1996, and the number of families supported grew to 18,361 during the same period. The average annual cash subsidy payment to a United States family was $2,331 in 1996. Texas and Michigan, however, accounted for more than half of all subsidy payments in the country that year. The largest programs on the basis of per capita spending for cash subsidies were in Michigan, Texas, North Dakota, and Kansas. Other than Michigan and Texas, only Minnesota, Illinois, Iowa, Kansas, Oklahoma, and Louisiana budgeted in excess of $1 million annually for subsidy payments. The interest in most states to experiment with cash subsidy programs is apparently tempered by a reluctance to expand the size of subsidy programs beyond the pilot stage.

Supported Employment

Supported employment refers to MR/DD state agency programs and projects for the long-term support of individuals in integrated work settings, work stations in industry, enclaves, or work crews where the goal is development of independent work skills and the ability to earn wages commensurate with those earned by individuals without disabilities doing similar work.

In the early 1980s, state MR/DD agencies began providing long-term support for workers with developmental disabilities. These services were provided in addition to the employment service options that were available in states' vocational rehabilitation agencies, which are not reported in the present study. Research since that time, along with advances in employment services and legislative mandates such as the Americans with Disabilities Act of 1990 (P.L. 101-336), have reinforced the need for supported employment (Blanck, 1998; Wehman, West, & Kane-Johnston, 1997). For example, one study examined 85,000 individuals in segregated and integrated services, and their employment-related outcomes (Kiernan, McGaughey, & Schalock, 1986), and found that quarterly incomes for individuals in supported employment were 95% higher than sheltered workshop incomes. Coker, Osgood, and Clouse (1995) matched clients in sheltered and supported employment by age, gender, intelligence, and primary and secondary disability. They found that average hourly wages in supported employment were approximately 2.25 times the average hourly wage in sheltered employment ($3.95 vs. $1.72).

Longitudinal studies of people moving from sheltered to supported employment have pointed to benefits for both consumers and taxpayers (Helms, Moore, & McSewyn, 1991; Hill & Wehman, 1983; Kregel, Wehman, & Banks, 1989; Lagomarcino, 1986; L. Thompson, Powers, & Houchard, 1992; Vogelsberg, Ashe, & Williams, 1986). However, in 1992 state MR/DD service systems still placed 81% of vocational/day program participants with developmental disabilities in sheltered employment, day activity, or day habilitation programs, and only 19% in supported or competitive employment (Braddock, 1994; McGaughey, Kiernan, McNally, & Gilmore, 1993). In 1996 the latter percentage increased slightly to 20%. The portion of total day-work participants receiving supported employment services in 1996 ranged from 6% or less in Arkansas, DC, Idaho, Illinois, and Mississippi, to 40% or more in Iowa, New Mexico, Utah, and Washington.

Supported employment spending grew by 47% in inflation-adjusted terms during 1992–1996—from $250 million to $409 million per year. Individuals supported increased from 62,158 to 90,745. The largest programs in terms of per capita spending (general population) were identified in Connecticut, New Hampshire, Maryland, Minnesota, South Dakota, and Wyoming. Large programs based on the number of workers supported as a proportion of state population were identified in South Dakota, Arizona, Iowa, and Wisconsin. In absolute terms, the largest programs were in New York, California, Ohio, Pennsylvania, Minnesota, Texas, Michigan, Wisconsin, and Washington. These nine states accounted for 55% of the supported employment activity across the United States in terms of funds budgeted.

Supported Living

Supported living incorporates personal choice by the individual with a developmental disability about where and with whom he or she lives, and distinctly separates ownership of the housing arrangement from the entity providing support services. The housing is owned by the individual with a disability, by the family, or by a housing cooperative, or the individual pays rent to a landlord. Supported living also implies that every person's need for support changes over time, and therefore periodic individualized support planning is required to address these changing needs (Howe, Horner, & Newton, 1998; Karan, Granfield, & Furey, 1992; Racino & Taylor, 1993; Smith, 1990; Smull, 1989).

Funding for supported living emerged as a priority in the states beginning in the early 1990s. Supported living was first initiated in Colorado, Florida, Missouri, North Dakota, Ohio, Oregon, and Wisconsin in the mid-1980s (Bauer & Smith, 1993; Pittsley, 1990; Smith, 1990). The increased funding to emphasize individual choice, control over housing, and individualized, person-centered planning reflected in large part the growing strength of self-advocacy organizations (Hayden & Senese, 1996; Longhurst, 1994). Self-advocates articulated where they wished to live and the types of support they preferred (e.g., Kennedy, 1990; Nelis, 1995; Nelis & Ward, 1995).

Forty-three states indicated that they were providing supported living services to 45,172 individuals in 1996, representing an increase from 21 states reporting in 1992 and 21,156 persons supported that year. Much of this supported living activity was being financed by the federal–state HCBS Waiver program. Total spending of $605 million in 1996 represented an increase of 173% in inflation-adjusted terms over the 1992 level. Substantial efforts to finance supported living were evident in 1996 in New Mexico, North Dakota, Washington, Alaska, Oklahoma, Maine, Missouri, Wyoming, Idaho, Connecticut, and Ohio. These states spent $5 or more per capita (state general population) for supported living and budgeted 47% of the nation's funds for supported living. The United States spent $2.29 per capita for supported living in 1996.

Supported living spending per participant varied greatly across the states from $71,969 in Oklahoma to $2,125 in Louisiana. This range highlights the fact that supported living plays different roles in the states' service systems, from major components in recent deinstitutionalization plans in Oklahoma and Washington to programs intended to provide more limited support to individuals with fewer needs (e.g., Arkansas and Louisiana). The national average supported living spending level per participant was $13,399 in 1996.

Personal assistance was defined as MR/DD state agencies' use of state funds, or federal–state HCBS Waiver or other Medicaid funds, to provide assistance for individuals in their own homes. Initiatives in personal assistance were identified in 14 states in 1996. The states were Washington, Oregon, New York, California, Idaho, Indiana, Wisconsin, South Carolina, Arkansas, Florida, West Virginia, Utah, Iowa, and Oklahoma. Total personal assistance funding was $59.9 million, up from $13.5 million in 1992. The number of persons served doubled from 5,906 persons in 1992 to 12,582 in 1996. Data reported for these states do not include personal assistance data for individuals participating in other state agency programs, such as those managed by states' Medicaid or social service agencies, or the personal assistance funding utilized in some states to augment traditional out-of-home residential placements, rather than to support individuals in their own homes.

THE FUTURE

Consolidated individual and family support spending in 1996 for family support, supported employment, and supported living/personal assistance totaled $1.6 billion nationally. This was 7% of the $22.8 billion in total MR/DD spending allocated in the United States that year, and 10% of total community spending. Seven states provided funding for individual and family support that exceeded 20% of total community spending in 1996. The states were Washington (54%), New Mexico (50%), Alaska (47%), Oklahoma (43%), Missouri (41%), North Dakota (30%), and Montana

(22%). The number of states and the proportion of community spending dedicated to individual and family support seems destined to grow rapidly into the next millennium.

On a national basis, 33% of total funding for individual and family support was allocated for family support, 42% for supported living and personal assistance, and 25% for supported employment. For many years, federal HCBS Waiver regulations restricted supported employment services to those individuals who were formerly institutionalized (Smith & Gettings, 1997). However, the Balanced Budget Act of 1997 (P.L. 105-33) removes this restriction, and The Arc (1997) estimates that approximately 150,000 HCBS Waiver participants have therefore become eligible for supported employment services.

A transformation has clearly been manifested in the United States toward family support, community living, and employment participation, and away from the segregated institutional model developed in the 19th century. The forces of change have included committed advocacy by The Arc and related organizations (Boggs, 1971; Jones & Barnes, 1987), extensive class action litigation (Herr, 1992), implementation of legislation such as the Individuals with Disabilities Education Act and the Americans with Disabilities Act (Blanck, 1998), and innovative progress in applied behavior analysis (T. Thompson & Grabowski, 1977; T. Thompson & Gray, 1994).

The nation today, however, still exhibits much disparity across the states in the degree of public commitment to innovative family and community mental retardation services versus institutional care. Some states have chosen to maximize acquisition of ICF/MR reimbursement to sustain ever more expensive state-operated institutions. In recent years, however, most states have aggressively pursued HCBS Medicaid Waiver funds, closed institutions, and significantly expanded community living. Some states have tried to address both institutional and community living objectives simultaneously, but few have done so with equal dedication to both objectives due to the high costs involved in operating dual systems.

By the year 2000, it is highly probable that fewer than 50,000 persons will reside in the nation's state-operated institutions. The census of these institutions will likely continue to decline by 6% or more per year well into the next millennium until all state-operated institutions are ultimately closed. The number of states committed to operate institution-free service delivery systems should easily increase from seven states today to a dozen or more states within 5 years. By the year 2000 or shortly thereafter, the first heavily populated state—possibly Michigan, Minnesota, or Arizona—is also likely to close its remaining institution(s), supplying additional momentum among the nation's larger states to close their remaining institutions while accelerating the development of community services and supports. It is unlikely, however, that all state-operated mental retardation institutions in the United States will close prior to the second decade of the new millennium. In any event, responsible deinstitutionalization entails the continuing development of a comprehensive community services infrastructure in each state *before* all state-operated institutions are closed. The community infrastructure must include appropriately trained and compensated support staff, flexible and individualized funding that supports individuals in a variety of residential settings, individualized service coordination, accessible transportation, employment training and support, basic and specialized health care services, behavior management support, recreation and leisure services, and comprehensive support for families.

In addition to reducing their reliance on state-operated institutions, the states will also continue to reduce reliance on state-funded, privately-operated facilities for 16 or more persons, including ICFs/MR, nursing homes, and other large private settings. In 1996 approximately 80,000 persons with developmental disabilities were residing in such settings. However, the average annual rate of reduction in the census of these facilities over the 1992–1996 period (-3%) is significantly less rapid than the annual rate of decline in state-operated institution population (-6%). Projecting the large private sector's 3% rate of decline forward suggests that in 15 years fewer than 50,000 persons will be residing in privately operated facilities for 16 or more persons.

Many states are aggressively utilizing the HCBS Waiver to develop supported living and other community integrated living arrangements for six or fewer individuals. Barring an economic recession of serious nationwide proportions, financial resources for community services will continue to grow rapidly over the next decade, although probably not quite as rapidly as the 9% real average annual growth rate achieved during the 1992–1996 period. By the second decade of the 21st century, we predict that 80% to 90% of individuals with developmental disabilities residing in out-of-home care in the United States will live in settings for six or fewer persons.

The continuing transformation of state service delivery systems will be influenced in the future by six dominant trends: (1) an emphasis on providing support for people with developmental disabilities that is flexibly tailored to meet individual and family needs rather than facility or group needs (Braddock, Hemp, & Parish, 1997); (2) the continuing privatization of the management and delivery of developmental services, which, over the past two decades, has advanced from private sector control of 29% of the available financial resources in the field to nearly 80% of resources today (Braddock, 1994); (3) the growth of specialized publicly traded proprietary service providers, which, in less than a decade, may constitute 10% or more of the field as opposed to 3% today; (4) the growth of managed health care organizations in the states (Hemp & Braddock, 1998); (5) a redirection in the states' utilization of the Medicaid ICF/MR program coupled with the expansion of the HCBS Waiver (Braddock & Hemp, 1997); and (6) growing waiting lists for residential care—particularly for personal assistance and supported living, but also for family support and employment-related services. The already intense demand for residential and day services (Davis, 1997; Lakin, 1998) will be accelerated by the aging of our society, which will strengthen political support for the expansion of community mental retardation services (Braddock, in press-a, in press-b). In Maryland, for example, 39% of the 4,682 persons on the waiting list for long-term residential care in 1997 were living in homes in which the family caregiver was 60 years of age or older. Fourteen percent of the family caregivers were at least 80 years of age (State of Maryland, 1997). If the Maryland data are only moderately representative of national trends, as the baby boom generation ages during the next 30 years, growing demand for MR/DD services will severely strain state capacities.

The aging of our society is correlated not only with baby boom demographics and significantly improved longevity, but also with a declining fertility rate, which will reduce the number of working-age taxpayers entering the workforce. By 2010, 14% of the U.S. population will be 65 or older and the figure will increase to over 20% of our population in the year 2030 (U.S. Bureau of the Census, 1996). Provider agencies will be challenged for a generation by the impact of this powerful demographic trend on the demand for community services and supports. The Arc's leadership and advocacy will be just as essential to the future well-being of people with mental retardation and their families as it has been for the past 50 years.

REFERENCES

Agosta, J. M., & Bradley, V. J. (Eds.). (1985). *Family care for persons with developmental disabilities: A growing commitment.* Cambridge, MA: Human Services Research Institute.

Americans with Disabilities Act of 1990, 42 U.S.C. § 12101 *et seq.*

The Arc/United States. (1997). *Budget reconciliation* (memorandum to state chapters of July 31st). Washington, DC: Author.

Balanced Budget Act of 1997, 42 U.S.C. § 1396n(c)(5).

Bauer, L., & Smith, G. (1993). Community living for the developmentally disabled. *State Legislative Report* (An information service of the National Conference of State Legislatures), *18*(12), 1–6.

Blanck, P. (1998). *The emerging workforce: Employment integration, economic opportunity, and the Americans with Disabilities Act: Empirical study 1990–1996.* Washington, DC: American Association on Mental Retardation.

Boggs, E. M. (1971). Federal legislation in J. Wortis (Ed.), *Mental retardation: An annual review* (pp. 103–127). New York: Grune & Stratton.

Braddock, D. (1994). Presidential address 1994: New frontiers in mental retardation *Mental Retardation, 32,* 434–443.

Braddock, D. (in press-a). Aging and developmental disabilities: Demographic and policy issues affecting American families. *Can we rest in peace? The anxiety of elderly parents caring for baby boomers with disabilities.* A Forum of the U.S. Senate Special Committee on Aging, September 18, 1998. Washington, DC: U.S. Government Printing Office.

Braddock, D. (in press-b). Aging and developmental disabilities: Demographic and policy issues affecting American families. *Mental Retardation.*

Braddock, D., & Heller, T. (1985). The closure of mental retardation institutions: I. Trends in the United States. *Mental Retardation, 23,* 168–176.

Braddock, D., & Hemp, R. (1997). Toward family and community: Mental retardation services in Massachusetts, New England, and the United States. *Mental Retardation, 35,* 241–256.

Braddock, D., Hemp, R, & Parish, S. (1997). Trends and milestones: Emergence of individual and family support in state service-delivery systems. *Mental Retardation, 35,* 497–498.

Braddock, D., Hemp, R, Parish, S., & Westrich, J. (1998). *The state of the states in developmental disabilities* (5th ed.). Washington, DC: American Association on Mental Retardation.

Braddock, D., & Mitchell, D. (1992). *Residential services and developmental disabilities in the United States.* Washington, DC: American Association on Mental Retardation.

Coker, C. C., Osgood, K., & Clouse, K. R. (1995). *A comparison of job satisfaction and economic benefits of four different employment models for persons with disabilities.* Menomonie: University of Wisconsin–Stout, Rehabilitation Research and Training Center on Improving Community-Based Rehabilitation Programs.

Davis, S. (1997). *A status report to the nation on people with mental retardation waiting for community services.* Arlington, TX: The Arc of the United States. (www.thearc.org/misc/WaitPage.html)

Fujiura, G. T., Garza, J., & Braddock, D. (1990). *National survey of family support services in developmental disabilities.* Chicago: University of Illinois at Chicago, University Affiliated Program in Developmental Disabilities.

Hayden, M. F., & Senese, D. (1996). *Self-advocacy groups: 1996 directory for North America.* Minneapolis: University of Minnesota, Research and Training Center on Community Living, Institute on Community Integration.

Heller, T. (1997). Older adults with mental retardation and their families. In N. Bray (Ed.), *International review of research in mental retardation* (Vol. 20, pp. 99–136). San Diego: Academic Press.

Helms, B. J., Moore, S. C., & McSewyn, C. A. (1991). Supported employment in Connecticut: An examination of integration and wage outcomes. *Career Development of Exceptional Individuals, 14*, 159–166.

Hemp, R, & Braddock, D. (1998). Medicaid managed care and individuals with disabilities: Status report. *Mental Retardation, 36*, 84, 85.

Hemp, R., Braddock, D., Lakin, K. C., & Smith, G. (1994). The growth of family support: Trends and milestones. *Mental Retardation, 32*, 319.

Herman, S. E. (1991). Use and impact of a cash subsidy program. *Mental Retardation, 29*, 253–258.

Herr, S. S. (1992). Beyond benevolence: Legal protection for persons with special needs. In L. Rowitz (Ed.), *Mental retardation in the year 2000* (pp. 279–298). New York: Springer-Verlag.

Hill, M., & Wehman, P. (1983). Cost benefit analysis of placing moderately and severely handicapped individuals into competitive employment. *Journal of The Association for Persons with Severe Handicaps, 8*, 30–38.

Howe, J., Horner, R. H., & Newton, J. S. (1998). Comparison of supported living and traditional residential services in the State of Oregon. *Mental Retardation, 36*, 1–11.

Jones, L. A., & Barnes, P. A. (1987). *Doing justice: Fifty years of parent advocacy in mental retardation.* Olympia: Association for Retarded Citizens of Washington.

Karan, O. C., Granfield, J. M., & Furey, E. M. (1992). Supported living: Rethinking the rules of residential services. *AAMR News and Notes, 5*(1), 5.

Kennedy, M. J. (1990). What quality assurance means to me: Expectations of consumers. In V. J. Bradley & H. A. Bersani (Eds.), *Quality assurance for individuals with developmental disabilities: It's everybody's business* (pp. 35–45). Baltimore: Brookes.

Kiernan, W. E., McGaughey, M. J., & Schalock, R. C. (1986). *National employment survey for adults with developmental disabilities.* Boston: Children's Hospital, Developmental Evaluation Clinic.

Kregel, J., Wehman, P., & Banks, P. D. (1989). The effects of consumer characteristics and type of employment model on individual outcomes in supported employment. *Journal of Applied Behavior Analysis, 22*, 407–415.

Lagomarcino, T. R. (1986). Community services: Using the supported work model with an adult service agency. In F. R. Rusch (Ed.), *Competitive employment issues and strategies* (pp. 65–75). Baltimore: Brookes.

Lakin, K. C. (1979). *Demographic studies of residential facilities for mentally retarded people: A historical review of methodologies and findings.* Minneapolis: Center for Residential and Community Services.

Lakin, K. C. (1998). On the outside looking in: Attending to waiting lists in systems of services for people with developmental disabilities. *Mental Retardation, 36*, 157–162.

Longhurst, N. (1994). *The self-advocacy movement by persons with developmental disabilities: A demographic study and directory of groups in the United States.* Washington, DC, and Chicago: American Association on Mental Retardation, in cooperation with People First of Illinois and the Institute on Disability and Human Development (UAP).

McGaughey, M. J., Kiernan, W. E., McNally, L. C., & Gilmore, D. S. (1993). *National perspectives on integrated employment: State MR/DD agency trends.* Boston: Children's Hospital, Institute for Community Inclusion.

Meyers, J. C., & Marcenko, M. O. (1989). Impact of a cash subsidy program for families of children with severe developmental disabilities. *Mental Retardation, 27,* 383–387.

Nelis, T. (1995). The realities of institutions. *Impact,* 9(1), 1, 27. Minneapolis: University of Minnesota, Institute on Community Integration.

Nelis, T., & Ward. N. (1995). Operation Close the Doors: Working for freedom. *Impact, 9,* 12. Minneapolis: University of Minnesota, Institute on Community Integration.

Pittsley, R. (1990). North Dakota: Individualized supported living arrangement. *DD Network News,* 3(3), 7, 8.

Racino, J. A., & Taylor, S. J. (1993). "People first": Approaches to housing and support. In J. A. Racino, P. Walker, S. O'Connor, & S. J. Taylor (Eds.), *Housing, support, and community: Choices and strategies for adults with disabilities* (pp. 33–56). Baltimore: Brookes.

Smith, G. A. (1990). *Supported living: New directions in services to people with developmental disabilities.* Alexandria, VA: National Association of State Mental Retardation Program Directors.

Smith, G. A., & Gettings, R. M. (1997). *Medicaid Home and Community-Based Waiver services and supports for people with developmental disabilities: Trends through 1997.* Alexandria, VA: National Association of State Directors of Developmental Disabilities Services.

Smull, M. (1989). *Crisis in the community.* Baltimore: University of Maryland at Baltimore, Applied Research and Evaluation Unit, Department of Pediatrics, School of Medicine.

State of Maryland. (1997). *Waiting list report data.* Baltimore: Mental Retardation/Developmental Disabilities Administration, Department of Health and Mental Hygiene.

Thompson, L., Powers, G., & Houchard, B. (1992). The wage effects of supported employment. *Journal of The Association for Persons with Severe Handicaps, 17,* 87–94.

Thompson, T., & Grabowski, J. (Eds.). (1977). *Behavior modification of the mentally retarded* (2nd ed.). New York: Oxford University Press.

Thompson, T., & Gray, D. B. (Eds.). (1994). *Destructive behavior in developmental disabilities: Diagnosis and treatment.* Thousand Oaks, CA: Sage.

U.S. Bureau of the Census. (1996, December). *Population Estimates Program, Population Division.* Washington, DC: Author.

Vogelsberg, R. T., Ashe, W., & Williams, W. (1986). Community based service delivery in rural Vermont. In R. H. Horner, L. H. Meyer, & H. D. Fredericks (Eds.), *Education of learners with severe handicaps: Exemplary service strategies* (pp. 29–59). Baltimore: Brookes.

Wehman, P., West, M., & Kane-Johnston, K. (1997). Improving access to competitive employment for persons with disabilities as a means of reducing social security expenditures. *Focus on Autism and Other Developmental Disabilities, 12*(1),23–30.

Social Constructions of Mental Retardation: Impersonal Histories and the Hope for Personal Futures

J. David Smith

I n *The Conquest of Mental Retardation*, Burton Blatt (1987) wrote of the importance of stories. He asserted that

> Every story can enhance life or destroy it. Every story can lift us or depress us. Every story can make a hero or a scapegoat. Stories sustain if not make a person's world. And thus, the storyteller holds a certain power (and responsibility). (p. 141)

In very important ways the stories of mental retardation have nourished and sustained the development of the field. The stories of Itard and Victor, of Samuel Gridley Howe and Edward Seguin, for example, have inspired generations of parents and professionals, and have provided them with hope and direction. On the other hand, many negative stories have been told that have proven to be damaging to people described as having mental retardation. The pessimistic and limiting stories of the Kallikaks and the Jukes, for example, questioned the efficacy of providing education for persons with retardation (Smith, 1985). The story of Carrie Buck, as another example, became central to the argument for the necessity of institutionalizing and sterilizing thousands of people perceived to be "defective" (Smith & Nelson, 1989).

In his book *Inventing the Feeble Mind*, James Trent (1994) introduced his examination of the changing American story of mental retardation with the illustration of the *simpleton* of postrevolutionary America. The Simple Simon nursery rhyme shows us that during that time period a person with retardation, a simpleton, might be ridiculed or teased, but was not feared. In fact, according to Trent, these people were a known and expected part of rural and village life. As America became more industrialized and urbanized during the 19th century, however, retardation was pathologized and the need to create a place for retardation to be contained became a social and political concern. That place became the asylum. The asylum, the institution, was a construction, says Trent, of the physician–superintendents who would dominate the field for the rest of that century and beyond. They would largely define the public image of retardation.

In speaking of social construction of the meaning of the term mental retardation, Trent (1994) described it as a "construction whose changing meaning is shaped both by individuals who initiate and administer policies, programs and practices, and by the social context to which these individuals are responding" (p. 2). He argued that the construction of the meaning of retardation is sometimes done in the name of science, sometimes in the name of caring for people, and sometimes in the name of social or economic necessity. Each of these reasons for defining people and their differences, however, has often been used for the purpose of controlling a group of people perceived to be a threat or an inconvenience to society. The construction of the meaning of mental retardation has, from this perspective, been motivated more by a search for social control than by a concern for the best interests of the individuals defined.

In his book *Abandoned to Their Fate*, Philip Ferguson (1994) spoke of people who have been judged "unfixable." Through his study of mental retardation in the 19th and early 20th centuries, Ferguson found that the judgment of "chronicity" has the most profound impact on the lives of people. To be judged "chronic" has meant to be socially abandoned. The judgment of chronicity is reached when, in Ferguson's words, "badness becomes incorrigible, ugliness becomes inhuman, and uselessness becomes untrainable" (p. 16). It is the status of chronicity, he argued, not that of retardation or other comparable terms, that has determined the fate of generations of people.

TWENTIETH-CENTURY DEFINITIONS OF MENTAL RETARDATION

As formal definitions of mental retardation were developed during the first half of the 20th century, they tended to reflect the judgment of chronicity. The most important of these, and the one that continues to influence the defining of mental retardation, was authored by the psychologist Edgar Doll (1941). His pioneering definition included six elements that he considered essential to the concept of mental retardation:

> (1) Social incompetence, (2) due to mental subnormality, (3) which has been developmentally arrested, (4) which obtains at maturity, (5) is of constitutional origin, and (6) is essentially incurable. (p. 215)

The first four of these elements have continued to be overtly central to the prevailing conceptualization of mental retardation. Social incompetence associated with deficits in mental ability is a thread that runs from Doll's definition through subsequent definitions to the most current. The same is true for his emphasis on mental retardation as a disability that originates during the developmental period.

The last two elements of Doll's definition, however, are not found as formal elements of contemporary definitions of mental retardation. Retardation is no longer viewed as always resulting from "constitutional" factors. It has long been recognized that environmental variables also are important as causes of mental retardation. Much retardation, for example, is associated with the depriving effects of poverty. This recognition, however, is not operative in many community and school contexts where "true" retardation is still considered to be physiological in origin. Mental retardation is also no longer considered to be an "incurable" condition in official definitions. The goal of educational services for many students, in fact, is to help those students achieve a level of competence at which it would no longer be appropriate to describe them as having mental retardation. The attitude of incurability about children and adults with mental retardation has continued to be a reality, however, in the minds of many people.

The legacy of Doll's conceptualization of mental retardation can be seen most clearly in definitions that have been developed during the second half of the 20th century by the American Association on Mental Retardation (AAMR). The definitions published by this professional organization have always included the criteria of low measured intelligence and deficits in social competence. They have also consistently described mental retardation as a developmental disability.

In 1959 the AAMR, at that time called the American Association on Mental Deficiency, published a definition of mental retardation that read as follows:

> Mental retardation refers to subaverage general intellectual functioning which originates during the developmental period and is associated with impairment in adaptive behavior. (Heber, 1959)

The definition was revised in 1961. That revision specified the meaning of the term *subaverage general intellectual functioning* in a manner that was to have considerable impact on the field of mental retardation. One standard deviation below the mean on an intelligence test was delineated as the point at which intellectual functioning should be considered *subnormal* (Heber, 1961). This specification meant that on an IQ test with a mean of 100 and a standard deviation of 15, any score below 85 would be diagnostic of mental retardation. If the total population was tested and classified on this basis, almost 16% would be diagnosed as having mental retardation. Even higher percentages would be expected to be found in subpopulations where minority status, language factors, or socioeconomic background depresses intelligence test scores.

There were criticisms of the concept of adaptive behavior as it appeared in the 1961 definition. The argument was made that adaptive behavior as it was presented in the definition was not actually functional for the diagnosis of mental retardation. In reality, it was argued, the determination of retardation continued to be based on intelligence tests and the idea that intelligence was not significantly "associated" with adaptive behavior in this process (Clausen, 1972).

In 1973 an AAMR committee again revised the definition. The committee constructed this revision with criticism of the 1961 definition in mind. It specified that *sig-*

nificantly subaverage general intellectual functioning was to be determined by a score of at least *two standard deviations* below the mean on an intelligence test (Grossman, 1973). This meant that the cutoff point for mental retardation was essentially moved downward from 85 to 70. This change lowered the percentage of the population that might be identified as having mental retardation from 16% to approximately 2.25%. This revision meant that fewer people would be labeled retarded because of language differences, socioeconomic factors, or minority status. It also meant, however, that fewer students were eligible for special education services. This is a particularly important consideration since the 1973 AAMR definition was adopted for defining mental retardation under the Education for All Handicapped Children Act of 1975 (P.L. 94-142). This definition also placed more emphasis on the importance of adaptive behavior and extended the developmental period upward from 16 to 18 years of age.

In 1977 the AAMR published another manual on mental retardation terminology and classification (Grossman, 1977). Although there were no substantive changes to the definition in this manual, the role of clinical judgment was given greater emphasis. Allowance was made as well for diagnosing people with IQs up to 10 points above the 70 cutoff as having mental retardation of they also showed marked deficits in adaptive behavior. A 1983 AAMR definition further expanded the developmental period from conception (instead of birth) to age 18 (Grossman, 1983). This change officially made persons with mental retardation resulting from prenatal factors eligible to be classified.

The 1992 Revision of the AAMR Definition

The AAMR published the most recent revision of its manual on the definition and classification of mental retardation in 1992. The definition itself includes dramatic changes. It reads as follows:

> Mental retardation refers to substantial limitations in present functioning. It is characterized by significantly subaverage intellectual functioning, existing concurrently with related limitations in two or more of the following applicable adaptive skill areas: communication, self-care, home living, social skills, community use, self-direction, health and safety, functional academics, leisure, and work. Mental retardation manifests before age 18. (Lukasson et al., 1992, p. 1)

This conception of mental retardation is presented by AAMR as a paradigm shift. Retardation is no longer to be viewed as being characteristic of an individual. It is the product of interactions between a person, and the nature and demands of that person's environment. The phrase "limitations in present functioning" is used to indicate that mental retardation is a current state, rather than a permanent trait. This change is meant to emphasize that mental retardation may be a transitory condition.

There are other distinctly different elements in the AAMR's new perspective on mental retardation. The global term adaptive behavior has been extended to 10 specific adaptive skill areas, each of which is discussed at some length in the manual. The four levels of severity of mental retardation are replaced by a system that classifies the intensities and patterns of support required by individuals: *intermittent needs*, which are episodic in nature and do not always require support; *limited needs*, which are consistent over time but limited in intensity; *extensive needs*, which are long term and serious; and *pervasive needs*, which are constant and intense throughout life (Lukasson et al., 1992).

Four assumptions are presented as being essential to the application of the definition:

1. Valid assessment considers cultural and linguistic diversity as well as differences in communication and behavioral factors.

2. The existence of limitations in adaptive skills occurs within the context of community environments typical of the individual's age peers and is indexed to the person's individualized needs for support.

3. Specific adaptive limitations often coexist with strengths in other adaptive skills or other personal capabilities.

4. With appropriate supports over a sustained period, the life functioning of the person with mental retardation will generally improve.

The 1992 AAMR revision also emphasizes leeway in the use of IQ scores in diagnosing mental retardation. It calls for a score of "approximately 70 to 75 or below" (Lukasson el al., 1992, p. 5).

MENTAL RETARDATION, THE AAMR CONSTRUCT, AND THE CRITICS

A great deal of professional and academic controversy has been generated by the 1992 revision of the AAMR definition and its changes in the classification guidelines on mental retardation. Even within the AAMR there have been sharp differences of opinion concerning the revised definition. John Jacobson, former president of the AAMR Psychology Division, was quoted as saying, "The new AAMR manual is a political manifesto, not a clinical document" (Michaelson, 1993, p. 34). He described the changes in diagnosing mental retardation as being politically motivated rather than research based. This position, and other criticisms of the revisions, have appeared elsewhere in professional literature (Jacobson & Mulick, 1993; MacMillan, Gresham, & Siperstein, 1993; MacMillan, Gresham, & Siperstein, 1995).

Greenspan (1995) observed that the AAMR revision represents a "less defectology-oriented approach to conceptualizing disorder, a view that is reflective of both new treatment approaches as well as new social trends" (pp. 684–685). On the other hand, he pointed out that the new definition was not grounded on a research base of any kind. He argued that this is a vulnerability that makes the definition subject to major criticisms. According to Greenspan, "relatively full acceptance of any radical new classificatory scheme (no matter how much philosophical or practical merit it might have) is likely to occur only if the promoters of the scheme are able to advance the illusion, if not the reality, that the field it serves is driven by scientific methods and findings" (p. 685).

SHIFTING PARADIGMS

The authors of the most recent AAMR manual (Lukasson et al., 1992) have characterized their revisions as a paradigm shift in the field of mental retardation. This paradigm shift is presented as consisting of two facets. The first of these is a change in the conception of mental retardation from a trait existing in an individual to an expression of the interaction between a person with limited intellectual and adaptive skills, and that individual's environment. The second element of the paradigm shift is the emphasis on the pattern of the person's needs rather than a focus on that person's deficits (Schalock et al., 1994).

Paradigm shifts may be critical to advancement and improvement in any field of endeavor. Thomas Kuhn (1962), in his classic book *The Structure of Scientific Revolutions*, defined paradigms as the shared world views of scientists, as shared ways of viewing certain realities. Kuhn argued that these shared views eventually become so strong and institutionalized that only a sudden and dramatic break from these conventional perspectives can bring on a positive revolution in thinking.

It must be recognized, however, that unlike physics, where a paradigm shift from the world view of Newton to that of Einstein did nothing to change the reality of the physical universe, a paradigm shift in the field of mental retardation is likely to have profound implications for the education, care, and treatment of millions of human beings.

What is the purpose of defining mental retardation? If it is to create greater understanding of the people whose lives are touched by retardation, Robert Edgerton's (1993) words from the newest edition of *The Cloak of Competence* are important to consider:

> There are many cognitively limited people in the United States and the rest of the world who live in dramatically different social cultural worlds. Until we enter those worlds and learn from the people who live in them, we will not know what mental retardation is or what people with it can accomplish, and that what they can accomplish can enlighten and enlarge us all. (p. 234)

The effort to define mental retardation in a way that is as scientifically accurate as possible continues. The effort to define it in a way that promotes greater sensitivity to the needs of people with mental retardation also continues. The successful resolution of the tension between meeting these two goals will determine the future of a social construct that promotes care rather than control for the people whose lives are central to this construction.

HISTORICAL GLIMPSES OF THE IMPERSONALIZATION OF RETARDATION

The eminent American psychologist Seymour Sarason (1985) observed, "Mental retardation is never a thing or characteristic of an individual, but rather a social invention stemming from time-bound societal values and ideology that makes diagnosis and management seem both necessary and socially desirable" (p. 233).

The fact that social values are "time-bound" is powerfully illustrated by a statement from Oliver Wendell Holmes. In his book *The Common Law*, published in 1881, Holmes wrote, "The life of the law has not been logic; it has been experience. The felt necessities of the time . . . [are the sources of law]" (p. 1). When Holmes spoke for the majority of the Supreme Court in 1927 supporting the right of the Commonwealth of Virginia to sterilize people who had been diagnosed as "feebleminded," he was upholding a "felt necessity" of his time and culture. He was also acting in accordance with a "felt necessity" that has a long history in American society. The life of Laura Bridgman provides a striking example of this history.

Laura Bridgman and Mental Retardation

Laura Bridgman was born into a prominent Massachusetts family in 1829. At the age of 2 she was rendered deaf and blind by scarlet fever. In 1837 she came to live at Perkins Institute for the Blind in Boston. There, she was tutored by the founder, Dr. Samuel Gridley Howe. Howe devised a teaching method that built on her ability to feel the differences in shapes of objects. Through drill and practice in distinguishing shapes, he led her to understand that these objects could be given names. At first he used labels with raised print on them to assign names that Laura could comprehend. He then taught her to form words using movable letters. He was thus teaching her by methods similar to those that were used for other students at Perkins who were blind. Eventually, however, he shifted to a communication method that had been developed for students who were deaf. He began teaching her words using finger spelling. He spelled words into her hand, and then associated them with objects and actions. This was the method, of course, that later came to be associated with Anne Sullivan's teaching of Helen Keller.

Laura's fame was eventually eclipsed by the extraordinary accomplishments of Helen and Anne. It is ironic that little note has been taken of the fact that Anne Sullivan, herself a student at Perkins, learned to communicate this way with Laura Bridgman, and then applied what she had learned to her teaching of Helen Keller (Smith, 1987).

For several decades during the 19th century, however, Laura Bridgman attracted international attention and Samuel Gridley Howe's work with her was heralded with as much admiration as the "Miracle Worker" would later receive. To many American intellectuals she became a symbol, "exemplifying the power of enlightened educational techniques and their capacity to transform seemingly hopeless cases" (Gallaher, 1995, p. 282).

As Howe began to communicate with Laura about abstract ideas, he found that her mind was not a blank slate. He described her internal life as a soul jailed in a body that was "active, and struggling continually not only to put itself in communication with things without, but to manifest what is going on within itself" (S. Howe, 1893, p. 9). Howe described Laura's internal life, as he discovered it in its natural and untouched state, as being of the highest moral character. He found that "her moral sense, is remarkably acute; few children are so affectionate or so scrupulously conscientious, few are so sensible of their own rights or regardful of the rights of others" (S. Howe, 1893, p. 50).

To support his argument that Laura was innately moral, he described her behavior toward other people after she had been liberated by his teaching and was enabled to communicate. He reported that she was always eager to share with others and to help take care of sick people. He also said that she showed a keen sense of sympathy for people with disabilities. Howe noted, however, one exception to Laura's expressions of natural altruism. He said that she showed an "unamiable" lack of respect for the children at the Perkins Institution whom she considered to be mentally inferior to herself. Interpreting this as an understandable manifestation of her Anglo-Saxon heritage, he excused the advantage she took of these children when she expected them to "wait on her" (S. Howe, 1893, p. 20).

One of the most famous of Laura's powerful and influential visitors at Perkins was Charles Dickens. His admiration for her began with his reading Howe's accounts of his instruction of Laura. It increased when he visited her in Boston. For Dickens, Laura Bridgman was "both charming and inspirational: a merry, graceful, and intelligent young girl, she seemed also to symbolize the possibility of spiritual awakening and redemption" (Gitter, 1991, p. 163). Dickens described his visit to Laura at Perkins in *American Notes*. He relayed his impressions of her and he also quoted from Howe's reports. In his account he repeats Howe's observation that she had disdain for those children whom she believed to be intellectually inferior (Dickens, 1842).

Samuel Gridley Howe is, of course, a person of importance in the history of mental retardation. In addition to his work with students with blindness and deaf–blindness, he was an early advocate for the education of students with these disabilities. He convinced the legislature of Massachusetts to provide funding for a school for the "teaching and training of idiotic children" in October of 1848 (M. Howe & Hall, 1904, p. 229). The school was initially housed at Perkins Institute. According to two of his daughters, however, Dr. Howe soon discovered that his blind students resented deeply the presence of the students with mental retardation under their roof. His daughters interpreted this resentment as an expression of fear that they might come to be associated with the retardation of these "weaker brethren" (p. 231). They quoted Laura Bridgman's journal as evidence of this feeling of resentment. Laura expressed the hope that the students with mental retardation would not actually come to Perkins and the fear that if they did they would "have our rooms . . . [and] our nice sitting room in a few days" (M. Howe & Hall, 1904, p. 231).

Laura's fears regarding the perceived association between herself and her "weaker brethren" may not have been unfounded. Indeed a literature has developed around the very notion of the transferability of social stigma, the process in which a "normal" person is seen by others as possessing the characteristics of a stigma merely by a close association with a stigmatized other (Goffman, 1963).

There is evidence to suggest that mental retardation carries the most debilitating socially constructed stigma. Gibbons (1985) contends that persons with mental retardation themselves are acutely aware of this stigma and tend to react with derogation to their own peers' lack of social competence and physical attractiveness.

Laura Bridgman may have been acutely aware of the very real potential of being perceived as incompetent by association and of the social consequences inherent in that perception. The threat of a devalued identity provides a powerful incentive for maintaining both physical and social distance from people more seriously stigmatized. As Goffman (1963) suggested, "In general, the tendency for a stigma to spread from the stigmatized individual . . . provides a reason why such relations tend either to be avoided or to be terminated, where existing" (p. 30). Perhaps it was this attempt to avoid stigma by association that explains the attitude of Laura Bridgman toward mental retardation. It may also explain the phenomenon of what might be called differential advocacy (Smith & Anton, 1997).

Helen Keller and Mental Retardation

Another example of the differential advocacy that has worked against people described as being mentally retarded is found in Helen Keller's life. It is particularly striking given her role as a great advocate for the rights of people with disabilities.

A fascinating book titled *The Black Stork* (Pernick, 1996) concerns the work of a physician who openly practiced euthanasia on "defective" newborns beginning in 1915. Dr. Harry Haiselden not only allowed infants with severe disabilities to die, he administered drugs to speed the deaths of several of these newborns. He also campaigned for the widespread adoption of these practices, and produced and starred in a movie promoting euthanasia, "The Black Stork." The film was based on Haiselden's eugenic arguments, and was shown in commercial movie theaters from 1916 through the 1920s.

Helen Keller supported Haiselden's eugenic campaign. In the December 18, 1915, issue of *The New Republic*, Helen Keller expressed the following opinions:

> It is the possibilities of happiness, intelligence and power that give life its sanctity, and they are absent in the case of a poor, misshapen, paralyzed, unthinking creature. . . . The toleration of such anomalies tends to lessen the sacredness in which normal life is held.

It seems to me that the simplest, wisest thing to do would be to submit cases like that of the malformed idiot baby to a jury of expert physicians. . . . A mental defective . . . is almost sure to be a potential criminal. The evidence before a jury of physicians considering the case of an idiot would be exact and scientific. Their findings would be free from the prejudice and inaccuracy of untrained observation. They would act only in case of true idiocy, where there could be no hope of mental development. (pp. 173–174)

Helen Keller's development as an intellectual and as an advocate took place within the context of the eugenics movement. It also occurred within the environment of political progressivism. Progressive thought held that most of the problems of society, and those of individuals, could and should be reduced to scientific terms, and resolved by scientific means. Helen's trust of a "jury" of physicians is very consistent with the faith in scientific progress that characterized the cultural climate of her formative years as a social activist. Her opinion that "true idiocy" lessens the sanctity of "normal life" reflects the eugenic principles to which she was certainly exposed.

In addition to being an advocate for people with disabilities, Helen Keller also became a political activist and a spokesperson for victims of poverty, economic exploitation, gender discrimination, and other forms of oppression (Foner, 1967). Helen's voice of advocacy was bold for its time. It was focused, however, on the potential for social intercourse and productivity in the lives of ignored, misunderstood, and exploited people. In that regard she moved beyond a social context that devalued many people with blindness, deafness, and other physical disabilities, for example, and she crusaded for their right to earn a place in society. She did not believe, however, that this right extended to those people who might never "earn" their own way in society.

WHOLENESS AND PERSONHOOD: LEAVING MENTAL RETARDATION BEHIND

In *Coming of Age in Samoa*, Margaret Mead (1928) included a discussion of people with disabilities in the Samoan culture she described in that book. She not only provided profiles of those Samoans with disabilities but, perhaps more importantly, she described a Samoan society that possessed "more charity towards weakness than towards misdirected strength" (p. 182).

Mead returned to this theme many years later. In 1959 she spoke to a conference sponsored by the American Association on Mental Deficiency (AAMD). In her remarks she referred to a statement made by a group of Catholic nuns who worked with children with mental retardation. She quoted them as saying that they were attempting to make it possible for the children whom they cared for to make a "contribution in time as well as in eternity" (Mead, 1959, p. 253).

Later in her speech she returned to the example of the work of the Catholic Church and persons with mental retardation. She gave the example of a child with

Down syndrome who had been tested, diagnosed, and given every opportunity for the best skill training. In her early teens, however, the child was given religious instruction, and Mead described the change that took place in the girl's life in terms of "wholeness." She said that at the same time the girl "became Catholic, she became a human being in a way that she had not been one before. . . . I think that what happened on the secular side with this little girl was that for the first time she met a situation where people were willing to teach her the *whole* instead of saying, 'you are defective and you can only learn a part'" (Mead, 1959, p. 260).

Mead concluded her address to the AAMD by elaborating on the concept of education for "wholeness." She distinguished between societies where everyone participates in all aspects of the culture (e.g., Samoa) and segmented, socially stratified societies that no longer attempt to teach the "whole" to all people (e.g., the United States). She emphasized that what makes for a culture of full participants are genuine opportunities for most people to learn how to wholly participate. She warned of the "risks of complicating sections of our culture so much that we define them as things most people can't learn" (pp. 258–259).

Margaret Mead's insights, unfamiliar to most people concerned about mental retardation and previously overlooked in my own reading of her work, added new meaning to my understanding that, in order for people with what we call mental retardation to be genuinely included in our culture, we must strive to make accessible to them the essential "wholeness" of citizenship (Smith & Johnson, 1997). That part of people that we have referred to as mental retardation, feeblemindedness, or some other diagnostic term must no longer be allowed to overshadow the "wholeness" of individuals.

THE REJECTION OF TOPOLOGICAL THINKING: ABANDONING THE "STOCKS" OF MENTAL RETARDATION

Steven Gelb recently examined the persistence of typological thinking in the field of mental retardation (Gelb, 1997). Typological thinking is the belief that individual differences diverge into underlying types or essences. Gelb explained that definitions of mental retardation, regardless of their differences or particulars, have been founded on the assumptions of typological thought. The axis or core of the field of mental retardation is the assumption that somehow there is an "essence of mental retardation" that eclipses all of the individual differences that characterize the people who are described by the term.

A glance at the panoply of causes that are associated with mental retardation is illustrative of the allure and power of typological thinking. In 1992 the AAMR listed more than 350 conditions in which mental retardation occurs (Lukasson et al., 1992). This list of etiologies does not, of course, take into account the varying degrees or specific types of disabilities associated with these etiologies. If these variables were taken into account, the contexts and expressions of what is called mental retardation would be staggering. The only "glue" that holds mental retardation together as a category is the typological notion that there is some underlying essence to the characteristics and needs of the people identified by this term. Clearly, mental retardation is a term used for an aggregation of life conditions. The only rationale for this aggregation has been the typological definitions that Gelb describes.

In his book *Wayward Puritans*, Kai Erikson (1965) observed that the amount of punishable deviancy that was recorded in 17th-century Quaker New England corresponded neatly with the supply of stocks and whipping posts that were available. If a community had an ample supply of stocks, it convicted and punished a corresponding number of persons for their deviations from the norm. If stocks were in short supply, the rate of deviations detected and punished in that community dropped. Erikson argued that it is a simple logistic fact that the degree of deviance that a community perceives and acts on is largely determined by the kinds of equipment it uses to detect and manage different forms of deviancy. The magnitude of deviation found in a community is at least in part, then, a function of the size and complexity of its social control mechanisms (Erikson, 1965).

Mechanisms of social control will, as has been discussed previously, be influenced by the "felt necessities" of the time and place. They will also be influenced, however, by the tolerance or intolerance for certain traits or for degrees of certain attributes. In *The Rules of Sociological Method*, Emile Durkheim (1895/1964) invited his readers to

> imagine a society of saints, a perfect cloister of exemplary individuals. Crimes properly so called, will there be unknown; but faults which appear venial to the layman will create there the same scandal that the ordinary offense does in ordinary consciousness. If, then, this society has the power to judge and punish, it will *define* these acts as criminal and will treat them as such. (p. 63)

During the 20th century in the United States, the number of individuals defined as being mentally retarded has shifted dramatically. As the emphasis on intelligence test performance has changed, there have been dramatic fluctuations in the demographics of mental retardation. The same is true of the other changes in the accepted definitions of mental retardation. In a sense we have established changing patterns of "intellectual and adaptive saintliness" and have thereby created the less than "exemplary individuals" that society has the power to define as "retarded." In this way, and usually with the best of intentions, we have created the social equivalent of the Puritans' stocks. We have created mechanisms of social control waiting to be used.

In his book, *Miles To Go: A Personal History of Social Policy*, Daniel Patrick Moynihan (1996) included a chapter titled "Defining Deviancy Down." In that chapter Moynihan described three ways that various forms of social deviance have been redefined. Moynihan commented that *altruistic redefinitions* may be the attempts of "good" people to do the "right" thing. These attempts, however, sometimes lead to losses that have a dramatic impact on those who are redefined (Moynihan's example is deinstitutionalization). *Opportunistic redefinitions*, according to Moynihan, may result in the growth of the numbers of people defined as deviant and an increase in the resources and power available to those who "control" the deviant population affected. Moynihan described a *normalizing redefinition* as a form of denial. The result of such a denial may be the neglect of the real needs of the persons who have been redefined. Moynihan's analysis of redefinitions makes evident the caution that must be used in redefining mental retardation.

Perhaps it is time, however, to abandon the term mental retardation. it may, in fact be a manifestation of typological thinking that inevitably creates a false and unhelpful categorization of people with very diverse needs and characteristics. Perhaps even the most recent AAMR definition of mental retardation does not go far enough to diminish the tendency of society to place people in the social stocks we create.

As we consider the alternatives for conceptualizing the needs of people currently referred to as having mental retardation, however, it may be helpful to use Moynihan's redefinition model as a way of asking ourselves questions about what changes in terms, categories, and definitions can mean in the lives of individuals and families. (What are the altruistic implications of redefinition?) We must also ask ourselves what redefining mental retardation might mean for the resource allocations and the provision of services to people who need them. (What are the opportunistic redefinition consequences?) Finally, we must consider the impact of a definition in terms of the dichotomies of need versus norm. How much segregation is necessary to meet needs? How much service is justified with the risk of stigma associated with these services? How can we achieve a balance between the need for assistance and the value of independence? These are the questions associated with a normalizing redefinition of mental retardation.

With the approach of the millennium, however, the time is overdue for a fundamental questioning of the concepts, terms, and practices associated with mental retardation. The millions of people with the myriad of developmental disabilities that have been subsumed under that term deserve this questioning of the manner in which they are being regarded and treated. A disassembling of the aggregation that mental retardation is may enhance our vision of what it should be.

REFERENCES

Blatt, B. (1987). *The conquest of mental retardation*. Austin, TX: PRO-ED.

Clausen, J. A. (1972). The continuing problem of defining mental deficiency. *Journal of Special Education*, 6, 97–106.

Dickens, C. (1842). *American notes*. London: Oxford University Press.

Doll, E. A. (1941). The essentials of an inclusive concept of mental deficiency. *American Journal of Mental Deficiency*, 46, 214–229.

Durkheim, E. (1964). *The rules of sociological method* (A. Birenbaum & H. Lesieur, trans.). New York: The Free Press. (Original work published 1895)

Edgerton, R. B. (1993). *The cloak of competence: Revised and updated*. Berkely: University of California Press.

Erikson, K. T. (1965). *Wayward puritans*. New York: Wiley.

Ferguson, P. M. (1994). *Abandoned to their fate: Social policy and practice toward severely retarded people in America, 1820–1920*. Philadephia: Temple University Press.

Foner, P. (1967). *Helen Keller: Her socialist years, writings and speeches*. New York: International Publishers.

Gallaher, D. (1995). *Voices for the mad: The life of Dorothea Dix*. New York: Free Press.

Gelb, S. A. (1997). The problem of typological thinking in mental retardation. *Mental Retardation, 35*, 448–457.

Gibbons, F. X. (1985). Stigma perception: Social comparison among mentally retarded persons. *American Journal of Mental Deficiency, 90*, 98—106.

Gitter, E. (1991). Charles Dickens. *Dickens Quarterly, 8*, 162–168.

Goffman, E. (1963). *Stigma: Notes on the management of spoiled identity*. Englewood Cliffs, NJ: Prentice-Hall.

Greenspan, S. (1995). Selling DSM: The rhetoric of science in psychiatry. *American Journal on Mental Retardation, 99*, 683–685.

Grossman, H. J. (1973). *Classification in mental retardation*. Washington, DC: American Association on Mental Deficiency.

Grossman, H. J. (Ed.). (1977). *Manual on terminology and classification in mental retardation*. Washington, DC: American Association on Mental Deficiency.

Grossman, H. J. (1983). *Classification in mental retardation*. Washington, DC: American Association on Mental Deficiency.

Heber, R. F. (1959). A manual on terminology and classification in mental retardation. *Monograph Supplement, American Journal of Mental Deficiency, 62*.

Heber, R. F. (1961). A manual on terminology and classification in mental retardation. *Monograph Supplement, American Journal of Mental Deficiency, 63*.

Holmes, O. W. (1881). *The common law*. Boston: Little, Brown.

Howe, S. (1893). *The education of Laura Bridgman*. Boston: Perkins Institute.

Howe, M., & Hall, F. (1904). *Laura Bridgman: Dr. Howe's famous pupil and what he taught her*. London: Hodden & Stoughton.

Jacobson, J., & Mulick, J. (1993). APA takes a step forward in professional practice. *Psychology in Mental Retardation and Developmental Disabilities, 19*, 4–8.

Keller, H. (1915, December 18). Physicians' juries for defective babies. *The New Republic*, pp. 173–174.

Kuhn, T. (1962). *The structure of scientific revolutions*. Chicago: The University of Chicago Press.

Lukasson, R., Coulter, D. L., Polloway, E. A., Reiss, S., Schalock, L. L., Snell, M. E., Spitalnik, D. M., & Stark, J. A. (1992). *Mental retardation: Definition, classification, and systems of supports*. Washington, DC: American Association on Mental Retardation.

MacMillan, D., Gresham, F., & Siperstein, G. (1993). Conceptual and psychometric concerns about the 1992 AAMR definition of mental retardation. *American Journal on Mental Retardation, 98*, 325–335.

MacMillan, D., Gresham, F., & Siperstein, G. (1995). Heightened concerns over the 1992 AAMR definition: Advocacy versus precision. *American Journal on Mental Retardation, 100*, 87–97.

Mead, M. (1928). *Coming of age in Samoa: A psychological study of primitive youth for Western civilization*. New York: William Morrow.

Mead, M. (1959). Research cult: or cure? *American Journal on Mental Deficiency, 64*, 253–164.

Michaelson, R. (1993). Tug-of-war is developing over defining retardation. *APA Monitor, 24*(5), 34.

Moynihan, D. P. (1996). *Miles to go: A personal history of social policy*. Cambridge, MA: Howard University Press.

Pernick, M. (1996). *The black stork: Eugenics and the death of "defective" babies in American medicine and motion pictures since 1915*. New York: Oxford University Press.

Sarason, S. (1985). *Psychology and mental retardation: Perspectives in change.* Austin, TX: PRO-ED.

Schalock, R., Coulter, D., Polloway, E., Reiss, S., Snell, M., Spitalnik, D., & Stark, J. (1994). The changing conception of mental retardation: Implications for the field. *Mental Retardation, 32,* 181–193.

Smith, J. D. (1985). *Minds made feeble: The myth and the legacy of the Kallikaks.* Rockville, MD: Aspen.

Smith, J. D. (1987). *The other voices: Profiles of women in the history of special education.* Seattle: Special Child Publications.

Smith, J. D., & Anton, M. (1997). Laura Bridgman, mental retardation, and the question of differential advocacy. *Mental Retardation, 35,* 398–401.

Smith, J. D., & Johnson, G. (1997). Margaret Mead and mental retardation: Words of understanding, concepts of inclusiveness. *Mental Retardation, 35,* 306–309.

Smith, J. D., & Nelson, K. (1989). *The sterilization of Carrie Buck.* Far Hill, NJ: New Horizon Press.

Trent, J. W. (1994). *Inventing the feeble mind: A history of mental retardation in the United States.* Berkeley: University of California Press.

Criminal Justice and Mental Retardation: A Journalist's Notebook

Robert Perske

> I suppose I am a pretty good representative of the judiciary because the truth is that judges, by and large, don't know much about mental retardation. I think that's also true of lawyers. Even criminal defense lawyers don't know a great deal about mental retardation. This is what I see as the great need, so far as the courts are concerned—a need to know. (Chief Justice James G. Exum, North Carolina Supreme Court, cited in Conley, Luckasson, & Bouthilet, 1992, p. 1)

Judge Exum opened the Presidential Forum on Offenders with Mental Retardation with this bold admission. He could have said the same thing about police, correction, probation, and victim's rights officers. Also, veteran court observers can testify that many psychological and psychiatric evaluators who appear on the witness stand do not understand mental retardation either.

THE BLEAK PAST

Three "witches" with retardation are reprieved (1693).

In 1692 the Puritans of Salem Village, Massachusetts, suddenly believed that their town had become "the battleground between God and the Devil." During that stormy year, they sentenced 20 citizens as witches and executed them. The convictions were based on "spectral evidence" supplied by a small group of hysterical maidens. For example, a teenager claimed that she saw a neighbor flying through the air. That type of evidence was enough to include the "flyer" in the town's frenzied attempt to cleanse itself.

On January 3, 1693, however, Governor William Phips ordered the Superior Court of Massachusetts to eliminate spectral evidence as a basis of conviction. With that order, the cases against 49 other defendants melted like butter on a hot summer day. Even so, Chief Justice William Stoughton, not happy with the order, suddenly signed the death warrants for three "feebleminded" women—Elizabeth Johnson, Mary Post, and Elizabeth Wardwell. After all, they had not been convicted by spectral evidence. They, unlike the others, had been forced to *confess* to being witches.

As soon as Governor Phips learned of the warrants, he reprieved the three along with five others who had been convicted earlier. Chief Justice Stoughton then lamented that the battle with the Devil was lost. Records show that he became ill and took to his bed (Hill, 1995, pp. 201–203; Starkey, 1949, pp. 242–243).

Criminality is ascribed to persons with retardation (1912).

Vineland, New Jersey, researcher Henry H. Goddard (1912) published a study of the long-reaching effects of one man's sexual intercourse with two different women. The man was Martin Kallikak, a Revolutionary soldier of "good English blood" who in "an unguarded moment" impregnated a feebleminded woman. From that sex act, Goddard found a six-generation lineage of 480 derelict offspring—prostitutes, epileptics, criminals, paupers, perverts, welfare clients, whorehouse madams, horse thieves, and one "of the Mongolian type." Then Goddard focused on Kallikak's later marriage to a "respectable girl of good family." He found 496 upper-crust offspring who possessed "nothing but good representative citizenship."

Thanks to psychologist–investigator J. David Smith (1985), Goddard's study was found to be a preposterous fraud. Goddard, nevertheless, instilled a phobia in society that lingers today. He even created the term *moron*. According to him, morons were "feebleminded persons" who could pass for normal—making them the most dangerous and despicable of all. The only way to find these people with "diseased germ plasm" was to identify them via intelligence tests and lock them away (Goddard, 1912).

State's attorney drops an "airtight case against a moron" (1924).

Early in 1924 a well-loved priest, Reverend Hubert Dahme, was gunned down on the sidewalk in downtown Bridgeport, Connecticut. Within hours, every available policeman began searching for clues. Eight days later, Harold Israel, a man described as a "transient indigent" and a "person of low mentality of the moron type" was arrested for the murder. The arrest was based on a powerful 10-point report that included seven eyewitnesses, a pistol, and an empty shell. Most important, the police got Israel to *confess* to murdering the priest.

On May 28, 1924, Fairfield County State's Attorney Homer Cummings appeared in court and dropped the case. Speaking without notes for 1 1/2 hours, he described his personal investigation that discredited every piece of evidence against Israel. At the finish, the courtroom remained deadly silent for a time. Then the audience stood and applauded.

Not everyone, however, applauded Cummings's surprise move. For example, Police Superintendent Patrick Flanagan took the case to the newspapers, stating angrily that Israel was indeed the vicious killer of the priest. Also, Cummings, a national committeeman for the Democratic party, received a snub by not being invited to a dinner in honor of Assistant Secretary of the Navy Franklin D. Roosevelt later in 1924.

Even so, in 1933 President-elect Roosevelt made Homer Cummings his Attorney General. Then in 1954 Bridgeport resident Ralph DeNigris broke a 30-year silence.

He admitted to witnessing the killing and being threatened with death by the murderer if he ever spoke out about it. That real murderer was not Harold Israel (Zeldes, 1994).

Supreme Court orders sterilization of "unfit" citizens (1927).

In 1924 Harry Laughlin, a leader at the Eugenic Records Office, guided the development of a law for the State of Virginia that called for the sterilization of all "hereditary defectives." To him, they were the "tramps, beggars, alcoholics, criminals, the feeble-minded, the insane, epileptics, the physically deformed, the blind and the deaf" (Smith, 1985, p. 138). The law came to the state courts as *Buck v. Bell* and it focused on Carrie Buck, an inmate of the Virginia Colony for Epileptics and the Feeble-minded. In 1927 the U.S. Supreme Court heard the case, and Chief Justice Oliver Wendell Holmes amplified the fears of leaders like Goddard and Laughlin. Holmes wrote,

> It is better for all the world, if instead of waiting to execute degenerate offspring for crime, or let them starve for their imbecility, society can prevent those who are manifestly unfit from continuing their kind . . . . Three generations of imbeciles are enough. (*Buck v. Bell*, 1927, p. 50)

The "three generations" Justice Holmes alluded to were Carrie Buck; her mother, Emma; and Carrie's daughter, Doris. Again, J. David Smith (1985) performed a valuable service to the mental retardation field by showing that neither Emma nor Carrie nor Doris had any retardation or debilitating illnesses at all (1985, pp. 150–155). He also showed how Holmes's ruling led to 4,000 sterilizations in Virginia, 50,000 nationally, and 56,000 in Germany. In 1936, Harry Laughlin received a Hitler-inspired honorary doctor's degree from Heidelberg University for his services to the science of eugenics and his efforts to purify "the human seed stock" (p. 157).

Warden fights to keep from executing a man labeled an "imbecile" (1939).

To all appearances, five-foot-four, 130-pound Joe Arridy, the son of Syrian immigrants, was one of those persons with so-called diseased protoplasm that had been so much in the news. He was kicked out of a Pueblo, Colorado, elementary school at an early age. He was tested and labeled an "imbecile" and was placed in the Grand Junction State Home and Training School for Mental Defectives. Then he ran away and became a scroungy but avid railroad boxcar rider during the summer of 1936.

When 15-year-old Dorothy Drain was raped and axed to death in Pueblo, Frank Aguilar, the murderer, was identified along with the weapon—but he refused to confess. This may have set the stage for a famous sheriff to become more famous by pulling Arridy off a boxcar in Cheyenne and questioning him about the murder in Pueblo. After an always-changing series of guided admissions—-most of them in two- and three-word sentences—Arridy said what Aguilar would not. Arridy was finally led into saying he committed the murder "with Frank." With the case completed, both went to death row at Canon City, Colorado. Many saw Arridy as merely an expendable tagalong.

On the other hand, Canon City Warden Roy Best did not. He befriended Arridy. He supplied picture books and cut-out scissors and toys for him to play with in his cell. During the Christmas of 1938, Warden Best even gave Arridy a toy train set. After that, his shouts of "train wreck!" and his unabashed laughter could be heard throughout the cell block. When reporters asked Best about Joe, he usually began by saying, "Joe Arridy is the happiest man who ever lived on death row." Best openly joined in court appeal efforts that brought nine stays in a single year.

Then Governor Teller Ammons called the warden and flatly told him to execute his friend—and Best broke down and cried. On January 6, 1939, Joe Arridy was racing his train over "it's tinny tracks" when the warden and other officials came for him, took him to a special chamber, and snuffed out his life (Perske, 1995).

THE WAVERING PRESENT

The foregoing cases show how a neighborhood—or even a nation—could become hysterical over a certain social situation and then try to cleanse themselves of it by finding and killing—or colonizing—scapegoats. At times like that, people with retardation often became

- the easiest to bear false witness against

- the easiest from whom to coerce a confession

- the easiest to demonize in the press

- the easiest to ignore when it comes to fighting for their Constitutional rights

Today we see through such primitive urges, but do we always?

Remember the famous Boston Murder of Carol Stuart in 1989?

Loving husband Charles Stuart, lost in the city, frantically called for help on a cellular phone in his car. He said that an African American had just killed his wife and shot him. Remember how he kept talking on the cellular phone until a police dispatcher pinpointed his location? Remember the national uproar?

The police and press quickly zeroed in on Willie Bennett, in Boston's Mission District, as the prime suspect. The Stuarts were described by the media as "the Camelot couple," and Bennett was labeled an "urban savage." Much was made of Willie's public school records that listed him as a "mental defective." Three testings resulted in reported IQs of 64, 65, and 62.

The whole country seemed to want Willie dead—until husband Charles, the real killer, suddenly committed suicide by jumping off the Tobin Bridge (Perske, 1991).

Remember the 1990 mutilation murders of five University of Florida at Gainesville students?

The police quickly focused on a freshman named Edward Humphrey because he was arrested for fighting with his grandmother, and records showed that at one time he had been labeled "manic-depressive." After long hours of intense interrogation, Edward confessed that his "alter ego John" was the killer. One cannot help wondering whether this "confession" might have led to a conviction if DNA testing had not cleared Edward, and connected the crimes to Danny Harold Rolling (Rohter, 1994).

Remember the 1996 Daytona Beach "Spring Break" murder?

On a Friday in March, Canadian student Mark Fyke was fatally shot in the back of the head. On Saturday, the police picked up odd, loquacious, happy-go-lucky, beach-loving, 18-year-old Donnie Shoup. Police said that they received a full confession from Donnie at 3 a.m. on Sunday morning. On Sunday afternoon, the police gave Shoup's confession to the press. They also added that he had an IQ of 52 (Ditzler, 1996).

Three weeks later, the real shooter and two accomplices were charged. Even so, Shoup was not released until August (Holland, 1996).

Remember Barry Fairchild, who was executed in Arkansas in 1995?

Did you know that there were 13 affidavits signed by African Americans who swore that Sheriff Tommy Robinson and his men brutally beat them in an unsuccessful attempt to get a confession for the 1983 rape–murder of Air Force nurse Greta Mason? Barry Fairchild was the 14th to be beaten. Barry Fairchild had mental retardation. Barry Fairchild, with his head wrapped in bandages, finally "confessed" (ABC TV, 1991).

By 1995 judicial authorities claimed that all of Fairchild's Constitutional protections were exhausted. Consequently, on August 31, he was executed as an *accomplice* to the murder of Ms. Mason, even though the real shooter has never even been identified.

Remember how Johnny Lee Wilson was pardoned in Missouri in 1995?

Johnny, a 20-year-old recent graduate of special education classes in the Aurora public schools, was intensely interrogated for the 1986 murder of 79-year-old Pauline Martz. Police officers at headquarters, who talked freely in the hall about Johnny being a "f_____ retard," questioned him repeatedly until he confessed.

Later, the trial judge warned Johnny that if he pled innocent and went through a trial, he could get death. Scared, Johnny quickly pled guilty and the judge quickly sentenced him to life without parole. Still later, the real killer, Chris Brownfield, from a prison cell in Kansas, confessed to the murder. Even so, Johnny continued to lose all of his appeals (Perske, 1991).

On September 29, 1995, Governor Carnahan, after studying the case for better than a year, found Johnny's confession to be totally false and coerced—and he pardoned him.

TURNING POINTS

As society becomes more complex, so does the criminal justice system. Today, it is a monstrous, many-departmented behemoth. It is so large that only the brightest thinkers can come close to defining it. Even so, more and more persons with a background in mental retardation are daring to move into the monster. They, in the midst of all this largeness, are finding small but powerful areas in which to work and do good. They are bringing about turning points that may seem minor now but that could prove to be monumental later.

Ellis and Luckasson monograph breaks new ground in two fields.

James Ellis, a law professor, and Ruth Luckasson, a lawyer and professor of special education, felt that a 1983 draft of the ABA Criminal Justice Mental Health Standards failed to deal adequately with defendants having mental retardation. They joined with others to change them for the better. Then, not content to leave them as mere standards, they produced "a preliminary overview" of the mental retardation issues found in the standards. That 78-page overview, "Mentally Retarded Criminal Defendants," printed in *The George Washington Law Review* (Ellis & Luckasson, 1985), has, without a doubt, become the most illuminating and the most widely read document by both lawyers and mental retardation professionals.

Drawing from case law and clinical practice, Ellis and Luckasson presented (a) a rich history of the treatment of persons with retardation in the criminal justice system, (b) vivid descriptions of characteristics of these persons and their consequences, (c) a discussion of the extent to which these persons should be exculpatory of criminal responsibility, and (d) the critical importance of competency issues. They concluded with thoughtful discussions on how persons in the field of retardation might aid the criminal justice system, and vice versa. This document still serves as the best introductory reader one can find on this subject. It remains one of the most quoted references in legal briefs filed on behalf of defendants with retardation.

Bowden, Smith, and The Arc of Georgia bring about the first modern death penalty law for persons with retardation.

On October 11, 1976, Kathryn Stryker was brutally beaten and stabbed to death in her Columbus, Georgia, home. The killer, without a reasonable doubt, was 16-year-old Jamie Graves. The motive, all of the evidence, and even the pawnbroker's records pointed to him. But Graves said 24-year-old Jerome Bowden was with him. Bowden was taken into intensive interrogation and he finally signed a confession. Graves was given a life sentence. Bowden was sentenced to death (Perske, 1991).

As Bowden's execution drew near, Patricia Smith, the president of The Arc of Georgia and a recent graduate of law school, got involved. After joining with others on an 11th-hour investigation, she wrote and filed a brief with the Board of Pardons and Appeals. The brief made three powerful points:

1. Jerome Bowden has mental retardation and is intellectually incapable of comprehending the meaning of death.

2. The question of Jerome Bowden's competency was never tried.

3. No evidence linked Jerome to the crime, and he could not have read or understood the confession drafted for him by the police. (p. 29)

That brief stopped the board dead in its tracks, but only for a while. His death warrant would expire soon, on June 24, 1986. So the board quickly contracted with Dr. Irwin Knopf, chairman of Emory University's psychology department, to test Bowden, which he did on the morning of June 23. After 3 hours of tests, Knopf reported that Bowden had a verbal IQ of 71, a nonverbal IQ of 62, and a full scale IQ of 65. Knopf added that Bowden would need an IQ of 45 or less in order to be spared electrocution and sent to an institution for persons with retardation.

The next day, June 24, Jerome Bowden was executed at 10:05 a.m. In his last call to his lawyers, he discussed the IQ test he had just taken. "I tried real hard," he said. "I did the best I could" (p. 33).

After that, citizens of Georgia, spearheaded by Arc members throughout the state, moved on the legislature. One year and 7 months after Jerome Bowden's execution, Governor Joe Frank Harris signed into law the first bill in the nation that banned the execution of persons with mental retardation (p. 37).

Norley agitates for police training.

Today, many volunteer and professional agencies are designing helps for police officers—brochures, wallet cards, and curricula for police academies. Whether they know it or not, they are operating in a furrow plowed long ago by the mother of a son with retardation—who also served as a professor of communications, a police trainer, and a practicing lawyer.

During the 1960s Dolores Norley taught at police academies; logged hours in patrol cars; voluntarily visited in the cells of prisoners with retardation; wrote training manuals for officers, attorneys, and judges; and helped to develop some of the first laws designed to protect persons with disabilities. Those who knew her then can still describe the pressures she put on others to join her. When most were repelled by such pursuits, she went it alone.

In the late 1960s, under the aegis of the national Arc and the President's Committee on Mental Retardation, Norley developed a special "training key" for the International Association of Police Chiefs (IAPC): *Contacts with Individuals Who Are Mentally Retarded* (IAPC, 1980). It includes a remarkable street test that officers can use with a suspect or person in need. It contains 23 simple questions related to physical appearance (e.g., "Can the individual easily button his or her coat?"); speech and language (e.g., "Can the person give coherent directions from one place to another?"); educational level (e.g., "Can the person recognize coins and make change?"); and social maturity (e.g., "Does the person answer yes or no questions affirmatively, even if the yes answer seems inappropriate?"). "Keep in mind," she writes, "the purpose of street testing is not to affix a prejudicial label to the individual . . . it permits the officer to recognize appropriate helping responses." This key was the springboard for many similar efforts that now take place across the nation (Perske, 1991, pp. 24–27).

Wood and White uphold the "right" to be arrested.

Hubert Wood and David White readily admit that "some individuals, because of their incompetence, are unable to be prosecuted," but they bounce back quickly to say that most persons with retardation should have the "right" to be arrested. According to them, when some persons are brought into the police station for less than heinous crimes and are recognized as retarded, all they get is a Pepsi, a kind lecture, a pat on the head, and a ride home in a patrol car. "If not arrested, citizens with mental retardation may feel they are above the law because of their disability. What needs to be taught is that citizens with retardation, like others, are accountable and responsible for their actions" (Wood & White, 1992, p. 154).

Consequently, in 1980, the twosome brought together two probation officers from the criminal justice system and two case managers from the mental health and mental retardation system. They developed The Lancaster, Pennsylvania, Office of Special Offenders Services. The goal of this joint system is "to enable offenders with mental retardation to successfully complete probation and parole." So they set up special programs for an annual average of 50 adults and 35 juveniles with retardation—each designed to help a person pay a debt to the court and society for a crime they committed. Their recidivism rate is only 5%. Retardation organizations, which talk increasingly about developing alternative sentencing programs, may want to begin by considering the work of Wood and White (1992, pp. 153–165).

Supreme Court ruling in Penry case serves as a wake-up call.

It began in Livingston, Texas, on the morning of October 29, 1979. Johnny Paul Penry rode his bicycle to the home of Pamela Mosely Carpenter. He knocked. They talked. He said he liked her. He forced his way into the house. There was a fight. Carpenter stabbed Penry in the back with scissors. Then she was brutally beaten and stabbed to death with the same scissors. Penry then rode home on his bicycle.

Penry was mentally retarded, with an early history of vicious torture as a child and a later and longer history in Texas institutions. It also did not help Penry that Carpenter was the sister of Mark Mosely, the star kicker for the Washington Redskins and the National Football League's most valuable player. People in Livingston were so aroused by the crime that the trial was held in Groveton, 40 miles to the northwest. But to East Texans, that distance equated to a city dweller's 10-block walk, and the courtroom was filled for every hearing.

On April 1, 1980, the judge ruled that the jury needed to answer three questions: (1) Did Penry deliberately commit the crime? (2) Was the crime committed without provocation? (3) Will Penry be dangerous in the future? It took 46 minutes for the jury to come up with three yes answers.

As Penry's execution drew near, the U.S. Supreme Court agreed to hear the case since retardation had not figured in the verdict. In *Penry v. Lynaugh* (1989), the court chose to rule on two questions: (1) Should juries consider mental retardation as a mitigating factor in death penalty cases? (2) Is it cruel and unusual punishment to execute persons with mental retardation?

The case was heightened to national awareness by a remarkable brief of *amicus curiae* written by attorneys James Ellis and Ruth Luckasson. Amazingly, the American Association on Mental Retardation, The Arc of the United States, and nine other national organizations signed the brief (Conley et al., 1992, pp. 257–276).

Even so, the court's ruling was a sharply divided shocker. It voted 5 to 4 that retardation as a mitigating factor must be considered in the lower court. Then, with Justice Sandra Day O'Connor moving to the other side, the court voted 5 to 4 that it was not cruel or unusual punishment to execute persons with mental retardation. O'Connor claimed that, until a consensus of states banned such an execution, she would not either (Perske, 1991, pp. 63–81).

That ruling moved many in the field to get to work. For example, at the time of the decision, only three states were against such executions. Now, the federal government and 12 of the 38 death penalty states have such laws. They are Alaska, Colorado, Georgia, Indiana, Kansas, Kentucky, Maryland, Nebraska, New Mexico, New York, Tennessee, and Washington. More are expected to adopt such legislation soon.

Glen Ridge, New Jersey, case raises awareness of victims.

On March 1, 1989, a 17-year old girl with retardation was coerced into the basement of a Glen Ridge, New Jersey, home by 13 high school males. They promised her a date with a high school athlete. There a broomstick, a miniature baseball bat, and a stick were inserted in her vagina. The girl, wanting so much to be liked by the guys, seemed to have gone along with what they were telling her to do.

Three days later, the girl approached her high school swimming coach, told her what had happened, and asked for advice on how to say no if she is approached again. The coach told the principal, who after a delay, called the police. Five students were charged.

During the 4 years that followed, the whole nation seemed to rise up and argue over whether or not a rape took place in that basement. Then, on April 23, 1993, three of the defendants were sentenced to indeterminate terms of up to 15 years in a state facility for youthful offenders. That victimization, constantly aided by the media, was raised to a higher awareness in almost everyone's mind. A victimization in North Dakota, however, may have provided a more coherent, turning-point model.

Men acquitted of gang rape, and a Grand Forks Arc rises up.

On September 16, 1990, in Grand Forks, North Dakota, a group of men began drinking in the afternoon. At 7:00 p.m. they met and talked to an attractive 18-year-old woman on the street. Fifteen minutes later, they drove the woman to an abandoned farmhouse. There, according to charges, four of them raped and sodomized her and then drove her back to town.

At the trial, expert witnesses described her as having an IQ of 65. They said she had been a virgin and she suffered tears in her rectum. They also said that she did not look retarded, but "as soon as people talked to her they would know."

Testifying on her own behalf for 1 1/2 hours, the woman knew where she worked, but could not say how long she worked there or how much she got paid an hour, and did not understand what the money was for. She could not tell what time it was on the prosecutor's watch. When the prosecutor asked her to talk about "the bad thing" that had happened to her, she began to cry. The men had asked her to go "cruising." She thought that meant going around the block. The sexual acts "hurt," she said, but they kept on. At one point, they put a blanket over her head, she said.

The defendants swore repeatedly they did not know she was retarded. They said she was more than willing. One even characterized her as being "horny." The defendants were charged under a statute stating that "a reasonable person would have known that the woman suffered from a mental disease or defect that made her incapable of understanding the nature of her conduct." The regular rape statute could not be applied, because the woman—like many persons with retardation—did not resist or fight back. The jury deliberated for 2 hours before giving a verdict of "not guilty."

A few days later, the Valley Chapter Arc called a press conference and voiced anger over the verdict. Arc President Nancy O'Connor claimed, "The real crime, apparently, was the woman did not look retarded." Prosecutor Rick Brown claimed there was "overwhelming evidence" that a reasonable person would know or at least suspect that the woman was mentally retarded. Executive Director Dianne Sheppard claimed that the statute favored the defendants and not the victim. She called for a language change in the statute (Sweney, 1991).

That press conference proved to be only the beginning. The Arc sponsored an all-day seminar on the case. They engaged attorneys to provide the legal help. They lobbied. They pushed a bill with better language, but the legislature refused to make the changes. Consequently, The Arc gathered around the victim and her family and brought a civil case against the four men—and they won.

OPPORTUNITIES AND ATTITUDES FOR THE 21ST CENTURY

Respect needs to be developed for criminal justice laws and lawmaking.

Know that an ever-changing criminal justice system is needed. When one walks into a police station, that person walks into a place that legal expert Yale Kamisar described as *The Gatehouse* of the criminal system (Kamisar, LaFave, & Israel, 1994). Mistakes may be made in this building that need correction. But one should also recognize and feel respect for those who work there and for the protection they give. When one sits in a courtroom, he or she is present in what Kamisar called *The Mansion* of criminal justice. Here errors are made that need to be appealed. But know also that the walls of this place echo powerful statements from the Magna Carta and the Constitution that are forever being reapplied in this ever-changing world. In Robert Bolt's 1990 play, *A Man for All Seasons*, an impatient young man rails against a law. He longs to cut down every law in England in his pursuit of the Devil, to which Thomas More replies, "And when the last law was down, and the Devil turned around on *you*—where would you hide?"

There is a place for citizens' groups, but there are limits to what they can do.

Without a citizens' group, Johnny Lee Wilson would have quietly disappeared in the penitentiary at Jefferson City, Missouri. A small handful of people kept hope alive for the young man who confessed falsely to the murder of Pauline Martz. Bumper stickers, fund raisers, a large billboard, petitions, letters from self-advocates, and even a march on the state capitol kept the innocent young man's plight uppermost in people's minds. Even the national media amplified the situation. Nevertheless, when it actually comes down to trying to win in a court of law, *only lawyers* can talk to the judge and *only lawyers* can put on the stand witnesses who can talk to the judge and jury. Also, *only lawyers* can write the brief that finally convinced a governor to grant a pardon like Mel Carnahan did.

Arcs can be natural home bases for citizens' groups, but it can be costly.

The board of directors of The Arc of Connecticut learned about a citizens' group fighting to free Richard Lapointe, a man with Dandy Walker syndrome who was in prison for a murder many believe he could not have committed. They discussed the case and voted to back this organization in any way they could (Perske, 1996). Later, one of the assistant state attorneys with a connection to the prosecution of Lapointe became the president of a local Arc. It was then communicated to the state executive director, Margaret Dignoti, that if the state board did not drop the Lapointe case, that local would pull out. Dignoti discussed the situation with the state board and they voted to keep backing Lapointe's citizens' group as one of their valued efforts. The local did indeed do what they promised. They withdrew.

An increasing number of windows of service for caring professionals are opening.

Again, there is a price to be paid for such actions. For example, Johnny Lee Wilson's two pro-bono attorneys—while working on the pardon brief and its appendix for the governor—suddenly felt uneasy about an earlier psychiatric evaluation. On a Thursday evening, the evaluation was read word for word over the telephone to Professor Denis Keyes in Charleston, South Carolina. On Friday evening, Keyes flew to Jefferson City, Missouri. He spent Saturday and Sunday in the state penitentiary, testing Wilson. At home, Keyes gave 2 weeks worth of late-night hours producing his report.

Although many others were called in for other emergency pro-bono services as well, it was, in the legal team's opinion, Keyes's report that helped make a difference.

> *Arcs can show that people with retardation who are executed are not exactly the most culpable.*

Although this was mentioned earlier, fresh ways of showing it will be needed in the new century. If there is a death penalty, it should be reserved for the most cunning, the most premeditating, the most vicious, the most aware of what they were doing, the most sure of the punishment if they were caught—the most culpable. Yet, of the 33 persons with retardation who were executed since 1976 (Keyes, Edwards, & Perske, 1997), they were easy to kill, but they certainly were not the most culpable.

When Morris Mason was taken away for execution, he told his fellow inmates he would be back for the basketball game in the recreation yard. Robert Wayne Sawyer told the board of pardons he was sorry for lying to them about being a river boat pilot and for making the prosecutor so angry. Barry Fairchild told a fellow inmate that he thought the reading of the Miranda warning was an "opening devotions" the police did before getting down to work. Jerome Bowden felt he had gotten into the fix he was in because he could not read and write. Walter Correll curled up in a corner and cried every time two appointed lawyers came to him and asked about the crime. Ricky Ray Rector left the pie from his last meal on his window sill—to eat after he got back from where they were taking him. On and on it goes.

These, of course, are personal observations that colleagues are quick to share, but they would not mean much in a court of law. The powerful legal foundation of this point can be found in the *Penry v. Lynaugh* (1989) amicus brief. The following is a paraphrasing of the arguments in the brief:

I. *Mental retardation is directly relevant to criminal responsibility and the choice of punishment.* First, it impairs the capacity to understand and control actions. Second, it should have a bearing on the choice of punishment.

II. *The reduction of blameworthiness caused by retardation makes the death penalty unconstitutional.* That is so because the death penalty is reserved for a few who should be selected according to their true blameworthiness and guilt. Also, persons with retardation simply do not have the degree of culpability needed for a death penalty.

III. *The execution of a person with retardation is cruel and unusual.* The Eighth Amendment of the Constitution bars such an act.

IV. *Executing a person with retardation serves no penological purpose.*

The foregoing does not do justice to the detailed language of the actual brief. Therefore, know that nonlegals have a rich opportunity to read it in its entirety in Conley et al. (1992, pp. 246–278).

Miranda does not always protect persons with mental retardation.

In 1966 *Miranda v. Arizona* was instituted to put a stop to beating confessions out of suspects. The reading of the Miranda warning, however, has proved to be of great comfort to many seasoned criminals. After the warning has been read to that kind of suspect, he or she can respond, "Thanks for reading that to me, guys, but you know I'm not talking until my lawyer is sitting beside me." To which the police must reply, "Okay, Bucky. You can go. See you again sometime." The suspect walks out into freedom.

But when Miranda is read to people with retardation, different responses can be expected. Some possible examples.

- *On the right to remain silent:* "That's okay. I'll talk. You guys are my friends."

- *On the right to know that anything you say can be used against you in a court of law:* "That's okay, too. I'm not afraid. I don't have anything to hide."

- *On the right to have a lawyer present:* "I haven't done anything wrong. So what do I need a lawyer for?"

These answers are honest and trusting. People with retardation are that way because that is the way we have helped them to be. Then in the police station they are asked to sign a "waiver sheet" and to put their initials at the end of each "right," even if they cannot read. After they sign and initial that sheet, a psychological and physical trap door is slammed shut between them and freedom. For hours after that they can be subject to the most vicious dehumanization and accusations and lies and threats and trickery they will ever experience in their lives. We see this happening on TV shows all the time, and we cheer on the interrogators. But when it happens to people we work with, it hurts!

Self-advocate groups have picked up on this danger. Many now role-play such situations. In one group, the goal is to get everyone to shout, "I want a lawyer," then to sit down and shut up. Somehow, that runs across the grain of what they have been taught, but they now may have to do it to protect themselves. In the new century, someone in the field may take a fresh look at *Miranda* and work for fairer alternatives.

Arcs need to understand what can happen in police interrogation rooms.

After signing the waiver sheet, a suspect is often taken to a room in the most out-of-the-way area of the station. The suspect's chair is far from the door and the farthest away from light switches, thermostats, and other control devices. Bathroom and eating privileges must be asked for. Here, the suspect becomes "a depersonalized 'subject' to be 'sized up' and subjected to 'interrogation tactics and techniques most appropriate for the occasion'; he is 'game' to be stalked and cornered" (Kamisar et al., 1994, p. 445). Forensic psychologist Saul Kassin (1997) sees three problems associated with the gathering of confession evidence today:

(a) The police routinely used deception, trickery, and psychologically coercive methods of interrogation; (b) these methods may, at times, cause innocent people to confess to crimes they did not commit; and (c) when coerced self-incriminating statements are presented in the courtroom, juries do not sufficiently discount the evidence in reaching a verdict. (p. 221)

Most interrogators today have been well trained in any of a large number of 3- to 5-day, graduated skill-enhancement courses. For some, becoming a skilled interrogator is much like going for a black belt in Karate. If an interrogator is trained according to Inbau, Reid, and Buckley (1986), everything possible is done by the interrogator to promote feelings of social isolation, sensory deprivation, and a lack of control in the suspect. Then the interrogator becomes a confident behavior analyst and the sole *stimulus* in the room, delivering a wide range of statements and questions and receiving every verbal and nonverbal *response* the suspect gives. The interrogator follows nine well-planned steps, a technique that leads many to incriminate themselves. Some interrogators even claim success rates as high as 90%. Such techniques are great for catching tricky criminals, but if an interrogator does not understand—really *understand*— people with retardation, watch out!

Arcs need to lobby for the nonstop videotaping of interrogations.

In Judge Harold Rothwax's recent controversial book (1996), he calls for "sweeping changes" in the criminal justice system. In one of them, he claims that *Miranda* can be replaced by the recording of an arrest and interrogation through videotapes, tape recorders, and other technology. That is quite a jump, but why not? This is the electronic era, and a 1993 national survey estimated that one third of all large police and sheriff's departments now videotape at least some interrogations. The survey also showed that 97% of those departments found them helpful (Geller, 1993).

There is nothing more anguishing than sitting in a courtroom and observing the "swearing contest" that goes on between articulate detectives and an inarticulate person with a disability, when there is *no record* of what was actually said and done in the interrogation room. In every case like this, the defendant with retardation loses.

Someone needs to work at solving the IQ number shibboleth.

Some courts get carried away with IQ numbers. Arguments can take place over whether a defendant measures above or below, say, an IQ of 70. It is hard to believe that in some cases, a 69 IQ can mean life and a 71 IQ can mean death. Mental retardation is the only disability that is sometimes measured with a number. After the IQ number issue is settled, the forensic witness can sometimes talk at length about adaptive behaviors—while the judge, jury, and lawyers almost go to sleep. The IQ makes such a vivid impression, they lose interest in everything else that is said. This is the very thing Alfred Binet, the father of this numbering system, warned against (Gould, 1981, p. 155). Some in the field long to see this problem solved, once and for all. Others do not.

EPILOGUE

Not so very long ago, I left a courtroom trial in a far west state. I noticed that all the seats behind the defendant with retardation and his lawyer were vacant. The seats behind the prosecutor were packed. Having witnessed this phenomenon before, I visited the executive director of an agency who at one time served and supported the defendant. When the exec was told about that day in court, he suddenly responded like a cow watching a passing train. Then after a long silence, he said, "John isn't in our population anymore. He belongs to the police now."

That response is understandable. Most people in the field of mental retardation feel that way. I felt that way once—until a painful arrest and conviction of a person with a mental disability in my own neighborhood grabbed me and refused to let me go.

So it goes.

REFERENCES

ABC TV. (1991, March 29). Confession at gunpoint. *20/20*.

Buck v. Bell. (1927). 274 U.S. 200, 47 S. Ct. 584.

Conley, R., Luckasson, R., & Bouthilet, G. (Eds.). (1992). *The criminal justice system and mental retardation*. Baltimore: Brookes.

Ditzler, J. (1996, March 18). Man admits killing breaker during robbery. *The Daytona Beach News Journal*, p. 1A.

Ellis, J., & Luckasson, R. (1985, March–May). Mentally retarded criminal defendants. *The George Washington Law Review*, 53(3 & 4), 414–492.

Geller, W. A. (1993, March). Videotaping interrogations and confessions. *National Institute of Justice: Research in Brief*. Washington, DC: U.S. Department of Justice.

Goddard, H. H. (1912). *The Kallikak family*. New York: MacMillan.

Gould, S. J. (1981). *The mismeasure of man*. New York: Norton.

Hill, F. (1995). *A delusion of Satan*. New York: Doubleday.

Holland, J. (1996, August 1). Former spring break murder suspect freed. *The Daytona Beach News Journal*, p. 1A.

Inbau, F. E., Reid, J. E., & Buckley, J. P. (1986). *Criminal interrogation and confessions* (3rd ed.). Baltimore: Williams & Wilkins.

International Association of Police Chiefs. (1980). *Contacts with individuals who are mentally retarded: Training key #253*. Gaithersburg, MD: Author.

Kamisar, Y., LaFave, W., & Israel, J. (1994). *Modern criminal procedure*. St. Paul: West Publishing.

Kassin, S. M. (1997, March). The psychology of confession evidence. *American Psychologist*, 53(3), 221–233.

Keyes, D., Edwards, W., & Perske, R. (1997, February). People with mental retardation are dying, legally. *Mental Retardation*, 35(1), 59–63.

Miranda v. Arizona, 384 U.S. 336 (1966).

Penry v. Lynaugh, 492 U.S. 302 (1989).

Perske, R. (1991). *Unequal justice?* Nashville, TN: Abingdon Press.

Perske, R. (1995). *Deadly innocence?* Nashville, TN: Abingdon Press

Perske, R. (1996, October). The battle for Richard Lapointe's life. *Mental Retardation*, 34(5).

Rohter, L. (1994, February 16). Suspect offers surprise guilty plea in Florida student killings. *New York Times*, p. A10.

Rothwax, H. J. (1996). *Guilty: The collapse of criminal justice*. New York: Random House.

Smith, J. D. (1985). *Minds made feeble: The myth and legacy of the Kallikaks*. Austin, TX: PRO-ED.

Starkey, M. L. (1949). *The devil in Massachusetts*. New York: Time.

Sweney, K. (1991, March 7). Arc blasts legal system: Many are outraged, say system failed GF rape victim. *Grand Forks (ND) Herald*, p. 1

Wood, H. R., & White, D. L. (1992). A model for habilitation and prevention for offenders with mental retardation—The Lancaster County (PA) Office of Special Offenders Services. In R. Conley, R. Luckasson, & G. Bouthilet (Eds.), *The criminal justice system and mental retardation* (pp. 153–165). Baltimore: Brookes.

Zeldes, J. D. (1994, December). *Connecticut Bar Journal*, 68(6), 443–455.

Epilogues

Newly in Pursuit of an Old Philosophy: Rebalancing Liberty, Equality, and Community

H. Rutherford Turnbull III and Ann P. Turnbull

W e want to briefly scan some American history, wander across the land-scape of contemporary political philosophy, and finally land on the solid ground that, we hope, will connect our concerns for people with mental retardation and related developmental disabilities to the United States of the millennium. We begin by reviewing premodern policy concerning people with mental retardation (some of which we discuss in Chapter 1 of this book on family support); then we review policies of the first and second generations of the modern era, showing how the dominant philosophies of liberty and equality affected people with mental retardation. Next, we address today's debate about the balance between liberty, equality, and community. We contrast the individualistic perspective (based on liberty) and the communal perspec-tive. To bolster our argument in favor of the communal imperative, we describe some of the factors that make today's context for people with mental retardation especially supportive of the communal perspective. We conclude by arguing, again, for a rebal-ancing of public and personal philosophies, one that favors the communal perspective. As The Arc enters its second half century and the new millennium arrives, we are espe-cially persuaded that advocates for citizens with mental retardation no longer can posit their arguments so much on liberty and equality, but instead need to conceptualize, articulate, and advance the communal imperative.

We are grateful to the following indivduals for conversations with us that led to some of the ideas in this chapter: Al Abeson, Bob Bernstein, Val Bradley, Bo Burt, Bill Kiernan, Paul Marchand, John Parry, Mike Ruef, Colleen Weick, and Michael Wehmeyer. They and others (Doug Guess, Earle Knowlton, Ruth Luck-asson, Holly Riddle, Wayne Sailor, and Steve Taylor) contributed to an earlier version presented to The Arc's governmental affairs retreat in the fall of 1997.

HISTORY

Premodern Policy

Early on, in colonial America, mental retardation was a "private" problem. If there were a single descriptive phrase, it would have to be this: Families bear all. The burden—economic, physical, emotional, and social—of disability was allocated singularly and pointedly to the family. A sense of public or communal responsibility was noticeably absent.

Given that disability carries a stigma of ancient origin, when public policy did respond, it not surprisingly did so in ways that strike familiar chords, even today: banishment from the colonies and their towns. If the fact of disability could not be cast out, then the person with the disability would become the outcast. A sense of communal commitment was wholly lacking. Private pain evoked no ameliorating public response.

From these two postures—families bearing all and banishment—public policy moved, early in the 20th century, to a truly enlightened posture. The earliest communal response took the form of asylum. The underlying philosophy was communal, the asylum being emblematic of altruism and collectivism. In a phrase, beneficence reigned.

It was not long, however, before the asylum and beneficence were perverted. Rather than being a place of refuge where kindliness was the leitmotiv, the asylum became a place of horror where degradation was the leitmotiv. In a phrase, maltreatment, even maleficence, reigned.

Closely associated in point of time and attitude with the creation and then perversion of the asylum was the science of "intelligence." The early developers of the intelligence tests, Terman, Yerkes, and Goddard (1905–1921), may not have intended their methods to become instruments of dominance, yet that is precisely what happened. Simultaneously, public policy took yet another perverse form. Special education was established as much for the purpose of educating the few who were regarded as "educable" as for the purpose of Americanizing the recent Eastern European immigrants.

Those who tested at the low end of the intelligence scale were involuntarily committed, sterilized, denied the civil rights of other citizens (including African Americans and women), and refused medical treatment. Indeed, some "leaders" of the "charity" movement even suggested that it is defensible to use the "chloroform" route for eliminating them (Johnson, 1901; cited in Herr, 1974; Murdoch, 1906). In the words of Justice Oliver Wendell Holmes, Jr. (*Buck v. Bell*, 1927), "three generations of imbeciles are enough." Those who, in Holmes's words, "sap the strength of the state," had no claim on the state and, in the eyes of some, had no claim to life.

If one had to find a single phrase for the eugenics era, it would have to be this: Social Darwinism. Underlying the survival of the fittest approach was, of course, a distinctly noncommunal, highly individualistic philosophy. The contrast between the early asylums, the communal response, and beneficence on the one hand, and the perverted asylums, individualistic response, and maleficence ob the other is sharp and disturbing.

With the end of World War II and for about three decades thereafter, two concurrent and complementary models of policy existed: "parentectomy" and "society-ectomy." The parentectomy model argued for removing the member who has a disability from the family. Even to this day, the ghost of Bruno Bettelheim reminds us of that approach. The "society-ectomy" model argued for institutionalizing—that is, segregating and purging from our midst—those who have disabilities. The "developmental centers," cosmetically renamed institutions, are not ghosts but rather living reminders of that approach. The underlying policy was, strangely, grounded on "liberty"—the liberty to be free of certain people. The irony—that some should lose their liberty so that others may have more of their own—is biting and without anesthesia.

The First Generation of the Modern Era

We need not be reminded, but neither should we discuss our future without recalling, that the disability rights movement owes a great and still unpaid debt to the civil rights movement on behalf of African Americans. In his argument on behalf of the state of South Carolina in *Brown v. Board of Education* (1954), the state's lawyer prophesied that, if the Supreme Court were to require the state to integrate its schools by race, it would not be long before the state would have to integrate its schools by disability, too. That of course proved to be entirely accurate. The equal protection doctrine, as applied in *Brown*, soon wound its way into gender-discrimination law and then into disability-discrimination law. As the majority schools were opened to racial minorities, so they were slowly opened to other minorities. The underlying public philosophy was, of course, equality. One must applaud that change: Equality evokes a far more kindly response to disability than "individualism" and its concomitant "liberty."

From *Brown* came two complementary, interdependent, interactive, and concurrent rights movements. One called for access to a free appropriate public education, provoked the two frontier-setting lawsuits that we know as *PARC* (*Pennsylvania Association for Retarded Children v. Commonwealth*, 1971, 1972) and *Mills* (1972), and resulted in the Individuals with Disabilities Education Act (IDEA) (P.L. 94-142 of 1975, P.L. 105-17 of 1997).

The other equal protection–related development addressed access to the community, although it also incorporated other public philosophy. Under theories of cruel and inhuman punishment (barred by the 8th Amendment) and due process and equal protection (assured by the 14th Amendment), courts created rights against harm and to treatment. They also created a right to deinstitutionalization and community placement. The three-pronged strategy proved powerful: Institutional reform (*Wyatt v. Stickney*, 1971), the institutional prevention (*Parham v. J.R.*, 1979), and finally institutional discharge and community support (*Pennhurst State School and Hospital v. Halderman*, 1981; Social Security Act Title XIX waivers; and family support and Supplemental Security Income [SSI]) evidenced a communal response—a sense that people with disabilities should have not only equal treatment but also opportunities to be integrated and included, to be part of our and their communities. With those opportunities came the liberty rights—rights to be free of professionally directed dominance in education (the parent-participation right) and to be free of discrimination based on disability alone (Sec. 504 of the Rehabilitation Act Amendments of 1975 and the Americans with Disabilities Act [ADA]).

During the 10 or so years beginning in the early 1970s and concluding somewhere in the mid-1980s, there was rare and magnificent concurrence of philosophies: Equality was the seedbed for community and inclusion, and both of these advanced liberty.

At the same time, during this Age of Aquarius, the advances in political and legal philosophy that combined equality with community inclusion and liberty were accompanied by advances in political philosophy and human services philosophy. Egalitarianism was the political philosophy initiated by the Kennedy and Johnson administrations. Normalization—making the normal ebb and flow of life characterized by nondisability available to those with disabilities—was the human service ideology. If there is a dominant strain, a recurring theme, it was one of equality; community and liberty were important, but they seem to have been subsumed under or to be by-products of equality.

The Second Generation of the Modern Era

The Age of Aquarius was short-lived. Officially, it ended the moment Ronald Reagan was sworn in as President; unofficially, it ended with his election in the fall of 1980. Among the Reagan administration's very first human service policies was the "deregulation" of IDEA. That, of course, was simply a stalking horse for defederalization of human services, including the elimination of the U.S. Department of Education. Kindly, the historian will speak of "defederalization" when, truthfully, we in the disability movement should speak about "destatism" and even "antistatism." The Cowboy Presidency called for Morning in America, but for people with disabilities and their families, his call conjured up Midnight in America. His Midnight in America call revisited the public policy and philosophy that perverted the asylum and shunned beneficence for maleficence.

Rugged individualism, reminiscent of frontier America, took on a new and problematic look. Stockbrokers, Baby Boomers—name your exemplars—glorified greed; gelt was the new god. Unfettered liberty, a rugged individualism, affected the disability cause in a way that was most peculiar. On the one hand, the notion of liberty and rights proved to be helpful to our constituency; on the other, it posed and continues to pose long-term challenges.

Within the disability movement, as within America generally, the principles of individualism and liberty created a whole new class of "rights-bearers," including our own constituents. An explosion in disability litigation resulted, with cases under IDEA, Section 504, the Developmental Disabilities Assistance and Bill of Rights (DD) Act, and, soon, ADA establishing and refining rights.

In a different forum of public policy, namely the legislative one, the DD Act proclaimed that the national policy for people with disabilities is independence, productivity, and integration, and IDEA was amended in the mid-1980s and again in 1997 to emphasize outcome-based special education. The Technology-Related Assistance to Individuals with Disabilities Act of 1988 (Tech Act), the Rehabilitation Act, and IDEA all place a great deal of value on independence. That is not at all objectionable and certainly is consistent with the post-Reagan era. That is so because these laws reflected a doctrine of equal treatment and equal access; the new equal access doctrine held that people with disabilities should have equal access to the same and different resources for the same, not different, results.

Making use of the equality philosophy, we argued not only that people with disabilities should be treated at least as equally as those who do not have disabilities but, in many cases, more equally. The Individualized Education Program exemplifies the "more equal" posture we took, and the current discipline safeguards in IDEA remind us how effective we have been in securing more than equal treatment.

Our justification for equal treatment and more was historical and constitutional. Historically, people with disabilities had been the victims of a great deal of discrimination; as five justices of the Supreme Court noted in the *Cleburn* decision (*City of Cleburne v. Cleburne Living Center*, 1985), their history was "grotesque." Constitutionally, we stood on good ground, too: Governments should not parcel out benefits and burdens on the basis of unalterable traits (as mental retardation is), and similarly situated people (students, employees, and users of public accommodations) should be treated equally.

As we argued for equal treatment, we also advocated for liberty/independence. The two were interdependent: The more of equal opportunity or more-than-equal opportunity we had, the more we would be able to be independent. The more independent we could become, the more self-directing, the more "normal," the more empowered. The two are difficult to separate; independence will enhance equality, and equality will produce independence. But the overriding theme, the strain that begins this era and is still loudly heard, is that of liberty, of individualism, of "rights bearers" seeking to establish and strengthen not only the existing rights but those that have yet to be acknowledged.

We in the disability movement have participated in and benefited from the individualistic rights-bearer tie; but, although we are not entirely misguided, we have gone somewhat astray. Recent commentary on public philosophy has confirmed our wariness of "individualistic liberty" and even equality as the best basis for our future approach to people with disabilities.

TODAY'S DEBATE: THE COMMUNAL IMPERATIVE

There is another tradition, another public philosophy, that we should emphasize, arguably in preference to those of equality and liberty/independence. It is an old one, and its dominant theme is "community." There are other terms by which we know this tradition—"fraternity" in the terms of the French Revolution, or "communitarianism" in the terms of today's sociology. This spirit of mutuality, of reciprocity, holds that those who have much have an obligation to those who have little. Today, we begin to detect how great is the appeal of the doctrine of community, and how useful the communal imperative can be.

Jonathan Rawls's (1971) 30-year-old theory of distributive justice—an early basis for equal treatment— calls for a public philosophy in which the "minimal rights and needs" of every one of us are met by every other one of us. If each of us were ignorant of our futures, we would be quite willing to give up all that we might have in order to assure that none of us would be without that which we minimally need (e.g., health care and education).

Similarly, sociologists such as Titmuss (1968) and Rein (1976) long have called for value-based public policy, with the value being that which enhances the moral transactions and social relationships among us all. More recently, Bellah and Sullivan (1985, 1996) have reminded us that there are habits of our hearts that public policy and philosophy should nurture to achieve the good society. Among those habits are those of caring for the welfare of others. The purpose of the modern state, they suggest, should be to reconstruct the Aristotelian concept of civic republicanism, a sense that we are all in this—in this community, state, nation, and world—together. This is a profoundly religious approach, too: Doing unto others as we would have them do unto us calls for us to act on a sense of our interdependence, our reciprocity. The human ecology is, in both a biological and philosophical sense, one of connectivity.

Within our own field of disability advocacy, Martha Minnow (1990) has written compellingly about inclusion and exclusion in American law, asking us to decide the disputes between us on the basis of how the result will advance our relationships with each other. Don't label each other; don't use terms that divide us, she pleads. Instead, seek those traits that connect—those aspects of each other that connect us to each other as human beings. Use law to establish, solidify, and resolve disputes within a framework of our relationships with each other.

Another disability advocate/scholar, R. A. (Bo) Burt (personal communication, 1997) sounds a similar note. The purpose of law, he says, it to put us into a position where we must confront our differences and resolve them on terms that advance our connection with each other. We must seek, he writes, a "vocabulary of mutuality" (1997), looking for a communal commitment to vulnerable people and finding language that provides "self-evidently convincing reasons why the strong are obligated to help the weak." For him, the parable of the Good Samaritan is especially apt.

The appeal of mutuality exists outside the disability advocacy community in surprisingly different ways. Mary Ann Glendon (1991) worries that the "rights-bearer" approach, with its emphasis on individuality, independence, and self-sufficiency, makes it difficult to give voice to the moral institutions that are hospitable to "losers," to the most vulnerable. Michael Sandel (1996) worries about "democracy's discontent," arguing that government should not be merely tolerant of diversity and independence but should cultivate a pluralism of mutual appreciation.

Despite an emerging sense of communitarianism, we all sometimes feel especially vulnerable to forces over which we have increasing influence. Those feelings of vulnerability include a sense that public policy and the operating philosophy of the next several decades should be one of communal, reciprocal, and mutual care. As abhorrent as assisted suicide is to many of us, its advocates give voice to a sense that we are also profoundly vulnerable to the power of technology. Being kept "alive" by machines is not "living" when we want to die and when we have to ask the help of others to assist us to die. Even in the act of dying, some of us want to call on our fellow citizens for their aid and comfort.

Let us now try to connect our sense about the communal, mutual, and reciprocal as the basis for policy, to the last 7 years. What was the significance of the 1992 election? Some call it the year of the Clinton Revolution. If there was a revolution, it was short-lived. Consider the hallmark of the Clinton Revolution, namely the Clinton health care proposal. The philosophy underlying that plan, and herein lay its appeal, was that we should all share in satisfying each other's health needs. A distribution of assets, a distribution of justice, would have become our national policy. That communal sense, however, not only justified the plan but also doomed it. In the end, we were unwilling to share assets, risks, and benefits with each other.

Only 2 years later, we experienced a wholly dichotomous revolution, the "Gingrich Revolution." Standing on the steps of the Capitol and holding an enlarged copy of the Contract for America were the individualists, the survivalists, the heirs of Ronald Reagan. It was not long before their welfare reform took shape, and it is only now that its effects, its Darwinian sharpness, are being felt by families who now are ineligible for SSI. Yes, welfare reform was not so severe as it might have been and Medicare was "saved"—for the time being. But there was something terribly ominous about the Gingrich Revolution and its highly individualistic appeal.

In 1996 we had the revolution of the moderates. Yes, the public still wanted to "devolve" programs, balance the budget, and possibly even eliminate our national debt. But they wanted to do so gradually and incrementally. Yes, we wanted to protect our health and invest in our children; we remain, however, divided on how to do so.

Our disagreements are about the role of government and more fundamentally about the philosophy that should guide our policies. Some favor individualistic liberty, but others favor communal and reciprocal obligation. Nowadays, we ask whether government is a help or a hindrance in our pursuit of our desires, and should government rest on a philosophy of one for him- or herself or all for each other?

Let us just look at a cutting-edge issue in those terms: long-term care. It is not merely an issue involving how we who are working will care for our elder parents, or how our working children will care for us when we are frail and elderly. It is an issue about whether we should care for each other. Two responses exist and both involve the role of government. Each is familiar, for we have already described them earlier in this epilogue. Having set out immediately above the essence of the call for a community imperative, we review these two responses and then turn to our fundamental argument in favor of the second of the two.

The Individualistic Perspective

One response takes a highly individualistic form. In its boiled-down form, it says: Let's privatize Social Security and allow Social Security Trust Funds to be invested into the market. Let's have health care IRAs and savings accounts. Let's also have education IRAs, vouchers, charter schools, and education credits. In short, let's have a "go it alone/individualistic/liberty" approach. After all, we have been cautioned by many "conservative" gurus that we cannot trust the "political class" and the welfare state, for both threaten our health and old age security. So, let us turn away from government and its programs. Indeed, while we are about it, let's reassert a nativism, a jingoism, an American firstism that is hostile to immigration issues. Let's be candid about our antipathy to constitutional rights of liberty. Indeed, let's recreate the orphanage and perform life-saving intervention for the institutions. Let's reduce taxes and eliminate deficits, not because those steps would free government to do more, but because those steps are the vanguards that will allow us eventually to dismantle and then eliminate the welfare state.

We are being argumentative, of course, putting the least favorable gloss on the individualistic philosophy. But it does not need our argument—it is frightening enough on its own. Today's news is fill of ominous words and names: Militiamen, McVeigh/Nichols/Oklahoma City, Ruby Ridge, Waco, "people's courts." What we hear when we listen hard is evidence of a virulent antistatism, a profoundly modern version of secession.

The Communal Perspective

There is, of course, another and far more compelling response. It is a deliberately collective one. It asserts that we all need each other. It seeks to reform the present welfare state, improve it, incrementally adjust it, continue to share the wealth, and be guided by values that resonate in a communal approach. The communal approach sees government as a solution but not the only solution. It recognizes that government sets a philosophical stance, enacts policies, and carries out programs to advance the commonweal. It asks government to be interested in all the people, especially those who are most vulnerable. At its best, its programs create social security, graduate the income tax, and redistribute wealth; they achieve mental health parity, portability of health benefits, and child health initiatives. The communal response also acknowledges the fiscal challenge of living within our means, making services cost effective and beneficial, and even paying down our national debt.

The communal response, however, is larger than government; it sets a moral tone for the country, proclaiming a mutuality of need and reciprocity of vulnerability. It finds its expression in the good works of private citizens and private organizations. It is more than action, though it requires action—careful, deliberate, forceful, effective action. The communal approach is, at essence, a spiritual response. It calls us to let our spirits fly—not away from each other and not into themselves, but toward each other and into each other.

The communal response calls for all of us—people with disabilities, their families, the providers who serve them, the members of the communities in which they live, the researchers and trainers who work for them, the policy makers whose laws affect them—to assert that we are interdependent. We have to say over and over again how much we all depend on each other physically, emotionally, financially, and in all other ways. We have to say that those with disabilities make many positive contributions to those without, and that those without make many contributions to those with disabilities. The image must be one of a seamless web of mutuality and reciprocity.

At the same time, we also have to say that we do not abandon our insistence that people with mental retardation must have rights to equal opportunities (and, for some of them, more than equal and different opportunities) and to independence and liberty. The total quantum of the life of a person with mental retardation requires all three values, all three principles, to be at work simultaneously.

It is not a matter of having communal interests rise above the equality and liberty interests, but rather that there must be some new interaction, some transformation, of these interests. We have not yet divined how that interaction, that mutual transformation, will occur, only that it must and usually has. In that interaction, as various approaches to philosophy and the human condition compete for dominance, we have to emphasize the communal response.

Already we see evidence of the communal response. The L'Arche and Camp Hill communities and the movement known as "communitas" reflect the communal spirit; they are tangible evidence of the reciprocity that the communal imperative seeks. Likewise, person-centered planning that creates a reliable alliance for individuals around a person with disability (Turnbull & Turnbull, 1996) is a promising and communal approach that extends the traditional "circle of friends/supports."

The communal response—it and it alone—can and will assure that we can establish new, and preserve and enlarge existing, rights of equality and liberty. Without the sympathetic imagination and heartfelt support of those without disabilities—that is, without their subscribing to the communal response—the equality and liberty rights and values will be hard for us to attain. Why is this so? What is it about the end of the millennium that requires us to posit our advocacy on somewhat different grounds than we have used in the past 50 years?

There are several reasons. First, we have come to the end of the century. Have we also come to the end of the half century of civil rights? The question is not rhetorical. As we have noted, some popular and scholarly commentary argue for and give some evidence of the decline of individualism and individual rights-bearer approaches. If there is not an actual decline, there is at least some stabilization.

Second, we are witnesses to a tremendous splintering of America. Arguably, a rights-bearer approach, founded on the notion of the individual as the center of the law and society and on the principles of liberty and equality, has contributed to that splintering. At the same time, the rights-bearer approach has given people with disabilities power that they otherwise would not have had. The issue is not whether to jettison the rights-bearer approach and our traditional insistence on liberty and equality as values, in and of themselves and in instrumental ways, that we should pursue for people with disabilities. Rather the issue is how to enrich our rights-bearer approaches with another approach, the communal one.

Third, arguably we are at the end of an era in which basic rights are established and at the beginning of an era requiring a much more nuanced, incremental, and balanced approach to rights-creation, rights-implementation, and right-duty rebalancing. We may anticipate few additional new rights and hope for no drastic erosion of existing ones. We may see a "rights-exploration" approach.

Finally, the context in which people with mental retardation and their families find themselves is replete with challenges and opportunities. Thus, it seems that we will be more able to secure an enviable quality of life for people with disabilities if we seek and find, and then give voice and action to, a new way of thinking about an America that is already and will continue to be even more distinctly different from the one that marked the beginning of the last half of this century.

TODAY'S CONTEXT

The context for the communal imperative—for a rebalancing of liberty, equality, and community—calls for the rebalancing. A few examples will suffice to make that point.

Triaging the Population with Mental Retardation

Nearly 85% of all those with mental retardation have what is classically described as "mild" mental retardation. As the severity of retardation increases and a person's needs grow, the number and relative proportions of persons so affected decrease.

For the most part, the policies we have advocated have been based, correctly so, on the purely utilitarian premise of the greatest good for the greatest number. That means that most of our policies benefit and assume a "mild" or "moderate" degree of impairment (to use the now outmoded descriptors). By the same token, many of our policies may not be especially suitable for those with severe or multiple disabilities, or for those whose mental retardation coexists with other disabilities.

Take inclusion as an example of a policy. Do we support it? Yes. But—and here is the usual "yes, but" conundrum—when we speak of and advocate for inclusion, we must be cautious that the very concept itself does not lead to reduced attention to and services to support a person's needs. We must be especially cautious about that prospect because we live in an era of increasing concern about long-term care costs, education costs, and cost-benefit or cost-effectiveness criteria. These criteria are two-edged swords.

Under the compelling reclassification of mental retardation as proposed by the American Association on Mental Retardation (Lukasson et al., 1992), the traditional degrees or levels of mental retardation are jettisoned; "mild," "moderate," "severe," and "profound" have no meaning, for the issue is simply what the person's intellectual and adaptive capacities are, how the person interacts with his or her environment, and how much and what kind of support the person needs to be able to be more capable in those environments.

Nevertheless, the degrees still affect public policy and program administration in ways that relate to the rebalancing of liberty, equality, and community. Thus, a person who has "mild" disability may not "present" so well clinically; he may not display the required "need" for services and, as recources are allocated, he may be triaged out of the services. Some may think that he can be supported without services. That was the approach taken with respect to the SSI "reform" and may well be the one taken with respect to school inclusion and other services. And even when the person does receive services, the type of service can backfire. It is one thing for a person with a disability to live in a home of her own; but the backlash can be powerful if inclusion is into a high-priced neighborhood. The middle class worker may well say, "Why should she live there on my tax dollar when I can't get out of my trailer court?"

Outcome-Based Policy and Commodification

On the other hand, the person who has the greatest need may be regarded as least able to benefit and therefore least worthy of services. Indeed, the tangible benefit may be difficult to measure for these people; even if it is measurable, the benefit still may be so slight and so socially insignificant that it will not persuade policy makers and resource allocation and eligibility specialists to spend funds to benefit the person. The case involving Timothy W.—the educability case (*Timothy W. v. Rochester*, 1989)—demonstrates how triage can also affect those with the greatest need for support. Within managed medical care, outcome-based criteria—improvement alone, not also maintenance of level of functioning—may undercut a person's claim on services and resources. The prospects for custodial care—nothing more—are large and ominous.

That prospect is especially real as the person nears the end of life. One of the hidden attractions behind assisted suicide is the ending of life of people who are not deemed particularly worthy of continued life. The kind of thinking about "disposable Baby Doe" (on quality of life grounds) easily becomes Granny Doe thinking, especially as it relates to persons with mental retardation and within that class to those who have the greatest disability. A good case can be made that, for people such as Joseph Saikewicz (*Superintendent v. Saikewicz*, 1977), involving substitute consent for chemotherapy for a person with profound retardation in a state facility whose cancer would not by cured, the decision to withhold treatment is a purely economic one: The sooner Joseph and people like him die, the less money the state will have to spend to keep him alive and to treat him medically.

Whether we are dealing with persons who need little or great support, we have to be on guard. The risk, very simply, is commodification based on cost–benefit criteria: Treating individuals as "products" that have to meet certain "standards of performance" is risky business.

Another risk exists with respect to people with mental retardation, whatever degree of disability they have. It is one that is inherent in the community and is no greater or lesser, just different, than the risk that they face in institutions. The risk is one of abuse and neglect. There are problems in the community provider system; some people with retardation are in jeopardy on that account—namely, those who are entitled to services but who are denied them or are maltreated under the guise of receiving services. Likewise, simply being in the community can make an individual vulnerable from nonproviders. Indeed, everyone is vulnerable and our policy of home and community–based service is vulnerable because, if the community system fails (by whatever criteria constitute "fail"), the resurrection of the institutional system will not be far behind.

The point is very simply this: Inclusion in the community requires supports and supports cost money. As in school inclusion, so in community inclusion: Those with greater capabilities still need their own types and degrees of support, just as do those with greater impairment, so our policies must address both populations. We ourselves dare not triage those who depend on our advocacy.

STIGMA

We are vulnerable simply because of societal prejudice. Disability still carries stigma, and backlash against civil rights generally and disability rights specifically is an increasingly frequent phenomenon. NIMBYism (not in my backyard) can be found nearly everywhere.

The answer can be that, if discrimination can happen to us, it can happen to others whose traits are "undesirable." Ask citizens from culturally and linguistically diverse backgrounds, women, and people who are elderly if that is not true. Our cause is with them and theirs is with us.

Demographics

The number of people in our "cause" is small, relative to, say, such other claimants on the public fisc as elderly citizens. Yet our political power, our "oomph" as a constituency, is disproportionate to our numbers. Will it remain that way? What must we do to ensure that we continue to have the disproportionate power we have enjoyed in the past?

Part of what we have to do is to link our cause with the causes of other vulnerable people, to espouse theirs as well, and yet to be able to distinguish our issues and advance them and only them at the point when, say, the elderly begin to shape health care in ways that may disadvantage us. Common cause is needed and will take us far, but only so far if we do not also keep our own cause first and foremost in our minds.

In connection with demographics and common causes, it is significant that Baby Boomers, Generation Xers, citizens who are elderly, and those with disabilities could be on the brink of intergenerational warfare over a single issue: Who owes what, and how much, to whom? We stand to be badly hurt by these debates, unles we can somehow show that we have issues alike with the Baby Boomers and the Generation Xers. Sad to say, too few of them are fellow travelers in the cause of social justice.

The issue of common cause becomes even more relevant when we realize that there is a "darkening" of America and Americans. A country that is already a polyglot of racially and ethnically different people is becoming increasingly Hispanic, African American, and Asian. Communal interests among these diverse subcultures exist but are difficult to discern. Racial divides among minority groups and between traditional majority and minority populations can be fueled by economics, culture, and separatist policy.

It is familiar knowledge that Americans from culturally and linguistically diverse backgrounds always have been and are still overrepresented in special education but not in family support or other services. What is the message they get?

On another level of demographics, wealth is increasingly concentrated, the middle class is not growing, but the economically marginal class is expanding. The correlation between disability, poverty, race/ethnicity, and socioeconomic status is positive, and, given the demographics just cited, likely to be unabated.

Public and Private Fiscs

The fiscal resources of federal and state–local governments are relatively static. There is and will be no great growth of public revenues. Deficit reduction drives tax and expenditure decisions. If debt reduction ever catches hold, it too will reduce even more the disposable income of the federal government. (State and local governments are already limited by their constitutions to not deficit-finance themselves.) Taxpayers still resist expenditures at a local level. The upshot is that competition for disposable public revenues is fierce. Aging is the big "sleeper" that will dominate expenditure decisions, and long-term care is more concerned with those who are elderly than with those who have mental retardation. How do we make common cause with them, within the fiscal realities?

We live in an era of bean-counters and accountants, in an era when responsibility is valued and indeed is the quid pro quo of welfare benefits. In this era when cost containment, cost–benefits, and efficiency are the dominant criteria for policy making, we have to ask yet another question: What about effectiveness and accountability? The simple fact is that we have to do more with less and we have to do better with what we have earned.

Now, a word about ourselves. Personal habits of families (assuming they have discretionary disposable income) are, nationwide, not savings prone, and when disability impacts a family, fewer savings are possible. There will be an impact of low-savings habits and high-cost expectations for mental retardation and developmental disability services. This impact is that low savings impede capital investment and tax bases, both of which are essential to services for people with disabilities.

Wealth and power are increasingly concentrated in fewer hands. As the numbers of poor or financially marginal people grow and as the economic middle class bears the greatest share of tax burdens, our cause finds itself facing an economically different America than, say, in the 1970s or 1980s.

The challenge is manifold: to advocate for policies of wealth distribution and simultaneously to advocate for policies that create incentives for the wealthy to give their wealth away to our cause. Taxation and donation policies need to coexist, especially since the appeal of individual interests (wealth accumulation and preservation) over community and state interests is powerful; the individualistic and liberty-based philosophy is dominant and threatening.

Demassification

Finally, the changes with which we are most familiar are but evidence of an underlying type of change—change that is occurring at a pace so rapid we can barely discern it and in ways so subtle we can barely count them. Alvin Toffler (1990) wrote about this kind of change in *Powershift*.

According to Toffler, there are three shifts in power. First, there is a disintegration of the structures of power. Traditional institutions and those who have had power through them are losing ground. Just look at our own field. Huge public institutions are being closed under a theory of deinstitutionalization. Community-based mini-institutions are being downsized under a theory of defacilitation. Separate education is now regarded as a service, not a place to which students are sent. The legal doctrines of consent and of parent and self-determination and the political doctrine of participatory democracy have reduced professionals' power.

The second shift involves the very nature of power itself. That shift refers to who exercises power and how those individuals (nations, states, private entities, individuals) come to have power. In our own field, a system-centered service delivery model has yielded to a person-centered model. Those who once were patients and were expected to be compliant are now regarded as consumers and collaborators, with all the caveat vendor implications that the term "consumer" carries. In some programs (as we explain in Chapter 1 of this book), the focus of service provision is the family, not only the person with a disability. And despite the indispensable role that Congress plays in setting policy and funding programs, the states and increasingly local governments and private enterprises are the sources of innovation; a bubble-up of innovation has usually led to a state or federal response.

The third shift involves demassification and globalization of power. In the "pre-democratic era," power resided in local structures and entities. In the era of "mass democracy," the past 200-plus years, power has resided in the nation state and its local entities.

Now, Toffler (1990) argues, we are about to enter the "post–mass-democratic" era. That will be a time when power is decentralized; demassification will be the dominant characteristic of local–state–federal power. In our field, we see evidence of this already (Turnbull, 1992; C. Weick, personal correspondence, September 15, 1997):

- Defederalization and even antistatism are part of demassification.

- People with disabilities have become an important interest group with their own quasi-affirmative action rights and expectations.

- Professional associations, parent organizations such as The Arc and others, and self-advocacy groups have become policy players.

- There has been a dispersal of the entire disability interest group across a much larger number of entities and individuals than before; we have demassified ourselves.

- Bureaucracies now contract out services to private entities; these types of "by-passes" are consistent with deinstitutionalization and defacilitation, with the inclusion models that basically call for a universal design of human services—a sort of "Go Generic" approach.

- The location of "mind power" is also dispersed, from government to private industry and from institutions of higher education to parent training and information centers.

- The rights of parents under IDEA now explicitly devolve to their children when they reach the age of majority.

- Electronic activism occurs daily as our faxes and e-mails bring us a deluge of information and appeals.

- Vertical bureaucracies struggle to handle horizontal problems, and fail.

Along with demassification comes a tremendous opportunity. If the powershift means that people will be acting with greater latitude and in a much more face-to-face way in the future, under policies and technology that disperse power, then we have a tremendous opportunity to assert and advance the communal ideal. Perhaps no other philosophy, no other advocacy posture, will be as effective as one that explicitly asserts that we are all interdependent, we are all vulnerable in new and old ways, and the most vulnerable among us are the most worthy of a communal response. Less able does not mean less worthy. Under a communal response, it means just the opposite.

SUMMARY AND CONCLUSION

Throughout its history, The Arc has asserted that disability is a distinction that makes a difference in conceptualizing rights. The Arc—the "we" to whom we authors refer in this conclusion—have asserted, first, that people with mental retardation should have equal opportunities and, when their needs are such that they need special supports to have real opportunities, more than equal treatment or at least different but not invidious or damaging treatment.

We have asserted that people with mental retardation should have the same liberty rights as people who do not have disabilities. Involuntary commitment, sterilization, and guardianship, for example, are not so widespread or unwarranted as they have been.

And we have asserted that people with mental retardation have an interest in being part of their communities. Their interest is not only physical and psychological—actually being in the community—but feeling that they belong there, being welcomed there. Their interest is deeper than this, we have said. It is in having a special moral claim on those who are more able than they, a claim that arises from their inherent vulnerability.

The three themes of law reform of the last 50 years—equality, liberty, and community—will be indispensable to our cause for at least the foreseeable future, for another 25 years. What is different, however, is the emphasis that we and others should give to them.

As we face the backlash against affirmative action and class entitlements, we need to assert that our clients have a special claim to equality. The discrimination they have experienced as a class is not yet "cured," so it is not yet justified to retrench their class-entitlements and class-based claims. Moreover, simply treating each person with mental retardation in exactly the same way that policy treats each person who does not have mental retardation will not produce, for each of our clients, equal opportunities. Mental retardation always makes a difference.

Already, too, the concept of individual liberty is being critiqued. The criticism is that there are simply too many "rights-bearers," too many individualistic assertions that "my right trumps your claim or right." The fundamental liberties that the constitution guarantees to those who do not have disabilities are not yet fully established for those with disabilities. So we dare not retreat on our advocacy for liberty in its fullest constitutional sense.

But another approach is developing. This is, of course, the communal perspective. It sees government as a solution, but not the only one. It seeks to advance the commonweal, the common causes that all citizens have with each other. It sets a moral tone for the country, proclaiming a mutuality of need and reciprocity of vulnerability. It calls for action—for equality and liberty–based policies and programs. But it also emanates from and resonates in a moral response.

The present and future context for people with mental retardation and their families may be captured in a single word: vulnerability. They—and we their families and advocates—are vulnerable from so many perspectives today. Their/our vulnerability is not theirs/ours alone; others affected by disability and many who have no disability at all but whose immutable traits—their color, race, or place of birth—and whose economic condition are precarious to begin with are also in perilous condition. This equality of vulnerability is precisely the fact on which our search for a communal philosophy rests.

We can articulate and advance this sense of reciprocal vulnerability and, in doing so, find ways in which our cause can be linked, for advocacy purposes, to the causes of other vulnerable people. But we must also distinguish our needs from those of other vulnerable populations. We need to be extraordinarily careful, as we select the issues, forums, and strategies for our advocacy, that we do not provoke an even greater backlash than already exists. We need to show our protegees as being part of the natural fabric of America. We need to reassert, time and time again, that, as ADA and IDEA proclaim, disability is a natural consequence, and therefore not an unwelcome consequence, of the human condition.

It is, after all, the human condition to which we are called and to which we call others. Despite all of our efforts, the human condition is a compound of fragility and strength. We are fragile in all familiar ways—spiritual, physical, economic. But we also are strong—in those ways, and in an even more fruitful way. That way is the avenue into our hearts; it is our sympathetic imagination, our sense of commonality with others seemingly different from us; it is our empathy and compassion, responding instinctively to those among us who are especially vulnerable—those with mental retardation and other imperiling conditions.

The Arc's 50th Birthday is a fit occasion for revisiting and renewing our sense of mutual and reciprocal vulnerability within our "cause." And it is a proper occasion for asserting the communal imperative—for being in, and of, the wider community of America. Shall we yield our rights, so hard won? Never. Shall we try to restate our rights claims? Yes, with emphasis on our obligations to and claims upon fellow citizens. Only in that way will our claims to equality and liberty be honored in the law and on the streets of our many communities, and only in this way will we be safeguarded in our journey in this life.

REFERENCES

Bellah, R. M., Sullivan, J., et al. (1985, 1996). *Habits of the heart*. Berkeley, CA: The University of California Press.

Brown v. Board of Education, 347 U.S. 483 (1954).

Buck v. Bell, 274 U.S. 200 (1927).

City of Cleburne v. Cleburne Living Center, 473 U.S. 432 (1985).

Glendon, M. A. (1991). *Rights talk: The impoverishment of political discourse*. New York: The Free Press.

Herr, S. (1974). Civil rights, uncivil asylums, and the retarded. *University of Cincinnati Law Review, 43*, 679, 697–698.

Lukasson, R., Coulter, D. L., Polloway, E. A., Reiss, S., Schalock, L. L., Snell, M. E., Spitalnik, D. M., & Stark, J. A. (1992). *Mental retardation: Definition, classification, and systems of support.* Washington, DC: American Association on Mental Retardation.

Mills, v. D.C. Board of Education, 348 F. Supp. 866 (D.D. C. 1972).

Minnow, M. (1990). *Making all the difference: Inclusion, exclusion, and American law.* Ithaca, NY: Cornell University Press.

Murdoch, J. (1906). The psychic treatment of mental defectives. *Journal of Psycho-Asthenics, 10,* 224.

Parham v. J.R., 442 U.S. 582 (1979).

Pennhurst State School and Hospital v. Halderman, 451 U.S. 1 (1981), 465 U.S. 89 (1984).

Pennsylvania Association for Retarded Children (PARC) v. Commonwealth, 334 F. Supp. 1257 (E.D. Pa. 1971), 343 F. Supp. 279 (E.D. Pa. 1972).

Rawls, J. (1971). *A theory of justice.* Cambridge, MA: Harvard University Press.

Rehabilitation Act Amendments of 1975, codified at 42 U.S.C. § 794.

Rein, M. (1976). *Social science and public policy.* New York: Penguin.

Sandel, M. J. (1996). *Democracy's discontent: America in search of a public philosophy.* Cambridge, MA: The Belknap Press.

Superintendent v. Saikewicz, 373 Mass. 728, 370 N.E. 2d 417 (1977).

Timothy W. v. Rochester School Dist., 875 F. 2d 954 (1st Cir. 1989), cert. den. 465 U.S. 1006 (1989).

Titmuss, R. (1968). *Commitment to welfare.* London: Allen & Unwin.

Toffler, A. (1990). *Powershift: Knowledge, wealth, and violence at the edge of the 21st century.* New York: Bantam Books.

Turnbull, A, & Turnbull, H. R. (1996). Group action planning as a strategy for providing comprehensive family support. In L. K. Koegel, R. L. Koegel, & G. Dunlap (Eds.), *Community, school, family, and social inclusion through positive behavioral support* (pp. 99–114). Baltimore: Brookes.

Turnbull, H. R. (1992). *Families of persons with developmental disabilities.* Lawrence, KS: Beach Center on Families and Disabilities (for National Conference of State Legislatures, Denver, CO).

Wyatt v. Stickney, 325 F. Supp. 781 (M.D. Ala. 1971), 344 F. Supp. (M.D. Ala. 1972), *aff'd,* 503 F. 2d 1305 (5th Cir. 1974). The Wyatt litigation has been carried on for more than 25 years by the Judge David L. Bazelon Mental Health Law Center; the most recent decision in the case reiterated the rights that the court first enunciated in 1971 and found that, again, the state was in violation of those rights, Wyatt v. Rogers, Gv. Act. No. 3195-N, M.D. Ala., Dec. 15, 1997.

Mental Retardation in the 21st Century

Gunnar Dybwad

This book represents a comprehensive collection of work by an outstanding group of professional writers. A reader who has completed the text, or even glanced at the table of contents, is no doubt impressed, as was I. However, rather than making some well-deserved general laudatory comments, I would like to present some thoughts from the viewpoint of an 89-year-old with 64 years of experience in the fields of human services and disability, mostly in the areas under discussion in this book.

Thus I have a vivid memory of conditions that to most readers will only be historical facts that they have read. I saw firsthand the dismal conditions in the overcrowded institutions that originated in good intentions, to give asylum and protection, and quickly became warehouses to offer society protection from the so-called "mental defectives." I saw in the late 1930s overcrowding with all its dire consequences. In Letchworth Village, considered to be one of the "better" New York State institutions at that time, I found a dormitory with 100 beds and 125 children in those beds. Then came World War II with the consequent manpower problems and the postwar period with its radical economic and social changes.

I also vividly remember something else that rose out of the postwar period. Parents of children with intellectual limitations spontaneously came together and organized locally throughout the country, what became, in 1950, the National Association for Retarded Children (NARC). The strong voice of this new group was soon heard in Congress and statehouses across the nation, effectively challenging the prevailing perceptions of "mental deficiency," and demanding radical changes to meet the needs of the children, especially in education.

These efforts of the parent movement were eminently successful, as attested to by Dr. Samuel Kirk, Professor of Education at the University of Illinois and selected by President John F. Kennedy as the director of the newly established Division of Services to Handicapped Children in the U.S. Office of Education, who was quoted as follows in the *American Journal of Rehabilitation Literature* (November 1960):

> The public has gone so fast in their demands of what should be done with the mentally retarded in all areas—medical, social, educational, and otherwise—that today we find not so much a cultural lag, but really a professional lag. Those of us in the professional field find ourselves so overwhelmed with not only the demands but sometimes support that we don't have the proper people today to handle this at a high professional level; and I think that can be said for all the professional groups, rather than just one of them.

Empowered by the disclosure that President Kennedy's family had a member with mental retardation, parents grew stronger in their advocacy for their family members. It is indeed regrettable that the far-reaching effectiveness of the parent movement, just now celebrating 50 years of successful advocacy, has not been given the attention it deserves in much of the professional literature. As professionals, and friends of people who experience intellectual disabilities, we must never overlook the far-reaching effectiveness of the parent movement. Together with the activities recounted in this volume, they brought us to where we are today.

Parent leaders, such as Lotte Moise of California, Betty Pendler of New York, and Eleanor Elkin of Pennsylvania, have carried the movement from its early moments to the precipice of the 21st century. Under their leadership we witnessed a parent rebellion that became a worldwide movement.

Today, that movement is carried forward by Inclusion International, formerly the International League of Societies for Persons with Mental Handicap, a nongovernmental organization, accredited not only to the United Nations, but also to several of the UN Specialized Agencies, such as UNESCO (United Nations Educational, Scientific, and Cultural Organization), WHO (Word Health Organization), and ILO (International Labour Organization). In 1997 the League's name was changed to Inclusion International, thus emphasizing its worldwide overall goal.

Today, advocacy organizations across the globe advocate for and with people with intellectual impairments in uniform agreement of the importance of community inclusion for all. A clear part of their mission is the elimination of "mental retardation," not by prevention or cure, but by changing our words, our professional classification systems, and our attitudes by eliminating the term *mental retardation*.

Today, there are revisionist historians who seek to minimize the horror of the Nazi Holocaust, or even to deny its existence. Survivors keep the memory alive, and work to reconstruct a written record for posterity, chanting "never again!" We are confronted with our own holocaust in the area of intellectual disability. Parent associations like The Arc were successful in developing special education opportunities and, to a lesser extent, community services for adults with intellectual impairments.

However, and I think significantly, the parents' success in developing community services such as in sheltered workshops, recreation, and home care did not extend to the institutional field. To the contrary, during the very years of progress in the community, the large state institutions deteriorated to a truly unbelievable level of overcrowding, unsanitary conditions, and physical and sexual abuse (not infrequently committed by the staff, newly hired without any relevant training). This not only resembled concentration camp conditions, but there was a striking similarity to a much discussed aspect of the Holocaust, although every one of these state institutions had a considerable medical, psychological, educational, and social work staff who could not help but see, hear, and indeed smell what went on. Although practically everyone belonged to a professional organization with strong ethical standards, with one or two exceptions, no one felt impelled to protest that blatant abuse either directly or through a professional organization. These were sad days—days we must not forget. It was not until a group of lawyers found parents willing to act as plaintiffs in class action suits that the public became aware of what had been going on for years. Detailed accounts of these atrocities and inhumane conditions were preserved in literally thousands of pages of sworn testimony by expert witnesses from their often extensive visits to the facilities, but conveniently filed away in steel cabinets.

At the 1996 Congress of the International Association for the Scientific Study of Intellectual Disabilities, I suggested in a plenary session that the time had come for professionals to confess as well as profess, to acknowledge their responsibility for the past horrors of institutional management, and their responsibility toward those who have been (and too often still are) confined to these institutions. Acknowledgment of that must be a part of our planning for the 21st century.

The actual Holocaust story is kept alive because of a strong belief that this is necessary to prevent a repetition in years to come. Likewise, the institutional horrors must be kept alive by eyewitnesses, as it is in Burton Blatt's trailblazing *Christmas in Purgatory* (Blatt & Kaplan, 1966), which he published at great risk to his professional reputation. It must not be forgotten, it cannot be erased from our professional history.

REFERENCE

Blatt, B., & Kaplan, F. (1966). *Christmas in purgatory*. New York: Allyn & Bacon.

Author Index

Subject Index